PL
FOOTBALL
ANNUAL 1990-91

PLAYFAIR FOOTBALL ANNUAL 1990-91

EDITED BY JACK ROLLIN

Macdonald
Queen Anne Press

A Queen Anne Press BOOK

First published in Great Britain in 1990 by
Queen Anne Press, a division of
Macdonald & Co (Publishers) Ltd
Orbit House
1 New Fetter Lane
London EC4A 1AR

A member of Maxwell Macmillan Pergamon Publishing Corporation

Jacket photograph: Split Second

British Library Cataloguing in Publication Data
Playfair Football annual — 1990–91
1. Soccer — Periodicals
796.334'05 GV942
ISBN 0-356-19196-6

The Editor would like to thank Don Aldridge and Mavis Suckling for their contributions.

Typeset, printed and bound in Great Britain by
BPCC Hazell Books
Aylesbury, Bucks, England
Member of BPCC Ltd.

CONTENTS

Editorial 7

The Football League
Football League Clubs 9
Barclays League First, Second, Third and Fourth Division results, final tables, play-offs, leading scorers, title wins 63
League positions 1964–65 to 1988–89 72
League Championship honours 82
Barclays League attendances 91
Transfer trail 94

British cups
FA Cup 1989–90 results 100
FA Cup past finals 102
Littlewoods Challenge Cup 1989–90 results 107
Past League Cup finals 110
Zenith Data Systems Cup 1989–90 112
Leyland Daf Cup 1989–90 113
FA Charity Shield 1927–89 115

Scottish Football League
Scottish club directory 116
B & Q Scottish League Premier Division, First Division and Second Division results 128
B & Q Scottish League final tables 131
Scottish League honours, title wins, leading scorers 132
Skol Cup 1989–90 138
Skol Cup past finals 139
Scottish Cup 1989–90 140
Past Scottish Cup finals 141

Welsh and Irish Football
Northern Ireland table 144
Republic of Ireland table 144
Abacus Welsh League tables 144

European and International Football
European Cup 1989–90 146
European Cup Winners' Cup 1989–90 147
UEFA Cup 1989–90 149
European Super Cup 152
European Cup past finals 153
European Cup Winners' Cup past finals 154
Fairs Cup finals 154
UEFA Cup past finals 153
FIFA World Cup 1990 finals 155
World Cup qualifying results 164
World Cup past finals 187
European Championship past finals 190
South American football 191
World Club Championship 192
Olympic past finals 196
Other British and Irish International matches 1989–90 193
British post-war International appearances 197
Goalscorers (international) since 1946 229
European Under-16 football 235
European Under-18 football 236
European Under-21 football 238

Non-League Football

GM Vauxhall Conference results, final table and leading scorers 242
HFS Loans results, final table and leading scorers 244
Beazer Homes League Premier, Southern and Midland Division results, final tables and leading scorers 246
Vauxhall League Premier, First, Second North, Second South results, final tables and leading scorers 252
Other League tables 260
FA Challenge Vase 265
FA Challenge Trophy 266
FA Youth Cup 268
FA Sunday Cup 269

Information and Records

Referees 241
Football awards 271
Records 273
GM Vauxhall Conference fixtures 1990–91 277
Football League fixtures 1990–91 278
International and Cup fixtures 1990–91 286
Useful addresses 288

EDITORIAL

The International Football Association Board spent part of the World Cup tournament in Italy deciding on a change in the offside law. The new decision means that a player who is level with the second last opponent or with the last two opponents is not in an off-side position. This has merely changed the problem rather than solved it. They might have been better employed ridding the game of penalty kicks to decide not only World Cup matches but any cup-tie.

The 1990 World Cup was disappointing to say the least. Fewer goals were scored, more players sent off than previously. Inventive free-kicks were non-existent. Teams with as many as two attacking forwards were in a minority. Yet in the midst of all this caution, there were many excellent scoring opportunities missed often because allegedly top class footballers can apparently only kick the ball with one foot.

The Cameroon were the most enterprising team of all. Their football flowed freely and at times they matched the flair of the Brazilians of old. Had their individual and combined skills been matched by discipline and organisation they might easily have gone on to win the tournament. They were unlucky against England, leading 2-1 and throwing away the chance to put the game beyond a recovery through inexperience before losing 3-2. All this despite having four players out through suspension.

They had started the tournament off by beating Argentina 1-0 despite having two players sent off and the defending champions scrambled their way to the final unimpressively where they lost 1-0 to West Germany after themselves having two players dismissed in a bad tempered final. The Germans were just about the most consistent team, physically stronger than most of their opponents, but as usual inclined to intimidate referees by play-acting over fouls. However since the officials only seemed to decide whether a tackle was legitimate or not by the antics of the victim, surely this action was irrelevant.

England began poorly in a dreadful game with the Republic of Ireland, then survived by luck against Belgium who twice hit the woodwork and were embarrassed by the Cameroon before playing with more credit and conviction against West Germany in the semi-final and Italy in the match for third place after losing on penalty kicks to the Germans. This lottery was used in both semi-finals and deprived Italy of a chance of reaching the final on home soil.

Technically, the Italians were the best team, but were often naive in attack where the discovery of the tournament, Salvatore Schillaci was the most caught offside player in the World Cup, often because he was left alone up front. He did have the satisfaction of finishing as top scorer with six goals.

There were many disappointing teams and players. Holland headed the list with Marco van Basten, Ronald Koeman and Frank Rijkaard giving poor performances. There was no spirit in the Dutch camp, the players apparently wanting Johan Cruyff as coach, not Leo Beenhakker. Ruud Gullit was also below his best, but had the excuse of being out of action for almost a year with injury.

Austria, Sweden and Spain also did less than expected, though few gave either the United States, the United Arab Emirates or South Korea much chance. Costa Rica gave Scotland a fright and this cost the Scots dearly, despite improved performances in their other two games. The Irish, under Jack Charlton, thoroughly enjoyed themselves and deserved to reach the quarter-finals, even though they won through on penalty kicks against Rumania who impressed in beating the Soviet Union.

The USSR, in fact, had a curious tournament. They were slow and out of touch against Rumania, but improved later only to be badly served by refereeing decisions against Argentina when they should have had a penalty following handball by Diego Maradona in his own area and they also had a player harshly dismissed. There were flashes from Costa Rica and Colombia and Uruguay and Egypt looked good in defence, poor in attack. The Czechs did better than expected and Yugoslavia improved after a wretched start. Belgium were desperately unlucky against England, twice hitting the woodwork and had in Enzo Scifo one of the outstanding players of the tournament.

Brazil should have beaten Argentina, but Maradona managed virtually one of his only real defence-splitting passes for Claudio Caniggia to score and were woefully short of punch despite dominating all their games. England were well served by Mark Wright, Des Walker, Gary Lineker and Paul Gascoigne and deserved their Fair Play award. Tragically Stuart Pearce and Chris Waddle missed penalties against the Germans and Peter Shilton, bowing out in his 125th international, was caught dallying on the ball in the third place game with Italy, having been badly positioned to recover from a wicked deflection in the game with West Germany.

Television coverage was infuriating. The number of action replays from a variety of angles often cut into subsequent play. Mercifully since the number of goalmouth incidents were rare, nothing much was missed of note. But the commentaries often annoyed and the opinions of studio experts grated. Perhaps everyone was as bored with the play as the television director, but did not like to admit it.

The first half of the final was all West Germany. They attacked relentlessly without much conviction and the second half degenerated into a stop-start affair punctuated by a series of Argentine fouls. Pedro Monzon became the first player to be sent off in a World Cup final and near the end Gustavo Dezotti became the second. Before this second dismissal, Roberto Sensini was adjudged to have brought down Rudi Voller and Andreas Brehme converted from the spot past Sergio Goycochea who had stood in for Nery Pumpido who had broken his leg in Argentina's second game.

On the domestic front, Rumbelows became the new sponsors of the League Cup with a £5 million four-year deal but Chester City were forced to sell their ground and move in with Macclesfield and Aldershot were tottering on the brink of extinction following a winding-up order in the High Court. The last club to be forced to quit the League was Accrington Stanley in 1962.

Swindon Town successfully appealed against a decision by the Football League to demote them from Division One to Division Three and they were allowed to remain in the Second Division following admitted charges of irregular payments to players. But the Football Association's ruling widened the gap between themselves and the Football League.

Attempts to return to a 22-team First Division also angered the FA, who were keen to retain a top echelon of just 20 clubs. But there had been a growing feeling that clubs were losing out on revenue from the loss of such fixtures.

The close season also saw a return of English clubs to Europe following the ban imposed on them after the Heysel Stadium disaster in 1985. Aston Villa entered the UEFA Cup and Manchester United the Cup Winner's Cup. Liverpool's continued suspension from Europe meant that they were unable to compete in the European Champion Clubs Cup after recording their 18th League Championship success.

English clubs can thank the conduct of the England players in Italy for their chance. Alas once again an element of the hooligan fringe disgraced itself and the country in Italy just to underline the problem which still exists underneath the surface of the game.

FOOTBALL LEAGUE CLUBS AND THEIR PLAYERS

ALDERSHOT DIV. 4

Banton, Dale C.
Beeks, Stephen J.
Brown, Kevan B.
Burvill, Glen
Coles, David A.
Coombs, Paul A.
Henry, Charlie
Holsgrove, Paul
Ogley, Mark A.
Puckett, David C.
Randall, Adrian J.
Stewart, Ian
Wignall, Steven L.
Williams, Jerry S. J.

League Appearances: Anderson, D. K. 10(6); Baker, G. 7; Banton, D. C. 16(7); Beeks, S. J. –(1); Beeney, M. R. 7; Brown, K. B. 41(1); Burvill, G. 29(4); Claridge, S. E. 21(4); Coles, D. A. 28; Coombs, P. A. 7(5); Coyne, P. D. 3; Devereux, J. A. –(1); Henry, C. 40; Hunt, R. A. 1(1); Ogley, M. A. 27(1); Phillips, I. A. 44; Powell, C. G. R. 11; Puckett, D. C. 46; Randall, A. J. 31(3); Sheffield, J. 11; Smith, C. R. 22(3); Stewart, I. 40(3); Wignall, S. L. 37(1); Williams, J. S. J. 27(1).
League Goals (49): Puckett 18 (7 pens), Claridge 10, Henry 5, Burvill 3, Baker 2, Brown 2, Phillips 2, Randall 2, Anderson 1, Banton 1, Coombs 1, Wignall 1, Williams 1.
Littlewoods Cup (6): Puckett 3 (1 pen), Coyne 1, Henry 1, own goal 1.
FA Cup (0).
Ground: Recreation Ground, High St., Aldershot GU11 1TW (0252–20211)
Nearest Station: Aldershot
Manager: Len Walker **Secretary:** Jon Pollard
Colours: Plain red shirts with blue trim; blue shorts
Record home gate: 19,138 v Carlisle, January 1970 (FA Cup)
Honours: Nil

ARSENAL DIV. 1

Adams, Tony A.
Ampadu, Kwame.
Bould, Stephen A.
Caesar, Gus C.
Campbell, Kevin J.
Carstairs, James
Cole, Andrew A.
Davis, Paul V.
Dixon, Lee M.
Groves, Perry
Hartfield, Charles J.
Hayes, Martin
Heaney, Neil A.
Hillier, David
Jonsson, Sigurdur
Lukic, Jovan
KcKeown, Gary J.
McKernon, Craig A.
Marwood, Brian
Merson, Paul C.
Miller, Alan J.
Morrow, Stephen J.
O'Leary, David A.
Pates, Colin G.
Richardson, Kevin
Rocastle, David
Scully, Patrick J.
Seaman, David A.
Smith, Alan M.
Thomas, Michael L.
Winterburn, Nigel

League Appearances: Adams, T. A. 38; Ampadu, K. –(2); Bould, S. A. 19; Caesar, G. C. –(3); Campbell, K. J. 8(7); Davis, P. V. 8(3); Dixon, L. M. 38; Groves, P. 20(10); Hayes, M. 8(4); Jonsson, S. –(6); Lukic, J. 38; Marwood, B. 17; Merson, P. C. 21(8); O'Leary, D.A. 28(6); Pates, C. G. 1(1); Quinn, N. J. 6; Richardson, K. 32(1); Rocastle, D. 28(5); Smith, A. M. 37(1); Thomas, M. L. 35(1); Winterburn, N. 36.
League Goals (54): Smith 10, Merson 7, Marwood 6 (1 pen), Adams 5, Dixon

5 (3 pens), Thomas 5, Groves 4, Hayes 3, Campbell 2, Quinn 2, Rocastle 2, Davis 1, Jonsson 1, O'Leary 1.
Littlewoods Cup (10): Smith 3, Thomas 3, Groves 1, Quinn 1, own goals 2.
FA Cup (1): Quinn 1.
Ground: Arsenal Stadium, Avenell Road, N5 1BU (071–226 0304)
Nearest Stations: Arsenal (Piccadilly Line), Drayton Park (British Rail) or Finsbury Park (BR, Piccadilly Line or Victoria Line)
Manager: George Graham **Secretary:** Ken Friar
Colours: Red shirts, with white sleeves; white shorts
Record home gate: 73,295 v Sunderland, March 1935 (League)
Honours – Champions: Division 1: 1930–1, 1932–3, 1933–4, 1934–5, 1937–8, 1947–8, 1952–3, 1970–71, 1988–9
FA Cup winners: 1929–30, 1935–6, 1949–50, 1970–71, 1978–9
League Cup winners: 1986–7
Fairs Cup winners: 1963–64, 1969–70

ASTON VILLA DIV. 1

Birch, Paul
Blake, Mark A.
Butler, Lee S.
Callaghan, Nigel
Cascarino, Tony G.
Comyn, Andrew J.
Cowans, Gordon S.
Daley, Anthony M.
Duffey, Darrel G.
Gage, Kevin W.
Gallacher, Bernard
Gray, Stuart
Jones, David
McGrath, Paul
Mountfield, Derek N.
Nielson, Kent
Olney, Ian D.
Ormondroyd, Ian
Parrott, Mark A.
Platt, David
Price, Christopher J.
Spink, Nigel P.
Williams, Gareth J.
Yorke, Dwight

League Appearances: Birch, P. 6(6); Blake, M. A. 6(3); Callaghan, N. 7(1); Cascarino, T. G. 10; Comyn, A. J. 3(1); Cowans, G. S. 34; Daley, A. M. 31(1); Gage, K. W. 22; Gallacher, B. 6(1); Gray, S. 26(3); Heath, A. P. 8(1); McGrath, P. 35; Mountfield, D. N. 32; Nielsen, K. 34(2); Olney, I. D. 27(8); Ormondroyd, I. 19(6); Platt, D. 37; Price, C. J. 33(1); Spink, N. P. 38; Williams, G. J. 4(6); Yorke, D. –(2).
League Goals (57): Platt 19 (1 pen), Olney 9, Daley 6, Cowans 4, Mountfield 4, Ormondroyd 4, Gage 3, Cascarino 2, Nielsen 2, McGrath 1, Price 1, own goals 2.
Littlewoods Cup (3): Gray 1, Mountfield 1, Platt 1.
FA Cup (13): Birch 2, Daley 2, Gray 2, Olney 2, Ormondroyd 2, Mountfield 1, Platt 1, own goal 1.
Ground: Villa Park, Birmingham B6 6HE (021–327 6604)
Nearest Station: Witton and Aston
Manager: Graham Taylor **Secretary:** Steven Stride
Colours: Claret and blue shirts; white shorts
Record home gate: 76,588 v Derby, March 1946 (FA Cup)
Honours – Champions: Division 1: 1893–4, 1895–6, 1896–7, 1898–9. 1899–1900, 1909–10, 1980–81; Division 2: 1937–8, 1959–60; Division 3: 1971–2
FA Cup winners: 1886–7, 1894–5, 1896–7, 1904–5, 1912–13, 1919–20, 1956–7. (Seven wins joint record with Spurs and Manchester U)
League Cup winners: 1960–61, 1974–5, 1976–7
European Cup winners: 1981–2
Super Cup Winners: 1982–3

BARNSLEY DIV. 2

Agnew, Stephen M.
Archdeacon, Owen D.
Baker, Clive E.
Banks, Ian F.
Cooper, Stephen B.
Cross, Paul
Deehan, John M.
Dobbin, James
Dunphy, Sean
Fleming, Gary J.
Futcher, Paul
Joyce, Joseph P.
Lowndes, Stephen R.
McCord, Brian J.
McGugan, Paul J.
Marshall, Colin
O'Connell, Brendan J.
Robinson, Mark J.
Saville, Andrew V.
Smith, Mark C.
Taggart, Gerald P.
Tiler, Carl
Wardle, Ian S.
Whitehead, Philip M.

League Appearances: Agnew, S. M. 46; Archdeacon, O. D. 17(4); Baker, C. E. 37; Banks, I. F. 33(4); Broddle, J. R. 20; Cooper, S. B. 26(4); Cross, P. 35(1); Currie, D. N. 24; Dobbin, J. 28; Dunphy, S. 5(1); Fleming, G. J. 12; Foreman, D. 11(6); Futcher, P. 28(1); Glover, E. L. 8; Gray, P. 3; Lowndes, S. R. 20(4); McCord, B. J. 16; McDonald, J. 3(1); Marshall, C. –(2); O'Connell, B. J. 2(9); Robinson, M. J. 18(6); Saville, A. V. 12(3); Shotton, M. 29; Smith M. C. 25; Taggart, G. P. 20(1); Thomas, D. G. 1(2); Tiler, C. 18(3); Wardle, I. S. 9.
League Goals (49): Agnew 8 (2 pens), Currie 7 (1 pen), Cooper 5, Lowndes 4, Archdeacon 3, Banks 3, Foreman 3, Saville 3, Smith 3, O'Connell 2, Taggart 2, Dobbin 1, McCord 1, McDonald 1, Shotton 1, Tiler 1, own goal 1.
Littlewoods Cup (2): Archdeacon 1, own goal 1.
FA Cup (6): Cooper 2, Currie 1, Lowndes 1, Smith 1, Taggart 1.
Ground: Oakwell, Grove Street, Barnsley S71 1ET (0226–295353)
Nearest Station: Barnsley
Manager: Mel Machin **Secretary:** Michael Spinks
Colours: Red shirts white trim; white shorts
Record home gate: 40,255 v Stoke 1936 (FA Cup)
Honours – Champions: Division 3 North: 1933–4, 1938–9, 1954–5
FA Cup winners: 1911–12

BIRMINGHAM CITY DIV. 3

Ashley, Kevin M.
Atkins, Ian L.
Bailey, Dennis
Bell, Douglas G.
Burton, Michael J.
Clarkson, Ian S.
Deakin, John
Fox, Matthew C.
Frain, John W.
Gleghorn, Nigel W.
Gordin, Colin K.
Harris, Andrew
Hopkins, Robert A.
Langley, Kevin J.
Masefield, Paul D.
Matthewson, Trevor
Overson, Vincent D.
Peer, Dean
Sproson, Philip J.
Sturridge, Simon A.
Tait, Paul R.
Thomas, Martin R.
Yates, Mark J.

League Appearances: Ashley, K. M. 31; Atkins, I. L. 45; Bailey, D. 40(3); Bell, D. G. 14(1); Clarkson, I. S. 15(5); Deakin, J. 3(4); Frain, J. W. 36(2); Gleghorn, N. W. 43; Gordon, C. K. 14(7); Hansbury, R. 1; Harris, A. –(1); Hopkins, R. A. 16(2); Langley, K. J. 33; Madden, D. J. 5; Matthewson, T. 46; Overson, V. D. 27(3); Peer, D. 22(5); Roberts, B. L. F. 9(1); Rutherford, M. R. –(2); Sproson, P. J. 12; Sturridge, S. A. 30(1); Tait, P. R. 7(7); Thomas, M. R. 42; Williams, D. 3; Yates, M. J. 12(8).
League Goals (60): Bailey 18 (5 pens), Sturridge 10, Gleghorn 9, Hopkins 6, Gordon 3, Peer 3, Atkins 2 (1 pen), Tait 2, Yates 2, Ashley 1, Frain 1, Madden 1, Matthewson 1, own goal 1.
Littlewoods Cup (5): Atkins 2, Bailey 2, Sproson 1.
FA Cup (4): Gleghorn 3, Sturridge 1.
Ground: St Andrews, Birmingham B9 4NH (021–772 0101 and 2689)
Nearest Station: Birmingham, New Street

Manager: Dave Mackay **Secretary:** H.J. Westmancoat FFA, MBIM.
Colours: Blue shirts with white trim; white shorts
Record home gate: 66,844 v Everton, February 1939 (FA Cup)
Honours – Champions: Division 2: 1892–3, 1920–21, 1947–8, 1954–5
League Cup winners: 1962–3

BLACKBURN ROVERS DIV. 2

Atkins, Mark M.
Collier, Darren
Finnigan, Anthony
Garner, Simon
Gayle, Howard A.
Gennoe, Terence W.
Hill, Keith J.
Irvine, James A.
Johnrose, Leonard
Kennedy, Andrew J.
Mail, David
May, David
Millar, John
Moran, Kevin B
Oliver, Neil
Reid, Nicholas A.
Sellars, Scott
Shepstone, Paul T.A
Skinner, Craig R.
Stapleton, Francis A.
Sulley, Christopher S.
Wilcox, Jason M.

League Appearances: Atkins, M. N. 41; Collier, D. 16; Dawson, A. J. (3); Finnigan, A. 8(11); Garner, S. 42(1); Gayle, H. A. 19(11); Gennoe, T. W. 28; Hendry, E. C. J. 5(2); Hildersley, R. 2(3); Hill, K. J. 25; Irvine, J. A. 13(12); Johnrose, L. 4(4); Kennedy, A. J. 26(8); Mail, D. 25; Marriott, A. 2; May, D. 17; Millar, J. 38(1); Moran, K. B. 19; Oliver, N. 3; Reid, N. S. 42; Sellars, S. 43; Stapleton, F. A. 42(1); Sulley, C. S. 36; Wilcox, J. M. 1.
League Goals (74): Garner 18, Sellars 14, Kennedy 13 (4 pens), Atkins 7 (1 pen), Gayle 5 (1 pen), Reid 4, Johnrose 3, Stapleton 3, Mail 2 (2 pens), Moran 2, Irvine 1, Millar 1, own goal 1.
Littlewoods Cup (2): Atkins 2.
FA Cup (3): Kennedy 1, Sellars 1, Stapleton 1.
Ground: Ewood Park, Nuttall Street, Blackburn BB2 4JF (0254–5432)
Nearest Station: Blackburn
Manager: Donald Mackay **Secretary:** John W. Howarth F.A.A.I.
Colours: Blue and white halved shirts; white shorts
Record home gate: 61,783 v Bolton Wanderers, March 1929 (FA Cup)
Honours – Champions: Division 1: 1911–12, 1913–14; Division 2: 1938–9; Division 3: 1974–5
FA Cup winners: 1883–4, 1884–5, 1885–6, 1889–90, 1980–91, 1927–8
Full Members' Cup winners: 1986–7

BLACKPOOL DIV. 4

Bradshaw, Mark
Briggs, Gary
Brook, Gary
Burgess, David J.
Costa, George
Coughlin, Russell
Davies, Michael J.
Diamond, Anthony J.
Elliott, Shaun
Eyres, David
Garner, Andrew
Gayle, Mark S. R.
Gore, Ian G.
Groves, Paul
Hawkins, Nigel S.
McIlhargey, Stephen
Matthews, Neil P.
Methven, Colin J.
Morgan, Stephen A.
Owen, Gordon
Richards, Carroll L.
Taylor, Peter M. R.
Wright, Alan G.

League Appearances: Bartram, V. L. 9; Bradshaw, M. 17(4); Briggs, G. 17; Brook, G. 23(2); Burgess, D. J. 19; Coughlin, R. 34(1); Davies, M. J. 14(9); Diamond, A. J. 2(1); Elliott, S. 25(1); Eyres, D. 30(5); Gabbiadini, R. 5; Garner, A. 45(1); Gore, I. G. 34; Gouck, A. S. 6(2); Groves, P. 18(1); Hawkins, N. S. 4(3); Jones, P. A. 6; McIlhargey, S. 22; Madden, C. A. (2); Matthews, N. P. 8(4); Methven, C. J. 44(1); Morgan, S. A. 36(2); Owen, G. 21(7); Rich-

ards, C. L. 16; Sinclair, T. L. 5(4); Thompson, C. D. 2(1); Wood, G. 15; Wright, A. G. 20(4).
League Goals (49): Garner 8 (6 pens), Eyres 7, Brook 6, Madden 4 (1 pen), Owen 4, Richards 4, Gabbiadini 3, Methven 3, Briggs 2, Bradshaw 1, Burgess 1, Coughlin 1, Diamond 1, Gouck 1, Groves 1, Morgan 1, own goal 1.
Littlewoods Cup (5): Briggs 2, Bradshaw 1, Gabbiadini 1, Garner 1.
FA Cup (9): Eyres 2, Owen 2, Brook 1, Burgess 1, Garner 1, Groves 1, Methven 1.
Ground: Bloomfield Road, Blackpool FY1 6JJ (0253–404331)
Nearest Station: Blackpool North
Manager: Graham Carr **Secretary:** D. Johnson
Colours: Tangerine shirts with white collar and cuffs; tangerine shorts
Record home gate: 38,098 v Wolves, September 1955 (League)
Honours – Champions: Division 2: 1929–30
FA Cup winners: 1952–3
Anglo–Italian Cup winners: 1970–1

BOLTON WANDERERS DIV. 3

Brown, Gary M.
Brown, Philip
Came, Mark R.
Comstive, Paul T.
Cowdrill, Barry J.
Crombie, Dean M.
Darby, Julian T.
Felgate, David W.
Fisher, Neil J.
Gray, Gareth
Green, Scott P.
Gregory, John C.
Henshaw, Gary
Hughes, Paul
Jeffrey, Michael R.
Neal, Philip G.
Oliver, Darren
Philliskirk, Anthony
Reeves, David
Rose, Kevin P.
Savage, Robert J.
Spooner, Nicholas
Stevens, Ian D.
Storer, Stuart J.
Thompson, Stephen J.
Winstanley, Mark A.

League Appearances: Brookman, N. A. –(2); Brown, P. 46; Came, M. R. 15(4); Chandler, J. G. –(1); Comstive, P. T. 30(1); Cowdrill, B. J. 43(1); Crombie, D. M. 36(2); Darby, J. T. 46; Felgate, D. W. 40; Green, S. P. 4(1); Gregory, J. C. 2(5); Henshaw, G. 9(5); Hughes, P. 1(1); Jeffrey, M. R. 1(3); Philliskirk, A. 45; Pike, M. R. 5; Reeves, D. 41; Rose, K. P. 6; Savage, R. J. 7(3); Stevens, I. D. 3(1); Storer, S. J. 38; Thompson, S. J. 45; Winstanley, M. A. 43.
League Goals (59): Philliskirk 18 (4 pens), Darby 10, Reeves 10, Thompson 6, Storer 4, Cowdrill 3, Green 2, Brown 1, Comstive 1, Crombie 1, Pike 1, Winstanley 1, own goal 1.
Littlewoods Cup (15): Philliskirk 5 (1 pen), Came 2, Brown 1, Comstive 1, Cowdrill 1, Darby 1, Henshaw 1, Reeves 1, Savage 1, Thompson 1 (pen).
FA Cup (1): Crombie 1.
Ground: Burnden Park, Manchester Rd., Bolton BL3 2QR (0204–389200)
Nearest Station: Bolton
Player/Manager: Phil Neal **Secretary:** Des McBain, F.A.A.I.
Colours: White shirts; navy blue shorts
Record home gate: 69,912 v Manchester City, February 1933 (FA Cup)
Honours – Champions: Division 2: 1908–9, 1977–8; Division 3: 1972–3
FA Cup winners: 1922–3, 1925–6, 1928–9, 1957–8
Associate Members Cup winners: 1988–9

AFC BOURNEMOUTH DIV. 3

Aylott, Trevor K. C.
Blissett, Luther L.
Bond, Kevin J.
Brooks, Shaun
Coleman, David H.
Ekoka, Efan
Holmes, Matthew J.
Kite, Philip D.
Lawrence, George R.
Miller, Paul R.
Mitchell, Paul R.
Morrell, Paul D. P.
Mundee, Denny W. J.
O'Driscoll, Sean M.
Peacock, Gavin K.
Peyton, Gerald J.
Rowland, Keith
Shearer, Peter A.
Teale, Shaun
Williams, William J.

League Appearances: Aylott, T. K. C. 10(8); Barnes, D. O. 1(3); Blissett, L. L. 46; Bond, K. J. 27(4); Brooks, S. 34(1); Cadette, R. 4(4); Coleman, D. H. 25(2); Holmes, M. J. 20(2); Kite, P. D. 7; Lawrence, G. R. 28(5); Miller, P. R. 29(2); Morrell, P. D. P. 21; Moulden, P. A. 32; Mundee, D. W. J. 8(2); Newson, M. J. 11(5); O'Connor, M. A. 5(1); O'Driscoll, S. M. 37(2); Peacock, G. K. 41; Peyton, G. J. 39; Redknapp, J. F. 1(3); Shearer, P. A. 27(7); Slatter, N. 5(1); Teale, S. 34; Williams, W. J. 14(2).
League Goals (57): Blissett 18 (3 pens), Moulden 13, Brooks 4, Peacock 4, Shearer 4, Lawrence 3, Aylott 2, Holmes 2,
Williams 2, Cadette 1, Coleman 1, Newson 1, own goals 2.
Littlewoods Cup (2): Moulden 1, Shearer 1.
FA Cup (0).
Ground: Dean Court, Bournemouth, Dorset BH7 7AF (0202–395381)
Nearest Station: Bournemouth
Manager: Harry Redknapp **Secretary:**
Colours: All red
Record home gate: 28,799 v Manchester United, March 1957 (FA Cup)
Honours – Champions: Division 3: 1986–7
Associate Members Cup winners: 1983–4

BRADFORD CITY DIV. 3

Abbott, Gregory S.
Adcock, Anthony C.
Aizlewood, Mark
Campbell, David A.
Costello, Peter
Davies, Alan
Duxbury, Lee E.
Ellis, Mark E.
Evans, David G.
Evans, Mark
Goddard, Karl
Graham, James
Jackson, Peter A.
Jewell, Paul
Lee, Christopher
Leonard, Mark A.
McCall, Ian
McHugh, Michael B.
Megson, Kevin C.
Mitchell, Charles B.
Oliver, Gavin R.
Pattison, Martin
Sinnott, Lee
Taylor, Craig
Timion, Brian
Tomlinson, Paul
Woods, Neil
Wroe, Derek

League Appearances: Abbott, G. S. 35; Adcock, A. C. 25(3); Aizlewood, M. 39; Campbell, D. A. 15(8); Chapman, G. A. 1(2); Costello, P. 8(4); Davies, A. 24(2); Duxbury, L. E. 9(3); Ellis, M. E. 3(3); Evans, D. G. 24; Evans, M. 5; Goddard, K. –(1); Graham, J. 6; Jackson, P. A. 25(1); Jewell, P. 20(10); Lawford, C. B. –(1); Leonard, M. A. 18(6); McCall, I. 11(1); Megson, K. C. 21(2); Mitchell, C. B. 32(3); Morgan, D. 2; Oliver, G. R. 19(3); Quinn, J. M. 23; Sinnott, L. 45; Tinnion, B. 37; Tomlinson, P. 41; Wharton, K. 5; Woods, N. 13(1).
League Goals (44): Quinn 6, Adcock 5, Leonard 5, Tinnion 5 (2 pens), Jewell 4, Abbott 3, Campbell 3, Jackson 2, Mitchell 2, Sinnott 2, Woods 2, Aizlewood 1, Davies 1, Duxbury 1, McCall 1, own goal 1.
Littlewoods Cup (6): Leonard 2, Abbott 1, Jewell 1, Megson 1, Quinn 1.
FA Cup (1): Tinnion 1 (pen).
Ground: Valley Parade, Bradford BD8 7DY (0274–306062)

Nearest Station: Bradford Exchange
Manager: John Docherty **Secretary:** T.F. Newman
Colours: Claret and amber striped shirts; black shorts
Record home gate: 39,146 v Burnley, March 1911 (FA Cup)
Honours – Champions: Division 2: 1907–8; Division 3: 1984–5; Division 3 North: 1928–9
FA Cup winners: 1910–11 (first holders of present trophy)

BRENTFORD DIV. 3

Bates, Jamie
Birch, Paul A.
Blissett, Gary D.
Buckle, Paul J.
Buttigieg, John
Cadette, Richard R.
Cockram, Allan C.
Cousins, Jason
Driscoll, Andrew
Evans, Terence W.
Fleming, Mark J.
Gayle, Marcus A.
Godfrey, Kevin
Holdsworth, Dean C.
Jones, Keith A.
May, Edward
Millen, Keith
Parks, Anthony
Peters, Robert A. G.
Ratcliffe, Simon
Smillie, Neil
Stanislaus, Roger E. P.

League Appearances: Ansah, A. –(1); Bates, J. 10(5); Bayes, A. J. 1; Blissett, G. D. 36(1); Branagan, K. G. 2; Buckle, P. J. 6(4); Buttigieg, J. 12(10); Cadette, R. R. 7(9); Cockram, A. C. 21(5); Cousins, J. 12(1); Driscoll, A. 10(2); Evans, T. W. 44; Fleming, M. J. 15(2); Gayle, M. A. 1(8); Godfrey, K. 16(11); Haag, K. J. 1(4); Holdsworth, D. C. 39; Jones, K. A. 42; May, E. 30; Millen, K. 32; Miller, P. R. 3; Moncur, J. F. 5; Parks, A. 37; Perryman, S. J. 3; Peters, R. A. G. 1(1); Ratcliffe, S. 35; Scott, C. 6; Smillie, N. 43; Sparham, S. 5; Stanislaus, R. E. P. 31.
League Goals (66): Holdsworth 24 (2 pens), Blissett 11, May 8, Smillie 5, Evans 3, Cockram 2, Driscoll 2, Godfrey 2, Jones 2, Ratcliffe 2, Cadette 1, Moncur 1, Sparham 1, Stanislaus 1, own goal 1.
Littlewoods Cup (7): Blissett 2, May 2, Evans 1, Godfrey 1, Millen 1.
FA Cup (0).
Ground: Griffin Park, Breamar Road, Brentford TW8 0NT (081–847 2511)
Nearest Station: Brentford (BR) or South Ealing (Piccadilly Line)
Manager: Steve Perryman **Secretary:** Polly Kates
Colours: Red and white striped shirts; black shorts
Record home gate: 39,626 v Preston North End, March 1938 (FA Cup)
Honours – Champions: Division 2: 1934–5; Division 3 South: 1932–3; Division 4: 1962–3

BRIGHTON & HOVE ALBION DIV. 2

Barham, Mark F.
Bissett, Nicholas
Bremner, Kevin J.
Chapman, Ian R.
Chivers, Gary P. S.
Codner, Robert A. G.
Crumplin, John L,.
Curbishley, Llewellyn C.
Digweed, Perry M.
Dublin, Keith B. L.
Gatting, Steven P.
Isaac, Robert C.
Keeley, John H.
McCarthy, Paul J.
McGrath, Derek B. J.
McKenna, Brian F. J.
Nelson, Garry P.
Owers, Adrian R.
Penney, Steven A.
Robinson, John R. C.
Stemp, Wayne D.
Wilkins, Dean M.

League Appearances: Barham, M. F. 16(1); Bissett, N. 28(1); Bremner, K. J. 42(1); Chapman, I. R. 41(1); Chivers, G. P. S. 41; Codner, R. A. G. 45; Crumplin, J. L. 14(11); Curbishley, L. C. 45; Digweed, P. M. 11; Dublin, K. B. L. 43; Edwards, A. M. 1; Gabbiadini, R. –(1); Gatting, S. P. 19; Gotsmanov, S. A. 14(2); Keeley, J. H. 35; Lambert, M. C. –(1); McCarthy, P. J. 2(1); McGrath,

D. B. J. 1; Nelson, G. P. 32(1); Owers, A. R. –(4); Robinson, J. R. C. 4(1); Stemp, W. D. 2; Wilkins, D. M. 46; Wood, P. A. 24(2).
League Goals (56): Bremner 13, Codner 9, Wilkins 6, Blissett 5, Nelson 5, Gotsmanov 4, Chivers 3, Wood 3, Barham 2, Crumplin 2, Curbishley 1, own goals 3.
Littlewoods Cup (1): Wilkins 1.
FA Cup (5): Barham 1, Codner 1, Curbishley 1, Dublin 1, Nelson 1.
Ground: Goldstone Ground, Old Shoreham Road, Hove, Sussex BN3 7DE (0273–739535)
Nearest Station: Hove
Manager: Barry Lloyd **Secretary:** Steve Rooke
Colours: Blue and white striped shirts; white shorts
Record home gate: 36,747 v Fulham, December 1958 (League)
Honours – Champions: Division 3 South: 1957–8; Division 4: 1964–5

BRISTOL CITY — DIV. 2

Bailey, John A.
Bent, Junior A.
Bromage, Russel
Bryant, Matthew
Eaton, Jason C.
Gavin, Mark W.
Honor, Christian R.
Humphreys, Glen
Leaning, Andrew J.
Llewellyn, Andrew
McQuilter, Ronald
Mardon, Paul J.
Melon, Michael
Morgan, Nicholas
Newman, Robert N.
Pender, John P.
Rennie, David
Shelton, Gary
Sinclair, Ronald M.
Smith, David A.
Taylor, Robert
Toshack, Jon C.
Turner, Robert P.

League Appearances: Bailey, J. A. 38; Bent, J. A. –(1); Bromage, R. 3; Eaton, J. C. 6(5); Ferguson, I. J. H. 8(3); Gavin, M. W. 36(4); Honor, C. R, 4(10); Horrix, D. V. 3; Humphries, G. 36(1); Jones, A. M. 2(2); Jordan, J. –(1); Leaning, A. J. 19; Llewellyn, A. 46; Mardon, P. J. 2(5); Melon, M. 7(2); Miller, P. A. –(3); Morgan, N. 7; Newman, R. N. 46; Pender, J. P. 10; Rennie, D. 45; Shelton, G. 43; Sinclair, R. M. 27; Smith, D. A. 45; Taylor, R. 37; Turner, R. P. 26(7); Wimbleton, P. P. 10(6).
League Goals (76): Taylor 27, Shelton 9, Newman 8, Turner 6, Morgan 4, Rennie 4, Smith 4 (1 pen), Gavin 3 (2 pens), Ferguson 2, Wimbleton 2 (2 pens), Bailey 1, Eaton 1, Honor 1, Jones 1, own goals 3.
Littlewoods Cup (4): Taylor 2, Smith 1, Wimbleton 1 (pen).
FA Cup (11): Taylor 5, Turner 3, Gavin 1, Newman 1, Wimbleton 1 (pen).
Ground: Ashton Gate, Bristol BS3 2EJ (0272–632812)
Nearest Station: Bristol Temple Meads
Manager: Joe Jordan **Secretary:** Jean Harris
Colours: Red shirts; white shorts
Record home gate: 43,335 v Preston North End, February 1935 (FA Cup)
Honours – Champions: Division 2: 1905–6; Division 3 South: 1922–3, 1926–7, 1954–5
Associate Members Cup winners: 1985–6

BRISTOL ROVERS — DIV. 2

Alexander, Ian
Bloomer, Robert
Browning, Marcus T.
Clark, William R.
Hazel, Ian
Holloway, Ian S.
Jones, Vaughan
McClean, Christian A.
Mehew, David S.
Nixon, Paul
Parkin, Brian
Purnell, Phillip
Reece, Andrew J.
Saunders, Carl S.
Sealey, Anthony J.
Twentyman, Geoffrey
White, Devon W.
Willmott, Ian M.
Yates, Steven

League Appearances: Alexander, I. 43; Browning, M. T. –(1); Byrne, D. S. –(2); Cawley, P. 1(2); Hazel, I. 2(6); Holloway, I. S. 46; Jones, V. 46; McClean, C. A. 10(5); Martyn, A. N. 16; Mehew, D. S. 46; Nixon, P. 21(6); Parkin, B. 30; Penrice, G. K. 12; Purnell, P. 17(5); Reece, A. J. 43; Saunders, C. S. 19(1); Sealy, A. J. 12(7); Twentyman, G. 46; White, D. W. 40(3); Willmott, I. M. 14(3); Yates, S. 42.
League Goals (71): Mehew 18, White 12, Holloway 8 (5 pens), Nixon 5, Saunders 5, McClean 4, Penrice 3, Sealy 3, Twentyman 3, Jones 2, Purnell 2, Reece 2, Alexander 1, own goals 3.
Littlewoods Cup (1): Penrice 1.
FA Cup (2): Mehew 1, Reece 1.
Ground: Twerton Park, Bath, Avon BA2 1DB (0272–352508)
Nearest Station: Bath Spa
Manager: Gerry Francis **Secretary:** R.C. Twyford
Colours: Blue and white quartered shirts; white shorts
Record home gate: 38,472 v Preston North End, January 1960 (FA Cup)
Honours – Champions: Division 3 South: 1952–3

BURNLEY DIV. 4

Davis, Steven P.
Deakin, Raymond J.
Deary, John S.
Eli, Roger
Farrell, Andrew J.
Francis, John A.
Futcher, Ronald
Grewcock, Neil
Hardy, Jason P.
Jakub, Yanek
Lawrie, Graham
McKay, Paul W.
Measham, Ian
Monington, Mark D.
Mumby, Peter
Pearce, Christopher L.
Smith, Nigel P.
White, Eric W.
Williams, David P.

League Appearances: Atkinson, P. G. 5(3); Bent, J. A. 7(2); Buckley, N. A. 5; Davis, S. M. 7(2); Davis, S. P. 31; Deakin, R. J. 32(1); Deary, J. S. 39(2); Eli, R. 24(5); Farrell, A. J. 36; Francis, J. A. 18(1); Futcher, R. 22(1); Gardner, S. G. 8(1); Grewcock, N. 4(3); Hancock, A. E. 9(8); Hardy, J. P. 20(2); Harris, M. A. 4; Howarth, N. –(1); Jakub, Y. 46; McGrory, S. P. 6(5); McKay, P. W. 8(4); Measham, I. 35; Monington, M. D. 13; Mumby, P. 20(5); O'Connell, B. 20(1); Pearce, C. L. 39; Rowell, G. –(1); Smith, N. P. 4(7); White, E. W. 37(3); Williams, D. P. 7.
League Goals (45): Futcher 7 (2 pens), White 7 (5 pens), Jakub 5, Francis 4, Mumby 4, O'Connell 4, Bent 3, Deary 2, Farrell 2, Grewcock 2, Davis S 1, own goals 4.
Littlewoods Cup (2): Mumby 1, White 1.
FA Cup (11): Eli 3, Futcher 3, Deary 1, Hardy 1, Mumby 1, O'Connell 1, White 1 (pen).
Ground: Turf Moor, Brunshaw Road, Burnley BB10 4BX (0282–27777)
Nearest Station: Burnley Central
Manager: Frank Casper **Secretary:** Albert Maddox
Colours: Claret shirts; white shorts
Record home gate: 54,775 v Huddersfield, February 1924 (FA Cup)
Honours – Champions: Division 1: 1920–21, 1959–60; Division 2: 1897–8, 1972–3; Division 3: 1981–2
FA Cup winners: 1913–14

BURY DIV. 3

Atkin, Paul A.
Bishop, Charles
Clements, Kenneth H.
Cunningham, Anthony
Davison, Aidan J.
Dunn, Shaun
Feeley, Andrew J.
Hill, Andrew
Hoyland, Jamie W.
Hulme, Kevin
Kelly, Gary A.
Knill, Alan R.
Lee, David
Parkinson, Philip J.
Patterson, Mark A.
Price, Gareth
Robinson, Spencer L.
Simms, Mark W.
Valentine, Peter
Walsh, Michael
Withe, Christopher

League Appearances: Atkin, P. A. 6(3); Beresford, M. 1; Bishop, C. 29(1); Clements, K. H. 14(14); Cunningham, A. 25; Farnworth, S. 7; Feeley, A. J. 26(4); Greenall, C. A. 3; Greenwood, N. P. 13(7); Hill, A. 46; Hoyland, J. W. 46; Hulme, K. 9(10); Kelly, G. A. 38; Knill, A. R. 43; Lee, D. 45; McIlroy, S. B. 7(5); Parkinson, P. J. 19(3); Patterson, M. A. 20; Price, G. –(1); Robinson, S. L. 43(2); Spink, D. P. 6; Valentine, P. 38; Withe, C. 22(9).
League Goals (70): Robinson 17 (5 pens), Hoyland 16 (2 pens), Cunningham 8 (1 pen), Lee 8, Greenwood 5, Patterson 4 (1 pen), Feeley 2, Hill 2, Parkinson 2, Atkin 1, Bishop 1, Hulme 1, Knill 1, Spink 1, Withe 1.
Littlewoods Cup (1): Robinson 1.
FA Cup (1): Bishop 1.
Ground: Gigg Lane, Bury BL9 9HR (061–764 4881/2)
Nearest Station: Bury Metro Interchange
Manager: Sam Ellis **Secretary:** John Heap
Colours: White shirts; navy blue shorts
Record home gate: 35,000 v Bolton, January 1960 (FA Cup)
Honours – Champions: Division 2: 1894–5; Division 3: 1960–61
FA Cup winners: 1899–1900, 1902–3

CAMBRIDGE UNITED DIV. 3

Baillie, Colin J.
Chapple, Phillip R.
Cheetham, Michael M.
Claridge, Stephen E.
Clayton, Gary
Cook, Michael J.
Daish, Liam S.
Dennis, John A.
Dublin, Dion
Fensome, Andrew B.
Kimble, Alan F.
Leadbitter, Christopher
O'Shea, Daniel E.
Philpot, Lee
Ryan, Laurie J.
Taylor, John P.
Vaughan, John
Welsh, Stephen

League Appearances: Bailie, C. J. 31(5); Beck, J. A. 2; Chapple, P. R. 45; Cheetham, M. M. 36; Claridge, S. E. 15(5); Clayton, G. 8(2); Cook, M. J. 11(4); Daish, L. S. 42; Dennis, J. A. 17; Dublin, D. 37(9); Fensome, A. B. 24; Kimble, A. F. 44; Leadbitter, C. 39(4); O'Shea, D. E. 14(12); Philpott, L. 37(5); Polston, A. A. 3; Robinson, M. J. 7(9); Ryan, L. J. 3(7); Smith, R. G. 4; Taylor, J. P. 41(4); Vaughan, J. 46.
League Goals (76): Dublin 15, Taylor 15, Cheetham 10 (3 pens), Kimble 8 (7 pens), Chapple 5, Philpott 5, Claridge 4, Leadbitter 4, Dennis 2, Clayton 1, Cook 1, Daish 1, Robinson 1, Ryan 1, own goals 3.
Littlewoods Cup (6): Dublin 2, Chapple 1, Leadbitter 1, Robinson 1, Taylor 1.
FA Cup (15): Taylor 5, Dublin 4, Leadbitter 2, Philpott 2, Cheetham 1, own goal 1.
Ground: Abbey Stadium, Newmarket Road, Cambridge CB5 8LL (0223–241237)
Nearest Station: Cambridge
Manager: John Beck **Secretary:** Terry Coad
Colours: Yellow and black shirts: Yellow and black shorts
Record home gate: 14,000 v Chelsea (friendly), May 1970
Honours – Champions: Division 4: 1976–7

CARDIFF CITY — DIV. 4

Abraham, Gareth J.
Barnard, Leigh K.
Chandler, Jeffrey G.
Daniel, Raymond C.
Fry, Christopher D.
Gibbins, Roger G.
Griffiths, Cohen
Hansbury, Roger
Kelly, Mark D.
Lewis, Alan
Lynex, Stephen C.
Morgan, Jonathan P.
Perry, Jason
Pike, Christopher
Rodgerson, Ian
Ward, Gavin J.
Wood, George

League Appearances: Abraham, G. J. 34(3); Barnard, L. K. 35; Blake, N. A. 3(3); Chandler, J. G. 21(3); Curtis, A. T. 8; Daniel, R. C. 43; Fry, C. D. 3(20); Gibbins, R. G. 38; Gilligan, J. M. 7; Griffith, C. 38; Gumner, J. C. –(1); Haig, R. N. 1(3); Hansbury, R. 35; Kelly, M. D. 41; Kevan, D. J. 6(1); Lewis, A. 3(8); Love, I. J. 1(1); Lynex, S. C. 22(4); Morgan, J. P. 29(3); Perry, J. 36; Pike, C. 41; Powell, C. G. –(1); Rodgerson, I. 45; Scott, M. J. 1(8); Sendall, R. A. 3(1); Thompson, C. D. 1(1); Tupling, S. –(1); Ward, G. J. 2; Wood, G. 9; Youds, E. P. –(1).
League Goals (51): Pike 18 (3 pens), Griffith 9, Barnard 8, Rodgerson 4, Morgan 3, Lynex 2, Abraham 1, Daniel 1, Fry 1, Gibbins 1, Gilligan 1, Kelly 1, own goal 1.
Littlewoods Cup (4): Scott 3, Pike 1.
FA Cup Ground: Ninian Park, Sloper Road, Cardiff CF1 8SX (0222–398636)
Nearest Station: Cardiff Central and Queens Street
Manager: Len Ashurst **Secretary:** Eddie Harrison
Colours: Blue shirts; white shorts
Record home gate: 61,566 Wales v England, October 1961 (Club record); 57,893 v Arsenal Division 1: 22 April, 1953
Honours – Champions: Division 3 South: 1946–7
FA Cup winners: 1926–7

CARLISLE UNITED — DIV. 4

Dalziel, Ian
Edwards, Robert W.
Fitzpatrick, Paul J.
Goldsmith, Craig S. W.
Graham, Michael A.
Halpin, John
Holliday, John R.
Jeffels, Simon
Jones, Alexander
Miller, David B.
Norris, Stephen M.
Priestley, Jason A.
Proudlock, Paul
Saddington, Nigel J.
Sendall, Richard A.
Shepherd, Anthony
Walsh, Derek
Walwyn, Keith

League Appearances: Cullen, A. 2; Dalziel, I. 24; Edwards, R. W. 12; Fitzpatrick, P. J. 45; Fyfe, T. 6(7); Goldsmith, C. S. W. 21(5); Gorman, P. A. 2; Graham, M. A. 43; Halpin, J. 17; Hetherington, R. B. 1(11); Jones, A. 36; McCall, S. H. 6; McKellar, D. 35; Miller, D. B. 42; Norris, S. M. 19(5); Ogley, M. A. 4; Proudlock, P. 34(6); Robertson, J. 1; Rose, K. P. 11; Saddington, N. J. 44; Sendall, R. A. 10(9); Shepherd, A. 30(1); Walsh, D. 21(7); Walwyn, K. 39(1); Wharton, K. 1.
League Goals (61): Walwyn 11, Saddington 10 (5 pens), Proudlock 6, Fitzpatrick 4, Fyfe 4, Jones 4, Sendall 4, Miller 3, Norris 3, Walsh 3, Hetherington 2, Shepherd 2, Cullen 1, Dalziel 1, Goldsmith 1, Ogley 1, own goal 1.
Littlewoods Cup (2): Shepherd 1, Walwyn 1.
FA Cup (3): Proudlock 2, Sendall 1.
Ground: Brunton Park, Warwick Road, Carlisle CA1 1LL (0228–26237)
Nearest Station: Carlisle Citadel
Manager: Clive Middlemass **Secretary:** Miss Alison Moore
Colours: Blue shirts; white shorts

Record home gate: 27,500 v Birmingham, January 1957 (FA Cup) and v Middlesbrough, February 1970 (FA Cup)
Honours – Champions: Division 3: 1964–5

CHARLTON ATHLETIC DIV. 2

Achampong, Kenneth
Bacon, Paul D.
Bolder, Robert J.
Caton, Thomas S.
Crooks, Garth A.
Gritt, Steven J.
Humphrey, John
Jones, Andrew M.
Leaburn, Carl W.
Lee, Jason
Lee, Robert M.
McLaughlin, Joseph
MacKenzie, Steven
Minto, Scott C.
Mortimer, Paul
Peake, Andrew M.
Pitcher, Darren E. J.
Reid, Mark
Salmon, Michael B.
Tivey, Mark R.
Walsh, Colin D.
Watson, Gordon W. G.
Watts, Matthew P.
Williams, Paul A.

League Appearances: Achampong, K. 2(8); Bennett, M. R. 2(4); Bolder, R. J. 38; Caton, T. S. 23(1); Ferguson, I. J. 1; Gritt, S. J. 2; Humphrey, J. 38; Jones, A. M. 23(2); Leaburn, C. W. 8(5); Lee, J. –(1); Lee, R. M. 37; McLaughlin, J. 31; Mackenzie, S. 11(6); Minto, S. C. 20(3); Mortimer, P. 35(1); Pates, C. G. 17; Peake, A. M. 36; Reid, M. 30(1).
League Goals (31): Williams 10, Jones 5, Mortimer 5, Minto 2, Walsh 2, Bennett 1, Caton 1, Lee R. 1, MacKenzie 1, own goals 3.
Littlewoods Cup (4): Jones 2, Walsh 1, Williams 1.
FA Cup (4): Jones 2, Lee 1, Williams 1.
Ground: Selhurst Park, London SE25 6PH (01–771 6321)
Nearest Station: Selhurst, Norwood Junction and Thornton Heath
Manager: Lennie Lawrence **Secretary:** Miss Anne Payne
Colours: Red shirts; white shorts
Record home gate: 75,031 v Aston Villa, February 1938 (FA Cup)
Honours – Champions: Division 3 South: 1928–9, 1934–5
FA Cup winners: 1946–7

CHELSEA DIV. 1

Beasant, David J.
Bumstead, John
Burley, Craig W.
Clarke, Stephen
Cundy, Jason V.
Davies, Roy M.
Dickens, Alan W.
Dixon, Kerry M.
Dorigo, Anthony R.
Durie, Gordon S.
Freestone, Roger
Hall, Gareth D.
Hitchcock, Kevin J.
Johnson, Erland
Lee, David J.
Le Saux, Graeme P.
McAllister, Kevin
Matthew, Damian
Mitchell, David S.
Monkou, Kenneth J.
Newton, Edward J. I.
Nicholas, Peter
Roberts, Graham P.
Sinclair, Frank M.
Stuart, Graham C.
West, Colin W.
Wilson, Clive
Wilson, Kevin J.
Winters, Jason

League Appearances: Beasant, D. J. 38; Bumstead, J. 21(8); Clarke, S. 24; Dickens, A. W. 20(2); Dixon, K. M. 38; Dorigo, A. R. 35; Durie, G. S. 14(1); Hall, G. D. 13; Hazard, M. 13; Johnsen, E. 18; Lee, D. J. 23(7); Le Saux, G. P. 4(3); McAllister, K. 21(3); Matthew, D. 2; Monkou, K. J. 34; Nicholas, P. 29; Roberts, G. P. 24; Stuart, G. C. 2; Wilson, C. 12(6); Wilson, K. J. 33(4).
League Goals (58): Dixon 20, Wilson K 14, Durie 5, Clarke 3, Dorigo 3, Roberts 3 (2 pens), Bumstead 2, Dickens 1, Hall 1, Lee 1, Le Saux 1, McAllister 1, Monkou 1, Stuart 1, own goal 1.
Littlewoods Cup (3): Clarke 1, Roberts 1, Wilson K 1.

FA Cup (4): Dixon 2, Clarke 1, Wilson K 1.
Ground: Stamford Bridge, Fulham Road, London SW6 1HS (071–385 5545)
Nearest Station: Fulham Broadway (District Line)
Manager: Bobby Campbell **Secretary:** Janet Wayth
Colours: All royal blue
Record home gate: 82,905 v Arsenal, October 1935 (League)
Honours – Champions: Division 1: 1954–5; Division 2: 1983–4, 1988–9
FA Cup winners: 1969–70
League Cup winners: 1964–5
European Cup Winners Cup winners: 1970–71
Full Members Cup winners: 1985–6, 1989–90

CHESTER CITY DIV. 3

Abel, Graham
Barrow, Graham
Bennett, Gary M.
Butler, Barry
Croft, Brian G. A.
Dale, Carl
Hinnigan, Joseph P.
Lane, Martin J.
Lightfoot, Christopher
Painter, Peter R.
Pugh, David
Reeves, Alan
Stewart, William I.
Woodthorpe, Colin

League Appearances: Abel, G. 41; Barrow, G. 28; Bennett, G. M. 8; Butler, B. 44; Croft, B. G. A. 41(3); Dale, C. 27(4); Danzey, M. –(2); Greer, R. 2; Hamilton, D. 26(2); Hayde, M. –(1); Hinnigan, J. P. 14(1); Hulme, K. 4; Lane, M. J. 36; Lightfoot, C. 38(2); Lundon, S. 5(6); Nassari, D. J. –(1); Newhouse, A. R. 15(3); O'Keefe, E. 1(2); Painter, P. R. 19(13); Parsley, N. 6; Pugh, D. 31(4); Reeves, A. 28(2); Senior, K. R. –(1); Stewart, W. I. 46; Woodthorpe, C. 46; Wynne, D. L. –(6).
League Goals (43): Dale 9, Abel 7 (2 pens), Butler 4, Newhouse 4 (1 pen), Painter 4, Croft 3, Pugh 3, Lundon 2, Reeves 2, Barrow 1, Bennett 1, Lightfoot 1, Woodthorpe 1, own goal 1.
Littlewoods Cup (0).
FA Cup (4): Abel 1 (pen), Butler 1, Croft 1, Painter 1.
Address: The Stadium, Sealand Road, Chester CH1 4LW (0244–371376)
Ground: Moss Rose Ground, Macclesfield
Nearest Station: Macclesfield
Manager: Harry McNally **Secretary:** R.A. Allan
Colours: Royal blue shirts; white shorts
Record home gate: 20,500 v Chelsea, January 1952 (FA Cup)
Honours: Nil

CHESTERFIELD DIV. 4

Allison, Michael
Brien, Anthony J.
Dyche, Sean M.
Gunn, Brynley C.
Hart, Nigel
Hewitt, James R.
Leonard, Michael C.
Morris, Andrew D.
Plummer, Calvin A.
Rogers, Lee J.
Rolph, Andrew J.P.
Ryan, John B.
Shaw, Adrian
Waller, David H.
Williams, Steven B.

League Appearances: Arnott, K. W. 16; Bloomer, R. 15(7); Brien, A. J. 43; Chiedozie, J. O. 5(2); Dyche, S. M. 21(1); Eley, K. 4(1); Francis, L. 2; Gunn, B. C. 46; Hart, N. 27; Hewitt, J. R. 42; Hoole, D. –(1); Hoyle, C. R. 3; Leonard, M. C. 46; Morris, A. D. 41(2); Plummer, C. A. 4; Rogers, L. J. 31(1); Rolph, A. J. P. 3(6); Ryan, J. B. 43; Shaw, A. 16(8); Slack, T. C. 2; Thompson, N. D. 9(1); Waller, D. H. 43; Williams, S. B. 4(7).
League Goals (63): Waller 16, Gunn 8 (7 pens), Plummer 8, Hewitt 6, Morris

4, Ryan 4, Arnott 3, Brien 3, Dyche 2, Hart 2, Shaw 2, Bloomer 1, Thompson 1, Williams 1, own goals 2.
Littlewoods Cup (2): Hewitt 1, Waller 1.
FA Cup (3): Gunn 1 (pen), Plummer 1, Waller 1.
Ground: Recreation Ground, Chesterfield S40 4SX (0246–209765)
Nearest Station: Chesterfield
Manager: Paul Hart **Secretary:** R.F. Pepper
Colours: Royal blue shirts; white shorts
Record home gate: 30,968 v Newcastle United, April 1939 (League)
Honours – Champions: Division 3 North: 1930–31, 1935–6; Division 4: 1969–70, 1984–5
Anglo-Scottish Cup: 1980–81

COLCHESTER UNITED GMVC

Bennett, Gary
Bruce, Marcelle E.
Collins, Eamonn
Daniels, Scott
English, Antony K.
Gilbert, William A.
Grace, John
Hicks, Stuart J.
Kinsella, Mark A.
Marmon, Neale G.
Morgan, Trevor J.
Radford, Mark
Stafford, Clive A.
Taylor, Leslie
Wilkins, Richard J.

League Appearances: Allison, I. J. R. 12(1); Ball, S. J. 3(1); Barrett, S. 13; Bennett, G. 26(10); Blake, M. C. 4; Bruce, M. E. 28(1); Collins, E. 39; Daniels, S. 46; Devereux, R. 1(1); English, A. K. 44; English, T. S. 12(1); Gilbert, W. A. 26(1); Goddard, K. E. 16; Grace, J. 19; Grainger, M. R. 4(3); Hagan, J. 2; Hansbury, R. 4; Hicks, S. J. 16(4); Kinsella, M. A. 1(5); Marmon, N. G. 22; Marriott, A. 10; Morgan, T. J. 31(1); Pollard, K. J. 1(6); Radford, M. 19(1); Restarick, S. L. J. –(1); Rooke, R. 4; Scott, R. 14(11); Stafford, C. A. 15(2); Taylor, L. 30(6); Warner, J. 1(1); Wilkins, R. J. 43.
League Goals (48): Morgan 12 (6 pens), Bennett 4 (1 pen), Marmon 4, Radford 4 (1 pen), Wilkins 4, Allinson 3 (2 pens), English T 3 (2 pens), Scott 3, Collins 2, English A 2, Grainger 2, Blake 1, Bruce 1, Goddard 1, Taylor 1, own goal 1.
Littlewoods Cup (4): Scott 2, Bennett 1, Collins 1.
FA Cup (1): Bennett 1.
Ground: Layer Road, Colchester CO2 7JJ (0206–574042)
Nearest Station: Colchester North (2 miles)
Manager: Ian Atkins. **Secretary:** Dee Elwood.
Colours: Sky blue and white striped shirts; sky blue shorts
Record home gate: 19,072 v Reading, November 1948 (FA Cup)
Honours: Nil

COVENTRY CITY DIV. 1

Billing, Peter G.
Booty, Martyn J.
Borrows, Brian
Clark, Howard, W.
Dobson, Anthony J.
Drinkell, Kevin S.
Edwards, Paul
Emerson, Dean
Gallacher, Kevin W.
Greenman, Christopher
Gynn, Michael
Harwood, Anthony
Hurst, Lee J.
Kilcline, Brian
Livingstone, Stephen
MacDonald, Kevin
McGrath, Lloyd A.
McGuire, Douglas J.
Middleton, Craig D.
Middleton, Lee J.
Ogrizovic, Steven
Peake, Trevor
Pearce, Andrew J.
Regis, Cyrille
Smith, David
Speedie, David R.
Thompson, Keith A.
Waugh, Keith

League Appearances: Bannister, G. 10(1); Billing, P. G. 16(2); Borrows, B. 37; Clark, H. W. 5(4); Dobson, A. J. 28(2); Downs, G. 16(1); Drinkell, K. S. 21(1);

Edwards, P. 6(2); Emerson, D. 12; Gallacher, K. W. 15; Gynn, M. 31(3); Kilcline, B. 11; Livingstone, S. 6(7); McGrath, L. A. 12(1); McGuire, D. J. 1(3); MacDonald, K. 19(3); Middleton, C. D. –(1); Middleton, L. J. –(2); Ogrizovic, S. 37; Peake, T. 33; Regis, C. 32(2); Smith, D. 37; Speedie, D. R. 32; Thompson, K. A. –(1); Titterton, D. S. J. –(1); Waugh, K. 1.
League Goals (39): Speedie 8, Smith 6, Drinkell 5, Regis 4, Gallacher 3, Gynn 3, Livingstone 3, Bannister 2, Borrows 1, Kilcline 1, own goals 3.
Littlewoods Cup (12): Livingstone 5, Drinkell 2, Downs 1, Kilcline 1 (pen), MacDonald 1, Regis 1, Speedie 1.
FA Cup (0).
Ground: Highfield Road Stadium, King Richard Street, Coventry CV2 4FW (0203–257171)
Nearest Station: Coventry
Manager: John Sillett **Secretary:** G.P. Hover
Colours: Sky blue and white stripes; navy blue shorts
Record home gate: 51,455 v Wolverhampton, April 1967 (League)
Honours – Champions: Division 2: 1966–7; Division 3: 1963–4; Division 3 South: 1935–6
FA Cup winners: 1986–7

CREWE ALEXANDRA DIV. 3

Callaghan, Aaron J.
Clayton, Paul S.
Curran, Christopher P.
Cutler, Christopher P.
Disley, Martin
Fishenden, Paul
Foreman, Darren
Gardiner, Mark C.
Greygoose, Dean
Gunn, Andrew C.
Hignett, Craig J.
Jasper, Dale W.
Jones, Robert
McKearnie, David
Murphy, Aiden J.
Naylor, Anthony J.
Rigby, Antony A.
Rose, Colin J.
Smart, Jason
Sussex, Andrew R.
Swain, Kenneth
Walters, Steven

League Appearances: Callaghan, A. J. 38(3); Clayton, P. S. 15(3); Curran, C. P. 1; Cutler, C. P. 24(14); Disley, M. –(1); Dyson, P. I. 30(1); Easter, G. P. –(3); Edwards, P. 8; Edwards, P. R. 27(1); Edwards, R. 1(3); Fishenden, P. 18(2); Foreman, D. 12(2); Gardiner, M. C. 24(2); Gayle, A. K. –(1); Greygoose, D. 32; Gunn, A. C. 1; Hignett, C. J. 30(5); Jasper, D. W. 39(1); Jones, R. 6(5); Joseph, F. 9(7); McKearney, D. 14(3); Murphy, A. J. 34(1); Naylor, A. J. –(2); Rees, M. J. 6; Rennie, P. 1(1); Smart, J. 40(1); Sussex, A. R. 26(7); Swain, K. 43; Walters, S. 27(3).
League Goals (56): Sussex 9 (1 pen), Hignett 8, Fishenden 6, Gardiner 6, Cutler 5, Clayton 4, Foreman 3, Murphy 3, Callaghan 2, Dyson 2, Joseph 2, Smart 2, Edwards P R 1, McKearney 1, Swain 1, Walters 1.
Littlewoods Cup (6): Gardiner 2, Clayton 1, Dyson 1, Murphy 1, Sussex 1.
FA Cup (6): Sussex 3, Cutler 1, Murphy 1 (pen), Walters 1.
Ground: Gresty Road, Crewe CW2 6EB (0270–213014)
Nearest Station: Crewe
Manager: Dario Gradi **Secretary:** Mrs G.C. Palin
Colours: Red shirts, white trim; white shorts
Record home gate: 20,000 v Tottenham, January 1960 (FA Cup)
Honours: Nil

CRYSTAL PALACE DIV. 1

Barber, Phillip A.
Bright, Mark A.
Burke, David I.
Carr, Darren
Dennis, Mark E.
Dyer, Alexander C.
Gray, Andrew A.
Hedman, Rudolph G.
Hopkins, Jeffrey
Jones, Murray L.
McGoldrick, Edward J. P.
Martyn, Antony N.
Newman, Richard A.
O'Reilly, Gary M.
Osborn, Simon E.
Pardew, Alan S.
Pemberton, John M.
Powell, Christopher G. R.
Salako, John A.
Shaw, Richard E.
Southgate, Gareth
Stevens, David K.
Suckling, Perry J.
Thomas, Geoffrey R.
Thompson, Garry
Thorn, Andrew C.
Whyte, David A.
Woodman, Andrew J.
Wright, Ian E.

League Appearances: Barber, Phillip A. 25(5); Bright, M. A. 36; Burke, D. I. 11; Dennis, M. E. 8; Dyer, A. C. 10; Gray, A. A. 35; Hedman, R. G. 8(4); Hopkins, J. 27; McGoldrick, E. J. P. 20(2); Madden, D J. 2(6); Martyn, A. N. 25; O'Reilly, G. M. 19(2); Pardew, A. S. 34(2); Parkin, B. 1; Pemberton, J. M. 34; Salako, J. A. 7(10); Shaw, R. E. 20(1); Suckling, P. J. 12; Thomas, G. R. 33(2); Thompson, G. 9; Thorn, A. C. 17; Wright, I. E. 25(1).
League Goals (42): Bright 12, Wright 8, Gray 6, Pardew 6, Hopkins 2, Salako 2, Thompson 2, Barber 1, Pemberton 1, Thomas 1, Thorn 1.
Littlewoods Cup (4): Bright 1, Hopkins 1, Thomas 1, Wright 1.
FA Cup (15): Bright 2, Gray 2 (1 pen), O'Reilly 2, Thomas 2, Wright 2, Barber 1, Hopkins 1, Pardew 1, Salako 1, own goal 1.
Ground: Selhurst Park, SE25 6PU (01–653 4462)
Nearest Station: Selhurst, Norwood Junction or Thornton Heath
Manager: Steve Coppell **Secretary:** Alan J. Leather
Colours: Red and blue shirts; red shorts
Record home gate: 51,482 v Burnley, May 1979 (League)
Honours – Champions: Division 2: 1978–9; Division 3 South: 1920–21

DARLINGTON DIV. 4

Ground: Feethams Ground, Darlington DL1 5JB (0325–465097 and 467712)
Nearest Station: Darlington
Manager: Brian Little **Secretary:** Brian Anderson
Colours: All white
Record home gate: 21,023 v Bolton, November 1960 (League Cup)
Honours – Champions: Division 3 North: 1924–5

DERBY COUNTY DIV. 1

Blades, Paul A.
Briscoe, Robert D.
Chalk, Martyn P. G.
Cross, Stephen C.
Davidson, Jonathan S.
Forsyth, Michael E.
Francis, Kevin M. D.
Gee, Phillip J.
Harford, Michael G.
Hayward, Steve L.
Hebberd, Trevor N.
Hindmarch, Robert
Kavanagh, Jason C.
McMinn, Kevin C.
Micklewhite, Gary
Patterson, Mark
Pickering, Nicholas
Ramage, Craig D.
Round, Stephen J.
Sage, Melvyn
Saunders, Dean N.
Shilton, Peter L.
Sleeuwenhoek, Kris
Straw, Robert G.
Symonds, John J.
Taylor, Martin J.
Taylor, Stephen M.
Williams, David G.
Williams, Paul D.
Wright, Mark

League Appearances: Blades, P. A. 18(1); Briscoe, R. D. 8(2); Cross, S. C. 2(6); Davidson, J. S. 4(2); Forsyth, M. E. 38; Francis, K. M. D. –(8); Gee, P. J. 4(4); Goddard, P. 18; Harford, M. G. 16; Hayward, S. L. 1(2); Hebberd, T. N. 21(2); Hindmarch, R. 26; McCord, B. J. 2(2); McMinn, K. C. 15; Micklewhite, G. 18; Patterson, M. 9; Pickering, N. 18(5); Ramage, C. D. 8(4); Sage, M. 33(1); Saunders, D. N. 38; Shilton, P. L. 35; Taylor, M. J. 3; Williams, D. G. 38; Williams, P. D. 9(1); Wright, M. 36.
League Goals (43): Saunders 11 (4 pens), Goddard 8, Wright 6, Harford 4, Hebberd 4, Pickering 3, Micklewhite 2, Briscoe 1, Gee 1, Ramage 1, Williams P 1, own goal 1.
Littlewoods Cup (12): Saunders 7 (1 pen), McMinn 3, Goddard 2.
FA Cup (3): Francis 1, Hebberd 1, Ramage 1.
Ground: The Baseball Ground, Shaftesbury Crescent, Derby DE3 8NB (0332–40105)
Nearest Station: Derby
Manager: Arthur Cox **Secretary:** M.J. Dunford
Colours: White shirts; black shorts
Record home gate: 41,826 v Tottenham, September 1969 (League)
Honours – Champions: Division 1: 1971–2, 1974–5; Division 2: 1911–12, 1914–15, 1968–9, 1986–7; Division 3 North: 1956–7
FA Cup winners: 1945–6

DONCASTER ROVERS DIV. 4

Adams, Stephen
Brevett, Rufus E.
Brockie, Vincent
Douglas, Colin F.
Gallagher, Nicholas
Harle, David
Jones Quartley, David
McKay, Mark
Morrow, Grant R.
Muir, Johnny G.
Noteman, Kevin S.
Rankine, Simon M.
Samways, Mark
Stiles, John C.
Turnbull, Lee M.

League Appearances: Adams, S. 23(7); Ashurst, J. 43; Brevett, R. E. 41(1); Brockie, V. 19(5); Cusack, D. S. 1; Cygan, P. –(1); Douglas, C. F. 45; Gallagher, N. –(1); Gaughan, S. E. 20(9); Grayson, N. 4(2); Harle, D. 10; Jones, G. 1(2); Jones-Quartey, D. 27; McGinley, J. 4(6); McKay, M. –(1); Morrow, G. 1(6); Muir, J. G. 15(1); Nicholson, M. 1(1); Noteman, K. S. 30; Raffell, S. C. 23(4); Rankine, S. M. 36; Reddish, S. –(1); Robinson, L. 32; Samways, M. 46; Stiles, J. C. 42; Sumner, J. T. 2; Turnbull, .L. M. 40(2).
League Goals (53): Jones D 12, Turnbull 10, Robinson 8 (6 pens), Muir 4, Brockie 3 (2 pens), Noteman 3, Douglas 2, Morrow 2, Rankine 2, Stiles 2, Adams 1, Gaughan 1, Grayson 1, own goals 2.
Littlewoods Cup (2): Turnbull 2.
FA Cup (1): Noteman 1.
Ground: Belle Vue Ground, Doncaster DN4 5HT (0302–539441)
Nearest Station: Doncaster
Manager: Billy Bremner **Secretary:** Mrs K.J. Oldale
Colours: White shirts with red trim; red shorts
Record home gate: 37,149 v Hull City, October 1948 (League)
Honours – Champions: Division 3 North: 1934–5, 1946–7, 1949–50; Division 4: 1965–6, 1968–9

EVERTON DIV. 1

Atteveld, Raymond
Beagrie, Peter S.
Cottee, Anthony R.
Ebbrell, John K.
Ebdon, Marcus
Jones, Philip A.
Kearton, Jason B.
Keown, Martin R.
McCall, Stuart M.
McDonald, Neil R.
Nevin, Patrick K. F.
Newell, Michael C.
Pointon, Neil G.
Powell, Gary
Quinlan, Philip E.
Ratcliffe, Kevin
Sharp, Graeme M.
Sheedy, Kevin M.
Snodin, Ian
Southall, Neville
Stowell, Michael
Watson, David
Whiteside, Norman
Wright, Mark A.
Youds, Edward P.

League Appearances: Atteveld, R. 16(2); Beagrie, P. S. 14(5); Cottee, A. R. 25(2); Ebbrell, J. K. 13(4); Keown, M. R. 19(1); McCall, S. M. 37; McDonald, N. R. 26(5); Nevin, P. K. F. 23(7); Newell, M. C. 20(6); Pointon, N. G. 19; Ratcliffe, K. 24; Rehn, J. S. 1(3); Sharp, G. M. 30(3); Sheedy, K. M. 33(4); Snodin, I. 25; Southall, N. 38; Watson, D. 28(1); Whiteside, N. 26(1); Wright, M. A. 1.
League Goals (57): Cottee 13 (1 pen), Sheedy 9 (3 pens), Whiteside 9, Newell 7, Sharp 6, Nevin 4, McCall 3, Atteveld 1, McDonald 1, Pointon 1, Watson 1, own goals 2.
Littlewoods Cup (7): Newell 3, Sheedy 2, Nevin 1, Whiteside 1.
FA Cup (8): Whiteside 3, Cottee 2, Sheedy 2 (1 pen), Sharp 1.
Ground: Goodison Park, Liverpool L4 4EL (051–521 2020)
Nearest Station: Liverpool Lime Street
Manager: Colin Harvey **Secretary:** Jim Greenwood
Colours: Royal blue shirts; white shorts
Record home gate: 78,299 v Liverpool, September 1948 (League)
Honours – Champions: Division 1: 1890–91, 1914–15, 1927–8, 1931–2, 1938–9, 1962–3, 1969–70, 1984–5, 1986–7; Division 2: 1930–31
FA Cup winners: 1905–6, 1932–3, 1965–6, 1983–4
European Cup Winners Cup winners: 1984–5

EXETER CITY DIV. 3

Bailey, Danny S.
Batty, Paul W.
Burgher, Symon G.
Cooper, Mark N.
Dryden, Richard A.
Eshelby, Paul
Harrower, Steven G.
Hiley, Scott P.
Kelly, Thomas J.
McDermott, Brian J.
McNichol, James A.
Miller, Kevin
Neville, Steven F.
Rogers, Lee
Rowbotham, Darren
Rowe, Benjamin P.
Taylor, Shaun
Walter, David W.
Whitehead, Clive R.
Young, Richard A.

League Appearances: Bailey, D. S. 46; Batty, P. W. 15(5); Benjamin, I. T. 10(2); Cooper, M. N. 1(4); Coyle, A. 1; Dryden, R. A. 30; Elkins, G. 5; Eshelby, P. 1; Frankland, T. 3(1); Goddard, K. E. –(1); Harrower, S. G. 3(4); Hiley, S. P. 45(1); Kelly, T. J. 11(1); McDermott, B. J. 38(3); McNicol, J. A. 33; McPherson, A. 11; Miller, K. 28; Neville, S. F. 42; Rogers, L. 13(3); Rowbotham, D. 31(1); Rowe, B. P. 4(6); Stafford, C. A. 2; Summerfield, K. 4; Taylor, S. 45; Vinnicombe, C. 14; Walter, D. W. 18; Whitehead, C. R. 36(2); Young, R. A. 16(12).
League Goals (83): Rowbotham 21 (6 pens), Neville 14, McNichol 8 (2 pens), Dryden 7, Young 6, Taylor 5, Whitehead 5, McDermott 3, Batty 2 (1 pen), Kelly 2 (2 pens), Rowe 2, Bailey 1, Benjamin 1, McPherson 1, Vinnicombe 1, own goals 4.

Littlewoods Cup (15): Rowbotham 6, McNichol 2, Neville 2, Benjamin 1, Dryden 1, McDermott 1, Vinnicombe 1, Young 1.
FA Cup (10): Rowbotham 4, Bailey 1, Batty 1, Cooper 1, Harrower 1, McDermott 1, Neville 1.
Ground: St James' Park, Exeter, Devon EX4 6PX (0392–54073)
Nearest Station: Exeter Central or St David's
Manager: Terry Cooper **Secretary:** M. Holladay
Colours: Red and white vertical striped shirts; black shorts
Record home gate: 20,984 v Sunderland, March 1931 (FA Cup)
Honours – Champions: Division 4: 1989–90

FULHAM DIV. 3

Barnett, Gary L.
Batty, Laurence
Cole, Michael W.
Davies, Gordon J.
Eckhardt, Jeffrey E.
Elkins, Gary
Gore, Shaun M.
Langley, Richard J.
Lewington, Raymond
Marshall, John P.
Mauge, Ronald C.
Milton, Stephen
Nebbeling, Gavin M.
Newson, Mark
Pike, Martin R.
Scott, Peter R.
Skinner, Justin
Stannard, James
Thomas, Glen A.
Walker, Clive

League Appearances: Barnett, G. L. 24(8); Batty, L. 2; Bremner, D. G. 7(9); Burns, H. 6; Cole, M. W. 1; Davies, G. J. 19(4); Donnellan, L. J. 8(3); Dowie, I. 5; Dowson, A. P. 4; Eckhardt, J. E. 39(1); Elkins, G. 9(1); Kimble, G. 1(2); Langley, R. J. 8(3); Lewington, R. 2(2); Marshall, J. P. 34(2); Mauge, R. C. 35(2); Milton, S. 27(7); Nebbeling, G. M. 36; Newson, M. 16; Peters, G. –(2); Pike, M. R. 20; Sayer, A. C. 25; Scott, P. R. 41; Skinner, J. 24(6); Stannard, J. 44; Thomas, G. A. 16(1); Vertannes, D. M. S. –(2); Walker, C. 41(4); Watson, J. M. 12(2).
League Goals (55): Walker 13 (3 pens), Milton 9, Davies 6, Sayer 5, Marshall 4, Skinner 4 (2 pens), Scott 3, Eckhardt 2, Mauge 2, Pike 2, Barnett 1, Dowie 1, Elkins 1, Stannard 1, Thomas 1.
Littlewoods Cup (6): Scott 2, Skinner 2 (1 pen), Walker 1, Watson 1.
FA Cup (5): Marshall 1, Peters 1, Scott 1, Walker 1, Watson 1.
Ground: Craven Cottage, Stevenage Road, Fulham SW6 6HH (071–736 6561)
Nearest Station: Putney Bridge (District) or Hammersmith (Metropolitan, District and Piccadilly)
Manager: Alan Dicks **Secretary:** Mrs Yvonne Haines
Colours: White shirts, black trim; black shorts
Record home gate: 49,335 v Millwall, October 1938 (League)
Honours – Champions: Division 2: 1948–9; Division 3 South: 1931–2.

GILLINGHAM DIV. 4

Beadle, Peter C.
Clarke, Brian R.
Docker, Ian
Eeles, Anthony G.
Guscott, Lindon
Haines, Ivan
Haylock, Paul
Heritage, Peter M.
Hillyard, Ronald W.
Johnson, Peter E.
Kimble, Garry L.
Lim, Harvey C.
Lovell, Stephen J.
Manuel, William A. J.
O'Connor, Mark A.
O'Shea, Timothy J.
Palmer, Lee J.
Place, Brendan A.
Pulis, Anthony R.
Trusson, Michael S.
Walker, Alan

League Appearances: Beadle, P. C. 4(6); Clarke, B. R. 3; Docker, I. 15(5); Eeles, A. G. 24(9); Gavin, P. J. 18(16); Haines, I. 23(3); Haylock, P. 44; Heri-

tage, P. M. 34(8); Hillyard, R. W. 42; Johnson, P. E. 45; Joseph, F. 2(1); Kimble, G. L. 12(2); Lim, H. C. 4; Lovell, S. J. 36(5); Manuel, W. A. J. 30(2); Norris, R. 2(3); O'Connor, M. A. 14(1);; O'Shea, T. J. 29(7); Palmer, L. J. 38(1); Pearson, R. 5(1); Place, B. A. 3(1); Pulis, A. R. 16; Smith, G. –(1); Thompson, S. 1(1); Trusson, M. S. 24(1); Walker, A. 38.
League Goals (46): Lovell 16 (9 pens), Heritage 9, Manuel 4, Palmer 3, Beadle 2, Eeles 2, Johnson 2, O'Shea 2, Trusson 2, Gavin 1, O'Connor 1, Walker 1, own goal 1.
Littlewoods Cup (1): Lovell 1.
FA Cup (0).
Ground: Priestfield Stadium, Gillingham, Kent ME7 4DD (0634–51854 and 576828)
Nearest Station: Gillingham
Manager: Damien Richardson **Secretary:** Barry Bright
Colours: Blue shirts, white trim; white shorts with blue trim
Record home gate: 23,002 v Queen's Park Rangers, January 1948 (FA Cup)
Honours – Champions: Division 4: 1963–4

GRIMSBY TOWN DIV. 3

Agnew, Paul
Alexander, Keith
Birtles, Garry
Childs, Gary P. C.
Cockerill, John
Cunnington, Shaun G.
Gilbert, David J.
Hargreaves, Christian
Jobling, Kevin A.
Knight, Ian J.
Lever, Mark
McDermott, John
Reece, Paul J.
Rees, Anthony A.
Sherwood, Stephen
Tillson, Andrew
Watson, Thomas R.
Willis, Roger C.

League Appearances: Agnew, P. 19(5); Alexander, K. 22(16); Birtles, G. 36(2); Childs, G. P. C. 44; Cockerill, J. 33; Cunnington, S. G. 44; Gabbiadini, R. 3; Gilbert, D. J. 45; Hargreaves, C. 5(14); Jobling, K. A. 30(3); Knight, I. J. 8(1); Lever, M. 35(3); McDermott, J. 39; Reece, P. J. 15; Rees, A. A. 35; Sherwood, S. 31; Smaller, P. A. 1; Stephenson, G. 7; Stoutt, S. P. 1; Tilson, A. 42; Watson, T. R. 10(6); Williams, T. –(1); Willis, R. C. 1(8).
League Goals (70): Rees 13, Alexander 12, Gilbert 10 (4 pens), Birtles 8, Childs 5, Cockerill 5 (2 pens), Cunnington 3, Tillson 3, Agnew 2, Hargreaves 2, Lever 2, Gabbiadini 1, Jobling 1, Knight 1, Watson 1, own goal 1.
Littlewoods Cup (5): Alexander 1, Birtles 1, Childs 1, Gilbert 1, Watson 1.
FA Cup (4): Hargreaves 2, Cockerill 1, Gilbert 1.
Ground: Blundell Park, Cleethorpes, DN35 7PY (0472–697111)
Nearest Station: Cleethorpes or Grimsby Town
Manager: Alan Buckley **Secretary:** I. Fleming
Colours: Black and white striped shirts; black shorts
Record home gate: 31,651 v Wolverhampton, February 1937 (FA Cup)
Honours – Champions: Division 2: 1900–1, 1933–4; Division 3 North: 1925–6, 1955–6; Division 3: 1979–80; Division 4: 1971–2

HALIFAX TOWN DIV. 4

Barr, William J.
Broadbent, Graham R.
Brown, David J.
Butler, Brian F.
Cook, Mitchel
Donnelly, Paul A.
Fleming, Craig
Fleming, Paul
Fyfe, Tony
Graham, Thomas
Hall, Derek R.
Hedworth, Christopher
Horner, Philip M.
McPhillips, Terence
Martin, Dean
Matthews, Neil
Naylor, Dominic J.
Richardson, Nicholas
Smith, Gareth S.
Watson, Andrew

League Appearances: Barr, W. J. 15(8); Bramhall, J. 23; Broadbent, G. R. 8(5); Brown, D. J. 27; Butler, B. F. 25(5); Cook, M. 36(1); Donnelly, P. A. 1; Fleming, C. 10; Fleming, P. 40; Fyfe, T. 10(2); Gannon, J. P. 2; Graham T. 21; Hall, D. R. 40(1); Harrison, F. 3(6); Hedworth, C. 27; Horner, P. M. 34; Juryeff, I. M. 15(2); McPhillips, T. 10(12); Martin, D. 37; Matthews, N. 38(1); Naylor D. J. 5(1); Richardson, N. 21(6); Smith, G. S. 6; Watson, A. 33(5); Whitehead, P. M. 19.
League Goals (57): Matthews 12, Watson 10, Juryeff 7, Richardson 6, Hall 4, Butler 3, McPhillips 3, Barr 2, Bramhall 2, Cook 2, Fleming P 1 (pen), Graham 1, Horner 1, Naylor 1, own goals 2.
Littlewoods Cup (3): Cook 1, Hall 1, Watson 1.
FA Cup (3): Horner 2, Fleming P 1.
Ground: The Shay, Halifax HX1 2YS (0422–53423)
Nearest Station: Halifax
Manager: Jim McCalliog **Secretary:** Mrs A. Pettifor
Colours: Blue and white shirts, blue shorts
Record home gate: 36,885 v Tottenham, February 1953 (FA Cup)
Honours: Nil

HARTLEPOOL UNITED DIV. 4

Allon, Joseph B.
Baker, David P.
Bennyworth, Ian R.
Dalton, Paul
Davies, Kenneth F.
Grayson, Simon D.
Honour, Brian
Hutchison, Donald
Lamb, Alan
MacDonald, Garry
McKinnon, Robert
Moverley, Robert
Nobbs, Alan K.
Olsson, Paul
Smith, Michael
Tinkler, John
Tupling, Stephen

League Appearances: Allon, J. B. 45; Atkinson, P. D. 3(5); Atkinson, P. 5(6); Baker, D. P. 43; Barrass, A. 8(1); Bennyworth, I. R. 27; Berryman, S. 1; Bowling, I. 1; Carr, G. G. J. 1; Curry, S. P. –(1); Dalton, P. 40(5); Davies, K. F. 3; Dearden, K. C. 10; Doig, R. 2(3); Dunbar, I. 1; Entwistle, W. P. 2; Grayson, S. D. 2; Honour, B. 4(5); Hutchison, D. 12(1); Lamb, A. 4(6); MacDonald, G. 9(7); McEwan, S. 14; McKinnon, R. 46; McStay, W. 3; Moverley, R. 6; Nobbs, A. K. 32; Ogden, P. 2; Olsson, P. 19(4); Plaskett, S. C. 7(1); Priestley, J. A. 16; Siddall, B. 11; Sinclair, J. 4; Smith, M. 35; Spiers, G. –(1); Stokes, W. D. 1; Stokle, D. 1; Tinkler, J. 45; Trewick, J. 8; Tupling, S. 26; Williams, P. A. 7(1); Wilson, P. M. –(1).
League Goals (66): Allon 18, Baker 16, Dalton 11, Smith 5, Bennyworth 2, Hutchison 2, McEwan 2 (2 pens), Olsson 2, Tinkler 2, Atkinson Paul 1, MacDonald 1, McKinnon 1, Tupling 1, own goals 3.
Littlewoods Cup (4): Grayson 2, Baker 1, Dalton 1.
FA Cup (0).
Ground: Victoria Ground, Clarence Road, Hartlepool TS24 8BZ (ground 0429–272584; office 0429–222077)
Nearest Station: Hartlepool
Manager: Cyril Knowles **Secretary:** M. Kirby
Colours: All blue
Record home gate: 17,426 v Manchester United, January 1957 (FA Cup)
Honours: Nil

HEREFORD UNITED DIV. 4

Benbow, Ian R.
Bradley, Russell
Devine, Steven B.
Elliott, Anthony R.
Hemming, Christopher
Jones, Mark
Jones, Mark A. W.
Jones, Richard
Juryeff, Ian M.
Narbett, Jonathan V
Peacock, Darren
Robinson, Colin R.
Tester, Paul L.
Wheeler, Paul.

League Appearances: Benbow, I. R. 21(6); Bowyer, G. D. 12(2); Bowyer, I. –(2); Bradley, R. 33; Burton, P. S. –(2); Devine, S. B. 31(3); Elliott, A. R. 29; Freestone, R. 8; Hemming, C. A. J. 34(1); Honor, C. R. 2(1); Jones, M. 40(2); Jones, M. A. W. 41; Jones, R. 16(3); Jones, S. G. 6(9); Juryeff, I. M. 22(3); Narbett, J. V. 36; Oghani, G. W. 7(1); Peacock, D. 35(1); Pejic, M. 34(4); Phillips, G. C. 6; Priday, M. A. 3; Robinson, C. R. 25(4); Starbuck, P. M. 6; Stevens, G. M. –(6); Tester, P. L. 24(2); Thomas, L. –(1); Wheeler, P. 21; Williams, B. 14.
League Goals (56): Wheeler 8, Jones M 8 (2 pens), Narbett 5, Pejic 5, Tester 5, Robinson 4, Jones R 3 (2 pens), Juryeff 3, Peacock 3, Bowyer G 2, Hemming 2, Oghani 2, Benbow 1, Bradley 1, Burton 1, Devine 1, Jones M A 1, own goal 1.
Littlewoods Cup (5): Jones R 3 (2 pens), Pejic 1, Robinson 1.
FA Cup (6): Jones M 1 (pen), Jones M A 1, Peacock 1, Pejic 1, Robinson 1, Tester 1.
Ground: Edgar Street, Hereford HR4 9JU (0432–276666)
Nearest Station: Hereford
Manager: Colin Addison **Secretary:** D.H. Vaughan
Colours: White shirts; black shorts
Record home gate: 18,114 v Sheffield Wednesday, 1958 (FA Cup)
Honours – Champions: Division 3: 1975–6

HUDDERSFIELD TOWN DIV. 3

Boothroyd, Adrian N.
Buyrne, Michael
Cecere, Michele J.
Charlton, Simon T.
Donovan, Kevin
Duggan, Andrew J.
Hardwick, Steven
Haylock, Gary A.
Hurst, Mark D.
Lewis, Dudley K.
Maguire, Peter J.
Marsden, Christopher
Martin, Lee B.
Maskell, Craig D.
May, Andrew M.
Mitchell, Graham L.
O'Doherty, Kenneth B.
Onuora, Iffem
O'Regan, Kieron
Smith, Mark C.
Trevitt, Simon
Wilson, Robert J.

League Appearances: Bent, J. A. 6(1); Boothroyd, A. N. 9(1); Bray, I. M. 13(1); Byrne, M. 17(2); Cecere, M. J. 22(1); Charlton, S. T. 1(2); Donovan, K. 1; Duggan, A. J. 15; Edwards, K. 6(4); Hardwick, S. 21; Hutchings, C. 46; Kelly, J. 9(1); Lewis, D. K. 28; Maguire, P. J. –(3); Marsden, C. 29(3); Martin, Lee B. 25; Maskell, C. D. 40(1); May, A. M. 40(1); Mitchell, G. L. 35(2); O'Connell, B. 11; O'Doherty, K. B. 17(1); Onuora, I. 3(17); O'Regan, K. 31(6); Smith, M. C. 39(5); Trevitt, S. 7; Wilson, R. J. 27(1); Withe, P. 8(4).
League Goals (61): Maskell 15 (2 pens), Smith 7, Wilson 6, Hutchings 5, Byrne 4, Cecere 4 (1 pen), Edwards 4, Onuora 3, O'Regan 3, Marsden 2, Bent 1, Duggan 1, Kelly 1, Mitchell 1, O'Connell 1, Withe 1, own goals 2.
Littlewoods Cup (7): Maskell 2, Wilson 2, Cecere 1, O'Doherty 1, Onuora 1.
FA Cup (7): Cecere 3 (3 pens), Maskell 2, Smith 1, own goal 1.
Ground: Kirklees Stadium, Leeds Road, Huddersfield HD1 6PE (0484–420335/6)
Nearest Station: Huddersfield

Manager: Eoin Hand **Secretary:** G.S. Binns
Colours: Blue and white striped shirts; white shorts
Record home gate: 67,037 v Arsenal, February 1932 (FA Cup)
Honours – Champions: Division 1: 1923–4, 1924–5, 1925–6; Division 2: 1969–70; Division 4: 1979–80
FA Cup winners: 1921–2

HULL CITY DIV. 2

Atkinson, Graeme
Bamber, John D.
Brown, Nicholas L.
Buckley, Neil A.
Calvert, Mark R.
Cleminshaw, David C.
Cooper, Mark A.
De Mange, Kenneth
Doyle, Stephen C.
Flynn, Gerard, J.
Hesford, Iain
Hunter, Paul
Jacobs, Wayne G.
Jenkinson, Leigh
Jobson, Richard I.
McParland, Ian J.
Mudd, Paul A.
Palin, Leigh
Payton, Andrew P.
Roberts, Garreth W.
Shotton, Malcolm
Smith, Michael K.
Swan, Peter H.
Thomas, David G.
Thompson, Leslie
Waites, Paul
Warren, Lee A.

League Appearances: Askew, W. 32; Atkinson, G. 6(7); Bamber, J. D. 19; Brown, N. L. 31(3); Buckley, N. A. 7(3); De Mange, K. J. P. P. 16(5); Doyle, S. C. 36; Edwards, K. 2; Hesford, I. 38; Hunter, P. 1(8); Jacobs, W. G. 46; Jenkinson, L. 9(13); Jobson, R. I. 45; Kelly, G. J. 8; McParland, I. J. 13(7); Murray, M. 3; Ngata, H. –(4); Palin, L. 9; Payton, A. P. 34(5); Roberts, G. W. 36; Shaw, R. E. 4; Shotton, M. 16; Smith, M. K. 1; Swan, P. H. 27(4); Terry, S. G. 29; Thomas, D. G. 11; Thompson, L. 1; Waites, P. 1; Warren, L. A. 10; Wheeler, P. –(5); Whitehurst, W. 15.
League Goals (58): Payton 17 (4 pens), Swan 11, McParland 5 (1 pen), Bamber 3, Hunter 3, Jacobs 3, Terry 3, Brown 2, Doyle 2, Jobson 2, Shotton 2, Askew 1, Atkinson 1, Buckley 1, Palin 1, own goal 1.
Littlewoods Cup (1): Payton 1.
FA Cup (0).
Ground: Boothferry Park, Hull HU4 6EU (0482–51119)
Nearest Station: Hull or Boothferry Park Halt
Manager: Stan Ternent **Secretary:** Frank Boughton
Colours: Black and amber striped shirts; black shorts
Record home gate: 55,019 v Manchester United, February 1949 (FA Cup)
Honours – Champions: Division 3 North: 1932–3, 1948–9; Division 3: 1965–6

IPSWICH TOWN DIV. 2

Bernal, Andrew
Donowa, Brian L.
Dozzell, Jason A. W.
Fearon, Ronald T.
Forrest, Craig L.
Gayle, Brian W.
Gregory, David S.
Hill, David M.
Honeywood, Lee B.
Humes, Anthony
Johnson, Gavin
Kiwomya, Christopher M.
Linighan, David
Lowe, David A.
Milton, Simon C.
Palmer, Stephen L.
Pennyfather, Glenn J.
Redford, Ian P.
Stockwell, Michael T.
Swailes, Christopher W.
Thompson, Neil
Wark, John
Yallop, Frank, W.
Zondervan, Romeo

League Appearances: Baltacha, S. 3(5); Cheetham, M. M. –(1); D'Avray, J. M. 8(4); Donowa, B. L. 17(6); Dozzell, J. A. W. 46; Forrest, C. L. 45; Gayle, B. W. 20; Gregory, D. S. 1(3); Harbey, G. K. –(1); Hill, D. M. 1(1); Humes, A. 17(7); Johnson, G. 3(3); Kiwomya, C. M. 19(10; Linighan, D. 41; Lowe, D. A.

31(3); Meade, R. –(1); Milton, S. C. 41; Neville, C. W. 1; Palmer, S. L. 3(2); Pennyfather, G. J. 7(1); Redford, I. P. 14(4); Stockwell, M. T. 34; Stuart, M. R. N. 5; Thompson, N. 44(1); Wark, J. 41; Woods, N. S. 3(4); Yallop, F. W. 31; Zondervan, R. 30.
League Goals (67): Lowe 13, Milton 10, Wark 10 (2 pens), Dozzell 8, Kiwomya 5, Humes 3, Stockwell 3, Thompson 3 (3 pens), Redford 2, Stuart 2, D'Avray 1, Donowa 1, Pennyfather 1, Woods 1, own goals 4.
Littlewoods Cup (0).
FA Cup (1): Dozzell 1.
Ground: Portman Road, Ipswich IP1 2DA (0473–219211)
Nearest Station: Ipswich
Manager: John Lyall **Secretary:** D.C.Rose
Colours: Royal blue shirts; white shorts
Record home gate: 38,010 v Leeds United, March 1975 (FA Cup)
Honours – Champions: Division 1: 1961–2; Division 2: 1960–61, 1967–8; Division 3 South: 1953–4, 1956–7
FA Cup winners: 1977–8
UEFA Cup winners: 1980–81

LEEDS UNITED DIV. 1

Batty, David
Beglin, James M.
Chapman, Lee R.
Davison, Robert
Day, Mervyn R.
Edmonds, Darren
Edwards, Neil R.
Fairclough, Courtney H.
Franklin, Darryl
Grayson, Simon N.
Haddock, Peter M.
Hendrie, John G.
Hilaire, Vincent M.
Jones, Vincent
Kamara, Christopher
Kerr, Dylan
Longstaff, Jason A.
McClelland, John
O'Donnell, Christopher
Pearson, John S.
Shorte, Grenville J.
Shutt, Carl S.
Snodin, Glynn
Speed, Gary A.
Sterland, Melvyn
Strachan, Gordon D.
Varadi, Imre
Whitlow, Michael
Williams, Andrew

League Appearances: Baird, I. J. 23(1); Batty, D. 39(3); Beglin, J. M. 18(1); Blake, N. L. G. 7; Chapman, L. R. 21; Davison, R. 25(4); Day, M. R. 44; Fairclough, C. H. 42; Haddock, P. M. 40; Hendrie, J. G. 22(5); Hilaire, V. M. –(2); Jones, V. 43(2); Kamara, C. 10(1); Kerr, D. 2(3); McClelland, J. 3; O'Donnell, C. –(1); Pearson, J. S. 2(5); Shutt, C. S. 6(14); Snodin, G. 3(1); Speed, G. A. 12(13); Sterland, M. 41(1); Strachan, G. D. 46; Thomas, M. R. 3; Turner, C. R. 2; Varadi, I. 12(1); Whitlow, M. 27(2); Williams, A. 13(3).
League Goals (79): Strachan 16 (7 pens), Chapman 12, Davison 11, Fairclough 8, Hendrie 5, Jones 5, Sterland 5, Baird 4, Speed 3, Shutt 2, Varadi 2, Williams 2, Kamara 1, Whitlow 1, own goals 2.
Littlewoods Cup (2): Fairclough 1, Strachan 1.
FA Cup (0).
Ground: Elland Road, Leeds LS11 0ES (0532–716037)
Nearest Station: Leeds
Manager: Howard Wilkinson **Secretary:** D.J. Dowse
Colours: All white
Record home gate: 57,892 v Sunderland, March 1967 (FA Cup)
Honours – Champions: Division 1: 1968–9, 1973–4; Division 2: 1923–4, 1963–4
FA Cup winners: 1971–2
League Cup winners: 1967–8
European Fairs Cup winners: 1967–8, 1970–71

LEICESTER CITY DIV. 2

Baraclough, Ian R.
Fitzpatrick, Gary
Gavin, Patrick J.
Hodge, Martin J.
Hyde, Gary S.
James, Anthony C.
Jeffrey, Andrew S.
Johnson, Robert S.
Kelly, David
Kitson, Paul
Linton, Desmond M.
Lyttle, Desmond
McAllister, Gary
Mauchlen, Alister H.
Mills, Gary R.
Morgan, Simon C.
Muggleton, Carl D.
North, Marc V.
Oakes, Scott J.
O'Connor, Paul D.
Oldfield, David C.
O'Toole, Christopher P.
Paris, Alan D.
Peake, Jason W.
Ramsey, Paul
Reid, Paul R.
Russell, Kevin J.
Smith, Richard G.
Spearing, Anthony
Walsh, Steven
Williams, Darren
Wright, Thomas E.

League Appearances: Campbell, K. J. 11; Clarke, W. 10(1); Evans, A. J. 14; Fitzpatrick, G. G. –(1); Glover, E. L. 3(2); Hodge, M. J. 46; James, A. C. 26(5); Johnson, R. S. 11(2); Kelly, D. 10; Kitson, P. 8(5); Linton, D. M. 1(1); McAllister, G. 43; Mauchlen, A. H. 38; Mills, G. R. 27(2); Moran, P. 10; Morgan, S. C. 14(3); North, M. V. 15(9); Oakes, S. J. –(2); Oldfield, D. C. 16(4); Paris, A. D. 33(5); Puttnam, D. 2(2); Ramsey, P. 31(4); Reid, P. R. 35(5); Russell, K. J. 4(6); Smith, R. G. –(4); Spearing, A. 19(1); Walsh, S. 34; Wilkinson, S. J. 2; Williams, D. 3(1); Wright, T. E. 40(1).
League Goals (67): McAllister 10 (4 pens), Reid 8, Kelly 7, North 6, Campbell 5, Oldfield 5, Mills 4, Ramsey 3, Walsh 3, Wright 3, James 2, Morgan 2, Paris 2, Clarke 1, Glover 1, Mauchlen 1, Moran 1, Spearing 1, Williams 1, own goal 1.
Littlewoods Cup (4): Clarke 1, Kitson 1, Paris 1, Reid 1.
FA Cup (1): Paris 1.
Ground: Filbert Street, Leicester LE2 7FL (0533–555000)
Nearest Station: London Road, Leicester
Manager: David Pleat **Secretary:** A.K. Bennett
Colours: Blue shirts; white shorts
Record home gate: 47,298 v Tottenham Hotspur, February 1928 (FA Cup)
Honours – Champions: Division 2: 1924–5, 1936–7, 1953–4, 1956–7, 1970–71, 1979–80
League Cup winners: 1963–4

LEYTON ORIENT DIV. 3

Baker, Stephen
Beesley, Paul
Berry, Greg J.
Burnett, Wayne
Carter, Darren S.
Castle, Stephen C.
Cooper, Mark D.
Day, Keith
Dickenson, Kevin J.
Hales, Kevin P.
Harvey, Lee D.
Heald, Paul A.
Hoddle, Carl
Howard, Terry
Hull, Alan E.
Nugent, Kevin P.
Pike, Geoffrey A.
Sayer, Andrew
Sitton, John E.
Whitbread, Adrian R.
Zoricich, Christopher V.

League Appearances: Baker, S. 27(5); Beesley, P. 32; Berry, G. J. 6(3); Burnett, W. 1(2); Campbell, G. 4(4); Carter, D. S. 29(2); Castle, S. C. 27; Cooper, M. D. 38(1); Day, K. 39; Dickenson, K. J. 31; Fashanu, J. S. 3(2); Hales, K. P. 36(3); Harvey, L. D. 36(1); Heald, P. A. 37; Hedman, R. G. 5; Hoddle, C. 19(7); Howard, T. 45; Hull, A. E. 15(9); Nugent, K. P. 5(6); Pike, G. A. 6(8); Rees, M. J. 9; Nugent, K. P. 5(6); Pike, G. A. 6(8); Rees, M. J. 9; Sayer, A. 9(1); Sitton, J. E. 36(1); Smalley, M. A. 1(2); Ward, P. T. 2(1); Whitbread, A. R. 8.
League Goals (52): Cooper 11, Castle 7 (1 pen), Howard 7, Harvey 6, Hull 6, Carter 5, Hales 2 (2 pens), Hoddle 2, Sitton 2, Beesley 1, Berry 1, Day 1, Sayer 1.

Littlewoods Cup (9): Carter 2, Castle 2, Cooper 1, Day 1, Harvey 1, Howard 1, Pike 1.
FA Cup (0).
Ground: Leyton Stadium, Brisbane Road, Leyton, E10 5NE (081–539 2223/4)
Nearest Station: Leyton (Central Line)
Manager: Frank Clark **Secretary:** Miss C. Stokes
Colours: Red shirts; white shorts
Record home gate: 34,345 v West Ham United, January 1964 (FA Cup)
Honours – Champions: Division 3: 1969–70; Division 3 South: 1955–6

LINCOLN CITY — DIV. 4

Bowling, Ian
Bressington, Graham
Brown, Grant A.
Carmichael, Matthew
Clarke, David A.
Davis, Darren J.
Gorton, Andrew W.
Hobson, Gordon
Lormor, Anthony
Nicholson, Shane M.
Puttnam, David P.
Roberts, Alan
Schofield, John D.
Scott, Keith
Smith, Neil
Smith, Paul M.
Stoutt, Stephen P.
Thompson, Steven P.
Wallington, Francis M.

League Appearances: Anderson, N. J. 1; Bressington, G. 43; Brown, G. A. 34; Brown, P. J. 1(4); Carmichael, M. 16(10); Casey, P. 12; Clarke, D. A. 30; Cook, M. R. 6; Cornforth, J. M. 9; Cumming, R. 11(1); Davis, D. J. 31(3); Gorton, A. W. 20; Groves, P. 8; Hobson, G. 29; James, A. C. 1; Lormor, A. 21; Nicholson, S. M. 18(5); Puttnam, D. P. 23; Roberts, A. 10; Schofield, J. D. 28(1); Scott, K. 6(4); Sertori, M. A. 21(3); Smith, N. 4; Smith, P. M. 32(1); Stoutt, S. P. 21; Thompson, S. P. 27; Waitt, M. H. 7(1); Wallington, F.M. 26; Williams, D. 7(2); Williams, P. D. 3.
League Goals (48): Hobson 8 (2 pens), Lormor 8, Carmichael 5, Sertori 5, Smith P 5, Bressington 2, Brown 2, Clarke 2 (2 pens), Schofield 2, Scott 2, Cornforth 1, Groves 1, Nicholson 1, Puttnam 1, Waitt 1, own goals 2.
Littlewoods Cup (0).
FA Cup (1): Nicholson 1.
Ground: Sincil Bank, Lincoln LN5 8LD (0522–22224 and 510263)
Nearest Station: Lincoln Central and St Mark's
Manager: Allan Clarke **Secretary:** G.R. Davey
Colours: Red and white striped shirts; black shorts
Record home gate: 23,196 v Derby, November 1967 (League Cup)
Honours – Champions: Division 3 North: 1931–2, 1947–8, 1951–2; Division 4: 1975–6

LIVERPOOL — DIV. 1

Ablett, Gary I.
Barnes, John C. B.
Beardsley, Peter A.
Burrows, David
Carroll, John G. M.
Collins, David D.
Gillespie, Gary T.
Grobbelaar, Bruce D.
Hansen, Alan D.
Harkness, Steven
Harrison, Wayne
Hooper, Michael D.
Houghton, Raymond J.
Hysen, Glen I.
Johnson, Craig P.
Jones, Barry
McMahon, Stephen
McManaman, Steven
Magilton, James
Marsh, Michael A.
Molby, Jan
Nicol, Stephen
Payne, Russell
Rush, Ian J.
Staunton, Stephen
Tanner, Nicholas
Venison, Barry
Watson, Alexander F.
Whelan, Ronald A.

League Appearances: Ablett, G. I. 13(2); Aldridge, J. W. –(2); Barnes, J. C. B. 34; Beardsley, P. A. 27(2); Burrows, D. 23(3); Dalglish, K. –(1); Gillespie,

G. T. 11(2); Grobelaar, B. D. 38; Hansen, A. D. 31; Houghton, R. J. 16(3); Hysen, G. I. 35; McMahon, S. 37(1); Marsh, M. A. –(2); Molby, J. 12(5); Nicol, S. 21(2); Rosenthal, R. 5(3); Rush, I. J. 36; Staunton, S. 18(2); Tanner, N. 2(2); Venison, B. 25; Whelan, R. A. 34.
League Goals (78): Barnes 22 (5 pens), Rush 18, Beardsley 10 (2 pens), Rosenthal 7, Nicol 6, McMahon 5, Gillespie 4, Aldridge 1 (pen), Houghton 1, Hysen 1, Molby 1, Whelan 1, own goal 1.
Littlewoods Cup (8): Staunton 3, Rush 2, Barnes 1, Beardsley 1, Hysen 1.
FA Cup (20): Rush 6, Barnes 5 (1 pen), Beardsley 4 (1 pen), Nicol 3, McMahon 1, Whelan 1.
Ground: Anfield Road, Liverpool L4 0TH (051–263 2361)
Nearest Station: All stations Liverpool
Manager: Kenny Dalglish MBE **Chief Executive/Secretary:** P.B. Robinson
Colours: All red
Record home gate: 61,905 v Wolverhampton, February 1952 (FA Cup)
Honours – Champions: Division 1: 1900–1, 1905–6, 1921–2, 1922–3, 1946–7, 1963–4, 1965–6, 1972–3, 1975–6, 1976–7, 1978–9, 1979–80, 1981–2, 1982–3, 1983–4, 1985–6, 1987–8, 1989–90 (record 18 titles); Division 2: 1893–4, 1895–6, 1904–5, 1961–2
FA Cup winners: 1964–5, 1973–4, 1985–6, 1988–9
Football League Cup winners: 1980–81, 1981–2, 1982–3, 1983–4
European Cup winners: 1976–7, 1977–8, 1980–81, 1983–4
UEFA Cup winners: 1972–3, 1975–6
Super Cup winners: 1977

LUTON TOWN — DIV. 1

Allpress, Timothy J.
Beaumont, David A.
Black, Kingsley
Breacker, Timothy S.
Chamberlain, Alec F. R.
Cooke, Richard E.
Crawshaw, Gary
Dowie, Iain
Dreyer, John B.
Elstrup, Lars
Farrell, Sean P.
Gillard, Kenneth J.
Gray, Robert P.
Harvey, Richard G.
Hughes, Ceri M.
James, Julian C.
Johnson, Marvin A.
Kennedy, Michael F. M.
McDonough, Darren K.
Nogan, Kurt
O'Brien, Michael T.
Pembridge, Mark A.
Petterson, Andrew K.
Preece, David W.
Rees, Jason
Rodger, Graham
Salton, Darren B.
Scott, Ian
Sealey, Leslie J.
Shanley, Kevin J.
Telfer, Paul N.
Tighe, Aaron P.
Williams, Steven C.
Wilson, Daniel J.

League Appearances: Allpress, T. J. 1; Beaumont, D. A. 16(3); Black, K. 36; Breacker, T. S. 38; Chamberlain, A. F. R. 38; Cooke, R. E. 3(8); Donaghy, M. 5; Dowie, I. 26(3); Dreyer, J. B. 38; Elstrup, L. 13(10); Farrell, S. P. –(1); Gray, R. P. 2(5); Harford, M. G. 1(3); Harvey, R. G. 17(9); Hughes, C. M. 1; James, J. C. 19(1); Johnson, M. A. 7(5); Kennedy, M. F. M. 30(2); McDonough, D. K. 15; Nogan, K. 10; Poutch, N. A. –(1); Preece, D. W. 30(2); Rees, J. 8(6); Rodger, G. 2; Wegerle, R. C. 13(2); Williams, S. C. 14; Wilson, D. J. 35.
League Goals (43): Black 11, Dowie 8, Wilson 7 (4 pens), Elstrup 4 (1 pen), Dreyer 2, Nogan 2, Wegerle 2 (1 pen), Breacker 1, Cooke 1, Gray 1, James 1, Preece 1, Williams 1, own goal 1.
Littlewoods Cup (11): Elstrup 5, Wegerle 4, Dreyer 1, Preece 1.
FA Cup (1): Wilson 1.
Ground: Kenilworth Road Stadium, Luton LU1 1DH (0582–411622)
Nearest Station: Luton
Manager: Jim Ryan **General-Manager-Secretary:** William J. Tomlins
Colours: White shirts with navy V-neck; navy shorts
Record home gate: 30,069 v Blackpool, March 1959 (FA Cup)

Honours – Champions: Division 2: 1981–2; Division 4: 1967–8
League Cup winners: 1987–8

MAIDSTONE UNITED DIV. 4

Barton, Warren D.
Beeney, Mark
Berry, Leslie D.
Butler, Stephen
Charlery, Kenneth
Cooper, Gary
Elsey, Karl W.
Gall, Mark I.
Galliers, Steven
Golley, Mark A.
Johns, Nicholas P.
Lillis, Jason W.
Oxbrow, Darren W.
Pritchard, Howard K.
Roast, Jesse
Rumble, Paul
Sorrell, Tony
Stebbing, Gary S.

League Appearances: Barton, W. D. 41(1); Beeney, M. 33; Berry, L. D. 37(1); Butler, S. 44; Charlery, K. 19(11); Cooper, G. 31(2); Elsey, K. W. 44; Gall, M. I. 33(8); Galliers, S. 7(1); Golley, M. A. 45; Johns, N. P. 13; Lillis, J. W. 26(7); Oxbrow, D. W. 24; Pamphlett, T. J. 7; Pearce, G. 24(3); Pritchard, H. K. 21(3); Roast, J. 15(1); Rumble, P. 19(4); Sorrell, T. 21(7); Stebbing, G. S. 2(4).
League Goals (77): Butler 21 (1 pen), Gall 18, Lillis 14 (1 pen), Cooper 4 (2 pens), Elsey 4, Pritchard 4, Golley 3, Sorrell 3, Charlery 2, Rumble 2, own goals 2.
Littlewoods Cup (1): Butler 1.
FA Cup (5): Gall 2, Barton 1, Butler 1, Elsey 1.
Ground: Watling Street, Dartford, Kent DA2 6EN (0622) 754403
Nearest Station: Dartford
Manager: Keith Peacock **Secretary:** W.T. Williams
Colours: Amber shirts, black shorts
Record home gate: (at The Stadium, London Road, Maidstone) 10,591 v Charlton, January 1979 (FA Cup)
Honours: Nil

MANCHESTER CITY DIV. 1

Allen, Clive
Beckford, Jason N.
Brightwell, David J.
Brightwell, Ian
Clarke, Wayne
Cooper, Paul D.
Dibble, Andrew
Harper, Alan
Heath, Adrian P.
Hendry, Edward C. J.
Hinchcliffe, Andrew G.
Hughes, Michael E.
Kelly, Paul
Lake, Paul A.
Megson, Gary J.
Quigley, Michael A.
Quinn, Niall
Redmond, Stephen
Reid, Peter
Seagraves, Mark
Thompstone, Ian P.
Wallace, Michael
Ward, Ashley S.
Ward, Mark W.
White, David

League Appearances: Allen, C. 23(7); Beckford, J. N. 1(4); Bishop, I. W. 18(1); Brightwell, I. 14(14); Clarke, W. 4(5); Cooper, P. D. 7; Dibble, A. 31; Fashanu, J. S. –(2); Fleming, G. J. 13(1); Gayle, B. W. 14; Gleghorn, N. W. 2; Harper, A. 21; Heath, A. P. 7(5); Hendry, E. C. J. 25; Hinchcliffe, A. G. 28(3); Lake, P. A. 31; McNab, N. 11(1); Megson, G. J. 19; Morley, T. W. 17; Oldfield, D. C. 10(5); Quinn, N. 9; Redmond, S. 38; Reid, P. 18; Seagraves, M. 2; Taggart, G. P. 1; Ward, A. S. –(1); Ward, M. W. 19; White, D. 35(2).
League Goals (43): Allen 10 (3 pens), White 8, Quinn 4, Hendry 3, Oldfield 3, Ward 3, Bishop 2, Brightwell 2, Heath 2, Hinchcliffe 2, Morley 2, Gleghorn 1, Reid 1.
Littlewoods Cup (8): Morley 2, Oldfield 2, White 2, Allen 1, Bishop 1.
FA Cup (2): Hendry 1, Lake 1.
Ground: Main Road, Moss Side, Manchester M14 7WN (061–226 1191/2)

Nearest Station: Manchester Piccadilly
Manager: Howard Kendall **Secretary:** J.B. Halford
Colours: Sky blue shirts; white shorts
Record home gate: 84,569 v Stoke City, March 1934 (FA Cup)
Honours – Champions: Division 1: 1936–7, 1967–8; Division 2: 1898–9, 1902–3, 1909–10, 1927–8, 1946–7, 1965–6
FA Cup winners: 1903–4, 1933–4, 1955–6, 1968–9
League Cup winners: 1969–70, 1975–6
European Cup Winners' Cup winners: 1969–70

MANCHESTER UNITED DIV. 1

Anderson, Vivian A.
Beardsmore, Russell P.
Blackmore, Clayton G.
Brazil, Derek M.
Bruce, Stephen R.
Bullimore, Wayne A.
Carey, Brian P.
Donaghy, Malachy M.
Gibson, Colin J.
Gill, Anthony G. D.
Graham, Deiniol W. T.
Hughes, Leslie M.
Ince, Paul E. C.
Leighton, James
McClair, Brian J.
McGuinness, Paul E.
Maiorana, Giuliano
Martin, Lee A.
Milne, Ralph
Pallister, Gary A.
Phelan, Michael C.
Rammell, Andrew V.
Robins, Mark G.
Robson, Bryan
Sharpe, Lee S.
Wallace, David L.
Walsh, Gary
Webb, Neil J.
Wilson, David G.
Wratten, Paul

League Appearances: Anderson, V. A. 14(2); Beardsmore, R. P. 8(13); Blackmore, C. G. 19(9); Bosnich, M. 1; Brazil, D. M. –(1); Bruce, S. R. 34; Donaghy, M. M. 13(1); Duxbury, M. 12(7); Gibson, C. J. 5(1); Graham, D. W. T. –(1); Hughes, L. M. 36(1); Ince, P. E. C. 25(1); Leighton, J. 35; McClair, B. J. 37; Maiorana, G. –(1); Martin, L. A. 28(4); Milne, R. –(1); Pallister, G. A. 35; Phelan, M. C. 38; Robins, M. G. 10(7); Robson, B. 20; Sealey, L. J. 2; Sharpe, L. S. 13(5); Wallace, D. L. 23(3); Webb, N. J. 10(1).
League Goals (46): Hughes 13, Robins 7, McClair 5, Bruce 3 (1 pen), Pallister 3, Wallace 3, Beardsmore 2, Blackmore 2, Robson 2, Webb 2, Gibson 1, Phelan 1, Sharpe 1, own goal 1.
Littlewoods Cup (3): Ince 2, Wallace 1.
FA Cup (15): McClair 3, Robins 3, Hughes 2, Robson 2, Wallace 2, Blackmore 1, Martin 1, Webb 1.
Ground: Old Trafford, Manchester M16 0RA (061–872 1661)
Nearest Station: All stations Manchester
Manager: Alex Ferguson **Secretary:** K.R. Merrett
Colours: Red shirts; white shorts
Record home gate: 76,962 FA Cup semi-final (Wolverhampton v Grimsby Town), March 1939; **club:** 70,504 v Aston Villa, December 1920 (League)
Honours – Champions: Division 1: 1907–8, 1910–11, 1951–2, 1955–6, 1956–7, 1964–5, 1966–7; Division 2: 1935–6, 1974–5
FA Cup winners: 1908–9, 1947–8, 1962–3, 1976–7, 1982–3, 1984–5, 1989–90 (seven wins joint record with Aston Villa and Spurs)
European Cup winners: 1967–8

MANSFIELD TOWN DIV. 3

Beasley, Andrew
Cassells, Keith B.
Charles, Stephen
Christie, Trevor
Davidson, Wayne
Fairclough, Wayne R.
Foster, George W.
Hathaway, Ian A.
Hodges, David
Hunt, David
Kearney, Mark J.
Kent, Kevin J.
Leishman, Graham
Lowery, Anthony W.
Murray, Malcolm
Pearcey, Jason
Prindiville, Steven
Smalley, Mark A.
Stringfellow, Ian R.
Wilkinson, Stephen J.

League Appearances: Beasley, A. 26; Chambers, S. 4(3); Charles, S. 42(1); Christie, T. 43(2); Clarke, M. J. 14; Coleman, S. 5; Cox, B. R. 15; Fairclough, W. R. 13; Foster, G. W. 42; Gray, K. J. 16; Hathaway, I. A. 11(11); Hodges, D. 8(11); Hunt, D. 21(1); Kearney, M. J. 41; Kent, K. J. 38; Kenworthy, A. D. 1; Leishman, G. 1(3); Lowery, A. W. 14; McDonald, G. 1(1); McKernon, C. A. 7; Murray, M. 28; O'Riordan, D. J. 6; Pearcey, J. 5; Place, M. 1; Prindiville, S. 22; Smalley, M. A. 28; Stringfellow, I. R. 17(2); Wilkinson, S. J. 36(1).
League Goals (50): Wilkinson 15, Christie 13 (2 pens), Charles 7 (1 pen), Kearney 3, Kent 3, Stringfellow 3, Clark 1, Hathaway 1, Hodges 1, Leishman 1, Smalley 1, own goal 1.
Littlewoods Cup (8): Christie 3, Stringfellow 3, Kearney 1, Wilkinson 1.
FA Cup (0).
Ground: Field Mill, Quarry Lane, Mansfield, Nottingham NG18 5DA (0624–23567)
Nearest Station: Mansfield, Alfreton Parkway
Manager: George Foster **Secretary:** J.D. Eaton
Colours: Amber shirts; blue shorts
Record home gate: 24,467 v Nottingham Forest, January 1953 (FA Cup)
Honours – Champions: Division 3: 1976–7; Division 4: 1974–5
Associate Members Cup winners: 1986–7

MIDDLESBROUGH DIV. 2

Arnold, Ian
Barid, Ian J.
Brennan, Mark R.
Burke, Mark S.
Coleman, Simon
Comfort, Alan
Cooper, Colin T.
Crosby, Lee D.
Davenport, Peter
Fletcher, Andrew M.
Hamilton, Gary J.
Hanford, Paul A.
Holmes, Daniel G.
Kernaghan, Alan N.
Kerr, Paul
Lake, Robert M.
McGee, Owen E.
Mohan, Nicholas
Mowbray, Anthony M.
Nesbitt, Mark T.
Parkinson, Gary A.
Pears, Stephen
Phillips, James N.
Poole, Kevin
Proctor, Mark G.
Putney, Trevor A.
Ripley, Stuart E.
Roxby, Lee
Russell, Martin
Slaven, Bernard
Sunley, Mark
Trotter, Michael
Tucker, Lee D.

League Appearances: Baird, I. J. 19; Brennan, M. R. 36(4); Burke, M. S. 3(9); Coleman, S. 33(3); Comfort, A. 15; Cooper, C. T. 18(3); Davenport, P. 30(5); Gill, G. 1; Kernaghan, A. N. 34(3); Kerr, P. 13(4); McGee, O. E. 12(1); Mohan, N. 21(1); Mowbray, A. M. 28; Pallister, G. A. 3; Parkinson, G. A. 40(1); Pears, S. 25; Phillips, J. N. 12; Poole, K. 21; Proctor, M. G. 45; Putney, T. A. 25; Ripley, S. E. 26(13); Slaven, B. 46.
League Goals (52): Slaven 21, Baird 5, Kernaghan 4, Proctor 4, Brennan 3, Davenport 3, Comfort 2, Cooper 2, Mowbray 2, Parkinson 2 (1 pen), Burke 1, Coleman 1, Kerr 1, Ripley 1.
Littlewoods Cup (6): Slaven 4, Comfort 1, Kernaghan 1.

FA Cup (1): Parkinson 1.
Ground: Ayresome Park, Middlesbrough TS1 4PB (0642–819659)
Nearest Station: Middlesbrough
Manager: Colin Todd **Secretary:** Tom Hughes
Colours: Red shirts; white shorts
Record home gate: 53,596 v Newcastle United, December 1949 (League)
Honours – Champions: Division 2: 1926–7, 1928–9, 1973–4
Amateur Cup: 1895, 1898
Anglo–Scottish Cup: 1975–6

MILLWALL DIV. 2

Allen, Malcolm
Babb, Philip A.
Branagan, Keith G.
Briley, Leslie
Carter, James W. C.
Coleman, Nicholas
Cunningham, Kenneth E.
Dawes, Ian R.
Dowson, Alan P.
Goddard, Paul
Horne, Brian S.
Hucker, Peter I.
Hurlock, Terence A.
McCarthy, Michael J.
McLeary, Alan T.
Magill, Manus P.,
Morgan, Darren J.
O'Callaghan, Kevin
Reid, Wesley A.
Sheringham, Edward P.
Sparham, Sean R.
Stephenson, Paul
Stevens, Keith H.
Thompson, David
Torpey, Stephen D. J.
Treacy, Darren R.
Waddock, Gary P.
Wood, Stephen A.

League Appearances: Allen, M. 6(2); Anthrobus, S. A. 13(2); Branagan, K. G. 16; Briley, L. 25(1); Carter, J. W. C. 25(3); Cascarino, A. G. 28; Coleman, N. 3; Cunningham, K. E. 5; Dawes, I. R. 38; Goddard, P. 13(1); Horne, B. S. 22; Horrix, D. V. –(1); Hurlock, T. A. 29; McCarthy, M. J. 6; McLeary, A. T. 30(1); Morgan, D. J. 1(1); Reid, W. A. 4(1); Salman, D. M. M. 7; Sheringham, E. P. 28(3); Sparham, S. R. 5(4); Stephenson, P. 19(4); Stevens, K. H. 28; Thompson, D. 25(2); Torpey, S. D. J. 3(4); Treacy, D. R. 4; Waddock, G. P. 14(4); Wood, S. A. 21.
League Goals (39): Cascarino 9, Sheringham 9, Anthrobus 4, Dawes 4, Allen 2, Briley 2, Carter 2, Stephenson 2, Thompson 2, Goddard 1, Morgan 1, own goal 1.
Littlewoods Cup (4): Burlock 2, Cascarino 1, Sheringham 1.
FA Cup (5): Sheringham 2, Carter 1, Cascarino 1, Goddard 1.
Ground: The Den, Cold Blow Lane, London SE14 5RH (01–639 3143/4)
Nearest Station: New Cross or New Cross Gate (SR and Metropolitan line)
Manager: Bruce Rioch **Secretary:** G.I.S. Hortop
Colours: Royal blue shirts; white shorts
Record home gate: 48,672 v Derby County, February 1937 (FA Cup)
Honours – Champions: Division 2: 1987–8; Division 3 South: 1927–8, 1937–8; Division 4: 1961–2
Football League Trophy: 1982–3

NEWCASTLE UNITED DIV. 2

Aitken, Robert S.
Anderson, John
Appleby, Matthew W.
Askew, William
Bradshaw, Darren S.
Brazil, Gary N.
Brock, Kevin S.
Burridge, John
Clark, Lee R.
Dillon, Kevin
Fereday, Wayne
Gallacher, John
Gourlay, Archibald M.
Howey, Steven N.
Kristensen, Bjorn
McGhee, Mark
Mason, Philip
O'Brien, Liam F.
Parkinson, Michael
Quinn, Michael
Ranson, Raymond
Robinson, David J.
Roche, David
Scott, Kevin W.
Stimson, Mark
Sweeney, Paul
Wright, Thomas J.

League Appearances: Aitken, R. S. 22; Anderson, J. 29(8); Askew, W. 4; Bradshaw, D. S. 9(3); Brazil, G. N. 4(12); Brock, K. S. 43(1); Burridge, J. 28; Dillon, K. 43; Fereday, W. 21(4); Gallacher, J. 21(7); Kelly, G. A. 4; Kristensen, B. 25(8); McGhee, M. 46; O'Brien, L. F. 14(5); Quinn, M. 45; Ranson, R. 33; Robinson, D. J. –(1); Scott, K. W. 42; Stimson, M. 35(2); Sweeney, P. 14(5); Thorn, A. 10; Wright, T. J. 14.
League Goals (80): Quinn 32 (3 pens), McGhee 19 (4 pens), Gallacher 6, Anderson 4, Kristensen 3, Scott 3, Brazil 2, Brock 2, O'Brien 2, Aitken 1, Stimson 1, Thorn 1, own goals 4.
Littlewoods Cup (5): Brazil 1 (pen), Brock 1, Gallacher 1, McGhee 1, Thorn 1.
FA Cup (10): McGhee 5 (1 pen), Quinn 2, O'Brien 1, Robinson 1, Scott 1.
Ground: St James' Park, Newcastle-upon-Tyne NE1 4ST (Tyneside 091–2328361)
Nearest Station: Newcastle Central (BR) or ST James' Park (Metro)
Manager: Jim Smith **Secretary:** R. Cushing
Colours: Black and white vertically striped shirts; black shorts
Record home gate: 68,386 v Chelsea, September 1930 (League)
Honours – Champions: Division 1: 1904–5, 1906–7, 1908–9, 1926–7; Division 2: 1964–5
FA Cup winners: 1909–10, 1923–4, 1931–2, 1950–1, 1951–2, 1954–5
European Fairs Cup winners: 1968–9
Anglo-Italian Cup winners: 1973

NORTHAMPTON TOWN DIV. 4

Barnes, David O.
Berry, Steven A.
Brown, Steven F.
Chard, Philip J.
Collins, Darren
Gernon, Frederick A. J.
Gleasure, Peter
McPherson, Keith A.
Quow, Trevor S.
Sandeman, Bradley R.
Scope, David F.
Terry, Steven
Thorpe, Adrian
Wilcox, Russell
Williams, Wayne
Wilson, Paul A.

League Appearances: Adcock, A. C. 8; Barnes, D. O. 37; Bell, M. 5(1); Berry, S. A. 41; Brown, S. F. 15(6); Chard, P. J. 29; Collins, D. 33(2); Culpin, P. 1(3); Donald, W. R. 20(7); Donegal, G. 1; Gernon, F. A. J. 12; Gleasure, P. 46; Johnson, D. 6(1); Leaburn, C. W. 9; McPherson, K. A. 43; McPhillips, T. –(1); Quow, T. S. 25(5); Sandeman, B. R. 20(9); Scope, D. F. 2(5); Singleton, M. D. 6(4); Terry, S. 17; Thomas, D. R. 31; Thorpe, A. 13; Wilcox, R. 46; Williams, W. 14(1); Wilson, P. A. 26(1).
League Goals (51): Barnes 18 (7 pens), Collins 8, Adcock 3 (2 pens), Thorpe 3, Wilcox 3, Berry 2, Chard 2, Donald 2, Terry 2, Thomas 2, Brown 1, Gernon 1, McPherson 1, Quow 1, Sandeman 1, own goal 1.
Littlewoods Cup (1): Adcock 1.
FA Cup (3): Barnes 1, Berry 1, Thomas 1.
Ground: County Ground, Abington Avenue, Northampton NN1 4PS (0604–234100)
Nearest Station: Northampton
Manager: Theo Foley **Secretary:** Philip Mark Hough
Colours: Yellow shirts claret trim, yellow shorts
Record home gate: 24,523 v Fulham, April 1966 (League)
Honours – Champions: Division 3: 1962–3: Division 4: 1986–7

NORWICH CITY DIV. 1

Bowen, Mark R.
Butterworth, Ian S.
Coney, Dean H.
Crook, Ian S.
Culverhouse, Ian B.
Fleck, Robert
Fox, Ruel A.
Gordon, Dale A.
Goss, Jeremy
Gunn, Bryan
Linighan, Andrew
Minett, Jason K.
Mortensen, Henrik
Pennock, Adrian B.
Phillips, David O.
Rosario, Robert M.
Sheffield, Jonathan
Sherwood, Timothy A.
Smith, David C.
Taylor, Robert A.
Theodosiou, Andy
Townsend, Andrew D.
Walton, Mark

League Appearances: Allen, M. 9(3); Bowen, M. R. 38; Butterworth, I. S. 22; Coney, D. H. 6(3); Cook, P. A. –(2); Crook, I. S. 34(1); Culverhouse, I. B. 31(1); Fleck, R. 25(2); Fox, R. A. 6(1); Gordon, D. A. 26; Goss, J. 3(4); Gunn, B. 37; Linighan, A. 37; Mortensen, H. 12(3); Pennock, A. B. 1; Phillips, D. O. 38; Power, L. M. –(1); Rosario, R. M. 29(2); Sherwood, T. A. 22(5); Smith, D. C. –(1); Tanner, N. 6; Townsend, A. D. 35; Walton, M. 1.
League Goals (44): Bowen 7, Fleck 7 (2 pens), Rosario 5, Phillips 4, Allen 3 (1 pen), Fox 3, Gordon 3, Sherwood 3, Townsend 3 (2 pens), Linighan 2, own goals 4.
Littlewoods Cup (4): Fleck 3, Gordon 1.
FA Cup (4): Fleck 2, Gordon 1, Rosario 1.
Ground: Carrow Road Stadium, Norwich NR1 1JE (0603–612131)
Nearest Station: Norwich Thorpe
Manager: Dave Stringer **Secretary:** A.R.W. Neville
Colours: Yellow shirts with green trim; green shorts with yellow trim
Record home gate: 43,984 v Leicester, March 1963 (FA Cup)
Honours – Champions: Division 2: 1971–2, 1985–6; Division 3 South: 1933–4
League Cup winners: 1961–2, 1984–5

NOTTINGHAM FOREST DIV. 1

Boardman, Craig G.
Carr, Franz A.
Cash, Stuart P.
Charles, Gary A.
Chettle, Stephen
Clark, Martin J.
Clough, Nigel H.
Crosby, Gary
Crossley, Mark G.
Currie, David N.
Fletcher, Jason L.
Gaynor, Thomas
Gemmill, Scot
Glover, Edward L.
Hodge, Stephen B.
Jemson, Nigel B.
Laws, Brian
Loughlan, Anthony J.
Lyne, Neil G. F.
McLoughlin, Steven R. G.
Marriott, Andrew
Orlygsson, Thorvaldur
Parker, Garry S.
Pearce, Stuart
Rice, Brian
Smith, Mark
Starbuck, Phillip M.
Stone, Steven B.
Sutton, Stephen J.
Walker, Desmond S.
Wassall, Darren P.
Williams, Brett
Wilson, Terry
Woan, Ian S.

League Appearances: Carr, F. A. 10(4); Chapman, L. R. 18; Charles, G. A. –(1); Chettle, S. 21(1); Clough, N. H. 38; Crosby, G. 34; Crossley, M. G. 8; Currie, D. N. 4(4); Foster, C. J. 6; Gaynor, T. 5(6); Hodge, S. B. 34; Jemson, N.B. 17(1); Laws, B. 38; Orlygsson, T. 11(1); Parker, G. S. 36(1); Pearce, S. 34; Rice, B. 15(3); Starbuck, P. M. –(2); Sutton, S. J. 30; Walker, D. S. 38; Wassall, D. P. 2(1); Williams, B. 1; Wilson, T. 18(3).
League Goals (55): Hodge 10, Clough 9 (3 pens), Chapman 7, Parker 6, Crosby 5, Pearce 5 (1 pen), Jemson 4, Laws 3, Rice 2, Carr 1, Chettle 1, Currie 1, Orlygsson 1.
Littlewoods Cup (18): Hodge 4, Clough 3 (1 pen), Crosby 3, Jemson 2, Pearce 2, Chapman 1, Gaynor 1, Parker 1, own goal 1.

FA Cup (0).
Ground: City Ground, Pavilion Road, Nottingham NG2 5FJ (0602–822202)
Nearest Station: Nottingham Midland
Manager: Brian Clough **Secretary:** P. White
Colours: Red shirts; white shorts
Record home gate: 49,945 v Manchester United, October, 1967 (League)
Honours – Champions: Division 1: 1977–8; Division 2: 1906–7, 1921–2; Division 3 South: 1950–1
FA Cup winners: 1897–8, 1958–9
League Cup winners: 1977–8, 1978–9, 1988–9, 1989–90
Full Members Cup winners: 1988–9, 1989–90
Super Cup winners: 1979–80
European Cup winners: 1978–9, 1979–80
Anglo-Scottish Cup winners: 1976–7.

NOTTS COUNTY DIV. 2

Bartlett, Kevin
Blackwell, Kevin P.
Chapman, Gary A.
Cherry, Steven R.
Cox, Paul R.
Dolan, Kenneth P.
Draper, Mark A.
Johnson, Thomas
Law, Nicholas
Lund, Gary J.
Machin, Scott J. L.
Norton, David W.
O'Riordan, Donald J.
Palmer, Charles A.
Platnauer, Nicholas R.
Robinson, Philip J.
Short, Jonathan C.
Snook, Edward K. G.
Stant, Philip R.
Telford, Mark A.
Thomas, Dean R.
Turner, Philip
Yates, Dean R.

League Appearances: Barnes, P. L. 10(3); Bartlett, K. 14; Chapman, G. A. 13(6); Cherry, S. R. 46; Chiedozie, J. –(1); Draper, M. A. 29(5); Fairclough, W. R. 5(3); Fleming, G. 3; Johnson, T. 34(6); Kevan, D. J. 1(2); Law, N. 2(1); Lund, G. J. 40; McStay, W. –(3); Norris, S. M. –(1); Norton, D. W. 11(4); O'Riordan, D. J. 15(2); Palmer, C. A. 36(1); Platnauer, N. R. 44; Robinson, P. J. 46; Short, J. C. 44; Stant, P. R. 14(8); Thomas, D. R. 10; Turner, P. 44; Yates, D. R. 45.
League Goals (73): Johnson 18 (3 pens), Lund 9, Bartlett 8, Stant 6, Turner 6, Yates 6, Palmer 5, Chapman 4, Draper 3 (1 pen), Robinson 2, Short 2, Barnes 1, Norton 1, Thomas 1, own goal 1.
Littlewoods Cup (3): Robinson 1, Short 1, Stant 1.
FA Cup (0).
Ground: Meadow Lane, Nottingham NG2 3HJ (0602–861155)
Nearest Station: Nottingham
Manager: Neil Warnock **Chief Executive:** N.E. Hook
Colours: Black and white striped shirts; black shorts
Record home gate: 47,310 v York, March 1955 (FA Cup)
Honours – Champions: Division 2: 1896–7, 1913–14, 1922–3; Division 3 South; 1930–31, 1949–50; Division 4: 1970–71
FA Cup winners: 1893–4

OLDHAM ATHLETIC DIV. 2

Adams, Neil J.
Barlow, Andrew J.
Barrett, Earl D.
Blundell, Christopher K.
Bunn, Frankie S.
Donachie, William
Halworth, Jonathan G.
Henry, Nicholas I.
Heseltine, Wayne A.
Holden, Andrew I.
Holden, Richard W.
Irwin, Denis J.
Kelly, Norman
McGarvey, Scott T.
Marshall, Ian P.
Milligan, Michael J.
Morgan, Stephen J.
Moulden, Paul
Palmer, Roger N.
Redfearn, Neil D.
Rhodes, Andrew C.
Ritchie, Andrew T.
Warhurst, Paul
Williams, Gary A.

League Appearances: Adams, N. J. 18(9); Barlow, A. J. 43(1); Barrett, E. D. 46; Bunn, F. S. 28(1); Donachie, W. 7; Hallworth, J. G. 15; Henry, N. I. 40(1); Heseltine, W. A. 1; Holden, A. I. 6; Holden, R. W. 45; Irwin, D. J. 42; McGarvey, S. T. 2(2); Marshall, I. P. 22(3); Milligan, M. J. 41; Moulden, P. 5(3); Palmer, R. N. 33(9); Redfearn, N. D. 15(2); Rhodes, A. C. 31; Ritchie, A. T. 37(1); Warhurst, P. 28(2); Williams, G. A. 1(2).
League Goals (70): Palmer 16, Ritchie 15 (4 pens), Holden R 9 (1 pen), Milligan 7, Bunn 5, Adams 4, Marshall 3, Barrett 2, Redfearn 2, Barlow 1, Irwin 1, McGarvey 1, Warhurst 1, own goals 3.
Littlewoods Cup (24): Ritchie 10, Bunn 7, Holden R 2, Adams 1, Barrett 1, Henry 1, Milligan 1, Palmer 1.
FA Cup (16): Marshall 3 (1 pen), Palmer 3, Ritchie 3 (1 pen), Holden R 2, Barrett 1, Bunn 1, McGarvey 1, Redfearn 1, own goal 1.
Ground: Boundary Park, Oldham OL1 2PA (061–624 4972)
Nearest Station: Oldham, Werneth and Oldham Mumps
Manager: Joe Royle **Secretary:** Terry Cale
Colours: All blue
Record home gate: 47,671 v Sheffield Wednesday, January 1930 (FA Cup)
Honours – Champions: Division 3 North: 1952–3; Division 3: 1973–4

OXFORD UNITED DIV. 2

Beauchamp, Joseph D.
Byrne, Paul B.
Durnin, John
Evans, Ceri L.
Evans, Paul
Ford, Michael P.
Foster, Stephen B.
Foyle, Martin J.
Greenall, Colin A.
Heath, Phillip A.
Hill, Richard W.
Jackson, Darren W.
Judge, Alan G.
Kee, Paul V.
Lewis, Michael
McClaren, Stephen
McDonnell, Matthew T.
Mustoe, Robbie
Muttock, Jonathan L.
Logan, Lee M.
Penney, David M.
Phillips, Leslie M.
Robinson, Leslie
Simpson, Paul D.
Smart, Garry
Stein, Earl M. S.
Waters, Graham J.

League Appearances: Bardsley, D. J. 3; Beauchamp, J. D. 2(1); Byrne, P. B. 2(1); Durnin, J. 39(3); Evans, C. L. 24; Ford, M. P. 25(6); Foster, S. B. 35; Foyle, M. J. 11(2); Greenall, C. A. 15; Heath, P. A. 16(5); Hucker, P. I. 8; Jackson, D. W. 1; Judge, A. G. 17; Kee, P. V. 21; Lewis, M. 45; McClaren, S. 17(5); Mustoe, R. 36(2); Muttock, J. L. 1; Nogan, L. M. 2(2); Penney, D. M. 20(9); Phillips, J. N. 34; Phillips, L. M. 6(2); Robinson, L. 1; Simpson, P. D. 38(4); Slatter, N. J. 10; Smart, G. 39(1); Stein, E. M. S. 38(3).
League Goals (57): Durnin 13, Simpson 9 (1 pen), Stein 9, Mustoe 7, Foster 4, Phillips J 3 (2 pens), Evans 2, Ford 2, Foyle 2, Penney 2, Lewis 1, own goals 3.
Littlewoods Cup (4): Simpson 2, Durnin 1, Foyle 1.
FA Cup (1): Simpson 1.
Ground: Manor Ground, Beech Road, Headington, Oxford OX3 7RS (0865–61503)
Nearest Station: Oxford
Manager: Brian Horton **Secretary:** John Clinkard
Colours: Gold shirts with navy blue sleeves; navy shorts
Record home gate: 22,750 v Preston, February 1964 (FA Cup)
Honours – Champions: Division 2: 1984–5; Division 3: 1967–8, 1983–4
League Cup winners: 1985–6

PETERBOROUGH UNITED DIV. 4

Butterworth, Garry J.
Crosby, Philip A.
Culpin, Paul
Graham, Milton M.
Halsall, Michael
Hine, Mark
Luke, Noel D.
McElhinney, Gerrard
Oakes, Keith B.
Osborne, Steven C.
Riley, David
Robinson, David A.
Sterling, Worrall R.

League Appearances: Andrews, G. M. 9(1); Barber, F. 6; Butterworth, G. J. 29(10); Crichton, P. A. 16; Crosby, P. A. 40(2); Culpin, P. 9(3); Godden, A. L. 24; Goldsmith, C. S. W. 5(1); Graham, M. M. 10(5); Halsall, M. 46; Harle, D. 14(1); Hine, M. 22; Jepson, R. F. 18; Longhurst, D. J. 14(7); Luke, N. D. 43; McElhinney, G. M. A. 34; Moore, M. 6(1); Oakes, K. B. 27(2); Osborne, S. C. 12(20; Richards, C. L. 16(4); Riley, D. 15; Robinson, D. A. 45; Sterling, W. R. 46; Watkins, D. A. –(1).
League Goals (59): Halsall 10, Jepson 5, Luke 5, Osborne 5, Richards 5, Riley 5, Sterling 5, Hine 4, Robinson 4 (1 pen), Butterworth 3, Culpin 2, Graham 2 (1 pen), Harle 2 (2 pens), Oakes 1, own goal 1.
Littlewoods Cup (4): Richards 2, Halsall 1, Sterling 1.
FA Cup (3): Andrews 1, Robinson 1, Sterling 1.
Ground: London Road Ground, Peterborough PE2 8AL (0733–63947)
Nearest Station: Peterborough
Manager: Mark Lawrenson **Secretary:** A.V. Blades
Colours: Royal blue shirts; white shorts
Record home gate: 30,096 v Swansea, February 1965 (FA Cup)
Honours – Champions: Division 4: 1960–61, 1973–4

PLYMOUTH ARGYLE DIV. 2

Barlow, Martin D.
Brimacombe, John
Broddle, Julian R.
Brown, Kenneth J.
Burrows, Adrian M.
Byrne, David S.
Damerell, Mark A.
Fiore, Mark J.
Garner, Darren J.
Hodges, Kevin
King, Adam
McCarthy, Sean C.
Marker, Nicholas R. T.
Morrison, Andrew C.
Pickard, Owen
Robinson, Paul
Rowbotham, Jason
Rowe, Paul D.
Salman, Danis M. M.
Stuart, Mark R. N.
Summerfield, Kevin
Thomas, Andrew M.
Whiston, Peter
Wilmot, Rhys J.

League Appearances: Barlow, M. D. –(1); Beglin, J. 5; Blackwell, D. R. 5(2); Brimacombe, J. 18(2); Broddle, J. R. 9; Brown, K. J. 44; Burrows, A. M. 46; Byrne, D. S. 28(4); Campbell, G. R. 15(7); Cooper, L. V. 2; Damerell, M. A. –(1); Fiore, M. J. 11(1); Garner, D. J. –(1); Gregory, J. C. 3; Hodges, K. 43(1); King, A. 5(3); McCarthy, S. C. 30(2); Marker, N. R. T. 43; Morrison, A. C. 18(1); Pickard, O. 1(4); Robson, M. A. 7; Salman, D. M. M. 10(1); Smith, M. C. 6; Stuart, M. R. N. 23(2); Summerfield, K. 8(2); Thomas, A. M. 33(3); Tynan, T. E. 44; Whiston, P. 3(5); Wilmot, R. J. 46.
League Goals (58): Tynan 15 (6 pens), Thomas 12, McCarthy 11, Stuart 6, Hodges 4, Campbell 3, Burrows 1, Byrne 1, Fiore 1, Marker 1, Morrison 1, Summerfield 1, own goal 1.
Littlewoods Cup (4): Tynan 3, McCarthy 1.
FA Cup (0).
Ground: Home Park, Plymouth, Devon PL2 3DQ (0752–562561)
Nearest Station: Plymouth North Road
Manager: David Kemp **Secretary:** Graham Little
Colours: Green shirts; black Shorts

Record home gate: 43,596 v Aston Villa, October 1936 (League)
Honours – Champions: Division 3 South: 1929–30, 1951–2; Division 3: 1958–9

PORTSMOUTH — DIV. 2

Anderton, Darren R.	Gilligan, James M.	Murray, Shaun
Aspinall, Warren	Gosling, Lee J.	Neill, Warren A.
Awford, Andrew T.	Gosney, Andrew R.	Powell, Darryl A.
Ball, Kevin A.	Gough, Alan T.	Ross, Michael P.
Beresford, John	Hall, Jason M.	Russell, Lee
Black, Kenneth G.	Hazard, Michael	Stevens, Gary A.
Chamberlain, Mark V.	Hogg, Graeme J.	Symons, Christopher J.
Connor, Terence F.	Kelly, Mark J.	Turner, Michael
Darby, Lee A.	Knight, Alan E.	White, Christopher J.
Fillery, Michael C.	Kuhl, Martin	Whittingham, Guy
Gale, Shaun M.	Maguire, Gavin T.	Wigley, Steven

League Appearances: Aspinall, W. 1(2); Ball, K. A. 36; Beresford, J. 27(1); Black, K. G. 36(5); Chamberlain, M. V. 34(4); Connor, T. F. 9(6); Fillery, M. C. 28(1); Gilligan, J. M. 24(8); Hazard, M. 8; Hogg, G. J. 36(3); Kelly, M. J. 6(7); Knight, A. E. 46; Kuhl, M. 30(10); Maguire, G. T. 29; Neill, W. A. 35(2); Russell, L. 2(1); Sandford, L. R. 13; Stevens, G. A. 21; Symons, C. J. 1; Whittingham, G. 39(3); Wigley, S. 45.
League Goals (62): Whittingham 23, Kuhl 9 (5 pens), Chamberlain 6, Gilligan 5, Fillery 4, Wigley 4, Connor 3, Ball 2, Black 2, Hazard 1, Hogg 1, Neill 1, Stevens 1.
Littlewoods Cup (4): Black 2, Fillery 1, Kuhl 1.
FA Cup (1): Whittingham 1.
Ground: Fratton Park, Frogmore Road, Portsmouth PO4 8RA (0705–731204)
Nearest Stations: Fratton, Portsmouth and Southsea
Manager: Frank Burrows **Secretary:** P. Weld
Colours: Blue shirts; white shorts
Record home gate: 51,385 v Derby County, February 1949 (FA Cup)
Honours – Champions: Division 1: 1948–9, 1949–50; Division 3 South; 1923–4; Division 3: 1961–2, 1982–3
FA Cup winners: 1938–9

PORT VALE — DIV. 2

Aspin, Neil	Glover, Dean V.	Mills, Brian
Atkinson, Paul	Grew, Mark S.	Mills, Simon
Beckford, Darren	Hughes, Darren J.	Parkin, Timothy J.
Booth, Matthew	Jeffers, John J.	Porter, Andrew M.
Cross, Nicholas J. R.	Jepson, Ronald F.	Walker, Raymond
Earle, Robert	McInstrey, Gary	Webb, Alan R.
Finney, Kevin	Millar, Paul W.	West, Gary
Ford, Gary	Miller, Ian	Wood, Trevor J.

League Appearances: Aspin, N. 41(1); Beckford, D. 40(2); Cross, N. J. R. 37(5); Earle, R. 43; Finney, K. 4(4); Futcher, R. 7(4); Glover, D. V. 44; Grew, M. S. 43; Hughes, D. J. 38; Jeffers, J. J. 38(2); Jepson, R. F. –(5); Millar, P. W. 11(12); Miller, I. 14(7); Mills, S. 45; Parkin, T. J. 9(3); Porter, A. M. 32(4); Riley, D. S. 2; Walker, R. 38(2); Webb, A. R. 14; West, G. 3; Wood, T. J. 3.
League Goals (62): Beckford 17, Cross 13 (1 pen), Earle 12, Millar 4, Glover 4

(3 pens), Futcher 3, Hughes 1, Jeffers 1, Miller 1, Mills 1, Parkin 1, Porter 1, own goals 3.
Littlewoods Cup (4): Beckford 3, Futcher 1.
FA Cup (4): Beckford 1, Cross 1, Walker 1, own goal 1.
Ground: Vale Park, Hamil Road, Burslem, Stoke-on-Trent ST6 1AW (0782–814134)
Nearest Stations: Longport, and Stoke-on-Trent
Manager: John Rudge **Secretary:** D.E. Barber J.P. AMITD
Colours: White shirts with black trim; black shorts
Record home gate: 50,000 v Aston Villa, February 1960 (FA Cup)
Honours – Champions: Division 3 North: 1929–30, 1953–4; Division 4: 1958–9

PRESTON NORTH END DIV. 3

Anderton, Steven D.
Atkins, Robert J.
Bogie, Ian
Flynn, Michael A.
Greenwood, Nigel P.
Hancock, Anthony E.
Harper, Steven J.
Hughes, Adrian F. S.
James, Martin J.
Joyce, Warren G.
Kelly, Alan T.
McIlroy, Samuel B.
Mooney, Brian J.
Rathbone, Michael J.
Shaw, Graham P.
Swann, Gary
Thomas, John W.
Tunks, Roy W.
Williams, Neil J. F.
Wrightson, Jeffrey G.

League Appearances: Anderton, S. D. –(1); Atkins, R. J. 27(1); Bennett, M. 10; Bogie, I. 30(5); Ellis, A. J. 17; Flynn, M. A. 23; Greenwood, N. P. 5; Harper, S. J. 28(8); Hughes, A. F. S. 29(6); Jones, A. 3; Joyce, W. G. 44; Kelly, A. T. 42; McIlroy, S. B. 20; Miller, D. B. 3; Mooney, B. J. 44(1); Patterson, M. A. 12(1); Rathbone, M. J. 3(5); Scully, P. J. 13; Shaw, G. P. 24(7); Snow, S. G. 1; Stowell, M. 2; Swann, G. 46; Thomas, J. W. 11; Tunks, R. W. 2; Williams, N. J. F. 41; Wrightson, J. G. 26.
League Goals (65): Joyce 11, Harper 10 (1 pen), Mooney 9, Swann 8, Shaw 5, Patterson 4 (1 pen), Bogie 3, Ellis 3, Thomas 3, Williams 3, Atkins 1, Flynn 1, Hughes 1, Scully 1, own goals 2.
Littlewoods Cup (4): Shaw 4 (1 pen).
FA Cup (1): Joyce 1.
Ground: Deepdale, Preston PR1 6RU (0772–795919)
Nearest Station: Preston
Manager: Les Chapman **Secretary:** D.J. Allan
Colours: All white
Record home gate: 42,684 v Arsenal, April 1938 (League)
Honours – Champions: Division 1: 1888–9, 1889–90; Division 2: 1903–4, 1912–13, 1950–51; Division 3: 1970–71
FA Cup winners: 1888–9, 1937–8

QUEEN'S PARK RANGERS DIV. 1

Allen, Bradley J.
Bardsley, David J.
Barker, Simon
Caldwell, Peter J.
Channing, Justin A.
Clarke, Colin J.
Crocker, Steven
Doyle, Maurice
Falco, Mark P.
Ferdinand, Leslie
Herrera, Roberto
Iorfa, Dominic
Joyce, Anthony J.
Law, Brian J.
MCarthy, Alan J.
McDonald, Alan
Macciochi, David A.
Maddix, Daniel S.
Meaker, Michael J.
Parker, Paul A.
Roberts, Anthony M.
Rutherford, Michael A.
Sansom, Kenneth G.
Sinton, Andrew
Vowles, Paul
Wegerle, Roy C.
Wilkins, Raymond C.

League Appearances: Allen, M. J. 2; Bardsley, D. J. 31; Barker, S. 24(4); Channing, J. A. 19(4); Clarke, C. J. 27(7); Falco, M. P. 11(10); Ferdinand, L. 6(3); Francis, T. J. 3(1); Herrera, R. 1; Iorfa, D. –(1); Kerslake, D. –(1); Law, B. J. 10; McDonald, A. 34; Maddix, D. S. 28(4); Parker, P. A. 32; Reid, P. 15; Roberts, A. M. 5; Rutherford, M. A. 1(1); Sansom, K. G. 36; Seaman, D. A. 33; Sinton, A. 38; Spackman, N. J. 11(2); Stein, E. M. S. 1(1); Wegerle, R. C. 18(1); Wilkins, R. C. 23; Wright, P. H. 9(6).
League Goals (45): Clarke 6, Sinton 6, Wegerle 6 (1 pen), Falco 5, Francis 5, Wright 5 (2 pens), Barker 3, Maddix 3, Channing 2, Ferdinand 2, Bardsley 1, Wilkins 1.
Littlewoods Cup (3): Clarke 1, Spackman 1, Wright 1 (pen).
FA Cup (11): Barker 2 (1 pen), Clarke 2, Sansom 2, Sinton 2, Wilkins 2, Wegerle 1.
Ground: Rangers Stadium, South Africa Road, Shepherds Bush, W12 7PA (081-743 0262)
Nearest Stations: Shepherds Bush (Metropolitan and Central lines); White City (Central line)
Chief coach: Don Howe **Secretary:** Miss S.F. Marson
Colours: Blue and white hooped shirts; white shorts
Record home gate: 35,353 v Leeds United, April 1974 (League)
Honours – Champions: Division 2: 1982–3; Division 3 South; 1947–8; Division 3: 1966–7
League Cup winners: 1966–7

READING DIV. 3

Beavon, Michael S.
Burns, Philip M.
Conroy, Michael K.
Francis, Stephen S.
Friel, George P.
Gilkes, Michael E.
Gooding, Michael C.
Hicks, Martin
Jones, Linden
Knight, Keith
Leworthy, David J.
Moran, Steven J.
Payne, Lee J.
Richardson, Steven E.
Senior, Trevor J.
Taylor, Scott D.
Whitlock, Mark
Williams, Adrian
Wood, Darren

League Appearances: Bashir, N. 1(2); Beavon, M. S. 29(3); Conroy, M. K. 27(7); Francis, S. S. 46; Friel, G. P. 2(1); Gernon, F. A. J. 3; Gilkes, M. E. 40(2); Gooding, M. C. 27; Hicks, M. 44; Jones, L. 38(1); Knight, K. 13; Lemon, P. A. 3; Leworthy, D. J. 16(12); Moran, S. J. 23(5); Payne, L. J. 10(2); Richardson, S. E. 43; Senior, T. J. 35; Tait, M. P. 27(1); Taylor, S. D. 22(7); Whitlock, M. 10; Williams, A. 16; Wood, D. 31(1).
League Goals (57): Senior 14, Moran 11 (3 pens), Leworthy 7, Beavon 3 (1 pen), Gooding 3, Tait 3, Conroy 2, Gilkes 2, Hicks 2, Taylor 2, Williams 2, Wood 2, Bashir 1, Knight 1, own goals 2.
Littlewoods Cup (8): Gilkes 4, Senior 3, Taylor 1.
FA Cup (12): Senior 4, Jones 3, Moran 2, Beavon 1 (pen), Conroy 1, Gilkes 1.
Ground: Elm Park, Norfolk Road, Reading RG3 2EF (0734–507878)
Nearest Station: Reading
Manager: Ian Porterfield **Secretary:**
Colours: Sky blue with white centre panel; sky blue shorts
Record home gate: 33,042 v Brentford, February 1927 (FA Cup)
Honours – Champions: Division 3: 1985–6; Division 3 South: 1925–6; Division 4: 1978–9
Full Members Cup winners: 1987–8

ROCHDALE DIV. 4

Brown, Antony J.
Burns, William
Chapman, Vincent J.
Cole, David A.
Dawson, Jason
Elliott, Stephen B.
Goodison, Christopher W.
Hill, Jonathon W.
Holmes, Michael A.
Hughes, Zacari D.
Johnson, Stephen A.
Milner, Andrew J.
O'Shaughnessy, Stephen
Stonehouse, Kevin
Ward, Peter
Welch, Keith J.

League Appearances: Ainscow, A. 19(1); Brown, A. J. 43; Burns, W. 42(2); Chapman, V. J. 4; Cole, D. A. 41(2); Dawson, J. 25(2); Duxbury, L. E. 9(1); Edmonds, N. A. 2(2); Elliott, S. B. 19(3); Goodison, C. W. 45; Graham, J. 11; Hasford, J. M. –(1); Henshaw, G. 8(1); Hill, J. W. 22(3); Holmes, M. A. 33(5); Johnson, S. A. 20(4); Lockett, P. B. –(1); Milligan, S. J. F. 5; Milner, A. J. 14(2); O'Shaughnessy, S. 27(3); Small, C. 5(2); Stonehouse, K. 13(1); Walling, D. 9(10); Ward, P. 39(1); Welch, K. J. 46; Whellans, R. 5(6).
League Goals (52): O'Shaughnessy 8 (1 pen), Elliott 6, Cole 5, Ward 5, Goodison 4 (4 pens), Johnson 4, Milner 4, Walling 3, Dawson 2, Holmes 2, Stonehouse 2 (2 pens), Burns 1 (pen), Henshaw 1, Milligan 1, Small 1, Whellans 1, own goals 2.
Littlewoods Cup (3): Burns 1, Goodison 1, Holmes 1.
FA Cup (8): Johnson 2, O'Shaughnessy 2, Dawson 1, Goodison 1 (pen), Stonehouse 1, Ward 1.
Ground: Spotland, Sandy Lane, Rochdale OL11 5DS (0706–44648/9)
Nearest Station: Rochdale
Manager: Terry Dolan **Secretary:** Bill Kenyon JP
Colours: All royal blue
Record home gate: 24,231 v Notts County, December 1949 (FA Cup)
Honours Nil

ROTHERHAM UNITED DIV. 3

Barnsley, Andrew
Buckley, John W.
Dempsey, Mark J.
Evans, Stewart J.
Ford, Stuart T.
Goater, Leonard S.
Goodwin, Shaun L.
Haycock, Thomas P.
Hazel, Desmond L.
Johnson, Nigel M.
Mendonca, Clive P.
Mercer, William
O'Hanlon, Kelham G.
Pepper, Nigel C.
Pickering, Albert G
Richardson, Neil T.
Robinson, Ronald
Russell, William M.
Scott, Martin
Thompson, Simon L.
Williamson, Robert

League Appearances: Ainscow, A. P. –(1); Barnsley, A. 31(6); Buckley, J. W. 40; Cash, S. P. 8; Dempsey, M. J. 22; Evans, S. J. 12(8); Ford, S. T. 1; Goater, L. S. 5(7); Goodwin, S. L. 35(3); Grealish, A. P. 31(2); Haycock, T. P. 2(1); Hazel, D. L. 22(11); Heard, T. P. 13(1); Johnson, N. M. 40(3); Mendonca, C. P. 30(2); Mercer, W. 2; O'Hanlon, K. G. 43; Pepper, N. C. 15(4); Pickering, A. G. 9(1); Richardson, N. T. 2; Robinson, R. 43; Russell, W. M. 28(1); Scott, M. 28; Thompson, S. L. 3(8); Williamson, R. 41(1).
League Goals (71): Williamson 19 (6 pens), Mendonca 14, Buckley 7, Goodwin 6, Evans 4, Barnsley 3, Dempsey 3, Heard 3, Goater 2, Hazel 2, Johnson 2, Cash 1, Pepper 1, Robinson 1, Scott 1, own goals 2.
Littlewoods Cup (3): Williamson 2 (1 pen), Mendonca 1.
FA Cup (2): Evans 1, Hazel 1.
Ground: Millmoor, Rotherham S60 1HR (0709–562434)
Nearest Station: Rotherham
Manager: Billy McEwan **Secretary:** N. Darnill

Colours: Red shirts; white shorts
Record home gate: 25,000 v Sheffield United, December 1952 and Sheffield Wednesday, January 1952 (League)
Honours – Champions: Division 3: 1980–81; Dividion 3 North: 1950–51; Division 4: 1988–9

SCARBOROUGH DIV. 4

Ash, Mark C.
Clarke, Michael D.
Dobson, Paul
Hirst, Lee
Ironside, Ian
Kamara, Alan
MacDonald, John
Matthews, Michael
Meyer, Adrian M.
Oghani, George W.
Richards, Stephen C.
Richardson, Barry
Saunders, Steven J.
Short, Christian M.
Slingsby, Lee

League Appearances: Ash, M. C. 7(4); Bennyworth, I. R. 15; Blackwell, K. P. 8; Brook, G. 10(5); Butler, M. C. 1(5); Clarke, M. D. 30(6); Dixon, K. L. 3; Dobson, P. 34(3); Fyfe, T. 6; Graham, T. 20(4); Hirst, L. 10; Holmes, D. J. 1(1); Ironside, I. 14; Kamara, A. 45; Law, N. 12; MacDonald, J. 29; Matthews, M. 21; Meyer, A. M. 18; Morris, C. –(1); Norris, S. M. 8(6); Oghani, G. W. 13(1); Olsson, P. 9(7); Richards, S. C. 35; Richardson, B. 24; Robinson, P. J. 13(7); Russell, M. C. 31; Saunders, S. J. 23(9); Short, C. M. 40(1); Slingsby, L. –(1); Spink, D. P. 3; Wilson, P. 23(1).
League Goals (60): Dobson 15, Russell 7 (2 pens), MacDonald 5, Norris 4, Oghani 4 (2 pens), Richards 4, Brook 3, Matthews 3, Robinson 3, Meyer 2, Spink 2, Clarke 1, Fyfe 1, Kamara 1, Olsson 1, Saunders 1, Short 1, Wilson 1, own goal 1.
Littlewoods Cup (7): Brook 1, Dobson 1, Graham 1, Richards 1, Robinson 1, Russell 1 (pen), own goal 1.
FA Cup (0).
Ground: The Athletic Ground, Seamer Road, Scarborough Y012 4HF (0723–375094)
Nearest Station: Scarborough
Manager: Ray McHale **General Manager/Secretary:** G.J. Alston
Colours: All red
Record home gate: 11,130 v Luton T., January 1938 (FA Cup)
Honours: Nil

SCUNTHORPE UNITED DIV. 4

Alexander, Graham
Bramhall, John
Cotton, Perry
Cowling, David R.
Cox, Neil J.
Daws, Anthony
Flounders, Andrew J.
Hall, Richard A.
Hamilton, Ian R.
Lillis, Mark A.
Lister, Stephen H.
Litchfield, Peter
Longden, David P.
Marshall, Gary
Musselwhite, Paul S.
Smalley, Paul T.
Stevenson, Andrew J.
Taylor, Kevin
Tucker, Gordon
Ward, Paul T.

League Appearances: Bramhall, J. 21; Butler, M. 2; Cotton, P. 14(3); Cowling, D. R. 29(3); Daws, A. 28(5); Flounders, A. J. 37(7); Hall, R. A. 1; Hamilton, I. R. 42(1); Hodkinson, A. J. 21; Knight, I. J. 2; Lillis, M. A. 27(2); Lister, S. H. 5(1); Litchfield, P. 17; Longden, D. P. 45(1); Marshall, G. 31(3); Money, R. 1; Musselwhite, P. S. 29; Nicol, P. J. 17(1); Smalley, P. T. 43(1); Stevenson, A. J. 19(5); Taylor, K. 37(2); Tucker, G. 14(1); Ward, P. T. 24(1).
League Goals (69): Flounders 18 (2 pens), Lillis 13 (2 pens), Daws 11, Taylor 8

(1 pen), Hamilton 6, Ward 4 (1 pen), Marshall 3, Cotton 1, Lister 1 (pen), Nicol 1, Stevenson 1, Tucker 1, own goal 1.
Littlewoods Cup (1): Flounders 1.
FA Cup (7): Lillis 3, Taylor 2, Daws 1, Hodkinson 1.
Ground: Glanford Park, Scunthorpe DN15 7RH (0724–848077)
Nearest Station: Scunthorpe
Manager: Mick Buxton **Secretary:** A.D. Rowing
Colours: All claret and blue
Record home gate: 28,775 v Rotherham U, May 1989 (League)
Honours – Champions: Division 3 North: 1957–8

SHEFFIELD UNITED DIV. 1

Agana, Patrick A. O.
Barnes, David
Benstead, Graham M.
Booker, Robert
Bradshaw, Carl
Bryson, James I. C.
Carr, Darren
Deane, Brian C.
Duffield, Peter
Flower, Johannes G.
Gannon, John S.
Hill, Colin F.
Lake, Michael C.
Lucas, Richard
Morris, Mark J.
Powell, Clifford G.
Smith, Brian
Stancliffe, Paul I.
Todd, Mark K.
Tracey, Simon P.
Ward, Mitchum D.
Webster, Simon P.
Whitehouse, Dane L.
Whitehurst, William
Wilder, Christopher J.
Winter, Julian
Wood, Paul A.

League Appearances: Agana, P. A. O. 26(5); Barnes, D. 24; Booker, R. 38(4); Bradshaw, C. 20(10); Bryson, J. I. C. 39; Deane, B. C. 45; Duffield, P. 2(3); Francis, J. A. 11(9); Gannon, J. S. 39; Hill, C. F. 42(1); Lake, M. C. 2(2); Morris, M. J. 41(1); Pike, M. R. 2(1); Roberts, A. 6(1); Rostron, J. W. 24(2); Stancliffe, P. I. 40; Todd, M. K. 10(6); Tracey, S. P. 46; Webster, S. P. 9(11); Whitehouse, D. L. 8(4); Whitehurst, W. 9(5); Wilder, C. J. 8; Wood, P. A. 15(2).
League Goals (78): Deane 21, Agana 10, Bryson 9 (2 pens), Booker 8, Francis 5, Bradshaw 3, Gannon 3 (1 pen), Morris 3, Rostron 3, Wood 3, Duffield 2 (2 pens), Whitehurst 2, Stancliffe 1, Todd 1, Whitehouse 1, own goals 3.
Littlewoods Cup (1): Deane 1.
FA Cup (8): Agana 2 (1 pen), Bryson 2, Bradshaw 1, Deane 1, Stancliffe 1, own goal 1.
Ground: Bramall Lane, Sheffield S2 4SU (0742–738955)
Nearest Station: Sheffield
Manager: Dave Bassett **Secretary:** D. Capper
Colours: Red and white striped shirts; black shorts
Record home gate: 68,287 v Leeds, February 1936 (FA Cup)
Honours – Champions: Division 1: 1897–8; Division 2: 1952–3; Division 4: 1981–2
FA Cup winners: 1898–9, 1901–2, 1914–15, 1924–5

SHEFFIELD WEDNESDAY DIV. 2

Atkinson, Dalian
Barrick, Dean
Bennett, David
Beresford, Marlon
Cam, Scott H.
Fee, Gregory
Francis, Trevor J.
Goodacre, Samuel D.
Gregory, Anthony G.
Hirst, David E.
Hyde, Graham
Johnson, David A.
Key, Lance
King, Phillip G.
Lycett, David R.
McCall, Stephen H.
Madden, Lawrence D.
Newsome, Jon
Nilsson, Nils L. R.
Palmer, Charlton L.
Pearson, Nigel G.
Pressman, Kevin P.
Sheridan, John J.
Shirtliff, Peter A.
Sowden, Shaun
Taylor, Robert M.
Turner, Christopher R.
Wetherall, David
Whitton, Stephen P.
Wood, Darren .
Worthington, Nigel

League Appearances: Atkinson, D. 38; Barrick, D. 3; Bennett, D. 10(8); Carr, F. A. 9(3); Fee, G. 1(1); Francis, T. J. 10(2); Harper, A. 9(2); Hirst, D. E. 36(2); King, P. G. 25; McCall, S. H. 1(2); Madden, L. D. 18(7); Newsome, J. 5(1); Nilsson, N. L. R. 20; Palmer, C. L. 34; Pearson, N. G. 33; Pressman, K. P. 15; Shakespeare, C. R. 15(2); Sheridan, J. J. 27; Shirtliff, P. A. 33; Taylor, R. M. 8(1); Turner, C. R. 23; Varadi, I. –(2); Whitton, S. P. 10(9); Wood, D. T. 3; Worthington, N. 32.
League Goals (35): Hirst 14 (1 pen), Atkinson 10, Sheridan 2, Shirtliff 2, Worthington 2, Pearson 1, Whitton 1, own goals 3.
Littlewoods Cup (9): Whitton 4, Atkinson 3, Hirst 1 (pen), Shakespeare 1.
FA Cup (3): Atkinson 1, Hirst 1, Shirtliff 1.
Ground: Hillsborough, Sheffield S6 1SW (0742–343122)
Nearest Station: Sheffield
Manager: Ron Atkinson **Secretary:** G.H. Mackrell FCCA
Colours: Blue and white striped shirts; black shorts
Record home gate: 72,841 v Manchester City, February 1934 (FA Cup)
Honours – Champions: Division 1: 1902–3, 1903–4, 1928–9, 1929–30; Division 2: 1899–1900, 1925–6, 1951–2, 1955–6, 1958–9
FA Cup winners: 1895–6, 1906–7, 1934–5

SHREWSBURY TOWN DIV. 3

Brown, Michael A.
Finley, Alan
Gorman, Paul A.
Green, Richard E.
Griffiths, Carl B.
Hartford, Richard A.
Hughes, Kenneth D.
Kelly, Anthony G.
Lynch, Thomas
McGinlay, John
Moyes, David W.
Naughton, William B. S.
Perks, Stephen J.
Spink, Dean P.
Weir, William
Wimbleton, Paul P.
Worsley, Graeme

League Appearances: Bell, D. 9; Blake, M. C. 10; Brown, M. A. 42(1); Cornforth, J. M. 3; Finley, A. 28(1); Gorman, P. A. 17(2); Green, R. E. 40; Griffiths, C. B. 10(8); Hartford, R. A. 14(3); Kasule, V. 3(2); Kelly, A. G. 43; Lynch T. 22; McGinlay, J. 44; Melrose, J. M. 5(14); Moyes, D. W. 46; Naughton, W. B. S. 40(3); Ormsby, B. T. 1; Parrish, S. –(2); Perks, S. J. 46; Pittman, S. 20; Pratley, R. G. 7; Priest, P. 7(4); Purdie, J. 9(3); Spink, D. P. 13; Wassall, K. D. –(2); Weir, W. 4(5); Wimbleton, P. P. 16; Worsley, G. 7(8).
League Goals (59): McGinlay 22 (3 pens), Moyes 8, Kelly 5, Spink 5, Griffiths 4, Bell 3, Naughton 3 (1 pen), Pittman 2, Brown 1, Finley 1, Gorman 1, Pratley 1, Purdie 1, own goals 2.
Littlewoods Cup (5): Naughton 2 (1 pen), Green 1, Melrose 1, Pratley 1.
FA Cup (2): McGinlay 2 (2 pens).
Ground: Gay Meadow, Shrewsbury SY2 6AB (0743–60111)
Nearest Station: Shrewsbury
Manager: Asa Hartford **Secretary:** M.J. Starkey
Colours: White shirts with blue trim; blue shorts
Record home gate: 18,917 v Walsall, April 1961 (League)
Honours – Champions: Division 3: 1978–9

SOUTHAMPTON DIV. 1

Adams, Michael R.
Andrews, Ian E.
Banger, Nicholas L.
Benali, Francis V.
Blake, Mark C.
Case, James R.
Cherednik, Alexsey
Cockerill, Glenn
Cook, Andrew C.
Davis, Stephen M.
Dodd, Jason R.
Flowers, Timothy D.
French, Gary R.
Horne, Barry
Kenna, Jeffrey J.
Lee, Samuel
Le Tissier, Matthew P.
Luscombe, Lee J.
Maddison, Neil S.
Moore, Kevin T.
Osman, Russell C.
Radford, Dean
Rideout, Paul D.
Rowland, Andrew J.
Ruddock, Neil
Shearer, Alan
Wallace, Raymond G.
Wallace, Rodney S.
Widdrington, Thomas

League Appearances: Adams, M. R. 15; Andrews, I. E. 3; Baker, G. 2(1); Benali, F. V. 23(4); Case, J. R. 33; Cherednik, A. 7(1); Cockerill, G. 35(1); Cook, A. C. 2(2); Davis, S. M. 4; Dodd, J. R. 21(1); Flowers, T. D. 35; Forrest, G. 1; Horne, B. 28(1); Lee, S. –(2); Le Tissier, M. P. 35; Maddison, N. S. –(2); Moore, K. T. 18(3); Osman, R. C. 34(1); Rideout, P. D. 30(1); Ruddock, N. 25(4); Shearer, A. 19(7); Wallace, D. L. 5; Wallace, R. G. 8(1); Wallace, R. S. 35(3).
League Goals (71): Le Tissier 20 (7 pens), Wallace Rod 18, Rideout 7, Osman 5, Cockerill 4, Horne 4, Case 3, Shearer 3, Ruddock 3, Wallace D 2, Cook 1, Moore 1.
Littlewoods Cup (8): Le Tissier 3 (1 pen), Wallace Rod 2, Cockerill 1, Horne 1, Rideout 1.
FA Cup (4): Horne 1, Le Tissier 1, Ruddock 1, Wallace Rod 1.
Ground: The Dell, Milton Road, Southampton SO9 4XX (0703–220505)
Nearest Station: Southampton
Manager: Chris Nicholl **Secretary:** B.P. Truscott
Colours: Red and white striped shirts; black shorts
Record home gate: 31,044 v Manchester United, October 1969 (League)
Honours – Champions: Division 3 South: 1921–2; Division 3: 1959–60
FA Cup winners: 1975–6

SOUTHEND UNITED DIV. 3

Ansah, Andrew
Austin, Dean B.
Benjamin, Ian
Butler, Peter J.
Clark, Paul P.
Cook, Jason P.
Crown, David I.
Daley, Peter J.
Edinburgh, Justin
Edwards, Andrew D.
Hyslop, Christian
Ling, Martin
McDonough, Roy
Martin, David
Newell, Paul .C
Prior, Spencer J.
Sansome, Paul E.
Smith, Paul W.
Tilson, Stephen B.
Walsh, Mario
West, Adrian P.

League Appearances: Ansah, A. 6(1); Austin, D. B. 7; Benjamin, I. 15; Bennett, G. M. 20(5); Brush, P. 28(3); Butler, P. J. 40(1); Butters, G. 16; Clark, P. P. 24(1); Cook, J. P. 29; Cooper, M. N. 4(1); Crown, D. I. 41; Daley, P. J. –(5); Dixon, A. 24; Edinburgh, J. 22; Edwards, A. D. 7(1); Jones, M. L. 2(2); Ling, M. 24(1); McDonough, R. 27(6); Martin, D. 38(1); O'Connell, I. A. –(4); Prior, S. J. 15; Roberts, P. 30(1); Sansome, P. E. 46; Smith, N. L. 12(2); Smith, P. W. 8(2); Tilson, S. B. 11(5); Walsh, M. 10(1).
League Goals (61): Crown 19 (3 pens), Ling 10, McDonough 5, Bennett 4, Benjamin 4, Butters 3, Martin 3, Butler 2, Walsh 2, Ansah 1, Cook 1, Daley 1, Prior 1, Smith N 1, Smith P 1, own goals 3.
Littlewoods Cup (9): Bennett 4, Crown 3 (1 pen), Martin 2.

FA Cup (0).
Ground: Roots Hall Football Ground, Victoria Avenue, Southend SS2 6NQ (0702 340707)
Nearest Stations: Pittlewell or Southend Central
Manager: David Webb **Secretary:** J.W. Adams
Colours: Blue shirts; yellow shorts with blue trim
Record home gate: 31,090 v Liverpool, January 1979 (FA Cup)
Honours – Champions: Division 4: 1980–81

STOCKPORT COUNTY DIV. 4

Angell, Brett
Beaumont, Christopher P.
Brabin, Gary
Brookman, Nicholas A.
Brown, Malcolm
Bullock, Stephen
Downes, Christopher
Edwards, Keith
Frain, David
Gannon, James P.
Hope, Darren
Knowles, Darren T.
Logan, David
McInerney, Ian
Mannion, John P.
Payne, Mark R. C.
Redfern, David
Ritchie, David M.
Robertson, Paul
Thorpe, Andrew
Williams, Paul R. C.
Williams, William R.

League Appearances: Angell, B. 43(1); Barrett, S. 10; Beaumont, C. P. 19(3); Brabin, G. 1; Brookman, N. A. 4(2); Brown, M. 37; Bullock, S. 23(4); Caldwell, A. –(2); Cecere, M. J. –(1); Cooke, J. 23(1); Downes, C. B. 10(1); Edwards, K. 26(1); Frain, D. 25(4); Gannon, J. P. 7; Hart, N. 1; Hope, D. 4; Howard, M. E. 1; Jones, P. B. 25; Knowles, D. T. 7(2); Leonard, G. A. 4(2); Logan, D. 25; MacDonald, G. 1; McInerney, I. 36(4); Matthews, M. 16; Muggleton, C. D. 4; Oghani, G. 5(3); Payne, M. R. C. 33(1); Redfern, D. 11; Ritchie, D. M. –(1); Robertson, P. 6(3); Siddall, B. 21; Thorpe, A. 39(1); Williams, P. R. C. 2(5); Williams, W. R. 37.
League Goals (68): Angell 23 (3 pens), Edwards 10, McInerney 8, Payne 6, Beaumont 5, Logan 4, Brown 2, Frain 2, Matthews 2, Oghani 2 (1 pen), Cooke 1, Downes 1, Gannon 1, own goal 1.
Littlewoods Cup (3): McDonald 1, McInerney 1, Matthews 1.
FA Cup (2): Angell 1, Edwards 1.
Ground: Edgeley Park, Stockport SK3 9DD (061–480 8888)
Nearest Station: Stockport
Manager: Danny Bergara **Secretary:** J.D. Simpson
Colours: White shirts: royal blue shorts
Record home gate: 27,833 v Liverpool, February 1950 (FA Cup)
Honours – Champions: Division 3 North: 1921–2, 1936–7; Division 4: 1966–7

STOKE CITY DIV. 3

Barnes, Paul L.
Barrett, Scott
Beeston, Carl F.
Biggins, Wayne
Blake, Noel L. G.
Boughey, Darren J.
Butler, John E.
Carr, Clifford P.
Cranson, Ian
Ellis, Anthony J.
Fowler, Lee E.
Fox, Peter D.
Higgins, Mark N.
Kelly, Anthony
Kevan, David J.
Noble, Daniel W. T.
Rennie, Paul A.
Sandford, Lee R.
Scott, Ian
Statham, Derek J.
Ware, Paul D.

League Appearances: Bamber, J. D. 20; Barnes, P. L. 4(1); Barrett, S. 7; Beagrie, P. S. 13; Beeston, C. F. 38; Berry, G. F. St. J. 15(1); Biggins, W. 35; Boughey, D. J. 4(3); Butler, J. E. 44; Blake, N. L. G. 18; Brooke, G. J. 6(2);

Carr, C. P. 22; Cranson, I. 17; Ellis, A. J. 24; Farrell, S. –(2); Fowler, L. E. 13(2); Fox, P. D. 38; Gallimore, A. M. –(1); Hackett, G. S. 18(8); Higgins, M. N. 4(2); Hilaire, V. M. 5; Holmes, A. J. 5(1); Kamara, C. 22; Kelly, A. 5(4); Kevan, D. J. 17; Morgan, N. 6(7); Noble, D. W. T. 1; Palin, L. G. 17(2); Sale, M. D. –(2); Sandford, L. R. 23; Saunders, C. S. 12(10); Scott, I. 14(5); Smith, M. 2; Statham, D. J. 19; Thomas, M. R. 8; Ware, P. D. 9(7); Wright, I. M. 1.
League Goals (35): Biggins 10 (1 pen), Ellis 6, Palin 3 (2 pens), Bamber 2, Beeston 2, Cranson 2, Hackett 2, Sandford 2, Berry 1 (pen), Hilaire 1, Kamara 1, Morgan 1, Saunders 1, Scott 1.
Littlewoods Cup (1): Morgan 1.
FA Cup (0).
Ground: Victoria Ground, Stoke-on-Trent ST4 4EG (0782–413511)
Nearest Station: Stoke-on Trent
Manager: Alan Ball **Secretary:** M.J. Potts
Colours: Red and white striped shirts; white shorts
Record home gate: 51,380 v Arsenal, March 1937 (League)
Honours – Champions: Division 2: 1932–3, 1962–3; Division 3 North: 1926–7
League Cup winners: 1971–2

SUNDERLAND DIV. 1

Agboola, Rueben O. F.
Armstrong, Gordon I.
Atkinson, Brian
Bennett, Gary E.
Bracewell, Paul W.
Brady, Kieron
Carter, Timothy D.
Cornforth, John M.
Cullen, Anthony
Gabbiadini, Marco
Gabbiadini, Ricardo
Gray, Martin
Hardyman, Paul G.
Hauser, Thomas
Hawke, Warren R.
Heathcote, Michael
Kay, John
Lemon, Paul A.
MacPhail, John
Norman, Anthony J.
Ord, Richard J.
Owers, Gary
Pascoe, Colin J.
Rush, David
Sams, Andrew G.
Trigg, Jonathan M.
Williams, Paul L.

League Appearances: Agboola, R. O. F. 30(6); Armstrong, G. I. 46; Atkinson, B. 11(2); Bennett, G. E. 36; Bracewell, P. W. 36(1); Brady, K. 9(2); Carter, T. D. 18; Cornforth, J. M. 1(1); Cullen, A. 5(11); Gabbiadini, M. 46; Gabbiadini, R. –(1); Gates, E. L. 34(2); Hardyman, P. G. 42; Hauser, T. 6(12); Hawke, W. R. 1(7); Heathcote, M. 6(2); Kay, J. 31(1); MacPhail, J. 38; Norman, A. J. 28; Ord, R. J. 6(1); Owers, G. 43; Pascoe, C. J. 32(1); Williams, P. L. 1.
League Goals (70): Gabbiadini 21, Owers 9, Armstrong 8, Hardyman 7 (4 pens), Gates 6, Hauser 6, Bennett 3, Bracewell 2, Brady 2, MacPhail 2, Hawke 1, Ord 1, Pascoe 1, own goal 1.
Littlewoods Cup (13): Gabbiadini 4, Armstrong 3, Gates 3, Hardyman 2 (1 pen), Pascoe 1.
FA Cup (1): Armstrong 1.
Ground: Roker Park, Grantham Road, Sunderland SR6 9 SW (091–5140332)
Nearest Stations: Sunderland or Seaburn
Manager: Denis Smith **Secretary:** G. Davidson F.C.A.
Colours: Red and white striped shirts; black shorts
Record home gate: 75,118 v Derby, March 1933 (FA Cup)
Honours – Champions: Division 1: 1891–2, 1892–3, 1894–5, 1901–2, 1912–13, 1935–6; Division 2: 1975–6; Division 3: 1987–8
FA Cup winners: 1936–7, 1972–3

SWANSEA CITY DIV. 3

Boyle, Terence D. J.
Bracey, Lee M. I.
Chalmers, Paul
Coleman, Christopher P.
D'Auria, David
Davey, Simon
Evans, Philip
Harris, Mark A.
Heeps, James A.
Hough, David J.
Hughes, John
James, Robert M.
Legg, Andrew
Melville, Andrew K.
Phillips, Stewart G.
Raynor, Paul J.
Thornber, Stephen J.
Trick, Desmond
Walker, Keith C.

League Appearances: Boyle, T. D. J. 27; Bracey, L. M. I. 31; Chalmers, P. 13(3); Cobb, G. E. 5; Coleman, C. P. 46; Curtis, A. T. 21(5); D'Auria, D. A. 6(1); Davey, S. 16(2); Freestone, R. 14; Harris, M. A. 41; Heeps, J. 1; Hough, D. J. 32; Hughes, J. 16(8); Hutchison, T. 31(5); James, R. M. 25(5); Legg, A. 20(6); Melville, A. K. 46; Phillips, S. G. 6(8); Raynor, P. J. 38(2); Salako, J. A. 13; Thornber, S. J. 34; Trick, D. 11(3); Wade, B. A. 2(9); Walker, K. C. 11(2).
League Goals (45): Raynor 6, Melville 5, Chalmers 4, Hughes 4, James 4 (2 pens), Curtis 3, Legg 3, Salako 3, Coleman 2, Davey 2, Harris 2, Hutchison 2, Boyle 1, Hough 1, Phillips 1, Thornber 1, Wade 1.
Littlewoods Cup (1): Raynor 1.
FA Cup (6): Chalmers 2, Melville 2, Davies 1, Raynor 1 (pen).
Ground: Vetch Field, Swansea SA1 3SU (0792–474114)
Nearest Station: Swansea
Manager: Terry Yorath **Secretary:** George Taylor
Colours: All white
Record home gate: 32,796 v Arsenal, February 1968 (FA Cup)
Honours – Champions: Division 3 South: 1924–5, 1948–9

SWINDON TOWN DIV. 2

Bodin, Paul J.
Calderwood, Colin
Close, Shaun C.
Cornwell, John A.
Coyne, Peter D.
Digby, Fraser C.
Foley, Steven
Galvin, Anthony
Gittens, Jon
Hammond, Nicholas D.
Hockaday, David
Hunt, Paul C.
Jones, Tom
Kerslake, David
MacLaren, Ross
McLoughlin, Alan .F
Shearer, Duncan M.
Simpson, Fitzroy
Summerbee, Nicholas J.
Tomlinson, Neil R.
Trollope, Paul J.
Viveash, Adrian L.
White, Stephen J.

League Appearances: Ardiles, O. –(2); Barnard, L. K. 5; Bodin, P. J. 38(3); Calderwood, C. 46; Close, S. C. 4(7); Cornwell, J. A. 2(17); Dearden, K. C. 1; Digby, F. C. 45; Foley, S. 20(3); Galvin, A. 6(5); Gittens, J. 40; Hockaday, D. 11(9); Hunt, P. C. 2(2); Jones, T. 43(1); Kerslake, D. 28; King, P. G. 14; McLoughlin, A. F. 46; MacLaren, R. 46; Parkin, T. J. 6; Shearer, D. N. 42; Simpson, F. 19(11); Summerbee, N. J. –(1); White, S. J. 42(1).
League Goals (79): Shearer 20, White 18, McLoughlin 12, Bodin 5 (2 pens), Foley 4, Gittens 4, Calderwood 3, MacLaren 3, Jones 2, Simpson 2, King 1, Parkin 1, own goals 4.
Littlewoods Cup (15): White 5, McLoughlin 4, Shearer 4, MacLaren 2.
FA Cup (1): Shearer 1.
Ground: County Ground, Swindon SN1 2ED (0793–22118 and 36170)
Nearest Station: Swindon
Manager: Ossie Ardiles **Secretary:** Lisa Maberly
Colours: All red

Record home gate: 32,000 v Arsenal, January 1972 (FA Cup)
Honours – Champions: Division 4: 1985–6
League Cup winners: 1968–9
Anglo-Italian Cup winners: 1970

TORQUAY UNITED DIV. 4

Bastow, Ian J.
Edwards, Dean S.
Elliott, Matthew S.
Hay, Alan B.
Holmes, Paul
Joyce, Sean W.
Lloyd, Philip R.
Loram, Mark J.
Matthews, John M.
Morrison, John
Smith, Paul
Uzzell, John E.
Veysey, Kenneth J.

League Appearances: Airey, C. 11(1); Bastow, I. J. 6(3); Caldwell, D. W. 17; Cookson, S. J. 7(3); Curran, C. –(1); Davis, A. J. 6(4); Edwards, D. S. 26(4); Elliott, M. S. 32(1); Hall, P. A. 7(3); Hannigan, A. J. 5(2); Hay, A. B. 8; Hirons, P. T. 9(7); Holmes, P. 44; Joyce, S. W. 38(3); Lloyd, P. R. 45(1); Loram, M. J. 39(3); Matthews, J. M. 22(3); Miller, A. J. 3(1); Morrison, J. 11(3); Mundee, D. W. J. 9; Pugh, D. J. 3; Smith, J. 2(8); Smith, P. 31(2); Taylor, R. S. 11(7); Uzzell, J. E. 35(1); Veysey, K. J. 46; Weston, I. P. 25; Whiston, P. M. 8.
League Goals (53): Loram 12 (4 pens), Airey 8, Smith P. 6, Caldwell 6, Joyce 5, Edwards 3, Elliott 2, Holmes 2, Uzzell 2, Cookson 1, Lloyd 1, Smith J. 1, Taylor 1, Whiston 1, own goals 2.
Littlewoods Cup (0).
FA Cup (9): Elliott 2, Smith J 2, Hirons 1, Lloyd 1, Loram 1, Uzzell 1, own goal 1.
Ground: Plainmoor, Torquay, Devon TQ1 3PS (0803–328666/7)
Nearest Stations: Torquay or Torre
Manager: Dave Smith **Secretary:** D.F. Turner
Colours: All white with yellow and blue trim
Record home gate: 21,908 v Huddersfield, January 1955 (FA Cup)
Honours: Nil

TOTTENHAM HOTSPUR DIV. 1

Allen, Paul K.
Amar, Mohamed A. (Nayim)
Bergsson, Gudni
Butters, Guy
Dearden, Kevin C.
Edwards, Matthew D.
Fenwick, Terence W.
Garland, Peter J.
Gascoigne, Paul J.
Gilzean, Ian R.
Gray, Philip
Hendon, Ian M.
Howells, David
Howells, Gareth J.
Hughton, Christopher
Lineker, Gary W.
McDonald, David H.
Mabbutt, Gary V.
Mimms, Robert A.
Moncur, John F.
Moran, Paul
Polston, Andy A.
Polston, John D.
Robson, Mark A.
Samways, Vincent
Sedgley, Steven P.
Statham, Brian
Stewart, Paul A.
Thomas, Mitchell A.
Thorstvedt, Erik
Stuttle, David
Van Den Hauwe, Patrick
Walker, Ian M.
Walsh, Paul A.

League Appearances: Allen, P. K. 29(3); Amar, M. A. 18(1); Bergsson, G. 17(1); Butters, G. 7; Fenwick, T. W. 10; Gascoigne, P. J. 34; Howells, D. 33(1); Hughton, C. W. G. 8; Lineker, G. W. 38; Mabbutt, G. V. 36; Mimms, R. A. 4; Moncur, J. F. 2(3); Moran, P. –(5); Polston, A. A. –(1); Polston, J. D. 11(2); Robson, M. A. –(3); Samways, V. 18(5); Sedgley, S. P. 31(1); Stevens, G. A. 4(3); Stewart, P. A. 24(4); Thomas, M. A. 17(9); Thorstvedt, E. 34; Van Den Hauwe, P. W. R. 31; Walsh, P. A. 12(14).

League Goals (59): Lineker 24 (2 pens), Stewart 8, Allen 6, Gascoigne 6, Howells 5, Samways 3, Walsh 2, Moncur 1, Moran 1, Polston J 1, Thomas 1, own goal 1.
Littlewoods Cup (16): Nayim 3, Allen 2, Lineker 2, Fenwick 1, Gascoigne 1, Howells 1, Mabbutt 1, Samways 1, Sedgley 1, Stewart 1, Walsh 1, own goal 1.
FA Cup (1): Howells 1.
Ground: White Hart Lane, 748 High Road, Tottenham, N17 0AP (01–808 8080)
Nearest Stations: White Hart Lane (BR), Northumberland Park (BR), or Seven Sisters (Victoria Lane) thence by bus
Manager: Terry Venables **Secretary:** Peter Barnes
Colours: White shirts; navy blue shorts
Record home gate: 75,038 v Sunderland, March 1938 (FA Cup)
Honours – Champions: Division 1: 1950–51, 1960–61; Division 2: 1919–20, 1949–50
FA Cup winners: 1900–1, 1920–21, 1960–61, 1961–62, 1966–7, 1980–81, 1981–2 (seven wins joint record with Aston Villa and Manchester U)
League Cup winners: 1970–71, 1972–3
European Cup Winners' Cup winners: 1962–3
UEFA Cup winners: 1971–2, 1983–4

TRANMERE ROVERS DIV. 3

Bauress, Gary J.
Bishop, Edward M.
Collings, Paul W.
Garnett, Shaun M.
Harvey, James
Higgins, David A.
Hughes, Mark
Irons, Kenneth
McCarrick, Mark B.
McNab, Neil
Malkin, Christopher G.
Martindale, David
Morrissey, John J.
Muir, Ian J.
Mungall, Steven H.
Nixon, Eric W.
Smith, John
Stell, William J.
Thomas, Tony
Vickers, Stephen H.

League Appearances: Bauress, G. J. 1; Bishop, E. M. 13(15); Fairclough, D. 3(11); Garnett, S. M. 4; Harvey, J. 45(1); Higgins, D. A. 45; Hughes, M. 45; Irons, K. –(3); McCarrick, M. B. 32; McNab, N. 22; Malkin, C. G. 36(4); Martindale, D. 13(6); Morrissey, J. J. 24(3); Muir, I. J. 46; Mungall, S. H. 16(1); Nixon, E. W. 46; Pike, M. R. 2; Steel, W. J. 29(7); Thomas, T. 42; Vickers, S. H. 42.
League Goals (86): Muir 23 (4 pens), Malkin 18, Bishop 7, Harvey 7, Steel 5, McCarrick 4, Morrissey 4, Hughes 4, Vickers 3, Martindale 2, Thomas 2, Mungall 1, Fairclough 1, Higgins 1, McNab 1, own goals 3.
Littlewoods Cup (14): Malkin 4, Muir 4 (2 pens), Bishop 2, Steele 2, McCarrick 1, Vickers 1.
FA Cup (0).
Ground: Prenton Park, Birkenhead, L42 9PN (051–608 4194)
Nearest Stations: Central Station Birkenhead and Rock Ferry
Manager: John King **Secretary:** C.N. Wilson F.A.A.I.
Colours: All white
Record home gate: 24,424 v Stoke, February 1972 (FA Cup)
Honours – Champions: Division 3 North: 1937–8
Associate Members Cup – Winners: 1989–90

WALSALL DIV. 4

Barber, Frederick
Bertschin, Keith E.
Forbes, Graeme S. A.
Goldsmith, Martin
Green, Ronald R.
Kelly, John
Littlejohn, Adrian S.
Marsh, Christopher J.
Mower, Kenneth M.
O'Hara, Stephen
Rimmer, Stuart A.
Skipper, Peter D.
Smith, Dean
Taylor, Alexander
Whitehouse, Phillip

League Appearances: Barber, F. 25; Bertschin, K. E. 29(6); Bremner, D G. 2(4); Dornan, A. 18; Forbes, G. S. A. 44; Ford, G. 13; Goldsmith, M. –(1); Goodwin,

M. A. 22(2); Green, R. R. 21; Gritt, S. J. 20; Hart, P. O. 10; Hawker, P. N. 22(8); Jones, P. A. 3; Kelly, J. 24(2); Lemon, P. A. 2; Littlejohn, A. S. 11; Lyne, N. 6(1); Marsh, C. J. 8(1); Mower, K. M. 29(1); O'Hara, S. 14(4); Pritchard, H. K. 4; Rees, M. 7; Rimmer, S. A. 38(3); Saville, A. V. 16(10); Shaw, G. 4(5); Skipper, P. D. 40; Smith, D. 7; Taylor, A. 30(2); Thorpe, A. 24(3); Whitehouse, P. 9; Wilder, C. J. 4.
League Goals (40): Rimmer 10 (2 pens), Bertschin 9, Shaw 3 (1 pen), Taylor 3, Forbes 2, Ford 2, Dornan 1, Gritt 1, Hawker 1, Kelly 1, Pritchard 1, Rees 1, Saville 1 (pen), Skipper 1, Thorpe 1, own goals 2.
Littlewoods Cup (1): Pritchard 1.
FA Cup (5): Bertschin 2, Rimmer 2, Forbes 1.
Ground: Bescot Stadium, Bescot Crescent, Walsall WS1 4SA (0922–22791)
Nearest Stations: Walsall or Bescott then 15 min walk
Manager: Ken Hibbitt **Secretary:** K.R. Whalley
Colours: Red shirts; white shorts
Record home gate: 25,453 v Newcasle, August 1961 (League)
Honours – Champions: Division 4: 1959–60

WATFORD DIV. 2

Allison, Wayne
Ashby, Barry J.
Coton, Anthony P.
Drysdale, Jason
Evans, David W.
Falconer, William
Gibbs, Nigel J.
Harrison, Gerald R.
Henry, Liburd A.
Hodges, Glyn P.
Holdsworth, David G.
Jackett, Kenneth F.
James, David
Penrice, Gary K.
Porter, Gary M.
Price, Jonathan
Pullan, Christopher J.
Rees, Melvyn J.
Richardson, Lee J.
Roberts, Iwan W.
Roeder, Glenn V.
Soloman, Jason R.
Thomas, Roderick C.
Towler, Paul A.
Wilkinson, Paul
Williams, Gary

League Appearances: Allison, W. 6(1); Ashby, B. J. 14(4); Bazeley, D. S. –(1); Coton, A. P. 46; Drysdale, J. 18(2); Falconer, W. 23(7); Gibbs, N. J. 41; Harrison, G. R. 2(1); Henry, L. A. 7(2); Hodges, G. P. 35; Holdsworth, D. G. 44; Holdsworth, D. C. –(4); Jackett, K. F. 16(1); McClelland, J. 1; Penrice, G. K. 29; Porter, G. M. 31(1); Pullan, C. J. 1(3); Redfearn, N. D. 10(2); Richardson, L. J. 31(1); Roberts, I. W. 8(1); Robson, M. A. 1; Roeder, G. V. 44(1); Thomas, R. C. 30(2); Thompson, G. L. 7(6); Wilkinson, P. 43; Williams, G. 18.
League Goals (58): Wilkinson 15, Penrice 13, Hodges 7 (3 pens), Thomas 6, Porter 4 (2 pens), Falconer 3, Holdsworth David 3, Ashby 1, Henry 1, Holdsworth Dean 1, Redfearn 1, Richardson 1, Roeder 1, Thompson 1.
Littlewoods Cup (2): Roberts 2.
FA Cup (4): Hodges 1, Penrice 1, Porter 1 (pen), Roeder 1.
Ground: Vicarage Road Stadium, Watford WD1 8ER (0923–30933)
Nearest Stations: Watford Junction, Watford High Street or Watford Stadium Halt
Manager: Colin Lee **Chief Executive:** E. Plumley F.A.A.I.
Colours: Yellow shirts with black and red trim; black shorts
Record home gate: 34,099 v Manchester United, February 1969 (FA Cup)
Honours – Champions: Division 3: 1968–9; Division 4: 1977–8

WEST BROMWICH ALBION DIV. 2

Allardyce, Samuel
Anderson, Colin R.
Bannister, Gary
Bradley, Darren M.
Burgess, Daryl
Cartwright, Neil A.
Dobbins, Lionel W.
Ford, Tony
Foster, Adrian M.
Goodman, Donald R.
Hackett, Gary S.
Harbey, Graham K.
Hodson, Simeon P.
McNally, Bernard A.
Naylor, Stuart W.
North, Stacey S.
Parkin, Stephen
Raven, Paul D.
Robson, Gary
Rogers, Darren J.
Shakespeare, Craig R.
Talbot, Brian E.
West, Colin
Whyte, Christopher A.

League Appearances: Allardyce, S. –(1); Anderson, V. –(1); Anderson, C. R. 13; Bannister, G. 13; Barham, M. F. 4; Bartlett, K. F. 15(5); Bennett, M. 1; Bradley, D. M. 25(2); Bradshaw, P. W. 4; Burgess, D. 31(3); Cartwright, N. A. 2(5); Dobbins, L. W. 5; Ford, T. 42; Foster, A. M. 7(7); Goodman, D. R. 39; Hackett, G. S. 9(5); Harbey, G. K. 30; Hodson, S. P. 10; McNally, B. A. 41; Marriott, A. 3; Naylor, S. W. 39; North, S. S. 32(2); Parkin, S. 14; Raven, P. D. 7; Robson, G. 21(4); Shakespeare, C. R. 18; Talbot, B. E. 12(8); Thomas, J. W. 8(10); West, C. 18(3); Whyte, C. A. 43(1).
League Goals (67): Goodman 21 (1 pen), Ford 8, Bartlett 7, McNally 5 (3 pens), Robson 5, West 4, Whyte 4, Bannister 2, Bradley 2, Hackett 2, Foster 1, Parkin 1, Shakespeare 1, Talbot 1, Thomas 1, own goals 2.
Littlewoods Cup (7): Thomas 3, Whyte 2, McNally 1, Talbot 1.
FA Cup (3): Bartlett 1, Ford 1, Robson 1.
Ground: The Hawthorns, West Bromwich B71 4LF (021–525 8888)
Nearest Stations: Smethwick Rolfe Street or Birmingham New Street
Manager: Brian Talbot **Secretary:** Dr J.J. Evans
Colours: Navy blue and white striped shirts; navy blue shorts
Record home gate: 64,815 v Arsenal, March 1937 (FA Cup)
Honours – Champions: Division 1: 1919–20; Division 2: 1901–2, 1910–11
FA Cup winners: 1887–8, 1891–2, 1930–31, 1953–4, 1967–8
League Cup winners: 1965–6

WEST HAM UNITED DIV. 2

Allen, Martin J.
Banks, Steven
Bishop, Ian W.
Clarke, Simon N.
Dicks, Julian A.
Dolan, Eamonn J.
Foster, Colin J.
Gale, Anthony P.
Harwood, Christopher T.
Keen, Kevin I.
Kelly, Paul M.
Livett, Simon R.
McAvennie, Francis
McKnight, Allen
McQueen, Thomas F.
Martin, Alvin E.
Miklosko, Ludek
Morley, Trevor W.
Parkes, Phillip B. F.
Parris, George M. R.
Potts, Steven J.
Quinn, James M.
Robson, Stewart I.
Rosenior, Leroy D. G.
Rush, Matthew J.
Slater, Stuart I.
Stewart, Raymond S.
Strodder, Gary J.

League Appearances: Allen, M. J. 39; Bishop, I. W. 13(4); Brady, W. L. 25(8); Devonshire, A. E. 3(4); Dicks, J. A. 40; Dolan, E. J. 8(2); Fashanu, J. S. 2; Foster, C. J. 20(2); Gale, A. P. 36; Ince, P. E. C. 1; Keen, K. I. 43(1); Kelly, D. T. A. 8(8); Kelly, P. M. –(1); McAvennie, F. 1(4); McQueen, T. F. 5(2); Martin, A. E. 31; Morley, T. W. 18(1); Miklosko, L. 18; Parkes, P. B. F. 22; Parris, G. M. R. 35(3); Potts, S. J. 30(2); Quinn, J. M. 18(3); Robson, S. I. 7; Rosenior, L. D. G. 4(1); Slater, S. I. 40; Strodder, G. J. 16; Suckling, P. J. 6; Ward, M. W. 17(2).
League Goals (80): Quinn 12 (1 pen), Keen 10, Morley 10, Allen 9, Dicks 9 (7 pens), Slater 7, Ward 5 (1 pen), Dolan 3, Bishop 2, Brady 2, Parris 2, Rosenior 2, Foster 1, Gale 1, Kelly 1, Robson 1, Strodder 1, own goals 2.

Littlewoods Cup (11): Dicks 4 (1 pen), Allen 2, Slater 2, Keen 1, Kelly 1, Martin 1.
FA Cup (0).
Ground: Boleyn Ground, Green Street, Upton Park E13 9AZ (01–472 2740)
Nearest Station: Upton Park (District line)
Manager: Billy Bonds **Chief Executive Secretary:** T.M. Finn
Colours: Claret shirts with blue trim; white shorts
Record home gate: 42,322 v Tottenham H, October 1970 (League)
Honours – Champions: Division 2: 1957–8, 1980–81
FA Cup winners: 1963–4, 1974–5, 1979–80
European Cup Winners' Cup winners: 1964–5

WIGAN ATHLETIC DIV. 3

Adkins, Nigel H.
Andrews, Simon P.
Atherton, Peter
Carberry, James
Daley, Philip
Griffiths, Bryan
Hughes, Philip
Johnson, Alan K.
Page, Donald R.
Parkinson, Joseph S.
Patterson, Darren J.
Pilling, Andrew J.
Rimmer, Neill
Rogerson, Lee A.
Tankard, Allen J.
Thompson, David S.
Woods, Raymond G.

League Appearances: Adkins, N. H. 13; Atherton, P. 45(1); Baraclough, I. R. 8(1); Beesley, P. 11; Carberry, J. 15(17); Crompton, J. D. 1; Daley, P. 32(1); Fallon, S. 1(1); Griffiths, B. 40(5); Hilditch, M. 20(1); Hughes, P. 33; Johnson, A. K. 26(7); Kelly, N. –(4); McGarvey, S. T. 3; Nugent, S. –(1); Page, D. R. 18(7); Parkinson, J. S. 33; Patterson, D. J. 12(17); Pilling, A. J. 21(5); Rimmer, N. 38; Rogerson, L. A. 1(2); Senior, S. 43; Tankard, A. J. 45; Taylor, R. G. –(1); Thompson, D. S. 38(1); Ward, A. 8(3); Whitworth, N. A. 1(1).
League Goals (48): Griffiths 7 (3 pens), Hilditch 7, Pilling 6, Daley 6, Thompson 5, Carberry 3, Baraclough 2, Parkinson 2, Ward 2, Johnson 1, Patterson 1, Rimmer 1, Tankard 1 (pen), own goals 4.
Littlewoods Cup (7): Thompson 2, Griffiths 1, Hilditch 1, Page 1, Parkinson 1, Senior 1.
FA Cup (4): Griffiths 1, Hilditch 1, Johnson 1, Page 1.
Ground: Springfield Park, Wigan WN6 7BA (0942–44433)
Nearest Stations: Wigan Wallgate and Wigan North West
Manager: Bryan Hamilton **Secretary:** Mark A. Blackbourne
Colours: Blue shirts; white shorts
Record home gate: 27,500 v Hereford United, December 1953 (FA Cup)
Honours: Nil
Associate Members Cup winners: 1984–5

WIMBLEDON DIV. 1

Anthrobus, Stephen A.
Bennett, Michael R.
Blackwell, Dean R.
Cooper, David A.
Cork, Alan G.
Cotterill, Stephen
Curle, Keith
Dobbs, Gerald F.
Fairweather, Carlton
Fashanu, John
Fitzgerald, Scott
Gayle, John
Gibson, Terence B.
Goodyear, Clive
Joseph, Roger A.
Kruszynsky, Zbigniew
McAllister, Brian
McGee, Paul
Miller, Paul A.
Newhouse, Aidan
Phelan, Terry M.
Quamija, Mark E.
Ryan, Vaughan W.
Sanchez, Lawrence P.
Scales, John R.
Segers, Johannes C. A.
Sullivan, Neil
Wise, Dennis F.
Young, Eric

League Appearances: Anthrobus, S. A. 10; Bennett, M. R. 6(1); Blackwell, D. R. –(3); Brooke, G. J. –(2); Cork, A. G. 12(19); Cotterill, S. 2; Curle, K. 38; Fair-

weather, C. 20(1); Fashanu, J. 24; Fitzgerald, S. –(1); Gayle, J. 8(3); Gibson, T. B. 16(2); Goodyear, C. 4; Joseph, R. A. 15(4); Kruszynsky, Z. 26(1); McAllister, B. 1(2); McGee, P. 11(2); Miller, P. A. 11(4); Newhouse, A. 1(1); Phelan, T. M. 34; Ryan, V. W. 28(3); Sanchez, L. P. 16(2); Scales, J. R. 27(1); Segers, J. C. A. 38; Wise, D. F. 35; Young, E. 35.
League Goals (47): Fashanu 11 (4 pens), Wise 8, Cork 5, Gibson 5, Young 5, Curle 2 (1 pen), Kryszynski 2, Miller 2, Scales 2, Bennett 1, Cotterill 1, Fairweather 1, Gayle 1, Sanchez 1.
Littlewoods Cup (7): Gibson 3, Fashanu 2 (1 pen), Fairweather 1, McGee 1.
FA Cup (0).
Ground: Plough Lane Ground, Durnsford Road, Wimbledon, SW19 (01–946 6311)
Nearest Stations: Wimbledon or Haydons Road (BR) Wimbledon Park (District)
Manager: Bobby Gould **Secretary:** Adrian Cook
Colours: All blue with yellow trim
Record home gate: 18,000 v HMS Victory, 1934–5 (FA Amateur Cup)
Honours – Champions: Division 4: 1982–3
FA Cup winners: 1987–8

WOLVERHAMPTON WANDERERS DIV. 2

Bartram, Vincent L.
Bellamy, Gary
Bennett, Thomas M.
Bull, Stephen G.
Clarke, Nicholas J.
Cook, Paul A.
Dennison, Robert
Downing, Keith G.
Jones, Paul A.
Lange, Anthony S.
McLoughlin, Paul B.
Mutch, Andrew
Paskin, William J.
Steele, Timothy W.
Taylor, Colin D.
Thompson, Andrew R.
Venus, Mark
Westley, Shane L. M.

League Appearances: Bellamy, G. 39; Bennett, T. M. 30; Bull, S. G. 42; Chard, P. J. 4(2); Clarke, N. J. 3; Cook, P. A. 28; Dennison, R. 46; Downing, K. G. 26(5); Gooding, M. C. 13; Jones, P. A. 7(6); Kendall, M. 41; Lange, A. S. 5; McLoughlin, P. B. 7(12); Mutch, A. 35(2); Paskin, W. J. 10(7); Robertson, A. 5; Steele, T. W. 13(2); Streete, F. A. 17; Thompson, A. R. 31(2); Vaughan, N. M. 23(2); Venus, M. 44; Westley, S. L. M. 37.
League Goals (67): Bull 24, Mutch 11, Dennison 8, McLaughlin 4, Thompson 4 (4 pens), Bellamy 3, Downing 3, Cook 2, Paskin 2, Venus 2, Steele 1, own goals 3.
Littlewoods Cup (5): Bull 2, Dennison 1, Mutch 1, Westley 1.
FA Cup (1): Bull 1.
Ground: Molineux Grounds, Wolverhampton WV1 4QR (0902–712181)
Nearest Station: Wolverhampton
Manager: Graham Turner **Secretary:** K.D. Pearson A.C.I.S.
Colours: Gold shirts; black shorts
Record home gate: 61,315 v Liverpool, February 1939 (FA Cup)
Honours – Champions: Division 1: 1953–4, 1957–8, 1958–9; Division 2: 1931–32, 1976–7; Division 3 North: 1923–4; Division 3: 1988–9; Division 4: 1987–8
FA Cup winners: 1892–3,1907–8, 1948–9, 1959–60
League Cup winners: 1973–4, 1979–80
Associate Members Cup winners: 1987–8

WREXHAM DIV. 4

Armstrong, Christopher
Barnes, Robert A.
Beaumont, Nigel
Bowden, Jon L.
Cooper, Graham
Flynn, Brian
Hunter, Geoffrey
Jones, Joseph P.
Morris, Mark
O'Keefe, Vincent J.
Phillips, Wayne
Reck, Sean M.
Sertori, Mark A.
Thackeray, Andrew J.
Watkin, Stephen
Williams, Michael
Worthington, Gary L.
Wright, Darren J.

League Appearances: Armstrong, C. 10(12); Barnes, R. A. 8; Beaumont, N. 43; Bowden, J. L. 31(2); Buxton, S. C. 16(5); Cooper, G. 16(2); Filson, R. M. –(1); Flynn, B. 19(4); Hardy, P. 1; Hunter, G. 21; Jones, J. P. 23(1); Jones, R. S. –(1); Kearns, O. A. 10(2); Kennedy, A. P. 6(1); Madden, C. A. 6(2); Morgan, S. 7; Morris, M. 3; O'Keefe, V. J. 43; Owen, G. 8(5); Phillips, W. 2(3); Preece, A. P. 4(3); Preece, R. 27(5); Reck, S. M. 28(4); Salathiel, D. N. 29; Sertori, M. A. 18; Thackeray, A. J. 29(5); Williams, M. 13; Worthington, G. L. 39(3); Wrench, M. N. 2; Wright, D. J. 24; Youds, E. P. 20.
League Goals (51): Worthington 12 (1 pen), Thackeray 7, Buxton 4 (3 pens), Armstrong 3, Beaumont 3, Cooper 3, Hunter 3, Flynn 2, Kearns 2, Sertori 2, Youds 2, Bowden 1, Jones 1, Morgan 1, Preece A 1, Preece R 1, Reck 1, Wright 1, own goal 1.
Littlewoods Cup (0).
FA Cup (0).
Ground: The Racecourse, Mold Road, Wrexham LL1 2AN (0978–262129)
Nearest Station: Wrexham General
Manager: Brian Flynn **Secretary:** D.L. Rhodes
Colours: Red shirts; white shorts
Record home gate: 34,445 v Manchester United, January 1957 (FA Cup)
Honours – Champions: Division 3: 1977–8

YORK CITY DIV. 4

Barratt, Anthony
Canham, Anthony
Crossley, Richard M.
Dunn, Iain G. W.
Hall, Wayne
Helliwell, Ian
Himsworth, Gary P.
Howlett, Gary P.
Kiely, Dean
Longhurst, David J.
McMillan, Lyndon A.
Marples, Christopher
Naylor, Glenn
Reid, Shaun
Spooner, Stephen A.
Tutill, Stephen A.
Warburton, Ray

League Appearances: Barratt, A. 46; Canham, A. 28(6); Colville, R. J. 17(7); Crossley, R. M. 1; Dixon, K. L. 15(4); Dunn, I. G. W. 10(8); Greenough, R. A. 2(1); Hall, W. 22(5); Heathcote, M. 3; Helliwell, I. 44(2); Himsworth, G. P. 15(8); Howlett, G. P. 41(2); Kelly, T. J. 35; Longhurst, D. J. 4; McMillan, L. A. 21(4); Madden, C. 3(1); Marples, C. 46; Naylor, G. –(1); Ord, R. J. 3; Reid, S. 24(1); Spooner, S. A. 41; Tutill, S. A. 42; Warburton, R. 43.
League Goals (55): Helliwell 14, Spooner 6 (1 pen), Barratt 4, Canham 4, Dixon 4, Himsworth 4, Howlett 4, Reid 4 (1 pen), Hall 3, Dunn 2, Kelly 2 (2 pens), Longhurst 2, Warburton 2.
Littlewoods Cup (7): Spooner 3, Colville 2, Helliwell 1, Warburton 1.
FA Cup (1): Warburton 1.
Ground: Bootham Crescent, York YO3 7AQ (0904–624447)
Nearest Station: York
Manager: John Bird **Secretary:** Keith Usher
Colours: Red shirts, navy blue shorts
Record home gate: 28,123 v Huddersfield T, March 1938 (FA Cup)
Honours – Champions: Division 4: 1983–4

LEAGUE TITLE WINS

League Division I 18 Liverpool; 9 Arsenal, Everton; 7 Aston Villa, Manchester U; 6 Sunderland; 4 Newcastle, Sheffield Wednesday; 3 Huddersfield, Wolves; 2 Blackburn R, Burnley, Derby Co, Leeds, Manchester C, Portsmouth, Preston NE, Tottenham; 1 Chelsea, Ipswich, Nottingham F, Sheffield U, West Bromwich Albion.

League Division II 6 Manchester C, Leicester; 5 Sheffield Wednesday; 4 *Birmingham, Derby C, Liverpool; 3 Middlesbrough, Notts Co, Preston; 2 Aston Villa, Bolton, Burnley, Chelsea, Grimsby, Ipswich, Leeds, Manchester U, Norwich C, Nottingham F, Stoke, Tottenham, West Bromwich, West Ham U, Wolverhampton W; 1 Blackburn R, Blackpool, Bradford C, Brentford, Bristol C, Bury, Coventry, Crystal P, Everton, Fulham, Huddersfield, Leeds U, Luton, Millwall, Newcastle, Oxford U, QPR, Sheffield U, Sunderland.

**Once as Small Heath.*

League Division III 2 Oxford U, Portsmouth; 1 Aston Villa, Blackburn R, Bolton, Bournemouth, Bradford C, Bristol R, Burnley, Bury, Carlisle, Coventry, Grimsby T, Hereford U, Hull, Mansfield, Northampton, Oldham Ath, Orient, Plymouth, Preston NE, Queen's Park Rangers, Reading, Rotherham U, Shrewsbury T, Southampton, Sunderland, Watford, Wolverhampton W, Wrexham.

League Division IV 2 Chesterfield, Doncaster R, Peterborough U; 1 Brentford, Brighton, Cambridge, Exeter C, Gillingham, Grimsby, Huddersfield T, Lincoln C, Luton, Mansfield T, Millwall, Northampton T, Notts Co, Port Vale, Reading, Rotherham U, Sheffield U, Southend U, Southport, Swindon T, Walsall, Watford, Wimbledon, Wolverhampton W, York C.

To 1957–58
Division III (South): Bristol C; 2 Charlton, Ipswich, Millwall, Notts Co, Plymouth, Swansea; 1 Brentford, Brighton, Bristol R, Cardiff, Coventry, Crystal P, Fulham, Leyton Orient, Luton, Newport, Nottingham F, Norwich, Portsmouth, Queen's Park Rangers, Reading, Southampton.
Division III (North): 3 Barnsley, Doncaster, Lincoln; 2 Chesterfield, Grimsby, Hull, Port Vale, Stockport; 1 Bradford, Bradford C, Darlington, Derby, Nelson, Oldham, Rotherham, Scunthorpe, Stoke, Tranmere, Wolverhampton.

PROMOTED AFTER PLAY-OFFS

1986–7 Aldershot, Div 4 to Div 3.
1987–8 Swansea C, Div 4 to Div 3.
1988–9 Leyton Orient, Div 4 to Div 3.
1989–90 Cambridge U, Div 4 to Div 3
1989–90 Sunderland Div 2 to Div 1

BARCLAYS LEAGUE – DIVISION 1

	Arsenal	Aston Villa	Charlton Ath	Chelsea	Coventry C	Crystal Palace	Derby Co	Everton	Liverpool	Luton T	Manchester C	Manchester U	Millwall	Norwich C	Nottingham F	QPR	Sheffield W	Southampton	Tottenham H	Wimbledon
Arsenal	—	0-1	1-0	0-1	2-0	4-1	1-1	1-0	1-1	3-2	4-0	1-0	2-0	4-3	3-0	3-0	5-0	2-1	1-0	0-0
Aston Villa	2-1	—	1-1	1-0	4-1	2-1	1-0	6-2	1-1	2-0	1-2	3-0	1-0	3-3	2-1	1-3	1-0	2-1	2-0	0-3
Charlton Ath.	0-0	0-2	—	3-0	1-1	1-2	0-0	0-1	0-4	2-0	1-1	2-0	1-1	0-1	1-1	1-0	1-2	2-4	1-3	1-2
Chelsea	0-0	0-3	3-1	—	1-0	3-0	1-1	2-1	2-5	1-0	1-1	1-0	4-0	0-0	2-2	1-1	4-0	2-2	1-2	2-5
Coventry C.	0-1	2-0	1-2	3-2	—	1-0	1-0	2-0	1-6	1-0	2-1	1-4	3-1	1-0	0-2	1-1	1-4	1-0	0-0	2-1
Crystal Palace	1-1	1-0	2-0	2-2	0-1	—	1-1	2-1	0-2	1-1	2-2	1-1	4-3	1-0	1-0	0-3	1-1	3-1	2-3	2-0
Derby Co.	1-3	0-1	2-0	0-1	4-1	3-1	—	0-1	0-3	2-3	6-0	2-0	2-0	0-2	0-2	2-0	2-0	0-1	2-1	1-1
Everton	3-0	3-3	2-1	0-1	2-0	4-0	2-1	—	1-3	2-1	0-0	3-2	2-1	3-1	4-0	1-0	2-0	3-0	2-1	1-1
Liverpool	2-1	1-1	1-0	4-1	0-1	9-0	1-0	2-1	—	2-2	3-1	0-0	1-0	0-0	2-2	2-1	2-1	3-2	1-0	2-1
Luton T	2-0	0-1	1-0	0-3	3-2	1-0	1-0	2-2	0-0	—	1-1	1-3	2-1	4-1	1-1	1-1	2-0	1-1	0-0	1-1
Manchester C	1-1	0-2	1-2	1-1	1-0	3-0	0-1	1-0	1-4	3-1	—	5-1	2-0	1-0	0-3	1-0	2-1	1-2	1-1	1-1
Manchester U	4-1	2-0	1-0	0-0	3-0	1-2	1-2	0-0	1-2	4-1	1-1	—	5-1	0-2	1-0	0-0	0-0	2-1	0-1	0-0
Millwall	1-2	2-0	2-2	1-3	4-1	1-2	1-1	1-2	1-2	1-1	1-1	1-2	—	0-1	1-0	1-2	2-0	2-2	0-1	0-0
Norwich C	2-2	2-0	0-0	2-0	0-0	2-0	1-0	1-1	0-0	2-0	0-1	2-0	1-1	—	1-1	0-0	2-1	4-4	2-2	0-1
Nottingham F	1-2	1-1	2-0	1-1	2-4	3-1	2-1	1-0	2-2	3-0	1-0	4-0	3-1	0-1	—	2-2	0-1	2-0	1-3	0-1
QPR	2-1	1-1	0-1	4-2	1-1	2-0	0-1	1-0	3-2	0-0	1-3	1-2	0-0	2-1	2-0	—	1-0	1-4	3-1	2-3
Sheffield W	1-0	1-0	3-0	1-1	0-0	2-2	1-0	1-1	2-0	1-1	2-0	1-0	1-1	0-2	0-3	2-0	—	0-1	2-4	0-1
Southampton	1-0	2-1	3-2	2-3	3-0	1-1	2-1	1-1	4-1	6-3	2-1	0-2	1-2	4-1	2-0	0-2	2-2	—	1-1	2-2
Tottenham H	2-1	0-2	3-0	1-4	3-2	0-1	1-2	2-1	1-0	2-1	1-1	2-1	3-1	4-0	2-3	3-2	3-0	2-1	—	0-1
Wimbledon	1-0	0-2	3-1	0-1	0-0	0-1	1-1	3-1	1-2	1-2	1-0	2-2	2-2	1-1	1-3	0-0	1-1	3-3	1-0	—

1989–90 RESULTS
Final results season 1989–90

First Division			Home			Goals		Away			Goals			
		P	*W*	*D*	*L*	*F*	*A*	*W*	*D*	*L*	*F*	*A*	*GD*	*Pts*
1	Liverpool	38	13	5	1	38	15	10	5	4	40	22	+41	79
2	Aston Villa	38	13	3	3	36	20	8	4	7	21	18	+19	70
3	Tottenham H	38	12	1	6	35	24	7	5	7	24	23	+12	63
4	Arsenal	38	14	3	2	38	11	4	5	10	16	27	+16	62
5	Chelsea	38	8	7	4	31	24	8	5	6	27	26	+8	60
6	Everton	38	14	3	2	40	16	3	5	11	17	30	+11	59
7	Southampton	38	10	5	4	40	27	5	5	9	31	36	+8	55
8	Wimbledon	38	5	8	6	22	23	8	8	3	25	17	+7	55
9	Nottingham F	38	9	4	6	31	21	6	5	8	24	26	+8	54
10	Norwich C	38	7	10	2	24	14	6	4	9	20	28	+2	53
11	QPR	38	9	4	6	27	22	4	7	8	18	22	+1	50
12	Coventry C	38	11	2	6	24	25	3	5	11	15	34	−20	49
13	Manchester U	38	8	6	5	26	14	5	3	11	20	33	−1	48
14	Manchester C	38	9	4	6	26	21	3	8	8	17	31	−9	48
15	Crystal Palace	38	8	7	4	27	23	5	2	12	15	43	−24	48
16	Derby Co	38	9	1	9	29	21	4	6	19	14	19	+3	46
17	Luton T	38	8	8	3	24	18	2	5	12	19	39	−14	43
18	Sheffield W	38	8	6	5	21	17	3	4	12	14	34	−16	43
19	Charlton Ath	38	4	6	9	18	25	3	3	13	13	32	−26	30
20	Millwall	38	4	6	9	23	25	1	5	13	16	40	−26	26

Leading Goalscorers
Goals listed in following order: League, FA Cup, Littlewoods Cup, total.

John Barnes (Liverpool) 22, 5, 1, 0, 28; Gary Lineker *(Tottenham H)* 24, 0, 2, 0, 26; Ian Rush *(Liverpool)* 18, 6, 2, 0, 26; Kerry Dixon *(Chelsea)* 20, 2, 0, 3, 25; Matthew Le Tissier *(Southampton)* 20, 1, 3, 0, 24; David Platt *(Aston Villa)* 19, 1, 1, 3, 24; Dean Saunders *(Derby Co)* 11, 0, 7, 3, 21; Rodney Wallace *(Southampton)* 18, 1, 2, 0, 21; Kevin Wilson *(Chelsea)* 14, 1, 1, 4, 20; Mark Bright *(Crystal Palace)* 12, 2, 1, 2, 17; David Hirst *(Sheffield W)* 14, 1, 1, 0, 16; Dalian Atkinson *(Sheffield W)* 10, 1, 3, 1, 15; Peter Beardsley *(Liverpool)* 10, 4, 1, 0, 15; Tony Cottee *(Everton)* 13, 2, 0, 0, 15; Mark Hughes *(Manchester U)* 13, 2, 0, 0, 15; John Fashanu *(Wimbledon)* 11, 0, 2, 1, 14; Steve Hodge (Nottingham F) 10, 0, 4, 0, 14; Alan Smith *(Arsenal)* 10, 0, 3, 0, 13; Tony Cascarino *(Aston Villa)* 11, 1, 1, 0, 13 *(Including all but 2 League for Millwall)*; Paul Goddard *(Millwall)* 9, 1, 2, 1, 13 *(Including all but 1 League, 1 FA Cup for Derby Co)*; Kevin Sheedy *(Everton)* 9, 2, 2, 0, 13; Roy Wegerle *(QPR)* 8, 1, 4, 0, 13 *(Including 2 League, 4 Littlewoods for Luton T)*; Norman Whiteside *(Everton)* 9, 3, 1, 0, 13.

BARCLAYS LEAGUE – DIVISION 2

	Barnsley	Blackburn R	Bournemouth	Bradford C	Brighton & HA	Hull C	Ipswich T	Leeds U	Leicester C	Middlesbrough	Newcastle U	Oldham Ath	Oxford U	Plymouth Arg	Portsmouth	Port Vale	Sheffield U	Stoke C	Sunderland	Swindon T	Watford	WBA	West Ham U	Wolverhampton W
Barnsley	—	0-0	0-1	2-0	1-0	1-1	0-1	1-0	2-2	1-1	1-1	1-0	1-0	1-1	0-1	0-3	1-2	3-2	1-0	0-1	0-1	2-2	1-1	2-2
Blackburn R	5-0	—	1-1	2-2	1-1	0-0	2-2	1-2	2-4	2-4	2-0	1-0	2-2	2-0	2-0	1-0	0-0	3-0	1-1	2-1	2-2	2-1	5-4	2-3
Bournemouth	2-1	2-4	—	1-0	0-2	5-4	3-1	0-1	2-3	2-2	2-1	2-0	0-1	2-2	0-1	1-0	0-1	2-1	0-1	1-2	0-0	1-1	1-1	1-1
Bradford C	0-0	0-1	1-0	—	2-0	2-3	1-0	0-1	2-0	0-1	3-2	1-1	1-2	0-1	1-1	2-2	1-4	1-0	0-1	1-1	2-1	2-0	2-1	1-1
Brighton & HA	1-1	1-2	2-1	2-1	—	2-0	1-0	2-2	1-0	1-0	0-3	1-1	0-1	2-1	0-0	2-0	2-2	1-4	1-2	1-2	1-0	0-3	3-0	1-1
Hull C	1-2	2-0	1-4	2-1	0-2	—	4-3	0-1	1-1	0-0	1-3	0-0	1-0	3-3	1-2	2-1	0-0	0-0	3-2	2-3	0-0	0-2	1-1	2-0
Ipswich T	3-1	3-1	1-1	1-0	2-1	0-1	—	2-2	2-2	3-0	2-1	1-1	1-0	3-0	0-1	3—2	1-1	2-2	1-1	1-0	1-0	3-1	1-0	1-3
Leeds U	1-2	1-1	3-0	1-1	3-0	4-3	1-1	—	2-1	2-1	1-0	1-1	2-0	2-1	2-0	0-0	4-0	2-0	2-0	4-0	2-1	2-2	3-2	1-0
Leicester C	2-2	0-1	2-1	1-1	1-0	2-1	0-1	4-3	—	2-1	2-2	3-0	0-0	1-1	1-1	2-0	2-5	2-1	2-3	2-1	1-1	1-3	1-0	0-0
Middlesbrough	0-1	0-3	2-1	2-0	2-2	1-0	1-2	0-2	4-1	—	4-1	1-0	1-0	0-2	2-0	2-3	3-3	0-1	3-0	0-2	1-2	0-0	0-1	4-2
Newcastle U	4-1	2-1	3-0	1-0	2-0	2-0	2-1	5-2	5-4	2-2	—	2-1	2-3	3-1	1-0	2-2	2-0	3-0	1-1	0-0	2-1	2-1	2-1	1-4
Oldham Ath	2-0	2-0	4-0	2-2	1-1	3-2	4-1	3-1	1-0	2-0	1-1	—	4-1	3-2	3-3	2-1	0-2	2-0	2-1	2-2	1-1	2-1	3-0	1-1
Oxford U	2-3	1-1	1-2	2-1	0-1	0-0	2-2	2-4	4-2	3-1	2-1	0-1	—	3-2	2-1	0-0	3-0	3-0	0-1	2-2	1-1	0-1	0-2	2-2
Plymouth Arg	2-1	2-2	1-0	1-1	2-1	1-2	1-0	1-1	3-1	1-2	1-1	2-0	2-0	—	0-2	1-2	0-0	3-0	3-0	0-3	0-0	2-2	1-1	0-1
Portsmouth	2-1	1-1	2-1	3-0	3-0	2-2	2-3	3-3	2-3	3-1	1-1	2-1	2-1	0-3	—	2-0	3-2	0-0	3-3	1-1	1-2	1-1	0-1	1-3
Port Vale	2-1	0-0	1-1	3-2	2-1	1-1	5-0	0-0	2-1	1-1	1-2	2-0	0-2	3-0	1-1	—	1-1	0-0	1-2	2-0	1-0	2-1	2-2	3-1
Sheffield U	1-2	1-2	4-2	1-1	5-4	0-0	2-0	2-2	1-1	1-1	1-1	2-1	2-1	1-0	2-1	2-1	—	2-1	1-3	2-0	4-1	3-1	0-2	3-0
Stoke C	0-1	0-1	0-0	1-1	3-2	1-1	0-0	1-1	0-1	0-0	2-1	1-2	1-2	0-0	1-2	1-1	0-1	—	0-2	1-1	2-2	2-1	1-1	2-0
Sunderland	4-2	0-1	3-2	1-0	2-1	0-1	2-4	0-1	2-2	2-1	0-0	2-3	1-0	3-1	2-2	2-2	1-1	2-1	—	2-2	4-0	1-1	4-3	1-1
Swindon T	0-0	4-3	2-3	3-1	1-2	1-3	3-0	3-2	1-1	1-1	1-1	3-2	3-0	3-0	2-2	3-0	0-2	6-0	0-2	—	2-0	2-1	2-2	3-1
Watford	2-2	3-1	2-2	7-2	4-2	3-1	3-3	1-0	3-1	1-0	0-0	3-0	0-1	1-2	1-0	1-0	1-3	1-1	1-1	0-2	—	0-2	0-1	3-1
WBA	7-0	2-2	2-2	2-0	3-0	1-1	1-3	2-1	0-1	0-0	1-5	2-2	3-2	0-3	0-0	2-3	0-3	1-1	1-1	1-2	2-0	—	1-3	1-2
West Ham U	4-2	1-1	4-1	2-0	3-1	1-2	2-0	0-1	3-1	2-0	0-0	0-2	3-2	3-2	2-1	2-2	5-0	0-0	5-0	1-1	1-0	2-3	—	4-0
W'hampton W	1-1	1-2	3-1	1-1	2-4	1-2	2-1	1-0	5-0	2-0	0-1	1-1	2-0	1-0	5-0	2-0	1-2	0-0	0-1	2-1	1-1	2-1	1-0	—

1989–90 RESULTS
Final results season 1989–90

Second Division			*Home*			*Goals*		*Away*			*Goals*			
		P	*W*	*D*	*L*	*F*	*A*	*W*	*D*	*L*	*F*	*A*	*GD*	*Pts*
1	Leeds U	46	16	6	1	46	18	8	7	8	33	34	+27	85
2	Sheffield U	46	14	5	4	43	27	10	8	5	35	31	+20	85
3	Newcastle U	46	17	4	2	51	26	5	10	8	29	29	+25	80
4	Swindon T	46	12	6	5	49	29	8	8	7	30	30	+20	74
5	Blackburn R	46	10	9	4	43	30	9	8	6	31	29	+15	74
6	Sunderland	46	10	8	5	41	32	10	6	7	29	32	+6	74
7	West Ham	46	14	5	4	50	22	6	7	10	30	35	+23	72
8	Oldham Ath	46	15	7	1	50	23	4	7	12	20	34	+13	71
9	Ipswich T	46	13	7	3	38	22	6	5	12	29	44	+1	69
10	W'hampton W	46	12	5	6	37	20	6	8	9	30	40	+7	67
11	Port Vale	46	11	9	3	37	20	4	7	12	25	37	+5	61
12	Portsmouth	46	9	8	6	40	34	6	8	9	22	31	−3	61
13	Leicester C	46	10	8	5	34	29	5	6	12	33	50	−12	59
14	Hull C	46	7	8	8	27	31	7	8	8	31	34	−7	58
15	Watford	46	11	6	6	41	28	3	9	11	17	32	−2	57
16	Plymouth Arg	46	9	8	6	30	23	5	5	13	28	40	−5	55
17	Oxford U	46	8	7	8	35	31	7	2	14	22	35	−9	54
18	Brighton & HA	46	10	6	7	28	27	5	3	15	28	45	−16	54
19	Barnsley	46	7	9	7	22	23	6	6	11	27	48	−22	54
20	WBA	46	6	8	9	35	37	6	7	10	32	34	−4	51
21	Middlesbrough	46	10	3	10	33	29	3	8	12	19	34	−11	50
22	AFC B'mouth	46	8	6	9	30	31	4	6	13	27	45	−19	48
23	Bradford C	46	9	6	8	26	24	0	8	15	18	44	−24	41
24	Stoke C	46	4	11	8	20	24	2	8	13	15	39	−28	37

PLAY-OFFS: Semi-finals – Blackburn R 1, 1, Swindon T 2, 2; Sunderland 0, 2, Newcastle U 0, 0; Final – Swindon T 1, Sunderland 0. **Sunderland promoted to First Division** (*after Swindon T relegated to Third Division, then reinstated to Second Division on appeal to FA*).

Leading Goalscorers

Goals listed in following order: League, FA Cup, Littlewoods Cup, total.

Mick Quinn (Newcastle U) 32, 2, 0, 2, 36; Bernie Slaven (Middlesbrough) 21, 0, 4, 7, 32; Andy Ritchie *(Oldham Ath)* 15, 3, 10 , 0, 28; Steve Bull *Wolverhampton W)* 24, 1, 2, 0, 27; Duncan Shearer *(Swindon T)* 20, 1, 4, 1, 26; Marco Gabbiadini *(Sunderland)* 21, 0, 4, 0, 25; Mark McGhee *(Newcastle U)* 19, 5, 1, 0, 25; Steve White (Swindon T) 18, 0, 5, 2, 25; Brian Deane *(Sheffield U)* 21, 1, 1, 1, 24; Guy Whittingham *(Portsmouth)* 23, 1, 0, 0, 24; Paul Hunter*(Hull C)* 16, 4, 2, 0, 22 *Including all but 3 League for East Fife)*; Darren Beckford *(Port Vale)* 17, 1, 3, 0, 21; Don Goodman *(WBA)* 21, 0, 0, 0, 21; Lee Chapman *(Leeds U)* 19, 0, 1, 0, 20 *(Including 7 League, 1 Littlewoods for Nottingham F)*; Roger Palmer *(Oldham Ath)* 16, 3, 1, 0, 20; Luther Blissett *(Bournemouth)* 18, 0, 0, 1, 19; Gary Penrice *(Watford)* 16, 1, 1, 1, 19 *(Including 3 League, 1 Littlewoods for Bristol R)*; Jimmy Quinn *(West Ham U)* 18, 0, 1, 0, 19 *(Including 6 League, 1 Littlewoods for Bradford C)*; Simon Garner *Blackburn R)* 18, 0, 0, 0, 18; Andy Payton *(Hull C)* 17, 0, 1, 0, 18; Gordon Strachan *(Leeds U)* 16, 0, 1, 1, 18; Tommy Tynan *(Plymouth Arg)* 15, 0, 3, 0, 18.

BARCLAYS LEAGUE – DIVISION 3

	Birmingham C	Blackpool	Bolton W	Brentford	Bristol C	Bristol R	Bury	Cardiff C	Chester C	Crewe Alex	Fulham	Huddersfield T	Leyton Orient	Mansfield T	Northampton T	Notts C	Preston NE	Reading	Rotherham U	Shrewsbury T	Swansea C	Tranmere R	Walsall	Wigan Ath
Birmingham C	—	3-1	1-0	0-1	0-4	2-2	0-0	1-1	0-0	3-0	1-1	0-1	0-0	4-1	4-0	1-2	3-1	0-1	4-1	0-1	2-0	2-1	2-0	0-0
Blackpool	3-2	—	2-1	4-0	1-3	0-3	0-1	1-0	1-3	1-3	0-1	2-2	1-0	3-1	1-0	0-0	2-2	0-0	1-2	0-1	2-2	0-3	4-3	0-0
Bolton W	3-1	2-0	—	0-1	1-0	1-0	3-1	3-1	1-0	0-0	0-0	2-2	2-1	1-1	0-3	3-0	2-1	3-0	0-2	0-1	0-0	1-1	1-1	3-2
Brentford	0-1	5-0	1-2	—	0-2	2-1	0-1	0-1	1-1	0-2	2-0	2-1	4-3	2-1	3-2	0-1	2-2	1-1	4-2	1-1	2-1	2-4	4-0	3-1
Bristol C	1-0	2-0	1-1	2-0	—	0-0	1-0	1-0	1-0	4-1	5-1	1-1	2-1	1-1	3-1	2-0	2-1	0-1	0-0	2-1	1-3	1-3	4-0	3-0
Bristol R	0-0	1-1	1-1	1-0	3-0	—	2-1	2-1	2-1	1-1	2-0	2-2	0-0	1-1	4-2	3-2	3-0	0-0	2-0	1-0	2-0	2-0	2-0	6-1
Bury	0-0	2-0	2-0	0-2	1-1	0-0	—	2-0	1-0	0-3	0-0	6-0	2-0	3-0	1-0	3-2	1-2	4-0	1-1	0-0	3-2	1-2	0-2	2-2
Cardiff C	0-1	2-2	0-2	2-2	0-3	1-1	3-1	—	1-1	0-0	3-3	1-5	1-1	1-0	2-3	1-3	3-0	3-2	2-0	0-1	0-2	0-0	3-1	1-1
Chester C	4-0	2-0	2-0	1-1	0-3	0-0	1-4	1-0	—	2-1	0-2	2-1	1-0	0-2	0-1	3-3	3-1	1-1	2-0	1-0	1-0	2-2	1-1	0-0
Crewe Alex	0-2	2-0	2-2	2-3	0-1	1-0	2-1	1-1	0-0	—	2-3	3-0	0-1	2-1	2-1	1-0	1-0	1-1	0-0	1-1	1-1	2-2	3-1	3-2
Fulham	1-2	0-0	2-2	1-0	0-1	1-2	2-2	2-5	1-0	1-1	—	0-0	1-2	1-0	1-1	5-2	3-1	1-2	1-1	2-1	2-0	1-2	0-0	4-0
Huddersfield T	1-2	2-2	1-1	1-0	2-1	1-1	2-1	2-3	4-1	0-1	0-1	—	2-0	1-0	2-2	1-2	0-2	0-1	2-1	1-1	1-0	1-0	1-0	2-0
Leyton Orient	1-2	2-0	0-0	0-1	1-1	0-1	2-3	3-1	0-3	2-1	1-1	1-0	—	3-1	1-1	0-1	3-1	4-1	1-1	1-0	0-2	0-1	1-1	1-0
Mansfield T	5-2	0-3	0-1	2-3	1-0	0-1	1-0	1-0	1-0	2-1	3-0	1-2	1-0	—	1-2	1-3	2-2	1-1	3-1	2-1	4-0	1-0	0-2	1-0
Northampton T	2-2	4-2	0-2	0-2	2-0	1-2	0-1	1-1	1-0	3-1	2-2	1-0	0-1	1-2	—	0-0	1-2	2-1	1-2	2-1	1-1	0-4	1-1	1-1
Notts C	3-2	0-1	2-1	3-1	0-0	3-1	0-4	2-1	0-0	2-0	2-0	1-0	1-0	4-2	3-2	—	2-1	0-0	2-0	4-0	2-1	1-0	2-0	1-1
Preston NE	2-2	2-1	1-4	4-2	2-2	0-1	2-3	4-0	5-0	0-0	1-0	3-3	0-3	4-0	0-0	2-4	—	1-0	0-1	2-1	2-0	2-2	2-0	1-1
Reading	0-2	1-1	2-0	1-0	1-1	0-1	1-0	0-1	1-1	1-1	3-2	0-0	1-1	1-0	3-2	1-1	6-0	—	3-2	3-3	1-1	1-0	1-0	2-0
Rotherham U	5-1	1-1	1-0	2-1	1-2	3-2	1-3	4-0	5-0	1-3	2-1	0-0	5-2	0-0	2-0	1-2	3-1	1-1	—	4-2	2-2	0-0	2-2	1-2
Shrewsbury T	2-0	1-1	3-3	1-0	0-1	2-3	3-1	0-0	2-0	0-0	2-0	3-3	4-2	0-1	2-0	2-2	2-0	1-1	1-1	—	1-1	3-1	2-0	1-3
Swansea C	1-1	0-0	0-0	2-1	0-5	0-0	0-1	0-1	2-1	3-2	4-2	1-3	0-1	1-0	1-1	0-0	2-1	1-6	1-0	0-1	—	1-0	2-0	3-0
Tranmere R	5-1	4-2	1-3	2-2	6-0	1-2	2-4	3-0	0-0	1-1	2-1	4-0	3-0	1-1	0-0	2-0	2-1	3-1	2-1	3-1	3-0	—	2-1	2-0
Walsall	0-1	1-1	2-1	2-1	0-2	1-2	2-2	0-2	1-1	1-1	0-0	2-3	1-3	1-0	1-0	2-2	1-0	1-1	1-1	0-2	0-1	2-1	—	1-2
Wigan Ath	1-0	1-1	2-0	2-1	2-3	1-2	0-0	1-1	1-0	1-0	2-1	1-2	0-2	4-0	0-0	1-1	0-1	3-1	0-3	0-0	2-0	1-3	3-0	—

1989–90 RESULTS
Final results season 1989–90

Third Division			*Home*			*Goals*		*Away*			*Goals*			
		P	*W*	*D*	*L*	*F*	*A*	*W*	*D*	*L*	*F*	*A*	*GD*	*Pts*
1	Bristol R	46	15	8	0	43	14	11	7	5	28	21	+36	93
2	Bristol C	46	15	5	3	40	16	12	5	6	36	24	+36	91
3	Notts Co	46	17	4	2	40	18	8	8	7	33	35	+20	87
4	Tranmere R	46	15	5	3	54	22	8	6	9	32	27	+37	80
5	Bury	46	11	7	5	35	19	10	4	9	35	30	+21	74
6	Bolton W	46	12	7	4	32	19	6	8	9	27	29	+11	69
7	Birmingham C	46	19	7	6	33	19	8	5	10	27	40	+1	66
8	Huddersfield T	46	11	5	7	30	23	6	9	8	31	39	−1	65
9	Rotherham U	46	12	6	5	48	28	5	7	11	23	34	+9	64
10	Reading	46	10	9	4	33	21	5	10	8	24	32	+4	64
11	Shrewsbury T	46	10	9	4	38	24	6	6	11	21	30	+5	63
12	Crewe Alex	46	10	8	5	32	24	5	9	9	24	29	+3	62
13	Brentford	46	11	4	8	41	31	7	3	13	25	35	0	61
14	Leyton Orient	46	9	6	8	28	24	7	4	12	24	32	−4	58
15	Mansfield T	46	13	2	8	34	25	3	5	15	16	40	−15	55
16	Chester C	46	11	7	5	30	23	2	8	13	13	32	−12	54
17	Swansea C	46	10	6	7	25	27	4	6	13	20	36	−18	54
18	Wigan Ath	46	10	6	7	29	22	3	8	12	19	42	−16	53
19	Preston NE	46	10	7	6	42	30	4	3	16	23	49	−14	52
20	Fulham	46	8	8	7	33	27	4	7	12	22	39	−11	51
21	Cardiff C	46	6	9	8	30	35	6	5	12	21	35	−19	50
22	Northampton T	46	7	7	9	27	31	4	7	12	24	37	−17	47
23	Blackpool	46	8	6	9	29	33	2	10	11	20	40	−24	46
24	Walsall	46	6	8	9	23	30	3	6	14	17	42	−32	41

PLAY-OFFS: Semi-finals – Bolton W 1, 0, Notts Co 1, 2; Bury 0, 0, Tranmere R 0, 2; Final – Notts Co 2, Tranmere R 0. **Notts Co promoted to Second Division.**

Leading Goalscorers
Goals listed in following order: League, FA Cup, Littlewoods Cup, total.

Bob Taylor (Bristol C), 27, 5, 2, 0, 34; Ian Muir *(Tranmere R)* 23, 0, 4, 6, 33; Dean Holdsworth *(Brentford)* 25, 0, 0, 4, 29 *(Including 1 League for Watford)*; John McGinlay *(Shrewsbury T)* 22, 2, 0, 2, 26; Tony Philliskirk *(Bolton W)* 18, 0, 5, 1, 24; Chris Malkin *(Tranmere R)* 17, 0, 4, 2, 23; Bobby Williamson *(Rotherham U)* 19, 0, 2, 1, 22; Craig Maskell *(Huddersfield T)* 15, 2, 2, 2, 21; David Mehew *(Bristol R)* 18, 1, 0, 2, 21; Trevor Senior *(Reading)* 14, 3, 3, 1, 21; Dennis Bailey *(Birmingham C)* 18, 0, 2, 0, 20; Bobby Barnes *(Northampton T)* 18, 1, 0, 1, 20; Chris Pike *(Cardiff)* 18, 1, 1, 0, 20; Tommy Johnson *(Notts Co)* 18, 0, 0, 0, 18; Stuart Rimmer *(Walsall)* 10, 2, 0, 6, 18; Liam Robinson *(Bury)* 17, 0, 1, 0, 18; Trevor Christie *(Mansfield T)* 13, 0, 3, 1, 17; Kevin Bartlett *(Notts Co)* 15, 1, 0, 0, 16 *(Including 7 League, 1 FA Cup for WBA)*; Jamie Hoyland *(Bury)* 16, 0, 0, 0, 16; Clive Mendonca *(Rotherham U)* 14, 0, 1, 1, 16; Steve Wilkinson *(Mansfield T)* 15, 0, 1, 0, 16.

BARCLAYS LEAGUE – DIVISION 4

	Aldershot	Burnley	Cambridge U	Carlisle U	Chesterfield	Colchester U	Doncaster R	Exeter C	Gillingham	Grimsby T	Halifax T	Hartlepool U	Hereford U	Lincoln C	Maidstone U	Peterborough U	Rochdale	Scarborough	Scunthorpe U	Southend U	Stockport Co	Torquay U	Wrexham	York C
Aldershot	—	1-1	2-2	1-0	0-0	4-0	1-1	0-1	1-0	0-0	2-0	6-1	0-2	0-1	0-2	0-1	1-1	1-1	4-2	0-5	2-1	1-2	1-0	2-2
Burnley	0-0	—	1-3	2-1	0-0	0-0	0-1	1-0	1-2	1-1	1-0	0-0	3-1	0-0	1-1	1-2	0-1	3-0	0-1	0-0	5-0	1-0	2-3	1-1
Cambridge U	2-2	0-1	—	1-2	0-1	4-0	1-0	3-2	2-1	2-0	1-0	2-1	0-1	2-1	2-0	3-2	0-3	5-2	5-3	2-1	0-2	5-2	1-1	2-2
Carlisle U	1-3	1-1	3-1	—	4-3	1-0	1-0	1-0	3-0	1-1	1-1	1-0	2-1	1-2	3-2	0-0	0-1	3-1	0-1	3-0	3-1	2-0	1-0	2-1
Chesterfield	2-0	0-1	1-1	3-0	—	1-1	0-1	2-1	2-0	2-0	4-3	3-1	2-1	0-0	3-1	1-1	2-1	2-2	1-1	1-1	1-1	5-1	3-0	0-0
Colchester U	1-0	1-2	1-2	4-0	1-0	—	2-0	0-1	2-0	1-0	2-2	3-1	1-1	0-1	4-1	0-1	1-2	0-0	1-0	0-2	0-1	0-3	1-3	0-2
Doncaster R	0-1	2-3	2-1	1-1	1-0	2-0	—	2-1	0-0	0-0	3-4	2-2	0-1	0-1	1-1	0-3	4-0	1-1	1-2	0-1	2-1	2-1	2-2	1-2
Exeter C	2-0	2-1	3-2	0-0	2-1	2-1	1-0	—	3-0	2-1	2-0	3-1	2-0	3-0	2-0	2-0	5-0	3-2	1-0	2-1	1-1	3-0	1-1	3-1
Gillingham	0-0	0-0	1-0	2-1	3-0	3-3	3-1	1-1	—	1-2	3-1	2-0	0-1	1-1	1-2	0-0	1-0	2-0	0-3	5-0	0-3	0-2	1-0	0-0
Grimsby T	2-1	4-2	0-0	1-0	0-1	4-1	2-1	1-0	2-0	—	1-1	0-0	0-2	1-0	2-3	1-2	1-2	3-0	2-1	2-0	4-2	0-0	5-1	3-0
Halifax T	4-1	0-0	0-0	1-1	0-1	1-1	0-2	1-2	0-1	2-2	—	4-0	1-3	0-1	1-2	2-2	1-0	1-2	0-1	1-2	1-2	3-1	4-2	2-2
Hartlepool U	2-0	3-0	1-2	1-0	3-1	0-2	0-0	0-3	1-2	4-2	2-0	—	1-2	1-1	4-2	2-2	2-1	4-1	3-2	1-1	5-0	1-1	3-0	1-2
Hereford U	4-1	0-1	0-2	2-2	3-2	2-0	0-1	2-1	1-2	0-1	0-1	4-1	—	2-2	3-0	1-2	1-3	3-1	1-2	0-3	1-2	0-0	0-0	1-2
Lincoln C	0-1	1-0	4-3	1-3	1-1	2-1	2-1	1-5	1-1	1-1	2-1	4-1	1-0	—	1-2	1-0	1-2	0-0	1-0	2-0	2-0	2-2	1-0	0-0
Maidstone U	5-1	1-2	2-2	5-2	0-1	4-1	1-0	1-0	0-1	2-2	1-2	4-2	2-0	2-0	—	1-1	2-0	4-1	1-1	3-0	0-1	5-1	2-0	1-0
Peterborough U	1-1	4-1	1-2	3-0	1-1	1-0	2-1	4-3	1-1	1-1	3-0	0-2	1-1	1-0	1-0	—	0-1	1-2	1-1	1-2	2-0	1-1	3-1	1-1
Rochdale	2-0	2-1	2-0	1-2	0-0	2-2	1-3	1-0	1-0	0-1	0-2	0-0	5-2	1-0	3-2	1-2	—	1-0	3-0	0-1	1-1	0-0	0-3	0-1
Scarborough	1-0	4-2	1-1	2-1	2-3	2-2	1-2	1-3	0-1	3-1	2-3	4-1	0-1	2-0	0-1	2-0	2-1	—	0-0	1-1	2-0	0-0	2-1	1-2
Scunthorpe U	3-2	3-0	1-0	2-3	0-1	4-0	4-1	5-0	0-0	2-1	1-1	0-1	3-3	1-1	1-0	0-5	0-1	0-1	—	1-1	5-0	2-0	3-1	1-1
Southend U	5-0	3-2	0-0	2-0	0-2	0-2	2-0	1-2	2-0	0-2	2-0	3-0	2-0	2-0	0-1	0-0	3-2	1-0	0-0	—	2-0	1-0	2-1	2-0
Stockport Co	1-1	3-1	3-1	3-1	3-1	1-1	3-1	2-1	1-0	2-4	0-1	6-0	2-1	1-1	1-2	0-0	2-1	3-2	4-2	1-0	—	1-1	0-2	2-2
Torquay U	1-2	0-1	3-0	1-2	1-0	4-1	2-5	0-2	0-2	0-3	1-0	4-3	1-1	0-3	2-1	2-1	1-0	3-2	0-3	3-0	3-0	—	0-1	1-0
Wrexham	2-2	1-0	2-3	1-0	0-2	3-2	0-0	1-1	2-1	0-1	2-1	1-2	0-0	0-2	4-2	2-1	1-1	0-2	0-0	3-3	0-1	1-1	—	2-0
York C	2-2	1-3	4-2	0-1	4-0	3-1	2-1	3-0	1-0	0-1	0-2	1-1	1-2	0-0	0-0	1-0	1-0	1-2	0-1	2-1	0-3	1-1	1-0	—

1989–90 RESULTS

Final results season 1989–90

Fourth Division		Home			Goals		Away			Goals			
	P	W	D	L	F	A	W	D	L	F	A	GD	Pts
1 Exeter C	46	20	3	0	50	14	8	2	13	33	34	+35	89
2 Grimsby T	46	14	4	5	41	20	8	9	6	29	27	+23	79
3 Southend U	46	15	3	5	35	14	7	6	10	26	34	+13	75
4 Stockport C	46	13	6	4	45	27	8	5	10	23	35	+6	74
5 Maidstone U	46	14	4	5	49	21	8	3	12	28	40	+16	73
6 Cambridge U	46	14	3	6	45	30	7	7	9	31	36	+10	73
7 Chesterfield	46	12	9	2	41	19	7	5	11	22	31	+13	71
8 Carlisle U	46	15	4	4	38	20	6	4	13	23	40	+1	71
9 Peterborough U	46	10	8	5	35	23	7	9	7	24	23	+13	68
10 Lincoln C	46	11	6	6	30	27	7	8	8	18	21	0	68
11 Scunthorpe U	46	9	9	5	42	25	8	6	9	27	29	+15	66
12 Rochdale	46	11	4	8	28	23	9	2	12	24	32	−3	66
13 York C	46	10	5	8	29	24	6	11	6	26	29	+2	64
14 Gillingham	46	9	8	6	28	21	8	3	12	18	27	−2	62
15 Torquay U	46	12	2	9	33	29	3	10	10	20	37	−13	57
16 Burnley	46	6	10	7	19	18	8	4	11	26	37	−10	56
17 Hereford U	46	7	4	12	31	32	8	6	9	25	30	−6	55
18 Scarborough	46	10	5	8	35	28	5	5	13	25	45	−13	55
19 Hartlepool U	46	12	4	7	45	33	3	6	14	21	55	−22	55
20 Doncaster R	46	7	7	9	29	29	7	2	14	24	31	−7	51
21 Wrexham	46	8	8	7	28	28	5	4	14	23	39	−16	51
22 Aldershot	46	8	7	8	28	26	4	7	12	21	43	−20	50
23 Halifax T	46	5	9	9	31	29	7	4	12	26	36	−8	49
24 Colchester U	46	9	3	11	26	25	2	7	14	22	50	−27	43

PLAY-OFFS: Semi-finals – Cambridge U 1, 2, Maidstone U 1, 0; Chesterfield 4, 2, Stockport Co 0, 0; Final – Cambridge U 1, Chesterfield 0. **Cambridge U promoted to Third Divison.**

Leading Goalscorers

Goals listed in following order: League, FA Cup, Littlewoods Cup, total.

Darren Rowbotham (Exeter C) 20, 4, 6, 0, 30; Brett Angell *(Stockport Co)* 23, 1, 0, 4, 28; Steve Butler *(Maidstone U)* 21, 1, 1, 3, 26; Mark Gall *(Maidstone U)* 18, 2, 0, 6, 26; David Crown *(Southend U)* 19, 0, 3, 1, 23; David Puckett *(Aldershot)* 18, 0, 3, 1, 22; Dion Dublin *(Cambridge U)* 15, 4, 2, 0, 21; John Taylor *(Cambridge U)* 15, 5, 1, 0, 21; Andy Flounders *(Scunthorpe U)* 18, 0, 1, 1, 20; Mike Helliwel *(York C)* 14, 0, 1, 4, 19; Joe Allon *(Hartlepool U)* 18, 0, 0, 0, 18; Paul Baker *(Hartlepool U)* 16, 0, 1, 1, 18; Steve Lovell *(Gillingham)* 16, 0, 1, 1, 18; Steve Neville *(Exeter C)* 14, 1, 2, 1, 18; Dave Waller *(Chesterfield)* 16, 1, 1, 0, 18; Steve Claridge *(Cambridge U)* 14, 0, 0, 2, 16 *(Including all but 4 League for Aldershot)*; Paul Dobson *(Scarborough)* 15, 0, 1, 0, 16; Mark Lillis *(Scunthorpe)* 13, 3, 0, 0, 16.

LEAGUE POSITIONS 1964–65 to 1988–89 – DIVISION 1

	1988–89	1987–88	1986–87	1985–86	1984–85	1983–84	1982–83	1981–82	1980–81	1979–80	1978–79	1977–78	1976–77	1975–76	1974–75	1973–74	1972–73	1971–72	1970–71	1969–70	1968–69	1967–68	1966–67	1965–66	1964–65
Arsenal	1	6	4	7	7	6	10	5	3	4	7	5	8	17	16	10	2	5	1	12	4	9	7	14	13
Aston Villa	17	–	22	16	10	10	6	11	1	7	8	8	4	16	–	–	–	–	–	–	–	–	21	16	16
Birmingham C	–	–	–	21	–	20	17	16	13	–	21	11	13	19	17	19	10	–	–	–	–	–	–	–	22
Blackburn R	–	–	–	–	–	–	–	–	–	–	–	–	–	–	–	–	–	–	–	–	–	–	–	22	10
Blackpool	–	–	–	–	–	–	–	–	–	–	–	–	–	–	–	–	–	–	22	–	–	–	22	13	17
Bolton W	–	–	–	–	–	–	–	–	–	22	17	–	–	–	–	–	–	–	–	–	–	–	–	–	–
Brighton & HA	–	–	–	–	–	–	22	13	19	16	–	–	–	–	–	–	–	–	–	–	–	–	–	–	–
Bristol C	–	–	–	–	–	–	–	–	–	20	13	17	18	–	–	–	–	–	–	–	–	–	–	–	–
Burnley	–	–	–	–	–	–	–	–	–	–	–	–	–	21	10	6	–	–	21	14	14	14	14	3	12
Carlisle U	–	–	–	–	–	–	–	–	–	–	–	–	–	–	22	–	–	–	–	–	–	–	–	–	–
Charlton Ath	14	17	19	–	–	–	–	–	–	–	–	–	–	–	–	–	–	–	–	–	–	–	–	–	–
Chelsea	–	18	14	6	6	–	–	–	–	–	22	16	–	–	21	17	12	7	6	3	5	6	9	5	3
Coventry C	7	10	10	17	18	19	19	14	16	15	10	7	19	14	14	16	19	18	10	6	20	20	–	–	–
Crystal Palace	–	–	–	–	–	–	–	–	22	13	–	–	–	–	–	–	21	20	18	20	–	–	–	–	–
Derby Co	5	15	–	–	–	–	–	–	–	21	19	12	15	4	1	3	7	1	9	4	–	–	–	–	–
Everton	8	4	1	2	1	7	7	8	15	19	4	3	9	11	4	7	17	15	14	1	3	5	6	11	4
Fulham	–	–	–	–	–	–	–	–	–	–	–	–	–	–	–	–	–	–	–	–	–	22	18	20	20
Huddersfield T	–	–	–	–	–	–	–	–	–	–	–	–	–	–	–	–	–	22	15	–	–	–	–	–	–
Ipswich T	–	–	–	20	17	12	9	2	2	3	6	18	3	6	3	4	4	13	19	18	12	–	–	–	–
Leeds U	–	–	–	–	–	–	–	20	9	11	5	9	10	5	9	1	3	2	2	2	1	4	4	2	2
Leicester C	–	–	20	19	15	15	–	–	21	–	–	22	11	7	18	9	16	12	–	–	21	13	8	7	18
Liverpool	2	1	2	1	2	1	1	1	5	1	1	2	1	1	2	2	1	3	5	5	2	3	5	1	7
Luton T	16	9	7	9	13	16	18	–	–	–	–	–	–	–	20	–	–	–	–	–	–	–	–	–	–

Manchester C	–	–	21	15	–	–	20	10	12	17	15	4	2	8	8	14	11	4	11	10	13	1	15	–	–
Manchester U	11	2	11	4	4	4	3	3	8	2	9	10	6	3	–	21	18	8	8	8	11	2	1	4	1
Middlesbrough	18	–	–	–	–	–	–	22	14	9	12	14	12	13	7	–	–	–	–	–	–	–	–	–	–
Millwall	10	–	–	–	–	–	–	–	–	–	–	–	–	–	–	–	–	–	–	–	–	–	–	–	–
Newcastle U	20	8	17	11	14	–	–	–	–	–	–	21	5	15	15	15	9	11	12	7	9	10	20	15	–
Northampton T	–	–	–	–	–	–	–	–	–	–	–	–	–	–	–	–	–	–	–	–	–	–	–	21	–
Norwich	4	14	5	–	20	14	14	–	20	12	16	13	16	10	–	22	20	–	–	–	–	–	–	–	–
Nottingham F	3	3	8	8	9	3	5	12	7	5	2	1	–	–	–	–	–	21	16	15	18	11	2	18	5
Notts Co	–	–	–	–	–	21	15	15	–	–	–	–	–	–	–	–	–	–	–	–	–	–	–	–	–
Oxford U	–	21	18	18	–	–	–	–	–	–	–	–	–	–	–	–	–	–	–	–	–	–	–	–	–
Portsmouth	–	19	–	–	–	–	–	–	–	–	–	–	–	–	–	–	–	–	–	–	–	–	–	–	–
QPR	9	5	16	13	19	5	–	–	–	–	20	19	14	2	11	8	–	–	–	–	22	–	–	–	–
Sheffield U	–	–	–	–	–	–	–	–	–	–	–	–	–	22	6	13	14	10	–	–	–	21	10	9	19
Sheffield W	15	11	13	5	8	–	–	–	–	–	–	–	–	–	–	–	–	–	–	22	15	19	11	17	8
Southampton	13	12	12	14	5	2	12	7	6	8	14	–	–	–	–	20	13	19	7	19	7	16	19	–	–
Stoke C	–	–	–	–	22	18	13	18	11	18	–	–	21	12	5	5	15	17	13	9	19	18	12	10	11
Sunderland	–	–	–	–	21	13	16	19	17	–	–	–	20	–	–	–	–	–	–	21	17	15	17	19	15
Swansea City	–	–	–	–	–	–	21	6	–	–	–	–	–	–	–	–	–	–	–	–	–	–	–	–	–
Tottenham H	6	13	3	10	3	8	4	4	10	14	11	–	22	9	19	11	8	6	3	11	6	7	3	8	6
Watford	–	20	9	12	11	11	2	–	–	–	–	–	–	–	–	–	–	–	–	–	–	–	–	–	–
WBA	–	–	–	22	12	17	11	17	4	10	3	6	7	–	–	–	22	16	17	16	10	8	13	6	14
West Ham U	19	16	15	3	16	9	8	9	–	–	–	20	17	18	13	18	6	14	20	17	8	12	16	12	9
Wimbledon	12	7	6	–	–	–	–	–	–	–	–	–	–	–	–	–	–	–	–	–	–	–	–	–	–
W'hampton W	–	–	–	–	–	22	–	21	18	6	18	15	–	20	12	12	5	9	4	13	16	17	–	–	21

LEAGUE POSITIONS 1964–65 to 1988–89 – DIVISION 2

	1988–89	1987–88	1986–87	1985–86	1984–85	1983–84	1982–83	1981–82	1980–81	1979–80	1978–79	1977–78	1976–77	1975–76	1974–75	1973–74	1972–73	1971–72	1970–71	1969–70	1968–69	1967–68	1966–67	1965–66	1964–65
Aston Villa	–	2	–	–	–	–	–	–	–	–	–	–	–	–	2	14	3	–	–	21	18	16	–	–	–
Barnsley	7	14	11	12	11	14	10	6	–	–	–	–	–	–	–	–	–	–	–	–	–	–	–	–	–
Birmingham C	23	19	19	–	2	–	–	–	–	3	–	–	–	–	–	–	–	2	9	18	7	4	10	10	–
Blackburn R	5	5	12	19	5	6	11	10	4	–	22	5	12	15	–	–	–	–	21	8	19	8	4	–	–
Blackpool	–	–	–	–	–	–	–	–	–	–	–	20	5	10	7	5	7	6	–	2	8	3	–	–	–
Bolton W	–	–	–	–	–	–	22	19	18	–	–	1	4	4	10	11	–	–	22	16	17	12	9	9	3
Bournemouth	12	17	–	–	–	–	–	–	–	–	–	–	–	–	–	–	–	–	–	–	–	–	–	–	–
Bradford C	14	4	10	13	–	–	–	–	–	–	–	–	–	–	–	–	–	–	–	–	–	–	–	–	–
Brighton & HA	19	–	22	11	6	9	–	–	–	–	2	4	–	–	–	–	22	–	–	–	–	–	–	–	–
Bristol C	–	–	–	–	–	–	–	–	21	–	–	–	–	2	5	16	5	8	19	14	16	19	15	5	–
Bristol R	–	–	–	–	–	–	–	–	22	19	16	18	15	18	19	–	–	–	–	–	–	–	–	–	–
Burnley	–	–	–	–	–	–	21	–	–	21	13	11	16	–	–	–	1	7	–	–	–	–	–	–	–
Bury	–	–	–	–	–	–	–	–	–	–	–	–	–	–	–	–	–	–	–	–	21	–	22	19	16
Cambridge U	–	–	–	–	–	22	12	14	13	8	12	–	–	–	–	–	–	–	–	–	–	–	–	–	–
Cardiff C	–	–	–	–	21	15	–	20	19	15	9	19	18	–	21	17	20	19	3	7	5	13	20	20	13
Carlisle U	–	–	–	20	16	7	14	–	–	–	–	–	20	19	–	3	18	10	4	12	12	10	3	14	–
Charlton Ath	–	–	–	2	17	13	17	13	–	22	19	17	7	9	–	–	–	21	20	20	3	15	19	16	18
Chelsea	1	–	–	–	–	1	18	12	12	4	–	–	2	11	–	–	–	–	–	–	–	–	–	–	–
Coventry C	–	–	–	–	–	–	–	–	–	–	–	–	–	–	–	–	–	–	–	–	–	–	1	3	10
Crystal Palace	3	6	6	5	15	18	15	5	–	–	1	9	–	–	–	20	–	–	–	–	2	11	7	11	7
Derby Co	–	–	1	–	–	20	13	16	6	–	–	–	–	–	–	–	–	–	–	–	1	18	17	8	9
Fulham	–	–	–	22	9	11	4	–	–	20	10	10	17	12	9	13	9	20	–	–	22	–	–	–	–
Grimsby T	–	–	21	15	10	5	19	17	7	–	–	–	–	–	–	–	–	–	–	–	–	–	–	–	–
Hereford U	–	–	–	–	–	–	–	–	–	–	–	–	22	–	–	–	–	–	–	–	–	–	–	–	–
Huddersfield T	–	23	17	16	13	12	–	–	–	–	–	–	–	–	–	–	21	–	–	1	6	14	6	4	8
Hull	21	15	14	6	–	–	–	–	–	–	–	22	14	14	8	9	13	12	5	13	11	17	12	–	–

Ipswich T	8	8	5	–	–	–	–	–	–	–	–	–	–	–	–	–	–	–	–	–	–	1	5	15	5
Leeds U	10	7	4	14	7	10	8	–	–	–	–	–	–	–	–	–	–	–	–	–	–	–	–	–	–
Leicester C	15	13	–	–	–	–	3	8	–	1	17	–	–	–	–	–	–	–	1	3	–	–	–	–	–
Leyton Orient	–	–	–	–	–	–	–	22	17	14	11	14	19	13	12	4	15	17	17	–	–	–	–	22	19
Luton T	–	–	–	–	–	–	–	1	5	6	18	13	6	7	–	2	12	13	6	–	–	–	–	–	–
Manchester C	2	9	–	–	3	4	–	–	–	–	–	–	–	–	–	–	–	–	–	–	–	–	–	1	11
Manchester U	–	–	–	–	–	–	–	–	–	–	–	–	–	–	1	–	–	–	–	–	–	–	–	–	–
Mansfield T	–	–	–	–	–	–	–	–	–	–	–	21	–	–	–	–	–	–	–	–	–	–	–	–	–
Middlesbrough	–	3	–	21	19	17	16	–	–	–	–	–	–	–	–	1	4	9	7	4	4	6	–	21	17
Millwall	–	1	16	9	–	–	–	–	–	–	21	16	10	–	20	12	11	3	8	10	10	7	8	–	–
Newcastle U	–	–	–	–	–	3	5	9	11	9	8	–	–	–	–	–	–	–	–	–	–	–	–	–	1
Northampton T	–	–	–	–	–	–	–	–	–	–	–	–	–	–	–	–	–	–	–	–	–	–	21	–	2
Norwich C	–	–	–	1	–	–	–	3	–	–	–	–	–	–	3	–	–	1	10	11	13	9	11	13	6
Nottingham F	–	–	–	–	–	–	–	–	–	–	–	–	3	8	16	7	14	–	–	–	–	–	–	–	–
Notts Co	–	–	–	–	20	–	–	–	2	17	6	15	8	5	14	10	–	–	–	–	–	–	–	–	–
Oldham Ath	16	10	3	8	14	19	7	11	15	11	14	8	13	17	18	–	–	–	–	–	–	–	–	–	–
Oxford U	17	–	–	–	1	–	–	–	–	–	–	–	–	20	11	18	8	15	14	15	20	–	–	–	–
Plymouth Arg	18	16	7	–	–	–	–	–	–	–	–	–	21	16	–	–	–	–	–	–	–	22	16	18	15
Portsmouth	20	–	2	4	4	16	–	–	–	–	–	–	–	22	17	15	17	16	16	17	15	5	14	12	20
Preston NE	–	–	–	–	–	–	–	–	20	10	7	–	–	–	–	21	19	18	–	22	14	20	13	17	12
QPR	–	–	–	–	–	–	1	5	8	5	–	–	–	–	–	–	2	4	11	9	–	2	–	–	–
Reading	–	22	13	–	–	–	–	–	–	–	–	–	–	–	–	–	–	–	–	–	–	–	–	–	–
Rotherham	–	–	–	–	–	–	20	7	–	–	–	–	–	–	–	–	–	–	–	–	–	21	18	7	14
Sheffield U	–	21	9	7	18	–	–	–	–	–	20	12	11	–	–	–	–	–	2	6	9	–	–	–	–
Sheffield W	–	–	–	–	–	2	6	4	10	–	–	–	–	–	22	19	10	14	15	–	–	–	–	–	–
Shrewsbury T	22	18	18	17	8	8	9	18	14	13	–	–	–	–	–	–	–	–	–	–	–	–	–	–	–
Southampton	–	–	–	–	–	–	–	–	–	–	–	2	9	6	13	–	–	–	–	–	–	–	–	2	4
Stoke C	13	11	8	10	–	–	–	–	–	–	3	7	–	–	–	–	–	–	–	–	–	–	–	–	–
Sunderland	11	–	20	18	–	–	–	–	–	2	4	6	–	1	4	6	6	5	13	–	–	–	–	–	–
Swansea C	–	–	–	–	–	21	–	–	3	12	–	–	–	–	–	–	–	–	–	–	–	–	–	–	22
Swindon T	6	12	–	–	–	–	–	–	–	–	–	–	–	–	–	22	16	11	12	5	–	–	–	–	21
Tottenham H	–	–	–	–	–	–	–	–	–	–	–	3	–	–	–	–	–	–	–	–	–	–	–	–	–
Walsall	24	–	–	–	–	–	–	–	–	–	–	–	–	–	–	–	–	–	–	–	–	–	–	–	–
Watford	4	–	–	–	–	–	–	2	9	18	–	–	–	–	–	–	–	22	18	19	–	–	–	–	–

	1988–89	1987–88	1986–87	1985–86	1984–85	1983–84	1982–83	1981–82	1980–81	1979–80	1978–79	1977–78	1976–77	1975–76	1974–75	1973–74	1972–73	1971–72	1970–71	1969–70	1968–69	1967–68	1966–67	1965–66	1964–65
WBA	9	20	15	–	–	–	–	–	–	–	–	–	–	3	6	8	–	–	–	–	–	–	–	–	–
West Ham U	–	–	–	–	–	–	–	–	1	7	5	–	–	–	–	–	–	–	–	–	–	–	–	–	–
Wimbledon	–	–	–	3	12	–	–	–	–	–	–	–	–	–	–	–	–	–	–	–	–	–	–	–	–
Wolv'hampton W	–	–	–	–	22	–	2	–	–	–	–	–	1	–	–	–	–	–	–	–	–	–	2	6	–
Wrexham	–	–	–	–	–	–	–	21	16	16	15	–	–	–	–	–	–	–	–	–	–	–	–	–	–
York C	–	–	–	–	–	–	–	–	–	–	–	–	–	21	15	–	–	–	–	–	–	–	–	–	–

LEAGUE POSITIONS 1964–65 to 1988–89 – DIVISION 3

	1988–89	1987–88	1986–87	1985–86	1984–85	1983–84	1982–83	1981–82	1980–81	1979–80	1978–79	1977–78	1976–77	1975–76	1974–75	1973–74	1972–73	1971–72	1970–71	1969–70	1968–69	1967–68	1966–67	1965–66	1964–65
Aldershot	24	20	–	–	–	–	–	–	–	–	–	–	–	21	20	8	–	–	–	–	–	–	–	–	–
Aston Villa	–	–	–	–	–	–	–	–	–	–	–	–	–	–	–	–	–	1	4	–	–	–	–	–	–
Barnsley	–	–	–	–	–	–	–	–	2	11	–	–	–	–	–	–	–	22	12	7	10	–	–	–	24
Barrow	–	–	–	–	–	–	–	–	–	–	–	–	–	–	–	–	–	–	–	23	19	8	–	–	–
Blackburn R	–	–	–	–	–	–	–	–	–	2	–	–	–	–	1	13	3	10	–	–	–	–	–	–	–
Blackpool	19	10	9	12	–	–	–	–	23	18	12	–	–	–	–	–	–	–	–	–	–	–	–	–	–
Bolton W	10	–	21	18	17	10	–	–	–	–	–	–	–	–	–	–	1	7	–	–	–	–	–	–	–
Bournemouth	–	–	1	15	10	17	14	–	–	–	–	–	–	–	21	11	7	3	–	21	4	12	20	18	11
Bradford C	–	–	–	–	1	7	12	–	–	–	–	22	–	–	–	–	–	24	19	10	–	–	–	–	–
Brentford	7	12	11	10	13	20	9	8	9	19	10	–	–	–	–	–	22	–	–	–	–	–	–	23	5
Brighton & HA	–	2	–	–	–	–	–	–	–	–	–	–	2	4	19	19	–	2	14	5	12	10	19	15	–
Bristol C	11	5	6	9	5	–	–	23	–	–	–	–	–	–	–	–	–	–	–	–	–	–	–	–	2
Bristol R	5	8	19	16	6	5	7	15	–	–	–	–	–	–	–	2	5	6	6	3	16	15	5	16	6

Burnley	–	–	–	–	21	12	–	1	8	–	–	–	–	–	–	–	–	–	–	–	–	–	–	–	–
Bury	13	14	16	20	–	–	–	–	–	21	19	15	7	13	14	–	–	–	22	19	–	2	–	–	–
Cambridge U	–	–	–	–	24	–	–	–	–	–	–	2	–	–	–	21	–	–	–	–	–	–	–	–	–
Cardiff C	16	–	–	22	–	–	2	–	–	–	–	–	–	2	–	–	–	–	–	–	–	–	–	–	–
Carlisle U	–	–	21	–	–	–	–	2	19	6	6	13	–	–	–	–	–	–	–	–	–	–	–	–	1
Charlton Ath	–	–	–	–	–	–	–	–	3	–	–	–	–	–	3	14	11	–	–	–	–	–	–	–	–
Chester C	8	15	15	–	–	–	–	24	18	9	16	5	13	17	–	–	–	–	–	–	–	–	–	–	–
Chesterfield	22	18	17	17	–	–	24	11	5	4	20	9	18	15	15	5	16	13	5	–	–	–	–	–	–
Colchester U	–	–	–	–	–	–	–	–	22	5	7	8	–	22	11	–	–	–	–	–	–	22	13	–	23
Crewe Alex	–	–	–	–	–	–	–	–	–	–	–	–	–	–	–	–	–	–	–	–	23	–	–	–	–
Crystal Palace	–	–	–	–	–	–	–	–	–	–	–	–	3	5	5	–	–	–	–	–	–	–	–	–	–
Darlington	–	–	22	13	–	–	–	–	–	–	–	–	–	–	–	–	–	–	–	–	–	–	22	–	–
Derby Co	–	–	–	3	7	–	–	–	–	–	–	–	–	–	–	–	–	–	–	–	–	–	–	–	–
Doncaster R	–	24	13	11	14	–	23	19	–	–	–	–	–	–	–	–	–	–	23	11	–	–	23	–	–
Exeter C	–	–	–	–	–	24	19	18	11	8	9	17	–	–	–	–	–	–	–	–	–	–	–	22	17
Fulham	4	9	18	–	–	–	–	3	13	–	–	–	–	–	–	–	–	–	2	4	–	–	–	–	–
Gillingham	23	13	5	5	4	8	13	6	15	16	4	7	12	14	10	–	–	–	24	20	20	11	11	6	7
Grimsby T	–	22	–	–	–	–	–	–	–	1	–	–	23	18	16	6	9	–	–	–	–	21	17	11	10
Halifax T	–	–	–	–	–	–	–	–	–	–	–	–	–	24	17	9	20	17	3	18	–	–	–	–	–
Hartlepool U	–	–	–	–	–	–	–	–	–	–	–	–	–	–	–	–	–	–	–	–	22	–	–	–	–
Hereford U	–	–	–	–	–	–	–	–	–	–	–	23	–	1	12	18	–	–	–	–	–	–	–	–	–
Huddersfield T	14	–	–	–	–	–	3	17	4	–	–	–	–	–	24	10	–	–	–	–	–	–	–	–	–
Hull C	–	–	–	–	3	4	–	–	24	20	8	–	–	–	–	–	–	–	–	–	–	–	–	1	4
Lincoln C	–	–	–	21	19	14	6	4	–	–	24	16	9	–	–	–	–	–	–	–	–	–	–	–	–
Luton T	–	–	–	–	–	–	–	–	–	–	–	–	–	–	–	–	–	–	–	2	3	–	–	–	21
Mansfield T	15	19	10	–	–	–	–	–	–	23	18	–	1	11	–	–	–	21	7	6	15	20	9	19	3
Middlesbrough	–	–	2	–	–	–	–	–	–	–	–	–	–	–	–	–	–	–	–	–	–	–	2	–	–
Millwall	–	–	–	–	2	9	17	9	16	14	–	–	–	3	–	–	–	–	–	–	–	–	–	2	–
Newport Co	–	–	23	19	18	13	4	16	12	–	–	–	–	–	–	–	–	–	–	–	–	–	–	–	–
Northampton T	20	6	–	–	–	–	–	–	–	–	–	–	22	–	–	–	–	–	–	–	21	17	–	–	–
Notts Co	9	4	7	8	–	–	–	–	–	–	–	–	–	–	–	–	2	4	–	–	–	–	–	–	–
Oldham Ath	–	–	–	–	–	–	–	–	–	–	–	–	–	–	–	1	4	11	–	–	24	16	10	20	20
Leyton Orient	–	–	–	–	22	11	20	–	–	–	–	–	–	–	–	–	–	–	–	1	18	18	14	–	–
Oxford U	–	–	–	–	–	1	5	5	14	17	11	18	17	–	–	–	–	–	–	–	–	1	16	14	–

	1988–89	1987–88	1986–87	1985–86	1984–85	1983–84	1982–83	1981–82	1980–81	1979–80	1978–79	1977–78	1976–77	1975–76	1974–75	1973–74	1972–73	1971–72	1970–71	1969–70	1968–69	1967–68	1966–67	1965–66	1964–65
Peterborough U	–	–	–	–	–	–	–	–	–	–	21	4	16	10	7	–	–	–	–	–	–	24	15	13	8
Plymouth Arg	–	–	–	2	15	19	8	10	7	15	15	19	–	–	2	17	8	8	15	17	5	–	–	–	–
Portsmouth	–	–	–	–	–	–	1	13	6	–	–	24	20	–	–	–	–	–	–	–	–	–	–	–	–
Port Vale	3	11	12	–	–	23	–	–	–	–	–	21	19	12	6	20	6	15	17	–	–	–	–	–	22
PNE	6	16	–	–	23	16	16	14	–	–	–	3	6	8	9	–	–	–	1	–	–	–	–	–	–
QPR	–	–	–	–	–	–	–	–	–	–	–	–	–	–	–	–	–	–	–	–	–	–	1	3	14
Reading	18	–	–	1	9	–	21	12	10	7	–	–	21	–	–	–	–	–	21	8	14	5	4	8	13
Rochdale	–	–	–	–	–	–	–	–	–	–	–	–	–	–	–	24	13	18	16	9	–	–	–	–	–
Rotherham U	–	21	14	14	12	18	–	–	1	13	17	20	4	16	–	–	21	5	8	14	11	–	–	–	–
Scunthorpe U	–	–	–	–	–	21	–	–	–	–	–	–	–	–	–	–	24	–	–	–	–	23	18	4	18
Sheffield U	2	–	–	–	–	3	11	–	21	12	–	–	–	–	–	–	–	–	–	–	–	–	–	–	–
Sheffield W	–	–	–	–	–	–	–	–	–	3	14	14	8	20	–	–	–	–	–	–	–	–	–	–	–
Shrewsbury T	–	–	–	–	–	–	–	–	–	–	1	11	10	9	–	22	15	12	13	15	17	3	6	10	16
Southend U	21	17	–	–	–	22	15	7	–	22	13	–	–	23	18	12	14	–	–	–	–	–	–	21	12
Southport	–	–	–	–	–	–	–	–	–	–	–	–	–	–	–	23	–	–	–	22	8	14	–	–	–
Stockport Co	–	–	–	–	–	–	–	–	–	–	–	–	–	–	–	–	–	–	–	24	9	13	–	–	–
Sunderland	–	1	–	–	–	–	–	–	–	–	–	–	–	–	–	–	–	–	–	–	–	–	–	–	–
Swansea C	12	–	–	24	20	–	–	–	–	–	3	–	–	–	–	–	23	14	11	–	–	–	21	17	–
Swindon T	–	–	3	–	–	–	–	22	17	10	5	10	11	19	4	–	–	–	–	–	2	9	8	7	–
Torquay U	–	–	–	–	–	–	–	–	–	–	–	–	–	–	–	–	–	23	10	13	6	4	7	–	–
Tranmere R	–	–	–	–	–	–	–	–	–	–	23	12	14	–	22	16	10	20	18	16	7	19	–	–	–
Walsall	–	3	8	6	11	6	10	20	20	–	22	6	15	7	8	15	17	9	20	12	13	7	12	9	19
Watford	–	–	–	–	–	–	–	–	–	–	2	–	–	–	23	7	19	–	–	–	1	6	3	12	9
Wigan Ath	17	7	4	4	16	15	18	–	–	–	–	–	–	–	–	–	–	–	–	–	–	–	–	–	–
Wimbledon	–	–	–	–	–	2	–	21	–	24	–	–	–	–	–	–	–	–	–	–	–	–	–	–	–
Wolv'hampton W	1	–	–	23	–	–	–	–	–	–	–	–	–	–	–	–	–	–	–	–	–	–	–	–	–
Workington	–	–	–	–	–	–	–	–	–	–	–	–	–	–	–	–	–	–	–	–	–	–	24	5	15
Wrexham	–	–	–	–	–	–	22	–	–	–	–	1	5	6	13	4	12	16	9	–	–	–	–	–	–
York City	–	23	20	7	8	–	–	–	–	–	–	–	24	–	–	3	18	19	–	–	–	–	–	24	–

LEAGUE POSITIONS 1964–65 to 1988–89 – DIVISION 4

	1988–89	1987–88	1986–87	1985–86	1984–85	1983–84	1982–83	1981–82	1980–81	1979–80	1978–79	1977–78	1976–77	1975–76	1974–75	1973–74	1972–73	1971–72	1970–71	1969–70	1968–69	1967–68	1966–67	1965–66	1964–65
Aldershot	–	–	6	16	13	5	18	16	6	10	5	5	17	–	–	–	4	17	13	6	15	9	10	17	18
Barnsley	–	–	–	–	–	–	–	–	–	–	4	7	6	12	15	13	14	–	–	–	–	2	16	16	–
Barrow	–	–	–	–	–	–	–	–	–	–	–	–	–	–	–	–	–	22	24	–	–	–	3	12	21
Blackpool	–	–	–	–	2	6	21	12	–	–	–	–	–	–	–	–	–	–	–	–	–	–	–	–	–
Bolton W	–	3	–	–	–	–	–	–	–	–	–	–	–	–	–	–	–	–	–	–	–	–	–	–	–
Bournemouth	–	–	–	–	–	–	–	4	13	11	18	17	13	6	–	–	–	–	2	–	–	–	–	–	–
Bradford PA	–	–	–	–	–	–	–	–	–	–	–	–	–	–	–	–	–	–	–	24	24	24	23	11	7
Bradford C	–	–	–	–	–	–	–	2	14	5	15	–	4	17	10	8	16	–	–	–	4	5	11	23	19
Brentford	–	–	–	–	–	–	–	–	–	–	–	4	15	18	8	19	–	3	14	5	11	14	9	–	–
Brighton & HA	–	–	–	–	–	–	–	–	–	–	–	–	–	–	–	–	–	–	–	–	–	–	–	–	1
Bristol C	–	–	–	–	–	4	14	–	–	–	–	–	–	–	–	–	–	–	–	–	–	–	–	–	–
Burnley	16	10	22	14	–	–	–	–	–	–	–	–	–	–	–	–	–	–	–	–	–	–	–	–	–
Bury	–	–	–	–	4	15	5	9	12	–	–	–	–	–	–	4	12	9	–	–	–	–	–	–	–
Cambridge U	8	15	11	22	–	–	–	–	–	–	–	–	1	13	6	–	3	10	20	–	–	–	–	–	–
Cardiff C	–	2	13	–	–	–	–	–	–	–	–	–	–	–	–	–	–	–	–	–	–	–	–	–	–
Carlisle U	12	23	–	–	–	–	–	–	–	–	–	–	–	–	–	–	–	–	–	–	–	–	–	–	–
Chester C	–	–	–	2	16	24	13	–	–	–	–	–	–	–	4	7	15	20	5	11	14	22	19	7	8
Chesterfield	–	–	–	–	1	13	–	–	–	–	–	–	–	–	–	–	–	–	–	1	20	7	15	20	12
Colchester U	22	9	5	6	7	8	6	6	–	–	–	–	3	–	–	3	22	11	6	10	6	–	–	4	–
Crewe Alex	3	17	17	12	10	16	23	24	18	23	24	15	12	16	18	21	21	24	15	15	–	4	5	14	10
Darlington	24	13	–	–	3	14	17	13	8	22	21	19	11	20	21	20	24	19	12	22	5	16	–	2	17
Doncaster R	23	–	–	–	–	2	–	–	3	12	22	12	8	10	17	22	17	12	–	–	1	10	–	1	9
Exeter C	13	22	14	21	18	–	–	–	–	–	–	–	2	7	9	10	8	15	9	18	17	20	14	–	–
Gillingham	–	–	–	–	–	–	–	–	–	–	–	–	–	–	–	2	9	13	–	–	–	–	–	–	–
Grimsby T	9	–	–	–	–	–	–	–	–	–	2	6	–	–	–	–	–	1	19	16	23	–	–	–	–

	1988–89	1987–88	1986–87	1985–86	1984–85	1983–84	1982–83	1981–82	1980–81	1979–80	1978–79	1977–78	1976–77	1975–76	1974–75	1973–74	1972–73	1971–72	1970–71	1969–70	1968–69	1967–68	1966–67	1965–66	1964–65
Halifax	21	18	15	20	21	21	11	19	23	18	23	20	21	–	–	–	–	–	–	–	2	11	12	15	23
Hartlepool U	19	16	18	7	19	23	22	14	9	19	13	21	22	14	13	11	20	18	23	23	–	3	8	18	15
Hereford U	15	19	16	10	5	11	24	10	22	21	14	–	–	–	–	–	2	–	–	–	–	–	–	–	–
Huddersfield T	–	–	–	–	–	–	–	–	–	1	9	11	9	5	–	–	–	–	–	–	–	–	–	–	–
Hull C	–	–	–	–	–	–	2	8	–	–	–	–	–	–	–	–	–	–	–	–	–	–	–	–	–
Lincoln C	10	–	24	–	–	–	–	–	2	7	–	–	–	1	5	12	10	5	21	8	8	13	24	22	22
Luton T	–	–	–	–	–	–	–	–	–	–	–	–	–	–	–	–	–	–	–	–	–	1	17	6	–
Mansfield T	–	–	–	3	14	19	10	20	7	–	–	–	–	–	1	17	6	–	–	–	–	–	–	–	–
Millwall	–	–	–	–	–	–	–	–	–	–	–	–	–	–	–	–	–	–	–	–	–	–	–	–	2
Newport Co	–	24	–	–	–	–	–	–	–	3	8	16	19	22	12	9	5	14	22	21	22	12	18	9	16
Northampton T	–	–	1	8	23	18	15	22	10	13	19	10	–	2	16	5	23	21	7	14	–	–	–	–	–
Notts Co	–	–	–	–	–	–	–	–	–	–	–	–	–	–	–	–	–	–	1	7	19	17	20	8	13
Oldham Ath	–	–	–	–	–	–	–	–	–	–	–	–	–	–	–	–	–	–	3	19	–	–	–	–	–
Leyton Orient	6	8	7	5	–	–	–	–	–	–	–	–	–	–	–	–	–	–	–	–	–	–	–	–	–
Oxford U	–	–	–	–	–	–	–	–	–	–	–	–	–	–	–	–	–	–	–	–	–	–	–	–	4
Peterborough U	7	7	10	17	11	7	9	5	5	8	–	–	–	–	–	1	19	8	16	9	18	–	–	–	–
Portsmouth	–	–	–	–	–	–	–	–	–	4	7	–	–	–	–	–	–	–	–	–	–	–	–	–	–
Port Vale	–	–	–	4	12	–	3	7	19	20	16	–	–	–	–	–	–	–	–	4	13	18	13	19	–
Preston NE	–	–	2	23	–	–	–	–	–	–	–	–	–	–	–	–	–	–	–	–	–	–	–	–	–
Reading	–	–	–	–	–	3	–	–	–	–	1	8	–	3	7	6	7	16	–	–	–	–	–	–	–
Rochdale	18	21	21	18	17	22	20	21	15	24	20	24	18	15	19	–	–	–	–	–	3	19	21	21	6
Rotherham U	1	–	–	–	–	–	–	–	–	–	–	–	–	–	3	15	–	–	–	–	–	–	–	–	–
Scarborough	5	12	–	–	–	–	–	–	–	–	–	–	–	–	–	–	–	–	–	–	–	–	–	–	–
Scunthorpe U	4	4	8	15	9	–	4	23	16	14	12	14	20	19	24	18	–	4	17	12	16	–	–	–	–
Sheffield U	–	–	–	–	–	–	–	1	–	–	–	–	–	–	–	–	–	–	–	–	–	–	–	–	–
Shrewsbury T	–	–	–	–	–	–	–	–	–	–	–	–	–	–	2	–	–	–	–	–	–	–	–	–	–
Southend U	–	–	3	9	20	–	–	–	1	–	–	2	10	–	–	–	–	2	18	17	7	6	6	–	–
Southport	–	–	–	–	–	–	–	–	–	–	–	23	23	23	11	–	1	7	8	–	–	–	2	10	20

Stockport Co	20	20	19	11	22	12	16	18	20	16	17	18	14	21	20	24	11	23	11	–	–	–	1	13	24
Swansea C	–	6	12	–	–	–	–	–	–	–	–	3	5	11	22	14	–	–	–	3	10	15	–	–	–
Swindon T	–	–	–	1	8	17	8	–	–	–	–	–	–	–	–	–	–	–	–	–	–	–	–	–	–
Torquay U	14	5	23	24	24	9	12	15	17	9	11	9	16	9	14	16	18	–	–	–	–	–	–	3	11
Tranmere R	2	14	20	19	6	10	19	11	21	15	–	–	–	4	–	–	–	–	–	–	–	–	4	5	5
Walsall	–	–	–	–	–	–	–	–	–	2	–	–	–	–	–	–	–	–	–	–	–	–	–	–	–
Watford	–	–	–	–	–	–	–	–	–	–	–	1	7	8	–	–	–	–	–	–	–	–	–	–	–
Wigan Ath	–	–	–	–	–	–	–	3	11	6	6	–	–	–	–	–	–	–	–	–	–	–	–	–	–
Wimbledon	–	–	–	–	–	–	1	–	4	–	3	13	–	–	–	–	–	–	–	–	–	–	–	–	–
Wolv'hampton W	–	1	4	–	–	–	–	–	–	–	–	–	–	–	–	–	–	–	–	–	–	–	–	–	–
Workington	–	–	–	–	–	–	–	–	–	–	–	–	24	24	23	23	13	6	10	20	12	23	–	–	–
Wrexham	7	11	9	13	15	20	–	–	–	–	–	–	–	–	–	–	–	–	–	2	9	8	7	24	14
York C	11	–	–	–	–	1	7	17	24	17	10	22	–	–	–	–	–	–	4	13	21	21	22	–	3

LEAGUE CHAMPIONSHIP HONOURS

**Won on goal average. †Won on goal difference.*
No championships during WWI and WWII.

First Division

	First	Pt	Second	Pt	Third	Pt
1888–9 *a*	Preston NE	40	Aston Villa	29	Wolverhampton	28
1889–90	Preston NE	33	Everton	31	Blackburn R	27
1890–1	Everton	29	Preston NE	27	Wolverhampton / Notts Co	26
1891–2 *b*	Sunderland	42	Preston NE	37	Bolton W	36
1892–3 *c*	Sunderland	48	Preston NE	37	Everton	36
1893–4	Aston Villa	44	Sunderland	38	Derby Co	36
1894–5	Sunderland	47	Everton	42	Aston Villa	39
1895–6	Aston Villa	45	Derby Co	41	Everton	39
1896–7	Aston Villa	47	Sheffield U	36	Derby Co	36
1897–8	Sheffield U	42	Sunderland	37	Wolverhampton W	35
1898–9 *d*	Aston Villa	45	Liverpool	43	Burnley	39
1899–1900	Aston Villa	50	Sheffield U	48	Sunderland	41
1900–1	Liverpool	45	Sunderland	43	Notts Co	40
1901–2	Sunderland	44	Everton	41	Newcastle U	37
1902–3	Sheffield W	42	Aston Villa	41	Sunderland	41
1903–4	Sheffield W	47	Manchester C	44	Everton	43
1904–5	Newcastle U	48	Everton	47	Manchester C	46
1905–6 *e*	Liverpool	51	Preston NE	47	Sheffield W	44
1906–7	Newcastle U	51	Bristol C	48	Everton	45
1907–8	Manchester U	52	Aston Villa	43	Manchester C	43
1908–9	Newcastle U	53	Everton	46	Sunderland	44
1909–10	Aston Villa	53	Liverpool	48	Blackburn R	45
1910–11	Manchester U	52	Aston Villa	51	Sunderland	45
1911–12	Blackburn R	49	Everton	46	Newcastle U	44
1912–13	Sunderland	54	Aston Villa	50	Sheffield W	49
1913–14	Blackburn	51	Aston Villa	44	Middlesbrough	43
1914–15	Everton	46	Oldham Ath	45	Blackburn R	43
1919–20 *f*	WBA	60	Burnley	51	Chelsea	49
1920–1	Burnley	59	Manchester C	54	Bolton W	55
1921–2	Liverpool	57	Tottenham H	51	Burnley	49
1922–3	Liverpool	60	Sunderland	54	Huddersfield T	53
1923–4	*Huddersfield T	57	Cardiff C	57	Sunderland	43
1924–5	Huddersfield T	58	WBA	56	Bolton W.	55
1925–6	Huddersfield T	57	Arsenal	52	Sunderland	48
1926–7	Newcastle U	56	Huddersfield T	51	Sunderland	49
1927–8	Everton	53	Huddersfield T	51	Leicester C	48
1928–9	Sheffield W	52	Leicester C	51	Aston Villa	50
1929–30	Sheffield W	60	Derby Co	50	Manchester C	47
1930–1	Arsenal	66	Aston Villa	59	Sheffield W	52
1931–2	Everton	56	Arsenal	54	Sheffield W	50
1932–3	Arsenal	58	Aston Villa	54	Sheffield W	51
1933–4	Arsenal	59	Huddersfield T	56	Tottenham H	49
1934–5	Arsenal	58	Sunderland	54	Sheffield W	49
1935–6	Sunderland	56	Derby Co	48	Huddersfield T	48
1936–7	Manchester C	57	Charlton Ath	54	Arsenal	52
1937–8	Arsenal	52	Wolverhampton W	51	Preston NE	49
1938–9	Everton	59	Wolverhampton W	55	Charlton Ath	50
1946–7	Liverpool	57	Manchester U	56	Wolverhampton W	56
1947–8	Arsenal	59	Manchester U	52	Burnley	52

	First		Second		Third	
1948–9	Portsmouth	58	Manchester U	53	Derby Co	53
1949–50	*Portsmouth	53	Wolverhampton W	53	Sunderland	52
1950–1	Tottenham H	60	Manchester U	56	Blackpool	50
1951–2	Manchester U	57	Tottenham H	53	Arsenal	53
1952–3	*Arsenal	54	Preston NE	54	Wolverhampton W	51
1953–4	Wolverhampton W	57	WBA	53	Huddersfield T	51
1954–5	Chelsea	52	Wolverhampton W	48	Portsmouth	48
1955–6	Manchester U	60	Blackpool	49	Wolverhampton W	49
1956–7	Manchester U	64	Tottenham H	56	Preston NE	56
1957–8	Wolverhampton W	64	Preston NE	59	Tottenham H	51
1958–9	Wolverhampton W	61	Manchester U	55	Arsenal	50
1959–60	Burnley	55	Wolverhampton W	54	Tottenham H	53
1960–1	Tottenham H	66	Sheffield W	58	Wolverhampton W	57
1961–2	Ipswich T	56	Burnley	53	Tottenham H	52
1962–3	Everton	61	Tottenham H	55	Burnley	54
1963–4	Liverpool	57	Manchester U	53	Everton	52
1964–5	*Manchester U	61	Leeds U	61	Chelsea	56
1965–6	Liverpool	61	Leeds U	55	Burnley	55
1966–7	Manchester U	60	Nottingham F	56	Tottenham H	56
1967–8	Manchester C	58	Manchester U	56	Liverpool	55
1968–9	Leeds U	67	Liverpool	61	Everton	57
1969–70	Everton	66	Leeds U	57	Chelsea	55
1970–1	Arsenal	65	Leeds U	64	Tottenham H	52
1971–2	Derby Co	58	Leeds U	57	Liverpool	57
1972–3	Liverpool	60	Arsenal	57	Leeds U	53
1973–4	Leeds U	62	Liverpool	57	Derby Co	48
1974–5	Derby Co	53	Liverpool	51	Ipswich T	51
1975–6	Liverpool	60	QPR	59	Manchester U	56
1976–7	Liverpool	57	Manchester C	56	Ipswich T	52
1977–8	Nottingham F	64	Liverpool	57	Everton	55
1978–9	Liverpool	68	Nottingham F	60	WBA	59
1979–80	Liverpool	60	Manchester U	58	Ipswich T	53
1980–1	Aston Villa	60	Ipswich T	56	Arsenal	53
1981–2 *g*	Liverpool	87	Ipswich T	83	Manchester U	78
1982–3	Liverpool	82	Watford	71	Manchester U	70
1983–4	Liverpool	80	Southampton	77	Nottingham F	74
1984–5	Everton	90	Liverpool	77	Tottenham H	77
1985–6	Liverpool	88	Everton	86	West Ham U	84
1986–7	Everton	86	Liverpool	77	Tottenham H	71
1987–8 *h*	Liverpool	90	Manchester U	81	Nottingham F	73
1988–9 *i*†	Arsenal	76	Liverpool	76	Nottingham F	64
1989–90 *i*	Liverpool	79	Aston Villa	70	Tottenham	63

Maximum points: *a*, 44; *b*, 56; *c*, 60; *d*, 58; *e*, 76; *f*, 84; *g*, 126; *h*, 120; *i*, 114

Second Division

	First		Second		Third	
1892–3 *a*	Small Heath	36	Sheffield U	35	Darwen	30
1893–4 *b*	Liverpool	50	Small Heath	42	Notts Co	39
1894–5 *c*	Bury	48	Notts Co	39	Newton Heath	38
1895–6	*Liverpool	46	Manchester C	46	Grimsby T	42
1896–7	Notts Co	42	Newton Heath	39	Grimsby T	38
1897–8	Burnley	48	Newcastle	45	Manchester C	39
1898–9 *d*	Manchester C	51	Glossop NE	46	Leicester Fosse	45
1899–1900	Sheffield W	54	Bolton W	52	Small Heath	46
1900–1	Grimsby T	49	Small Heath	48	Burnley	44
1901–2	WBA	55	Middlesbrough	51	Preston NE	42
1902–3	Manchester C	54	Small Heath	51	W'lwich Arsenal	48
1903–4	Preston NE	50	W'lwich Arsenal	49	Manchester U	48
1904–5	Liverpool	58	Bolton W	56	Manchester U	53
1905–6 *e*	Bristol C	66	Manchester U	62	Chelsea	53
1906–7	Nottingham F	60	Chelsea	57	Leicester Fosse	48
1907–8	Bradford C	54	Leicester Fosse	52	Oldham	50

1908–9	Bolton W 52	Tottenham H 51	WBA..................51
1909–10	Manchester C.......54	Oldham Ath 53	Hull C 53
1910–11	WBA..................53	Bolton W 51	Chelsea 49
1911–12	*Derby Co 54	Chelsea 54	Burnley................52
1912–13	Preston NE..........53	Burnley................50	Birmingham..........46
1913–14	Notts Co 53	Bradford 49	W'lwich Arsenal ...49
1914–15	Derby Co 53	Preston NE...........50	Barnsley..............47
1919–20*f*	Tottenham H........70	Huddersfield T......64	Birmingham C 56
1920–1	*Birmingham.........58	Cardiff C 58	Bristol C 51
1921–2	Nottingham F.......56	Stoke C...............52	Barnsley..............52
1922–3	Notts Co 53	West Ham U........51	Leicester C 51
1923–4	Leeds U 54	Bury....................51	Derby Co 51
1924–5	Leicester C 59	Manchester U 57	Derby Co 55
1925–6	Sheffield W..........60	Derby Co 57	Chelsea 52
1926–7	Middlesbrough 62	Portsmouth 54	Manchester C.......54
1927–8	Manchester C.......59	Leeds U 57	Chelsea 54
1928–9	Middlesbrough 55	Grimsby T 53	Bradford C 48
1929–30	Blackpool 58	Chelsea 55	Oldham Ath 53
1930–1	Everton...............61	WBA..................55	Tottenham H 51
1931–2	Wolverhampton W56	Leeds U 54	Stoke C...............52
1932–3	Stoke C...............56	Tottenham H 55	Fulham 50
1933–4	Grimsby..............59	Preston NE...........52	Bolton W 51
1934–5	Brentford 61	Bolton W 56	West Ham U........56
1935–6	Manchester U 56	Charlton Ath 55	Sheffield U 52
1936–7	Leicester C 56	Blackpool 55	Bury...................52
1937–8	Aston Villa..........57	Manchester U 53	Sheffield U 53
1938–9	Blackburn R 55	Sheffield U 54	Sheffield W..........53
1946–7	Manchester C.......62	Burnley...............58	Birmingham 55
1947–8	Birmingham.........59	Newcastle U 56	Southampton........52
1948–9	Fulham 57	WBA..................56	Southampton........55
1949–50	Tottenham H 61	Sheffield W..........52	Sheffield U 52
1950–1	Preston NE..........57	Manchester C.......52	Cardiff C.............50
1951–2	Sheffield W..........53	Cardiff C.............51	Birmingham C......51
1952–3	Sheffield U 60	Huddersfield T 58	Luton T 52
1953–4	*Leicester C 56	Everton...............56	Blackburn R 55
1954–5	*Birmingham C......54	Luton 54	Rotherham U.......54
1955–6	Sheffield W..........55	Leeds U 52	Liverpool 48
1956–7	Leicester C 61	Nottingham F.......54	Liverpool 53
1957–8	West Ham U........57	Blackburn R 56	Charlton Ath 55
1958–9	Sheffield W..........62	Fulham 60	Sheffield U 53
1959–60	Aston Villa..........59	Cardiff C.............58	Liverpool 50
1960–1	Ipswich T 59	Sheffield U 58	Liverpool 52
1961–2	Liverpool 62	Leyton O 54	Sunderland 53
1962–3	Stoke C...............53	Chelsea 52	Sunderland 52
1963–4	Leeds U 63	Sunderland 61	Preston NE..........56
1964–5	Newcastle U 57	Northampton T 56	Bolton W 50
1965–6	Manchester C.......59	Southampton........54	Coventry C..........53
1966–7	Coventry C..........59	Wolverhampton W58	Carlisle U............52
1967–8	Ipswich T 59	QPR...................58	Blackpool 58
1968–9	Derby Co 63	Crystal P 56	Charlton Ath 50
1969–70	Huddersfield T 60	Blackpool 53	Leicester C 51
1970–1	Leicester C 59	Sheffield U 56	Cardiff C.............53
1971–2	Norwich C 57	Birmingham C......56	Millwall...............55
1972–3	Burnley...............62	QPR...................61	Aston Villa..........50
1973–4	Middlesbrough 65	Luton 50	Carlisle 49
1974–5	Manchester U 61	Aston Villa..........58	Norwich C 53
1975–6	Sunderland 56	Bristol C 53	WBA..................53
1976–7	Wolverhampton W57	Chelsea 55	Nottingham F.......52
1977–8	Bolton W 58	Southampton........57	Tottenham H 56
1978–9	Crystal P 57	Brighton & HA 56	Stoke C...............56
1979–80	Leicester C 55	Sunderland 54	Birmingham C......53

1980–1	West Ham U........66	Notts Co 53	Swansea C...........50
1981–2 *g*	Luton T 88	Watford 80	Norwich C...........71
1982–3	QPR...................85	Wolverhampton W75	Leicester C..........70
1983–4 †	Chelsea 88	Sheffield W..........88	Newcastle U 80
1984–5	Oxford U 84	Birmingham C......82	Manchester C.......74
1985–6	Norwich C...........84	Charlton Ath 77	Wimbledon..........76
1986–7	Derby Co 84	Portsmouth..........78	Oldham Ath 75
1987–8 *h*	Millwall...............82	Aston Villa..........78	Middlesbrough 78
1988–9 *i*	Chelsea 99	Manchester C.......82	Crystal P 81
1989–90	Leeds 85	Sheffield U 85	Newcastle U 80

Maximum points: *a*, 44; *b*, 56; *c*, 60; *d*, 58; *e*,76; *f*,84; *g*,126; *h*,132; *i* 138

Third Division

1958–9 *a*	Plymouth A 62	Hull C 61	Brentford 57
1959–60	Southampton........61	Norwich C...........59	Shrewsbury..........52
1960–1	Bury....................68	Walsall................62	QPR....................60
1961–2	Portsmouth..........65	Grimbsy T...........62	Bournemouth........59
1962–3	Northampton T 62	Swindon T...........58	Port Vale 54
1963–4	*Coventry C.........60	Crystal P 60	Watford 58
1964–5	Carlisle U............60	Bristol C 59	Mansfield T 59
1965–6	Hull C 69	Millwall...............65	QPR....................57
1966–7	QPR....................67	Middlesbrough 55	Watford 54
1967–8	Oxford U 57	Bury....................56	Shrewsbury T.......55
1968–9	*Watford 64	Swindon T...........64	Luton T 61
1969–70	Orient.................62	Luton T 60	Bristol R 56
1970–1	Preston NE.........61	Fulham 60	Halifax................56
1971–2	Aston Villa..........70	Brighton & HA 65	Bournemouth.......62
1972–3	Bolton W 61	Notts Co 57	BLackburn R 55
1973–4	Oldham Ath 62	Bristol R 61	York C 61
1974–5	Blackburn R 60	Plymouth Arg 59	Charlton Ath 55
1975–6	Hereford U..........63	Cardiff C.............57	Millwall...............56
1976–7	Mansfield T 64	Brighton & HA 61	Crystal P 59
1977–8	Wrexham 61	Cambridge U 58	Preston NE..........56
1978–9	Shrewsbury T.......61	Watford 60	Swansea C...........60
1979–80	Grimsby T...........62	Blackburn R 59	Sheffield W..........58
1980–1	Rotherham U.......61	Barnsley..............59	Charlton Ath 59
1981–2 *b*	Burnley...............80	Carlisle U............80	Fulham 78
1982–3	Portsmouth..........91	Cardiff C.............86	Huddersfield T.....82
1983–4	Oxford U 95	Wimbledon..........87	Sheffield U 83
1984–5	Bradford C..........94	Millwall...............90	Hull C 87
1985–6	Reading 94	Plymouth Arg 87	Derby Co 84
1986–7	Bournemouth.......97	Midlesbrough.......94	Swindon T...........87
1987–8	Sunderland 93	Brighton & HA 84	Walsall................82
1988–9	Wolverhampton W92	†Sheffield U 84	Port Vale 84
1989–90	Bristol R 93	Bristol C 91	Notts Co 87

Maximum points *a* 92; *b* 138

Third Division (Southern Section)

1920–1 *a*	Crystal P 59	Southampton........54	QPR....................53
1921–2	*Southampton........61	Plymouth Arg 61	Portsmouth..........53
1922–3	Bristol C 59	Plymouth Arg 53	Swansea 53
1923–4	Portsmouth..........59	Plymouth Arg 55	Millwall...............54
1924–5	Swansea C...........57	Plymouth Arg 56	Bristol C 53
1925–6	Reading 57	Plymouth Arg 56	Millwall...............53
1926–7	Bristol C 62	Plymouth Arg 60	Millwall...............56
1927–8	Millwall...............65	Northampton T 55	Plymouth Arg 53
1928–9	Charlton Ath 54	Crystal P 54	Northampton T 52
1929–30	Plymouth Arg 68	Brentford 61	QPR....................51
1930–1	Notts Co 59	Crystal P 51	Brentford 50
1931–2	Fulham 57	Reading 55	Southend U 53
1932–3	Brentford 62	Exeter 58	Norwich C...........57

Season	First	Second	Third
1933–4	Norwich C 61	Coventry C 54	Reading 54
1934–5	Charlton Ath 61	Reading 53	Coventry C 51
1935–6	Coventry C 57	Luton T 56	Reading 54
1936–7	Luton T 58	Notts Co 56	Brighton & HA 53
1937–8	Millwall 56	Bristol C 55	QPR 53
1938–9	Newport C 55	Crystal P 52	Brighton & HA 49
1946–7	Cardiff 66	QPR 57	Bristol C 51
1947–8	QPR 61	Bournemouth 57	Walsall 51
1948–9	Swansea 62	Reading 55	Bournemouth 52
1949–50	Notts Co 58	Northampton T 51	Southend U 51
1950–1 *b*	Nottingham F 70	Norwich C 64	Reading 57
1951–2	Plymouth Arg 66	Reading 61	Norwich C 61
1952–3	Bristol R 64	Northampton T 62	Millwall 62
1953–4	Ipswich T 64	Brighton & HA 61	Bristol C 56
1954–5	Bristol C 70	Leyton O 61	Southampton 59
1955–6	Leyton O 66	Brighton & HA 65	Ipswich T 64
1956–7	*Ipswich T 59	Torquay U 59	Colchester U 58
1957–8	Brighton & HA 60	Brentford 58	Plymouth Arg 58

Maximum points: *a*, 84; *b* 92

Third Division (Northern Section)

Season	First	Second	Third
1921–2 *a*	Stockport C 56	Darlington 50	Grimsby 50
1922–3	Nelson 51	Bradford 47	Walsall 46
1923–4 *b*	Wolverhampton W 63	Rochdale 62	Chesterfield 54
1924–5	Darlington 58	Nelson 53	New Brighton 53
1925–6	Grimsby T 61	Bradford 60	Rochdale 59
1926–7	Stoke C 63	Rochdale 58	Bradford 55
1927–8	Bradford 63	Lincoln C 55	Stockport C 54
1928–9	Bradford C 63	Stockport C 62	Wrexham 52
1929–30	Port Vale 67	Stockport C 63	Darlington 50
1930–1	Chesterfield 58	Lincoln C 57	Wrexham 54
1931–2 *c*	*Lincoln C 57	Gateshead 57	Chester 50
1932–3 *b*	Hull C 59	Wrexham 57	Stockport C 54
1933–4	Barnsley 62	Chesterfield 61	Stockport C 59
1934–5	Doncaster R 57	Halifax T 55	Chester 54
1935–6	Chesterfield 60	Chester 55	Tranmere R 55
1936–7	Stockport C 60	Lincoln C 57	Chester 53
1937–8	Tranmere R 56	Doncaster R 54	Hull C 53
1938–9	Barnsley 67	Doncaster R 56	Bradford C 52
1946–7	Doncaster R 72	Rotherham U 64	Chester 56
1947–8	Lincoln C 60	Rotherham U 59	Wrexham 50
1948–9	Hull C 65	Rotherham U 62	Doncaster R 50
1949–50	Doncaster R 55	Gateshead 53	Rochdale U 51
1950–1 *d*	Rotherham U 71	Mansfield T 64	Carlisle U 62
1951–2	Lincoln C 69	Grimsby T 66	Stockport C 59
1952–3	Oldham Ath 59	Port Vale 58	Wrexham 56
1953–4	Port Vale 69	Barnsley 58	Scunthorpe 57
1954–5	Barnsley 65	Accrington S 61	Scunthorpe 58
1955–6	Grimsby T 68	Derby Co 63	Accrington S 59
1956–7	Derby Co 63	Hartlepool 59	Accrington S 58
1957–8	Scunthorpe U 66	Accrington S 59	Bradford C 57

Maximum points: *a*, 70; *b*, 84; *c*, 80; *d*, 90.

Fourth Division

Season	First	Second	Third
1958–9 *a*	Port Vale 64	Coventry C 60	York C 60
1959–60	Walsall 65	Notts Co 60	Torquay 60
1960–1	Peterborough 66	Crystal P 64	Northampton T 60
1961–2	Millwall 56	Colchester U 55	Wrexham 53
1962–3	Brentford 62	Oldham Ath 59	Crewe Alex 59
1963–4	*Gillingham U 60	Carlisle U 60	Workington T 59
1964–5	Brighton & HA 63	Millwall 62	York C 62

1965–6	*Doncaster R 59	Darlington 59	Torquay 58
1966–7	Stockport C 64	Southport C 59	Barrow 59
1967–8	Luton T 66	Barnsley..............61	Hartlepool...........60
1968–9	Doncaster R 59	Halifax T.............57	Rochdale.............56
1969–70	Chesterfield 64	Wrexham 61	Swansea T...........60
1970–1	Notts Co 69	Bournemouth.......60	Oldham Ath 59
1971–2	Grimsby T...........63	Southend U 60	Brentford 59
1972–3	Southport 62	Hereford U...........58	Cambridge U 57
1973–4	Peterborough U....65	Gillingham...........62	Colchester U........60
1974–5	Mansfield T 68	Shrewsbury T.......62	Rotherham U.......59
1975–6	Lincoln C............74	Northampton T 68	Reading 60
1976–7	Cambridge U 65	Exeter C 62	Colchester 59
1977–8	Watford 71	Southend U 60	Swansea C...........56
1978–9	Reading 65	Grimsby T...........61	Wimbledon..........61
1979–80	Huddersfield T.....66	Walsall................64	Newport Co.........61
1980–1	Southend U 67	Lincoln C............65	Doncaster R 56
1981–2 *b*	Sheffield U..........96	Bradford C..........91	Wigan Ath...........91
1982–3	Wimbledon..........98	Hull C 90	Port Vale 88
1983–4	York C.............101	Doncaster R 85	Reading 82
1984–5	Chesterfield 91	Blackpool............86	Darlington...........85
1985–6	Swindon T.........102	Chester C............84	Mansfield T 81
1986–7	Northampton T 99	Preston NE..........90	Southend U 80
1987–8	Wolverhampton W90	Cardiff................85	Bolton W 78
1988–9	Rotherham U.......82	Tranmere R.........80	Crewe Alex 78
1989–90	Exeter C 89	Grimsby T 79	Southend U 75

Maximum points *a*, 92; *b*, 138

RELEGATED CLUBS

(Since inception of automatic promotion and relegation in 1898–9)
**Relegated after play–offs*

Season	**Division I to Division II**	**Division II to Division III**
1989–90	Sheffield W, Charlton Ath, Millwall	AFC Bournemouth, Bradford C, Stoke C
1988–9	Middlesbrough, West Ham U, Newcastle U	Shrewsbury T, Birmingham C, Walsall
1987–8	Oxford U, Watford, Portsmouth, Chelsea*	Huddersfield T, Reading, Sheffield U*
1986–7	Leicester C, Manchester C, Aston Villa	Sunderland*, Grimsby T, Brighton & HA
1985–6	Ipswich T, Birmingham C, WBA	Carlisle U, Middlesbrough, Fulham
1984–5	Norwich C, Sunderland Stoke C	Notts Co, Cardiff C, Wolverhampton W
1983–4	Birmingham C, Notts Co, Wolverhampton W	Derby Co, Swansea C, Cambridge U
1982–3	Manchester C, Swansea C, Brighton & HA	Rotherham U, Burnley, Bolton W
1981–2	Leeds U, Middlesbrough, Wolverhampton W	Cardiff, Wrexham, Orient
1980–1	Norwich C, Leicester C, Crystal P	Preston NE, Bristol C, Bristol R
1979–80	Bristol C, Derby Co, Bolton W	Fulham, Burnley, Charlton Ath
1978–9	QPR, Birmingham, Chelsea	Sheffield U, Millwall, Blackburn

1977–8	West Ham, Newcastle, Leicester	Blackpool, Mansfield, Hull C
1976–7	Sunderland, Stoke, Tottenham	Carlisle, Plymouth, Hereford
1975–6	Wolves, Burnley, Sheffield U	Oxford, York, Portsmouth
1974–5	Luton, Chelsea, Carlisle	Millwall, Cardiff, Sheff. W
1973–4	So'ton, Man. U, Norwich	C. Palace, Preston, Swindon
1972–3	Crystal P and WBA	Huddersfield and Brighton
1971–2	Huddersfield and Nottingham F	Charlton and Watford
1970–1	Burnley and Blackpool	Blackburn and Bolton
1969–70	Sunderland and Sheffield W	Aston Villa and Preston
1968–9	Leicester and QPR	Bury and Fulham
1967–8	Sheffield U and Fulham	Rotherham and Plymouth
1966–7	Aston Villa and Blackpool	Northampton and Bury
1965–6	Blackburn and Northampton	Leyton O and Middlesbrough
1964–5	Birmingham and W'hampton	Swindon and Swansea
1963–4	Bolton and Ipswich	Grimsby and Scunthorpe
1962–3	Manchester C and Leyton O	Walsall and Luton
1961–2	Cardiff and Chelsea	Bristol R and Brighton
1960–1	Newcastle and Preston	Portsmouth and Lincoln
1959–60	Leeds and Luton	Hull and Bristol C
1958–9	Aston V and Portsmouth	Grimsby and Barnsley
1957–8	Sunderland and Sheffield W	Notts Co and Doncaster
1956–7	Cardiff and Charlton	Bury and Port Vale
1955–6	Huddersfield and Sheffield U	Plymouth and Hull
1954–5	Leicester and Sheffield W	Ipswich and Derby
1953–4	Middlesbrough and Liverpool	Brentford and Oldham
1952–3	Stoke and Derby	Southampton and Barnsley
1951–2	Fulham and Huddersfield	Coventry and QPR
1950–1	Sheffield W and Everton	Chesterfield and Grimsby
1949–50	Manchester C and Birmingham	Plymouth and Bradford
1948–9	Preston and Sheffield U	Lincoln and Nottingham F
1947–8	Blackburn and Grimsby	Doncaster and Millwall
1946–7	Brentford and Leeds	Swansea and Newport
1938–9	Birmingham and Leicester	Norwich and Tranmere
1937–8	Manchester C and WBA	Barnsley and Stockport
1936–7	Manchester U and Sheffield W	Doncaster and Bradford C
1935–6	Aston Villa and Blackburn	Port Vale and Hull
1934–5	Leicester and Tottenham	Oldham and Notts Co
1933–4	Newcastle and Sheffield U	Millwall and Lincoln
1932–3	Bolton and Blackpool	Chesterfield and Charlton
1931–2	Grimsby and West Ham	Barnsley and Bristol City
1930–1	Leeds and Manchester U	Reading and Cardiff
1929–30	Burnley and Everton	Hull and Notts Co
1928–9	Bury and Cardiff	Port Vale and Clapton O
1927–8	Tottenham and Middlesbrough	Fulham and South Shields
1926–7	Leeds and WBA	Darlington and Bradford C
1925–6	Manchester C and Notts Co	Stoke and Stockport
1924–5	Preston and Nottingham F	Crystal Palace and Coventry
1923–4	Chelsea and Middlesbrough	Nelson and Bristol City
1922–3	Stoke and Oldham	Rotherham and W'hampton
1921–2	Bradford C and Manchester U	Bradford and Bristol City
1920–1	Derby Co and Bradford	Stockport
1919–20	Notts Co and Sheffield W	
1916–18	*During the War the Football League competition was suspended. Previously the clubs relegated from Div. I to Div. II were:*	
1914–15	Tottenham and Chelsea	
1913–14	Preston NE and Derby Co	
1912–13	Notts Co and Woolwich Arsenal	
1911–12	Preston NE and Bury	
1910–11	Bristol City and Nottingham F	
1909–10	Bolton W and Chelsea	
1908–9	Manchester C and Leicester Fosse	

1907–8	Bolton W and Birmingham
1906–7	Derby Co and Stoke
1905–6	Nottingham F and Wolverhampton W
1904–5	*League extended*. Bury and Notts Co, two bottom clubs in First Division, re-elected.
1903–4	Liverpool and West Bromwich Albion
1902–3	Grimsby and Bolton
1901–2	Small Heath and Manchester C
1900–1	Preston NE and West Bromwich
1899–1900	Burnley and Glossop
1898–9	Bolton and Sheffield Wednesday

Season	**Relegation from Division III to Division IV**
1989–90	Cardiff C, Northampton T, Blackpool, Walsall
1988–9	Southend U, Chesterfield, Gillingham, Aldershot
1987–8	Doncaster R, York C, Grimsby T, Rotherham U*
1986–7	Bolton W*, Carlisle U, Darlington, Newport Co
1985–6	Lincoln C, Cardiff C, Wolverhampton W, Swansea C
1984–5	Burnley, Orient, Preston NE, Cambridge U
1983–4	Scunthorpe U, Southend U, Port Vale, Exeter C
1982–3	Reading, Doncaster R, Wrexham, Chesterfield
1981–2	Wimbledon, Swindon T, Bristol C, Chester
1980–1	Sheffield U, Colchester U, Hull C, Blackpool
1979–80	Bury, Southend U, Mansfield T and Wimbledon
1978–9	Peterborough, Walsall, Tranmere and Lincoln
1977–8	Port Vale, Bradford, Hereford and Portsmouth
1976–7	Reading, Northampton, Grimsby and York
1975–6	Aldershot, Colchester, Southend U, and Halifax T
1974–5	Bournemouth, Tranmere, Watford and Huddersfield
1973–4	Cambridge, Shrewsbury, Southport and Rochdale
1972–3	Rotherham, Brentford, Swansea and Scunthorpe
1971–2	Mansfield, Barnsley, Bradford C and Torquay
1970–1	Reading, Bury, Doncaster and Gillingham
1969–70	Bournemouth, Southport, Barrow and Stockport
1968–9	Northampton, Hartlepool, Crewe and Oldham
1967–8	Grimsby, Colchester, Scunthorpe and Peterborough†
1966–7	Swansea, Darlington, Workington and Doncaster
1965–6	Southend, Exeter, Brentford, and York
1964–5	Luton, Port Vale, Colchester and Barnsley
1963–4	Millwall, Crewe, Wrexham and Notts Co
1962–3	Bradford, Brighton, Carlisle and Halifax
1961–2	Torquay, Lincoln, Brentford and Newport
1960–1	Tranmere, Bradford C, Colchester and Chesterfield
1959–60	York, Mansfield, Wrexham and Accrington
1958–9	Stockport, Doncaster, Notts Co and Rochdale

†Expelled to Fourth Division by League

APPLICATION FOR RE-ELECTION TO THIRD DIVISION UNTIL 1957–58

Seven times: Walsall
Six: Exeter, Halifax, Newport
Five: Accrington, Barrow, Gillingham, New Brighton, Southport
Four: Norwich, Rochdale
Three: Crewe, Crystal P, Darlington, Hartlepool, Merthyr T, Swindon
Two: Aberdare Ath, Aldershot, Ashington, Bournemouth, Brentford, Chester, Colchester, Millwall, Durham C, Nelson, Queen's Park Rangers, Rotherham, Southend, Tranmere, Watford, Workington
One: Bradford, Bradford C, Brighton, Bristol R, Cardiff, Carlisle, Charlton, Gateshead, Grimsby, Mansfield, Shrewsbury, Thames, Torquay, York

APPLICATION FOR RE-ELECTION TO FOURTH DIVISION UNTIL 1985–86

Eleven times: Hartlepool
Seven: Crewe
Six: Barrow, Halifax T, Rochdale, Southport and York
Five: Chester C, Darlington, Lincoln, Stockport Co and Workington
Four: Bradford, Newport Co and Northampton T
Three: Doncaster R and Hereford U
Two: Bradford C, Exeter C, Oldham, Scunthorpe and Torquay U
One: Aldershot, Blackpool, Cambridge U, Colchester, Gateshead, Grimsby, Port Vale, Preston NE, Swansea C, Tranmere R, and Wrexham.

Gateshead not re-elected, their place being taken by Peterborough in the 1960–1 season.
Accrington resigned March 1962, and Oxford U elected to replace them in 1962–3 season.
Bradford not re-elected, their place being taken by Cambridge U in the 1970–1 season.
Barrow not re-elected, their place being taken by Hereford U in the 1972–3 season.
Workington not re-elected, their place being taken by Wimbledon in the 1977–8 season.
Southport not re-elected, their place being taken by Wigan in the 1978–9 season.

LEAGUE STATUS FROM 1986–87

1986–7 *Relegated*: Lincoln C *Promoted*: Scarborough
1987–8 *Relegated*: Newport C *Promoted*: Lincoln C
1988–9 *Relegated*: Darlington *Promoted*: Maidstone U
1989–90 *Relegated:* Colchester U *Promoted:* Darlington

BARCLAYS LEAGUE ATTENDANCES 1989–90

TOTAL LEAGUE ATTENDANCES SINCE 1946–47

Season	*Matches*	*Total*	*Season*	*Matches*	*Total*
1946–47	1848	35,604,606	1968–69	2028	29,382,172
1947–48	1848	40,259,130	1969–70	2028	29,600,972
1948–49	1848	41,271,414	1970–71	2028	28,194,146
1949–50	1848	40,517,865	1971–72	2028	28,700,729
1950–51	2028	39,584,967	1972–73	2028	25,448,642
1951–52	2028	39,015,866	1973–74	2027	24,982,203
1952–53	2028	37,149,966	1974–75	2028	25,577,977
1953–54	2028	36,174,590	1975–76	2028	24,896,053
1954–55	2028	34,133,103	1976–77	2028	26,182,800
1955–56	2028	33,150,809	1977–78	2028	25,392,872
1956–57	2028	32,744,405	1978–79	2028	24,540,627
1957–58	2028	33,562,208	1979–80	2028	24,623,975
1958–59	2028	33,610,985	1980–81	2028	21,907,569
1959–60	2028	32,538,611	1981–82	2028	20,006,961
1960–61	2028	28,619,754	1982–83	2028	18,766,158
1961–62	2015	27,979,902	1983–84	2028	18,358,631
1962–63	2028	28,885,852	1984–85	2028	17,849,835
1963–64	2028	28,535,022	1985–86	2028	16,488,577
1964–65	2028	27,641,168	1986–87	2028	17,379,218
1965–66	2028	27,206,980	1987–88	2030	17,959,732
1966–67	2028	28,902,596	1988–89	2036	18,464,192
1967–68	2028	30,107,298	1989–90	2036	19,445,442

	TOTAL ATTENDANCES	AVERAGE ATTENDANCES
TOTAL	19,445,442	9550
DIVISION 1	7,883,039	20,744
DIVISION 2	6,867,674	12,441
DIVISION 3	2,803,551	5078
DIVISION 4	1,891,178	3426

DIVISION ONE STATISTICS

	Average gate			*Season 1989/90*	
	1988/89	*1989/90*	*+/−%*	*Highest*	*Lowest*
Arsenal	35,595	33,713	−5.3	46,133	23,732
Aston Villa	23,310	25,544	+9.6	41,247	14,170
Charlton Athletic	9398	10,748	+14.4	17,806	5679
Chelsea	15,731	21,531	+36.9	31,285	13,114
Coventry City	16,040	14,312	−10.8	23,204	8294
Crystal Palace	10,655	17,105	+60.5	29,870	10,051
Derby County	17,536	17,426	−0.6	24,190	13,694
Everton	27,765	26,280	−5.3	41,443	17,591
Liverpool	38,574	36,589	−5.1	38,730	33,319
Luton Town	9504	9886	+4.0	12,620	8244
Manchester City	23,500	27,975	+19.0	43,246	23,354
Manchester United	36,488	39,077	+7.1	47,245	29,281
Millwall	15,416	12,413	−19.5	17,265	10,267
Norwich City	16,785	16,737	−0.3	20,210	12,640
Nottingham Forest	20,785	20,606	−0.9	26,766	16,437
Queens Park Rangers	12,281	13,218	+7.6	18,997	8437
Sheffield Wednesday	20,037	20,930	+4.5	33,260	13,728
Southampton	15,590	16,463	+5.6	20,510	12,904
Tottenham Hotspur	24,467	26,588	+8.7	33,944	17,668
Wimbledon	7824	7756	−0.9	14,738	3 618

DIVISION TWO STATISTICS

	Average gate			*Season 1989/90*	
	1988/89	*1989/90*	*+/−%*	*Highest*	*Lowest*
AFC Bournemouth	8087	7454	−7.8	9970	5506
Barnsley	7215	9033	+25.2	16,629	5524
Blackburn Rovers	8891	9624	+8.2	15,633	7494
Bradford City	10,524	8777	−16.6	12,527	4903
Brighton & Hove Albion	9048	8679	−4.1	12,689	5504
Hull City	6666	6518	−2.2	11,620	4207
Ipswich Town	12,650	12,913	+2.1	25,326	9430
Leeds United	21,811	28,210	+29.3	32,697	21,884
Leicester City	10,694	11,716	+9.6	21,134	8199
Middlesbrough	19,999	16,269	−18.7	23,617	11,428
Newcastle United	22,921	21,590	−5.8	31,665	15,163
Oldham Athletic	7204	9727	+35.0	17,451	4940
Oxford United	6352	5820	−8.4	8397	3863
Plymouth Argyle	8628	8749	+1.4	11,702	6793
Portsmouth	10,201	8959	−12.2	14,204	6496
Port Vale	6943	8978	+29.3	22,075	6168
Sheffield United	12,222	16,989	+39.0	31,602	12,653
Stoke City	9817	12,449	+26.8	27,004	8139
Sunderland	14,878	17,728	+19.2	28,499	13,014
Swindon Town	8687	9394	+8.1	16,208	6540
Watford	12,292	10,353	−15.8	15,682	7289
West Bromwich Albion	12,757	11,308	−11.4	21,316	8017
West Ham United	20,738	20,311	−2.1	25,892	14,960
Wolverhampton W.	14,392	17,045	+18.4	24,475	12,338

DIVISION THREE STATISTICS

	Average gate 1988/89	1989/90	+/−%	Season 1989/90 Highest	Lowest
Birmingham City	6265	8558	+36.6	14,278	5473
Blackpool	4276	4075	−4.7	8108	1842
Bolton Wanderers	5705	7286	+27.7	11,098	4679
Brentford	5681	5662	−0.3	7962	4537
Bristol C	8120	11,544	+42.2	19,483	6365
Bristol Rovers	5259	6202	+17.9	9813	4350
Bury	3367	3450	+2.5	6551	2327
Cardiff City	4384	3642	−16.9	8356	2086
Chester City	3055	2506	−18.0	4218	1730
Crewe Alexandra	3296	4008	+21.6	6900	3165
Fulham	4938	4484	−9.2	7141	2652
Huddersfield Town	5821	5630	−3.3	8483	3514
Leyton Orient	3793	4365	+15.1	7273	3040
Mansfield Town	4005	3129	−21.9	6384	2231
Northampton Town	3918	3187	−18.7	4346	2119
Notts County	5675	6151	+8.4	10,151	4586
Preston North End	7737	6313	−18.4	9105	4480
Reading	5105	4060	−20.5	6147	3009
Rotherham United	5063	5612	+10.8	7724	3420
Shrewsbury Town	4706	3521	−25.2	5319	2297
Swansea City	5088	4223	−17.0	12,244	2474
Tranmere Rovers	5331	7449	+39.7	12,723	4912
Walsall	6108	4077	−33.3	6036	2903
Wigan Athletic	3151	2758	−12.5	6850	1934

DIVISION FOUR STATISTICS

	Average gate 1988/89	1989/90	+/−%	Season 1989/90 Highest	Lowest
Aldershot	2609	2022	−22.5	3208	1139
Burnley	7062	6222	−11.9	12,277	3959
Cambridge United	2653	3359	+26.6	4963	1990
Carlisle United	3176	4740	+49.2	8462	3059
Chesterfield	3717	4181	+12.5	7501	2822
Colchester United	2893	3150	+8.9	5283	1720
Doncaster Rovers	2158	2706	+25.4	4336	1806
Exeter City	2679	4859	+81.4	8271	2754
Gillingham	3675	3887	+5.8	11,605	2382
Grimsby Town	4302	5984	+39.1	11,894	3447
Halifax Town	1946	1895	−2.6	4744	1233
Hartlepool United	2048	2503	+22.2	3724	1379
Hereford United	2132	2676	+25.5	7302	1567
Lincoln City	3887	4071	+4.7	6251	2470
Maidstone United	1037	2427	+134.0	5006	1299
Peterborough United	3264	4804	+47.3	9257	2813
Rochdale	1968	2027	+3.0	5420	1216
Scarborough	2961	2325	−21.5	3602	1623
Scunthorpe United	4547	3524	−22.5	8384	2226
Southend United	3699	3836	+3.7	7070	2584
Stockport County	2792	3899	+39.6	6593	2356
Torquay United	2349	2147	−8.6	3389	1521
Wrexham	2636	2368	−10.2	4653	1225
York City	2613	2615	+0.1	3665	2061

TRANSFER TRAIL

1989–90 Transfers involving First Division Clubs

(from July 1989 to May 1990)

July 1989

28 Beglin, James M. – Liverpool to Leeds United
26 Bradley, Russell – Nottingham Forest to Hereford United
27 Clarke, Wayne – Everton to Leicester City
25 Cranson, Ian – Sheffield Wednesday to Stoke City
13 Foster, Stephen B. – Luton Town to Oxford United
17 Harkness, Steven – Carlisle United to Liverpool
31 Nebbeling, Gavin M. – Crystal Palace to Fulham
27 Newell, Michael C. – Leicester City to Everton
1 Phelan, Michael C. – Norwich City to Manchester United
31 Phillips, David O. – Coventry City to Norwich City
6 Salman, Michael B. – Wrexham to Charlton Athletic
10 Scott, Ian – Manchester City to Stoke City
28 Sedgley, Stephen P. – Coventry City to Tottenham Hotspur
18 Sherwood, Timothy A. – Watford to Norwich City
26 Shirtliff, Peter A. – Charlton Athletic to Sheffield Wednesday
24 Webb, Neil J. – Nottingham Forest to Manchester United
20 Wilmot, Rhys J. – Arsenal to Plymouth Argyle

August 1989

16 Adams, Neil J. – Everton to Oldham Athletic
24 Allen, Martin J. – Queens Park Rangers to West Ham United
3 Bailey, Dennis L. – Crystal Palace to Birmingham City
10 Biggins, Wayne – Manchester City to Stoke City
2 Bishop, Ian W. – A.F.C. Bournemouth to Manchester City
18 Dennis, Mark E. – Queens Park Rangers to Crystal Palace
18 Dickens, Alan W. – West Ham United to Chelsea
4 Dodds, William – Chelsea to Dundee
17 Fleming, Gary J. – Nottingham Forest to Manchester City
18 Galvin, Anthony – Sheffield Wednesday to Swindon Town
18 Gray, Andrew A. – Queens Park Rangers to Crystal Palace
29 Gregory, John C. – Derby County to Portsmouth
18 Johnson, Robert S. – Luton Town to Leicester City
18 Kennedy, Michael F. – Leicester City to Luton Town
7 Keown, Martin R. – Aston Villa to Everton
18 Lawrence, George R. – Millwall to A.F.C. Bournemouth
3 McGrath, Paul – Manchester United to Aston Villa
17 McLaughlin, Joseph – Chelsea to Charlton Athletic
2 Moulden, Paul A. – Manchester City to A.F.C. Bournemouth
29 Palliser, Garry A. – Middlesbrough to Manchester United
14 Putney, Trevor A. – Norwich City to Middlesbrough
18 Reeves, Alan – Norwich City to Chester City
17 Reeves, David – Sheffield Wednesday to Bolton Wanderers
1 Rodger, Graham – Coventry City to Luton Town
3 Sheridan, John J. – Leeds United to Nottingham Forest
18 Statham, Derek J. – Southampton to Stoke City
25 Van Den Hauwe, Patrick W. R. – Everton to Tottenham Hotspur

15 Walton, Mark A. – Colchester United to Norwich City
18 Waugh, Keith – Bristol City to Coventry City
1 Whiteside, Norman – Manchester United to Everton

Temporary Transfers
25 Beresford, Marlon – Sheffield Wednesday to Bury
23 Bracewell, Paul W. – Everton to Sunderland
14 Cobb, Gary E. – Luton Town to Swansesa City
31 Dearden, Kevin C. – Tottehham Hotspur to Hartlepool United
7 Harris, Mark A. – Crystal Palace to Burnley
17 Knight, Ian J. – Sheffield Wednesday to Scunthorpe United
14 Salako, John A. – Crystal Palace to Swansea City

September 1989
15 Bardsley, David J. – Oxford United to Queens Park Rangers
29 Bracewell, Paul W. – Everton to Sunderland
2 Carey, Brian P. – Cork City to Manchester United
22 Foster, Colin J. – Nottingham Forest to West Ham United
9 Gleghorn, Nigel W. – Manchester City to Birmingham City
22 Harris, Mark A. – Crystal Palace to Swansea City
14 Ince, Paul E. C. – West Ham United to Manchester United
8 Jonsson, Sigurdur – Sheffield Wednesday to Arsenal
21 Lillis, Mark A. – Aston Villa to Scunthorpe United
15 Stein, Earl M. S. – Queens Park Rangers to Oxford United
18 Wallace, David L. – Southampton to Manchester United

Temporary Transfers
29 Beresford, Marlon – Sheffield Wednesday to Ipswich Road
5 Blake, Mark C. – Southampton to Colchestesr United
7 Bradshaw, Carl – Manchester City to Sheffield United
15 Clark, Martin J. – Nottingham Forest to Falkirk
29 Cobb, Gary E. – Swansea City to Luton Town (Tr. Back)
13 Dowie, Iain – Luton Town to Fulham
29 Freestone, Roger – Chelsea to Swansea City
14 Glover, Edward L. – Nottingham Forest to Leicester City
2 Gormley, Edward J. – Tottenham Hotspur to Shrewsbury Town
21 Lamb, Alan – Nottingham Forest to Hartlepool United
6 Marriott, Andrew – Nottingham Forest to West Bromwich Albion
19 Rostron, John W. – Sheffield Wednesday to Sheffield United
7 Scully, Patrick J. – Arsenal to Preston North End
22 Sheffield, Jonathon – Norwich City to Aldershot
6 Williams, Brett – Nottingham Forest to Hereford United

October 1989
5 Bradshaw, Carl – Manchestesr City to Sheffield United
3 Burridge, John – Southampton to Newcastle United
3 Drinkell, Kevin – Glasgow Rangers to Coventry City
13 Lamb, Alan – Nottingham Forest to Hartlepool United
25 Pennyfather, Howard K. – Crystal Palace to Ipswich Town

Temporary Transfers
18 Beresford, Marlon – Ipswich Town to Sheffield Wednesday (Tr. Back)
25 Goater, Leonard S. – Manchester United to Rotherham United
12 Johns, Nicholas P. – Queens Park Rangers to Maidstone United
30 Kiely, Dean L. – Coventry City to Ipswich Town
19 Moncur, John F. – Tottenham Hotspur to Brentford

November 1989

2 Beagrie, Peter S. – Stoke City to Everton
1 Cook, Paul A. – Norwich City to Wolverhampton Wanderers
20 Fashanu, Justinus S. – Manchester City to West Ham United
16 Hendry, Edward C. J. – Blackburn Rovers to Manchestesr City
16 Hucker, Peter I. – Oxford United to Millwall
24 Kerslake, David – Queens Park Rangers to Swindon Town
30 King, Philip G. – Swindon Town to Sheffield Wednesday
21 Martyn, Antony N. – Bristol Rovers to Crystal Palace
3 Sheridan, John J. – Nottingham Forest to Sheffield Wednesday
30 Spackman, Nigel J. – Queens Park Rangers to Glasgow Rangers

Temporary Transfers

24 Branagan, Keith G. – Millwall to Brentford
8 Campbell, Kevin J. – Arsenal to Leicester City
21 Davis, Stephen M. – Southampton to Burnley
29 Ferguson, Iain J. H. – Heart of Midlothian to Charlton Athletic
30 Jones, Andrew M. – Charlton Athletic to Bristol City
2 King, Philip G. – Swindon Town to Sheffield Wednesday
16 McCord, Brian J. – Derby County to Barnsley
17 Martyn, Antony N. – Bristol Rovers to Crystal Palace
2 Moran, Paul – Tottenham Hotspur to Leicester City
11 Parkin, Brian – Crystal Palace to Bristol Rovers
22 Rees, Melvyn J. – Watford to Southampton
20 Spink, Dean P. – Ason Villa to Scarborough
15 Turner, Christopher R. – Sheffield Wednesday to Leeds United
9 Williams, Paul D. – Derby County to Lincoln City

December 1989

28 Bishop, Ian W. – Manchester City to West Ham United
4 Flynn, Michael A. – Norwich City to Preston North End
29 Goddard, Paul – Derby County to Millwall
15 Harper, Alan – Sheffield Wednesday to Manchester City
22 Heseltine, Wayne A. – Manchestesr United to Oldham Athletic
22 McKernon, Craig A. – Mansfield Town to Arsenal
28 Morley, Trevor W. – Manchester City to West Ham United
15 Reid, Peter – Queens Park Rangers to Manchester City
5 Thorn, Andrew – Newcastle United to Crystal Palace
29 Ward, Mark W. – West Ham United to Manchester City
14 Wegerle, Roy C. – Luton Town to Queen's Park Rangers

Temporary Transfers

22 Andrews, Ian E. – Celtic to Southampton
13 Branagan, Keith G. – Brentford to Millwall (Tr. Back)
22 Carr, Franz A. – Nottingham Forest to Sheffield Wednesday
14 Dearden, Kevin C. – Tottentham Hotspur to Oxford United
14 Donaghy, Malachy – Manchester United to Luton Town
15 Hedman, Rudolph G. – Crystal Palace to Leyton Orient
29 Marriott, Andrew – Nottingham Forest to Blackburn Rovers
22 Robson, Mark A. – Tottehham Hotspur to Plymouth Argyle
6 Rostron, John W. – Sheffield United to Sheffield Wednesday (Tr. Back)
14 Sealey, Leslie J. – Luton Town to Manchester United
14 Shaw, Richard E. – Crystal Palace to Hull City
15 Suckling, Perry J. – Crystal Palace to West Ham United
29 Youds, Edward P. – Everton to Cardiff City

January 1990

9 Bennett, Michael R. – Charlton Athletic to Wimbledon
11 Chapman, Lee R. – Nottingham Forest to Leeds United
12 Clarke, Wayne – Leicester City to Manchestesr City
19 Currie, David N. – Barnsley to Nottingham Forest
29 Gallacher, Kevin W. – Dundee United to Coventry City
19 Gayle, Brian W. – Manchester City to Ipswich Town
19 Goater, Leonard S. – Manchester United to Rotherham United
18 Harford, Michael G. – Luton Town to Derby County
11 Hazard, Michael – Chelsea to Portsmouth
5 McNab, Neil – Manchester City to Tranmere Rovers
18 Milner, Andrew J. – Manchester City to Rochdale
12 Oldfield, David C. – Manchester City to Leicestesr City
11 Parkin, Brian – Crystal Palace to Bristol Rovers
22 Pates, Colin G. – Charlton Athletic to Arsenal
10 Taggart, Gerald P. – Manchester City to Barnsley

Temporary Transfers

13 Butters, Guy – Tottenham Hotspur to Southend United
15 Crossley, Mark G. – Nottingham Forest to Manchester United
11 Dowson, Alan P. – Millwall to Fulham
11 Edinburgh, Justin C. – Southend United to Tottenham Hotspur
18 Glover, Edward L. – Nottingham Forest to Barnsley
17 Gray, Philip – Tottenham Hotspur to Barnsley
16 Howells, Gareth J. – Tottenham Hotspur to Swindon Town
11 Knight, Ian J. – Sheffield Wednesday to Grimsby Town
25 Madden, David J. – Crystal Palace to Birmingham City
11 Miller, Paul A. – Wimbledon to Bristol City
22 Milne, Ralph – Manchester United to West Ham United
11 Powell, Christopher G. R. – Crystal Palace to Aldershot
19 Shaw, Richard E. – Hull City to Crystal Palace (Tr. Back)
11 Stevens, Gary A. – Tottenham Hotspur to Portsmouth
22 Suckling, Perry J. – West Ham United to Crystal Palace (Tr. Back)

February 1990

15 Andrews, Ian E. – Celtic to Southampton
16 Anthrobus, Stephen A. – Millwall to Wimbledon
20 Gritt, Stephen J. – Walsall to Charlton Athletic
23 Heath, Adrian P. – Aston Villa to Manchester City
26 Knight, Ian J. – Sheffield Wednesday to Grimsby Town
22 Newhouse, Aidan – Chester City to Wimbledon
16 Varadi, Imre – Sheffield Wednesday to Leeds United

Temporary Transfers

9 Anthrobus, Stephen A. – Millwall to Southend United
13 Anthrobus, Stephen A. – Southend United to Millwall (Tr. Back)
27 Danzey, Michael – Nottingham Forest to Chester City
16 Davis, Stephen M. – Burnley to Southampton (Tr. Back)
1 Dyche, Sean M. – Nottingham Forest to Chesterfield
8 Hedman, Rudolph G. – Leyton Orient to Crystal Palace (Tr. Back)
8 Hoyle, Colin R. – Arsenal to Chesterfield
10 Hurst, Mark D. – Nottingham Forest to Huddersfield Town
8 McCall, Stephen H. – Sheffield Wednesday to Carlisle United
16 Mimms, Robert A. – Tottenham Hotspur to Aberdeen
22 Powell, Christopher G. R. – Crystal Palace to Aldershot
17 Robson, Mark A. – Plymouth Argyle to Tottenham Hotspur (Tr. Back)
8 Shakespeare, Craig R. – Sheffield Wednesday to West Bromwich A.

1 Spink, Dean P. – Aston Villa to Bury
19 Starbuck, Philip M. – Nottingham Forest to Hereford United
8 Stowell, Michael – Everton to Preston North End
20 Stowell, Michael – Preston North End to Everton (Tr. Back)
8 Veradi, Imre – Sheffield Wednesday to Leeds United
8 Youds, Edward P. – Everton to Wrexham

March 1990
20 Allen, Malcolm – Norwich City to Millwall
9 Bannister, Gary – Coventry City to West Bromwich Albion
16 Cascarino, Anthony G. – Millwall to Aston Villa
1 Dyche, Sean – Nottingham Forest to Chesterfield
16 Edwards, Paul R. – Crewe Alexandra to Coventry City
16 Fiore, Mark J. – Wimbledon to Plymouth Argyle
23 Fleming, Gary J. – Manchester City to Barnsley
17 Green, Scott P. – Derby County to Bolton Wanderers
2 Horrix, Dean V. – Millwall to Bristol City
12 Johns, Nicholas – Queens Park Rangers to Maidstone United
21 Quinn, Niall – Arsenal to Manchester City
20 Salman, Danis M. M. – Millwall to Plymouth Argyle
6 Shakespeare, Craig R. – Sheffield Wednesday to West Bromwich Albion
27 Smith, Mark – Dunfermline to Nottingham Forest
15 Spink, Dean P. – Aston Villa to Shrewsbury Town
22 Stevens, Gary A. – Tottenham Hotspur to Portsmouth
24 Thompson, Garry – Watford to Crystal Palace
2 Wright, Paul H. – Queens Park Rangers to Hibernian

Temporary Transfers
22 Baker, Graham – Southampton to Aldershot
15 Blackwell, Dean R. – Wimbledon to Plymouth Argyle
22 Blake, Mark C. – Southampton to Shrewsbury Town
1 Brooke, Garry J. – Wimbledon to Stoke City
22 Cash, Stuart P. – Nottingham Forest to Rotherham United
15 Clarke, Martin J. – Nottingham Forest to Mansfield Town
20 Dearden, Kevin C. – Tottenham Hotspur to Swindon Town
8 Fleming, Gary J. – Manchestesr City to Notts. County
22 Fleming, Gary J. – Notts. County to Manchester City (Tr. Back)
17 Francis, Lee C. – Arsenal to Chesterfield
22 Freestone, Roger – Chelsea to Hereford United
21 Hannigan, Al J. – Arsenal to Torquay United
16 Hilaire, Vincent M. – Leeds United to Charlton Athletic
21 Howells, Gareth – Tottenham Hotspur to Leyton Orient
22 Hurst, Mark – Huddersfield Town to Nottingham Forest (Tr. Back)
22 Jones, Philip A. – Everton to Blackpool
9 Kiely, Dean – Coventry City to York City
22 Leaburn, Carl W. – Charlton Athletic to Northampton Town
22 Lyne, Neil – Nottingham Forest to Walsall
21 Marriott, Andrew – Nottingham Forest to Colchester United
22 Morgan, Darren – Millwall to Bradford City
22 Poutch, Neil – Luton Town to Leicester City
21 Sealey, Leslie J. – Luton Town to Manchester United
21 Sheffield, Jon – Norwich City to Ipswich Town
22 Sparham, Sean – Millwall to Brentford
1 Tanner, Nicholas – Liverpool to Norwich City

April 1990 Temporary Transfers
30 Blackwell, Dean R. – Plymouth Argyle to Wimbledon (Tr. Back)

26 Brooke, Garry J. – Stoke City to Wimbledon (Tr. Back)
25 Freestone, Roger – Hereford United to Chelsea (Tr. Back)
20 Johnston, Richard W. – Tottenham Hotspur to Dunfermline Athletic
13 Mimms, Robert A. – Aberdeen to Tottenham Hotspur (Tr. Back)
23 Morgan, Darren J. – Bradford City to Millwall (Tr. Back)

May 1990
18 Kiely, Dean L. – Coventry City to York City
18 Seaman, David A. – Queens Park Rangers to Arsenal

Summer moves
Ian Thompstone, Manchester C – Oldham Ath; Warren Barton, Maidstone U – Wimbledon; Colin Clarke, QPR – Portsmouth; Lee Francis, Arsenal – Chesterfield; Rod Hindmarsh, Derby Co to Wolverhampton W; John Humphrey, Charlton Ath – Crystal Palace; Denis Irwin, Oldham Ath – Manchester U; John Lukic, Arsenal – Leeds U; Mike Stowell, Everton – Wolverhampton W; Dennis Wise, Wimbledon – Chelsea; Andy Linighan, Norwich C – Arsenal; Andy Townsend, Norwich C – Chelsea; Clive Wilson, Chelsea – QPR; Kevin Ball, Portsmouth – Sunderland; Peter Davenport, Middlesbrough – Sunderland; Mike Heathcote, Sunderland – Shrewsbury T; Andy Hinchcliffe, Manchester C – Everton; Glyn Hodges, Watford – Crystal Palace; Jamie Hoyland, Bury – Sheffield U; Neil Pointon, Everton – Manchester C; Colin Woodthorpe, Chester C – Norwich C; Tony Coton, Watford – Manchester C; Mark Brennan, Middlesbrough – Manchester C; John Pemberton, Crystal Palace – Sheffield U; Paul Beesley, Leyton Orient – Sheffield U; Kevin Richardson, Arsenal – Real Sociedad; Martin Hayes. Arsenal – Celtic.

FA CUP 1989–90

First Round

Aldershot	0	Cambridge U	1
Marine	0	Rochdale	1
Aylesbury	1	Southend U	0
Basingstoke	3	Bromsgrove	0
Bishop Auckland	2	Tow Law T	0
Blackpool	2	Bolton W	1
Brentford	0	Colchester U	1
Bristol C	2	Barnet	0
Bristol R	1 1 0	Reading	1 1 1
Burnley	1 2	Stockport Co	1 1
Cardiff C	1	Halesowen	0
Carlisle U	3	Wrexham	0
Crewe Alex	2	Congleton	0
Darlington	6	Northwich	2
Dartford	1 1	Exeter C	1 4
Doncaster R	1	Notts Co	0
Farnborough	0	Hereford U	1
Gillingham	0 0	Welling	0 1
Gloucester	1	Dorchester	0
Hartlepool U	0	Huddersfield T	2
Kettering	0	Northampton T	1
Kidderminster	2	Swansea	3
Leyton Orient	0	Birmingham C	1
Lincoln C	1	Billingham Syn	0
Macclesfield	1 2	Chester C	1 3
Peterborough U	1 1	Hayes	1 0
Preston NE	1	Tranmere R	0
Redditch	1	Merthyr	3
Rotherham U	0 2	Bury	0 1
Scarborough	0	Whitley Bay	1
Scunthorpe U	4	Matlock	1
Shrewsbury T	2	Chesterfield	3
Slough	1	Woking	2
Stafford R	2	Halifax T	3
Sutton U	1 0	Torquay U	1 4
Telford U	0	Walsall	3
York C	1	Grimsby T	2
Bath C	2 1	Fulham	2 2
Maidstone U	2	Yeovil	1
Wigan Ath	2	Mansfield T	0

Second Round

Basingstoke	2	Torquay U	3
Blackpool	3	Chester	0
Bristol C	2	Fulham	1
Cambridge U	3	Woking	1
Cardiff C	2 1	Gloucester	2 0
Chesterfield	0	Huddersfield T	2
Colchester U	0	Birmingham C	2
Crewe Alex	1 2	Bishop Auckland	1 0
Darlington	3	Halifax T	0
Grimsby T	1	Doncaster R	0

Home	Score	Away	Score
Hereford U	3	Merthyr	2
Maidstone U	1 2	Exeter C	1 3
Northampton T	0 1	Aylesbury	0 0
Reading	0 1 0 2	Welling	0 1 0 1
Rochdale	3	Lincoln C	0
Scunthorpe U	2 1 0	Burnley	2 1 5
Swansea C	3	Peterborough U	1
Walsall	1	Rotherham U	0
Whitley Bay	2	Preston NE	0
Wigan Ath	2	Carlisle U	0

Third Round

Home	Score	Away	Score
Birmingham C	1 0	Oldham Ath	1 1
Blackburn R	2 1	Aston Villa	2 3
Blackpool	1	Burnley	0
Brighton & HA	4	Luton T	1
Bristol C	2	Swindon T	1
Cambridge U	0 3	Darlington	0 1
Cardiff C	0 0	QPR	0 2
Chelsea	1 2	Crewe Alex	1 0
Crystal Palace	2	Portsmouth	1
Exeter C	1 0	Norwich C	1 2
Hereford U	2	Walsall	1
Huddersfield T	3	Grimsby T	1
Hull C	0	Newcastle U	1
Leeds U	0	Ipswich T	1
Leicester C	1	Barnsley	2
Manchester C	0 1 1	Millwall	0 1 3
Middlesbrough	0 1 0	Everton	0 1 1
Northampton T	1	Coventry C	0
Plymouth Arg	0	Oxford U	1
Reading	2	Sunderland	1
Rochdale	1	Whitley Bay	0
Sheffield U	2	Bournemouth	0
Stoke C	0	Arsenal	1
Swansea C	0 0	Liverpool	0 8
Torquay U	1	West Ham U	0
Tottenham H	1	Southampton	3
Watford	2	Wigan Ath	0
WBA	2	Wimbledon	0
Wolverhampton W	1	Sheffield W	2
Charlton Ath	1 3	Bradford C	1 0
Nottingham F	0	Manchester U	1
Port Vale	1 3	Derby Co	1 2

Fourth Round

Home	Score	Away	Score
Arsenal	0 0	QPR	0 2
Aston Villa	6	Port Vale	0
Barnsley	2	Ipswich T	0
Blackpool	1	Torquay U	0
Bristol C	3	Chelsea	1
Crystal Palace	4	Huddersfield T	0
Millwall	1 0	Cambridge U	1 1
Oldham Ath	2	Brighton & HA	1
Reading	3 1	Newcastle U	3 4
Rochdale	3	Northampton T	0
Sheffield U	1 2	Watford	1 1

Southampton	1	Oxford U	0
WBA	1	Charlton Ath	0
Hereford U	0	Manchester U	1
Norwich C	0 1	Liverpool	0 3
Sheffield W	1	Everton	2

Fifth Round

Bristol C	0 1 1	Cambridge U	0 1 5
Liverpool	3	Southampton	0
Crystal Palace	1	Rochdale	0
Oldham Ath	2 1 2	Everton	2 1 1
WBA	0	Aston Villa	2
Blackpool	2 0 0	QPR	2 0 3
Newcastle U	2	Manchester U	3
Sheffield U	2 0 1	Barnsley	2 0 0

Sixth Round

Cambridge U	0	Crystal Palace	1
QPR	2 0	Liverpool	2 1
Sheffield U	0	Manchester U	1
Oldham Ath	3	Aston Villa	0

Semi-Finals

Crystal Palace	4	Liverpool	3
Manchester U	3 2	Oldham Ath	3 1

Final at Wembley, 29 May 1990, att. 80,000

Crystal Palace (1) 3 *(O'Reilly, Wright 2)* Manchester U (1) 3 *(Robson, Hughes 2)*

Crystal Palace: Martyn; Pemberton, Shaw, Gray (Madden), O'Reilly, Thorn, Barber (Wright), Thomas, Bright, Salako, Pardew.
Manchester U: Leighton; Ince, Martin (Blackmore), Bruce, Phelan, Pallister (Robins), Robson, Webb, McClair, Hughes, Wallace.
Referee: A. Gunn (South Chailey).

Replay at Wembley, 17 May, 1990, att. 80,000

Crystal Palace (0) 0 Manchester U (0) 1 *(Martin)*

Crystal Palace: Martyn; Pemberton, Shaw, Gray, O'Reilly, Thorn, Barber (Wright), Thomas, Bright, Salako (Madden), Pardew.
Manchester U: Sealey; Ince, Martin, Bruce, Phelan, Pallister, Robson, Webb, McClair, Hughes, Wallace. *Referee:* A. Gunn (South Chailey).

PAST FA CUP FINALS

Details of some goalscorers are not available for the early years

1872	The Wanderers *Betts*	1	Royal Engineers	0
1873	The Wanderers *Kinnaird, Wollaston*	2	Oxford University	0
1874	Oxford University *Mackarness, Patton*	2	Royal Engineers	0
1875	Royal Engineers *Unknown*	1	Old Etonians *Bonsor*	1*
	Royal Engineers *Scorers in replay: Renny-Tailyour, Stafford*	2	Old Etonians	0
1876	The Wanderers *Edwards*	1	Old Etonians *Bonsor*	1*
	The Wanderers *Wollaston, Hughes 2*	3	Old Etonians	0
1877	The Wanderers *Kenrick, Heron*	2	Oxford University *Kinnaird (og)*	1*
1878	The Wanderers *Kenrick 2, unknown*	3	Royal Engineers *Unknown*	1

Year	Winners		Runners-up	
1879	Old Etonians	1	Clapham Rovers	0
	Clerke			
1880	Clapham Rovers	1	Oxford University	0
	Lloyd-Jones			
1881	Old Carthusians	3	Old Etonians	0
	Page, Wynard, Tod			
1882	Old Etonians	1	Blackburn Rovers	0
	Anderson			
1883	Blackburn Olympic	2	Old Etonians	1*
	Costley, Mathews		*Goodhart*	
1884	Blackburn Rovers	2	Queen's Park	1
	Forrest, Brown		*Christie*	
1885	Blackburn Rovers	2	Queen's Park	0
	Forrest, Brown			
1886	Blackburn Rovers	0	West Bromwich Albion	0
	Blackburn Rovers	2	West Bromwich Albion	0
	Brown, Sowerbutts			
1887	Aston Villa	2	West Bromwich Albion	0
	Hunter, Hodgetts			
1888	West Bromwich Albion	2	Preston NE	1
	Woodall, Bayliss		*Goodall*	
1889	Preston NE	3	Wolverhampton W	0
	Ross, Dewhurst, Thomson			
1890	Blackburn Rovers	6	Sheffield Wednesday	1
	Dewar, Lofthouse, John Southworth, Townley 3		*Bennett*	
1891	Blackburn Rovers	3	Notts Co	1
	Dewar, John Southworth Townley		*Oswald*	
1892	West Bromwich Albion	3	Aston Villa	1
	Reynolds, Nicholls, Geddes			
1893	Wolverhampton W	1	Everton	0
	Allen			
1894	Notts Co	4	Bolton W	1
	Watson, Logan 3		*Cassidy*	
1895	Aston Villa	1	West Bromwich Albion	0
	Chatt			
1896	Sheffield Wednesday	2	Wolverhampton W	1
	Spiksley		*Black*	
1897	Aston Villa	3	Everton	2
	Crabtree, Campell, Weldon		*Boyle, Bell*	
1898	Nottingham F	3	Derby Co	1
	McPherson, Capes 2		*Bloomer*	
1899	Sheffield U	4	Derby Co	1
	Bennett, Beers, Almond, Priest		*Boag*	
1900	Bury	4	Southampton	0
	Wood, McLuckie 2, Plant			
1901	Tottenham H	2	Sheffield U	2
	Brown		*Bennett, Priest*	
	Tottenham H	3	Sheffield U	1
	Cameron, Smith, Brown		*Priest*	
1902	Sheffield U	1	Southampton	1
	Common		*Wood*	
	Sheffield U	2	Southampton	1
	Hedley, Barnes		*Brown*	
1903	Bury	6	Derby Co	0
	Wood, Sagar, Ross, Plant, Leeming 2			
1904	Manchester C	1	Bolton W	0
	Meredith			

Year	Winner		Runner-up	
1905	Aston Villa	2	Newcastle U	0
	Hampton			
1906	Everton	1	Newcastle U	0
	Young			
1907	Sheffield Wednesday	2	Everton	1
	Stewart, Simpson		*Sharp*	
1908	Wolverhampton W	3	Newcastle U	1
	Hunt, Harrison, Hedley		*Howie*	
1909	Manchester U	1	Bristol C	0
	A. Turnbull			
1910	Newcastle U	1	Barnsley	1
	Rutherford		*Tuffnell*	
	Newcastle U	2	Barnsley	0
	Shepherd (1 pen)			
1911	Bradford C	0	Newcastle U	0
	Bradford C	1	Newcastle U	0
	Spiers			
1912	Barnsley	0	West Bromwich Albion	0
	Barnsley	1	West Bromwich Albion	0*
	Tuffnell			
1913	Aston Villa	1	Sunderland	0
	Barber			
1914	Burnley	1	Liverpool	0
	Freeman			
1915	Sheffield U	3	Chelsea	0
	Simmons, Fazackerley, Kitchen			
1920	Aston Villa	1	Huddersfield T	0*
	Kirton			
1921	Tottenham H	1	Wolverhampton W	0
	Dimmock			
1922	Huddersfield T	1	Preston NE	0
	Smith (pen)			
1923	Bolton W	2	West Ham U	0
	Jack, J.R. Smith			
1924	Newcastle U	2	Aston Villa	0
	Harris, Seymour			
1925	Sheffield U	1	Cardiff C	0
	Tunstall			
1926	Bolton W	1	Manchester C	0
	Jack			
1927	Cardiff C	1	Arsenal	0
	Ferguson			
1928	Blackburn Rovers	3	Huddersfield T	1
	Roscamp 2, McLean		*A. Jackson*	
1929	Bolton W	2	Portsmouth	0
	Butler, Blackmore			
1930	Arsenal	2	Huddersfield Town	0
	Lambert, James			
1931	West Bromwich Albion	2	Birmingham C	1
	W.G. Richardson		*Bradford*	
1932	Newcastle U	2	Arsenal	1
	Allen		*John*	
1933	Everton	3	Manchester C	0
	Dunn, Dean, Stein			
1934	Manchester C	2	Portsmouth	1
	Tilson		*Rutherford*	
1935	Sheffield Wednesday	4	West Bromwich Albion	2
	Hooper, Palethorpe, Rimmer 2		*Sandford, Boyes*	
1936	Arsenal	1	Sheffield U	0
	Drake			

Year	Winner		Runner-up	
1937	Sunderland	3	Preston NE	1
	Carter, Gurney, Burbanks		*F. O'Donnell*	
1938	Preston NE	1	Huddersfield T	0*
	Mutch (pen)			
1939	Portsmouth	4	Wolverhampton W	1
	Anderson, Barlow, Parker 2		*Dorsett*	
1946	Derby Co	4	Charlton Ath	1*
	H. Turner (og), Stamps 2, Doherty		*H. Turner*	
1947	Charlton Ath	1	Burnley	0*
	Duffy			
1948	Manchester U	4	Blackpool	2
	Anderson, Rowley 2, Pearson		*Shimwell (pen), Mortensen*	
1949	Wolverhampton W	3	Leicester C	1
	Smyth, Pye 2		*Griffiths*	
1950	Arsenal	2	Liverpool	0
	Lewis			
1951	Newcastle	2	Blackpool	0
	Milburn			
1952	Newcastle	1	Arsenal	0
	G. Robledo			
1953	Blackpool	4	Bolton W	3
	Mortensen 3, Perry		*Bell, Moir, Lofthouse*	
1954	West Bromwich Albion	3	Preston NE	2
	Griffin, Allen 2		*Wayman, Morrison*	
1955	Newcastle U	3	Manchester C	1
	Milburn, Hannah, Mitchell		*Johnstone*	
1956	Manchester C	3	Birmingham C	1
	Johnstone, Hayes, Dyson		*Kinsey*	
1957	Aston Villa	2	Manchester U	1
	McParland		*T. Taylor*	
1958	Bolton W	2	Manchester U	0
	Lofthouse			
1959	Nottingham F	2	Luton T	1
	Dwight, Wilson		*Pacey*	
1960	Wolverhampton W	3	Blackburn Rovers	0
	Deeley 2, McGrath (og)			
1961	Tottenham H	2	Leicester C	0
	Smith, Dyson			
1962	Tottenham H	3	Burnley	1
	Blanchflower (pen), Smith, Greaves		*Robson*	
1963	Manchester U	3	Leicester C	1
	Herd 2, Law		*Keyworth*	
1964	West Ham U	3	Preston N E	2
	Boyce, Hurst, Sissons		*Dawson, Holden*	
1965	Liverpool	2	Leeds U	1*
	Hunt, St John		*Bremner*	
1966	Everton	3	Sheffield Wednesday	2
	Trebilcock 2, Temple		*McCalliog, Ford*	
1967	Tottenham H	2	Chelsea	1
	Robertson, Saul		*Tambling*	
1968	West Bromwich Albion	1	Everton	0*
	Astle			
1969	Manchester C	1	Leicester C	0
	Young			
1970	Chelsea	2	Leeds U	2*
	Houseman, Hutchinson		*Charlton, Jones*	
	Chelsea	2	Leeds U	1*
	Webb, Osgood		*Jones*	

Year	Winner		Runner-up	
1971	Arsenal	2	Liverpool	1*
	Kelly, George		*Heighway*	
1972	Leeds U	1	Arsenal	0
	Clarke			
1973	Sunderland	1	Leeds U	0
	Porterfield			
1974	Liverpool	3	Newcastle U	0
	Keegan 2, Heighway			
1975	West Ham U	2	Fulham	0
	A. Taylor			
1976	Southampton	1	Manchester U	0
	Stokes			
1977	Manchester U	2	Liverpool	1
	Pearson, J. Greenhoff		*Case*	
1978	Ipswich T	1	Arsenal	0
	Osborne			
1979	Arsenal	3	Manchester U	2
	Talbot, Stapleton, Sunderland		*McQueen, McIlroy*	
1980	West Ham U	1	Arsenal	0
	Brooking			
1981	Tottenham H	1	Manchester C	1*
	Hutchison (og)		*Hutchison*	
	Tottenham H	3	Manchester C	2
	Crooks, Villa 2		*Mackenzie, Reeves (pen)*	
1982	Tottenham H	1	QPR	1*
	Hoddle		*Fenwick*	
	Tottenham H	1	QPR	0
	Hoddle (pen)			
1983	Manchester U	2	Brighton & HA	2*
	Stapleton, Wilkins		*Smith, Stevens*	
	Manchester U	4	Brighton & HA	0
	Robson 2, Whiteside, Muhren (pen)			
1984	Everton	2	Watford	0
	Sharp, Gray			
1985	Manchester U	1	Everton	0*
	Whiteside			
1986	Liverpool	3	Everton	1
	Rush 2, Johnston		*Lineker*	
1987	Coventry C	3	Tottenham H	2*
	Bennett, Houchen, Mabbutt (og)		*C. Allen, Kilcline (og)*	
1988	Wimbledon	1	Liverpool	0
	Sanchez			
1989	Liverpool	3	Everton	2
	Aldridge, Rush 2		*McCall 2*	
1990	Manchester U	3	Crystal P	3
	Robson, Hughes 2		*O'Reilly, Wright 2*	
	Manchester U	1	Crystal P	0
	Martin			

**After extra time*

FA CUP WINNERS SINCE 1871

Club	Wins
Aston Villa	7
Manchester United	7
Tottenham Hotspur	7
Blackburn Rovers	6
Newcastle United	6
Arsenal	5
Wanderers	5
West Bromwich Albion	5
Bolton Wanderers	4
Everton	4
Liverpool	4
Manchester City	4
Sheffield United	4
Wolverhampton Wanderers	4
Sheffield Wednesday	3
West Ham United	3
Bury	2
Nottingham Forest	2
Old Etonians	2
Preston North End	2
Sunderland	2
Barnsley	1
Blackburn Olympic	1
Blackpool	1
Bradford City	1
Burnley	1
Cardiff City	1
Charlton Athletic	1
Chelsea	1
Clapham Rovers	1
Coventry City	1
Leeds United	1
Derby County	1
Huddersfield Town	1
Ipswich Town	1
Notts County	1
Old Carthusians	1
Oxford University	1
Portsmouth	1
Royal Engineers	1
Southampton	1
Wimbledon	1

APPEARANCES IN FA CUP FINAL

Club	Appearances
Arsenal	11
Everton	11
Newcastle United	11
Manchester United	11
West Bromwich Albion	10
Aston Villa	9
Liverpool	9
Blackburn Rovers	8
Manchester City	8
Tottenham Hotspur	8
Wolverhampton Wanderers	8
Bolton Wanderers	7
Preston North End	7
Old Etonians	6
Sheffield United	6
Huddersfield Town	5
Sheffield Wednesday	5
Wanderers	5
Derby Country	4
Leeds United	4
Leicester City	4
Oxford University	4
Royal Engineers	4
West Ham United	4
Blackpool	3
Burnley	3
Chelsea	3
Southampton	3
Portsmouth	3
Sunderland	3
Barnsley	2
Birmingham City	2
Cardiff City	2
Bury	2
Charlton Athletic	2
Clapham Rovers	2
Nottingham Forest	2
Notts County	2
Queen's Park (Glasgow)	2
Blackburn Olympic	1
Bradford City	1
Brighton & Hove Albion	1
Bristol City	1
Coventry City	1
Crystal Palace	1
Fulham	1
Ipswich Town	1
Luton Town	1
Old Carthusians	1
Queen's Park Rangers	1
Watford	1
Wimbledon	1

LITTLEWOODS CHALLENGE CUP 1989–90

First round (*2 legs*)

Birmingham C	2 1	Chesterfield	1 1
Blackpool	2 1	Burnley	2 0
Bristol C	2 2	Reading	3 2
Cambridge U	3 1	Maidstone U	1 0
Cardiff C	0 2	Plymouth Arg	3 0
Colchester U	3 1	Southend U	4 2
Crewe Alex	4 2	Chester C	0 0
Gillingham	1 0	Leyton Orient	4 3
Halifax T	3 0	Carlisle U	1 1
Huddersfield T	1 2	Doncaster R	1 1
Hull C	1 0	Grimsby T*	0 2
Mansfield T	1 2	Northampton T	1 0
Preston NE	3 1	Tranmere R	4 3
Rochdale	2 1	Bolton W	1 5
Sheffield U	1 0	Rotherham U	1 1
Shrewsbury T	3 1	Notts Co	0 3
Stockport C	1 1	Bury	0 1
Torquay U	0 0	Hereford U	1 3
Walsall	1 0	Port Vale	2 1
Wolverhampton W	1 2	Lincoln C	0 0
Wrexham	0 0	Wigan Ath	0 5
Brighton & HA	0 1	Brentford	3 1
Bristol R	1 0	Portsmouth	0 2
Exeter C	3 1	Swansea C	0 1
Fulham	0 5	Oxford U	1 3
Hartlepool U	3 1	York C	3 4
Peterborough U	2 2	Aldershot*	0 6
Scarborough	2 1	Scunthorpe U	0 1

Second round (*2 legs*)

Port Vale	1 0	Wimbledon	2 3
Arsenal	2 6	Plymouth Arg	0 1
Barnsley	1 1	Blackpool†	1 1
Birmingham C	1 1	West Ham U	2 1
Bolton W	2 1	Watford	1 1
Brentford	2 1	Manchester C	1 4
Cambridge U	2 0	Derby Co	1 5
Chelsea	1 2	Scarborough	1 3
Crewe Alex	0 0	Bournemouth	1 0
Crystal Palace	1 3	Leicester C	2 2
Grimsby T	3 0	Coventry C	1 3
Ipswich T	0 0	Tranmere R	1 1
Leyton O	0 2	Everton	2 2
Liverpool	5 3	Wigan Ath	2 0
Mansfield T	3 2	Luton T	4 7
Oldham Ath	2 2	Leeds U	1 1
Reading	3 0	Newcastle U	1 4
Shrewsbury T	0 1	Swindon T	3 3
Stoke C	1 0	Millwall	0 2
Sunderland	1 3	Fulham	1 0
Aston Villa	2 1	Wolverhampton W	1 1
Charlton Ath	3 1	Hereford U	1 0

Exeter C	3 1	Blackburn R	0 2
Middlesbrough	4 1	Halifax T	0 0
Norwich C	1 2	Rotherham U	1 0
Nottingham F	1 3**	Huddersfield T	1 3
Portsmouth	2 0	Manchester U	3 0
QPR	2 0	Stockport Co	1 0
Sheffield W	0 8	Aldershot	0 0
Tottenham H	1 2**	Southend U	0 3
WBA	1 5**	Bradford C	3 3
York C	0 0	Southampton	1 2

Third Round

Tranmere R	3	Millwall	2
Crystal Palace	0 0	Nottingham F	0 5
Everton	3	Luton T	0
Southampton	1	Charlton Ath	0
Sunderland	1 1	Bournemouth	1 0
Swindon T	3 1*1*2*	Bolton W	3 1 1 1
Arsenal	1	Liverpool	0
Aston Villa	0 0	West Ham U	0 1
Derby Co	2	Sheffield W	1
Exeter C	3	Blackpool	0
Manchester C	3	Norwich C	1
Manchester U	0	Tottenham H	3
Middlesbrough	1 0	Wimbledon	1 1
Newcastle U	0	WBA	1
Oldham Ath	7	Scarborough	0
QPR	1	Coventry C	2

Fourth Round

Derby Co	2	WBA	0
Manchester C	0	Coventry C	1
Nottingham F	1	Everton	0
Oldham Ath	3	Arsenal	1
Tranmere R	2 0	Tottenham H	2 4
West Ham U	1	Wimbledon	0
Exeter C	2 2	Sunderland	2 5
Swindon T	0 2	Southampton	0 4

Fifth Round

Nottingham F	2 3	Tottenham H	2 2
Sunderland	0 0	Coventry C	0 5
West Ham U	1 0 2	Derby Co	1 0 1
Southampton	2 0	Oldham Ath	2 2

Semi-finals *(2 legs)*

Nottingham F	2 0	Coventry C	1 0
Oldham Ath	6 0	West Ham U	0 3

Final at Wembley, 29 April 1990, att. 74,343
Nottingham F (0) 1 *(Jemson)* Oldham Ath (0) 0

Nottingham F: Sutton; Laws, Pearce, Walker, Chettle, Hodge, Crosby, Parker, Clough, Jemson, Carr.
Oldham Ath: Rhodes; Irwin, Barlow, Henry, Barrett, Warhurst, Adams, Ritchie, Bunn (Palmer), Milligan, Holden R.
Ref: J. Martin (Alton)

* *After extra time* † *Won on penalties* ** *Won on away goals*

PAST LEAGUE CUP FINALS

Played as two legs up to 1966

1961	Rotherham U *Webster, Kirkman*	2	Aston Villa	0
	Aston Villa *O'Neill, Burrows, McParland*	3	Rotherham U	0*
1962	Rochdale	0	Norwich C *Lythgoe 2, Punton*	3
	Norwich C *Hill*	1	Rochdale	0
1963	Birmingham C *Leek 2, Bloomfield*	3	Aston Villa *Thomson*	1
	Aston Villa	0	Birmingham C	0
1964	Stoke C *Bebbington*	1	Leicester C *Gibson*	1
	Leicester C *Stringfellow, Gibson, Riley*	3	Stoke C *Viollet, Kinnell*	2
1965	Chelsea *Tambling, Venables (pen), McCreadie*	3	Leicester C *Appleton, Goodfellow*	2
	Leicester C	0	Chelsea	0
1966	West Ham U *Moore, Byrne*	2	WBA *Astle*	1
	WBA *Kaye, Brown, Clark, Williams*	4	West Ham U *Peters*	1
1967	QPR *Morgan R., Marsh, Lazarus*	3	WBA *Clark C.*	2
1968	Leeds U *Cooper*	1	Arsenal	0
1969	Swindon T *Smart, Rogers 2*	3	Arsenal *Gould*	1
1970	Manchester C *Doyle, Pardoe*	2	WBA *Astle*	1
1971	Tottenham Hotspur *Chivers*	2	Aston Villa	0
1972	Chelsea *Osgood*	1	Stoke C *Conroy, Eastham*	2
1973	Tottenham Hotspur *Coates*	1	Norwich C	0
1974	Wolverhampton W *Hibbitt, Richards*	2	Manchester C *Bell*	1
1975	Aston Villa *Graydon*	1	Norwich C	0
1976	Manchester C *Barnes, Tueart*	2	Newcastle U *Gowling*	1
1977	Aston Villa	0	Everton	0
Replay	Aston Villa *Kenyon (og)*	1	Everton *Latchford*	1*
Replay	Aston Villa *Little 2, Nicholl*	3	Everton *Latchford, Lyons*	2*

1978	Nottingham F	0	Liverpool	0*
Replay	Nottingham F	1	Liverpool	0
	Robertson (pen)			
1979	Nottingham F	3	Southampton	2
	Birtles 2, Woodcock		*Peach, Holmes*	
1980	Wolverhampton W	1	Nottingham F	0
	Gray			
1981	Liverpool	1	West Ham U	1*
	Kennedy, A		*Stewart (pen)*	
Replay	Liverpool	2	West Ham U	1
	Dalglish, Hansen		*Goddard*	
1982	Liverpool	3	Tottenham	1*
	Whelan 2, Rush		*Archibald*	
1983	Liverpool	2	Manchester U	1*
	Kennedy, Whelan		*Whiteside*	
1984	Liverpool	0	Everton	0*
Replay	Liverpool	1	Everton	0
	Souness			
1985	Norwich C	1	Sunderland	0
	Chisholm (og)			
1986	Oxford U	3	QPR	0
	Hebberd, Houghton, Charles			
1987	Arsenal	2	Liverpool	1
	Nicholas		*Rush*	
1988	Luton T	3	Arsenal	2
	Stein, B. 2, Wilson		*Hayes, Smith*	
1989	Nottingham F	3	Luton T	1
	Clough 2, Webb		*Harford*	

**After extra time*

ZENITH DATA SYSTEMS CUP
(formerly Full Members' Cup and Simod Cup)
1989–90

First Round
Coventry C 1, Wimbledon 3 (aet)
Leeds U 1, Blackburn R 0
Sheffield U 1, Wolverhampton W 0
Oxford U 2, Luton T 3 (aet)
Sunderland 1, Port Vale 2

Second Round
Charlton Ath 2, Leicester C 1
Ipswich T 4, Watford 1
Sheffield W 3, Sheffield U 2 (aet)
Crystal Palace 4, Luton T 1
Barnsley 1, Leeds U 2
Bournemouth 2, Chelsea 3 (aet)
Hull C 1, Aston Villa 2
Newcastle U 2, Oldham Ath 0
Stoke C 2, Bradford C 1
Middlesbrough 3, Port Vale 1
Norwich C 5, Brighton & HA 0
Nottingham F 3, Manchester C 2
WBA 0, Derby Co 5
West Ham U 5, Plymouth Arg 2 (aet)
Portsmouth 0, Wimbledon 1
Swindon T 2, Millwall 1

Third Round
Crystal Palace 2, Charlton Ath 0
Stoke C 2, Leeds U 2 (aet)
Leeds U won 5-4 on penalties
Middlesbrough 4, Sheffield W 1
Newcastle U: 3, Derby Co 2 (aet)
Ipswich T 3, Wimbledon 1
Aston Villa 2, Nottingham F 1
Chelsea 4, West Ham U 3
Swindon T 4, Norwich C 1

Semi-Finals – (Southern Area)
Crystal Palace 1, Swindon T 0
Ipswich T 2, Chelsea 3

Semi-Finals (Northern Area)
Aston Villa 2, Leeds U 0
Middlesbrough 1, Newcastle U 0

Southern Area Final – First Leg
Crystal Palace (0) 0 Chelsea (2) 2 *(Dixon, Wilson K)* att. 14,839

Southern Area Final – Second Leg
Chelsea (0) 2 (*Bumstead, Hall*) Crystal Palace (0) 0 att. 15,061
Chelsea won 4-0 on aggregate.

Northern Area Final – First Leg
Aston Villa (1) 1 *(Birch)* Middlesbrough (1) 2 *(Slaven, Brennan)* att. 16,547

Northern Area Final – Second Leg
Middlesbrough (0) 2 *(Slaven, Kerr)* Aston Villa (0) 1 *(Gray) aet* att. 20,806
Middlesbrough won 4-2 on aggregate.

Final at Wembley, 25 March 1990, att. 76,369
Chelsea (1) 1 *(Dorigo)* Middlesbrough (0) 0

LEYLAND DAF CUP 1989–90

(formerly Freight Rover Trophy and Sherpa Van Trophy)

Southern Area
Brentford 3, Leyton Orient 0
Cardiff C 3, Walsall 5
Colchester U 0, Northampton T 3
Southend U 1, Gillingham 0
Torquay U 1, Bristol R 1
Hereford U 3, Aldershot 2
Peterborough U 1, Fulham 0
Aldershot 3, Birmingham 0
Fulham 0, Notts Co 1
Gillingham 2, Cambridge U 0
Leyton Orient 2, Mansfield T 0
Northampton T 2, Maidstone U 4
Walsall 0, Shrewsbury T 1
Bristol C 2, Swansea C 1
Mansfield T 2, Brentford 1
Birmingham C 1, Hereford U 0
Cambridge U 3, Southend U 3
Notts Co 2, Peterborough U 2
Shrewsbury T 4, Cardiff C 0
Mansfield T 2, Leyton Orient 1
Mansfield T won play-off match to reach First Round.
Aldershot 1, Walsall 4
Maidstone U 2, Colchester U 1
Peterborough U 0, Hereford U 1
Exeter C 2, Torquay U 0
Reading 1, Bristol C 1
Bristol R 3, Exeter C 0
Swansea C 1, Reading 2
Maidstone U 2, Mansfield T 1
Southend U 2, Northampton T 1
Brentford 2, Reading 1
Bristol C 0, Notts Co 1
Bristol R 1, Gillingham 0
Shrewsbury 0, Exeter C 1
Walsall 4, Southend U 1
Brentford 2, Bristol R 2 (aet)
Bristol R won 4-3 on penalties.
Hereford U 1, Notts Co 1 (aet)
Notts Co won 4-3 on penalties.
Maidstone U 2, Exeter C 0

Southern Area
Semi-Finals
Bristol R 0, Walsall 0 (aet)
Bristol R won 3-2 on penalties.
Maidstone U 0, Notts Co 1 (aet)

Final – First Leg
Bristol R 1, Notts Co 0

Final – Second Leg
Notts Co 0, Bristol R 0 (aet)
Bristol R won 1-0 on aggregate.

Northern Area
Halifax T 3, Lincoln C 0
Huddersfield T 2, Doncaster R 2
Preston NE 3, Burnley 0
Scunthorpe U 1, Scarborough 0
Tranmere R 1, Chester C 0
Wrexham 1, Blackpool 0
York C 7, Hartlepool U 1
Blackpool 4, Bury 0
Bolton W 2, Crewe Alex 0
Burnley 0, Stockport Co 2
Chester C 0, Rochdale 0
Doncaster R 1, Grimsby T 0
Hartlepool U 1, Rotherham U 4
Lincoln C 3, Chesterfield 0
Scarborough 0, Carlisle U 1
Wigan Ath 1, Bolton W 0
Bury 4, Wrexham 1
Chesterfield 2, Halifax T 1,
Grimsby T 3, Huddersfield T 3
Rochdale 0, Tranmere R 1
Rotherham U 3, York C 1
Stockport Co 2, Preston NE 4
Crewe Alex 1, Wigan Ath 0
Rochdale 1, Chester C 2
Chester C won play-off match to reach First Round
Carlisle U 1, Scunthorpe U 1
Bolton W 2, Lincoln C 1
Carlisle U 1, Stockport Co 2 (aet)
Doncaster R 2, Bury 0
Halifax T 1, York C 1 (aet)
Halifax T won 7-6 on penalties.
Preston NE 1, Wigan Ath 2
Rotherham U 3, Huddersfield T 0
Tranmere R 2, Scunthorpe U 1
Halifax T 3, Stockport Co 1 (aet)
Wigan Ath 1, Doncaster R 2 (aet)
Bolton W 1, Rotherham U 0
Tranmere R 3, Chester C 0
Blackpool 0, Chester C 1

Northern Area
Semi-Finals
Doncaster R 3, Halifax T 0
Tranmere R 2, Bolton W 1

Northern Area Final
First Leg
Tranmere R 2, Doncaster R 0

Northern Area Final
Second Leg
Doncaster R 1, Tranmere R 1

FINAL at Wembley, 20 May, att 48,402
Bristol R (0) 1 *(White)* Tranmere R (1) 2 *(Muir, Steel)*

FA CHARITY SHIELD 1927–89

Year	Winner	Score	Opponent	Score
1927	Cardiff C	2	Corinthians	1
1928	Everton	2	Blackburn R	1
1929	Professionals	3	Amateurs	0
1930	Arsenal	2	Sheffield W	1
1931	Arsenal	1	WBA	0
1932	Everton	5	Newcastle U	3
1933	Arsenal	3	Everton	0
1934	Arsenal	4	Manchester C	0
1935	Sheffield W	1	Arsenal	0
1936	Sunderland	2	Arsenal	1
1937	Manchester C	2	Sunderland	0
1938	Arsenal	2	Preston NE	1
1948	Arsenal	4	Manchester U	3
1949	Portsmouth	1	Wolverhampton W	1*
1950	World Cup Team	4	Canadian Touring Team	2
1951	Tottenham H	2	Newcastle U	1
1952	Manchester U	4	Newcastle U	2
1953	Arsenal	3	Blackpool	1
1954	Wolverhampton W	4	WBA	4*
1955	Chelsea	3	Newcastle U	0
1956	Manchester U	1	Manchester C	0
1957	Manchester U	4	Aston Villa	0
1958	Bolton W	4	Wolverhampton W	1
1959	Wolverhampton W	3	Nottingham F	1
1960	Burnley	2	Wolverhampton W	2
1961	Tottenham H	3	FA X1	2
1962	Tottenham H	5	Ipswich T	1
1963	Everton	4	Manchester U	0
1964	Liverpool	2	West Ham U	2*
1965	Manchester U	2	Liverpool	2*
1966	Liverpool	1	Everton	0
1967	Manchester U	3	Tottenham H	3*
1968	Manchester C	6	WBA	1
1969	Leeds U	2	Manchester C	1
1970	Everton	2	Chelsea	1
1971	Leicester C	1	Liverpool	0
1972	Manchester C	1	Aston Villa	0
1973	Burnley	1	Manchester C	0
1974	Liverpool	1†	Leeds U	1
1975	Derby Co	2	West Ham U	0
1976	Liverpool	1	Southampton	0
1977	Liverpool	0	Manchester U	0*
1978	Nottingham F	5	Ipswich T	0
1979	Liverpool	3	Arsenal	1
1980	Liverpool	1	West Ham U	0
1981	Aston Villa	2	Tottenham H	2*
1982	Liverpool	1	Tottenham H	0
1983	Manchester U	2	Liverpool	0
1984	Everton	1	Liverpool	0
1985	Everton	2	Manchester U	0
1986	Everton	1	Liverpool	1*
1987	Everton	1	Coventry C	0
1988	Liverpool	2	Wimbledon	1
1989	Liverpool	1	Arsenal	0

**Each club retained shield for six months.* *†Won on Penalties.*

SCOTTISH CLUBS

ABERDEEN
PREM. DIV.

Ground: Pittodrie Stadium, Aberdeen AB2 1QH (0224–632328)
Colours: All red with white trim.
Year formed: 1903. **Managers:** Alex Smith and Jocky Scott.
League appearances: Bett, J. 30; Booth, S. 1(1); Cameron, I. 6(5); Connor, R. 34; Dodds, D. (1); Gillhaus, H. 19(1); Grant, B. 28(3); Harvie, S. (1); Irvine, B. 28(3); Jess, E. 7(4); Mason, P. 33(1); McKimmie, S. 33; McLeish, A. 32; Miller, W. 15; Mimms, R. 6; Nicholas, C. 32(1); Robertson, C. 10(12); Robertson, D. 20; Robertson, I. 5; Simpson, N. 5 (4); Snelders, T. 23; Van der Ark, W. 15(11); Watson, Graham 3(1); Watson, Gregg 3(1); Watt, M. 7; Wright, S. (1).
Goals – League: (56): Nicholas 11 (1 pen), Mason 9, Gillhaus 8, Van der Ark 7, Grant 6, Bett 3 (1 pen), Jess 3, McLeish 2, Robertson C 2, Connor 1, Irvine 1, Robertson D 1, Graham Watson 1, own goal 1.
Scottish Cup: (16): Gillhaus 3, Van der Ark 3, Irvine 2, Nicholas 2, Bett 1, Grant 1, Mason 1, own goals 3.
Skol Cup: (12): Mason 5, Bett 2, Cameron 2, Robertson D 1, Van der Ark 1, own goal 1.

AIRDRIEONIANS
DIV. 1

Ground: Broomfield Park, Gartlea Road, Airdrie ML6 9JL (0236–62067)
Colours: White shirts with red diamond, white shorts.
Year formed: 1878. **Manager:** Jim Bone.
League appearances: Auld, S. 25; Balfour, E. 34(2); Boyle, J. 30(1); Butler, J. 17(2); Conn, S. 29(2); Coyle, O. 10; Grant, D. 20(5); Gray, S. 30(1); Harvey, G. 20(7); Hendry, A. 1(3); Irvine, W. 11(10); Jack, P. 24(2); Kelly, J. 1; Lawrence, A. 29(5); Lawrie, D. (1); MacDonald, I. 30(7); MacDonald, K. 5(3); Martin, J. 39; McAdam, T. 15; McKeown, B. 21; McPhee, I. 19; Speirs, G. 6(3); Stewart, A. (8); Walsh, R. 3(1); Watson, J. 10(1).
Goals – League: (77): Coyle 10 (1 pen), Lawrence 9, Gray 8 (4 pens), Harvey 8, Irvine 7 (2 pens), Balfour 5, Macdonald K 5, MacDonald I 4, Stewart 3, Butler 2, Conn 2, Grant 2, Jack 2, Auld 1, Boyle 1, McAdam 1, McPhee 1, Speirs 1 (pen), Watson 1, own goals 4.
Scottish Cup: (3): Gray 1, Harvey 1, Lawrence 1.
Skol Cup:

ALBION ROVERS
DIV. 2

Ground: Cliftonhill Stadium, Main Street, Coatbridge ML5 9XX (0236–32350)
Colours: Yellow shirts with red and white trim, red shorts with yellow stripes.
Year formed: 1882. **Manager:** David Provan
League appearances: Bishop, J. (1); Cadden, S. 29(2); Chapman, J. 35; Clark, G. 25; Clark, R. 31(1); Cormack, D. 1; Cougan, C. 7(8); Cowan, S. 6; Diver, D. 6(4); Edgar, D. 9(3); Graham, A. 28(3); Granger, C. 5(6); Haddow, L. 5(10); Irvine, W. 5; Lauchlan, G. (4); McAnenay, M. 23(10); McCulloch, R. 38; McDonald, D. 24(1); McGowan, M. 20; McKenzie, P. 16; McKeown, D. 16; McTeague, G. 30; Millar, G. 12(4); Oliver, M. 22; Teevan, P. 4(7); Watson, E. 32(4).
Goals – League: (50): McAnenay 10, Clark G 8, Graham 7, Chapman 6 (5 pens), Cougan 3, Watson 3, Cowan 2, Irvine 2, Edgar 1, Haddow 1, Lauchlan 1, McKenzie 1, McKeown 1, McTeague 1, Oliver 1, own goals 2.
Scottish Cup: (0).
Skol Cup: (0).

ALLOA

DIV. 2

Ground: Recreation Park, Alloa FK10 1RR (0259–722695)
Colours: Gold shirts with black trim, black shorts.
Year formed: 1883. **Manager:** Hugh McCann
League appearances: Blackie, W. 3(1); Currie, M. 6(6); Erwin, H. 26(4); Gibson, J. 30(2); Haggart, L. 18(3); Hayton, G. 13(11); Holmes, J. 8; Irvine, J. 23(7); Lamont, P. 33(2); Lee, D. 19(2); Lee, I. 35(1); Lee, R. 35; Lowrie, R. 38; Lytwyn, C. 14(5); McCallum, M. 13(2); McCulloch, K. 17(1); McGuiness, S. 1; Millen, A. 37; Miller, S. 5(3); Ormond, J. 2(4); Paxton, W. 8(1); Ramsay, S. 20(4); Robertson, R. 13(4); Shanks, D. 3; Sorbie, S. 9.
Goals – League: (41): Lamont 9, Irvine 8, McCallum 8 (1 pen), Gibson 4, Lee I 4, Millen 2, Ramsay 2, Sorbie 2, Hayton 1, Lytwyn 1.
Scottish Cup: (2): Irvine 2.
Skol Cup: (0).

ARBROATH

DIV. 2

Ground: Gayfield Park, Arbroath DD11 1QB (0241–72157)
Colours: Maroon shirts, white shorts.
Year formed: 1878. **Manager:** Ian Gibson
League appearances: Balfour, D. 13; Bennett, M. 20; Bennett, W. 26(1); Brand, R. 15(3); Carlin, G. 25; Dewar, G. 19(3); Farnan, C. 2; Fleming, J. 35; Florence, S. 9; Fotheringham, J. 25(6); Gallagher, J. 18(4); Gibson, I. 23(1); Hamilton, J. 34(2); Jackson, D. 26; Kerr, B. 7(6); Marshall, J. 27(2); McKillop, A. 13; McNab, S. 1; Mitchell, B. 36(1); Richardson, A. 28; Smith, R. 12(5); Stewart, I. 6(5); Tindal, K. 9(3).
Goals – League: (47): Marshall 12, Brand 9 (2 pens), Fotheringham 6, Richardson 4, Smith 4, Bennett M 3, Carlin 3, Hamilton 2, Gibson 1, Kerr 1, McKillop 1, Stewart 1.
Scottish Cup: (1): Fotheringham 1.
Skol Cup: (1) Fotheringham 1.

AYR UNITED

DIV. 1

Ground: Somerset Park, Ayr KA8 9NB (0292–263435)
Colours: White shirts with black trim, black shorts.
Year formed: 1910. **Manager:** Ally MacLeod.
League appearances: Brown, R. 5; Bryce, T. 34(1); Conlan, P. 3(1); Cowell, J. 3(2); Ellis, C. 1; Evans, S. 34(1); Fraser, A. 5(3); Furphy, W. 34; Gillespie, A. 6(1); Gilmour, G. 2; Henderson, J. 1; Hughes, J. 21; Kennedy, D. 36; Lewis, D. 2; Love, J. 4(3); McAllister, I. 31; McCann, J. 19; McCracken, D. 11(6); McIntyre, S. 21(1); Purdie, D. 22; Ross, B. 7; Rough, A. 1; Scott, R. 12; Sludden, J. 6(3); Shaw, G. 2(1); Smyth, D. 3; Templeton, H. 31(2); Walker, T. 32(1); Watson, G. 16; Willock, A. 20(7); Wilson, K. 4(13).
Goals – League: (41): Bryce 10 (1 pen), Templeton 8, Walker 8, McCracken 3, Kennedy 2, McAllister 2, McIntyre 2 (1 pen), Scott 2, Conlan 1, McCann 1, Sludden 1, Willock 1.
Scottish Cup: (1): McCracken 1.
Skol Cup: (0).

BERWICK RANGERS DIV. 2

Ground: Shielfield Park, Berwick-on-Tweed TD15 2EF (0289–307424)
Colours: Black and gold striped shirts, black shorts.
Year formed: 1881. **Manager:** Ralph Callachan.
League appearances: Ainslie, G. 1(1); Bickmore, S. 19(3); Callacham, R. 30(1); Cass, M. 21(5); Davidson, G. 31; Fraser, S. 37; Frizell, I. 1; Graham, T. 9(3); Hughes, J. 14; Leetion, P. (2); Leitch, G. 11(7); Locke, S. 24; Marshall, B. 19(1); Maxwell, D. 3(3); McLaren, P. 6(6); Muir, L. 11; Neil, M. 8(2); Neilson, D. 34; O'Donnell, J. 38(1); Porteous, S. 7(5); Scally, D. 2 (9); Sloan, S. 32(3); Sokoluk, J. 18(4); Tait, G. 25(1); Telford, M. (1); Thorpe, B. 21(4); Watson, S. 5; Wharton, K. 2.
Goals – League: (66): Sloan 16, Bickmore 7, Sokoluk 7, Thorpe 5, Hughes 4, Tait 4, Cass 3, Fraser 3 (1 pen), Graham 3, Porteous 3, Frizell 2, Locke 2, Callachan 1, Davidson 1 (pen), McLaren 1, Neil 1, Wharton 1, own goals 2.
Scottish Cup: (1): Neil 1.
Skol Cup: (3): Sloan 2, Thorpe 1.

BRECHIN CITY DIV. 1

Ground: Glebe Park, Brechin DD9 6BJ (03562–2856)
Colours: All red.
Year formed: 1906. **Manager:** John Ritchie.
League appearances: Baillie, R. 4(5); Brash A. 36; Brown, R. 28; Buckley, G. 5(1); Candlish, C. 20; Conway, F. 22; Grant, B. 1; Hamilton, R. 6(2); Hill, H. 36(1); Hutt, G. 27(4); Lawrie, D. 38; Lees, G. 32(1); Moffat J. 1; Paterson I. A. 23(6); Paterson I. G. 20(2); Pryde, I. 22(6); Ritchie, P. 25(13); Sexton, P. 28(1); Scott, D. 28(5); Stevens, G. 7; Wardell, S. 14(12); Watt, D. 5; Wilkie, S. (3); Yule, R. 1.
Goals – League: (59): Lees 12, Ritchie 9, Pryde 6, Paterson I A 5, Sexton 5, Brash 4, Candlish 4 (4 pens), Brown 3, Hutt 3, Hill 2, Wardell 2, Buckley 1, Conway 1, Scott 1, own goal 1.
Scottish Cup: (13): Lees 5, Hutt 3, Ritchie 3, Brown 1, Paterson I A 1.
Skol Cup: (4): Hill 1, Paterson I G 1, Ritchie 1, Sexton 1.

CELTIC PREM. DIV.

Ground: Celtic Park, Glasgow G40 3RE (041–554 2611)
Colours: Green and white hooped shirts, white shorts.
Year formed: 1888. **Manager:** Billy McNeill.
League appearances: Aitken R. 18; Bonner, P. 36; Burns, T. 8(1); Coyne, T. 17(6); Creaney, G. 2(4); Dziekanowski, D. 31(2); Elliott, P. 25(2); Fulton, S. 13(3); Galloway, M. 29(4); Grant, P. 24(2); Hewitt, J. 8(4); Mathie, A. 5(1); McCahill S. 2; McStay, P. 35; Miller, J. 16(8); Morris, C. 32; Rogan, A. 16(2); Stark, W. 2; Walker, A. 19(13); Wdowczyk, D. 23; Whyte, D. 35.
Goals – League: (37): Dziekanowski 8, Coyne 7 (1 pen), Walker 6 (1 pen), Miller 5, McStay 3, Aitken 2, Galloway 2, Creaney 1, Morris 1, Wdowczyk 1, Whyte 1.
Scottish Cup: (8): Coyne 2, Walker 2, Dziekanowski 1, McStay 1, Miller 1, Morris 1 (pen).
Skol Cup: (7): Dziekanowski 3, Burns 1, Grant 1, McStay 1, Walker 1.

CLYDE DIV. 1

Ground: Firhill Park, Glasgow G20 7AL (041–946 9000)
Colours: White shirts with red and black trim, black shorts.
Year formed: 1878. **Manager:** John Clark.

League appearances: Atkins, D. 21; Callaghan, W. 5; Clarke, S. 28; Cowell, J. 4(6); Fairlie, J. 19(6); Knox, K. 34(5); Mallan, S. 8(2); McCabe, G. 31(4); McFarlane, R. 33; McGlashan, C. 39; McGuiness, B. 16(3); McVie, Gary (2); McVie, Graeme 20(1); Nolan, M. 32(5); Nugent, S. (2); Quinn, S. 2(2); Reid, W. 24(1); Robertson, S. 6; Rooney, J. 24(3); Ross, S. 12; Scott, M. 1(1); Shanks, D. 8(3); Speirs, C. 38; Spence, T. 12; Thompson, D. 12; Tracey, P. (1).
Goals – League: (39): McGlashan 11 (2 pens), Clarke 7, McCabe 5, Thompson 4, Speirs 3, Callaghan 2, Fairlie 2, Knox 2, Nolan 1, Rooney 1, Shanks 1.
Scottish Cup: (0).
Skol Cup: (1): McCabe 1.

CLYDEBANK DIV. 1

Ground: Kilbowie Park, Clydebank G81 2PB (041–952 2887)
Colours: White with red band, white shorts.
Year formed: 1965. **Manager:** John Steedman.
League appearances: Arrol, A. 1; Auld, S. 7(1); Bryce, T. 1; Caffrey, H. 12(6); Campbell, K. 2(2); Coyle, O. 27; Coyle, T. 26(1); Crawford, J. 14 (9); Davies, J. 31; Dick, I. 2(1); Dickson, J. 30; Duncanson, J. 5(1); Eadie, K. 37; Ferguson, W. 2(4); Gallacher, J. 34; Hamilton, L. 1; Harvey, P. 34; Hughes, J. 10(1); Kelly, P. 13(4); Lansdown, A. 5(3); Maher, J. 28; McGurn, G. 4(1); O'Brien, J. 1; Robertson, J. 1(7); Rodger, J. 28; Rowe, G. 25(4); Smith, B. 11(5); Stevenson, H. 1; Sweeney, S. 33(1); Thomson, W. 2; Traynor, J. 1.
Goals – League: (74): Eadie 21 (3 pens), Coyle O 17, Coyle T 7, Kelly 7, Davies 5, Harvey 3, Hughes 3, Rowe 3, Auld 1, Caffrey 1, Crawford 1, Dickson 1, Sweeney 1, own goals 3.
Scottish Cup: (8): Davies 4, Eadie 2, Kelly 1, own goal 1.
Skol Cup: (3): Eadie 2, McGurn 1.

COWDENBEATH DIV. 2

Ground: Central Park, Cowdenbeath KY4 9EY (0383–511205)
Colours: Royal blue shirts with white stripes, white shorts.
Year formed: 1881. **Manager:** John Brownlie.
League appearances: Allan, R. 4; Archibald, E. 26(3); Baillie, R. 4(1); Buckley, G. 10(5); Callaghan, W. 4; Cullen, D. (1); Douglas, H. 14(7); Duffy, D. 6(8); Frith, J. 2(5); Hamill, K. 24(3); Herd, W. 12; Kerr, G. 39; Lamont, W. 35; MacKenzie, A. 11 (9); McConville, J. 12(2); McGovern, D. 22; Mailer, J. 14(2); Malone, G. 34(1); Rae, J. 3; Ross, A. 30(4); Scott, C. 33; Smith, M. 11; Spence, W. 26(4); Watt, D. 36; Wright, J. 17(7).
Goals – League: (58): Ross 16, Buckley 7 (3 pens), Malone 7 (1 pen), Spence 7, Scott 6, Wright 4, MacKenzie 3, Mailer 3, Hamill 2, Archibald 1, Duffy 1, Herd 1.
Scottish Cup: (6): Ross 4, Wright 1, own goal 1.
Skol Cup: (0).

DUMBARTON DIV. 2

Ground: Boghead Park, Dumbarton G82 2JA (0389–62569 and 67864)
Colours: Gold with white band, black shorts.
Year formed: 1872. **Manager:** Billy Lamont
League appearances: Boyd, J. 16; Cairney, P. 18(1); Dempsey, J. 29; Dickie, G. 14(5); Doyle, J. 18(3); Gibson, C. 36; Gow, S. 11(1); Grant, B. 7; Hughes, J. 24(1); MacIver, S. 32(2); Meechan, J. 12(1); McGinley, J. 1; McGrogan, P. 3(3); McQuade, A. 38; McQuade, J. 8(8); Morrison, S. 17; Quinn, P. 17(11); Reid, W. 23(6); Spence, C. 38; Stevens, G. 8; Stevenson, H. 11; Strachan, B. 28; Wharton, P. 19(5); Wilson, D. 1.

Goals – League: (70): Gibson 20, MacIver 19, Hughes 7 (2 pens), Spence 5, Morrison 4 (3 pens), McQuade J 3 (1 pen), Boyd 2, Cairney 2, McQuade A 2, Quinn 2, Doyle 1, Reid 1, own goals 2.
Scottish Cup: (2): McQuade J 1, Quinn 1.
Skol Cup: (3): MacIver 2, Gibson 1.

DUNDEE DIV. 1

Ground: Dens Park, Dundee DD1 7JY (0382–826104)
Colours: Dark blue shirts with red and white trim, white shorts.
Year formed: 1893. **Manager:** Gordon Wallace.
League appearances: Albiston, A. 9(1); Angus, I. 4; Bain, K. (1); Beedie, S. 19(2); Campbell, A. 8(7); Campbell, D. 6 (9); Campbell, S. (2); Carson, T. 16; Chisholm, G. 34; Craib, M. 20(2); Craig, A. 12(8); Dinnie, A. 21(1); Dodds, W. 29(1); Duffy, J. 8; Ferguson, D. 4; Forsyth, S. 33(1); Frail, S. 6; Geddes, R. 12; Harvey, G. 4(2); Holt, J. 2; Jamieson, W. 14; Kerr, M. (2); Mathers, P. 8; McBride, J. 10(8); McGeachie, G. 2; McLeod, G. 24(3); McMartin, G. 3(1); McQuillan, J. 1(1); McSkimming, S. 6(1); Saunders, W. 7(2); Shannon, R. 36; Smith, J. 4; Wright, K. 34.
Goals – League: (41): Dodds 13 (4 pens), Wright 11, Beedie 3, Chisholm 3, Campbell A 2, Craig 2, Campbell D 1, Craib 1, Forsyth 1, Harvey 1, McBride 1, Saunders 1, Shannon 1.
Scottish Cup: (0).
Skol Cup: (5): Harvey 2, McBride 2, Wright 1.

DUNDEE UNITED PREM. DIV.

Ground: Tannadice Park, Dundee DD3 7JW (0382–833166)
Colours: Tangerine shirts with black trim, black shorts.
Year formed: 1909 as Dundee Hibernians, Dundee United from 1923.
Manager: Jim McLean.
League appearances: Bowman, D. 20(4); Clark, J. 18(11); Cleland, A. 12(3); Connolly, P. 12(3); French, H. 7(5); Gallacher, K. 17; Hegarty, P. 5; Hinds, P. 7(6); Irvine, J. A. 1; Jackson, D. 24(1); Krivokapic, M. 25(1); Main, A. 27; Malpas, M. 30; McGinnis, G. 4(3); McInally, J. 35; McKinlay, W. 13; McKinnon, R. 7(3); McLeod, J. (2); Narey, D. 31; O'Neil, J. 6(4); O'Neill, M. 15(3); Paatelainan, M. 27(4); Preston, A. 8; Thomson, S. 2; Thomson, W. 7; Van der Hoorn, F. 31; Welsh, B. 5.
Goals – League: (36): Jackson 7, Paatelainan 7 (4 pens), Connolly 5, O'Neill M 5 (1 pen), McInally 3, French 2, Malpas 2, Van der Hoorn 2, Bowman 1, Clark 1, Gallacher 1.
Scottish Cup: (4): Clark 1, Connolly 1, Jackson 1, Paatelainan 1.
Skol Cup: (2): Hinds 1, O'Neill M 1.

DUNFERMLINE ATHLETIC PREM. DIV.

Ground: East End Park, Dunfermline KY12 7RB (0383–724295)
Colours: Black and white striped shirts, black shorts.
Year formed: 1885. **Manager:** Jim Leishman.
League appearances: Abercromby, W. 5(4); Bonnyman, P. 1; Clark, A. 3(1); Farningham, R. 11(6); Gallagher, E. 4 (1); Irons, D. 13(10); Jack, R. 34(2); Kozma, I. 32(1); McCathie, N. 36; Nicholl, J. 17; O'Boyle, G. 28; Rafferty, S. 31(1); Robertson, G. 15(2); Rougvie, D. 28; Sharp, R. 22(5); Sinclair, C. 1; Smith, P. 32(1); Tierney, G. 33; Westwater, I. 36; Williamson, A. 1; Wilson, T. 13(2).
Goals – League: (37): Jack 16 (4 pens), Kozma 6, Smith P 4, O'Boyle 3 (1 pen), Irons 2, Robertson 2, Tierney 2, Gallagher 1, Rafferty 1.
Scottish Cup: (3): Jack 2 (1 pen), O'Boyle 1.
Skol Cup: (7): Jack 3, Rougvie 2, Abercromby 1, Smith P 1.

EAST FIFE

DIV. 2

Ground: Bayview Park, Methil, Fife KY8 3AG (0333–26323)
Colours: Black and gold striped shirts, black shorts.
Year formed: 1903. **Manager:** Gavin Murray.
League appearances: Atkins, D. 2; Banner, A. 2; Bell, G. 22(3); Brown, I. 18(8); Brown, W. 24(3); Bryce, G. 1(11); Charles, R. 33; Collins, N. 1; Crolla, C. 22(7); Gallacher, W. 23(4); Hall, A. 15(2); Halliday, D. 12(2); Harrow, A. 8; Hogarth, G. 0(1); Hope, D. 20(12); Hunter, P. 28(1); Lennox, S. 33; McGonigal, A. 17(2); McPhee, W. 1(1); Mitchell, A. 35; Moffat J. 2; Prior, S. 8; Reid, G. 9; Rogerson, S. 25(1); Taylor, P. 38; Taylor, P. H. 21; Wilson, S. 9.
Goals – League: (60): Hunter 14, Mitchell 12, Brown W 9, Taylor P 5 (5 pens), Lennox 3, Wilson 3, Brown I 2, Hope 2, McGonigal 2, Bell 1, Charles 1, Crolla 1, Rogerson 1, own goals 4.
Scottish Cup: (8): Hunter 4, Brown I 1, Brown W 1, Crolla 1, Mitchell 1.
Skol Cup:

EAST STIRLING

DIV. 2

Ground: Firs Park, Falkirk FK2 7AY (0324–23583)
Colours: White shirts with black band, white shorts.
Year formed: 1881. **Manager:** Alan Mackin.
League appearances: Bateman, A. 26(3); Brannigan, K. 24; Brown, G. 1; Bryne, W. 15; Cairns, M. 6; Carr, P. 2; Diver, D. 21; Drew, D. 12(3); Durie, C. 18(4); Feeney, P. 4(12); Gilchrist, A. 6; Granger, C. 7; Grant, Arthur 27 (9); Grant, Lex (5); Henderson, J. 10; Kelly, C. 12; Lauchlan, G. 1(1); Love, D. 4; Mackin, A. 6; McCulley, R. 4; McEntegart, T. 8(1); McGraw, A. 3; McIntosh, S. 18; McLaren, P. 4(3); McNeill, W. 23(4); O'Brien, P. 16(1); Peters, A. 4; Purdie, B. 14; Russell, G. 30(1); Scott, R. 3(4); Watson, G. 17; Wilcox, D. 29; Wilson, C. 25(4); Wood, D. (3); Workman, J. 24.
Goals – League: (34): McNeill 4, Wilcox 4 (1 pen), Wilson 4, Diver 3, Durie 3, O'Brien 3, Bateman 2 (1 pen), Byrne 2, Lex Grant 2, Workman 2 (1 pen), Brannigan 1, Feeney 1, Arthur Grant 1, Henderson 1, own goal 1.
Scottish Cup: (3): Armstrong 1, Arthur Grant 1, Wilson 1.
Skol Cup: (0).

FALKIRK

DIV. 1

Ground: Brockville Park, Falkirk FK1 5AX (0324–24121)
Colours: Dark blue shirts with white trim, white shorts.
Year formed: 1876. **Manager:** Jim Jefferies.
League appearances: Baptie, C. 32(2); Beaton, D. 21(2); Brannigan, K. 10; Burgess, G. 28; Callaghan, T. 9(1); Clark, M. 21(1); Cowell, J. 3(6); Hamilton, G. (1); Hay, G. 25; Hetherston, P. 14 (9); Holmes, J. 7(2); Houston, P. 28(3); Logan, S. 15(6); Marshall, G. 39; Melvin, M. 14(1); McCoy, G. 18(1); McGivern, S. 12(3); McKenzie, P. 10(4); McKinnon, C. 3(8); McNair, C. 6(1); McWilliams, D. 33; Mooney, M. 8(7); Rae, A. 34; Robertson, D. 4(1); Rutherford, P. 18(10); Smith, G. 36.
Goals – League: (59): McWilliams 17 (7 pens), Baptie 8, Rae 8, Rutherford 6, McCoy 4, Beaton 2, Burgess 2, Hetherston 2, McGivern 2, Mooney 2, Callaghan 1, Clark 1, Hay 1, Logan 1, McKinnon 1, Robertson 1.
Scottish Cup: (0).
Skol Cup: (4): Burgess 2 (1 pen), Beaton 1, McGivern 1.

P.F.A. 90/91—6

FORFAR ATHLETIC DIV. 1

Ground: Station Park, Forfar, Angus DD8 3BT (0307–63576)
Colours: Sky blue shirts, navy shorts.
Year formed: 1885. **Manager:** Bobby Glennie
League appearances: Adam, C. 9; Allan, R. 32; Bennett, W. 2; Brazil, A. 29(1); Brewster, C. 32(6); Clark, J. 11(6); Clinging, I. 20(4); Dolan, S. (1); Glennie, R. 20; Grant, B. 4(2); Hamill, A. 38; Hendry, J. 10; Hutton, G. 21; Kennedy, S. 3; Leslie, A. 2(10); Lorimer, R. 15(5); Mennie, V. 1; McCafferty, T. 32; McNaughton, B. (4); Moffat, J. 4; Morland, D. 3(2); Morris, R. 36; Morton, J. 17(4); Ormond, J. 1(6); Peacock, B. 1; Robertson, D. 1; Smith, P. 6(2); Thompson, G. 11(3); Ward, K. 1(1); Whyte, G. 35(2); Winter, G. 32(1).
Goals – League: (51): Brewster 8 (3 pens), Clinging 6, Hendry 6, Whyte 6, Clark 5, Morton 4 (1 pen), Leslie 3, Adam 2, Grant 2, McCafferty 2, Winter 2 (2 pens), Brazil 1, Glennie 1, Lorimer 1, Mennie 1, Morris 1.
Scottish Cup: (1): Brewster 1.
Skol Cup: (0).

HAMILTON ACADEMICAL DIV. 1

Ground: Douglas Park, Hamilton ML3 0DF (0698–286103)
Colours: Red and white hooped shirts, white shorts.
Year formed: 1875. **Manager:** Billy McLaren
League appearances: Archer, S. 19(2); Carr, S. 3(3); Donaghy, P. 7(7); Ferguson, A. 34; Gordon, S. 4(3); Harris, C. 35; Hillcoat, C. 14; Jamieson, W. 19; Kasule, V. 7(5); Martin, P. 21(2); McCluskey, G. 27(1); McDonald, P. 37(1); McFarlane, I. 1; McGachie, J. 21(5); McGrinlay, M. 3(1); McGuigan, R. 6(10); McKee, K. 39; McLean, S. (2); Miller, C. 37; Moore, S. 2(8); Morrison, S. 17(2); Murdoch, A. 4; Napier, C. 39; Prentice, A. 4(1); Smith, M. 5; Smith, T. 3; Weir, J. 21 (9);.
Goals – League: (52): Harris 9 (2 pens), McCluskey 8, Morrison 7 (1 pen), Napier 6, McGachie 5, McDonald 3, Smith 3, Archer 1, Donaghy 1, Gordon 1, McGinlay 1, McKee 1, Martin 1, Miller 1, Weir 1, own goals 3.
Scottish Cup: (0).
Skol Cup: (3): Carr 1, McDonald 1, McKee 1.

HEART OF MIDLOTHIAN PREM. DIV.

Ground: Tynecastle Park, Gorgie Road, Edinburgh EH11 2NL (031–337 6132)
Colours: Maroon shirts, white shorts.
Year formed: 1874. **Manager:** Alex MacDonald.
League appearances: Bannon, E. 31(2); Berry, N. 10; Colquhoun, J. 36; Crabbe, S. 27(8); Ferguson, I. 1(10); Foster, W. 14(3); Kidd, W. 12(5); Kirkwood, D. 10 (9); Levein C. 35; Mackay, G. 31(2); McCreery, D. 20(2); McKinlay, T. 29; McLaren, A. 26(1); McPherson, D. 35; Musemic, H. 4(2); Robertson, J. 25(7); Sandison, J. 8(4); Smith, H. 36; Whittaker, B. 6; Wright, G. (1).
Goals – League: (54): Robertson 17 (2 pens), Crabbe 12, Colquhoun 6, McPherson 4, Musemic 3, Bannon 2, Sandison 2, Berry 1, Ferguson 1, Foster 1, Kidd 1, Mackay 1, McKinlay 1, McLaren 1, own goal 1.
Scottish Cup: (7): Robertson 4, Colquhoun 2, Crabbe 1.
Skol Cup: (9): Crabbe 4, Bannon 1, Kidd 1, Kirkwood 1, Musemic 1, Robertson 1.

HIBERNIAN

PREM. DIV.

Ground: Easter Road Stadium, Edinburgh EH7 5QG (031–661 2159)
Colours: Green shirts with white sleeves and collar, white shorts.
Year formed: 1875. **Manager:** Alex Miller.
League appearances: Archibald, S. 8(5); Collins, J. 35; Cooper, N. 27; Evans, G. 23(5); Fellenger, D. 8(4); Findlay, W. 5(5); Goram, A. 34; Hamilton, B. 26(2); Houchen, K. 27(2); Hunter, G. 34; Kane, P. 31; McGinlay, P. 20(8); Miller, W. 11; Milne, C. 3; Mitchell, G. 28(3); Orr, N. 24(5); Rae, G. 2; Reid, C. 2; Sneddon, A. 28(1); Tortolano, J. 6(1); Weir, M. 12(6); Wright, P. 2(1).
Goals – League: (34): Houchen 8, Collins 6, Evans 3, Kane 3 (1 pen), McGinlay 3, Weir 3, Archibald 2, Sneddon 2, Fellenger 1, Hamilton 1, Orr 1, Wright 1.
Scottish Cup: (7): Houchen 3, McGinlay 2, Collins 1, Orr 1.
Skol Cup: (3): Sneddon 2, Collins 1.

KILMARNOCK

DIV. 1

Ground: Rugby Park, Kilmarnock KA1 2DP (0563–25184)
Colours: Blue and white hooped shirts, blue shorts.
Year formed: 1869. **Manager:** Jim Fleeting.
League appearances: Burns, T. 22; Callaghan, T. 20(1); Cody, S. 12(8); Curran, P. 12(4); Davidson, F. 3; Flexney, P. 34; Geddes, R. 10; Geraghty, M. 2 (9); Jenkins, E. 7(6); MacCabe, D. 4; MacFarlane, D. 5(2); MacKinnon, D. 33; Marshall, S. 1; McArthur, M. 2(1); McCulloch, A. 24; McKellar, D. 5; McLean, S. 19(2); Montgomerie, R. 32(3); Porteous, I. 5(2); Quinn, S. (3); Reilly, R. 30(1); Sludden, J. 22; Spence, T. 17; Tait, T. 37(1); Thompson, D. 8(7); Thompson, H. 4(3); Walker, David 13(1); Watters, W. 35(3); Wilson, K. 6(1); Wylde, G. 5(6).
Goals – League: (67): Watters 23, Sludden 7, Tait 6, Curran 4, Reilly 4, Burns 3, Montgomerie 3, Thompson H 3, Callaghan 2, Flexney 2, MacKinnon 2 (1 pen), Thompson D 2, McArthur 1, MacCabe 1, MacFarlane 1, Marshall 1, Porteous 1, own goal 1.
Scottish Cup: (1): Watters 1.
Skol Cup:

MEADOWBANK THISTLE

DIV. 1

Ground: Meadowbank Stadium, Edinburgh EH7 6AE (031-661 5351)
Colours: Amber with black trim, black shorts.
Year formed: 1943 as Ferranti Thistle, Meadowbank Thistle from 1974.
Manager: Terry Christie.
League appearances: Armstrong, G. 39; Banks, A. 3(4); Boyd, W. 13(17); Bullan, L. 5(4); Carswell, A. 1; Christie, M. 13; Forrest, R. 19(8); Inglis, J. 37(1); Irvine, N. 29(1); Logan, S. 9; McCormack J. T. 25; McGachie, J. 5(1); McNaughton, B. 24(4); McQueen, J. 38; Park, D. 9(11); Perry, J. 21(5); Prentice, A. 20; Roseburgh, D. 35; Scott, G. 12(1); Sprott, A. 37(2); Williamson, S. 35.
Goals – League: (41): McNaughton 8, Roseburgh 7 (1 pen), Forrest 6, Boyd 4, Park 4, Inglis 3, Williamson 2, Armstrong 1 (pen), Irvine 1, McGachie 1, Scott 1, Sprott 1, own goals 2.
Scottish Cup: (1): Armstrong 1.
Skol Cup: (1): Roseburgh 1.

MONTROSE

DIV. 2

Ground: Links Park, Montrose DD10 8QD (0674–73200)
Colours: Blue with white trim, white shorts.

Year formed: 1879. **Manager:** Ian Stewart.
League appearances: Allan, M. 32(3); Brown, K. 28(1); Dolan, A. 11(5); Duffy, A. 5(4); Greig, I. 4(6); Halley, K. 4; King, S. 38; Larter, D. 39; Lyons, A. 33(3); Mackay, H. 14(15); Maver, C. 37; McGlashan, J. 33; McLelland, C. 3(2); Morrison, B. 32; Murray, G. 22(10); Paterson, D. 32(1); Powell, D. 23 (9); Price, R. 1; Selbie, A. 15(6); Sheran, J. 21(1); Walker, A. 1; Wright, A. (1); Young, J. 1.
Goals – League: (53): Powell 11, Murray 10, McGlashan 9, Maver 7, Allan 6, Brown 5 (2 pens), Dolan 1, King 1, Paterson 1, Sheran 1, own goal 1.
Scottish Cup: (1): Allan 1.
Skol Cup: (4): Murray 4.

MORTON DIV. 1

Ground: Cappielow Park, Greenock PA15 2TY (0475–23571)
Colours: Blue and white hooped shirts, white shorts.
Year formed: 1874. **Manager:** Allan McGraw.
League appearances: Alexander, R. 38; Boag, Jim 6(7); Boag, John 29(3); Collins, D. 36(2); Cowie, G. 5; Deeney, M. 17(5); Fowler, J. 24(1); Goodwin, J. (4); Gourlay, A. 4; Hopkin, D. 3(5); Hunter, J. 36; Kelly, G. 1(3); McCrystal, R. 1; McDonald, I. 22(3); McGoldrick, K. (2); McGraw, M. 5(6); McInnes, D. 15(8); McNeil, J. 7(1); O'Hara, A. 19(10); Pickering, M. 30; Reid, B. 36; Roberts, P. 4(4); Robertson, D. 7(1); Ronald, G. 13(2); Strain, B. 2; Turner, T. 30; Wylie, D. 39.
Goals – League: (38): Alexander 11, Turner 6, McGraw 3, O'Hara 3, Pickering 3, Deeney 2, Fowler 2 (1 pen), Jim Boag 1, McDonald 1, McInnes 1, McNeil 1, Reid 1, Roberts 1, Robertson 1, Ronald 1.
Scottish Cup: (6): Alexander 3, Fowler 1, O'Hara 1, Turner 1.
Skol Cup: (2): Alexander 1, Turner 1.

MOTHERWELL PREM. DIV.

Ground: Fir Park, Motherwell ML1 2QN (0698–614378)
Colours: Amber shirts with claret band, claret shorts.
Year formed: 1886. **Manager:** Tommy McLean.
League appearances: Arnott, D. 23(7); Boyd, T. 33; Burley, G. 34; Bryce, S. (3); Cooper, D. 31; Cusack, N. 29(2); Dolan, J. 5(7); Gahagan, J. 7(19); Gardner, J. 1; Griffin, J. 6(5); Kirk, S. 32(2); MacCabe, D. (1); Mair, G. 7(2); Maxwell, A. 36; McAdam, T. 6; McBride, M. 1; McCart, C. 33(1); McLean, P. (2); McNair, C. 1(1); O'Neill, C. 24; Paterson, C. 33; Philliben, J. 19(5); Reilly, M. 3(1); Russell, R. 32(1).
Goals – League: (43): Cusack 11, Kirk 8, Cooper 6 (3 pens), Arnott 5, Gahagan 3, Paterson 3, Russell 3, Boyd 1, McCart 1, O'Neill 1 (pen), own goal 1.
Scottish Cup: (7): Arnott 1, Bryce 1, Cooper 1 (pen), Gahagan 1, Kirk 1, McCart 1, Russell 1.
Skol Cup: (4): Cusack 2, Dolan 1, Kirk 1.

PARTICK THISTLE DIV. 1

Ground: Firhill Park, Glasgow G20 7AL (041–946 2673)
Colours: Amber shirts with red trim, red shorts.
Year formed: 1876. **Manager:** John Lambie.
League appearances: Adam, C. 6(2); Campbell, C. 34; Charnley, J. 29; Clarke, S. 1(2); Collins, G. 8; Corrie, T. 4(2); Craig, D. 6(3); Dempsey, J. 1; Dinnie, A. 14; Duncan, C. 25; English, I. 3(3); Flood, J. 26(7); Gallagher, B. 15(7); Graham, P. 1; Grant, A. 1(2); Jardine, I. 12; Kennedy, A. 22; Kerr, J. 33(2); Law, R. 27(1); MacDonald, R. 17; MacFarlane, D. 5(4); McCoy, G. 6(2); McGuire, W. 4(4); McStay, W. 4(1); Mitchell, J. 14(7); Murdoch, A. 13; Peebles, G. 22(2); Rae, G. 9; Smith, R. 29(1); Wright, B. 36; Wylie, R. 2.

Goals – League: (62): Campbell 18, Charnley 11 (7 pens), Flood 9, Wright 5, McCoy 3, Adam 2, Dinnie 2, English 2, Craig 1, Kennedy 1, Kerr 1, Law 1, MacFarlane 1, Mitchell 1, Peebles 1, Smith 1, own goals 2.
Scottish Cup: (2): Campbell 1, Charnley 1 (pen).
Skol Cup: (0).

QUEEN OF THE SOUTH DIV. 2

Ground: Palmerston Park, Dumfries DG2 9BA (0387–54853)
Colours: Royal blue shirts, white shorts.
Year formed: 1919. **Manager:** Frank McGarvey.
League appearances: Andrews, G. 14(10); Archer, S. 5; Bain, A. 1(1); Davidson, A. 24; Dawson, L. 1; Donaldson, S. 1; Fraser, G. 17; Gordon, S. 25; Gray, W. 4; Hetherington, K. 33(1); Holland, B. 7; Johnston, G 31; McCafferty, T. 27(2); McGhie, W. 35; McGuire, J. 12(1); McLean, A. 8; Mills, D. 23(3); Moore, S. 4; Possee, M. 5(8); Robertson, J. 17(1); Shanks, M. 18(3); Sim, W. 30(4); Sloan, T. 39; Stewart, R. 1(6); Telfer, G. (1); Thomson, A. 20(6); Thomson, I. 27.
Goals – League: (58): Gordon 8, Sloan 7, Andrews 6, Thomson A 6, Fraser 5 (3 pens), Robertson 5 (3 pens), McGhie 4, McGuire 4, Moore 3, Sim 3, Johnston 2, Possee 2, Thomson I 2, Mills 1.
Scottish Cup: (7): Gordon 3, Fraser 1, McGhie 1, Sloan 1, Thomson A 1.
Skol Cup: (1): Fraser 1 (pen).

QUEEN'S PARK DIV. 2

Ground: Hampden Park, Glasgow G42 9BA (041–632 1275)
Colours: Black and white hooped shirts, white shorts.
Year formed: 1867. **Coach:** Eddie Hunter
League appearances: Armstrong, P. 29; Caven, R. 31(1); Elder, G. 39; Elliot, D. 28(7); Flannigan, M. 3(5); Greig, D. 1(6); Hendry, M. 30(1); Jack, S. 26; Kinnie, R. 1; McEntegart, S. 19(6); McFadyen, J. 1(4); McKenzie, K. 27(6); McLean, S. 32; McNamee, P. 29; Mirner, E. 1(1); Monaghan, M. 39; Morton, C. (3); O'Brien, J. 18(1); O'Brien, P. 39; Ogg, G. 31(1); Rodden, J. 5(14).
Goals – League: (40): Hendry 10, O'Brien P 9 (1 pen), Caven 4, McKenzie 4, Ogg 4, Elliot 2, McEntegart 2, Armstrong 1, Elder 1, McFadyen 1, McNamee 1, Rodden 1.
Scottish Cup: (1): Rodden 1.
Skol Cup: (2): McKenzie 1, O'Brien P 1.

RAITH ROVERS DIV. 1

Ground: Stark's Park, Pratt Street, Kirkcaldy KY1 1SA (0592–263514)
Colours: Royal blue shirts, white shorts.
Year formed: 1883. **Manager:** Frank Connor.
League appearances: Arthur, G. 39; Buchanan, N. 2(1); Burn, P. 25(4); Coyle, R. 28; Dalziel, G. 39; Dennis, S. 18; Ferguson, I. 12(20); Fraser, C. 23; Glennie, R. 7; Logan, A. 16(10); Macdonald, K. 25(1); Mcleod, I. 37; McGeachie, G. 14; McStay, J. 38; Murray, D. 28(1); Nelson, M. 27(5); Romaines, S. 26(3); Simpson, S. 20(7); Sorbie, S. 5 (9).
Goals – League: (57): Dalziel 20, Macdonald 10 (3 pens), Ferguson 6, Logan 6, Nelson 4, McStay 3, Coyle 2, Fraser 2 (1 pen), Burn 1, Romaines 1, Simpson 1, Sorbie 1.
Scottish Cup: (3): Dalziel 1, Logan 1, own goal 1.
Skol Cup: (0).

RANGERS PREM. DIV.

Ground: Ibrox Stadium, Glasgow G51 2XD (041–427 5232)
Colours: Royal blue shirts, white shorts.
Year formed: 1873. **Player Manager:** Graeme Souness.
League appearances: Brown, J. 24(3); Butcher, T. 34; Cooper, N. 2(1); Cowan, T. 1(2); Dodds, D. 4 (10); Drinkell, K. 2(2); Ferguson, D. 3(2); Ferguson, I. 21(3); Ginzburg, B. 4; Gough, R. 26; Johnston, M. 36; McCall, I. 2(2); McCoist, A. 32(2); Munro, S. 36; Nisbet, S. 4(3); Robertson, A. (1); Souness, G. (1); Spackman, N. 21; Steven, T. 34; Stevens, G. 35; Vinnicombe, C. 1(6); Walters, M. 27; Wilkins, R. 15; Woods, C. 32.
Goals – League: (48): Johnston 15 (1 pen), McCoist 14 (1 pen), Walters 5 (1 pen), Dodds 4, Butcher 3, Steven T 3, Brown 1, Munro 1, Spackman 1, Stevens G 1.
Scottish Cup: (3): Brown 1, Johnston 1, Walters 1.
Skol Cup: (15): McCoist 5, Walters 4 (2 pens), Ferguson I 2, Steven 2, Johnston 1, own goal 1.

ST JOHNSTONE PREM. DIV.

Ground: McDiarmid Park, Crieff Road, Perth PH1 2SJ (0738–26961)
Colours: Royal blue shirts with white trim, blue shorts.
Year formed: 1884. **Manager:** Alex Totten.
League appearances: Balavage, J. 38; Barron, D. 16(1); Bingham, D. 1; Blackie, W. 2(8); Butter, J. 1; Cherry, P. 38(1); Curran, H. 26(5); Grant, R. 33(4); Heddle, I. 38(1); Hegarty, P. 14; Jenkins, G. 20(8); Johnston, S. 34(3); Maher, G. (1); Maskrey, S. 22(7); McGinnis, G. 10(1); McKillop, A. 5; McVicar, D. 35; Moore, A. 33; Newbigging, W. 1; Nicolson, K. 1; Smith, M. (2); Sorbie, S. (3); Thompson, G. 1(6); Thomson, K. 24; Treanor, M. 30; Ward, K. 6(12).
Goals – League: (81): Grant 19, Moore 13, Maskrey 12, Johnston 7, Heddle 5, Cherry 4, Treanor 4 (2 pens), Ward 4, Curran 3, Jenkins 3, McVicar 3 (2 pens), Hegarty 1, own goals 3.
Scottish Cup: (0).
Skol Cup: (0)

ST MIRREN PREM. DIV.

Ground: St Mirren Park, Paisley PA3 2EJ (041–889 2558 and 041-840 1337)
Colours: White shirts with black vertical stripes, black shorts.
Year formed: 1877. **Manager:** Tony Fitzpatrick.
League appearances: Black, T. 31; Chalmers, P. 2(7); Davies, W. 22(7); Dawson, R. 1; Fridge, L. 8; Godfrey, P. 22; Hutchinson, T. (1); Kinnaird, P. 22(3); Lambert, P. 19(6); Manley, R. 30; Martin, B. 35; McDowall, K. 20(3); McEwan, A. 2; McGarvey, F. 2(1); McGill, D. 1(1); McGowne, K. 1(1); McIntosh, M. 1(1); McWalter, M. 13(9); McWhirter, N. 20(1); Money, C. 28; Shaw, G. 18(5); Stickroth, T. 6(1); Torfason, G. 29; Walker, K. 10; Weir, P. 9(3); Wilson, T. 9; Winnie, D. 16(1); Wishart, F. 19(1).
Goals – League: (28): Torfason 12 (1 pen), Lambert 3, McDowall 3, Godfrey 2, Martin 2, Shaw 2, Walker 2, Black 1, Davies 1.
Scottish Cup: (5): Davies 2, McDowall 1, McWalter 1, Shaw 1.
Skol Cup: (4): Kinnaird 1, McDowall 1, Shaw 1, Torfason 1.

STENHOUSEMUIR DIV. 2

Ground: Ochilview Park, Stenhousemuir FK5 5QL (0324–562992)
Colours: Maroon shirts with white trim, white shorts.

Year formed: 1884. **Manager:** James Meakin.
League appearances: Aitchison, T. 15(7); Aitkin, N. 13(2); Anderson, P. 19; Bell, A. 21 (9); Cairney, H. 39; Clark, R. 7(2); Clouston, B. 31(1); Condie, T. 5(3); Elliott, T. 27(1); Gavin, S. 2(7); Hoggan, K. 2; Kelly, C. 13; Kemp, B. 39; McCormick, S. 33(1); McGurn, J. 9; McKeown, K. 11; McKinlay, J. (1); McNab, J. 1; Milligan, J. 10(2); Nelson, M. 19; Paterno, J. 15; Quinton, I. 15(19); Speirs, A. 20(5); Tracey, K. 34; Walker, C. 24(1); Yardley, K. 5(1).
Goals – League: (60): McCormick 15 (5 pens), Speirs 10, Walker 7, Nelson 5, Kemp 4, McGurn 4, Bell 3, Aitchison 2, Anderson 2, Cairney 2, Clouston 2, Milligan 1, Quinton 1, Tracey 1, Yardley 1.
Scottish Cup: (2): McCormick 1, Speirs 1.
Skol Cup: (0).

STIRLING ALBION DIV. 2

Ground: Annfield Park, Stirling FK8 2HE (0786–50399)
Colours: Red shirts with white sleeves, white shorts.
Year formed: 1945. **Manager:** John Brogan
League appearances: Blackwood, I. 1; Brown, M. 2(1); Conway, M. 23(4); Docherty, R. 39; George, D. 15(15); Gilmour, J. 7(12); Given, J. 31(1); Graham, A. 5; Hamilton, L. 5; Hannigan, P. (5); Hughes, M. 1(4); Lawrie, D. 27; Lloyd, D. 31(3); McConville, R. 22(4); McGeown, M. 29; Mitchell, C. 39; Mooney, M. 2; Moore, V. 36; Reid, J. 28(7); Robertson, S. 33; Tennant, S. 23; Walker, David 3(4); Walker, Derek 9 (9); Woods, J. 18.
Goals – League: (73): Reid 16, Lloyd 15, Moore 14 (4 pens), George 6, Docherty 5, Derek Walker 4, Lawrie 3, Robertson 3, Gilmour 2, Mitchell 2, Conway 1, Tennant 1, own goal 1.
Scottish Cup: (15): Lloyd 7, Docherty 2, Gilmour 2, Moore 2 (1 pen), George 1, Reid 1.
Skol Cup: (0).

STRANRAER DIV. 2

Ground: Stair Park, Stranraer DG9 8BS (0776–3271)
Colours: Royal blue shirts with amber band, blue shorts.
Year formed: 1870. **Manager:** Alex McAnespie
League appearances: Barr, R. 2(1); Cook, D. 32(6); Corrie, T. 8(2); Cuthbertson, S. 6(2); Doherty, J. (1); Dougan, M. (1); Duffy, B. 39; Duncan, G. 24(14); Ewing, A. 23(2); Gallagher, A. 36; Hamilton, D. (1); Harkness, C. 28(1); Henderson, D. 30(1); Lindsay, C. 30; Lowe, L. 25(2); Martin, P. 1; McCutcheon, D. 34; McInnes, I. 15(15); McMillan, G. 18(10); McNiven, J. 35; Millar, D. (2); Muir, W. 3(2); Shirkie, S. 8(1); Spittal, I. 24(4); Teevan, P. 3; Workman, J. 5.
Goals – League: (57): Harkness 13, Cook 11, Henderson 10, McNiven 7, Duncan 6, McCutcheon 5 (1 pen), Ewing 2, Lindsay 2, McMillan 1.
Scottish Cup: (2): Harkness 2.
Skol Cup: (3): Harkness 2, Cuthbertson 1.

B & Q SCOTTISH LEAGUE PREMIER DIVISION RESULTS 1989–90

Note: *In the Scottish League Divisions I and II, the teams play each other twice and after a draw made at the beginning of the season, half of the fixtures are repeated once.*

	Aberdeen	Celtic	Dundee	Dundee U	Dunfermline Ath	Hearts	Hibernian	Motherwell	Rangers	St Mirren
Aberdeen	—	1-1 1-1	1-0 5-2	2-0 1-0	2-1 4-1	1-3 2-2	1-0 1-2	1-0 2-0	1-0 0-0	5-0 2-0
Celtic	1-0 1-3	—	4-1 1-1	0-1 3-0	1-0 0-2	2-1 1-1	3-1 1-1	1-1 0-1	1-1 0-1	1-1 0-3
Dundee	1-1 1-1	1-3 0-0	—	4-3 1-1	1-2 1-0	2-2 0-1	0-0 2-0	2-1 1-2	0-2 2-2	3-3 1-2
Dundee U	2-0 1-1	2-2 2-0	0-0 1-2	—	2-1 1-0	2-1 1-1	1-0 1-0	1-1 1-1	1-1 0-1	0-0 2-0
Dunfermline Ath	0-3 2-4	2-0 0-0	2-1 1-0	1-1 0-1	—	0-2 0-1	0-0 1-1	1-1 0-5	1-1 0-1	5-1 1-0
Hearts	1-1 1-0	1-3 0-0	6-3 0-0	1-1 3-2	1-2 0-2	—	1-0 2-0	3-0 2-0	1-2 1-1	4-0 0-0
Hibernian	0-3 3-2	0-3 1-0	3-2 1-1	2-0 0-0	2-2 2-1	1-1 1-2	—	3-2 1-2	2-0 0-0	3-1 0-1
Motherwell	0-0 2-2	0-0 1-1	3-0 3-1	3-2 0-1	1-1 1-3	1-3 0-3	0-2 1-0	—	1-0 1-1	3-1 2-0
Rangers	1-0 2-0	1-0 3-0	2-2 3-0	2-1 3-1	3-0 2-0	1-0 0-0	3-0 0-1	3-0 2-1	—	0-1 1-0
St Mirren	0-2 1-0	1-0 0-2	3-2 0-0	1-0 0-0	2-0 1-2	1-2 2-0	0-0 0-1	2-2 0-0	0-2 0-0	—

B & Q SCOTTISH LEAGUE DIVISION 1 RESULTS 1989–90

	Airdrie	Albion R.	Alloa	Ayr U	Clyde	Clydebank	Falkirk	Forfar Ath.	Hamilton A.	Meadowbank Th.	Morton	Partick Th.	Raith R.	St. Johnstone
Airdrie	—	1-0	2-1 3-1	1-1 6-0	1-0	2-2 3-4	1-1	4-1	1-0 3-1	3-1 1-1	4-1	1-1 3-2	3-2 0-1	2-2
Albion R	0-2 1-2	—	1-1	3-1	2-0	3-4 1-2	2-1 2-2	0-2 2-2	0-0	0-0 1-2	1-1	5-4 2-2	2-2	1-3 2-5
Alloa	0-2	4-1 3-4	—	1-1 0-0	1-1 1-0	1-4 1-1	1-1 0-0	0-2	0-2 1-1	0-1	1-1	1-0	2-0 0-4	0-1
Ayr U	1-3	2-0 0-2	3-0	—	1-0 1-0	3-2	3-3 1-1	1-1 1-1	0-1	0-0	2-3	0-0 2-1	1-0	2-2 0-2
Clyde	1-0 0-1	0-0 2-1	2-4	2-2	—	2-0	2-0 0-0	0-0	1-1 0-1	0-3 1-1	1-1	3-3	1-0 0-0	0-2
Clydebank	0-3	1-3	3-1	4-1 0-1	2-1 2-1	—	3-3	3-2 3-2	2-2	1-1 2-1	3-1 0-1	1-2	3-1 2-2	4-0
Falkirk	3-1 3-1	6-0	1-0	0-1	3-0	2-1 0-1	—	4-0 2-2	3-3	1-1	1-0 2-0	1-1 2-0	0-2	3-3 1-0
Forfar Ath	1-1 2-3	3-0	3-3 3-2	1-0	1-1 2-2	2-2	1-2	—	0-1 2-0	1-3	0-1	0-3 2-0	2-2 2-2	1-5
Hamilton A	3-2	0-0 1-2	1-0	4-0 2-1	0-1	2-1 1-3	1-0 2-2	1-1	—	2-0	2-2 2-0	1-4	3-2	3-3 2-3
Meadowbank Th.	0-1	3-2	1-3	1-2 1-1	2-1 1-0	1-1	1-2	3-1 1-0	1-0 0-3	—	0-0	1-1 1-0	1-2 1-1	1-3
Morton	0-1 1-1	0-0 3-0	3-2 2-0	1-1 0-1	0-1 2-3	2-2	0-2	1-1 2-0	0-0	0-0	—	2-2	1-1	0-0 1-2
Partick Th.	2-1	4-0	3-3 1-0	1-2	2-2 0-3	1-1 4-0	1-0	0-0	3-1 4-1	2-0	1-2 0-1	—	3-1 1-1	0-1 0-2
Raith R.	0-4	2-1 3-2	1-1	2-0 5-2	0-2	1-0	4-0 1-1	1-0	1-3 0-0	1-3 3-0	2-0 2-1	1-1	—	0-2
St. Johnstone	1-2 3-1	2-1	3-0 6-0	4-0	2-0 1-1	2-1 1-3	2-0	3-1 1-0	3-0	1-0 1-2	1-1	2-1	1-2 0-0	—

B & Q SCOTTISH LEAGUE DIVISION 2 RESULTS 1989–90

	Arbroath	Berwick R.	Brechin C.	Cowdenbeath	Dumbarton	East Fife	East Stirling	Kilmarnock	Queen of South	Queen's Park	Montrose	Sten'muir	Stirling Alb.	Stranraer
Arbroath	—	1-0	0-1 0-2	0-0 0-1	2-1	3-0	2-0	1-1 2-4	1-0 1-0	2-2 1-1	2-2 3-0	2-1	1-2	2-0
Berwick	3-1 5-0	—	1-1 1-0	2-0	1-2 3-2	1-1 2-0	1-0	3-2 1-4	1-1	2-0	2-0	0-2 1-0	1-1	3-1 2-1
Brechin	2-2	1-0	—	1-0 1-3	4-0 3-0	2-1	2-1 0-0	3-1	3-1	1-0 1-0	1-1 2-2	1-2	3-1 1-5	1-0 0-0
Cowdenbeath	1-1	2-1 3-1	1-1	—	1-5	0-1 2-2	4-0 3-3	2-1	4-2 2-1	0-0	0-1 2-4	0-1	4-0 1-1	3-4
Dumbarton	0-0 2-0	1-5	1-1	2-2 1-3	—	3-1	3-0 2-1	0-2 1-3	2-1	2-1	3-2	1-0	2-2 1-2	5-2 1-1
East Fife	3-0 2-3	2-2	3-1 1-3	0-0	2-2 3-1	—	1-1 1-1	4-2	2-2 1-2	1-1 3-2	4-1	2-3	1-0	1-2
East Stirling	1-1 1-0	3-1 2-1	2-0	1-1	1-2	0-2	—	2-1	1-0	1-0	0-2 1-1	0-3 4-2	0-2 0-2	0-3 0-1
Kilmarnock	3-0	2-0	0-2 2-2	0-0 2-1	3-0	1-0 2-1	2-0 2-0	—	2-0 4-1	2-0 3-0	1-1	2-2	1-2 1-0	0-1
Queen of South	2-2	4-2 3-2	3-1 2-2	2-4	1-4 1-1	5-1	2-2 1-1	2-1	—	3-1 0-0	3-2	1-1 0-4	3-1	2-2
Queen's Park	1-2	3-1 0-3	0-3	0-0 0-2	2-2 1-0	2-1	3-2 2-1	1-0	0-0	—	2-1	0-0 1-1	2-1 3-1	0-2 3-0
Montrose	4-2	2-1 0-2	0-1	2-0	2-2 1-2	2-2 0-2	3-0	0-1 1-3	0-0 1-1	4-1 0-1	—	0-2 1-1	3-3	2-2
Stenhousemuir	3-0 1-0	1-3	2-0 1-1	3-1 2-1	4-3 1-3	2-2 1-2	2-0	0-3 2-1	1-3	1-3	1-0	—	2-1	0-2
Stirling Alb.	2-3 3-2	3-2 4-0	2-0	1-1	4-1	3-1 2-0	4-0	0-1	5-0 1-1	1-0	2-0 2-3	1-1 1-3	—	1-0 2-1
Stranraer	2-1 2-1	1-3	2-4	3-1 1-2	4-4	1-1 0-2	1-1	1-0 2-1	0-2 3-0	0-1	1-2 2-0	2-2 4-1	0-2	—

B & Q SCOTTISH LEAGUE FINAL TABLES 1989–90

Premier Division			*Home*			*Goals*		*Away*			*Goals*			
		P	*W*	*D*	*L*	*F*	*A*	*W*	*D*	*L*	*F*	*A*	*GD*	*Pts*
1	Rangers	36	14	2	2	32	7	6	9	3	16	12	+29	51
2	Aberdeen	36	12	4	2	33	13	5	6	7	23	20	+23	44
3	Hearts	36	8	6	4	28	17	8	6	4	26	18	+19	44
4	Dundee U	36	8	8	2	21	12	3	5	10	15	27	−3	35
5	Celtic	36	6	6	6	21	20	4	8	6	16	17	0	34
6	Motherwell	36	7	6	5	23	21	4	6	8	20	26	−4	34
7	Hibernian	36	8	5	5	25	23	4	5	9	9	18	−7	34
8	Dunfermline Ath	36	5	6	7	17	23	6	2	10	20	27	−13	30
9	St Mirren	36	6	6	6	14	15	4	4	10	14	33	−20	30
10	Dundee	36	4	8	6	23	26	1	6	11	18	39	−24	24

First Division 1			*Home*			*Goals*		*Away*			*Goals*			
		P	*W*	*D*	*L*	*F*	*A*	*W*	*D*	*L*	*F*	*A*	*GD*	*Pts*
1	St Johnstone	39	13	3	4	40	16	12	5	2	41	23	+42	58
2	Airdrieonians	39	12	6	2	45	23	11	2	6	32	22	+32	54
3	Clydebank	39	10	4	5	39	29	7	6	7	35	35	+10	44
4	Falkirk	39	11	5	3	38	17	3	10	7	21	29	+13	43
5	Raith Rovers	39	10	4	5	30	22	5	8	7	27	28	+7	42
6	Hamilton A	39	9	5	5	33	27	5	8	7	19	26	−1	41
7	Meadowbank Th	39	7	6	7	22	25	6	7	6	19	21	−5	39
8	Partick Th	39	9	5	6	33	22	3	9	7	29	31	+9	38
9	Clyde	39	5	9	5	18	20	5	6	9	21	26	−7	35
10	Ayr U	39	6	8	5	24	23	5	5	10	17	39	−21	35
11	Morton	39	4	10	6	21	20	5	6	8	17	26	−8	34
12	Forfar Ath*	39	5	7	7	29	33	3	8	9	22	32	−14	29
13	Albion R	39	4	8	8	31	38	4	3	12	19	40	−28	27
14	Alloa	39	4	8	8	18	27	2	5	12	23	43	−29	25

Second Division			*Home*			*Goals*		*Away*			*Goals*			
		P	*W*	*D*	*L*	*F*	*A*	*W*	*D*	*L*	*F*	*A*	*GD*	*Pts*
1	Brechin C	39	12	5	3	33	20	7	6	6	26	24	+15	49
2	Kilmarnock	39	14	3	3	35	11	8	1	10	32	28	+28	48
3	Stirling A	39	13	3	4	44	20	7	4	8	29	30	+23	47
4	Stenhousemuir	39	10	2	7	30	29	8	6	6	30	24	+7	44
5	Berwick R	39	13	4	3	36	19	5	1	13	30	38	+9	41
6	Dumbarton	39	9	5	5	33	29	6	5	9	37	44	−3	40
7	Cowdenbeath	39	7	6	6	35	30	6	7	7	23	24	+4	39
8	Stranraer	39	8	4	8	32	31	7	4	8	25	28	−2	38
9	East Fife	39	7	7	5	37	29	5	5	10	23	34	−3	36
10	Queen of the S	39	8	8	3	40	34	3	6	11	18	35	−11	36
11	Queen's Park	39	10	5	5	26	23	3	5	11	14	28	−11	36
12	Arbroath	39	9	5	5	26	18	3	5	12	21	43	−14	34
13	Montrose	39	5	7	8	28	29	5	5	9	25	34	−10	32
14	East Stirling	39	8	3	8	20	25	0	7	13	14	41	−32	26

** 2 points deducted for breach of rules.*

Scottish League Leading Scorers 1989–90

Listed in order of League goals. Columns indicate League, Scottish Cup, Skol Cup.

Premier Division				
John Robertson (Hearts)	17	4	1	22
Ross Jack (Dunfermline Ath)	16	2	3	21
Mo Johnston (Rangers)	15	1	1	17
Ally McCoist (Rangers)	14	0	5	19
Billy Dodds (Dundee)	13	0	0	13
First Division				
Ken Eadie (Clydebank)	21	2	2	25
Gordon Dalziel (Raith R)	20	1	0	21
Roddy Grant (St Johnstone)	19	0	0	19
Calum Campbell (Partick Th)	18	1	0	19
Derek McWilliams (Falkirk)	17	0	0	17
Second Division				
Willie Watters (Kilmarnock)	23	1	0	24
Charles Gibson (Dumbarton)	20	0	1	21
Sandy Ross (Cowdenbeath)	16	4	0	20
Joe Reid (Stirling Alb)	16	1	0	17
Scott Sloan (Berwick R)	16	0	2	18

Scottish League and Cup honours

Championship wins

40 – Rangers (including one shared); 35 – Celtic; 4 – Aberdeen, Hearts, Hibernian; 2 – Dumbarton (including one shared); 1 – Dundee, Dundee U, Kilmarnock, Motherwell, Third Lanark.

Scottish FA Cup

29 – Celtic; 24 – Rangers; 10 – Queen's Park; 7 – Aberdeen; 5 – Hearts; 3 – Clyde, St Mirren, Vale of Leven; 2 – Dunfermline Ath, Falkirk, Hibernian, Kilmarnock, Renton, Third Lanark; 1 – Airdrieonians, Dumbarton, Dundee, East Fife, Morton, Motherwell, Partick Th, St Bernard's.

Scottish League/Skol Cup

15 – Rangers; 9 – Celtic; 5 – Aberdeen, Hearts; 3 – Dundee, East Fife; 2 – Dundee U; 1 – Hibernian, Motherwell, Partick Th.

SCOTTISH LEAGUE HONOURS LIST

Premier Division (maximum points: *a*, 72; *b*, 88)

		First	Pt	Second	Pt	Third	Pt
1975–76	*a*	Rangers	54	Celtic	48	Hibernian	43
1976–77	*a*	Celtic	55	Rangers	46	Aberdeen	43
1977–78	*a*	Rangers	55	Aberdeen	53	Dundee U	40
1978–79	*a*	Celtic	48	Rangers	45	Dundee U	44
1979–80	*a*	Aberdeen	48	Celtic	47	St Mirren	42
1980–81	*a*	Celtic	56	Aberdeen	49	Rangers	44
1981–82	*a*	Celtic	55	Aberdeen	53	Rangers	43
1982–83	*a*	Dundee U	56	Celtic	55	Aberdeen	55
1983–84	*a*	Aberdeen	57	Celtic	50	Dundee U	47
1984–85	*a*	Aberdeen	59	Celtic	52	Dundee U	47
1985–86	*a*	Celtic	50	Hearts	50	Dundee U	47
1986–87	*b*	Rangers	69	Celtic	63	Dundee U	60
1987–88	*b*	Celtic	72	Hearts	62	Rangers	60
1988–89	*a*	Rangers	56	Aberdeen	50	Celtic	46
1989–90	*a*	Rangers	51	Aberdeen	44	Hearts	44

First Division (maximum points: *a*, 52; *b*, 78; *c*, 88)

		First	Pt	Second	Pt	Third	Pt
1975–76	*a*	Partick Th	41	Kilmarnock	35	Montrose	30
1976–77	*b*	St Mirren	62	Clydebank	58	Dundee	51
1977–78	*b**	Morton	58	Hearts	58	Dundee	57
1978–79	*b*	Dundee	55	*Kilmarnock	54	Clydebank	54
1979–80	*b*	Hearts	53	Airdrieonians	51	Ayr U	44
1980–81	*b*	Hibernian	57	Dundee	52	St Johnstone	51
1981–82	*b*	Motherwell	61	Kilmarnock	51	Hearts	50
1982–83	*b*	St Johnstone	55	Hearts	54	Clydebank	50
1983–84	*b*	Morton	54	Dumbarton	51	Partick Th	46
1984–85	*b*	Motherwell	50	Clydebank	48	Falkirk	45
1985–86	*b*	Hamilton Acad.	56	Falkirk	45	Kilmarnock	44
1986–87	*c*	Morton	57	Dunfermline Ath	56	Dumbarton	53
1987–88	*c*	Hamilton Acad.	56	Meadowbank Th	52	Clydebank	49
1988–89	*b*	Dunfermline Ath	54	Falkirk	52	Clydebank	48
1989–90	*b*	St Johnstone	58	Airdrieonians	54	Clydebank	44

Second Division (maximum points: *a*, 52; *b*, 78)

		First	Pt	Second	Pt	Third	Pt
1975–76	*a**	Clydebank	40	Raith Rovers	40	Alloa	35
1976–77	*b*	Stirling Albion	55	Alloa	51	Dunfermline Ath.	50
1977–78	*b**	Clyde	53	Raith Rovers	53	Dunfermline Ath.	48
1978–79	*b*	Berwick	54	Dunfermline Ath.	52	Falkirk	50
1979–80	*b*	Falkirk	50	E. Stirlingshire	49	Forfar Ath	46
1980–81	*b*	Queen's Park	50	Q of S	46	Cowdenbeath	45
1981–82	*b*	Clyde	59	*Alloa	50	Arbroath	50
1982–83	*b*	Brechin	55	Meadowbank Th.	54	Arbroath	49
1983–84	*b*	Forfar Ath	63	E. Fife	47	Berwick Rangers	43
1984–85	*b*	Montrose	53	Alloa	50	Dunfermline Ath.	49
1985–86	*b*	Dunfermline Ath.	57	Q of the S	55	Meadowbank Th	49
1986–87	*b*	Meadowbank Th.	55	*Raith Rovers	52	Stirling Albion	52
1987–88	*b*	Ayr U	61	St Johnstone	59	Queen's Park	51
1988–89	*b*	Albion R	50	Alloa	45	Brechin C	43
1989–90	*b*	Brechin C	49	Kilmarnock	48	Stirling A	47

First Division to 1974–75 (maximum points: *a*, 36; *b*, 44; *c*,40; *d*, 52; *e*, 60; *f*, 68; *g*, 76; *h*, 84; *j*, 60)

		First	Pt	Second	Pt	Third	Pt
1890–91	*a*	Dumbarton	29	Rangers	29	Celtic	24
1891–92	*b*	Dumbarton	37	Celtic	35	Hearts	30
1892–93	*a*	Celtic	29	Rangers	28	St Mirren	23
1893–94		Celtic	29	Hearts	26	St Bernards	22
1894–95		Hearts	31	Celtic	26	Rangers	21
1895–96		Celtic	30	Rangers	26	Hibernian	24
1896–97		Hearts	28	Hibernian	26	Rangers	25
1897–98		Celtic	33	Rangers	29	Hibernian	22
1898–99		Rangers	36	Hearts	26	Celtic	24
1899–1900		Rangers	32	Celtic	25	Hibernian	24
1900–1	*c*	Rangers	35	Celtic	29	Hibernian	25
1901–2	*a*	Rangers	28	Celtic	26	Hearts	22
1902–3	*b*	Hibernian	37	Dundee	31	Rangers	29
1903–4		Third Lanark	43	Hearts	39	*Rangers	38
1904–5	*d*	Celtic	41	Rangers	41	Third Lanark	35
1905–6	*e*	Celtic	49	Hearts	43	Airdrieonians	38
1906–7	*f*	Celtic	55	Dundee	48	Rangers	45
1907–8		Celtic	55	Falkirk	51	Rangers	50
1908–9		Celtic	51	Dundee	50	Clyde	48
1909–10		Celtic	54	Falkirk	52	Rangers	46
1910–11		Rangers	52	Aberdeen	48	Falkirk	44
1911–12		Rangers	51	Celtic	45	Clyde	42
1912–13		Rangers	53	Celtic	49	*Hearts	41
1913–14	*g*	Celtic	65	Rangers	59	*Hearts	54
1914–15	*g*	Celtic	65	Hearts	61	Rangers	50
1916–17	*g*	Celtic	64	Morton	54	Rangers	53
1917–18	*f*	Rangers	56	Celtic	55	Kilmarnock	43
1918–19		Celtic	58	Rangers	57	Morton	47
1919–20	*h*	Rangers	71	Celtic	68	Motherwell	57
1920–21		Rangers	76	Celtic	66	Hearts	56
1921–22		Celtic	67	Rangers	66	Raith Rovers	56
1922–23	*g*	Rangers	55	Airdrieonians	50	Celtic	46
1923–24		Rangers	59	Airdrieonians	50	Celtic	41
1924–25		Rangers	60	Airdrieonians	57	Hibernian	52
1925–26		Celtic	58	*Airdrieonians	50	Hearts	50
1926–27		Rangers	56	Motherwell	51	Celtic	49
1927–28		Rangers	60	*Celtic	55	Motherwell	55
1928–29		Rangers	67	Celtic	51	Motherwell	50
1929–30		Rangers	60	Motherwell	55	Aberdeen	53
1930–31		Rangers	60	Celtic	58	Motherwell	56
1931–32		Motherwell	66	Rangers	61	Celtic	48
1932–33		Rangers	62	Motherwell	59	Hearts	50
1933–34		Rangers	66	Motherwell	62	Celtic	47
1934–35		Rangers	55	Celtic	52	Hearts	50
1935–36		Celtic	66	*Rangers	61	Aberdeen	61
1936–37		Rangers	61	Aberdeen	54	Celtic	52
1937–38		Celtic	61	Hearts	58	Rangers	49
1938–39		Rangers	59	Celtic	48	Aberdeen	46
1946–47	*f*	Rangers	46	Hibernian	44	Aberdeen	39
1947–48	*j*	Hibernian	48	Rangers	46	Partick Th	36
1948–49		Rangers	46	Dundee	45	Hibernian	39
1949–50		Rangers	50	Hibernian	49	Hearts	43
1950–51		Hibernian	48	*Rangers	38	Dundee	38
1951–52		Hibernian	45	Rangers	41	E. Fife	37

	First	Pt	Second	Pt	Third	Pt
1952–53	*Rangers	43	Hibernian	43	E. Fife	39
1953–54	Celtic	43	Hearts	38	Partick Th	35
1954–55	Aberdeen	49	Celtic	46	Rangers	41
1955–56 *f*	Rangers	52	Aberdeen	46	*Hearts	45
1956–57	Rangers	55	Hearts	53	Kilmarnock	42
1957–58	Hearts	62	Rangers	49	Celtic	46
1958–59	Rangers	50	Hearts	48	Motherwell	44
1959–60	Hearts	54	Kilmarnock	50	*Rangers	42
1960–61	Rangers	51	Kilmarnock	50	Third Lanark	42
1961–62	Dundee	54	Rangers	51	Celtic	46
1962–63	Rangers	57	Kilmarnock	48	Partick Th	46
1963–64	Rangers	55	Kilmarnock	49	*Celtic	47
1964–65 *	Kilmarnock	50	Hearts	50	Dunfermline Ath	49
1965–66	Celtic	57	Rangers	55	Kilmarnock	45
1966–67	Celtic	58	Rangers	55	Clyde	46
1967–68	Celtic	63	Rangers	61	Hibernian	45
1968–69	Celtic	54	Rangers	49	Dunfermline Ath	45
1969–70	Celtic	57	Rangers	45	Hibernian	44
1970–71	Celtic	56	Aberdeen	54	St Johnstone	44
1971–72	Celtic	60	Aberdeen	50	Rangers	44
1972–73	Celtic	57	Rangers	56	Hibernian	45
1973–74	Celtic	53	Hibernian	49	Rangers	48
1974–75	Rangers	56	Hibernian	49	Celtic	45

Second Division to 1974–75 from 1921–22 (maximum points: *a*, 76; *b*, 72; *c*, 68; *d*, 52; *e*, 60)

	First	Pt	*Second*	Pt	*Third*	Pt
1921–22 *a*†*	Alloa	60	Cowdenbeath	47	Armadale	45
1922–23 *a*	Queen's Park	57	Clydebank	**50	St Johnstone	**45
1923–24 *a*	St Johnstone	56	Cowdenbeath	55	Bathgate	44
1924–25 *a*	Dundee U	50	Clydebank	48	Clyde	47
1925–26 *a*	Dunfermline Ath	59	Clyde	53	Ayr U	52
1926–27 *a*	Bo'ness	56	Raith Rovers	49	Clydebank	45
1927–28 *a*	Ayr U	54	Third Lanark	45	King's Park	44
1928–29 *b*	Dundee U	51	Morton	50	Arbroath	47
1929–30 *a**	Leith Ath	57	E. Fife	57	Albion Rovers	54
1930–31 *a*	Third Lanark	61	Dundee U	50	Dunfermline Ath	47
1931–32 *a**	E. Stirling	55	St Johnstone	55	*Raith Rovers	46
1932–33 *c*	Hibernian	54	Q of S	49	Dunfermline Ath	47
1933–34 *c*	Albion Rovers	45	*Dunfermline Ath	44	Arbroath	44
1934–35 *c*	Third Lanark	52	Arbroath	50	St Bernard's	47
1935–36 *c*	Falkirk	59	St Mirren	52	Morton	48
1936–37 *c*	Ayr U	54	Morton	51	St Bernard's	48
1937–38 *c*	Raith Rovers	59	Albion Rovers	48	Airdrieonians	47
1938–39 *c*	Cowdenbeath	60	*Alloa	48	E. Fife	48
1946–47 *d*	Dundee	45	Airdrieonians	42	E. Fife	31
1947–48 *e*	E. Fife	53	Albion Rovers	42	Hamilton Acad	40
1948–49 *e**	Raith Rovers	42	Stirling Albion	42	*Airdrieonians	41
1949–50 *e*	Morton	47	Airdrieonians	44	*St Johnstone	36
1950–51 *e**	Q of S	45	Stirling Albion	45	*Ayr U	36
1951–52 *e*	Clyde	44	Falkirk	43	Ayr U	39
1952–53 *e*	Stirling Albion	44	Hamilton Acad	43	Queen's Park	37
1953–54 *e*	Motherwell	45	Kilmarnock	42	*Third Lanark	36
1954–55 *e*	Airdrieonians	46	Dunfermline Ath	42	Hamilton Acad	39
1955–56 *b*	Queen's Park	54	Ayr U	51	St Johnstone	49
1956–57 *b*	Clyde	64	Third Lanark	51	Cowdenbeath	45

1957–58 *b*	Stirling Albion	55	Dunfermline Ath	53	Arbroath	47
1958–59 *b*	Ayr U	60	Arbroath	51	Stenhousemuir	46
1959–60 *b*	St Johnstone	53	Dundee U	50	Q of S	49
1960–61 *b*	Stirling Albion	55	Falkirk	54	Stenhousemuir	50
1961–62 *b*	Clyde	54	Q of S	53	Morton	44
1962–63 *b*	St Johnstone	55	E. Stirling	49	Morton	48
1963–64 *b*	Morton	67	Cylde	53	Arbroath	46
1964–65 *b*	Stirling Albion	59	Hamilton Acad	50	Q of S	45
1965–66 *b*	Ayr U	53	Airdrieonians	50	Q of S	49
1966–67 *b*	Morton	69	Raith Rovers	58	Arbroath	57
1967–68 *b*	St Mirren	62	Arbroath	53	E. Fife	40
1968–69 *b*	Motherwell	64	Ayr U	53	*E. Fife	47
1969–70 *b*	Falkirk	56	Cowdenbeath	55	Q of S	50
1970–71 *b*	Partick Th	56	E. Fife	51	Arbroath	46
1971–72 *b**	Dumbarton	52	Arbroath	52	Stirling Albion	50
1972–73 *b*	Clyde	56	Dunfermline Ath	52	*Raith Rovers	47
1973–74 *b*	Airdrieonians	60	Kilmarnock	59	Hamilton Acad	55
1974–75 *b*	Falkirk	54	*Q of S.	53	Montrose	53

** On goal average/difference. † Held jointly after indecisive play-off. ‡ Won on deciding match. †† Held jointly.** Two points deducted for fielding ineligible player.*† Only one club promoted. Competition suspended 1940–45.*

RELEGATED CLUBS

From Premier Division

1975–76 Dundee, St Johnstone
1976–77 Hearts, Kilmarnock
1977–78 Ayr U, Clydebank
1978–79 Hearts, Motherwell
1979–80 Dundee, Hibernian
1980–81 Kilmarnock, Hearts
1981–82 Partick Th. Airdrieonians
1982–83 Morton, Kilmarnock
1983–84 St Johnstone, Motherwell
1984–85 Dumbarton, Morton
1985–86 *No relegation due to League reorganisation*
1986–87 Clidebank, Hamilton Acad
1987–88 Falkirk, Dunfermline Ath, Morton
1988–89 Hamilton Acad
1989–90 Dundee

From First Division

1975–76 Dunfermline Ath, Clyde
1976–77 Raith R, Falkirk
1977–78 Alloa, E. Fife
1978–79 Montrose, Q of S
1979–80 Arbroath, Clyde
1980–81 Stirling A, Berwick R
1981–82 E. Stirling, Q of S
1982–83 Dunfermline Ath, Queen's Park
1983–84 Raith R, Alloa
1984–85 Meadowbank Th, St Johnstone
1985–86 Ayr U, Alloa
1986–87 Brechin City, Montrose
1987–88 E. Fife, Dumbarton
1988–89 Kilmarnock Q of S.
1989–90 Albion R, Alloa

Relegated from First Division to 1973–74

1921–22 *Queen's Park, Dumbarton, Clydebank
1922–23 Albion R, Alloa
1923–24 Clyde, Clydebank
1924–25 Third Lanark, Ayr U
1925–26 Raith R, Clydebank
1953–54 Airdrieonians, Hamilton Acad
1954–55 *No clubs relegated*
1955–56 Stirling A, Clyde
1956–57 Dunfermline Ath, Ayr U

1926–27 Morton, Dundee U
1927–28 Dunfermline Ath, Bo'ness
1928–29 Third Lanark, Raith R,
1929–30 St Johnstone, Dundee U
1930–31 Hibernian, E. Fife
1931–32 Dundee U, Leith Ath
1932–33 Morton, E. Stirling
1933–34 Third Lanark, Cowdenbeath
1934–35 St Mirren, Falkirk
1935–36 Airdrieonians, Ayr U
1936–37 Dunfermline Ath, Albion R
1937–38 Dundee, Morton
1938–39 Queen's Park, Raith R
1946–47 Kilmarnock, Hamilton Acad
1947–48 Airdrieonians, Queen's Park
1948–49 Morton, Albion R
1949–50 Q of S,Stirling A
1950–51 Clyde, Falkirk
1951–52 Morton, Stirling A
1952–53 Motherwell, Third Lanark
1957–58 E. Fife, Queen's Park
1958–59 Q of S, Falkirk
1959–60 Arbroath, Stirling A
1960–61 Ayr U, Clyde
1961–62 St Johnstone, Stirling A
1962–63 Clyde, Raith R
1963–64 Q of S, E. Stirling
1964–65 Airdrieonians, Third Lanark
1965–66 Morton, Hamilton Acad
1966–67 St Mirren, Ayr U
1967–68 Motherwell, Stirling A
1968–69 Falkirk, Arbroath
1969–70 Raith R, Partick Th
1970–71 St Mirren, Cowdenbeath
1971–72 Clyde, Dunfermline Ath
1972–73 Kilmarnock, Airdrieonians
1973–74 E. Fife, Falkirk
1974–75 *League reorganised at end of season*

*Season 1921–22 – only 1 club promoted, 3 clubs relegated.

SKOL (SCOTTISH LEAGUE) CUP 1989–90

First Round
Dumbarton 3, Stenhousemuir 0
Arbroath 1, East Stirling 0
Cowdenbeath 0, Montrose 4*
East Fife 2, Queen's Park 2*
Stirling Albion 0, Berwick R 3
Stranraer 3, Brechin C 4*

Second Round
Airdrieonians 4, Forfar Ath 0
Ayr U 0, Hamilton A 1
Berwick R 0, St Mirren 2
Dumbarton 0, Celtic 3
Dundee 5, Clyde 1
Dunfermline Ath 3, Raith R 0
Hibernian 2, Alloa 0
Kilmarnock 1, Motherwell 4
Queen's Park 0, Morton 1
Rangers 4, Arbroath 0
Albion R 0, Aberdeen 2
Brechin C 0, Falkirk 3
Clydebank 3, Meadowbank T 1
Dundee U 1, Partick T 0
Hearts 3, Montrose 0
Queen of the S 1, St Johnstone 0

Third Round
Celtic 2, Queen of the S 0
Hibernian 0, Clydebank 0*
Hibernian won 5-3 on penalties
Aberdeen 4, Airdrieonians 0
Dunfermline Ath 1, Dundee 0
Falkirk 1, Hearts 4
Hamilton A 2, Dundee U 1
Morton 1, Rangers 2
St Mirren 1, Motherwell 0

Quarter-finals
Hibernian 1, Dunfermline Ath 3*
Aberdeen 3, St Mirren 1
Hamilton A 0, Rangers 3
Hearts 2, Celtic 2*
Celtic won 3-1 on penalties

Semi-finals – at Hampden Park
Rangers 5, Dunfermline Ath 0
Aberdeen 1, Celtic 0

Final - at Hampden Park, 22 October, att. 61,190
Aberdeen (1) 2 (*Mason* 2), Rangers (1) 1 (*Walters (pen.)*)*

* *After extra time*

PAST SCOTTISH LEAGUE CUP FINALS

Season	Team	Score	Team	Score
1946–47	Rangers	4	Aberdeen	0
1947–48	East Fife	0 4	Falkirk	0 1
1948–49	Rangers	2	Raith Rovers	0
1949–50	East Fife	3	Dunfermine	0
1950–51	Motherwell	3	Hibernian	0
1951–52	Dundee	3	Rangers	2
1952–53	Dundee	2	Kilmarnock	0
1953–54	East Fife	3	Partick Thistle	2
1954–55	Hearts	4	Motherwell	2
1955–56	Aberdeen	2	St Mirren	1
1956–57	Celtic	0 3	Partick Thistle	0 0
1957–58	Celtic	7	Rangers	1
1958–59	Hearts	5	Partick Rangers	1
1959–60	Hearts	2	Third Lanark	1
1960–61	Rangers	2	Kilmarnock	0
1961–62	Rangers	1 3	Hearts	1 1
1962–63	Hearts	1	Kilmarnock	0
1963–64	Rangers	5	Morton	0
1964–65	Rangers	2	Celtic	1
1965–66	Celtic	2	Rangers	1
1966–67	Celtic	1	Rangers	0
1967–68	Celtic	5	Dundee	3
1968–69	Celtic	6	Hibernian	2
1969–70	Celtic	1	St Johnstone	0
1970–71	Rangers	1	Celtic	0
1971–72	Partick Thistle	4	Celtic	1
1972–73	Hibernian	2	Celtic	1
1973–74	Dundee	1	Celtic	0
1974–75	Celtic	6	Hibernian	3
1975–76	Rangers	1	Celtic	0
1976–77	Aberdeen	2	Celtic	1
1977–78	Rangers	2	Celtic	1
1978–79	Rangers	2	Aberdeen	1
1979–80	Aberdeen	0 0	Dundee U.	0 3
1980–81	Dundee	0	Dundee U.	3
1981–82	Rangers	2	Dundee U.	1
1982–83	Celtic	2	Rangers	1
1983–84	Rangers	3	Celtic	2
1984–85	Rangers	1	Dundee U	0
1985–86	Aberdeen	3	Hibernian	0
1986–87	Rangers	2	Celtic	1
1987–88	Rangers	3	Aberdeen	3
1988–89	Aberdeen	2	Rangers	3

**After extra time* †*Won on penalties*

SCOTTISH CUP 1989–90

First Round

Berwick R (*at Stenhousemuir*)	1	Stenhousemuir	1
Replay: Stenhousemuir	1	Berwick R	0
Brechin C	3	Montrose	1
Elgin City	2	Arbroath	1
Queen of the S	2	Cove Rangers	1
Queen's Park	1	Dumbarton	2
Stirling Albion (*at Alloa*)	4	Coldstream	0

Second Round

Dumbarton	0	Cowdenbeath	2
Elgin City	2	Brechin C	2
Replay: Brechin C	8	Elgin C	0
Gala Fairydean	2	Inverness Caledonian	2
Replay: Inverness Caledonian	4	Gala Fairydean	1
Stenhousemuir	0	Queen of the S	1
Stirling Albion (*at E. Stirling*)	3	Whitehill Welfare	0
Stranraer	1	Kilmarnock	1
Replay: Kilmarnock	0	Stranraer	0
(After extra time Stranraer won 4-3 on penalties)			
Vale of Leithen	1	East Stirling	3
Ross County	1	East Fife	4

Third Round

Airdrieonians	2	Inverness Caledonian	2
Replay: Inverness Caledonian	1	Airdrieonians	1
(After extra time Inverness Caledonian won 5-4 on penalties)			
Albion R	0	Clydebank	2
Ayr U	0	St Mirren	0
Replay: St Mirren	2	Ayr U	1
Brechin C	0	Hibernian	2
Cowdenbeath	3	Stranraer	1
Dundee	0	Dundee U	0
Replay: Dundee U	1	Dundee	0
Dunfermline Ath	0	Hamilton A	0
Replay: Hamilton A	0	Dunfermline Ath	1
East Fife	3	Meadowbank T	1
Forfar Ath	1	Celtic	2
Hearts	2	Falkirk	0
Morton	2	Raith R	2
Replay: Raith R	1	Morton	3
Motherwell	7	Clyde	0
Partick T	2	Aberdeen	6
Queen of the S	0	Alloa	0
Replay: Alloa	2	Queen of the S	3
Rangers	3	St Johnstone	0
East Stirling	0	Stirling Albion	1

Fourth Round

Aberdeen	2	Morton	1
Hearts	4	Motherwell	0

Hibernian	5	East Fife	1
Celtic	1	Rangers	0
Dundee U	2	Queen of the S	1
Cowdenbeath	1	Dunfermline Ath	2
St Mirren	1	Clydebank	1
Replay: Clydebank	3	St Mirren	2
Stirling Albion (*at Falkirk*)	6	Inverness Caledonian	2

Fifth Round

Aberdeen	4	Hearts	1
Clydebank	1	Stirling Albion	1
Replay: Stirling Alb	0	Clydebank	1
Dundee U	1	Hibernian	0
Dunfermline Ath	0	Celtic	0
Replay: Celtic	3	Dunfermline Ath	0

Semi-finals

Celtic	2	Clydebank	0
Aberdeen	4	Dundee U	0

FINAL at Hampden Park, 12 May 1990, att. 60,493
Aberdeen (0) 0 Celtic (0) 0
(After extra time; Aberdeen won 9-8 on penalties)

SCOTTISH CUP PAST FINALS

1874	Queen's Park	2	Clydesdale	0
1875	Queen's Park	3	Renton	0
1876	Queen's Park	1 2	Third Lanark	1 0
1877	Vale of Leven	0 1 3	Rangers	0 1 2
1878	Vale of Leven	1	Third Lanark	0
1879	Vale of Leven	1	Rangers	1
	Vale of Leven awarded cup, Rangers did not appear for replay			
1880	Queen's Park	3	Thornlibank	0
1881	Queen's Park	2 3	Dumbarton	1 1
	Replayed because of protest			
1882	Queen's Park	2 4	Dumbarton	2 1
1883	Dumbarton	2 2	Vale of Leven	2 1
1884	*Queen's Park awarded cup when Vale of Leven did not appear for the final*			
1885	Renton	0 3	Vale of Leven	0 1
1886	Queen's Park	3	Renton	1
1887	Hibernian	2	Dumbarton	1
1888	Renton	6	Cambuslang	1
1889	Third Lanark	3 2	Celtic	0 1
	Replayed because of protest			
1890	Queen's Park	1 2	Vale of Leven	1 1
1891	Hearts	1	Dumbarton	0
1892	Celtic	1 5	Queen's Park	0 1
	Replayed because of protest			

1893	Queen's Park	2	Celtic	1
1894	Rangers	3	Celtic	1
1895	St Bernards	2	Renton	1
1896	Hearts	3	Hibernian	1
1897	Rangers	5	Dumbarton	1
1898	Rangers	2	Kilmarnock	0
1899	Celtic	2	Rangers	0
1900	Celtic	4	Queen's Park	3
1901	Hearts	4	Celtic	3
1902	Hibernian	1	Celtic	0
1903	Rangers	1 0 2	Hearts	1 0 0
1904	Celtic	3	Rangers	2
1905	Third Lanark	0 3	Rangers	0 1
1906	Hearts	1	Third Lanark	0
1907	Celtic	3	Hearts	0
1908	Celtic	5	St Mirren	1
1909	*After two drawn games between Celtic and Rangers, 2–2, 1–1, there was a riot and the cup was withheld*			
1910	Dundee	2 0 2	Clyde	2 0 1
1911	Celtic	0 2	Hamilton	0 0
1912	Celtic	2	Clyde	0
1913	Falkirk	2	Raith Rovers	0
1914	Celtic	0 4	Hibernian	0 1
1920	Kilmarnock	3	Albion Rovers	2
1921	Partick Th	1	Rangers	0
1922	Morton	1	Rangers	0
1923	Celtic	1	Hibernian	0
1924	Airdrieonians	2	Hibernian	0
1925	Celtic	2	Dundee	1
1926	St Mirren	2	Celtic	0
1927	Celtic	3	East Fife	1
1928	Rangers	4	Celtic	0
1929	Kilmarnock	2	Rangers	0
1930	Rangers	0 2	Partick Th	0 1
1931	Celtic	2 4	Motherwell	2 2
1932	Rangers	1 3	Kilmarnock	1 0
1933	Celtic	1	Motherwell	0
1934	Rangers	5	St Mirren	0
1935	Rangers	2	Hamilton Acad	1
1936	Rangers	1	Third Lanark	0
1937	Celtic	2	Aberdeen	1
1938	East Fife	1 4	Kilmarnock	1 2
1939	Clyde	4	Motherwell	0
1947	Aberdeen	2	Hibernian	1
1948	Rangers	1 1	Morton	1 0
1949	Rangers	4	Clyde	1
1950	Rangers	3	East Fife	0
1951	Celtic	1	Motherwell	0
1952	Motherwell	4	Dundee	0
1953	Rangers	1 1	Aberdeen	1 0
1954	Celtic	2	Aberdeen	1
1955	Clyde	1 1	Celtic	1 0
1956	Hearts	3	Celtic	1
1957	Falkirk	1 2	Kilmarnock	1 1
1958	Clyde	1	Hibernian	0
1959	St Mirren	3	Aberdeen	1
1960	Rangers	2	Kilmarnock	0

1961	Dunfermline Ath	0 2	Celtic	0 0
1962	Rangers	2	St Mirren	0
1963	Rangers	1 3	Celtic	1 0
1964	Rangers	3	Dundee	1
1965	Celtic	3	Dunfermline Ath	2
1966	Rangers	0 1	Celtic	0 0
1967	Celtic	2	Aberdeen	0
1968	Dunfermline Ath	3	Hearts	1
1969	Celtic	4	Rangers	0
1970	Aberdeen	3	Celtic	1
1971	Celtic	1 2	Rangers	1 1
1972	Celtic	6	Hibernian	1
1973	Rangers	3	Celtic	2
1974	Celtic	3	Dundee U	0
1975	Celtic	3	Airdrieonians	1
1976	Rangers	3	Hearts	1
1977	Celtic	1	Rangers	0
1978	Rangers	2	Aberdeen	1
1979	Rangers	0 0 3	Hibernian	0 0 2
1980	Celtic	1	Rangers	0
1981	Rangers	0 4	Dundee U	0 1
1982	Aberdeen	4	Rangers	1
1983	Aberdeen	1	Rangers	0
1984	Aberdeen	2	Celtic	1
1985	Celtic	2	Dundee U	1
1986	Aberdeen	3	Hearts	0
1987	St Mirren	1	Dundee U	0
1988	Celtic	2	Dundee U	1
1989	Celtic	1	Rangers	0

IRISH LEAGUE

	P	W	D	L	F	A	Pts
Portadown	26	18	7	3	42	17	55
Glenavon	26	16	6	4	52	26	54
Glentoran	26	12	8	6	43	24	44
Linfield	26	14	2	10	54	40	44
Ballymena United	26	12	7	7	37	25	43
Bangor	26	11	5	10	26	22	28
Newry Town	26	11	4	11	42	37	37
Cliftonville	26	9	8	9	36	39	35
Larne	26	8	7	11	29	38	31
Carrick Rangers	26	8	6	12	33	36	30
Coleraine	26	8	6	12	36	44	30
Ards	26	5	6	15	25	43	21
Crusaders	26	4	8	14	27	55	20
Distillery	26	4	8	14	27	53	20

Irish Cup Final at Windsor Park, Belfast, 5 May, 1990, att. 12,000
Glentoran 3 *(Neill, Douglas, Morrison)*, Portadown 0

REPUBLIC OF IRELAND

	P	W	D	L	F	A	Pts
St. Patrick's	33	22	8	3	51	22	52
Derry City	33	20	9	4	72	18	49
Dundalk	33	17	8	8	50	26	42
Shamrock R	33	16	8	9	45	37	40
Cork City	33	14	7	12	35	24	35
Bohemians	33	14	7	12	35	32	35
Shelbourne	33	10	13	10	39	39	33
Galway Utd	33	10	9	14	39	61	29
Limerick City	33	7	8	18	28	50	22
Athlone Town	33	5	12	16	28	53	22
Drogheda Utd	33	5	8	20	20	44	18
UCD	33	6	5	22	25	61	17

Cup Final: Bray Wanderers 3, St Francis 0

ABACUS WELSH LEAGUE

National Division

	P	W	D	L	F	A	Pts
Haverfordwest County	30	19	5	6	70	25	62
Aberystwyth Town	30	18	7	5	69	31	61
Abergavenny Thur.	30	18	7	5	66	34	61
Cwmbran Town	30	19	3	8	55	33	60
Llanelli	30	16	6	8	61	38	54
Briton Ferry Athletic	30	16	6	8	58	43	54
AFC Cardiff	30	14	6	10	44	40	48
Pembroke Borough	30	13	7	10	46	38	46
Ton Pentre	30	11	6	13	44	54	39
Bridgend Town	30	9	8	13	38	49	35
Port Talbot Athletic	30	7	11	12	41	46	32
Brecon Corinthians	30	8	7	15	37	50	31
Maesteg Park Athletic	30	6	9	15	31	36	27
Ammanford Town	30	7	6	17	32	54	27
Pontllanfraith	30	3	7	20	33	73	16
Ebbw Vale	30	4	3	23	26	104	15

Premier Division

	P	W	D	L	F	A	Pts
Sully	34	24	6	4	120	38	78
Ferndale	34	22	7	5	73	34	73
Afan Lido	34	20	6	8	78	43	66
Milford United	34	19	6	9	73	38	63
Ynysybwl	34	18	5	11	67	56	59
Llanwern	34	17	5	12	62	51	56
Clydach United	34	15	8	11	63	60	53
Blaenrhondda	34	14	10	10	63	55	52
Seven Sisters	34	12	8	14	62	74	44
BP Llandarcy	34	12	7	15	48	59	43
Panteg	34	12	5	17	60	76	41
Garw	34	10	7	17	49	66	37
Morriston Town	34	10	7	17	56	81	37
Cardiff Corinthians	34	10	7	17	47	72	37
Newport YMCA	34	9	9	16	42	66	36
Caerleon	34	9	6	19	46	63	33
Tonyrefail Welfare	34	6	9	19	40	75	27
Trelewis	34	4	8	22	43	85	20

Division One

	P	W	D	L	F	A	Pts
Caldicot Town	32	20	5	7	66	32	65
Methyr Tydfil	32	21	1	10	118	50	64
Aberaman	32	18	9	5	87	43	63
Blaenavon Blues	32	20	2	10	83	49	62
Taffs Well	32	18	5	9	63	45	59
Carmarthen Town	32	16	3	13	69	56	51
South Wales Police	32	12	13	7	48	32	49
Treharris Athletic	32	15	4	13	65	41	49
Skewen Athletic	32	12	9	11	48	47	45
Pontlottyn	32	12	6	14	54	62	42
Caerau	32	11	5	16	39	74	38
Pontardawe	32	9	9	14	47	67	36
Pontyclun	32	8	10	14	57	65	34
SGIHE	32	9	6	17	40	63	33
Tondu Robins	32	9	5	18	57	68	32
Abercynon Athletic	32	7	8	17	48	90	29
Blaine West Side	32	3	4	25	28	122	13

Clydach United have withdrawn from the league for the season 1990–91. Blaina West Side failed to gain re-election. They will be replaced by Risca United and Cardiff Civil Service. AFC Cardiff and Sully have merged to form a new club – Inter Cardiff – which will play in the top division in season 1990–91. The three divisions will be retitled divisons 1, 2 and 3 in season 1990–91.

EUROPEAN CUP 1989–90

First Round, First Leg

Derry	(0) 1	Benfica	(0) 2
Dynamo Dresden	(0) 1	AEK Athens	(0) 0
Honved	(0) 1	Vojvodina	(0) 0
Linfield	(0) 1	Dnepr	(1) 2
Malmo	(0) 1	Internazionale	(0) 0
Marseille	(0) 3	Brondby	(0) 0
AC Milan	(2) 4	HJK Helsinki	(0) 0
PSV Eindhoven	(3) 3	Lucerne	(0) 0
Rangers	(1) 1	Bayern Munich	(1) 3
Rosenborg	(0) 0	Mechelen	(0) 0
Ruch Chorzow	(1) 1	CSKA Sofia	(1) 1
Sliema Wanderers	(0) 1	17 Nentori	(0) 0
Sparta Prague	(0) 3	Fenerbahce	(1) 1
Spora	(0) 0	Real Madrid	(1) 3
Steaua	(2) 4	Fram	(0) 0
Tirol	(2) 6	Omonia	(0) 0

First Round, Second Leg

AEK Athens	(3) 5	Dynamo Dresden	(1) 3
Bayern Munich	(0) 0	Rangers	(0) 0
Benfica	(1) 4	Derry	(0) 0
Brondby	(0) 1	Marseille	(0) 1
CSKA Sofia	(2) 5	Ruch Chorzow	(0) 1
Dnepr	(1) 1	Linfield	(0) 0
Fenerbahce	(0) 1	Sparta Prague	(1) 2
Fram	(0) 0	Steaua	(0) 1
HJK Helsinki	(0) 0	AC Milan	(1) 1
Internazionale	(0) 1	Malmo	(0) 1
Lucerne	(0) 0	PSV Eindhoven	(2) 2
Mechelen	(1) 5	Rosenborg	(0) 0
17 Nentori	(3) 5	Sliema Wanderers	(0) 0
Omonia	(1) 2	Tirol	(0) 3
Real Madrid	(3) 6	Spora	(0) 0
Vojvodina	(1) 2	Honved	(0) 1

Second Round, First Leg

Bayern Munich	(2) 3	17 Nentori	(1) 1
Dnepr	(1) 2	Tirol	(0) 0
Honved	(0) 0	Benfica	(1) 2
Malmo	(0) 0	Mechelen	(0) 0
Marseille	(0) 2	AEK Athens	(0) 0
AC Milan	(2) 2	Real Madrid	(0) 0
Sparta Prague	(0) 2	CSKA Sofia	(1) 2
Steaua	(1) 1	PSV Eindhoven	(0) 0

Second Round, Second Leg

AEK Athens	(0) 1	Marseille	(0) 1
Benfica	(3) 7	Honved	(0) 0
CSKA Sofia	(1) 3	Sparta Prague	(0) 0
Mechelen	(2) 4	Malmo	(0) 1
17 Nentori	(0) 0	Bayern Munich	(1) 3
PSV Eindhoven	(1) 5	Steaua	(1) 1

Real Madrid	(1) 1	AC Milan	(0) 0
Tirol	(1) 2	Dnepr	(1) 2

Quarter-Finals, First Leg

Bayern Munich	(0) 2	PSV Eindhoven	(0) 1
Benfica	(1) 1	Dnepr	(0) 0
CSKA Sofia	(0) 0	Marseille	(0) 1
Mechelen	(0) 0	AC Milan	(0) 0

Quarter-Finals, Second Leg

AC Milan	(0) 2	Mechelen	*aet* (0) 0
PSV Eindhoven	(0) 0	Bayern Munich	(0) 1
Marseille	(2) 3	CSKA Sofia	(0) 1
Dnepr	(0) 0	Benfica	(0) 3

Semi-Finals, First Leg

Marseille	(2) 2	Benfica	(1) 1
AC Milan	(0) 1	Bayern Munich	(0) 0

Semi-Finals, Second Leg

Bayern Munich	(0) 2	AC Milan	*aet* (0) 1
Benfica	(0) 1	Marseille	(0) 0

Final at Vienna, 23 May 1990, att. 57,500
AC Milan (0) 1, Benfica (0) 0

AC Milan: Galli G; Tassotti, Costacurta, Baresi, Maldini, Colombo (Galli F 89), Rijkaard, Ancelotti (Massaro 72), Evani, Gullit, Van Basten. *Scorer:* Rijkaard 68.

Benfica: Silvino; Jose Carlos, Aldair, Ricardo, Samuel, Vitor Paneira (Vata 76), Valdo, Thern, Hernani, Magnusson, Paceco (Brito 66).

Referee: Kohl (Austria).

EUROPEAN CUP-WINNERS' CUP 1989–90

Preliminary Round, First Leg

Chernomoretz	(1) 3	Dinamo Tirana	(0) 1

Preliminary Round, Second Leg

Dinamo Tirana	(0) 4	Chernomoretz	(0) 0

First Round, First Leg

Belenenses	(0) 1	Monaco	(0) 1
Ferencvaros	(3) 5	Valkeakosken Haka	(1) 1
Partizan	(1) 2	Celtic	(1) 1
Slovan Bratislava	(1) 3	Grasshoppers	(0) 0
Union Luxembourg	(0) 0	Djurgaarden	(0) 0
Valladolid	(2) 5	Hamrun Spartans	(0) 0
Anderlecht	(3) 6	Ballymena	(0) 0

Admira Wacker	(0) 3	AEL Limassol	(0) 0
Barcelona	(0) 1	Legia Warsaw	(1) 1
Besiktas	(0) 0	Borussia Dortmund	(1) 1
Brann Bergen	(0) 0	Sampdoria	(1) 2
Dinamo Tirana	(0) 1	Dinamo Bucharest	(0) 0
Groningen	(0) 1	Ikast	(0) 0
Panathinaikos	(1) 3	Swansea C	(0) 2
Torpedo Moscow	(4) 5	Cork C	(0) 0
Valur	(1) 1	Dynamo Berlin	(0) 2

First Round, Second Leg

Dinamo Bucharest	(2) 2	Dinamo Tirana	(0) 0
Grasshoppers	(1) 4	Slovan Bratislava	(0) 0
Monaco	(3) 3	Belenenses	(0) 0
Hamrun Spartans	(0) 0	Valladolid	(1) 1
AEL Limassol	(1) 1	Admira Wacker	(0) 0
Ballymena	(0) 0	Anderlecht	(1) 4
Borussia Dortmund	(1) 2	Besiktas	(0) 1
Celtic	(1) 5	Partizan	(1) 4
Cork C	(0) 0	Torpedo Moscow	(1) 1
Djurgaarden	(0) 5	Union Luxembourg	(0) 0
Dynamo Berlin	(1) 2	Valur	(0) 1
Valkeakosken Haka	(0) 1	Ferencvaros	(0) 1
Ikast	(0) 1	Groningen	(1) 2
Legia Warsaw	(0) 0	Barcelona	(1) 1
Sampdoria	(0) 1	Bran Bergen	(0) 0
Swansea C	(1) 3	Panathinaikos	(0) 3

Second Round, First Leg

Borussia Dortmund	(0) 1	Sampdoria	(0) 1
Monaco	(0) 0	Dynamo Berlin	(0) 0
Admira Wacker	(0) 1	Ferencvaros	(0) 0
Anderlecht	(1) 2	Barcelona	(0) 0
Groningen	(2) 4	Partizan	(2) 3
Panathinaikos	(0) 0	Dinamo Bucharest	(0) 2
Torpedo Moscow	(1) 1	Grasshoppers	(0) 1
Valladolid	(2) 2	Djurgaarden	(0) 0

Second Round, Second Leg

Barcelona	(0) 2	Anderlecht	(0) 1
Dinamo Bucharest	(3) 6	Panathinaikos	(1) 1
Djurgaarden	(1) 2	Valladolid	(0) 2
Dynamo Berlin	(0) 1	Monaco	(0) 1
Ferencvaros	(0) 0	Admira Wacker	(0) 1
Grasshoppers	(2) 3	Torpedo Moscow	(0) 0
Partizan	(1) 3	Groningen	(0) 1
Sampdoria	(0) 2	Borussia Dortmund	(0) 0

Quarter-Finals, First Leg

Dinamo Bucharest	(1) 2	Partizan	(0) 1
Sampdoria	(1) 2	Grasshoppers	(0) 0
Valladolid	(0) 0	Monaco	(0) 0
Anderlecht	(1) 2	Admira Wacker	(0) 0

Quarter-Finals, Second Leg

Grasshoppers	(0) 1	Sampdoria	(1) 2
Partizan	(0) 0	Dinamo Bucharest	(0) 2

Admira Wacker	(0) 1	Anderlecht	(0) 1
Monaco	(0) 0	Valladolid	(0) 0

Monaco won 3-1 on penalties aet

Semi-Finals, First Leg

Anderlecht	(0) 1	Dinamo Bucharest	(0) 0
Monaco	(1) 2	Sampdoria	(0) 2

Semi-Finals, Second Leg

Dinamo Bucharest	(0) 0	Anderlecht	(0) 1
Sampdoria	(0) 2	Monaco	(0) 0

Final at Gothenburg, 9 May 1990, att 20,103
Sampdoria (0) 2, Anderlecht (0) 0 *aet*

Sampdoria: Pagliuca; Pellegrini, Mannini, Vierchowod, Carboni, Pari, Katanec (Salsano 93), Invernizzi (Lombardo 53), Dossena, Vialli, Mancini. *Scorer:* Vialli 105, 107.

Anderlecht: De Wilde; Grun, Marchoul, Keshi, Kooiman, Vervoort, Musonda, Gudjohnsen, Jankovic (Oliveira 112), Degryse (Nilis 103), Van der Linden.

Referee: Galler (Switzerland).

UEFA CUP 1989–90

Preliminary Round, First Leg

Auxerre	(0) 0	Dinamo Zagreb	(0) 1

Preliminary Round, Second Leg

Dinamo Zagreb	(0) 1	Auxerre	(2) 3

First Round, First Leg

Akranes	(0) 0	Liege	(1) 2
Gornik Zabrze	(0) 0	Juventus	(0) 1
Hibernian	(1) 1	Videoton	(0) 0
Sochaux	(3) 7	Jeunesse Esch	(0) 0
Valletta	(0) 1	Vienna	(2) 4
Vitosha	(0) 0	Antwerp	(0) 0
Aberdeen	(0) 2	Rapid Vienna	(1) 1
Atalanta	(0) 0	Spartak Moscow	(0) 0
Atletico Madrid	(0) 1	Fiorentina	(0) 0
Auxerre	(1) 5	Apolonia	(0) 0
Glentoran	(0) 1	Dundee U	(1) 3
Hansa Rostock	(2) 2	Banik Ostrava	(0) 3
Iraklis	(1) 1	Sion	(0) 0
Karl-Marx-Stadt	(1) 1	Boavista	(0) 0
Kiev Dynamo	(3) 4	MTK Budapest	(0) 0
Cologne	(1) 4	Plastika Nitra	(1) 1
Kuusysi Lahti	(0) 0	Paris St Germain	(0) 0
Lillestrom	(0) 1	Werder Bremen	(2) 3
Orgryte	(0) 1	Hamburg	(1) 2
Porto	(1) 2	Flacari Moreni	(0) 0
Rad Belgrade	(1) 2	Olympiakos	(0) 1
RoPs Rovaniemi	(1) 1	Katowice	(1) 1

Stuttgart	(1) 2	Feyenoord	(0) 0
Twente	(0) 0	FC Brugge	(0) 0
Valencia	(0) 3	Victoria Bucharest	(1) 1
Wettingen	(2) 3	Dundalk	(0) 0
Zenit Leningrad	(1) 3	Naestved	(0) 1
Zhalgiris Vilnius	(1) 2	IFK Gothenburg	(0) 0
Apollon Limassol	(0) 0	Zaragoza	(1) 3
FK Austria	(1) 1	Ajax	(0) 0
Galatasaray	(1) 1	Red Star Belgrade	(1) 1
Sporting Lisbon	(0) 0	Napoli	(0) 0

First Round, Second Leg

Antwerp	(0) 4	Vitosha	(1) 3
Jeunesse Esch	(0) 0	Sochaux	(4) 5
Videoton	(0) 0	Hibernian	(1) 3
Vienna	(1) 3	Valletta	(0) 0
Zaragoza	(1) 1	Apollon Limassol	(0) 1
Olympiakos	(1) 2	Rad Belgrade	(0) 0
Ajax	(1) 1	FK Austria	(0) 1

(*aet; match abandoned 104 minutes after missiles thrown at Austrian goalkeeper*.

Apolonia	(0) 0	Auxerre	(2) 3
Banik Ostrava	(2) 4	Hansa Rostock	(0) 0
Boavista	(1) 2	Karl-Marx-Stadt	(0) 2
FC Brugge	(4) 4	Twente	(1) 1
Dundalk	(0) 0	Wettingen	(1) 2
Dundee U	(1) 2	Glentoran	(0) 0
Feyenoord	(1) 2	Stuttgart	(0) 1
Fiorentina	(1) 1	Atletico Madrid	(0) 0
Flacara Moreni	(0) 1	Porto	(1) 2
Katowice	(0) 0	RoPs Rovaniemi	(0) 1
Hamburg	(2) 5	Orgryte	(0) 1
IFK Gothenburg	(0) 1	Zhalgiris Vilnius	(0) 0
Juventus	(4) 4	Gornik Zabrze	(1) 2
Liege	(3) 4	Akranes	(1) 1
MTK Budapest	(0) 1	Kiev Dynamo	(1) 2
Naestved	(0) 0	Zenit Leningrad	(0) 0
Napoli	(0) 0	Sporting Lisbon	(0) 0
Paris St Germain	(1) 3	Kuusysi Lahti	(1) 2
Plastika Nitra	(0) 0	Cologne	(1) 1
Rapid Vienna	(1) 1	Aberdeen	(0) 0
Red Star Belgrade	(1) 2	Galatasaray	(0) 0
Sion	(0) 2	Iraklis	(0) 0
Spartak Moscow	(1) 2	Atalanta	(0) 0
Victoria Bucharest	(0) 1	Valencia	(1) 1
Werder Bremen	(0) 2	Lillestrom	(0) 0

Second Round, First Leg

Antwerp	(3) 4	Dundee U	(0) 0
Vienna	(1) 2	Olympiakos	(1) 2
FC Brugge	(1) 1	Rapid Vienna	(0) 2
Fiorentina	(0) 0	Sochaux	(0) 0
Hibernian	(0) 0	Liege	(0) 0
Kiev Dynamo	(1) 3	Banik Ostrava	(0) 0
Cologne	(2) 3	Spartak Moscow	(1) 1
Paris St Germain	(0) 0	Juventus	(0) 1
Porto	(1) 3	Valencia	(0) 1
Red Star Belgrade	(3) 4	Zhalgiris Vilnius	(0) 1

RoPs Rovaniemi	(0) 0	Auxerre	(1) 5
Sion	(0) 2	Karl-Marx-Stadt	(1) 1
Werder Bremen	(2) 5	FK Austria	(0) 0
Wettingen	(0) 0	Napoli	(0) 0
Zaragoza	(0) 1	Hamburg	(0) 0
Zenit Leningrad	(0) 0	Stuttgart	(0) 1

Second Round, Second Leg

Auxerre	(1) 3	RoPs Rovaniemi	(0) 0
Dundee U	(1) 3	Antwerp	(2) 2
FK Austria	(1) 2	Werder Bremen	(0) 0
Hamburg	(0) 2	Zaragoza	(0) 0
Liege	(0) 1	Hibernian	(0) 0
Banik Ostrava	(1) 1	Kiev Dynamo	(1) 1
Juventus	(1) 2	Paris St Germain	(1) 1
Karl-Marx-Stadt	(3) 4	Sion	(0) 1
Napoli	(0) 2	Wettingen	(1) 1
Rapid Vienna	(0) 4	FC Brugge	(1) 3
Sochaux	(1) 1	Fiorentina	(1) 1
Spartak Moscow	(0) 0	Cologne	(0) 0
Stuttgart	(4) 5	Zenit Leningrad	(0) 0
Valencia	(1) 3	Porto	(1) 2
Zhalgiris Vilnius	(0) 0	Red Star Belgrade	(0) 1
Olympiakos	(0) 1	Vienna	(0) 1

Third Round, First Leg

Antwerp	(1) 1	Stuttgart	(0) 0
Fiorentina	(0) 1	Kiev Dynamo	(0) 0
Hamburg	(0) 1	Porto	(0) 0
Juventus	(0) 2	Karl-Marx-Stadt	(0) 1
Napoli	(0) 2	Werder Bremen	(1) 3
Olympiakos	(1) 1	Auxerre	(1) 1
Rapid Vienna	(0) 1	Liege	(0) 0
Red Star Belgrade	(0) 2	Cologne	(0) 0

Third Round, Second Leg

Stuttgart	(0) 1	Antwerp	(0) 1
Auxerre	(0) 0	Olympiakos	(0) 0
Karl-Marx-Stadt	(0) 0	Juventus	(1) 1
Kiev Dynamo	(0) 0	Fiorentina	(0) 0
Cologne	(0) 3	Red Star Belgrade	(0) 0
Liege	(3) 3	Rapid Vienna	(0) 1
Porto	(1) 2	Hamburg	(1) 1
Werder Bremen	(1) 5	Napoli	(0) 1

Quarter-Finals, First Leg

Cologne	(1) 2	Antwerp	(0) 0
Fiorentina	(1) 1	Auxerre	(0) 0
Liege	(1) 1	Werder Bremen	(3) 4
Hamburg	(0) 0	Juventus	(0) 2

Quarter-Finals, Second Leg

Auxerre	(0) 0	Fiorentina	(0) 1
Juventus	(1) 1	Hamburg	(0) 2
Werder Bremen	(0) 0	Liege	(1) 2
Antwerp	(0) 0	Cologne	(0) 0

Semi-Finals, First Leg

Werder Bremen	(0) 1	Fiorentina	(0) 1
Juventus	(3) 3	Cologne	(0) 2

Semi-Finals, Second Leg

Fiorentina	(0) 0	Werder Bremen	(0) 0
Cologne	(0) 0	Juventus	(0) 0

Final First Leg, 2 May at Turin, att. 45,000
Juventus (1) 3, Fiorentina (1) 1

Juventus: Tacconi; Napoli, De Agostini, Galia, Brio (Alessio 46), Bonetti, Aleinikov, Rui Barros, Casiraghi, Marocchi, Schillaci. *Scorers:* Galia 3, Casiraghi 59, De Agostini 73.
Fiorentina: Landucci; Dell'Oglio, Volpecina, Dunga, Pin, Battistini, Nappi, Kubik (Malusci 87), Buso, Baggio, Di Chiara. *Scorer:* Buso 10.
Referee: Soriano (Spain).

Final Second Leg, 16 May at Avellino, att. 32,000
Fiorentina (0) 0, Juventus (0) 0

Fiorentina: Landucci; Dell'Oglio, Volpecina, Dunga, Pin, Battistini, Nappi, (Zironelli 71), Kubik, Buso, Baggio, Di Chiara.
Juventus: Tacconi; Napoli, De Agostini, Galia, Bruno, Alessio, Aleinikov, Rui Barros (Avallone 72), Casiraghi (Rosa 79), Marocchi, Schillaci.
Referee: Schmidhuber (West Germany).

EUROPEAN SUPER CUP

1972	Ajax	3 3	Glasgow Rangers	1 2
1973	Ajax	0 6	AC Milan	1 0
1974	Not contested			
1975	Dynamo Kiev	1 2	Bayern Munich	0 0
1976	Anderlecht	4 1	Bayern Munich	1 2
1977	Liverpool	1 6	SV Hamburg	1 0
1978	Anderlecht	1 3	Liverpool	1 2
1979	Nottingham Forest	1 1	Barcelona	0 1
1980	Nottingham Forest	2 0	Valencia**	1 1
1981	Not contested			
1982	Aston Villa	0 3	Barcelona	1 0
1983	SV Hamburg	0 0	Aberdeen	0 2
1984	Juventus	2	Liverpool	0
1985	Not contested due to UEFA ban on English clubs.			
1986	Steaua Bucharest	1	Dynamo Kiev	0
1987	FC Porto	1 1	Ajax	0 0
1988	Mechelen	3 0	PSV Eindhoven	0 1
1989	Barcelona	1 0	AC Milan	1 1

***Won on away goals*

UEFA CUP PAST FINALS

1972	Tottenham Hotspur	2 1	Wolverhampton W	1 1
1973	Liverpool	3 0	Borussia Moenchengladbach	0 2
1974	Feyenoord	2 2	Tottenham H	2 0
1975	Borussia Moenchengladbach	0 5	Twente Enschede	0 1
1976	Liverpool	3 1	FC Bruges	2 1
1977	Juventus**	1 1	Athletic Bilbao	0 2
1978	PSV Eindhoven	0 3	SEC Bastia	0 0
1979	Borussia Moenchengladbach	1 1	Red Star Belgrade	1 0
1980	Borussia Moenchengladbach	3 0	Eintracht Frankfurt**	2 1
1981	Ipswich T.	3 2	AZ 67 Alkmaar	0 4
1982	IFK Gothenburg	1 3	SV Hamburg	0 0
1983	RSC Anderlecht	1 1	Benfica	0 1
1984	Tottenham H †	1 1	RSC Anderlecht	1 1
1985	Real Madrid	3 0	Videoton	0 1
1986	Real Madrid	5 0	Cologne	1 2
1987	IFK Gothenburg	1 1	Dundee U	0 1
1988	Bayer Leverkusen †	0 3	Espanol	0 3
1989	Napoli	2 3	Stuttgart	1 3

**After extra time **Won on away goals †Won on penalties ††Aggregate score*

EUROPEAN CUP PAST FINALS

1956	Real Madrid	4	Stade de Rheims	3
1957	Real Madrid	2	Fiorentina	0
1958	Real Madrid	3	AC Milan	2*
1959	Real Madrid	2	Stade de Rheims	0
1960	Real Madrid	7	Eintracht Frankfurt	3
1961	SL Benfica	3	Barcelona	2
1962	SL Benfica	5	Real Madrid	3
1963	AC Milan	2	SL Benfica	1
1964	Inter Milan	3	Real Madrid	1
1965	Inter Milan	1	SL Benfica	0
1966	Real Madrid	2	Partizan Belgrade	1
1967	Celtic	2	Inter Milan	1
1968	Manchester U	4	SL Benfica	1*
1969	AC Milan	4	Ajax Amsterdam	1
1970	Feyenoord	2	Celtic	1*
1971	Ajax Amsterdam	2	Panathinaikos	0
1972	Ajax Amsterdam	2	Inter Milan	0
1973	Ajax Amsterdam	1	Juventus	0
1974	Bayern Munich	1 4	Atletico Madrid	1 0
1975	Bayern Munich	2	Leeds U	0
1976	Bayern Munich	1	St Etienne	0
1977	Liverpool	3	Borussia Moenchengladbach	1
1978	Liverpool	1	FC Bruges	0
1979	Nottingham F	1	Malmö	0
1980	Nottingham F	1	SV Hamburg	0
1981	Liverpool	1	Real Madrid	0
1982	Aston Villa	1	Bayern Munich	0
1983	SV Hamburg	1	Juventus	0
1984	Liverpool†	1	AS Roma	1
1985	Juventus	1	Liverpool	0
1986	Steaua Bucharest†	0	Barcelona	0

1987 FC Porto	2	Bayern	1
1988 PSV Eindhoven†	0	Benfica	0
1989 AC Milan	4	Steaua Bucharest	0

EUROPEAN CUP-WINNERS' CUP PAST FINALS

1961 Fiorentina	4	Rangers	1†
1962 Atletico Madrid	1 3	Fiorentina	1 0
1963 Tottenham Hotspur	5	Atletico Madrid	1
1964 Sporting Lisbon	3 1	MTK Budapest	3 0
1965 West Ham U	2	Munich 1860	0
1966 Borussia Dortmund	2	Liverpool	1*
1967 Bayern Munich	1	Rangers	0*
1968 AC Milan	2	SV Hamburg	0
1969 Slovan Bratislava	3	Barcelona	2
1970 Manchester C	2	Gornik Zabrze	1
1971 Chelsea	1 2	Real Madrid	1 1*
1972 Rangers	3	Dynamo Moscow	2
1973 AC Milan	1	Leeds U	0
1974 FC Magdeburg	2	AC Milan	0
1975 Dynamo Kiev	3	Ferencvaros	0
1976 RSC Anderlecht	4	West Ham U	2
1977 SV Hamburg	2	Anderlecht	0
1978 RSC Anderlecht	4	Austria Vienna	0
1979 Barcelona	4	Fortuna Dusseldorf	3
1980 Valencia†	0	Arsenal	0
1981 Dynamo Tbilisi	2	Carl Zeiss Jena	1
1982 Barcelona	2	Standard Liege	1
1983 Aberdeen	2	Real Madrid	1
1984 Juventus	2	FC Porto	1
1985 Everton	3	Rapid Vienna	1
1986 Dynamo Kiev	3	Atletico Madrid	0
1987 Ajax Amsterdam	1	Lokomotiv Leipzig	0
1988 Mechelen	1	Ajax Amsterdam	0
1989 Barcelona	2	Sampdoria	0

FAIRS CUP FINALS

1958 Barcelona	8	London	2††
1960 Barcelona	4	Birmingham C	1††
1961 AS Roma	4	Birmingham C	2††
1962 Valencia	7	Barcelona	3††
1963 Valencia	4	Dynamo Zagreb	1††
1964 Real Zaragoza	2	Valencia	1
1965 Ferencvaros	1	Juventus	0
1966 Barcelona	4	Real Zaragoza	3††
1967 Dynamo Zagreb	2	Leeds U	0††
1968 Leeds U	1	Ferencvaros	0††
1969 Newcastle U	6	Ujpest Dozsa	2††
1970 Arsenal	4	Anderlecht	3††
1971 Leeds U	3**	Juventus	3††

WORLD CUP 1990
FINAL TOURNAMENT IN ITALY

First Round
Group A
9 June, Rome, 72,303
Italy (0) 1 *(Schillaci 77)*
Austria (0) 0
Italy: Zenga; Maldini, Ferri, Baresi, Bergomi, De Napoli, Ancelotti (De Agostini 46), Donadoni, Giannini, Carnevale (Schillaci 74), Vialli.
Austria: Lindenberger; Russ, Streiter, Pecl, Aigner, Artner (Zsak 61), Herzog, Schottel, Linzmaier (Hortnagl 70), Ogris, Polster. Referee: Wright (Brazil).

10 June, Florence, 33,266
Czechoslovakia (2) 5 *(Skuhravy 25, 78, Bilek 39 (pen), Hasek 50, Luhovy 90).*
USA (0) 1 *(Caligiuri 61)*
Czechoslovakia: Stejskal; Hasek, Kocian, Kadlec, Straka, Moravcik (Weiss 84), Chovanec, Kubik, Bilek, Knoflicek (Luhovy 79), Skuhravy.
USA: Meola; Armstrong, Stollmeyer (Balboa 65), Windischmann, Trittschuh, Caligiuru, Ramos, Harkes, Wynalda*, Vermes, Murray (Sullivan 80).
Referee: Rothlisberger (Switzerland).

14 June, Rome, 73,423
Italy (1) 1 *(Giannini 11)*
USA (0) 0
Italy: Zenga; Bergomi, Ferri, Baresi, Maldini, De Napoli, Berti, Giannini, Donadoni, Carnevale (Schillaci 50), Vialli.
USA: Meola; Armstrong, Windischmann, Doyle, Banks (Stollmeyer 80), Ramos, Balboa,Caligiuri, Harkes,Vermes, Murray (Sullivan 82). *Referee:* Codesal (Mexico).

15 June, Florence, 38,962
Austria (0) 0
Czechoslovakia (0) 1 *(Bilek 30 (pen))*
Austria: Lindenberger; Russ (Ogris 46), Aigner, Pecl, Pfeffer, Hortnagl, Zsak, Schottel (Streiter 82), Herzog, Rodax, Polster.
Czechoslovakia: Stejskal; Hasek, Kadlec, Kocian, Nemecek, Moravcik, Chovanec (Bielik 31), Kubik, Bilek, Skuhravy, Knoflicek (Weiss 81). *Referee:* Smith (Scotland).

19 June, Rome, 73,303
Italy (1) 2 *(Schillaci 9, Baggio 77)*
Czechoslovakia (0) 0
*Italy:*Zenga; Bergomi, Ferri, Baresi, Maldini, Donadoni (De Agostini 50), De Napoli (Vierchowod 66), Giannini, Berti, Baggio, Schillaci.
Czechoslovakia: Stejskal; Hasek, Kadlec, Kinier, Nemecek (Bielik 46), Moravcik, Chovanec, Weiss (Griga 58), Bilek, Skuhravy, Knoflicek. *Referee:* Quiniou (France).

19 June, Florence, 34,857
Austria (0) 2 *(Ogris 51, Rodax 63)*
USA (0) 1 *(Murray 82)*
Austria: Lindenberger; Streiter, Aigner, Pecl, Pfeffer, Artner*, Zsak, Herzog, Rodax (Glatzmeyer 85), Polster (Reisinger 46), Ogris.
USA: Meola; Doyle, Windischmann, Banks (Wynalda 55), Armstrong, Caligiuri (Bliss 70), Harkes, Ramos, Balboa, Murray, Vermes.
Referee: Al-Sharif (Egypt).

	P	*W*	*D*	*L*	*F*	*A*	*Pts*
Italy	3	3	0	0	4	0	6
Czechoslovakia	3	2	0	1	6	3	4
Austria	3	1	0	2	2	3	2
USA	3	0	0	3	2	8	0

Group B

8 June, Milan 73,780

Argentina (0) 0

Cameroon (0) 1 *(Omam-Biyik 65)*

Argentina: Pumpido; Ruggeri (Caniggia 46), Fabbri, Simon, Lorenzo, Batista, Sensini (Calderon 69), Balbo, Basualdo, Burruchaga, Maradona.
Cameroon: Nkono; Tataw, Ebwelle, Massing*, Ndip, Kunde, Mbouh, Kana-Biyik*, Mfede (Libih 65), Makanaky (Milla 82), Omam-Biyik.
Referee: Vautrot (France)

9 June, Bari, 42,960

USSR (0) 0

Rumania (1) 2 *(Lacatus 40, 54 (pen))*

USSR: Dasayev; Kuznetsov, Khidiatulin, Gorlukovich, Rats, Aleinikov, Bessonov, Litovchenko (Yaremchuk 65), Zavarov, Protasov, Dobrovolski (Borodyuk 71).
Rumania: Lung; Rednic, Andone, Poescu, Klein, Rotariu, Timofte, Sabau, Lupescu, Lacatus (Dumitrescu 86), Raducioiu (Balint 79).
Referee: Cardellino (Uruguay).

13 June, Naples, 55,759

Argentina (1) 2 *(Troglio 27, Burruchaga 79)*

USSR (0) 0

Argentina: Pumpido (Goycochea 9); Monzon (Lorenzo 78), Serrizuela, Simon, Olarticoechea, Batista, Basualdo, Burruchaga, Troglio, Maradona, Caniggia.
USSR: Uvarov; Bessonov*, Kuznetsov, Khidiatulin, Gorlukovich, Zygmantovich, Aleinikov, Shalimov, Zavarov (Lyuti 85), Dobrovolski, Protasov (Litovchenko 75).
Referee: Fredricksson (Sweden).

14 June, Bari, 38,687

Cameroon (0) 2 *(Milla 76, 86)*

Rumania (0) 1 *(Balint 88)*

Cameroon: Nkono; Tataw, Onana, Ndip, Ebwelle, Kunde (Pagal 68), Mbouh, Mfede, Maboang (Milla 58), Makanaky, Omam-Biyik.
Rumania: Lung; Rednic, Andone, Popescu, Klein, Rotariu, Sabau, Timofte, Hagi (Dumitrescu 55), Raducioiu (Balint 79), Lacatus.
Referee: Silva (Chile).

18 June, Naples, 52,733

Argentina (0) 1 *(Monzon 61)*

Rumania (0) 1 *(Balint 67)*

Argentina: Goycochea; Simon, Serrizuela, Monzon, Troglio (Giusti 53), Batista, Burruchaga (Dezotti 60), Basualdo, Olarticoechea, Maradona, Caniggia.
Rumania: Lung; Rednic, Andone, Popescu, Klein, Rotariu, Sabau (Mateut 82), Lupescu, Hagi, Lacatus, Balint (Lupu 72).
Referee. Valente (Portugal).

18 June, Bari, 37,307

USSR (2) 4 *(Protasov 20, Zygmantovich 29, Zavarov 52, Dobrovolski 63)*

Cameroon (0) 0.

USSR: Uvarov; Khidiatulin, Kuznetzov, Demianenko, Gorlukovich, Aleinikov, Litovchenko (Yaremchuk 72), Zygmantovich, Shalimov (Zavarov 46), Protasov, Dobrovolski.
Cameroon: Nkono; Onana, Ebwelle, Kunde (Milla 34), Tataw, Ndip, Kana-Biyik, Mbouh, Mfede, Makanaky (Pagal 58), Omam-Biyik.
Referee. Wright (Brazil).

	P	*W*	*D*	*L*	*F*	*A*	*Pts*
Cameroon	3	2	0	1	3	5	4
Rumania	3	1	1	1	4	3	3
Argentina	3	1	1	1	3	2	3
USSR	3	1	0	2	4	4	2

Group C

10 June, Turin, 62,628

Brazil (1) 2 *(Careca 40, 62)*

Sweden (0) 1 *(Brolin 78)*

Brazil: Taffarel; Mauro Galvao, Mozer, Ricardo Gomes, Jorginho, Branco, Dunga, Alemao, Valdo (Silas 83), Muller, Careca.
Sweden: Ravelli; Nilsson R, Larsson P, Ljung (Stromberg 70), Limpar, Thern, Schwarz, Ingesson, Nilsson J, Brolin, Magnusson (Pettersson 46).
Referee: Lanese (Italy).

11 June, Genoa, 30,867

Costa Rica (0) 1 *(Cayasso 49)*

Scotland (0) 0

Costa Rica: Conejo; Chavarria, Flores, Marchena, Montero, Chavez, Gonzalez, Gomez, Ramirez, Jara (Medford 85), Cayasso.
Scotland: Leighton; Gough (McKimmie 46), McPherson, McLeish, Malpas, McStay, Aitken, McCall, Bett (McCoist 74), Johnston, McInally.
Referee: Lousta (Argentina).

16 June, Turin, 58,007

Brazil (1) 1 *(Muller 32)*

Costa Rica (0) 0

Brazil: Taffarel; Mauro Galvao, Jorginho, Mozer, Ricardo Gomes, Branco, Dunga, Alemao, Valdo (Silas 86), Careca (Bebeto 83), Muller.
Costa Rica: Conejo; Flores, Chavarria, Marchena, Gonzalez, Montero, Chavez, Gomez, Ramirez, Jara (Myers 72), Cayasso (Guimares 78).
Referee: Jouini (Tunisia).

16 June, Genoa, 31,823

Scotland (1) 2 *(McCall 10, Johnston 83 (pen))*

Sweden (0) 1 *(Stromberg 85)*

Scotland: Leighton; McPherson, Levein, McLeish, Malpas, Aitken, MacLeod, McCall, Fleck (McCoist 84), Durie (McStay 74), Johnston.
Sweden: Ravelli; Nilsson R, Larsson P (Stromberg 74), Hysen, Schwarz, Ingesson, Thern, Limpar, Nilsson J, Brolin, Pettersson (Ekstrom 65).
Referee: Maciel (Paraguay).

20 June, Turin, 62,502

Brazil (0) 1 *(Muller 81)*

Scotland (0) 0

Brazil: Taffarel; Jorginho, Mauro Galvao, Ricardo Rocha, Ricardo Gomes, Branco, Alemao, Dunga, Valdo, Careca, Romario (Muller 66).
Scotland: Leighton; McKimmie, McPherson, Aitken, McLeish, Malpas, McCall, McStay, MacLeod (Gillespie 39), Johnston, McCoist (Fleck 77).
Referee: Kohl (Austria).

20 June, Genoa, 30,223

Costa Rica (0) 2 *(Flores 75, Medford 87)*

Sweden (1) 1 *(Ekstrom 32)*

Costa Rica: Conejo; Marchena, Flores, Gonzalez, Montero, Chavarria, Gomez (Medford 62), Chaves, Cayasso, Ramirez, Jara.
Sweden: Ravelli; Nilsson R, Larsson P, Hysen, Schwarz, Pettersson, Stromberg (Engqvist 81), Ingesson, Nilsson J, Ekstrom, Brolin (Gren 34).
Referee: Petrovic (Yugoslavia).

	P	*W*	*D*	*L*	*F*	*A*	*Pts*
Brazil	3	3	0	0	4	1	6
Costa Rica	3	2	0	1	3	2	4
Scotland	3	1	0	2	2	3	2
Sweden	3	0	0	3	3	6	0

GROUP D

9 June, Bologna, 30,791

Colombia (0) 2 *(Redin 50, Valderrama 87)*

UAE (0) 0

Colombia: Higuita; Escobar, Gildardo Gomez, Herrera, Perea, Gabriel Gomez, Valderrama, Redin, Alvarez, Rincon, Iguaran (Estrada 75).

UAE: Faraj; Mubarak KG, Abdulrahman I, Abdulrahman E (Sultan 74), Mohamed Y, Juma'a, Abdullah Moh, Abbas, Mubarak N, Mubarak K (Bilal 58), Talyani.

Referee: Courtney (England).

10 June, Milan, 74,765

Yugoslavia (0) 1 *(Jozic 55)*

West Germany (2) 4 *(Matthaus 29, 63, Klinsmann 40, Voller 70)*

Yugoslavia: Ivkovic; Vulic, Hadzibegic, Jozic, Spasic, Katanec, Baljic, Susic (Brnovic 59), Savicevic (Prosinecki 56), Stojkovic, Vujovic.

West Germany: Illgner; Reuter, Berthold, Augenthaler, Brehme, Buchwald, Matthaus, Bein (Moller 74), Hassler (Littbarski 74), Klinsmann, Voller.

Referee: Mikkelsen (Denmark).

14 June, Bologna, 32,257

Yugoslovia (0) 1 *(Jozic 73)*

Colombia (0) 0

Yugoslavia: Ivkovic; Stanojkovic, Spasic, Hadzibegic, Jozic, Brnovic, Susic, Katanec (Jarni 46), Stojkovic, Sabanadzovic, Vujovic (Pancev 54).

Colombia: Higuita; Herrera, Perea, Gildardo Gomez, Escobar, Gabriel Gomez, Alvarez, Valderrama, Redin (Estrada 79), Rincon (Hernandez 67), Iguaran.

Referee: Agnolin (Italy).

15 June, Milan, 71,167

West Germany (2) 5 *(Voller 35, 76, Klinsmann 37, Matthaus 47, Bein 58)*

UAE (0) 1 *(Mubarak K 46)*

West Germany: Illgner; Reuter, Buchwald, Augenthaler, Brehme, Berthold (Littbarski 46), Matthaus, Hassler, Bein, Klinsmann (Riedle 72), Voller.

UAE: Faraj; Abdulrahman E, Mubarak KG, Mohamed Y, Abdulrahman I (Al Haddad 86), Abdullah Moh, Juma'a, Mubarak N, Mubarak K (Hussain 82), Abbas, Talyani. *Referee:* Spirin (USSR).

19 June, Milan, 72,510

West Germany (0) 1 *(Littbarski 88)*

Colombia (0) 1 *(Rincon 90)*

West Germany: Ilgner; Reuter, Buchwald, Augenthaler, Pflugler, Berthold, Matthaus, Hassler (Thon 88), Bein (Littbarski 46), Klinsmann, Voller.

Colombia: Higuita; Herrera, Escobar, Perea, Gildardo Gomez, Gabriel Gomez, Alvarez, Estrada, Valderrama, Rincon, Fajardo.

Referee: Snoddy (N. Ireland).

19 June, Bologna, 27,833

Yugoslavia (2) 4 *(Susic 4, Pancev 8, 46, Prosinecki 90)*

UAE (1) 1 *(Juma'a 21)*

Yugoslavia: Ivkovic; Stanojkovic, Spasic, Hadzibegic, Jozic, Brnovic, Susic, Stojkovic, Sabanadzovic (Prosinecki 78), Pancev, Vujovic (Vulic 63).

UAE: Faraj; Mubarak KG, Abdulrahman I, Abdulrahman E, Al Haddad, Juma'a (Mubarak FK 46), Abdullah Moh, Abbas, Mubarak N (Sultan 34), Mubarak I*, Talyani. *Referee:* Takada (Japan).

	P	*W*	*D*	*L*	*F*	*A*	*Pts*
West Germany	3	2	1	0	10	3	5
Yugoslavia	3	2	0	1	6	5	4
Colombia	3	1	1	1	3	2	3
UAE	3	0	0	3	2	11	0

Group E

12 June, Verona, 32,486

Belgium (0) 2 *(De Gryse 52, Dewolf 64)*

South Korea (0) 0

Belgium: Preud'homme; Gerets, Clijsters, Demol, Dewolf, Emmers, Van der Elst, Scifo, Versavel, De Gryse, Van der Linden (Ceulemans 46).
South Korea: Choi In-Young, Choi Kang-Hee, Chung Yong Hwan, Hong Myung-Bo, Park Kyung-Joon, Gu Sang-Bum, Lee Young-Jin (Cho Min-Kook 46), Noh Soon-Jin (Lee Tae-Hoo 62), Choi Soon-Ho, Hwang Seon-Hong, Kim Joo-Sung.
Referee: Mauro (USA).

13 June, Udine, 35,713

Spain (0) 0

Uruguay (0) 0

Spain: Zubizarreta; Chendo, Sanchis, Andrinua, Jimenez, Martin Vazquez, Roberto, Villaroya (Gorriz 79), Michel, Manolo (Rafa Paz), Butragueno.
Uruguay: Alvez; Herrera, Gutierrez, De Leon, Dominguez, Ruben Pereira (Correa 64), Perdomo, Paz, Alzamendi (Aguilera 64), Francescoli, Sosa.
Referee: Kohl (Austria).

17 June, Udine, 32,733

Spain (1) 3 *(Michel 23, 61, 81)*

South Korea (1) 1 *(Hwang Kwan-Bo 43)*

Spain: Zubizarreta; Chendo, Andrinua, Sanchis, Gorriz, Michel, Villaroya, Roberto (Bakero 81), Martin Vazquez, Butragueno (Fernando 76), Julio Salinas.
South Korea: Choi In-Young; Park Kyung-Joon (Chung Jong-Soo 68), Choi Kang-Hee, Hong Myung-Bo, Yoon Deuk-Yeo, Hwang Kwan-Bo, Chung Hae-Won (Noh Soo-Jin 52), Kim Joo-Sung, Gu Sang-Bum, Byun Byung-Joo, Choi Soon-Ho.
Referee: Guerrero (Ecuador).

17 June, Verona, 33,759

Belgium (2) 3 *(Clijsters 15, Scifo 22, Ceulemans 47)*

Uruguay (0) 1 *(Bengoechea 72)*

Belgium: Preud'homme; Gerets*, Grun, Clijsters (Emmers 46), Demol, Dewolf, Versavel (Vervoort 73), Van der Elst, Scifo, De Gryse, Ceulemans.
Uruguay: Alvez; Herrera, Gutierrez, De Leon, Dominguez, Ostolaza (Bengoechea 63), Perdomo, Paz, Alzamendi (Aguilera 63), Francescoli, Sosa.
Referee: Kirschen (East Germany).

21 June, Verona, 39,950

Spain (2) 2 *(Michel 26 (pen), Gorriz 38)*

Belgium (1) 1 *(Vervoort 29)*

Spain: Zubizarreta; Chendo, Sanchis, Andriuna, Villaroya, Gorriz, Michel, Roberto, Martin Vazquez, Butragueno (Alcorta 83), Julio Salinas (Pardeza 88).
Belgium: Preud'homme; Staelens (Van der Linden 79), Albert, Demol, Dewolf, Van der Elst, Emmers (Plovie 31), Vervoort, Scifo, De Gryse, Ceulemans.
Referee: Loustau (Argentina).

21 June, Udine, 29,039

Uruguay (0) 1 *(Fonseca 90)*

South Korea (0) 0

Uruguay: Alvez; Gutierrez, De Leon, Herrera, Dominguez, Perdomo, Ostolaza (Aguilera 46), Francescoli, Paz, Martines, Sosa (Fonseca 62).
South Korea: Choi In-Young; Park Kyung-Joon, Choi Kang-Hee, Chung Jong-Soo, Hong Myung-Bo, Yoon Deuk-Yeo*, Hwang Kwan-Bo (Chung Hae-Won 77), Lee Heung-Sil, Kim Joo-Sung (Hwang Seon-Hong 42), Byun Byung Joo, Choi Soon-Ho
Referee: Lanese (Italy).

	P	*W*	*D*	*L*	*F*	*A*	*Pts*
Spain	3	2	1	0	5	2	6
Belgium	3	2	0	1	6	3	4
Uruguay	3	1	1	1	2	3	3
South Korea	3	0	0	3	1	6	0

Group F

11 June, Cagliari, 35,238

England (1) 1 *(Lineker 8)*

Rep of Ireland (0) 1 *(Sheedy 72)*

England: Shilton; Stevens, Walker, Butcher, Pearce, Robson, Beardsley (McMahon 69), Gascoigne, Waddle, Barnes, Lineker (Bull 83).
Rep of Ireland: Bonner; Morris, McCarthy, Moran, Staunton, McGrath, Houghton, Sheedy, Aldridge (McLoughlin 64), Townsend, Cascarino.
Referee: Schmidhuber (West Germany).

12 June, Palermo, 33,288

Egypt (0) 1 *(Abdelghani 82 (pen))*

Holland (0) 1 *(Kieft 58)*

Egypt: Shoubeir; Hassan I, Yaken, Ramzi H, Yassine, Youssef, Ramzı A (Abdel Rahmane 68), Hassan H, Abdelhamid (Tolba 68), Abdelghani, Abdou.
Holland: Van Breukelen; Van Aerle, Rutjes, Koeman R, Van Tiggelen, Vanenburg (Kieft 46), Wouters, Rijkaard, Koeman E (Witschge 69), Van Basten, Gullit.
Referee: Aladren (Spain).

16 June, Cagliari, 35,267

England (0) 0

Holland (0) 0

England: Shilton; Parker, Walker, Wright, Butcher, Pearce, Robson (Platt 65), Waddle (Bull 59), Gascoigne, Barnes, Lineker.
Holland: Van Breukelen; Van Aerle, Rijkaard, Koeman R, Van Tiggelen, Wouters, Gullit, Witschge, Van't Schip (Kieft 74), Gillhaus, Van Basten.
Referee: Petrovic (Yugoslavia).

17 June, Palermo, 33,288

Egypt (0) 0

Rep of Ireland (0) 0

Egypt: Shoubeir; Hassan I, Yaken, Ramzi H, Yassine, Abdelghani, Orabi, Tolba (Abou Seid 59), Youssef, Abdou (Abdelhamid 76), Hassan H.
Rep of Ireland: Bonner; Morris, McCarthy, Moran, Staunton, McGrath, Houghton, Townsend, Sheedy, Aldridge (McLoughlin 84), Cascarino (Quinn 84).
Referee: Van Langehove (Belgium).

21 June, Cagliari, 34,959

England (0) 1 *(Wright 58)*

Egypt (0) 0

England: Shilton; Parker, Wright, Walker, Pearce, Waddle (Platt 86), McMahon, Gascoigne, Barnes, Lineker, Bull (Beardsley 84).
Egypt: Shoubeir; Hassan I, Yaken, Ramzi H, Yassine, Youssef, Abdelghani, Abdou (Soliman 81), Ramzi A, Abdelhamid (Adbel Rahmane 81), Hassan H.
Referee: Rothlisberger (Switzerland).

21 June, Palermo, 33,288

Rep of Ireland (0) 1 *(Quinn 71)*

Holland (1) 1 *(Gullit 10)*

Rep of Ireland: Bonner; Morris, McCarthy, Moran, Staunton, McGrath, Houghton, Townsend, Sheedy (Whelan 61), Aldridge (Cascarino 61), Quinn.
Holland: Van Breukelen; Van Aerle, Rijkaard, Koeman R, Van Tiggelen, Wouters, Witschge (Fraser 59), Van Basten, Gullit, Gillhaus, Kieft (Van Loen 78).
Referee: Vautrot (France).

	P	*W*	*D*	*L*	*F*	*A*	*Pts*
England	3	1	2	0	2	1	4
Rep of Ireland	3	0	3	0	2	2	3
Holland	3	0	3	0	2	2	3
Egypt	3	0	2	1	1	2	2

Second Round

23 June, Naples, 50,026

Cameroon (0) 2 *(Milla 106, 109)*

Colombia (0) 1 *(Redin 117)* aet

Cameroon: Nkono; Tataw, Ndip, Onana, Ebwelle, Kana-Biyik, Mbouh, Maboang, Mfede (Milla 54), Omam-Biyik, Makanaky (Djonkep 68).
Colombia: Higuita; Herrera, Perea, Escobar, Gildardo Gomez, Alvarez, Gabriel Gomez (Redin 79), Rincon, Fajardo (Iguaran 100), Valderrama, Estrada.
Referee: Lanese (Italy).

23 June, Bari, 47,673

Czechoslovakia (1) 4 *(Skuhravy 11, 63, 82, Kubik 76)*

Costa Rica (0) 1 *(Gonzalez 55)*

Czechoslovakia: Stejskal; Hasek, Kadlec, Kocian, Straka, Moravcik, Chovanec, Kubik, Bilek, Skuhravy, Knoflicek.
Costa Rica: Barrantes; Chavarria (Guimaraes 67), Marchena, Flores, Montero, Chavez, Ramirez, Gonzalez, Obando (Medford 46), Cayasso, Jara.
Referee: Kirschen (East Germany).

24 June, Turin, 61,381

Argentina (0) 1 *(Caniggia 80)*

Brazil (0) 0

*Argentina:*Goycochea; Basualdo, Monzon, Simon, Ruggeri, Olarticoechea, Giusti, Burruchaga, Maradona, Troglio (Calderon 62), Caniggia.
Brazil: Taffarel; Jorginho, Ricardo Rocha, Ricardo Gomes*, Mauro Galvao (Renato 85), Branco, Alemao (Silas 85), Dunga, Valdo, Careca, Muller.
Referee: Quiniou (France).

24 June, Milan, 74,559

West Germany (0) 2 *(Klinsmann 51, Brehme 85)*

Holland (0) 1 *(Koeman R 88 (pen))*

West Germany: Illgner; Reuter, Kohler, Augenthaler, Brehme, Buchwald, Berthold, Matthaus, Littbarski, Voller*, Klinsmann (Riedle 79).
Holland: Van Breukelen; Van Aerle (Kieft 56), Koeman R, Van Tiggelen, Wouters, Rijkaard*, Witschge (Gillhaus 79), Winter, Gullit, Van Basten, Van't Schip.
Referee: Loustau (Argentina).

25 June, Genoa, 31,818

Rep of Ireland (0) 0

Rumania (0) 0 aet

Rep of Ireland: Bonner; Morris, McCarthy, Moran, Staunton (O'Leary 93), Houghton, McGrath, Townsend, Sheedy, Quinn, Aldridge (Cascarino 21).
Rumania: Lung; Rednic, Andone, Popescu, Klein, Rotariu, Lupescu, Sabau (Timofte 97), Hagi, Raducioiu (Lupu 64), Balint.
Referee: Wright (Brazil).
Republic of Ireland won 5-4 on penalties.

25 June, Rome, 73,303

Italy (0) 2 *(Schillaci 67, Serena 85)*

Uruguay (0) 0

Italy: Zenga; Bergomi, Ferri, Baresi, Maldini, De Agostini, De Napoli, Berti (Serena 52), Giannini, Schillaci, Baggio (Vierchowod 80).
Uruguay: Alvez; Saldana, Gutierrez, De Leon, Dominguez, Ostolaza (Alzamendi 80), Perdomo, Francescoli, Ruben Pereira, Aguilera (Sosa 55, Fonseca.
Referee: Courtney (England).

26 June, Verona, 35,500

Spain (0) 1 *(Julio Salinas 83)*

Yugoslavia (0) 2 *(Stojkovic 77, 92)* aet

Spain. Zubizarreta; Chendo, Gorriz, Andrinua (Jimenez 50), Sanchis, Villaroya, Martin Vazquez, Roberto, Michel, Butragueno (Rafa Paz 78), Julio Salinas.
Yugoslavia: Ivkovic; Sabanadzovic, Spasic, Brnovic, Katanec (Vulic 78), Hadzibegic, Jozic, Susic, Stojkovic, Pancev (Savicevic 56), Vujovic.
Referee: Schmidhuber (West Germany).

26 June, Bologna, 34,520
England (0) 1 *(Platt 119)*
Belgium (0) 0 aet
England: Shilton; Parker, Butcher, Wright, Walker, Pearce, Waddle, Gascoigne, McMahon (Platt 71), Barnes (Bull 74), Lineker.
Belgium: Preud'homme; Gerets, Grun, Demol, Clijsters, Dewolf, Van der Elst, Scifo, Versavel (Vervoort 107), Ceulemans, De Gryse (Claesen 64).
Referee: Mikkelsen (Denmark).

Quarter-finals
30 June, Florence, 38,971
Yugoslavia (0) 0
Argentina (0) 0 aet
Yugoslavia: Ivkovic; Hadzibegic, Spasic, Brnovic, Vulic, Sabanadzovic*, Jozic, Susic (Savicevic 62), Prosinecki, Stojkovic, Vujovic.
Argentina: Goycochea; Simon, Ruggeri, Serrizuela, Basualdo, Olarticoechea (Troglio 52), Giusti, Burruchaga, Calderon (Dezotti 85), Caniggia, Maradona.
Referee: Rothlisberger (West Germany).
Argentina won 3-2 on penalties.

30 June, Rome, 73,303
Rep of Ireland (0) 0
Italy (1) 1 *(Schillaci 37)*
Rep of Ireland: Bonner; Morris, McCarthy, Moran, Staunton, McGrath, Houghton, Townsend, Sheedy, Quinn (Cascarino 52), Aldridge (Sheridan 77).
Italy: Zenga; Bergomi, Ferri, Baresi, Maldini, De Agostini, Donadoni, De Napoli, Giannini (Ancelotti 62), Baggio (Serena 70), Schillaci.
Referee: Valente (Portugal).

1 July, Milan, 73,347
Czechoslovakia (0) 0
West Germany (1) 1 *(Matthaus 24 (pen))*
Czechoslovakia: Stejskal; Hasek, Straka, Kocian, Kadlec, Moravcik*, Chovanec, Bilek (Nemecek 68), Kubik (Griga 79), Skuhravy, Knoflicek.
West Germany: Illgnerr; Berthold, Kohler, Augenthaler, Brehme, Buchwald, Matthaus, Bein (Moller 83), Littbarski, Riedle, Klinsmann.
Referee: Kohl (Austria).

1 July, Naples, 55,205
Cameroon (0) 2 *(Kunde 63 (pen), Ekeke 67)*
England (1) 3 *(Platt 25, Lineker 82, 104 (both pens))* aet
Cameroon: Nkono; Tataw, Massing, Kunde, Edwelle, Maboang (Milla 46), Libih, Pagal, Makanaky, Mfede (Ekeke 62), Omam-Biyik.
England: Shilton; Parker, Butcher (Steven 74), Wright, Walker, Pearce, Waddle, Platt, Gascoigne, Barnes (Beardsley 46), Lineker.
Referee: Codesal (Mexico).

Semi-finals
3 July, Naples, 59,978
Argentina (0) 1 *(Caniggia 67)*
Italy (1) 1 *(Schillaci 17)* aet
Argentina. Goycochea, Simon, Ruggeri, Serrizuela, Giusti*, Calderon (Troglio 46), Burruchaga, Basualdo (Batista 99), Olarticoechea, Caniggia, Maradona

Italy: Zenga; Bergomi, Baresi, Ferri, De Napoli, De Agostini, Donadoni, Maldini, Giannini (Baggio 73), Schillaci, Vialli (Serena 70).
Referee: Vautrot (France).
Argentina won 4-3 on penalties.

4 July, Turin, 62,628
West Germany (0) 1 *(Brehme 59)*
England (0) 1 *(Lineker 80)* aet
West Germany: Illgner; Berthold, Augenthaler, Buchwald, Kohler Hassler (Reuter 67), Matthaus, Thon, Brehme, Klinsmann, Voller (Riedle 38).
England: Shilton; Parker, Butcher (Steven 70), Wright, Walker, Pearce, Platt, Gascoigne, Waddle, Beardsley, Lineker.
Referee: Wright (Brazil).
West Germany won 4-3 on penalties.

Match for third place
7 July, Bari, 51,426
Italy (0) 2 *(Baggio 70, Schillaci 84 (pen))*
England (0) 1 *(Platt 80)*
Italy: Zenga; Bergomi, Baresi, Ferrara, Maldini, Vierchowod, De Agostini (Berti 67), Ancelotti, Giannini (Ferri 89), Baggio, Schillaci.
England: Shilton; Stevens, Wright (Waddle 72), Parker, Walker, Dorigo, Steven, Platt, McMahon (Webb 72), Beardsley, Lineker.
Referee: Quiniou (France).

Final
8 July, Rome, 73,603
West Germany (0) 1 *(Brehme 84 (pen))*
Argentina (0) 0
West Germany: Illgner; Berthold (Reuter 73), Kohler, Augenthaler, Buchwald, Brehme, Littbarski, Hassler, Matthaus, Voller, Klinsmann.
Argentina: Goycochea; Lorenzo, Serrizuela, Sensini, Ruggeri (Monzon 46*), Simon, Basualdo, Burruchaga (Calderon 53), Maradona, Troglio, Dezotti*.
Referee: Codesal (Mexico).
* denotes players sent off.
In the 1990 finals there were 164 bookings, 16 dismissals (170 players had been cautioned but six of those who were subsequently sent off had their sending-off recorded, not the booking).
Top scorer: Schillaci (Italy) 6 goals.

1990 FIFA WORLD CUP

Qualifying Results

EUROPE

Group 1 *(Denmark, Bulgaria, Rumania, Greece)*
19 October, Sofia, 52,000
Bulgaria (1) 1 *(Kolev 31)*
Rumania (1) 3 *(Mateut 25, Camataru 79, 89)*
Bulgaria: Mikhailov; Nikolov, Rankov, Vasev (Kiryakov 55), Iliev, Stoichkov, Sadkov, Yordanov, Getov, Alexandrov (Kolev 30), Penev.
Rumania: Lung; Iovan, Andone, Belodedici, Rotariu, Mateut (Klein 55), Sabau, Hagi, Popescu, Lacatus (Vaiscovici 66), Camataru.

19 October, Athens, 45,000
Greece (1) 1 *(Mitropoulos 41)*
Denmark (0) 1 *(Povlsen 56)*
Greece: Talikariadis; Hatziathanassiu, Manolas, Mavridis, Kolomitrousis, Skartados (Karapialis 74), Tsalouhidis, Bonovas, Mitropoulos (Georgamlis 56), Saravakos, Anastopoulos.
Denmark: Schmeichel; Heintze, Nielsen I, Olsen L, Sivebaek (Kristensen 46), Bartram, Helt, Jensen J, Povlsen, Laudrup, Brylle (Elstrup 75).

2 November, Copenhagen, 34,600
Denmark (1) 1 *(Elstrup 8)*
Bulgaria (1) 1 *(Sadkov 38)*
Denmark: Schmeichel; Olsen L, Sivebaek, Nielsen K, Kristensen, Heintze (Brylle 76), Helt (Bartram 65), Jensen J, Laudrup, Elstrup, Povlsen.
Bulgaria: Valov; Iliev, Kiryakov, Dochev, Ivanov, Penev, Sadkov, Kirov, Yordanov (Rakov 86), Stoichkov (Balkov 88), Bezinski.

2 November, Bucharest, 22,500
Rumania (2) 3 *(Mateut 26, Hagi 40 (pen), Sabau 84)*
Greece (0) 0
Rumania: Lung; Iovan, Belodedici, Andone, Ungureanu, Popescu, Hagi, Sabau (Klein 85), Mateut, Lacatus (Vaiscovici 77), Camataru.
Greece: Talikariadis; Hatziathanassiu, Kolomitroussis, Manolas, Mavridis, Tsalouhidis, Saravakos, Bonovas, Anastopoulos, Mitropoulos (Kutulas 46), Tsiantakis (Nioblias 68).

26 April, Athens, 30,000
Greece (0) 0
Rumania (0) 0
Greece: Economopoulos; Apostolakis, Hatziathanasiu, Manolas, Mavridis, Tsalouhidis, Saravakos, Papadopoulos (Bonovas 65), Samaras, Savidis, Tsiantakis.
Rumania: Lung; Iovan, Bumbescu, Klein, Rednic, Mateut, Popescu, Sabau, Camataru (Vaiscovici 89), Hagi, Lupescu (Dumitrescu 78).

26 April, Sofia, 45,000
Bulgaria (0) 0
Denmark (1) 2 *(Povlsen 41, Laudrup B 89)*
Bulgaria: Valov (Donev 55); Kiryakov, Dochev, Bezinski, Iliev, Rakov, Kirov, Sadkov (Simeonov 46), Stoichkov, Mikhtarski, Getov.
Denmark: Schmeichel; Heintze, Nielsen K, Olsen L, Sivebaek, Larsen J, Olsen M (Vilfort 74), Jensen J (Helt 84), Bartram, Povlsen, Laudrup B.

17 May, Copenhagen, 38,500
Denmark (1) 7 *(Laudrup B 24, Bartram 47, Nielsen K 55, Povlsen 56, Vilfort 79, Andersen H 85, Laudrup M 89 (pen))*

Greece (1) 1 *(Samaras 39)*
Denmark: Schmeichel; Sivebaek (Vilfort 30), Olsen L, Nielsen K, Larsen J, Bartram (Andersen H), Olsen M, Jensen J, Laudrup M, Povlsen, Laudrup B.
Greece: Economopoulos; Hatziathanasiu, Mavridis, Manolas, Apostolakis, Tsalouhidis, Tsiantakis, Mitropoulos (Kalitzakis 50), Papadopoulos, Saravakos, Samaras.

17 May, Bucharest, 20,000
Rumania (1) 1 *(Popescu 35)*
Bulgaria (0) 0
Rumania: Stelea; Iovan, Bumbescu, Rednic (Balint 64), Mateut, Sabau (Dumitrescu 85), Popescu, Rotariu, Hagi, Lacatus, Camataru.
Bulgaria: Valov (Donev 46); Dochev, Ivanov, Vasev, Mladenov D, Tinchev, Kostadinov E, Stoichkov, Mladenov S, Bakalov, Balekov.

11 October, Varna, 15,000
Bulgaria (0) 4 *(Ivanov 72, Bankov 76, Iskrenov 79, Stoichkov 88)*
Greece (0) 0
Bulgaria: Valov; Dimitrov, Ivanov, Tinchev, Bankov, Yordanov (Lechkov 84), Kostadinov (Penev 65), Stoichkov, Balakov, Georgiev, Iskrenov.
Greece: Pietsis; Kutulas, Hatzithanasiu, Vakalopoulos, Mavridis, Papaioannou, Saravakos, Stamatis (Noblias 65), Dimitriadis, Sandakis, Kofidis.

11 October, Copenhagen, 45,000
Denmark (2) 3 *(Neilsen K 4, Laudrup B 26, Povlsen 85)*
Rumania (0) 0
Denmark: Schmeichel; Sivebaek, Nielsen K, Olsen L, Nielsen I, Bartram, Jensen, Heintze, Povlsen, Laudrup M, Laudrup B.
Rumania: Lung; Iovan, Klein, Rednic, Mateut, Andone, Rotariu, Sabau (Lupu 68), Camataru, Hagi, Popescu.

15 November, Athens, 2500
Greece (0) 1 *(Noblias 49)*
Bulgaria (0) 0
Greece: Papadopoulos; Karageorghiu, Mustakidis, Manolas, Deliyannis, Papadopoulos D (Alexiu 75), Borbokis, Vutiritsas, Samaras (Stamatis 29), Noblias, Marangos.
Bulgaria: Valov; Dimitrov, Ivanov, Tinchev, Dochev (Stoyanov 81), Bankov, Yanchez, Stoichkov, Balakov, Yordanov, Iskrenov (Kostadinov 75).

15 November, Bucharest, 30,000
Rumania (2) 3 *(Balint 25, 61, Sabau 38)*
Denmark (1) 1 *(Povlsen)*
Rumania: Lung; Petrescu (Ungureanu 85), Iovan, Andone, Rotariu, Hagi, Sabau, Popescu, Lupu (Mateut 78), Lacatus, Balint.
Denmark: Schmeichel; Sivebaek (Elstrup 72), Olsen L, Nielsen K, Nielsen I, Jensen J, Laudrup M, Lerby, Bartram, Povlsen, Laudrup B.

Final table	*P*	*W*	*D*	*L*	*F*	*A*	*Pts*
Rumania	6	4	1	1	10	5	9
Denmark	6	3	2	1	15	6	8
Greece	6	1	2	3	3	15	4
Bulgaria	6	1	1	4	6	8	3

Rumania qualified

Group 2 *(England, Poland, Sweden, Albania)*
19 October, Wembley, 65,628
England (0) 0
Sweden (0) 0
England: Shilton; Stevens, Pearce, Webb, Adams (Walker 64), Butcher, Robson, Beardsley, Waddle, Lineker, Barnes (Cottee 79).
Sweden: Ravelli; Nilsson R (Schiller 77), Hysen, Larsson P, Ljung, Thern, Stromberg, Prytz, Nilsson J, Holmqvist (Ekstrom 63), Pettersson.

19 October, Chorzow, 30,000
Poland (0) 1 *(Warzycha K 78)*
Albania (0) 0
Poland: Wandzik; Warzycha R, Wojcicki, Lukasik, Wdowczyk, Matsik (Ziober 46), Warzycha K, Urban, Furtok (Komornicki 73), Rudy, Smolarek.
Albania: Mersini; Alimehmeti, Josa, Hodja, Gega, Iera, Shehu (Stoia 70), Lekbello, Millo, Minga, Demollari.

5 November, Tirana, 11,500
Albania (1) 1 *(Shehu 33)*
Sweden (0) 2 *(Holmqvist 68, Ekstrom 71)*
Albania: Mersini; Alimehmeti, Hodja, Lekbello, Stoia, Josa, Gega, Demollari, Millo, Shehu, Minga.
Sweden: Ravelli; Nilsson R, Larsson P, Hysen, Ljung, Thern, Prytz (Holmqvist 66), Stromberg, Nilsson J, Pettersson, Ekstrom.

8 March, Tirana, 30,000
Albania (0) 0
England (1) 2 *(Barnes 16, Robson 63)*
Albania: Mersini; Zmijani, Josa, Hodja, Gega, Jera, Shehu, Lekbello, Millo (Majaci 75), Minga, Demollari.
England: Shilton; Stevens, Pearce, Webb, Walker, Butcher, Robson, Rocastle, Waddle (Beardsley 79), Lineker (Smith 79), Barnes.

26 April, Wembley, 60,602
England (2) 5 *(Lineker 5, Beardsley 12, 64, Waddle 72, Gascoigne 88)*
Albania (0) 0
England: Shilton; Stevens (Parker 77), Pearce, Webb, Walker, Butcher, Robson, Rocastle (Gascoigne 67), Beardsley, Lineker, Waddle.
Albania: Nallbani; Zmijani, Bubeqi, Hodja, Gega, Jera, Shehu, Lekbello, Millo, Hasanpapa (Noga 31), Demollari.

7 May, Stockholm, 35,021
Sweden (0) 2 *(Ljung 76, Larsson N 89)*
Poland (0) 1 *(Tarasiewicz 86)*
Sweden: Ravelli T; Nilsson R, Lonn (Ravelli A 80), Ljung, Schiller, Limpar, Prytz, Thern, Nilsson J (Larsson N 58), Ekstrom, Magnusson.
Poland: Bako; Soczynski, Lukasik, Wojcicki, Wdowczyk (Tarasiewicz 15), Prusik, Matysik, Urban, Dziekanowski (Kosecki 60), Furtok, Warzycha K.

3 June, Wembley, 69,203
England (1) 3 *(Lineker 24, Barnes 69, Webb 82)*
Poland (0) 0
England: Shilton; Stevens, Pearce, Webb, Walker, Butcher, Robson, Waddle (Rocastle 75), Beardsley (Smith 75), Lineker, Barnes.
Poland: Bako; Wijas, Wojcicki, Wdowczyk, Lukasik, Matysik, Prusik, Urban (Tarasiewicz 70), Furtok, Warzycha K, Lesniak (Kosecki 58).

6 September, Stockholm, 38,588
Sweden (0) 0
England (0) 0
Sweden: Ravelli T; Nilsson R, Hysen, Larsson P, Ljung, Engqvist, Thern, Ingesson (Stromberg 72), Nilsson J (Limpar 77), Ekstrom, Magnusson.
England: Shilton; Stevens, Pearce, Walker, Butcher, McMahon, Waddle, Webb (Gascoigne 72), Beardsley, Lineker, Barnes (Rocastle 76).

8 October, Stockholm, 32,423
Sweden (1) 3 *(Magnusson 20, Ingesson 55, Engqvist 89)*
Albania (1) 1 *(Kushta 8 (pen))*
Sweden: Ravelli T; Nilsson R, Hysen, Larsson P, Ljung, Gren (Engqvist), Ingesson, Thern, Limpar, Ekstrom (Lindqvist 82), Magnusson.

Albania: Mersini; Hodja, Zmijani, Lekbello (Noga 75), Taho, Jera, Josa, Gega (Arberi 87), Demollari, Millo, Kushta.

11 October, Chorzow, 30,000
Poland (0) 0
England (0) 0
Poland: Bako; Czachowski, Kaczmarek, Wdowczyk, Warzycha R, Nawrocki, Tarasiewicz, Ziober, Kosecki, Dziekanowski, Warzycha K (Furtok 57).
England: Shilton; Stevens, Pearce, Walker, Butcher, McMahon, Robson, Rocastle, Beardsley, Lineker, Waddle.

25 October, Chorzow, 12,000
Poland (0) 0
Sweden (1) 2 *(Larsson P (pen) 34, Ekstrom 60)*
Poland: Bako; Czachowski, Kaczmarek, Warzycha R (Kubicki 67), Wdowczyk, Nawrocki (Gora 82), Tarasiewicz, Ziober, Kosecki, Dziekanowski, Warzycha K.
Sweden: Ravelli T; Nilsson R, Hysen, Larsson P, Ljung, Engqvist, Thern, Ingesson (Larsson N 72), Nilsson J, Ekstrom (Lindqvist 82), Magnusson.

15 November, Tirana, 10,000
Albania (0) 1 *(Kushta 63)*
Poland (1) 2 *(Tarasiewicz 45, Ziober 84)*
Albania: Nailbani; Zmijani, Hodja, Xhumba, Iljadhi, Josa (Arberi 60), Demollari, Pano (Kepa 74), Jera, Kushta, Bubeqi.
Poland: Bako; Kubicki, Czachowski, Wdowczyk, Kaczmarek, Warzycha R, Tarasiewicz, Kosecki, Szewczyk, Dziekanowski (Warzycha K 36), Ziober.

Final table	*P*	*W*	*D*	*L*	*F*	*A*	*Pts*
Sweden	6	4	2	0	9	3	10
England	6	3	3	0	10	0	9
Poland	6	2	1	3	4	8	5
Albania	6	0	0	6	3	15	0

Sweden and England qualified

Group 3 *(USSR, East Germany, Austria, Iceland, Turkey)*
31 August, Reykjavik, 8300
Iceland (1) 1 *(Gretarsson 11)*
USSR (0) 1 *(Litovchenko 75)*
Iceland: Sigurdsson; Bergsson, Saevar Jonsson, Edvaldsson, Thordarsson, Gislason, Ormslev, Siggi Jonsson, Sigurvinsson, Gudjohnsen, Gretarsson (Torfasson G 82).
USSR: Dasayev; Bessonov (Dobrovolski 65), Khidiatulin, Kuznetsov, Demianenko, Aleinikov, Litovchenko, Zavarov, Rats, Protasov, Mikhailichenko.

12 October, Istanbul, 25,680
Turkey (0) 1 *(Onal 73)*
Iceland (0) 1 *(Torfasson O 62)*
Turkey: Fatih; Recep (Feyyaz 57), Semih, Cuneyt, Mucahit, Gokhan G, Oguz, Ridvan, Onal, Tanju, Savas K.
Iceland: Fridriksson; Gislason, Edvaldsson, Arnthorsson (Askelsson 79), Bergsson, Siggi Jonsson, Margeirsson, Torfasson O, Torfasson G, Gudjohnsen, Thordarsson.

19 October, East Berlin, 12,000
East Germany (1) 2 *(Thom 34, 88)*
Iceland (0) 0
East Germany: Weissflog; Kreer, Schossler, Stahmann, Lindner, Doschner, Raab, Ernst, Stubner (Sammer 34), Kirsten, Thom.
Iceland: Sigurdsson; Saevar Jonsson, Bergsson, Edvaldsson, Gislason, Thordarsson, Torfasson O, Gudjohnsen, Sigurvinsson, Gretarsson, Torfasson G (Margeirsson 77).

19 October, Kiev, 100,000
USSR (0) 2 *(Mikhailichenko 47, Zavarov 69)*
Austria (0) 0
USSR: Dasayev; Ivanauskas (Gorlukovich), Khidiatulin, Zigmantovich, Demianenko, Aleinikov, Litovchenko, Zavarov, Rats, Mikhailichenko, Protasov (Savichev 83).
Austria: Lindenberger; Russ, Degeorgi, Pfeffer, Weber H, Zsak, Keglevits, Artner, Polster, Hormann (Herzog 63), Willfurth.

2 November, Vienna, 25,000
Austria (2) 3 *(Polster 38, Herzog 42, 54)*
Turkey (0) 2 *(Feyyaz 61, Tanju 81)*
Austria: Lindenberger, Weber G, Russ, Pfeffer, Artner, Willfurth (Pacult 55), Prohaska, Herzog (Glatzmayer 68), Degeorgi, Ogris, Polster.
Turkey: Fatih; Cuneyt, Recep, Gokhan G (Savas K), Semih, Mustafa, Unal, Oguz, Gokhan K, Ridvan, Feyyaz (Tanju).

30 November, Istanbul, 39,000
Turkey (1) 3 *(Tanju 23, 63, Oguz 69)*
East Germany (0) 1 *(Thom 75)*
Turkey: Fatih; Recep, Semih, Cuneyt, Gokhan G, Onal, Ugur, Ridvan, Oguz (Hassan 88), Tanju (Metin 78), Feyyaz.
East Germany: Weissflog; Kreer (Schossler 66), Stahmann, Lindner, Doschner, Pilz, Stubner, Steinmann, Kirsten, Ernst (Doll 46), Thom.

12 April, Magdeburg, 23,000
East Germany (0) 0
Turkey (1) 2 *(Tanju 21, Ridvan 88)*
East Germany: Muller; Hauptmann, Rohde, Trautmann, Lindner, Stubner (Wuckel 64), Sammer, Pilz (Doll 19), Kirsten, Minge, Thom.
Turkey: Engin; Recep, Cuneyt, Gokhan B, Semih, Yusuf, Ugur (Erdal 65), Oguz (Gokhan G 80), Unal, Ridvan, Tanju.

26 April, Kiev, 100,000
USSR (3) 3 *(Dobrovolski 3, Litovchenko 22, Protasov 40)*
East Germany (0) 0
USSR: Dasayev; Luzhny, Gorlukovich, Kuznetsov, Dobrovolski (Savichev 75), Aleinikov (Kulkov 80), Litovchenko, Mikhailichenko, Protasov, Rats, Zavarov.
East Germany: Weissflog; Hauptmann (Mertz 46), Lieberam, Kohler, Trautmann, Doschner, Sammer, Wosz, Scholz (Kirsten 55), Doll, Thom.

10 May, Istanbul, 42,500
Turkey (0) 0
USSR (1) 1 *(Mikhailichenko 40)*
Turkey: Engin; Recep, Cuneyt, Gokhan B, Semih, Yusuf, Ugur (Hasan Vezir 46) (Feyyez 60), Unal, Mustafa, Ridvan, Tanju.
USSR: Dasayev; Luzhny, Gorlukovich, Kuznetsov, Aleinikov (Ketaschvili 89), Rats, Mikhailichenko, Litovchenko, Zavarov, Protasov (Borodyuk 86), Dobrovolski.

20 May, Leipzig, 22,000
East Germany (0) 1 *(Kirsten 86)*
Austria (1) 1 *(Polster 3)*
East Germany: Weissflog; Stahmann, Lindner, Trautmann (Doll 46), Kreer, Rohde, Stubner, Sammer (Weidemann 68), Steinmann, Kirsten, Thom.
Austria: Lindenberger; Weber G, Russ, Pfeffer, Pecl, Rodax (Ogris 68), Prohaska, Zsak, Artner, Herzog (Stoger 60), Polster.

31 May, Moscow, 50,000
USSR (0) 1 *(Dobrovolski 62)*
Iceland (0) 1 *(Askelsson 86)*

USSR: Dasayev; Luzhny, Gorlukovich, Kuznetsov, Rats, Aleinikov, Bessonov (Ketaschvili 82), Dobrovolski, Litovchenko, Protasov (Savichev 82), Zavarov.
Iceland: Sigurdsson; Edvaldsson, Jonsson A, Bergsson, Gislason, Siggi Jonsson, Thordarsson, Torfason O (Kristiansson 82), Arnthorsson, Gretarsson, Torfason G (Askelsson 69).

14 June, Reykjavik, 15,000
Iceland (0) 0
Austria (0) 0
Iceland: Sigurdsson; Edvaldsson, Bergsson, Gislason (Thorkelsson 65), Siggi Jonsson, Thordarsson, Saevar Jonsson, Arnthorsson, Sigurvinsson, Gretarsson, Torfason G.
Austria: Lindenberger; Pecl, Weber, Pfeffer, Hortnagl (Herzog 36), Russ, Zsak, Artner, Prohaska, Polster, Rodax (Ogris 46).

23 August, Salzburg, 18,000
Austria (0) 2 *(Pfeifenberger 47, Szak 62)*
Iceland (0) 1 *(Margeirsson 48)*
Austria: Lindenberger; Weber, Russ, Peci (Streiter 30), Pfeffer, Linzmaier, Zsak, Herzog (Hortnagi 59), Rodax, Pfeiffenberger, Ogris A.
Iceland: Sigurdsson; Bergsson, Saevar Jonsson, Jonsson A, Gislasson, Thordarsson O, Margeirsson (Torfasson O 80), Arnthorsson (Kristinsson 70), Siggi Jonsson, Torfasson G, Gretarsson.

6 September, Reykjavik, 7124
Iceland (0) 0
East Germany (0) 3 *(Sammer 55, Ernst 63, Doll 65)*
Iceland: Fridriksson; Gislasson, Jonsson A, Torfasson O, Thorkelsson, Saevar Jonsson, Bergsson, Torfasson G, Gretarsson, Sigurvinsson, Gudjohnsen (Margeirsson 59).
East Germany: Heyne; Kreer, Steinmann, Lindner, Doschner, Sammer, Stubner, Reich, Kirsten, Ernst (Steinmann 76), Doll.

6 September, Vienna, 62,500
Austria (0) 0
USSR (0) 0
Austria: Lindenberger; Weber, Russ, Pfeffer, Streiter, Linzmaier, Artner, Zsak, Herzog (Hortnagi 78), Ogris A (Rodax 65), Polster.
USSR: Chanov; Khidiatulin, Gorlukovich, Kuznetsov, Bessonov, Mikhailichenko, Cherenkov (Aleinikov 78), Litovchenko, Zavarov, Dobrovolski, Protasov.

20 September, Reykjavik, 3500
Iceland (0) 2 *(Petursson 56, 72)*
Turkey (0) 1 *(Feyyaz 85)*
Iceland: Sigurdsson; Thordarsson, Bergsson, Gislasson, Oddsson, Orlygsson, Gudjohnsen, Kristinsson, Sigurvinsson, Gretarsson (Margeirsson 71), Petursson.
Turkey: Engin; Gokhan K, Recep, Cuneyt, Semih, Yusuf (Feyyaz 66), Ugur (Mustafa Yucedag 48), Oguz, Unal, Hasan Vesir, Hakan.

8 October, Karl-Marx-Stadt, 15,900
East Germany (0) 2 *(Thom 80, Sammer 82)*
USSR (0) 1 *(Litovchenko 74)*
East Germany: Heyne; Kreer, Stahmann, Lindner, Doschner, Steinmann (Weidemann 88), Stubner, Ernst (Doll 74), Sammer, Kirsten, Thom.
USSR: Chanov; Bessonov, Khidiatulin, Kuznetsov, Kotovchenko, Zavarov, Mikhailichanko, Dobrovolski, Gorlukovich, Protasov, Aleinikov.

25 October, Istanbul, 40,000
Turkey (1) 3 *(Ridvan 12, 52, Feyyaz 60)*
Austria (0) 0
Turkey: Engin; Riza, Semih, Cuneyt, Gokhan K, Unal, Ugur (Tanju 76), Ridvan, Mustafa, Oguz, Feyyaz (Metin Tecimer 87).

Austria: Lindenberger; Russ, Streiter, Pfeffer, Weber, Zsak, Ogris A, Linzmaier, Polster, Herzog (Glatzmayer 57), Artner (Rodax 46).

15 November, Vienna, 65,000
Austria (2) 3 *(Polster 2, 23 (pen), 61)*
East Germany (0) 0
Austria: Lindenberger; Aigner, Peci, Pfeffer, Artner, Keglevits, Linzmaier, Zsak, Hortnagi, Ogris A (Herzog 76, Pfeifenberger 83), Polster.
East Germany: Heyne; Stahmann, Kreer, Lindner, Schossler, Doschner (Doll 43), Stubner, Sammer (Weidemann 78), Steinmann, Kirsten, Thom.

15 November, Simferopol, 30,000
USSR (0) 2 *(Protasov 68, 79)*
Turkey (0) 0
USSR: Dasayev; Luzhny (Rats 46), Khidiatulin, Zigmantovich, Gorlukovich, Yaremchum, Mikhailichanko, Litovchenko, Zavarov, Protasov, Dobrovolski (Cherenkov 46).
Turkey: Engin; Recep, Kemal, Semih, Gokhan K, Mustafa (Metin 46), Oguz, Hakan (Tanju 77), Riza, Ridvan, Feyyaz.

Final table	*P*	*W*	*D*	*L*	*F*	*A*	*Pts*
USSR	8	4	3	1	11	4	11
Austria	8	3	3	2	9	9	9
Turkey	8	3	1	4	12	10	7
East Germany	8	3	1	4	9	13	7
Iceland	8	1	4	3	6	11	6

USSR and Austria qualified

Group 4 *(West Germany, Holland, Wales, Finland)*
31 August, Helsinki, 31,693
Finland (0) 0
West Germany (2) 4 *(Voller 6, 15, Matthaus 52, Riedle 86)*
Finland: Laukkanen; Europaeus, Hannikainen (Lipponen 43), Lahtinen, Petaja, Myyry, Pekonen, Ukkonen (Alatensio 62), Hjelm, Rantanen, Paatelainen.
West Germany: Illgner; Brehme, Gortz, Kohler, Fach, Buchwald (Rolff 26), Littbarski, Hassler, Voller, Matthaus, Eckstein (Riedle 75).

14 September, Amsterdam, 58,000
Holland (0) 1 *(Gullit 82)*
Wales (0) 0
Holland: Van Breukelen; Van Aerle, Rijkaard, Koeman R, Van Tiggelen, Vanenburg (Kieft 66), Wouters, Koeman E, Kruzen, Gullit, Van Basten.
Wales: Southall; Hall, Blackmore, Williams, Knill, Davies, Horne, Nicholas, Rush, Hughes (Saunders 76), Aizlewood.

19 October, Swansea, 9603
Wales (2) 2 *(Saunders (pen) 16, Lahtinen (og) 40)*
Finland (2) 2 *(Ukkonen 8, Paatelainen 45)*
Wales: Southall; Hall (Bowen 59), Blackmore, Nicholas, Van Den Hauwe, Ratcliffe, Horne, Saunders, Rush, Hughes, Pascoe.
Finland: Huttunen; Pekonen, Lahtinen, Europaeus, Kanerva, Myyry (Lipponen 86), Holmgren, Ukkonen, Petaja (Rantanen 61), Paatelainen, Hjelm.

19 October, Munich, 73,000
West Germany (0) 0
Holland (0) 0
West Germany: Illgner; Fach, Kohler, Buchwald, Berthold, Hassler, Matthaus, Thon, Brehme, Klinsmann (Mill 67), Voller.
Holland: Van Breukelen; Van Tiggelen, Koeman R, Rijkaard, Vanenburg, Van Aerle (Winter 20), Wouters, Koeman E, Silooy, Van Basten, Bosman.

26 April, Rotterdam, 53,000
Holland (0) 1 *(Van Basten 87)*
West Germany (0) 1 *(Riedle 68)*
Holland: Hiele; Van Aerle, Van Tiggelen, Koeman R, Rijkaard, Hofkens (Rutjes 84), Vanenburg, Koeman E, Van Basten, Winter, Huistra (Eykelkamp 75).
West Germany: Illgner; Berthold, Brehme, Kohler (Rolff 75), Reuter, Buchwald, Riedle, Moller, Voller (Klinsmann 33), Matthaus, Hassler.

31 May, Cardiff, 25,000
Wales (0) 0
West Germany (0) 0
Wales: Southall; Phillips, Blackmore (Bowen 82), Ratcliffe, Aizlewood, Nicholas, Saunders, Horne, Rush, Hughes, Williams (Pascoe 82).
West Germany: Illgner; Berthold, Reinhardt, Buchwald, Reuter, Fach, Hassler, Moller, Brehme, Riedle (Klinsmann 77), Voller.

31 May, Helsinki, 48,000
Finland (0) 0
Holland (0) 1 *(Kieft 87)*
Finland: Laukkanen; Kanerva, Europaeus, Heikkinen, Ikalainen, Holmgren, Ukkonen (Tornvall 68), Hjelm (Petaja 83), Lipponen, Paatelainen, Myyry.
Holland: Van Breukelen; Koeman R, Van Tiggelen, Rutjes, Van Aerle, Vanenburg (Huistra 83), Rijkaard, Koeman E, Ellerman (Gullit 66), Van Basten, Kieft.

6 September, Helsinki, 7480
Finland (0) 1 *(Lipponen 50)*
Wales (0) 0
Finland: Laukkanen; Lahtinen, Heikkinen, Europaeus, Holmgren, Tarkkio, Ukkonen (Tauriainen 82), Ikalainen, Paatelainen (Tornvall 65), Lipponen, Myyry.
Wales: Southall; Blackmore, Phillips, Nicholas (Maguire 88), Aizlewood, Ratcliffe, Saunders, Williams (Bowen 80), Rush, Hughes, Davies.

4 October, Dortmund, 40,000
West Germany (1) 6 *(Moller 12, 80, Littbarski 46, Klinsmann 52, Voller 62, Matthaus 85 (pen))*
Finland (0) 1 *(Lipponen 75)*
West Germany: Illgner; Reiter, Brehme, Buchwald, Augenthaler, Hassler (Bein 46), Littbarski, Moller (Mill 81), Voller, Matthaus, Klinsmann.
Finland: Laukkanen; Lahtinen, Heikkinen, Europaeus, Holmgren, Tarkkio, Ukkonen, Ikalainen (Hjelm 71), Myyry, Paatelainen (Lius 62), Lipponen.

11 October, Wrexham, 9025
Wales (0) 1 *(Bowen 89)*
Holland (1) 2 *(Rutjes 13, Bosman 79)*
Wales: Southall; Blackmore, Bowen, Nicholas, Hopkins, Maguire, Saunders, Phillips, Roberts (Jones 64), Williams (Pascoe 85), Allen.
Holland: Van Breukelen; Van Aerle, Rutjes, Koeman R, Koot, Wouters, Van't Schip, Hofkens, Kieft, Rijkaard (Bosman 46), Rob Witschge (Van Basten 71).

15 November, Rotterdam, 49,500
Holland (0) 3 *(Bosman 57, Koeman E 62, Koeman R 69 (pen))*
Finland (0) 0
Holland: Van Breukelen; Van Aerle, Koeman R, Rijkaard, Van Tiggelen, Van't Schip (Rob Witschge 78), Wouters, Koeman E (Hofkens 68), Ellerman, Bosman, Van Basten.
Finland: Laukkanen; Kanerva, Holmgren, Europaeus, Heikkinen, Ikalainen, Myyry, Ukkonen (Tauriainen 56), Tarkkio (Petaja 75), Lipponen, Paatelainen.

15 November, Cologne, 60,000
West Germany (1) 2 *(Voller 27, Hassler 48)*
Wales (1) 1 *(Allen 11)*

West Germany: Illgner; Augenthaler (Reinhardt A 46), Reuter, Buchwald, Brehme, Hassler, Dorfner, Moller (Bein 82), Littbarski, Klinsmann, Voller.
Wales: Southall; Bowen (Horne 65), Aizlewood, Phillips, Blackmore, Saunders, Melville (Pascoe 80), Nicholas, Hughes, Allen, Maguire.

Final table	*P*	*W*	*D*	*L*	*F*	*A*	*Pts*
Holland	6	4	2	0	8	2	10
West Germany	6	3	3	0	13	3	9
Finland	6	1	1	4	4	16	3
Wales	6	0	2	4	4	8	2

Holland and West Germany qualified

Group 5 *(France, Scotland, Yugoslavia, Norway, Cyprus)*
14 September, Oslo, 22,769
Norway (1) 1 *(Fjortoft 44)*
Scotland (1) 2 *(McStay 14, Johnston 62)*
Norway: Thorstvedt; Henriksen, Johnsen, Bratseth, Giske, Osvold, Brandhaug, Loken, Sorloth, Sundby (Berg 2, Jakobsen 84), Fjortoft.
Scotland: Leighton; Nicol, Malpas, Gillespie, McLeish, Miller, Aitken (Durrant 55), McStay, Johnston, McClair, Gallacher.

28 September, Paris, 25,000
France (0) 1 *(Papin 84 (pen))*
Norway (0) 0
France: Bats; Amoros, Boli (Kastendeuch 63), Casoni, Sonor, Sauzee, Bravo, Dib, Passi (Paille 76), Papin, Xuereb.
Norway: Thorstvedt; Henriksen (Halle), Johnsen, Kojedal, Giske, Osvold (Gulbrandsen 81), Brandhaug, Bratseth, Berg, Sorloth, Jakobsen.

19 October, Hampden Park, 42,771
Scotland (1) 1 *(Johnston 17)*
Yugoslavia (1) 1 *(Katanec 36)*
Scotland: Goram; Gough, Malpas, Nicol, McLeish, Miller, Aitken (Speedie 70), McStay, Johnston, McClair, Bett (McCoist 55).
Yugoslavia: Ivkovic; Stanojkovic, Spasic (Sabanadzovic 83), Jozic, Hadzibegic, Radanovic, Stojkovic, Katanec, Cvetkovic (Jankovic M 89), Bazdarevic, Zlatko Vujovic.

22 October, Nicosia, 3000
Cyprus (0) 1 *(Pittas (pen) 78)*
France (1) 1 *(Xuereb 44)*
Cyprus: Pantzarias; Christodolu, Stavru, Miamiliotis, Pittas, Petsas, Yiangudakis, Nikolau, Kantilos, Savva, Christofi (Ioannu 77).
France: Bats; Sonor, Casoni, Boli, Amoros, Bravo (Paille 80), Dib, Sauzee, Passi (Vercruysse 72), Papin, Xuereb.

2 November, Limassol, 7767
Cyprus (0) 0
Norway (0) 3 *(Sorloth 56, 78, Osvold 89)*
Cyprus: Pantzarias; Pittas, Miamiliotis, Christodolu (Kastanis 25), Stavrou, Yiangudakis, Kantilos (Koliandris 31), Savva, Savvides, Nikolau, Christofi.
Norway: Thorstvedt; Lokken, Kojedal, Bratseth, Halle, Osvold, Brandhaug, Halvorsen, Gulbrandsen, Sorloth, Agdestein.

19 November, Belgrade, 16,000
Yugoslavia (1) 3 *(Spasic 11, Susic 76, Stojkovic 82)*
France (1) 2 *(Perez 3, Sauzee 68)*
Yugoslavia: Ivkovic; Stanojkovic, Spasic (Juric 55), Hadzibegic, Jozic, Stojkovic, Susic, Bazdarevic, Katanec, Cvetkovic (Savicevic 70), Zlatko Vujovic.
France: Bats; Roche, Boli, Kastendeuch, Amoros, Ferreri (Papin 78), Dib, Sauzee, Tigana, Paille, Perez (Bravo 69).

11 December, Rijeka, 9000
Yugoslavia (3) 4 *(Savicevic 13, 33, 82, Hadzibegic 44 (pen))*
Cyprus (0) 0
Yugoslavia: Ivkovic; Stanojkovic, Spasic (Juric 46), Brnovic, Hadzibegic, Josic, Stojkovic, Susic, Savicevic, Bazdarevic, Zlatko Vujovic.
Cyprus: Pantzarias; Antonionios, Pittas, Papacoats, Stavrou, Yiangudakis, Savva, Nikolau, Christodolu (Kastanas 65), Ioannu (Petsas 77), Tsingis.

8 February, Limassol, 25,000
Cyprus (1) 2 *(Koliandris 14, Ioannu 47)*
Scotland (1) 3 *(Johnston 9, Gough 54, 96 – injury time)*
Cyprus: Pantzarias, Pittas, Miamiliotis, Christodolu, Socratous, Yiangudakis, Koliandris, Savva (Petsas 36), Savvides, Nikolau, Ioannu.
Scotland: Leighton; Gough, Malpas, Aitken, McLeish, Narey, Nicol (Ferguson I 9), McStay, McClair, Speedie (McInally 68), Johnston.

8 March, Hampden Park, 65,204
Scotland (1) 2 *(Johnston 28, 52)*
France (0) 0
Scotland: Leighton; Gough, Malpas, Aitken, McLeish, Gillespie, Nicol, McStay, McCoist (McClair 69), Ferguson (Strachan 56), Johnston.
France: Bats; Amoros, Silvestre, Sonor, Battiston, Sauzee, Durand (Paille 57), Laurey, Papin, Blanc, Xuereb (Perez 70).

26 April, Hampden Park, 50,081
Scotland (1) 2 *(Johnston 26, McCoist 63)*
Cyprus (0) 1 *(Nicolau 62)*
Scotland: Leighton; Gough, Malpas, Aitken, McLeish, McPherson, Nevin (Nicholas 74), McStay, Johnston, McCoist, Durie (Speedie 59).
Cyprus: Charitou; Castanas, Pittas (Elia 64), Christodolou, Michael, Yiangudakis, Petsas, Nicolau, Savvides, Ioannou Y, Kollandris.

29 April, Paris, 39,469
France (0) 0
Yugoslavia (0) 0
France: Bats; Amoros, Sonor, Boli, Battison, Sauzee, Xuereb (Deschamps 76), Durand (Cocard 46), Paille, Blanc, Perez.
Yugoslavia: Ivkovic; Stanojkovic, Spasic, Katanec, Hadzibegic, Josic, Zoran Vujovic, Susic, Bazdarevic, Stojkovic, Zlatko Vujovic (Brnovic 85).

21 May, Oslo, 10,273
Norway (3) 3 *(Osvold 17, Sorloth 34, Bratseth 35)*
Cyprus (1) 1 *(Kollandris 44)*
Norway: Thorstvedt; Halle, Kojedal, Bratseth, Giske, Lokken, Serkh (Gulbrandsen 82), Osvold, Jakobsen, Sorloth (Agdestein 61), Fjortoft.
Cyprus: Charitou; Kastanas, Pittas, Christodolou, Socratous, Yiangudakis, Kollandris (Andrelis 69), Nicolau, Savvides (Orfanides 87), Petsas, Ioannou.

14 June, Oslo, 22,740
Norway (0) 1 *(Fjortoft 90)*
Yugoslavia (1) 2 *(Stojkovic 22, Zlatko Vujovic 88)*
Norway: Ole By Rise; Halle, Bratseth, Kojedal, Giske, Lokken, Berg (Gulbrandsen 83), Osvold, Jakobsen, Sorloth (Agdestein 63), Fjortoft.
Yugoslavia: Ivkovic; Spasic, Stanojkovic, Jozic, Katanec, Hadzibegic, Zoran Vujovic, Susic (Vujavic 73), Bazdarevic, Stojkovic, Zlatko Vujovic.

5 September, Oslo, 8564
Norway (0) 1 *(Bratseth 84)*
France (1) 1 *(Papin 40 (pen))*
Norway: Thorstvedt; Halle, Kojedal, Bratseth, Bjornebye, Lokken, Brandhaug (Berg 75), Ahlsen, Jakobsen JI, Jorn Andersen, Fjortoft (Agdestein 75).

France: Bats; Amoros, Di Meco, Le Roux (Silvestre 55), Sauzee, Pardo, Deschamps, Perez, Papin, Ferreri (Blanc 75), Cantona.

6 September, Zagreb, 42,500
Yugoslavia (0) 3 *(Katanec 52, Nicol (og) 58, Gillespie og 59)*
Scotland (1) 1 *(Durie 37)*
Yugoslavia: Ivkovic; Spasic, Baljic, Katanec, Hadzibegic, Brnovic, Susic, Bazdarevic, Jakovljevic (Savicevic 73), Stojkovic, Zlatko Vujovic.
Scotland: Leighton; Gillespie, Malpas, Aitken, McLeish, Miller, Nicol, McStay, McCoist, MacLeod, Durie (McInally).

11 October, Sarajevo, 30,000
Yugoslavia (1) 1 *(Hadzibegic 44 (pen))*
Norway (0) 0
Yugoslavia: Ivkovic; Spasic, Baljic, Brnovic, Hadzibegic, Jozic, Stojkovic, Bazdarevic, Susic, Jakovljevic (Stanojkovic 84), Zlatko Vujovic.
Norway: Thorstvedt; Halle, Kojedal, Bratseth, Bjornebye, Lokken, Brandhaug, Ahlsen, Jakobsen, Jorn Andersen (Sorloth 70), Fjortoft.

11 October, Paris, 25,000
France (1) 3 *(Deschamps 25, Cantona 61, Nicol (og) 89)*
Scotland (0) 0
France: Bats; Silvestre, Le Roux (Casoni 46), Sauzee, Di Meco, Durand, Pardo, Deschamps, Ferreri, Cantona, Perez (Bravo 81).
Scotland: Leighton; Nicol, Gough, McLeish, Malpas, Aitken, Strachan (McInally 64), McStay, MacLeod (Bett 75), McCoist, Johnston.

28 October, Athens, 5000
Cyprus (1) 1 *(Pittas 38 (pen))*
Yugoslavia (1) 2 *(Stanojkovic 5, Pancev 49)*
Cyprus: Kouis; Pittas, Kostadinou, Scoratous, Yiangudakis, Koliandris, Miamiliotis, Petsas (Tsingis 69), Kastanas, Nikolau, Ioannu (Agas 84).
Yugoslavia: Omerovic; Stanojkovic, Marovic, Brnovic, Vulic, Spasic, Prosinecki (Mijakovic 70), Savicevic, Pancev, Stojkovic, Skoro.

15 November, Hampden Park, 70,000
Scotland (1) 1 *(McCoist 44)*
Norway (0) 1 *(Johnsen 89)*
Scotland: Leighton; McPherson, Malpas, Aitken, McLeish, Miller (MacLeod 66), Johnston, McStay, McCoist, Bett, Cooper (McClair 74).
Norway: Thorstvedt; Hansen H, Bratseth, Kojedal (Halvorsen 83), Johnsen, Gulbrandsen, Bjornebye, Ahlsen, Skammelsrud (Bohinen 58), Sorloth, Fjortoft.

18 November, Toulouse, 34,687 *(including 15,450 children admitted free)*
France (1) 2 *(Deschamps 25, Blanc 75)*
Cyprus (0) 0
France: Bats; Amoros, Silvestre, Casoni, Sauzee, Ferreri, Pardo, Deschamps, Perez (Blanc 17), Papin, Cantona.
Cyprus: Charitou; Kastanas, Pittas, Christodolu, Socratous, Constantinou, Nikolau, Christofi, Savva, Koliandris, Ioannu.

Final table	*P*	*W*	*D*	*L*	*F*	*A*	*Pts*
Yugoslavia	8	6	2	0	16	6	14
Scotland	8	4	2	2	12	12	10
France	8	3	3	2	10	7	9
Norway	8	2	2	4	10	9	6
Cyprus	8	0	1	7	6	20	1

Yugoslavia and Scotland qualified

Group 6 *(Spain, Hungary, Northern Ireland, Eire, Malta)*
21 May, Belfast, 9000
Northern Ireland (3) 3 *(Quinn 14, Penney 23, Clarke 25)*
Malta (0) 0
Northern Ireland: McKnight; Donaghy, Worthington, McClelland, McDonald, O'Neill, Penney (McNally 81), Wilson D, Clarke, Quinn, Dennison (Black).
Malta: Cluett; Camilleri E (Refalo 46), Azzopardi, Galea, Brincat, Buttigieg, Busuttil, Scerri, Carabott, Scicluna, Di Giorgio (Caruana 60).

14 September, Belfast, 19,873
Northern Ireland (0) 0
Eire (0) 0
Northern Ireland: McKnight; Donaghy (Rogan), Worthington, McClelland, McDonald, O'Neill, Penney, Wilson D, Clarke, Quinn, Black.
Eire: Peyton; Morris, Hughton, McGrath, McCarthy, Moran, Houghton, Whelan, Aldridge, Cascarino, Sheedy.

19 October, Budapest, 18,000
Hungary (0) 1 *(Vincze 84)*
Northern Ireland (0) 0
Hungary: Disztl P; Sallai, Nagy, Sass, Meszoly (Dajka 46), Garaba, Kiprich, Kozma, Bognar, Detari, Hajszan (Vincze 81).
Northern Ireland: McKnight; Rogan, Worthington, McClelland, McDonald, Donaghy, Dennison, Wilson D, Clarke (Quinn 81), O'Neill (Wilson K 58), Black.

16 November, Seville, 50,000
Spain (0) 2 *(Manolo 52, Butragueno 66)*
Eire (0) 0
Spain: Zubizarreta; Quique Flores (Solana 84), Jimenez, Andrinua, Sanchis, Gorriz, Michel, Roberto, Martin Vazquez, Manolo (Ramon 67), Butrageuno.
Eire: Bonner; Morris, McCarthy, Staunton, O'Leary, Moran, Houghton, Sheridan (O'Brien 82), Aldridge (Quinn 65), Cascarino, Galvin.

11 December, Valletta, 12,000
Malta (0) 2 *(Busuttil 46, 90)*
Hungary (1) 2 *(Vincze 5, Kiprich 56)*
Malta: Cluett; Camilleri E (Saliba 53), Azzopardi, Galea, Camilleri S, (Vella S 70), Busuttil, Vella R, Carabott, Gregory, De Giorgio, Woods.
Hungary: Disztl P; Kozma, Disztl L, Keller, Kekesi, Csuhay, Kiprich (Pinter 85), Kovacs, Czucsansky, Vincze (Fischer 70), Balog.

21 December, Seville, 70,000
Spain (1) 4 *(Rogan (og) 30, Butragueno 55, Michel 60 (pen), Roberto (64)*
Northern Ireland (0) 0
Spain: Zubizarreta; Quique Flores, Jimenez, Andrinua, Gorriz, Roberto, Manolo (Julio Salinas 78), Michel, Butragueno, Martin Vazquez, Beguiristain (Serna 65).
Northern Ireland: McKnight; Rogan, Worthington, McCreery (Quinn 54), McDonald, McClelland, Donaghy (O'Neill 72), Penney, Clarke, Wilson K, Black.

22 January, Valletta, 23,000
Malta (0) 0
Spain (1) 2 *(Michel (pen) 16, Beguiristain 51)*
Malta: Cluett; Camilleri S (Camilleri E 55), Galea, Buttigieg, Azzopardi, Brincat (Scerri 46), Vella R, Gregory, Carabott, De Giorgio, Busuttil.
Spain: Zubizarreta; Quique Flores, Sanchis, Andrinua, Jimenez, Michel, Roberto, Martin Vazquez, Manolo, Butragueno (Gorriz 76), Beguiristain (Eusebio 66).

8 February, Belfast, 20,000
Northern Ireland (0) 0
Spain (1) 2 *(Andrinua 3, Manolo 84)*

Northern Ireland: McKnight; Ramsey, Rogan, Donaghy, McClelland, Wilson D (Clarke 68), Dennison (O'Neill 63), Sanchez, Quinn, Wilson K, Black.
Spain: Zubizarreta; Chendo (Eusebio 44), Jimenez, Andrinua, Serna, Gorriz, Bakero (Manolo 75), Michel, Butragueno, Roberto, Martin Vazquez.

8 March, Budapest, 20,000
Hungary (0) 0
Eire (0) 0
Hungary: Disztl P; Kozma, Disztl L, Bognar Z, Sass, Kovacs E, Detari, Hajszan, Gregor (Boda 77), Kiprich, Meszaros (Bognar G 46).
Eire: Bonner; Morris, Hughton, McGrath, McCarthy, Moran, Whelan, Houghton, Aldridge (Brady 80), Cascarino (Quinn 80), Sheedy.

23 March, Seville, 50,000
Spain (1) 4 ***(Michel 38, 68 (pen), Manolo 71, 80)***
Malta (0) 0
Spain: Zubizarreta; Quique Sanchez, Jimenez, Andrinua, Roberto, Sanchis, Michel, Butragueno, Martin Vazquez (Eusebio 68), Beguiristain (Eloy 68), Manolo.
Malta: Cluett; Camilleri E, Azzopardi A (Cauchi 30), Buttigieg, Galea, Vella R, De Giorgio, Scerri C, Carabott, Gregory, Busuttil.

12 April, Budapest, 15,000
Hungary (0) 1 ***(Boda 49)***
Malta (1) 1 ***(Busuttil 7)***
Hungary: Disztl P; Kozma (Kiprich 57), Keller, Disztl L, Kovacs E, Bognar Z, Boda, Bognar G, Sass (Fischer 46), Detari, Hajszan.
Malta: Cluett; Camilleri E, Azzopardi A, Galea, Cauchi (Vella S 46), Buttigieg, Busuttil, Vella R, Carabott, Scerri, Gregory.

26 April, Valletta, 15,000
Malta (0) 0
Northern Ireland (0) 2 ***(Clarke 55, O'Neill 73)***
Malta: Cluett; Buttigieg, Camilleri E, Cauchi (Vella S 62), Galea, De Giorgio, Scerri, Vella R, Busuttil, Gregory, Carabott (Delia 78).
Northern Ireland: Wright; Donaghy, Worthington (Rogan 86), McCreery, McClelland, Dennison, Wilson D, Quinn, Clarke, Sanchez (O'Neill 70), Wilson K.

26 April, Dublin, 49,160
Eire (1) 1 ***(Michel (og) 15)***
Spain (0) 0
Eire: Bonner; Hughton, Staunton, McCarthy, Moran, Whelan, McGrath, Houghton, Stapleton (Townsend 69), Cascarino, Sheedy.
Spain: Zubizarreta; Quique Sanchez (Eusebio 69), Jimenez, Serna, Sanchis, Gorriz, Manolo, Michel, Butragueno (Julio Salinas 70), Roberto, Martin Vazquez.

28 May, Dublin, 49,000
Eire (1) 2 ***(Houghton 32, Moran 55)***
Malta (0) 0
Eire: Bonner; Hughton, Staunton, O'Leary, Moran, Whelan, McGrath, Houghton (Townsend 70), Stapleton (Aldridge 27), Cascarino, Sheedy.
Malta: Cluett; Camilleri E, Azzopardi (Carabott 65), Galea, Vella S, Buttigieg, Busuttil, Vella R, Scerri, De Giorgio, Gregory.

4 June, Dublin, 49,000
Eire (1) 2 ***(McGrath 33, Cascarino 80)***
Hungary (0) 0
Eire: Bonner; Hughton, Staunton, O'Leary, McGrath (Morris 80), Moran, Houghton, Townsend, Aldridge (Brady 74), Cascarino, Sheedy.
Hungary: Disztl P; Bognar Z, Fitos, Disztl L, Garaba, Kozma, Meszaros (Vincze 71), Detari, Czehi (Bognar G 66), Keller, Boda.

6 September, Belfast, 8000
Northern Ireland (0) 1 *(Whiteside 89)*
Hungary (2) 2 *(Kovacs K 13, Bognar G 44)*
Northern Ireland: Wright; Fleming, Worthington, Rogan, McDonald, McCreery, Wilson D, Quinn, (O'Neill M 64), Clarke, Whiteside, Black.
Hungary: Disztl P; Sallai, Keller, Disztl L, Kovacs E, Limperger, Bognar G (Istvan 84), Sass, Fischer (Bognar Z 89), Detari, Kovacs K.

11 October, Budapest, 40,000
Hungary (1) 2 *(Pinter 38, 82)*
Spain (2) 2 *(Julio Salinas 30, Michel 35)*
Hungary: Disztl P; Sallai, Keller (Lovasz 71), Pinter, Bognar Z, Roth (Kozma 46), Bognar G, Detari, Vincze, Kovacs K, Kiprich.
Spain: Zubizarreta; Chendo, Sanchis, Andrinua, Jimenez, Roberto, Michel, Martin Vazquez, Villaroya, Manolo (Hierro 84), Julio Salinas (Pardeza 67).

11 October, Dublin, 48,500
Eire (1) 3 *(Whelan 42, Cascarino 48, Houghton 57)*
Northern Ireland (0) 0
Eire: Bonner; Morris, Staunton (O'Leary 77), McCarthy, Moran, Whelan, Townsend, Houghton, Aldridge, Cascarino, Sheedy.
Northern Ireland: Dunlop; Fleming, Worthington, Donaghy, McDonald, McCreery (O'Neill C 72), Wilson D, O'Neill M (Wilson K 80), Clarke, Whiteside, Dennison.

15 November, Seville, 20,000
Spain (3) 4 *(Manolo 7, Butragueno 24, Juanito 40, Fernando 63)*
Hungary (0) 0
Spain: Zubizarreta; Chendo, Sanchis, MIlla, Jimenez, Michel (Eusebio 65), Juanito, Fernando, Manolo (Julio Salinas 65), Btragueno, Villaroya.
Hungary: Disztl P; Simon, Pinter, Keller, Bognar Z, Kovacs E, Bognar G, (Szalma 62), Kovacs K, Fischer (Bacsi 62), Szekeres, Kozma.

15 November, Valletta, 25,000
Malta (0) 0
Eire (1) 2 *(Aldridge 31, 68 (pen))*
Malta: Cini; Vella S, Azzopardi (Suda 68), Galea, Scerri, Buttigieg, Busuttil, Zerafa (Zarb 68), Carabott, De Giorgio, Gregory.
Eire: Bonner; McGrath, Moran (Morris 26), Staunton, O'Leary, Houghton, Sheedy, Townsend, Whelan, Aldridge, Cascarino.

Final table	*P*	*W*	*D*	*L*	*F*	*A*	*Pts*
Spain	8	6	1	1	20	3	13
Eire	8	5	2	1	10	2	12
Hungary	8	2	4	2	8	12	8
Northern Ireland	8	2	1	5	6	12	5
Malta	8	0	2	6	3	18	2

Spain and Eire qualified

Group 7 *(Belgium, Portugal, Czechoslovakia, Switzerland, Luxembourg)*
21 September, Luxembourg, 2500
Luxembourg (0) 1 *(Langers 80)*
Switzerland (3) 4 *(Sutter A 15 sec, Turkyilmaz 21 (pen), 53, Sutter B 28)*
Luxembourg: Van Rijswijk; Meunier, Bossi, Weis, Petry, Girres (Scuto 63), Hellers, Jeitz, Scholten, Langers, Krings (Morocutti 73).
Switzerland: Corminboeuf; Geiger, Tschuppert, Martin Weber, Mottiez, Andermatt (Lei-Ravello 70), Hermann, Favre, Sutter B, Turkyilmaz, Sutter A (Bonvin 79).

19 October, Brussels, 14,450
Belgium (1) 1 *(Vervoort 30)*
Switzerland (0) 0

Belgium: Bodart; Grun, Clijsters, Demol, Versavel, Emmers, Van der Elst F, Scifo, Vervoort, Ceulemans, Nilis (Severeyns 76).
Switzerland: Corminboeuf; Mottiez, Geiger, Weber, Schallibaum, Andermatt (Bonvin 76), Hermann, Favre, Zuffi, Sutter B, Turkyilmaz.

18 October, Esch-sur-Alzette, 2500
Luxembourg (0) 0
Czechoslovakia (2) 2 *(Hasek 25, Chovanec 35)*
Luxembourg: Van Rijswijk; Meunier, Scheuer, Petry, Bossi, Jeitz (Girres 82), Hellers, Weis, Scholten, Langers, Krings (Morocutti 61).
Czechoslovakia: Stejskal; Bielik, Kadlec, Hasek, Bilek, Nemecek, Fieber, Chovanec, Griga (Danek 81), Skuhravy, Weiss (Hyravy 75).

16 November, Bratislava, 48,000
Czechoslovakia (0) 0
Belgium (0) 0
Czechoslovakia: Stejskal; Bielik, Nemecek (Danek 87), Chovanec, Kadlec, Vlk, Weiss (Moravcik 80), Hasek, Bilek, Griga, Luhovy.
Belgium: Preud'homme; Demol, Gerets, Grun, Albert, Dewolf, Emmers, Veyt, Van der Elst F, Scifo (Van den Linden 75), Christiaens (Nilis 82).

16 November, Oporto, 29,000
Portugal (1) 1 *(Gomes 31)*
Luxembourg (0) 0
Portugal: Silvino; Jaime, Sobrinho, Morato, Alvaro, Rui Barros, Vitor Paneira, Nunes, Futre, Jordao (Jaime Magalhaes 46), Gomes.
Luxembourg: Van Rijswijk; Meunier, Scheuer, Petry, Bossi, Girres, Jeitz, Weis, Scholten (Thome 82), Krings (Malget 60), Langers.

15 February, Lisbon, 70,000
Portugal (0) 1 *(Paneira 53)*
Belgium (0) 1 *(Gerets 83)*
Portugal: Silvino; Joao Pinto, Oliveira, Sobrinho, Veloso, Nunes, Vitor Paneira (Cesar Brito 86), Sousa, Rui Barros, Futre (Pacheco 61), Semedo.
Belgium: Preud'homme; Gerets, Grun, De Wolf, Versavel, Emmers, Demol (Van der Linden 77), Scifo, Van der Elst, Ceulemans, De Gryse.

26 April, Lisbon, 15,000
Portugal (0) 3 *(Joao Pinto 48, Frederico 56, Vitor Paneira 69)*
Switzerland (0) 1 *(Zuffi 64)*
Portugal: Silvano; Joao Pinto, Sobrinho, Frederico (Oliveira 87), Veloso, Nunes, Andre, Vitor Paneira, Rui Barros, Sousa (Jorge Silva 46), Cesar Brito.
Switzerland: Brunner; Mottiez, Birrel (Ryf 73), Weber M, Koller, Marini, Sutter B, Hermann, Favre, Zuffi, Sutter A (Turkyilmaz 86).

29 April, Brussels, 21,000
Belgium (1) 2 *(Degryse 29, 77)*
Czechoslovakia (1) 1 *(Luhovy 41)*
Belgium: Preud'homme; Gerets, Demol, Grun, Albert, Versavel, Van der Elst F, Emmers, Ceulemans, Degryse, Nilis (Van der Linden 65).
Czechoslovakia: Stejskal; Bilek (Weiss 85), Chovanec, Kocian, Straka, Kadlec, Moravcik, Vik (Nemecek 83), Hasek, Griga, Luhovy.

9 May, Prague, 16,350
Czechoslovakia (1) 4 *(Griga 6, Skuhravy 76, 84, Bilek 81)*
Luxembourg (0) 0
Czechoslovakia: Stejskal; Bilek, Kadlec (Bielik 46), Hasek, Kocian, Nemecek (Weiss 71), Straka, Chovanec, Griga, Skuhravy, Moravcik.
Luxembourg: Van Rijswijk; Meunier, Scheuer, Petry, Bossi, Girres, Birsens, Weis, Jeitz (Salbene 76), Hellers, Krings (Malget 89).

7 June, Berne, 30,000
Switzerland (0) 0
Czechoslovakia (1) 1 *(Skuhravy 21)*
Switzerland: Brunner; Koller, Marini, Schepull, Weber, Hermann, Sutter R (Turkyilmaz 58), Geiger, Sutter A, Sutter B (Zuffi 71), Halter.
Czechoslovakia: Stejskal; Bielik, Kadlec, Kocian, Straka, Hasek, Chovanec (Nemecek 83), Moravcik, Bilek, Griga,Skuhravy (Danek 56).

1 June, Lille, 10,000
Luxembourg (0) 0
Belgium (1) 5 *(Van der Linden 13, 52, 62 (pen), 90, Vervoort 64)*
Luxembourg: Van Rijswijk; Meunier, Scheuer, Petry, Bossi, Girres, Birsens, Jeitz (Salbene 75), Scholten (Malget 83), Langers, Krings.
Belgium: Preud'homme; Gerets, Sanders, Versavel, Van der Elst F (Scifo 73), Emmers, Demol, Vervoort, De Gryse, Van der Linden, Ceulemans.

6 September, Brussels, 28,250
Belgium (1) 3 *(Ceulemans 34, Van der Linden 59, 69)*
Portugal (0) 0
Belgium: Preud'homme; Gerets, Grun, Demol, De Wolf, Emmers, Franky Van der Elst, Versavel, De Gryse, Ceulemans, Van der Linden (Nilis 86).
Portugal: Silvino; Joao Pinto; Sobrinho, Venancio, Veloso, Carlos Xavier, Vitor Paneira (Rui Aguas 60), Rui Barros, Cesar Brito, Futre, Andre.

20 September, Neuchatel, 16,500
Switzerland (1) 1 *(Turkyilmaz 28 (pen))*
Portugal (0) 2 *(Futre 74 (pen), Rui Aguas 77)*
Switzerland: Brunner; Rey, Weber, Baumann, Geiger, Piffaretti, Favre (Herr 78), Hermann, Chapuisat, Beat Sutter (Zuffi 69), Turkyilmaz.
Portugal: Silvino; Vitor Paneira (Sobrinho 89), Joao Pinto, Frederico, Venancio, Veloso, Andrea, Adelino Nunes, Jaime Magalhaes (Rui Aguas 44), Rui Barros, Futre.

6 October, Prague, 28,000
Czechoslovakia (1) 2 *(Bilek 11 (pen), 82)*
Portugal (0) 1 *(Rui Aguas 74)*
Czechoslovakia: Stejskal; Straka, Kadlec, Hasek, Kocian, Cabala (Nemecek 70), Bilek, Chovanec, Griga, Skuhravy, Moravcik (Kinier 89).
Portugal: Silvino; Frederico, Joao Pinto, Venancio, Veloso, Nunes (Lima 71), Sobrinho (Vitor Paneira 27), Rui Barros, Rui Aguas, Futre, Andre.

11 October, Basle, 5000
Switzerland (0) 2 *(Knup 50, Turkyilmaz 60)*
Belgium (0) 2 *(De Gryse 58, Geiger (og) 73)*
Switzerland: Brunner; Geiger, Piffaretti, Herr, Baumann, Koller, Hermann, Bickel, Douglas (Knup 46), Turkyilmaz, Chapuisat (Hottiger 80).
Belgium: Preud'homme; Demol, Gerets, Clijsters, Franky Van der Elst, Versavel, Emmers (Scifo 46), Vervoort, De Gryse, Ceulemans, Van der Linden.

11 October, Saarbrucken, 15,000
Luxembourg (0) 0
Portugal (1) 3 *(Rui Aguas 43, 53, Rui Barros 72)*
Luxembourg: Van Rijswijk; Bossi, Weiss, Birsens, Girres, Groff (Jeitz 70), Salbene, Langers, Malget, Hallers, Reiter (Scholten 58).
Portugal: Silvino; Joao Pinto, Venancio, Frederico, Fonseca (Pedro Xavier 33), Vitor Paneira, Nunes (Jaime Magalhaes 64), Veloso, Rui Barros, Rui Aguas, Lima.

25 October, Prague, 33,000
Czechoslovakia (1) 3 *(Skuhravy 17, Bilek 86, Moravcik 88)*
Switzerland (0) 0
Czechoslovakia: Stejskal; Straka, Kocian, Kadlec (Nemecek 60), Bilek, Weiss (Hyravy 73), Hasek, Chovanec, Moravcik, Luhovy, Skuhravy.

Switzerland: Brunner; Weber, Geiger, Herr, Baumann, Piffaretti (Andermatt 55), Hermann, Koller (Lorenz 70), Heldmann, Turkyilmaz, Bonvin.

25 October, Brussels, 20,000
Belgium (0) 1 *(Versavel 86)*
Luxemboug (0) 1 *(Hellers 88)*
Belgium: Preud'homme; Grun, Clijsters, Broeckart, Versavel, Emmers (Nilis 76), Van der Elst, Boffin (Claesen 76), De Gryse, Scifo, Ceulemans.
Luxembourg: Van Rijswijk; Bossi, Scheuer (Scholten 82), Weiss, Birsens, Girres, Hellers, Salbene (Jeitz 75), Groff, Langers, Malget.

15 November, Lisbon, 50,000
Portugal (0) 0
Czechoslovakia (0) 0
Portugal: Silvino; Joao Pinto (Vitor Paneira 46), Venancio, Frederico, Veloso, Jorge Ferreira, Pacheco, Sousa, Rui Barros, Cesar Brito (Pedro Xavier 80), Rui Aguas.
Czechoslovakia: Stejskal; Kocian, Straka, Kadlec, Nemecek, Bilek, Hasek, Chovanec, Moravcik (Kiniek 88), Skuhravy, Luhovy (Weiss 87).

15 November, St Gallen, 2500
Switzerland (0) 2 *(Bonvin 54, Turkyilmaz 62)*
Luxembourg (1) 1 *(Malget 14)*
Switzerland: Brunner; Geiger, Marini, Herr, Baumann, Koller, Heldmann (Schepull 59), Hermann, Sutter A (Bonvin 46), Turkyilmaz, Knup.
Luxembourg: Van Rijswijk; Bossi, Birsens, Weiss, Scheuer, Girres, Ellers, Salbene, Groff, Malget (Scholten 83), Morocutti.

Final table	*P*	*W*	*D*	*L*	*F*	*A*	*Pts*
Belgium	8	4	4	0	15	5	12
Czechoslovakia	8	5	2	1	13	3	12
Portugal	8	4	2	2	11	8	10
Switzerland	8	2	1	5	10	14	5
Luxembourg	8	0	1	7	3	22	1

Belgium and Czechoslovakia qualified

ASIA

First Round

Group 1

6.1.89 Qatar (1) 1 Jordan (0) 0
6.1.89 Oman (1) 1 Iraq (1) 1
13.1.89 Oman (0) 0 Qatar (0) 0
13.1.89 Jordan (0) 0 Iraq (0) 1
20.1.89 Jordan (2) 2 Oman (0) 0
20.1.89 Qatar (0) 1 Iraq (0) 0
27.1.89 Jordan (0) 1 Qatar (0) 1
27.1.89 Iraq (1) 3 Oman (0) 1
3.2.89 Qatar (1) 3 Oman (0) 0
3.2.89 Iraq (2) 4 Jordan (0) 0
10.2.89 Oman (0) 0 Jordan (0) 2
10.2.89 Iraq (1) 2 Qatar (1) 2

Group 2 *(Bahrain withdrew)*

10.3.89 Yemen AR (0) 0 Syria (1) 1
15.3.89 Saudi Arabia (2) 5 Syria (1) 4
20.3.89 Yemen AR (0) 0 Saudi Arabia (0) 1
25.3.89 Syria (1) 2 Yemen AR (0) 0
30.3.89 Syria (0) 0 Saudi Arabia (0) 0
5.4.89 Saudi Arabia (1) 1 Yemen AR (0) 0

Group 3 *(Yemen PDR withdrew)*

6.1.89 Pakistan (0) 0 Kuwait (0) 1
13.1.89 Kuwait (1) 3 UAE (0) 2
20.1.89 UAE (2) 5 Pakistan (0) 0
27.1.89 Kuwait (1) 2 Pakistan (0) 0
3.2.89 UAE (0) 1 Kuwait (0) 0
10.2.89 Pakistan (0) 1 UAE (3) 4

Group 4 *(India withdrew)*

23.5.89 Malaysia (0) 2 Nepal (0) 0
23.5.89 Singapore (0) 0 Korea Rep (2) 3
25.5.89 Malaysia (0) 1 Singapore (0) 0
25.5.89 Nepal (0) 0 Korea Rep (5) 9
27.5.89 Singapore (2) 3 Nepal (0) 0
27.5.89 Korea Rep (1) 3 Malaysia (0) 0
3.6.89 Singapore (2) 2 Malayasia (1) 2
3.6.89 Korea Rep (3) 4 Nepal (0) 0
5.6.89 Malaysia (0) 0 Korea Rep (0) 3
5.6.89 Nepal (0) 0 Singapore (4) 7
7.6.89 Singapore (0) 0 Korea Rep (1) 3
7.6.89 Malaysia (1) 3 Nepal (0) 0

Group 5

19.2.89 Thailand (0) 1 Bangladesh (0) 0
23.2.89 China (0) 2 Bangladesh (0) 0
23.2.89 Thailand (0) 0 Iran (2) 3
27.2.89 Bangladesh (0) 1 Iran (1) 2
28.2.89 Thailand (0) 0 China (0) 3
4.3.89 Bangladesh (0) 0 China (1) 2
8.3.89 Bangladesh (2) 3 Thailand (0) 1
17.3.89 Iran (0) 1 Bangladesh (0) 0
30.5.89 Iran (2) 3 Thailand (0) 0
15.7.89 China (0) 2 Iran (0)
22.7.89 Iran (2) 3 China (0) 0
29.7.89 China 2 Thailand 0

Group 6

21.5.89 Indonesia (0) 0 Korea DPR (0) 0
22.5.89 Hong Kong (0) 0 Japan (0) 0
27.5.89 Hong Kong (0) 1 Korea DPR (2) 2
28.5.89 Indonesia (0) 0 Japan (0) 0
4.6.89 Hong Kong (1) 1 Indonesia (0) 1
4.6.89 Japan (0) 2 Korea DPR (0) 1
11.6.89 Japan (4) 5 Indonesia (0) 0
18.6.89 Japan (0) 0 Hong Kong (0) 0
25.6.89 Indonesia (0) 3 Hong Kong (1) 2
25.6.89 Korea DPR (1) 2 Japan (0) 0
2.7.89 Korea DPR (2) 4 Hong Kong (1) 1
9.7.89 Korea DPR 2 Indonesia 1

Second Round *(in Singapore)*

12.10.89 UAE (0) 0 Korea DPR (0) 0
12.10.89 China (0) 2 Saudi Arabia (1) 1
13.10.89 Korea Rep (0) 0 Qatar (0) 0
16.10.89 Qatar (0) 1 Saudi Arabia (1) 1
16.10.89 Korea Rep (1) 1 Korea DPR (0) 0
17.10.89 China (0) 1 UAE (0) 2
20.10.89 China (0) 0 Korea Rep (0) 1
20.10.89 Korea DPR (2) 2 Qatar (0) 0
21.10.89 Saudi Arabia (0) UAE (0) 0
24.10.89 UAE (1) 1 Qatar (1) 1
24.10.89 Korea DPR (0) 0 China (0) 1
25.10.89 Saudi Arabia (0) 0 Korea Rep (1) 2

28.10.89 UAE (1) Korea Rep (1) 1
28.10.89 Saudi Arabia (1) 2 Korea DPR (0) 0
28.10.89 Qatar (0) 2 China (0) 1

AFRICA

First Round

Group 1

7.8.88 Angola (0) 0 Sudan (0) 0
11.11.88 Sudan (1) 1 Angola (0) 2
Lesotho withdrew; Zimbabwe walked over
Zambia walked over; Rwanda withdrew
16.7.88 Uganda (0) 1 Malawi (0) 0
30.7.88 Malawi (2) 3 Uganda (0) 1

Group 2

3.6.88 Libya (3) 3 Burkina Faso (0) 0
3.7.88 Burkina Faso (0) 2 Libya (0) 0
7.8.88 Ghana (0) 0 Liberia (0) 0
21.8.88 Liberia (1) 2 Ghana (0) 0
5.8.88 Tunisia (2) 5 Guinea (0) 0
21.8.88 Guinea (1) 3 Tunisia (0) 0
Togo withdrew; Gabon walked over

Second Round

Group A

6.1.89 Algeria (2) 3 Zimbabwe (0) 0
8.1.89 Ivory Coast (0) 1 Libya (0) 0
20.1.89 Libya v Algeria; *Libya refused to play on the grounds that a state of war existed with the USA. Algeria were awarded the game 2-0. Libya withdrew.*
22.1.89 Zimbabwe (0) 0 Ivory Coast (0) 0
11.6.89 Ivory Coast (0) 0 Algeria (0) 0
25.6.89 Zimbabwe (0) 1 Algeria (1) 2

Group B

6.1.89 Egypt (2) 2 Liberia (0) 0
7.1.89 Kenya (0) 1 Malawi (1) 1
21.1.89 Malawi (0) 1 Egypt (0) 1
22.1.89 Liberia (0) 0 Kenya (0) 0
10.6.89 Kenya (0) 0 Egypt (0) 0
11.6.89 Liberia (1) 1 Malawi (0) 0
24.6.89 Malawi (0) 1 Kenya (0) 0
25.6.89 Liberia (1) 1 Egypt (0) 0

Group C

7.1.89 Nigeria (1) 1 Gabon (0) 0
8.1.89 Cameroon (0) 1 Angola (1) 1
22.1.89 Gabon (1) 1 Cameroon (2) 3
22.1.89 Angola (1) 2 Nigeria (0) 2
10.6.89 Nigeria (1) 2 Cameroon (0) 0
11.6.89 Angola (2) 2 Gabon (0) 0
25.6.89 Angola (1) 1 Cameroon (0) 2
25.6.89 Gabon (2) 2 Nigeria (0) 1

Group D

8.1.89 Morocco (1) 1 Zambia (0) 0
8.1.89 Zaire (2) 3 Tunisia (1) 1

22.1.89 Tunisia (2) 2 Morocco (1) 1
22.1.89 Zambia (2) 4 Zaire (1) 2
11.6.89 Zaire (0) 0 Morocco (0) 0
11.6.89 Zambia (0) 1 Tunisia (0) 0
25.6.89 Tunisia (0) 1 Zaire (0) 0
25.6.89 Zambia (1) 2 Morocco (0) 1

Third Round

8.10.89 Algeria (0) 0 Egypt (0) 0
17.11.89 Egypt (1) 1 Algeria (0) 0
8.10.89 Cameroon (0) 2 Tunisia (0) 0
19.11.89 Tunisia (0) Cameroon (1) 1

OCEANIA

First Round

11.12.88 Chinese Taipei (0) 0 New Zealand (2) 4
15.12.88 New Zealand (3) 4 Chinese Taipei (0) 1
(both matches played in New Zealand)
26.11.88 Fiji (0) 1 Australia (0) 0
3.12.88 Australia (2) 5 Fiji (0) 1

Second Round

5.3.89 Israel (1) 1 New Zealand (0) 0
12.3.89 Australia (2) 4 New Zealand (0) 1
19.3.89 Israel (0) 1 Australia (0) 1
2.4.89 New Zealand (1) 2 Australia (0) 0
9.4.89 New Zealand (2) 2 Israel (2) 2
16.4.89 Australia (0) 1 Israel (1) 1

Israel qualified for matches against the winner of South American Group 2.

CONCACAF

First Round

17.4.88 Guyana (0) 0 Trinidad/Tobago (2) 4
8.5.88 Trinidad/Tobago (1) 1 Guyana (0) 0
30.4.88 Cuba (0) 0 Guatemala (1) 1
15.5.88 Guatemala (0) 1 Cuba (1) 1
12.5.88 Jamaica (1) 1 Puerto Rico (0) 0
29.5.88 Puerto Rico (0) 1 Jamaica (1) 2
19.6.88 Antigua (0) 0 Netherlands Antilles (0) 1
29.7.88 Netherlands Antilles (0) 0 Antigua (1) 1
(Netherlands Antilles won 3-1 on penalties after extra time)
17.7.88 Costa Rica (1) 1 Panama (1) 1
31.7.88 Panama (0) 0 Costa Rica (1) 2

Second Round

1.10.88 Netherlands Antilles (0) 0 El Salvador (0) 1
16.10.88 El Salvador (2) 5 Netherlands Antilles (0) 0
24.7.88 Jamaica (0) 0 USA (0) 0
13.8.88 USA (1) 5 Jamaica (0) 1
30.10.88 Trinidad/Tobago (0) 0 Honduras (0) 0
13.11.88 Honduras (1) 1 Trinidad/Tobago (0) 1
Costa Rica walked over; Mexico disqualified for playing over-age players in youth tournament
9.10.88 Guatemala (1) 1 Canada (0) 0
15.10.88 Canada (0) 3 Guatemala (2) 2

Third Round

19.3.89 Guatemala (1) 1 Costa Rica (0) 0
2.4.89 Costa Rica (1) 2 Guatemala (0) 1
16.4.89 Costa Rica (1) 1 USA (0) 0
30.4.89 USA (0) 1 Costa Rica (0) 0
13.5.89 USA (0) 1 Trinidad/Tobago (0) 1
28.5.89 Trinidad/Tobago (0) 1 Costa Rica (0) 1
11.6.89 Costa Rica (*) 1 Trinidad/Tobago (*) 0
30.7.89 Trinidad/Tobago (0) 2 El Salvador (0) 0
13.8.89 El Salvador (0) 0 Trinidad/Tobago (0) 0
20.8.89 Guatemala (0) 0 Trinidad/Tobago (0) 1
3.9.89 Trinidad/Tobago (1) 2 Guatemala (1) 1
17.9.89 El Salvador (0) 0 USA (0) 1
8.10.89 Guatemala (0) USA (0) 0
5.11.89 USA (0) 0 El Salvador (0) 0
19.11.89 Trinidad/Tobago (0) 0 USA (1) 1

Guatemala v El Salvador and El Salvador v Guatemala not played due to deterioration of political situation in El Salvador.

SOUTH AMERICA

Group 1

20 August, La Paz, 50,000
Bolivia (1) 2 *(Melgar 44 (pen), Ramallo 53)*
Peru (1) 1 *(Del Solar 43)*
Bolivia: Galarza; Fontana, Martinez, Perez, Soria, Borja, Melgar, Takeo (Sanchez 46), Romero, Pena (Roca 75), Ramallo.
Peru: Purizaga; Olivares (Manassero 46), Olaechea, Requena, Carranza, Suarez, Reinoso, Del Solar, Valencia, Navarro (Rey Munoz 46), Hirano.

27 August, Lima, 45,000
Peru (0) 0
Uruguay (0) 2 *(Sosa 46, Alzamendi 69)*
Peru: Purizaga; Carranza, Arteaga, Requena, Olivares (Manassero 73), Del Solar, Reinoso, Uribe, Dall'Orso, Hirano, Navarro.
Uruguay: Pereyra; Herrera, Guiterrez, De Leon, Dominquez, Ostolaza (Correa 80), Perdomo, Paz (Bengoechea 75), Alzamendi, Francescoli, Sosa.

3 September, La Paz, 52,000
Bolivia (1) 2 *(Dominguez (og) 38, Pena 47)*
Uruguay (0) 1 *(Sosa 49)*
Bolivia: Galarza; Martinez, Fontana, Ferrufino, Perez, Borja, Soria, Romero, Melgar, Ramallo, Pena (Sanchez 61).
Uruguay: Pereyra; Herrera (Bengoechea 82), Gutierrez, De Leon, Dominguez, Perdomo, Ostolaza, Paz, Alzamendi, Francescoli, Sosa.

10 September, Lima, 9500
Peru (0) 1 *(Gonzalez 53)*
Bolivia (1) 2 *(Ramallo 44, Sanchez 76)*
Peru: Purizaga; Arteaga, Requena, Del Solar, Olivares, Reinoso, Reyna (Yanez 46), Manassero (Torres 46), Rey Munoz, Gonzalez, Hirano.
Bolivia: Truco; Montano, Martinez, Vargas, Fontana, Soria, Ferrufino, Melgar, Romero (Sanchez 59), Crisaldo, Ramallo.

17 September, Montevideo, 70,000
Uruguay (2) 2 *(Sosa 31, Francescoli 38)*
Bolivia (0) 0
Uruguay: Pereyra; Herrera, Gutierrez, De Leon, Dominguez, Ostolaza, Perdomo (Correa 78), Paz (Bengoechea 66), Alzamendi, Francescoli, Sosa.
Bolivia: Truco; Fontana, Vargas, Ferrufino, Martinez, Montano (Sanchez 46), Borja, Villegas, Melgar, Romero (Pena 46), Ramallo.

24 September, Montevideo, 60,000
Uruguay (1) 2 *(Sosa 43, 57)*
Peru (0) 0
Uruguay: Pereyra; Herrera, Gutierrez, De Leon, Dominguez, Ostolaza, Correa, Bengoechea, Alzamendi, Paz, Sosa.
Peru: Purizaga; Guido, Sanjinez, Requena, Arteaga, Yanez (Manassero 62), Del Solar, Reinoso, Carranza, Gonzalez, Hirano (Bazalar 54).

Final table	*P*	*W*	*D*	*L*	*F*	*A*	*Pts*
Uruguay	4	3	0	1	7	2	6
Bolivia	4	3	0	1	6	5	6
Peru	4	0	0	4	2	8	0

Uruguay qualified

Group 2
20 August, Barranquilla, 60,000
Colombia (1) 2 *(Iguaran 32, 72)*
Ecuador (0) 0
Colombia: Higuita; Wilson Perez, Escobar, Perea, Villa, Ricardo Perez, Alvarez, Redin, Valderrama C, Uzurriaga (Hernandez 55), Iguaran (Fajardo 80).
Ecuador: Morales; Izquierdo, Quinonez, Macias, Capurro, Fajardo, Aguinaga, Rosero, Cuvi (Marsetti 77, Aviles, Benitez (Tenorio 57).

27 August, Asuncion, 50,000
Paraguay (0) 2 *(Javier Ferreira 58, Chilavert 90 (pen))*
Colombia (0) 1 *(Iguaran 87)*
Paraguay: Chilavert; Caceres, Zabala, Delgado, Torales, Romerito (Javier Ferreira 50), Guasch, Nunes, Neffa, Hicks (Buenaventura Ferreira 73), Mendoza.
Colombia: Higuita; Wilson Perez, Perea, Escobar, Hoyos, Alvarez, Ricardo Perez (Hernandez 67), Valderrama C, Redin, Iguaran, Galeano (Uzurriaga 55).

3 September, Guayaquil, 40,000
Ecuador (0) 0
Colombia (0) 0
Ecuador: Morales; Izquierdo, Quinteros, Quinonez, Capurro, Aguinaga, Rosero (Benitez 65), Fajardo, Cuvi (Verduga 72), Tenorio, Aviles.
Colombia: Higuita; Hoyos, Perea, Escobar, Wilson Perez, Fajardo (Uzurriaga 82), Gomez, Ricardo Perez, Valderrama C, Iguaran, Hernandez (Galeano 87).

10 September, Asuncion, 60,000
Paraguay (1) 2 *(Cabanas 36, Javier Ferreira 67)*
Ecuador (0) 1 *(Aviles 84)*
Paraguay: Chilavert; Caceres, Delgado, Zabala, Torales, Guasch, Nunes, Javier Ferreira, Hicks (Buenaventura Ferreira 58), Cabanas, Neffa (Romero 62).
Ecuador: Morales; Bravo, Quinteros, Quinonez, Capurro, Rosero (Cuvi), Fajardo, Aguinaga (Benitez 62), Munoz, Aviles, Guerrero.

17 September, Barranquilla, 60,000
Colombia (0) 2 *(Iguaran 55, Hernandez 66)*
Paraguay (1) 1 *(Mendoza 44)*
Colombia: Higuita; Wilson Perez, Perea, Escobar, Villa, Alvarez, Gomez (Fajardo 46), Redin, Valderrama C (Uzuriaga 46), Iguaran, Hernandez.
Paraguay: Fernandez; Caceres, Delgado, Zabala, Torales, Romero, Guasch, Nunes (Cabellero 63), Palacios (Neffa 25), Buenaventura Ferreira, Mendoza.

24 September, Asuncion, 16,000
Ecuador (1) 3 *(Aguinaga 26, Marsetti 71, Aviles 82)*
Paraguay (1) 1 *(Neffa 18)*
Ecuador: Mendoza; Bravo, Quinonez, Macias, Capurro, Fajardo, Marsetti (Veduga), Aguinaga, Munoz, Aviles, Guerrero (Tenorio).

Paraguay: Fernandez; Caceres (Guasch 75), Delgado, Zabala, Torales, Nunez, Canete (Hicks 67), Neffa, Buenaventura Ferreira, Cabanas, Mendoza.

Final table	*P*	*W*	*D*	*L*	*F*	*A*	*Pts*
Colombia	4	2	1	1	5	3	5
Paraguay	4	2	0	2	6	7	4
Ecuador	4	1	1	2	4	5	3

Colombia qualified

Group 3
30 July, Caracas, 20,000
Venezuela (0) 0
Brazil (1) 4 *(Branco 5, Romario 65, Bebeto 79, 81)*
Venezuela: Baena; Pacheco, Morovic, Acosta, Betancourt, Cavallo, Rivas, Anor (Carrero), Maldonaldo, Febles (Arreaza), Fernandez.
Brazil: Taffarel; Mazinho, Ricardo, Mauro Galvao, Aldair, Branco (Josimar), Dunga, Bebeto, Valdo, Romario, Careca (Silas).

6 August, Caracas, 25,000
Venezuela (0) 1 *(Fernandez 65)*
Chile (2) 3 *(Aravena 5, 34, Zamorano 71)*
Venezuela: Baena; Paz, Acosta, Betancourt (Anor), Cacallo, Febles (Fernandez), Maldonaldo, Rivas, Torres, Carrero, Gallardo.
Chile: Rojas; Hisis, Gonzalez, Astengo, Puebla, Pizzaro, Ormeno, Aravena, Basay (Zamorano), Rubio, Yanez.

13 August, Santiago, 65,000
Chile (0) 1 *(Basay 91)*
Brazil (0) 1 *(Gonzales (og) 63)*
Chile: Rojas; Hisis, Gonzalez, Astengo, Puebla, Pizarro, Ormeno, Aravena, Zamorano (Letelier 87), Rubio (Basay 58), Yanez.
Brazil: Taffarel; Mazinho (Andre Cruz 77), Mauro Galvao, Aldair, Ricardo, Dunga, Branco (Jorginho 9), Silas, Valdo, Romario, Bebeto.

20 August, Sao Paulo, 106,000
Brazil (4) 6 *(Careca 9, 16, 78, 86, Silas 36, Acosta 39)*
Venezuela (0) 0
Brazil: Taffarel; Ricardo II, Mauro Galvao, Ricardo I, Jorginho, Silas, Dunga (Alemao 65), Valdo (Tita 68), Branco, Careca, Bebeto.
Venezuela: Baena; Torres, Acosta, Paz, Pacheco, Rivas, Caballo, Carrero, Maldonaldo, Gallardo (Febles 71), Ariaza (Marazona 63).

27 August, Mendoza (Argentina), 20,000
Chile (3) 5 *(Letelier 14, 34, 68, Yanez 43, Vera 84)*
Venezuela (0) 0
Chile: Rojas; Hisis, Astengo (Contreras 46), Gonzalez, Puebla, Pizarro, Vera, Aravena, Yanez (Covarrubias 76), Letelier, Basay.
Venezuela: Gomez; Torres, Paz, Morovic, Cavallo, Carrero, Acosta (Gallardo 58), Lopez, Maldonaldo, Fernandez (Febles 50), Arreaza.

3 September, Rio de Janeiro, 141,072
Brazil (0) 1 *(Careca 49)*
Chile (0) 0
Brazil: Taffarel; Mauro Galvao, Aldair, Ricardo, Jorginho, Dunga, Silas, Valdo, Branco, Bebeto, Careca.
Chile: Rojas; Reyes, Gonzalez, Astengo, Puebla, Pizarro, Hisis, Vera, Aravena, Yanez, Letelier.
match abandoned after 65 minutes; Brazil awarded game 2-0

Final table	P	W	D	L	F	A	Pts
Brazil	4	3	1	0	13	1	7
Chile	4	2	1	1	9	4	5
Venezuela	4	0	0	4	1	18	0

Brazil qualified

Play-off between winner of Group 2 and winner of Oceania/Israel

15 October, Barranquilla, 50,000
Colombia (0) 1 *(Uzurriaga 73)*
Israel (0) 0
Colombia: Higuita; Wilson Perez, Escobar, Perea, Villa, Alvarez, Valderrama C, Fajardo, Redin (Uzurriaga 46), Iguaran, Ruben Hernandez.
Israel: Ginzburg; Alon, Amar, Avi Cohen, Barda, Klinger, Sinai, Tikva (Pizanti 55), Davidi, Ohana (Levin 75), Rosenthal.

30 October, Tel Aviv, 50,000
Israel (0) 0
Colombia (0) 0
Israel: Ginzburg; Avi Cohen, Amar, Alon, Schmueli (Pizanti 46), Davidi, Klinger, Sinai, Tikva, Rosenthal, Levin (Ohana 50).
Colombia: Higuita; Wilson Perez, Escobar, Mendoza, Villa, Alvarez, (Gomez), Valderrama C, Redin (Uzurriaga 46), Fajardo, Iguaran, Hernandez.

THE WORLD CUP FINALS

Uruguay 1930
URUGUAY 4, ARGENTINA 2 (1–2) *Montevideo*
Uruguay: Ballesteros; Nasazzi (capt), Mascheroni, Andrade, Fernandez, Gestido, Dorado, Scarone, Castro, Cea, Iriarte, **Scorers**: Dorado, Cea, Iriarte, Castro.
Argentina: Botasso; Della Torre, Paternoster, Evaristo, J., Monti, Suarez, Peucelle, Varallo, Stabile, Ferreira (capt), Evaristo, M. **Scorers**: Peucelle, Stabile.
Leading scorer: Stabile (Argentina) 8.

Italy 1934
ITALY 2, CZECHOSLOVAKIA 1 (0–0) (1–1)* *Rome*
Italy: Combi (capt), Monseglio, Allemandi, Ferraris IV, Monti, Bertolini, Guaita, Meazza, Schiavio, Ferrari, Orsi. **Scorers:** Orsi, Schiavio.
Czechoslovakia: Planicka (capt), Zenisek, Ctyroky, Kostalek, Cambal, Krcil, Junek, Svoboda, Sobotka, Nejedly, Puc. **Scorer:** Puc.
Leading scorers: Schiavio (Italy), Nejedly (Czechoslovakia), Conen (Germany) each 4.

France 1938
ITALY 4, HUNGARY 2 (3–1) *Paris*
Italy: Olivieri; Foni, Rava, Serantoni, Andreolo, Locatelli, Biavati, Meazza (capt), Piola, Ferrari, Colaussi. **Scorers:** Colaussi 2, Piola 2.
Hungary: Szabo; Polgar, Biro, Szalay, Szucs, Lazar, Sas, Vincze, Sarosi, (capt.), Szengeller, Titkos. **Scorers:** Titkos, Sarosi.
Leading scorer: Leonidas (Brazil) 8.

Brazil 1950
Final pool *(replaced knock-out system)*

Uruguay 2, Spain 2
Brazil 7, Sweden 1
Uruguay 3, Sweden 2
Brazil 6, Spain 1
Sweden 3, Spain 1
Uruguay 2, Brazil 1

Final positions	*P*	*W*	*D*	*L*	*F*	*A*	*Pts*
Uruguay	3	2	1	0	7	5	5
Brazil	3	2	0	1	14	4	4
Sweden	3	1	0	2	6	11	2
Spain	3	0	1	2	4	11	1

Leading scorers: Ademir (Brazil) 7, Schiaffino (Uruguay), Basora (Spain) 5.

Switzerland 1954
WEST GERMANY 3, HUNGARY 2 *(2–2) Berne*
West Germany: Turek; Posipal, Kohlmeyer, Eckel, Liebrich, Mai, Rahn, Morlock, Walter, O., Walter, F. (capt), Schaefer. **Scorers:** Morlock, Rahn 2.
Hungary: Grosics; Buzansky, Lantos, Bozsik, Lorant, Zakarias, Czibor, Kocsis, Hidegkuti, Puskas (capt), Toth, J. **Scorers:** Puskas, Czibor.
Leading scorer: Kocsis (Hungary) 11.

Sweden 1958
BRAZIL 5, SWEDEN 2 (2–1) *Stockholm*
Brazil: Gilmar; Santos, D., Santos, N., Zito, Bellini, Orlando, Garrincha, Didi, Vavà, Peìe, Zagalo. **Scorers:** Vavà 2, Pelé 2, Zagalo.
Sweden:Svensson; Bergmark, Axbom, Boerjesson, Gustavsson, Parling, Hamrin, Gren, Simonsson, Liedholm, Skoglund. **Scorers:** Liedholm, Simonsson.
Leading scorer: Fontaine (France) 13 (present record total).

Chile 1962
BRAZIL 3, CZECHOSLOVAKIA 1 (1–1) *Santiago*
Brazil: Gilmar; Santos, D., Mauro, Zozimo, Santos, N., Zito, Didi, Garrincha, Vavà, Amorildo, Zagalo. **Scorers:** Amarildo, Zito, Vavà.
Czechoslovakia: Schroiff; Tichy, Novak, Pluskal, Popluhar, Masopust, Pospichal, Scherer, Kvasniak, Kadraba, Jelinek. **Scorer:** Masopust.
Leading scorer: Jerkovic (Yugoslavia) 5.

England 1966
ENGLAND 4, WEST GERMANY 2 (1–1) (2–2)* *Wembley*
England: Banks; Cohen, Wilson, Stiles, Charlton, J., Moore, Ball, Hurst, Hunt, Charlton, R., Peters. **Scorers:** Hurst 3, Peters.
West Germany: Tilkowski; Hottges, Schulz, Weber, Schnellinger, Haller, Beckenbauer, Overath, Seeler, Held, Emmerich. **Scorers:** Haller, Weber.
Leading scorer: Eusebio (Portugal) 9.

Mexico 1970
BRAZIL 4, ITALY 1 (1–1) *Mexico City*
Brazil: Felix; Carlos Alberto, Brito, Piazza, Everaldo, Gerson, Clodoaldo, Jairzinho, Pelé, Tostão, Rivelino. **Scorers:** Pelé, Gerson, Jairzinho, Carlos Alberto.
Italy: Albertosi; Burgnich, Cera, Rosato, Facchetti, Bertini (Juliano), Riva, Domenghini, Mazzola, De Sisti, Boninsegna (Riveta). **Scorer:** Boninsegna.
Leading scorer: Müller (West Germany) 10.

West Germany 1974
WEST GERMANY 2, HOLLAND 1 (2–1) *Munich*
West Germany: Maier; Vogts, Schwarzenbeck, Beckenbauer, Breitner, Bonhof, Hoeness, Overath, Grabowski, Müller, Holzenbein. **Scorers:** Breitner *(pen)*, Müller.
Holland: Jongbloed; Suurbier, Rijsbergen (De Jong), Haan, Krol, Jansen, Van Hanegem, Neeskens, Rep (Nanninga), Cruyff, Rensenbrink (Van der Kerhof, R.).
Scorer: Nanninga (*pen*).
Leading scorer: Lato (Poland) 7.

Argentina 1978
ARGENTINA 3, HOLLAND 1 (1–1)* *Buenos Aires*
Argentina: Fillol; Olguin, Passarella, Galvan, Tarantini, Ardiles (Larrosa), Gallego, Ortiz (Houseman), Bertoni, Luque, Kempes. **Scorers:** Kempers 2, Bertoni.
Holland: Jongbloed; Poortvliet, Brandts, Krol, Jansen (Suurbier), Neeskens, Van der Kerkhof, W., Van der Kerkhof, R., Haan, Rep (Nanninga), Rensenbrink. **Scorer:** Nanninga.
Leading scorer: Kempes (Argentina) 6.

Spain 1982
ITALY 3, WEST GERMANY 1 (0–0) *Madrid*
Italy: Zoff; Bergomi, Cabrini, Collovati, Scirea, Gentile, Oriali, Tardelli, Conti, Graziani (Altobelli), Rossi (Causio). **Scorers:** Rossi, Tardelli, Altobelli.
West Germany: Schumacher; Kaltz, Forster, K-H. Stielike, Forster, B. Breitner, Dremmler (Hrubesch), Littbarski, Briegel, Fischer, Rummenigge (Müller). **Scorer:** Breitner.
Leading scorer: Rossi (Italy) 6.

Mexico 1986
ARGENTINA 3, WEST GERMANY 2 (1–0) *Mexico City*
Argentina: Pumpido; Cuciuffo, Olarticoechea, Ruggeri, Brown, Giusti, Burruchaga (Trobbiani), Batista, Valdano, Maradona, Enrique. **Scorers:** Brown, Valdano, Burruchaga.
West Germany: Schumacher; Berthold, Briegel, Jakobs, Forster, Eder, Brehme, Matthaus, Allofs (Voller), Magath (Hoeness), Rummenigge. **Scorers:** Rummenigge, Voller.
Leading scorer: Lineker (England) 6.

**After extra time*

EUROPEAN CHAMPIONSHIPS PAST FINALS

Paris, 10 July 1960 USSR 2, YUGOSLAVIA 1*
Ussr: Yachin; Tchekeli, Kroutikov, Voinov, Maslenkin, Netto, Metreveli, Ivanov, Ponedelnik, Bubukin, Meshki. **Scorers**: Metreveli, Ponedelnik.
Yugoslavia: Vidinic; Durkovic, Jusufi, Zanetic, Miladinovic, Perusic, Sekularac, Jerkovic, Galic, Matus, Kostic. **Scorer**: Netto (og).

Madrid, 21 June 1964 SPAIN 2, USSR 1
Spain; Iribar; Rivilla, Calleja, Fuste, Olivella, Zoco, Amancio, Pereda, Marcellino, Suarez, Lapetra. **Scorers**: Pereda, Marcellino.
USSR: Yachin; Chustikov, Mudrik, Voronin, Shesternjev, Anitchkin, Chislenko, Ivanov, Ponedelnik, Kornaev, Khusainov.**Scorer:** Khusainov.

Rome, 8 June 1968 ITALY 1, YUGOSLAVIA 1
Italy: Zoff; Burgnich, Facchetti, Ferrini, Guarneri, Castano, Domenghini, Juliano, Anatasi, Lodetti, Prati. **Scorer**: Domenghini.
Yugoslavia: Pandelic; Fazlagic, Damjanovic, Pavlovic, Paunovic, Holcer, Petkovic, Acimovic, Musemic, Trivic, Dzajic. **Scorer**: Dzajic.

Replay: Rome, 10 June 1968 ITALY 2, YUGOSLAVIA 0
Italy: Zoff; Burgnich, Facchetti, Rosato, Guarneri, Salvadore, Domenghini, Mazzola, Anastasi, De Sisti, Riva. **Scorers**: Riva, Anastasi.
Yugoslavia: Pantelic; Fazlagic, Damjanovic, Pavlovic, Paunovic, Holcer, Hosic, Acimovic, Meusemic, Trivic, Dzajic.

Brussels, 18 June 1972 WEST GERMANY 3, USSR 0
West Germany: Maier; Hottges, Schwarzenbeck, Beckenbauer, Breitner, Hoeness, Wimmer, Netzer, Heynckes, Muller, Kremers, **Scorers**: Muller 2, Wimmer.
USSR: Rudakov; Dzodzuashvili, Khurtsilava, Kaplichny, Istomin, Troshkin, Kolotov, Baidachni, Konkov (Dolmatov), Banishevski (Konzinkievits), Onishenko.

Belgrade, 20 June 1976 CZECHOSLOVAKIA 2, WEST GERMANY 2*
Czechoslovakia: Viktor; Dobias (Vesely, F.), Pivarnik, Ondrus, Capkovic, Gogh, Moder, Panenka, Svehlik (Jurkemik), Masny, Nehoda. **Scorers**: Svehlik, Dobias.
West Germany: Maier; Vogts, Beckenbauer, Schwarzenbeck, Dietz, Bonhof, Wimmer, (Flohe), Müller, D., Beer (Bongartz), Hoeness, Holzenbein. **Scorers**: Müller, Holzenbein.
Czechoslovakia won 5–3 on penalties.

Rome, 22 June 1980 WEST GERMANY 2, BELGIUM 1
West Germany: Schumacher; Briegel, Forster, K.Dietz, Schuster, Rummenigge, Hrubesch, Müller, Allofs, Stielike,
Kalz. **Scorer**: Hrubesch 2.
Belgium: Pfaff; Gerets, Millecamps, Meeuws, Renquin, Cools, Van der Eycken, Van Moer, Mommens, Van der Elst, Ceulemans. **Scorer**: Van der Eycken.

Paris, 27 June 1984 FRANCE 2, SPAIN 0
France: Bats; Battiston (Amoros), Le Roux, Bossis, Domergue, Giresse, Platini, Tigana, Fernandez, Lacombe (Genghini), Bellone. **Scorers:** Platini, Bellone
Spain: Arconada; Urquiaga, Salva (Roberto), Gallego, Camacho, Francisco, Julio Alberto (Sarabia), Senor, Victor, Carrasco, Santilana.

Munich, 25 June 1988 HOLLAND 2, USSR 0
Holland: Van Breukelen; Van Aerle, Van Tiggelen, Wouters, R. Koeman, Rijkaard, Vanenburg, Gullit, Van Basten, Muhren, E. Koeman. **Scorers:** Gullit, Van Basten.
USSR: Dassayev; Khidiatulin, Aleinikov, Mikhailichenko, Litovchenko, Demianenko, Belanov, Gotsmanov, (Blatcha), Protasov (Pasulko), Zavarov, Rats

**After extra time*

SOUTH AMERICAN CHAMPIONSHIP WINNERS

(Copa America)

1916 Uruguay
1917 Uruguay
1919 Brazil
1920 Uruguay
1921 Argentina
1922 Brazil
1923 Uruguay
1924 Uruguay
1925 Argentina
1926 Uruguay
1927 Argentina
1929 Argentina
1935 Uruguay
1937 Argentina
1939 Peru
1941 Argentina
1942 Uruguay
1945 Argentina
1946 Argentina
1947 Argentina
1949 Brazil
1953 Paraguay
1955 Argentina
1956 Uruguay
1957 Argentina
1959 Argentina
1959 Uruguay
1963 Bolivia
1967 Uruguay
1975 Peru
1979 Paraguay
1983 Uruguay
1987 Uruguay
1989 Brazil

SOUTH AMERICAN CUP WINNERS

(Copa Libertadores)

1960 Penarol (Uruguay)
1961 Penarol
1962 Santos (Brazil)
1963 Santos
1964 Independiente (Argentina)
1965 Independiente
1966 Penarol
1967 Racing Club (Argentina)
1968 Estudiantes (Argentina)
1969 Estudiantes
1970 Estudiantes
1971 Nacional (Uruguay)
1972 Independiente
1973 Independiente
1974 Independiente
1975 Independiente
1976 Cruzeiro (Brazil)
1977 Boca Juniors (Argentina)
1978 Boca Juniors
1979 Olimpia (Paraguay)
1980 Nacional
1981 Flamengo (Brazil)
1982 Penarol
1983 Gremio Porto Alegre (Brazil)
1984 Independiente
1985 Argentinos Juniors (Argentina)
1986 River Plate (Argentina)
1987 Penarol
1988 Nacional (Uruguay)
1989 Nacional (Colombia)

WORLD CLUB CHAMPIONSHIP

Played annually up to 1974 between the winners of the European Cup and the winners of the South American Champions Cup – known as the Copa Libertadores de America. Revived in February 1981 (for the calendar year 1980), but played on a single match basis on a neutral ground.

Year	*Winners*	*Runners-up*	*Score*
1960	Real Madrid	Penarol	0–0, 5–1
1961	Penarol (Uruguay)	Benfica	0–1, 5–0, 2–1
1962	Santos (Brazil)	Benfica	3–2, 5–2
1963	Santos	AC Milan	2–4, 4–2, 1–0
1964	Inter-Milan	Independiente	0–1, 2–0, 1–0
1965	Inter-Milan	Independiente	3–0, 0–0
1966	Penarol	Real Madrid	2–0, 2–0
1967	Racing Club (Argentina)	Celtic	0–1, 2–1, 1–0
1968	Estudiantes (Argentina)	Manchester United	1–0, 1–1
1969	AC Milan	Estudiantes	3–0, 1–2
1970	Feyenoord	Estudiantes	2–2, 1–0
1971	Nacional (Uruguay)	Panathinaikos	1–1, 2–1
1972	Ajax	Independiente	1–1, 3–0
1973	Independiente (Argentina)	Juventus	1–0
1974	Atletico Madrid	Independiente	0–1, 2–0
1980	Nacional	Nottingham Forest	1–0 (in Tokyo)
1981	Flamengo (Brazil)	Liverpool	3–0 (in Tokyo)
1982	Penarol	Aston Villa	2–0 (in Tokyo)
1983	Gremio Porto Alegre (Brazil)	SV Hamburg	2–1 (in Tokyo)
1984	Independiente	Liverpool	1–0 (in Tokyo)
1985	Juventus	Argentinos Juniors	2–2 (in Tokyo)
Juventus won 4–2 penalties			
1986	River Plate (Argentina)	Steaua Bucharest	1–0 (in Tokyo)
1987	FC Porto*	Penarol	2–1 (in Tokyo)
1988	Nacional*	PSV Eindhoven	2–2 (in Tokyo)
1989	AC Milan	Atletico Nacional	1–0 (in Tokyo)

Nacional won 7–6 on penalties.
**After extra time*

OTHER BRITISH AND IRISH INTERNATIONAL MATCHES 1989–90

Dublin, 6 September 1989, 48,000

Rep of Ireland (1) 1 *(Stapleton)*

West Germany (1) 1 *(Dorfner)*

Rep of Ireland: Bonner; Morris, Staunton, McCarthy, O'Leary, Brady (Townsend), McGrath, Aldridge (Cascarino), Stapleton (Byrne), Whelan, Galvin.
West Germany: Illgner (Aumann); Reuter, Pflugler, Buchwald (Reinhardt), Augenthaler, Dorfner (Bein), Moller, Thon, Wohlfarth, Littbarski, Hassler.

Wembley, 15 November 1989, 75,000

England (0) 0

Italy (0) 0

England: Shilton (Beasant); Stevens, Pearce (Winterburn), Walker, Butcher, McMahon (Hodge), Robson (Phelan), Beardsley (Platt), Barnes, Lineker, Waddle.
Italy: Zenga; Bergomi, Maldini, Baresi, Ferri, Berti, Donadoni, De Napoli, Vialli (Baggio), Giannini, Carnevale (Serena).

Wembley, 13 December 1989, 34,796

England (1) 2 *(Robson 2)*

Yugoslavia (1) 1 *(Skoro)*

England: Shilton (Beasant); Parker, Pearce (Dorigo), Thomas (Platt), Walker, Butcher, Robson (McMahon), Rocastle (Hodge), Bull, Lineker, Waddle.
Yugoslavia: Ivkovic; Stanojkovic, Spasic, (Petric), Brnovic (Panadic), Hadzibegic, Vulic, Skoro, Susic (Prosinecki), Mihajlovic, Stojkovic, Savevski.

Belfast, 27 March 1990, 3500

N. Ireland (1) 2 *(Quinn, Wilson K)*

Norway (0) 3 *(Skammelstrud, Anderson, Hansen)*

N. Ireland: Kee; Hill, Donaghy, McClelland, Taggart, McCreery (Rogan), Wilson D, Quinn, Clarke (Dowie), Wilson K, Black.
Norway: Thorstvedt; Hansen, Johnsen, Halvorsen, Halle, Loken, Ahlsen, Gulbrandsen, Skammelstrud, Andersen, Fjortoft (Jakobsen).

Wembley, 28 March 1990, 80,000

England (1) 1 *(Lineker)*

Brazil (0) 0

England: Shilton (Woods); Stevens, Pearce, McMahon, Walker, Butcher, Platt, Waddle, Beardsley (Gascoigne), Lineker, Barnes.
Brazil: Taffarel; Jorginho, Mozer (Aldair), Mauro Galvao, Branco, Ricardo, Bebeto (Muller), Dunga, Careca, Silas (Alemao), Valdo (Bismarck).

Dublin, 28 March 1990, 41,350

Rep of Ireland (0) 1 *(Slaven)*

Wales (0) 0

Rep of Ireland: Bonner; Morris, Staunton (Hughton), McCarthy, Moran (O'Leary), Whelan (Sheedy), Townsend, Byrne, Slaven, Cascarino, Sheridan.
Wales: Southall; Hall, Phillips, Nicholas, Aizlewood, Melville, Maguire, Horne, Rush, Allen, Davies.

Glasgow, 28 March 1990, 51,537

Scotland (1) 1 *(McKimmie)*

Argentina (0) 0

Scotland: Leighton; Gough, McKimmie, Levein, McLeish, MacLeod, Bett (Aitken), McCall, McInally (McClair), McStay, Fleck.
Argentina: Pumpido; Batista, Bauza, Sensini, Fabbri, Ruggeri (Monzon), Calderon, Basualdo, Burruchaga (Troglio), Valdano, Caniggia.

Wembley, 25 April 1990, 21,342

England (2) 4 *(Bull 2, Pearce, Gascoigne)*

Czechoslovakia (1) 2 *(Skuhravy, Kubik)*

England: Shilton (Seaman); Dixon, Pearce (Dorigo), Steven, Walker (Wright), Butcher, Robson (McMahon), Gascoigne, Bull, Lineker, Hodge.
Czechoslovakia: Miklosko; Bielik, Straka (Kadlec), Hasek, Kocian, Kinier, Bilek, Kubik, Knoflicek, Skuhravy (Weiss), Moravcik.

Glasgow, 25 April 1990, 21,868

Scotland (0) 0

East Germany (0) 1 *(Doll (pen))*

Scotland: Goram; Gillespie (McStay), MacLeod, Levein, McLeish, Gough, McAllister, McCall, Durie (McCoist), Johnston, Collins.
East Germany: Brautigam; Boger, Peschke, Lindner, Schuster, Sammer, Herzog, Steubner (Buttner), Kirsten, Ernst, Doll.

Stockholm, 25 April 1990, 13,981

Sweden (2) 4 *(Brolin 2, Ingesson 2)*

Wales (1) 2 *(Saunders 2)*

Sweden: Ravelli; Nilsson, Hysen, Larsson P, Ljung, Engqvist, Limpar, Ingesson, Schwarz, Brolin, Magnusson (Pettersson).
Wales: Southall; Phillips, Bowen, Melville, Law, Maguire, Nicholas, Horne, Allen, Saunders, Hodges.

Dublin, 25 April 1990, 43,990

Rep of Ireland (0) 1 *(Staunton)*

USSR (0) 0

Rep of Ireland: Peyton; Morris (Hughton), Staunton, McCarthy, O'Leary (Moran), Waddock, McGrath, Townsend, Quinn, Kelly D, Sheedy.
USSR: Uvarov; Fokin, Kuznetsov, Khidiatulin, Gorlukovich, Tishenko, Zigmantovich, Bzoshin, (Cherenkov), Bozodjuk, Ljuty (Savictav), Belanov.

Wembley, 15 May 1990, 27,643

England (0) 1 *(Lineker)*

Denmark (0) 0

England: Shilton (Woods); Stevens, Pearce (Dorigo), McMahon (Platt), Walker, Butcher, Hodge, Gascoigne, Waddle (Rocastle), Lineker (Bull), Barnes.
Denmark: Schmeichel; Sivebaek, Nielsen, Olsen, Andersen, Bartram, Jensen, Vilfort, Povlsen (Brunn), Laudrup M (Jakobsen), Laudrup B

Dublin, 16 May 1990, 31,556

Rep of Ireland (0) 1 *(Sheedy)*

Finland (0) 1 *(Tauriainen P)*

Rep of Ireland; Bonner; Hughton, Staunton (Morris), McCarthy, O'Leary, Brady (Townsend), McGrath, Houghton, Slaven (Aldridge), Cascarino, Byrne (Sheedy).
Finland: Huttunen; Vuorela, Sulonen, Heikkinen, Jantti (Turunen), Kanerva, Jorvinen, Tauriainen P, Litmanen (Tauriainen A), Myyry (Aaltonen), Paatelainen.

Aberdeen, 16 May 1990, 23,000

Scotland (0) 1 *(McCoist)*

Egypt (2) 3 *(Abdelhamid, Hassan H, Yousef)*

Scotland: Gunn; McKimmie (McCall), Malpas, Gillespie, McLeish (Levein), Gough, Durie, Bett, McCoist, McStay, Cooper.
Egypt: Shoubeir; Hassan I, Yakan, Yassin, Hassan H, El Kass (El Batel), Ramzy H, Abdelhany, Ramzy A, Youssef, Abdelhamid.

Belfast, 18 May 1990, 4000

N. Ireland (1) 1 *(Wilson K)*

Uruguay (0) 0

N. Ireland: Wright; Hill (Devine), Worthington, Taggart, McDonald, Rogan (Morrow), Dennison (McCreery), Wilson D, Wilson K, Dowie, Black.
Uruguay: Zeoli; Gutierrez, De Leon, Herrera (Saldana), Perdomo, Dominguez, Alzamendi (Aguilera), Ostolaza, Francescoli, Bengoechea (Paz), Sosa.

Glasgow, 19 May 1990, 25,142

Scotland (1) 1 *(Johnston)*

Poland (0) 1 *(Gillespie (og))*

Scotland: Goram; Gillespie, Malpas, Gough, Aitken, Levein, McCall, McAllister (McStay), McCoist, Johnston (McInally), MacLeod (Collins).
Poland: Bako; Kubicki, Lukasik (Soczynski), Wdowczyk, Kaczmarek, Prusik, Czachowski, Nawrocki (Pisz), Dziekanowski, Kosecki, Ziober.

Cardiff, 20 May 1990, 5977

Wales (1) 1 *(Saunders)*

Costa Rica (0) 0

Wales: Southall; Blackmore, Bodin, Aizlewood, Young (Melville), Hopkins, Horne, Nicholas, Saunders, Hughes (Allen), Hodges (Speed).
Costa Rica: Conejo; Flores, Medford (Marin), Chavel, Guimarez (Jaibel), Chavarria, David, Cayasso, Marchena, Montero, Ramirez.

Wembley, 22 May 1990, 38,751

England (0) 1 *(Barnes)*

Uruguay (1) 2 *(Ostolaza, Perdomo)*

England: Shilton; Parker, Pearce, Hodge (Beardsley), Walker, Butcher, Robson, Gascoigne, Waddle, Lineker (Bull), Barnes.
Uruguay: Pereira; Gutierrez, De Leon, Herrera, Perdomo, Dominguez, Alzamendi, Ostolaza, Francescoli, Paz, Sosa (Martinez).

Izmir, 27 May 1990, 5000

Turkey (0) 0

Rep of Ireland (0) 0

Turkey: Engin; Riza, Tugay, Gokhan B, Kemal (Gokhan K), Ogun, Mustafa (Heyrettin) Unal (Mehmet), Feyyaz (Savas), Oguz, Metin.
Rep of ireland: Bonner; Morris, Staunton (Hughton), McGrath, McCarthy, O'Leary (Slaven), Townsend (Sheridan), Waddock (Byrne), Aldridge, Cascarino, Sheedy.

Valetta, 28 May 1990, 3000

Malta (1) 1 *(Degiorgio)*

Scotland (1) 2 *(McInally 2)*

Malta: Cini; Vella S, Carabott, Calea (Camilleri), Laferia, Buttigieg, Zerafa, Vella R, Gregory (Zarb), Degiorgio, Licari (Scerri).
Scotland: Goram (Leighton); Gough, Aitken, McPherson, Gillespie (Levein), Malpas, McStay (Collins), McCall, Bett (McAllister), McInally, Johnston (McCoist)

Valetta, 2 June 1990, 800

Malta (0) 0

Rep of Ireland (1) 3 *(Quinn, Townsend, Stapleton)*

Malta: Cini; Vella S (Delia), Laferia, Galea (Camilleri), Gregory (Zarb), Buttigieg, Zerafa, Vella R, Carabott, Degiorgio, Licari.
Rep of Ireland: Peyton; Hughton, Staunton, O'Leary, Moran, McLoughlin, Sheridan, Byrne, Quinn, Kelly (Stapleton), Slaven (Townsend).

Tunis, 2 June 1990, 25,000

Tunisia (1) *(Hergal)*

England (0) 1 *(Bull)*

Tunisia: Zitouni; Mbadbi, Neji, Hishiri, Yahia, Mahjoubi, Sellimi, Tarak, Hergal (Dermach), Rouissi, Khemiri (Rashid).
England: Shilton; Stevens, Pearce, Hodge (Beardsley), Walker, Butcher (Wright), Robson, Gascoigne, Waddle (Platt), Lineker (Bull), Barnes.

OLYMPIC FOOTBALL

Previous winners

Year	Venue		
1896	Athens*	1.	Denmark
		2.	Greece
1900	Paris*	1.	England
		2.	France
1904	St Louis**	1.	Canada
		2.	USA
1908	London	1.	England
		2.	Denmark
		3.	Holland
1912	Stockholm	1.	England
		2.	Denmark
		3.	Holland
1920	Antwerp	1.	Belgium
		2.	Spain
		3.	Holland
1924	Paris	1.	Uruguay
		2.	Switzerland
		3.	Sweden
1928	Amsterdam	1.	Uruguay
		2.	Argentina
		3.	Italy
1932	Los Angeles		no competition
1936	Berlin	1.	Italy
		2.	Austria
		3.	Norway
1948	London	1.	Sweden
		2.	Yugoslavia
		3.	Denmark
1952	Helsinki	1.	Hungary
		2.	Yugoslavia
		3.	Sweden
1956	Melbourne	1.	USSR
		2.	Yugoslavia
		3.	Bulgaria
1960	Rome	1.	Yugoslavia
		2.	Denmark
		3.	Hungary
1964	Tokyo	1.	Hungary
		2.	Czechoslovakia
		3.	East Germany
1968	Mexico City	1.	Hungary
		2.	Bulgaria
		3.	Japan
1972	Munich	1.	Poland
		2.	Hungary
		3.	East Germany/ USSR joint bronze
1976	Montreal	1.	East Germany
		2.	Poland
		3.	USSR
1980	Moscow	1.	Czecholsovakia
		2.	East Germany
		3.	USSR
1984	Los Angeles	1.	France
		2.	Brazil
		3.	Yugoslavia
1988	Seoul	1.	USSR
		2.	Brazil
		3.	West Germany

POST-WAR INTERNATIONAL APPEARANCES
As at 30 June, 1990

ENGLAND

A'Court, A. (5) (Liverpool) 1957/8, 1958/9.
Adams, T.A. (17) (Arsenal) 1986/7, 1987/8, 1988/9.
Allen, C. (5) (QPR) 1983/4, 1986/7 (Tottenham Hotspur) 1987/8.
Allen, R. (5) (West Bromwich Albion) 1951/2, 1953/4, 1954/5.
Allen, T. (3) (Stoke City) 1959/60.
Anderson, S. (2) (Sunderland) 1961/2.
Anderson, V. (30) (Nottingham Forest) 1978/9, 1979/80, 1980/1, 1981/2, 1983/4, (Arsenal) 1984/5, 1985/6, 1986/7, (Manchester United).
Angus, J. (1) (Burnley) 1960/1.
Armfield, J. (43) (Blackpool) 1958/9, 1959/60, 1960/1, 1961/2, 1962/3, 1963/4, 1965/6.
Armstrong, D. (3) (Middlesbrough) 1979/80, (Southampton) 1982/3, 1983/4.
Armstrong, K. (1) (Chelsea) 1954/5.
Astall, G. (2) (Birmingham) 1955/6.
Astle, J. (5) (West Bromwich Albion) 1968/9, 1969/70.
Aston, J. (17) (Manchester United) 1948/9, 1949/50, 1950/1.
Atyeo, J. (6) (Bristol City) 1955/6, 1956/7.

Bailey, G.R. (2) (Manchester United) 1984/5.
Bailey, M. (2) (Charlton) 1963/4, 1964/5.
Baily, E. (9) (Tottenham Hotspur) 1949/50, 1950/1, 1951/2, 1952/3.
Baker, J. (8) (Hibernian) 1959/60, 1965/6, (Arsenal).
Ball, A. (72) (Blackpool) 1964/5, 1965/6, 1966/7, (Everton) 1967/8, 1968/9, 1969/70, 1970/1, 1971/2 (Arsenal) 1972/3, 1973/4, 1974/5.
Banks, G. (73) (Leicester) 1962/3, 1963/4, 1964/5, 1965/6, 1966/7, 1967/8, (Stoke) 1968/9, 1969/70, 1970/1, 1971/2.
Banks, T. (6) (Bolton Wanderers) 1957/8, 1958/9.
Barham, M. (2) (Norwich City) 1982/3.
Barlow, R. (1) (West Bromwich Albion) 1954/5.
Barnes, J. (58) (Watford) 1982/3, 1983/4, 1984/5, 1985/6, 1986/7, (Liverpool) 1987/8, 1988/9, 1989/90.
Barnes, P. (22) (Manchester City) 1977/8, 1978/9, 1979/80 (West Bromwich Albion) 1980/1, 1981/2 (Leeds United).
Barrass, M. (3) (Bolton Wanderers) 1951/2, 1952/3.
Baynham, R. (3) (Luton Town) 1955/6.
Beardsley P.A. (45) (Newcastle United) 1985/6, 1986/7 (Liverpool) 1987/8, 1988/9, 1989/90.
Beasant, D.J. (2) (Chelsea), 1989/90.
Beattie, T.K. (9) (Ipswich Town) 1974/5, 1975/6, 1976/7, 1977/8.
Bell, C. (48) (Manchester City) 1967/8, 1968/9, 1969/70, 1971/2, 1972/3, 1973/4, 1974/5, 1975/6.
Bentley, R. (12) (Chelsea) 1948/9, 1949/50, 1952/3, 1954/5.
Berry, J. (4) (Manchester United) 1952/3, 1955/6.
Birtles, G. (3) (Nottingham Forest) 1979/80, 1980/1 (Manchester United).
Blissett, L. (14) (Watford) 1982/3, 1983/4 (AC Milan).
Blockley, J. (1) (Arsenal) 1972/3.
Blunstone, F. (5) (Chelsea) 1954/5, 1956/7.
Bonetti, P. (7) (Chelsea) 1965/6, 1966/7, 1967/8, 1969/70.
Bowles, S. (5) (QPR) 1973/4, 1976/7.
Boyer, P. (1) (Norwich City) 1975/6.
Brabrook, P. (3) (Chelsea) 1957/8, 1959/60.

Bracewell, P.W. (3) (Everton) 1984/5, 1985/6.
Bradford, G. (1) (Bristol Rovers) 1955/6.
Bradley, W. (3) (Manchester United) 1958/9.
Bridges, B. (4) (Chelsea) 1964/5, 1965/6.
Broadbent, P. (7) (Wolverhampton Wanderers) 1957/8, 1958/9, 1959/60.
Broadis, I. (14) (Manchester City) 1951/2, 1952/3 (Newcastle United) 1953/4.
Brooking, T. (47) (West Ham United) 1973/4, 1974/5, 1975/6, 1976/7, 1977/8, 1978/9, 1979/80, 1980/1, 1981/2.
Brooks, J. (3) (Tottenham Hotspur) 1956/7.
Brown, A. (1) (West Bromwich Albion) 1970/1.
Brown, K. (1) (West Ham United) 1959/60.
Bull, S.G. (11) (Wolverhampton Wanderers) 1988/9, 1989/90.
Butcher, T. (77) (Ipswich Town) 1979/80, 1980/1, 1981/2, 1982/3, 1983/4, 1984/5, 1985/6, 1986/7 (Rangers) 1987/8. 1988/9, 1989/90.
Byrne, G. (2) (Liverpool) 1962/3, 1965/6.
Byrne, J. (11) (Crystal Palace) 1961/2, 1962/3, (West Ham United) 1963/4, 1964/5.
Byrne, R. (33) (Manchester United) 1953/4, 1954/5, 1955/6, 1956/7, 1957/8.

Callaghan, I. (4) (Liverpool) 1965/6, 1977/8.
Carter, H. (7) (Derby County) 1946/7.
Chamberlain, M. (8) (Stoke City) 1982/3, 1983/4, 1984/5.
Channon, M. (46) (Southampton) 1972/3, 1973/4, 1974/5, 1975/6, 1976/7, (Manchester City) 1977/8.
Charlton, J. (35) (Leeds United) 1964/5, 1965/6, 1966/7, 1967/8, 1968/9, 1969/70.
Charlton, R. (106) (Manchester United) 1957/8, 1958/9, 1959/60, 1960/1, 1961/2, 1962/3, 1963/4, 1964/5, 1965/6, 1966/7, 1967/8, 1968/9, 1969/70.
Charnley, R. (1) (Blackpool) 1961/2.
Cherry, T. (27) (Leeds United) 1975/6, 1976/7, 1977/8, 1978/9, 1979/80.
Chilton, A. (2) (Manchester United) 1950/1, 1951/2.
Chivers, M. (24) (Tottenham Hotspur) 1970/1, 1971/2, 1972/3, 1973/4.
Clamp, E. (4) (Wolverhampton Wanderers) 1957/8.
Clapton, D. (1) (Arsenal) 1958/9.
Clarke, A. (19) (Leeds United) 1969/70, 1970/1, 1972/3, 1973/4, 1974/5, 1975/6.
Clarke, H. (1) (Tottenham Hotspur) 1953/4.
Clayton, R. (35) (Blackburn Rovers) 1955/6, 1956/7, 1957/8, 1958/9, 1959/60.
Clemence, R. (61) (Liverpool) 1972/3, 1973/4, 1974/5, 1975/6, 1976/7, 1977/8, 1978/9, 1979/80, 1980/1, 1981/2, (Tottenham Hotspur) 1982/3, 1983/4.
Clement, D. (5) (QPR) 1975/6, 1976/7.
Clough, B. (2) (Middlesbrough) 1959/60.
Clough, N.H. (1) (Nottingham Forest) 1988/9.
Coates, R. (4) (Burnley) 1969/70, 1970/1, (Tottenham Hotspur).
Cockburn, H. (13) (Manchester United) 1946/7, 1947/8, 1948/9, 1950/1, 1951/2.
Cohen, G. (37) (Fulham) 1963/4, 1964/5, 1965/6, 1966/7, 1967/8.
Compton, L. (2) (Arsenal) 1950/1.
Connelly J. (20) (Burnley) 1959/60, 1961/2, 1962/3, 1964/5 (Manchester United) 1965/6.
Cooper, T. (20) (Leeds United) 1968/9, 1969/70, 1970/1, 1971/2, 1974/5.
Coppell, S. (42) (Manchester United) 1977/8, 1978/9, 1979/80, 1980/1, 1981/2, 1982/3.
Corrigan J. (9) (Manchester City) 1975/6, 1977/8, 1978/9, 1979/80, 1980/1, 1981/2.
Cottee A.R. (7) (West Ham United) 1986/7, 1987/8, (Everton) 1988/9.
Cowans, G. (9) (Aston Villa) 1982/3, 1985/6 (Bari).
Crawford, R. (2) (Ipswich Town) 1961/2.
Crowe, C. (1) (Wolverhampton Wanderers) 1962/3.

Cunningham, L. (6) (West Bromwich Albion) 1978/9 (Real Madrid) 1979/80, 1980/1.
Currie, A. (17) (Sheffield United) 1971/2, 1972/3, 1973/4, 1975/6 (Leeds United) 1977/8, 1978/9.

Davenport, P. (1) (Nottingham Forest) 1984/5.
Deeley, N. (2) (Wolverhampton Wanderers) 1958/9.
Devonshire, A. (8) (West Ham United) 1979/80, 1981/2, 1982/3, 1983/4.
Dickinson, J. (48) (Portsmouth) 1948/9, 1949/50, 1950/1, 1951/2, 1952/3, 1953/4, 1954/5, 1955/6, 1956/7.
Ditchburn, E. (6) (Tottenham Hotspur) 1948/9, 1952/3, 1956/7.
Dixon, K.M. (8) (Chelsea) 1984/5, 1985/6, 1986/7.
Dixon, L.M. (1) (Arsenal) 1989/90.
Dobson, M. (5) (Burnley) 1973/4, 1974/5 (Everton).
Dorigo, A. R. (4) (Chelsea) 1989/90.
Douglas, B. (36) (Blackburn Rovers) 1957/8, 1958/9, 1959/60, 1960/1, 1961/2, 1962/3.
Doyle, M. (5) (Manchester City) 1975/6, 1976/7.
Duxbury, M. (10) (Manchester United) 1983/4, 1984/5.

Eastham, G. (19) (Arsenal) 1962/3, 1963/4, 1964/5, 1965/6.
Eckersley, W. (17) (Blackburn Rovers) 1949/50, 1950/1, 1951/2, 1952/3, 1953/4.
Edwards, D. (18) (Manchester United) 1954/5, 1955/6, 1956/7, 1957/8.
Ellerington, W. (2) (Southampton) 1948/9.
Elliott, W.H. (5) (Burnley) 1951/2, 1952/3.

Fantham, J. (1) (Sheffield Wednesday) 1961/2.
Fashanu, J. (2) (Wimbledon) 1988/9.
Fenwick, T. (20) (QPR) 1983/4, 1984/5, 1985/6 (Tottenham Hotspur) 1987/8.
Finney, T. (76) (Preston) 1946/7, 1947/8, 1948/9, 1949/50, 1950/1, 1951/2, 1952/3, 1953/4, 1954/5, 1955/6, 1956/7, 1957/8, 1958/9.
Flowers, R. (49) (Wolverhampton Wanderers) 1954/5, 1958/9, 1959/60, 1960/1, 1961/2, 1962/3, 1963/4, 1964/5, 1965/6.
Foster, S. (3) (Brighton) 1981/2.
Foulkes, W. (1) (Manchester United) 1954/5.
Francis, G. (12) (QPR) 1974/5, 1975/6.
Francis, T. (52) (Birmingham City) 1976/7, 1977/8 (Nottingham Forest) 1978/9, 1979/80, 1980/1, 1981/2 (Manchester City) 1982/3, (Sampdoria) 1983/4, 1984/5, 1985/6.
Franklin, N. (27) (Stoke City) 1946/7, 1947/8, 1948/9, 1949/50.
Froggatt, J. (13) (Portsmouth) 1949/50, 1950/1, 1951/2, 1952/3.
Froggatt, R. (4) (Sheffield Wednesday) 1952/3.

Garrett, T. (3) (Blackpool) 1951/2, 1953/4.
Gascoigne, P.J. (17) (Tottenham Hotspur) 1988/9, 1989/90.
Gates, E. (2) (Ipswich Town) 1980/1.
George, F.C. (1) (Derby County) 1976/7.
Gidman, J. (1) (Aston Villa) 1976/7.
Gillard, I. (3) (QPR) 1974/5, 1975/6.
Goddard, P. (1) (West Ham United) 1981/2.
Grainger, C. (7) (Sheffield United) 1955/6, 1956/7 (Sunderland).
Greaves, J. (57) (Chelsea) 1958/9, 1959/60, 1960/1, 1961/2 (Tottenham Hotspur) 1962/3, 1963/4, 1964/5, 1965/6, 1966/7.
Greenhoff, B. (18) (Manchester United) 1975/6, 1976/7, 1977/8, 1979/80.
Gregory, J. (6) (QPR) 1982/3, 1983/4.

Hagan, J. (1) (Sheffield United) 1948/9.
Haines, J. (1) (West Bromwich Albion) 1948/9.
Hall, J. (17) (Birmingham City) 1955/6, 1956/7.
Hancocks, J. (3) (Wolverhampton Wanderers) 1948/9, 1949/50, 1950/1.
Hardwick, G. (13) (Middlesbrough) 1946/7, 1947/8.
Harford, M.G. (2) (Luton Town) 1987/8, 1988/9.

Harris, G. (1) (Burnley) 1965/6.
Harris, P. (2) (Portsmouth) 1949/50, 1953/4.
Harvey, C. (1) (Everton) 1970/1.
Hassall, H. (5) (Huddersfield Town) 1950/1, 1951/2 (Bolton Wanderers) 1953/4.
Hateley, M. (31) (Portsmouth) 1983/4, 1984/5, (AC Milan) 1985/6, 1986/7, (Monaco) 1987/8.
Haynes, J. (56) (Fulham) 1954/5, 1955/6, 1956/7, 1957/8, 1958/9, 1959/60, 1960/1, 1961/2.
Hector, K. (2) (Derby County) 1973/4.
Hellawell, M. (2) (Birmingham City) 1962/3.
Henry, R. (1) (Tottenham Hotspur) 1962/3.
Hill, F. (2) (Bolton Wanderers) 1962/3.
Hill, G. (6) (Manchester United) 1975/6, 1976/7, 1977/8.
Hill, R. (3) (Luton Town) 1982/3, 1985/6.
Hinton, A. (3) (Wolverhampton W.) 1962/3, 1964/5 (Nottingham Forest).
Hitchens, G. (7) (Aston Villa) 1960/1 (Inter Milan) 1961/2.
Hoddle, G. (53) (Tottenham Hotspur) 1979/80, 1980/1, 1981/2, 1982/3, 1983/4, 1984/5, 1985/6, 1986/7 (Monaco) 1987/8.
Hodge, S.B. (22) (Aston Villa) 1985/6, 1986/7, (Tottenham Hotspur), (Nottingham Forest) 1988/9, 1989/90.
Hodgkinson, A. (5) (Sheffield United) 1956/7, 1960/1.
Holden, D. (5) (Bolton Wanderers) 1958/9.
Holliday, E. (3) (Middlesbrough) 1959/60.
Hollins, J. (1) (Chelsea) 1966/7.
Hopkinson, E. (14) (Bolton Wanderers) 1957/8, 1958/9, 1959/60.
Howe, D. (23) (West Bromwich Albion) 1957/8, 1958/9, 1959/60.
Howe, J. (3) (Derby County) 1947/8, 1948/9.
Hudson, A. (2) (Stoke City) 1974/5.
Hughes, E. (62) (Liverpool) 1969/70, 1970/1, 1971/2, 1972/3, 1973/4, 1974/5, 1976/7, 1977/8, 1978/9 (Wolverhampton Wanderers) 1979/80.
Hughes, L. (3) (Liverpool) 1949/50.
Hunt, R. (34) (Liverpool) 1961/2, 1962/3, 1963/4, 1964/5, 1965/6, 1966/7, 1967/8, 1968/9.
Hunt, S. (2) (West Bromwich Albion) 1983/4.
Hunter, N. (28) (Leeds United) 1965/6, 1966/7, 1967/8, 1968/9, 1969/70, 1970/1, 1971/2, 1972/3, 1973/4, 1974/5.
Hurst, G. (49) (West Ham United) 1965/6, 1966/7, 1967/8, 1968/9, 1969/70, 1970/1, 1971/2.

Jezzard, B. (2) (Fulham) 1953/4, 1955/6.
Johnson, D. (8) (Ipswich Town) 1974/5, 1975/6 (Liverpool) 1979/80.
Johnston, H. (10) (Blackpool) 1946/7, 1950/1, 1952/3, 1953/4.
Jones, M. (3) (Sheffield United) 1964/5 (Leeds United) 1969/70.
Jones, W.H. (2) (Liverpool) 1949/50.

Kay, A. (1) (Everton) 1962/3.
Keegan, K. (63) (Liverpool) 1972/3, 1973/4, 1974/5, 1975/6, 1976/7 (SV Hamburg) 1977/8, 1978/9, 1979/80 (Southampton) 1980/1, 1981/2.
Kennedy, A. (2) (Liverpool) 1983/4.
Kennedy, R. (17) (Liverpool) 1975/6, 1977/8, 1979/80.
Kevan, D. (14) (West Bromwich Albion) 1956/7, 1957/8, 1958/9, 1960/1.
Kidd, B. (2) (Manchester United) 1969/70.
Knowles, C. (4) (Tottenham Hotspur) 1967/8.

Labone, B. (26) (Everton) 1962/3, 1966/7, 1967/8, 1968/9, 1969/70.
Lampard, F. (2) (West Ham United) 1972/3, 1979/80.
Langley, J. (3) (Fulham) 1957/8.
Langton, R. (11) (Blackburn Rovers) 1946/7, 1947/8, 1948/9 (Preston North End) 1949/50 (Bolton Wanderers) 1950/1.
Latchford, R. (12) (Everton) 1977/8, 1978/9.
Lawler, C. (4) (Liverpool) 1970/1, 1971/2.

Lawton, T. (15) (Chelsea) 1946/7, 1947/8 (Notts County) 1948/9.
Lee, F. (27) (Manchester City) 1968/9, 1969/70, 1970/1, 1971/2.
Lee, J. (1) (Derby County) 1950/1.
Lee, S. (14) (Liverpool) 1982/3, 1983/4.
Lindsay, A. (4) (Liverpool) 1973/4.
Lineker, G. (58) (Leicester City) 1983/4, 1984/5 (Everton) 1985/6, 1986/7, (Barcelona) 1987/8, 1988/9 (Tottenham H) 1989/90.
Little, B. (1) (Aston Villa) 1974/5.
Lloyd, L. (4) (Liverpool) 1970/1, 1971/2 (Nottingham Forest) 1979/80.
Lofthouse, N. (33) (Bolton Wanderers) 1950/1, 1951/2, 1952/3, 1953/4, 1954/5, 1955/6, 1958/9.
Lowe, E. (3) (Aston Villa) 1946/7.

Mabbutt, G. (13) (Tottenham Hotspur) 1982/3, 1983/4, 1986/7, 1987/8.
Macdonald, M. (14) (Newcastle United) 1971/2, 1972/3, 1973/4, 1974/5; (Arsenal) 1975/6.
Madeley, P. (24) (Leeds United) 1970/1, 1971/2, 1972/3, 1973/4, 1974/5, 1975/6, 1976/7.
Mannion, W. (26) (Middlesbrough) 1946/7, 1947/8, 1948/9, 1949/50, 1950/1, 1951/2.
Mariner, P. (35) (Ipswich Town) 1976/7, 1977/8, 1979/80, 1980/1, 1981/2, 1982/3, 1983/4, 1984/5 (Arsenal).
Marsh, R. (9) (QPR) 1971/2 (Manchester City) 1972/3.
Martin, A. (17) (West Ham United) 1980/1, 1981/2, 1982/3, 1983/4, 1984/5, 1985/6, 1986/7.
Marwood, B. (1) (Arsenal) 1988/9.
Matthews, R. (5) (Coventry City) 1955/6, 1956/7.
Matthews, S. (37) (Stoke City) 1946/7 (Blackpool) 1947/8, 1948/9, 1949/50, 1950/1, 1953/4, 1954/5, 1955/6, 1956/7.
McDermott, T. (25) (Liverpool) 1977/8, 1978/9, 1979/80, 1980/1, 1981/2.
McDonald, C. (8) (Burnley) 1957/8, 1958/9.
McFarland, R. (28) (Derby County) 1970/1, 1971/2, 1972/3, 1973/4, 1975/6, 1976/7.
McGarry, W. (4) (Huddersfield Town) 1953/4, 1955/6.
McGuinness, W. (2) (Manchester United) 1958/9.
McMahon, S. (16) (Liverpool) 1987/8, 1988/9, 1989/90.
McNab, R. (4) (Arsenal) 1968/9.
McNeil, M. (9) (Middlesbrough) 1960/1, 1961/2.
Meadows, J. (1) (Manchester City) 1954/5.
Medley, L. (Tottenham Hotspur) 1950/1, 1951/2.
Melia, J. (2) (Liverpool) 1962/3.
Merrick, G. (23) (Birmingham City) 1951/2, 1952/3, 1953/4.
Metcalfe, V. (2) (Huddersfield Town) 1950/1.
Milburn, J. (13) (Newcastle United) 1948/9, 1949/50, 1950/1, 1951/2, 1955/6.
Miller, B. (1) (Burnley) 1960/1.
Mills, M. (42) (Ipswich Town) 1972/3, 1975/6, 1976/7, 1977/8, 1978/9, 1979/80, 1980/1, 1981/2.
Milne, G. (14) (Liverpool) 1962/3, 1963/4, 1964/5.
Milton, C.A. (1) (Arsenal) 1951/2.
Moore, R. (108) (West Ham United) 1961/2, 1962/3, 1963/4, 1964/5, 1965/6, 1966/7, 1967/8, 1968/9, 1969/70, 1970/1, 1971/2, 1972/3, 1973/4.
Morley, A. (6) (Aston Villa) 1981/2, 1982/3.
Morris, J. (3) (Derby County) 1948/9, 1949/50.
Mortensen, S. (25) (Blackpool) 1946/7, 1947/8, 1948/9, 1949/50, 1950/1, 1953/4.
Mozley, B. (3) (Derby County) 1949/50.
Mullen, J. (12) (Wolverhampton Wanderers) 1946/7, 1948/9, 1949/50, 1953/4.
Mullery, A. (35) (Tottenham Hotspur) 1964/5, 1966/7, 1967/8, 1968/9, 1969/70, 1970/1, 1971/2.

Neal, P. (50) (Liverpool) 1975/6, 1976/7, 1977/8, 1978/9, 1979/80, 1980/1, 1981/2, 1982/3, 1983/4.
Newton, K. (27) (Blackburn Rovers) 1965/6, 1966/7, 1967/8, 1968/9, 1969/70, (Everton).
Nicholls, J. (2) (West Bromwich Albion) 1953/4.
Nicholson, W. (1) (Tottenham Hotspur) 1950/1.
Nish, D. (5) (Derby County) 1972/3, 1973/4.
Norman, M. (23) (Tottenham Hotspur) 1961/2, 1962/3, 1963/4, 1964/5.

O'Grady, M. (2) (Huddersfield Town) 1962/3, 1968/9 (Leeds United).
Osgood, P. (4) (Chelsea) 1969/70, 1973/4.
Osman, R. (11) (Ipswich Town) 1979/80, 1980/1, 1981/2, 1982/3, 1983/4.
Owen, S. (3) (Luton Town) 1953/4.

Paine, T. (19) (Southampton) 1962/3, 1963/4, 1964/5, 1965/6.
Pallister, G. (2) (Middlesbrough) 1987/8.
Parker, P.A. (11) (QPR) 1988/9, 1989/90.
Parkes, P. (1) (QPR) 1973/4.
Parry, R. (2) (Bolton Wanderers) 1959/60.
Peacock, A. (6) (Middlesbrough) 1961/2, 1962/3, 1965/6 (Leeds United).
Pearce, S. (30) (Nottingham Forest) 1986/7, 1987/8, 1988/9, 1989/90.
Pearson, Stan (8) (Manchester United) 1947/8, 1948/9, 1949/50, 1950/1, 1951/2.
Pearson, Stuart (15) (Manchester United) 1975/6, 1976/7, 1977/8.
Pegg, D. (1) (Manchester United) 1956/7.
Pejic, M. (4) (Stoke City) 1973/4.
Perry, W. (3) (Blackpool) 1955/6.
Perryman, S. (1) (Tottenham Hotspur) 1981/2.
Peters, M. (67) (West Ham United) 1965/6, 1966/7, 1967/8, 1968/9, 1969/70, (Tottenham Hotspur) 1970/1, 1971/2, 1972/3, 1973/4.
Phelan, M.C. (1) (Manchester U) 1989/90.
Phillips, L. (3) (Portsmouth) 1951/2, 1954/5.
Pickering, F. (3) (Everton) 1963/4, 1964/5.
Pickering, N. (1) (Sunderland) 1982/3.
Pilkington, B. (1) (Burnley) 1954/5.
Platt, D. (11) (Aston Villa) 1989/90.
Pointer, R. (3) (Burnley) 1961/2.
Pye, J. (1) (Wolverhampton Wanderers) 1949/50.

Quixall, A. (5) (Sheffield Wednesday) 1953/4, 1954/5.

Radford, J. (2) (Arsenal) 1968/9, 1971/2.
Ramsey, A. (32) (Southampton) 1948/9, 1949/50, (Tottenham Hotspur) 1950/1, 1951/2, 1952/3, 1953/4.
Reaney, P. (3) (Leeds United) 1968/9, 1969/70, 1970/1.
Reeves, K. (2) (Norwich City) 1979/80.
Regis, C. (5) (West Bromwich Albion) 1981/2, 1982/3, (Coventry).
Reid, P. (13) (Everton) 1984/5, 1985/6, 1986/7.
Revie, D. (6) (Manchester City) 1954/5, 1955/6, 1956/7.
Richards, J. (1) (Wolverhampton Wanderers) 1972/3.
Rickaby, S. (1) (West Bromwich Albion) 1953/4.
Rimmer, J. (1) (Arsenal) 1975/6.
Rix, G. (17) (Arsenal) 1980/1, 1981/2, 1982/3, 1983/4.
Robb, G. (1) (Tottenham Hotspur) 1953/4.
Roberts, G. (6) (Tottenham Hotspur) 1982/3, 1983/4.
Robson, B. (87) (West Bromwich Albion) 1979/80, 1980/1, 1981/2, (Manchester United) 1982/3, 1983/4, 1984/5, 1985/6, 1986/7, 1987/8, 1988/9, 1989/90.
Robson, R. (20) (West Bromwich Albion) 1957/8, 1959/60, 1960/1, 1961/2.
Rocastle, D. (11) (Arsenal) 1988/9, 1989/90.
Rowley, J. (6) (Manchester United) 1948/9, 1949/50, 1951/2.
Royle, J. (6) (Everton) 1970/1, 1972/3, (Manchester City) 1975/6, 1976/7.

Sadler, D. (4) (Manchester United) 1967/8, 1969/70, 1970/1.
Sansom, K. (86) (Crystal Palace) 1978/9, 1979/80, 1980/1, (Arsenal) 1981/2, 1982/3, 1983/4, 1984/5, 1985/6, 1986/7, 1987/8.
Scott, L. (17) (Arsenal) 1946/7, 1947/8, 1948/9.
Seaman, D.A. (3) (QPR) 1988/9, 1989/90.
Sewell, J. (6) (Sheffield Wednesday) 1951/2, 1952/3, 1953/4.
Shackleton, L. (5) (Sunderland) 1948/9, 1949/50, 1954/5.
Shaw, G. (5) (Sheffield United) 1958/9, 1962/3.
Shellito, K. (1) (Chelsea) 1962/3.
Shilton, P. (125) (Leicester City) 1970/1, 1971/2, 1972/3, 1973/4, 1974/5, (Stoke City) 1976/7, (Nottingham Forest) 1977/8, 1978/9, 1979/80, 1980/1, 1981/2, (Southampton) 1982/3, 1983/4, 1984/5, 1985/6, 1986/7, (Derby County) 1987/8, 1988/9, 1989/90.
Shimwell, E. (1) (Blackpool) 1948/9.
Sillett, P. (3) (Chelsea) 1954/5.
Slater, W. (12) (Wolverhampton Wanderers) 1954/5, 1957/8, 1958/9, 1959/60.
Smith, A.M. (4) (Arsenal) 1988/9.
Smith, L. (6) (Arsenal) 1950/1, 1951/2, 1952/3.
Smith, R. (15) (Tottenham Hotspur) 1960/1, 1961/2, 1962/3, 1963/4.
Smith, Tom (1) (Liverpool) 1970/1.
Smith, Trevor (2) (Birmingham City) 1959/60.
Spink, N. (1) (Aston Villa) 1982/3.
Springett, R. (33) (Sheffield Wednesday) 1959/60, 1960/1, 1961/2, 1962/3, 1965/6.
Staniforth, R. (8) (Huddersfield Town) 1953/4, 1954/5.
Statham, D. (3) (West Bromwich Albion) 1982/3.
Stein, B. (1) (Luton Town) 1983/4.
Stepney, A. (1) (Manchester United) 1967/8.
Sterland, M. (1) (Sheffield Wednesday) 1988/9.
Steven, T.M.(29) (Everton) 1984/5, 1985/6, 1986/7, 1987/8, 1988/9 (Glasgow Rangers) 1989/90.
Stevens, G.A. (7) (Tottenham Hotspur) 1984/5, 1985/6.
Stevens, M.G. (41) (Everton) 1984/5, 1985/6, 1986/7, 1987/8, (Rangers) 1988/9, 1989/90.
Stiles, N. (28) (Manchester United) 1964/5, 1965/6, 1966/7, 1967/8, 1968/9, 1969/70.
Storey-Moore, I. (1) (Nottingham Forest) 1969/70.
Storey, P. (19) (Arsenal) 1970/1, 1971/2, 1972/3.
Streten B. (1) (Luton Town) 1949/50.
Summerbee, M. (8) (Manchester City) 1967/8, 1971/2, 1972/3.
Sunderland, A. (1) (Arsenal) 1979/80.
Swan, P. (19) (Sheffield Wednesday) 1959/60, 1960/1, 1961/2.
Swift, F. (19) (Manchester City) 1946/7, 1947/8, 1948/9.

Talbot, B. (6) (Ipswich Town) 1976/7, 1979/80.
Tambling, R. (3) (Chelsea) 1962/3, 1965/6.
Taylor, E. (1) (Blackpool) 1953/4.
Taylor, J. (2) (Fulham) 1950/51.
Taylor, P.H. (3) (Liverpool) 1947/8:.
Taylor, P.J. (4) (Crystal Palace) 1975/6.
Taylor, T. (19) (Manchester United) 1952/3, 1953/4, 1955/6, 1956/7, 1958/9.
Temple, D. (1) (Everton) 1964/5.
Thomas, Danny (2) (Coventry City) 1982/3.
Thomas, Dave. (8) (QPR) 1974/5, 1975/6.
Thomas, M.L. (2) (Arsenal) 1988/9, 1989/90.
Thompson, P.B. (42) (Liverpool) 1975/6, 1976/7, 1978/9, 1979/80, 1980/1, 1981/2, 1982/3.
Thompson, T. (2) (Aston Villa) 1951/2, (Preston) 1956/7.
Thomson, P. (16) (Liverpool) 1963/4, 1964/5 1965/6, 1967/8, 1969/70.
Thomson, R. (8) (Wolverhampton Wanderers) 1963/4, 1964/5.
Todd, C. (27) (Derby County) 1971/2, 1973/4, 1974/5, 1975/6, 1976/7.

Towers, T. (3) (Sunderland) 1975/6.
Tueart, D. (6) (Manchester City) 1974/5, 1976/7.

Ufton, D. (1) (Charlton Athletic) 1953/4.

Venables, T. (2) (Chelsea) 1964/5.
Viljoen, C. (2) (Ipswich Town) 1974/5.
Viollet, D. (2) (Manchester United) 1959/60, 1961/2.

Waddle, C.R. (59) (Newcastle United) 1984/5, (Tottenham Hotspur) 1985/6, 1986/7, 1987/8, 1988/9, (Marseille) 1989/90.
Waiters, A. (5) (Blackpool) 1963/4, 1964/5.
Walker, D.S.(25) (Nottingham Forest) 1988/9, 1989/90.
Wallace, D.L. (1) (Southampton) 1985/6.
Walsh, P. (5) (Luton Town) 1982/3, 1983/4.
Ward, P. (1) (Brighton) 1979/80.
Ward, T. (2) (Derby County) 1947/8, 1948/9.
Watson, D. (12) (Norwich City) 1983/4, 1984/5, 1985/6, 1986/7 (Everton) 1987/8.
Watson, D.V. (65) (Sunderland) 1973/4, 1974/5, 1975/6 (Manchester City) 1976/7, 1977/8 (Southampton) 1978/9 (Werder Bremen) 1979/80, (Southampton) 1980/1, 1981/2 (Stoke City).
Watson, W. (4) (Sunderland) 1949/50, 1950/1.
Webb, N. (20) (Nottingham Forest) 1987/8, 1988/9 (Manchester United) 1989/90.
Weller, K. (4) (Leicester City) 1973/4.
West, G. (3) (Everton) 1968/9.
Wheeler, J. (1) (Bolton Wanderers) 1954/5.
Whitworth, S. (7) (Leicester City) 1974/5, 1975/6.
Whymark, T. (1) (Ipswich Town) 1977/8.
Wignall, F. (2) (Nottingham Forest) 1964/5.
Wilkins, R. (84) (Chelsea) 1975/6, 1976/7, 1977/8, 1978/9, (Manchester United) 1979/80, 1980/1, 1981/2, 1982/3, 1983/4, 1984/5, (AC Milan) 1985/6, 1986/7.
Williams, B. (24) (Wolverhampton Wanderers) 1948/9, 1949/50, 1950/1, 1951/2, 1954/5, 1955/6.
Williams, S. (6) (Southampton) 1982/3, 1983/4, 1984/5.
Willis, A. (1) (Tottenham Hotspur) 1951/2.
Wilshaw, D. (12) (Wolverhampton Wanderers) 1953/4, 1954/5, 1955/6, 1956/7.
Wilson, R. (63) (Huddersfield Town) 1959/60, 1961/2, 1962/3, 1963/4, 1964/5, (Everton) 1965/6, 1966/7, 1967/8.
Winterburn, N. (1) (Arsenal) 1989/90.
Withe, P. (11) (Aston Villa) 1980/1, 1981/2, 1982/3, 1983/4, 1984/5.
Wood, R. (3) (Manchester United) 1954/5, 1955/6.
Woodcock, A. (42) (Nottingham Forest) 1977/8, 1978/9, 1979/80 (FC Cologne) 1980/1, 1981/2 (Arsenal) 1982/3, 1983/4, 1984/5, 1985/6.
Woods, C.C.E. (16) (Norwich City) 1984/5, 1985/6, 1986/7, (Rangers) 1987/8, 1988/9, 1989/90.
Worthington, F. (8) (Leicester City) 1973/4, 1974/5.
Wright M. (30) (Southampton) 1983/4, 1984/5, 1985/6, 1986/7, (Derby County) 1987/8, 1988/9, 1989/90.
Wright, T. (11) (Everton) 1967/8, 1968/9, 1969/70.
Wright, W. (105) (Wolverhampton Wanderers) 1946/7, 1947/8, 1948/9, 1949/50, 1950/1, 1951/2, 1952/3, 1953/4, 1954/5, 1955/6, 1956/7, 1957/8, 1958/9.

Young, G. (1) (Sheffield Wednesday) 1964/5.

NORTHERN IRELAND

Aherne, T. (4) (Belfast Celtic) 1946/7, 1947/8, 1948/9, 1949/50 (Luton Town).
Anderson, T. (22) (Manchester United) 1972/3, 1973/4, 1974/5, (Swindon Town) 1975/6, 1976/7, 1977/8 (Peterborough United) 1978/9.

Armstrong, G. (63) (Tottenham Hotspur) 1976/7, 1977/8, 1978/9, 1979/80, 1980/1, (Watford) 1981/2, 1982/3, (Real Mallorca) 1983/4, 1984/5, (West Bromwich Albion) 1985/6 (Chesterfield).

Barr, H. (3) (Linfield) 1961/2, 1962/3 (Coventry City).
Best, G. (37) (Manchester United) 1963/4, 1964/5, 1965/6, 1966/7, 1967/8, 1968/9, 1969/70, 1970/1, 1971/2, 1972/3, 1973/4 (Fulham) 1976/7, 1977/8.
Bingham, W. (56) (Sunderland) 1950/1, 1951/2, 1952/3, 1953/4, 1954/5, 1955/6, 1956/7, 1957/8, 1958/9 (Luton Town) 1959/60, 1960/1 (Everton) 1961/2, 1962/3, 1963/4 (Port Vale).
Black, K. (10) (Luton Town) 1987/8, 1988/9, 1989/90.
Blair, R. (5) (Oldham Athletic) 1974/5, 1975/6.
Blanchflower, D. (54) (Barnsley) 1949/50, 1950/1 (Aston Villa) 1951/2, 1952/3, 1953/4, 1954/5 (Tottenham Hotspur) 1955/6, 1956/7, 1957/8, 1958/9, 1959/60, 1960/1, 1961/2, 1962/3.
Blanchflower, J. (12) (Manchester United) 1953/4, 1954/5, 1955/6, 1956/7, 1957/8.
Bowler, G. (3) (Hull City) 1949/50.
Braithwaite, R. (10) (Linfield) 1961/2, 1962/3 (Middlesbrough) 1963/4, 1964/5.
Brennan, R. (5) (Luton Town) 1948/9, 1949/50 (Birmingham City) (Fulham), 1950/1.
Briggs, R. (2) (Manchester United) 1961/2, 1964/5 (Swansea).
Brotherston, N. (27) (Blackburn Rovers) 1979/80, 1980/1, 1981/2, 1982/3, 1983/4, 1984/5.
Bruce, W. (2) (Glentoran) 1960/1, 1966/7.

Campbell, A. (2) (Crusaders) 1962/3, 1964/5.
Campbell, D.A. (10) (Nottingham Forest) 1985/6, 1986/7, 1987/8 (Charlton Athletic).
Campbell, J. (2) (Fulham) 1950/1.
Campbell, R. M. (2) (Bradford City) 1981/2.
Campbell, W. (6) (Dundee) 1967/8, 1968/9, 1969/70.
Carey, J. (7) (Manchester United) 1946/7, 1947/8, 1948/9.
Casey, T. (12) (Newcastle United) 1954/5, 1955/6, 1956/7, 1957/8, 1958/9 (Portsmouth).
Caskey, A. (7) (Derby County) 1978/9, 1979/80, 1981/2 (Tulsa Roughnecks).
Cassidy, T. (24) (Newcastle United) 1970/1, 1971/2, 1973/4, 1974/5, 1975/6, 1976/7, 1979/80 (Burnley) 1980/1, 1981/2.
Caughey, M. (2) (Linfield) 1985/6.
Clarke, C.J. (24) (Bournemouth) 1985/6, 1986/7 (Southampton) 1987/8, 1988/9, 1989/90.
Cleary, J. (5) (Glentoran) 1981/2, 1982/3, 1983/4, 1984/5.
Clements, D. (48) (Coventry City) 1964/5, 1965/6, 1966/7, 1967/8, 1968/9, 1969/70, 1970/1, 1971/2 (Sheffield Wednesday) 1972/3 (Everton) 1973/4, 1974/5, 1975/6 (New York Cosmos).
Cochrane, D. (10) (Leeds United) 1946/7, 1947/8, 1948/9, 1949/50.
Cochrane, T. (26) (Coleraine) 1976, (Burnley) 1977/8, 1978/9, (Middlesbrough) 1979/80, 1980/1, 1981/2, (Gillingham) 1983/4.
Cowan, J. (1) (Newcastle United) 1969/70.
Coyle, F. (4) (Coleraine) 1955/6, 1956/7, 1957/8 (Nottingham Forest).
Coyle, L. (1) (Derry C) 1988/9.
Coyle, R. (5) (Sheffield Wednesday) 1972/3, 1973/4.
Craig, D. (25) (Newcastle United) 1966/7, 1967/8, 1968/9, 1969/70, 1970/1, 1971/2, 1972/3, 1973/4, 1974/5.
Crossan, E. (3) (Blackburn Rovers) 1949/50, 1950/1, 1954/5.
Crossan, J. (23) (Rotterdam Sparta) 1959/60, 1962/3 (Sunderland) 1963/4, 1964/5 (Manchester City) 1965/6, 1966/7, 1967/8 (Middlesbrough).
Cunningham, W. (30) (St Mirren) 1950/1, 1952/3, 1953/4, 1954/5, 1955/6, 1956/7 (Leicester City) 1957/8, 1958/9, 1959/60, 1960/1 (Dunfermline Athletic) 1961/2.
Cush, W. (26) (Glentoran) 1950/1, 1953/4, 1956/7, 1957/8 (Leeds United) 1958/9, 1959/60, 1960/1 (Portadown) 1961/2.

D'Arcy, S. (5) (Chelsea) 1951/2, 1952/3 (Brentford).
Dennison, R. (7) (Wolverhampton Wanderers) 1987/8, 1988/9, 1989/90.
Devine, J. (1) (Glentoran) 1989/90.
Dickson, D. (4) (Coleraine) 1969/70, 1972/3.
Dickson, T. (1) (Linfield) 1956/7.
Dickson, W. (12) (Chelsea) 1950/1, 1951/2, 1952/3 (Arsenal) 1953/4, 1954/5.
Doherty, L. (2) (Linfield) 1984/5, 1987/8.
Doherty, P. (6) (Derby County) 1946/7 (Huddersfield Town) 1947/8, 1948/9, (Doncaster Rovers) 1950/1.
Donaghy, M. (64) (Luton Town) 1979/80, 1980/1, 1981/2, 1982/3, 1983/4, 1984/5, 1985/6, 1986/7, 1987/8, (Manchester United) 1988/9, 1989/90.
Dougan, D. (43) (Portsmouth) 1957/8, 1959/60 (Blackburn Rovers) 1960/1, 1962/3 (Aston Villa); 1965/6 (Leicester City); 1966/7 (Wolverhampton Wanderers) 1967/8, 1968/9, 1969/70, 1970/1, 1971/2, 1972/3.
Douglas, J.P. (1) (Belfast Celtic) 1946/7.
Dowd, H. (3) (Glentoran) 1972/3, 1974/5 (Sheffield Wednesday).
Dowie, I. (2) (Luton Town) 1989/90.
Dunlop, G. (4) (Linfield) 1984/5, 1986/7.

Eglington, T. (6) (Everton) 1946/7, 1947/8, 1948/9.
Elder, A. (40) (Burnley) 1959/60, 1960/1, 1961/2, 1962/3, 1963/4, 1964/5, 1965/6, 1966/7, (Stoke City) 1967/8, 1968/9, 1969/70.

Farrell, P. (7) (Everton) 1946/7, 1947/8, 1948/9.
Feeney, J. (2) (Linfield) 1946/7 (Swansea City) 1949/50.
Feeney, W. (1) (Glentoran) 1975/6.
Ferguson, W. (2) (Linfield) 1965/6, 1966/7.
Ferris, R. (3) (Birmingham City) 1949/50, 1950/1, 1951/2.
Finney, T. (14) (Sunderland) 1974/5, 1975/6 (Cambridge United) 1979/80.
Fleming, J.G. (11) (Nottingham Forest) 1986/7, 1987/8, 1988/9 (Manchester City) 1989/90.
Forde, T. (4) (Ards) 1958/9, 1960/1.

Gallogly, C. (2) (Huddersfield Town) 1950/1.
Garton, R. (1) (Oxford United) 1968/9.
Gorman, W. (4) (Brentford) 1946/7, 1947/8.
Graham, W. (14) (Doncaster Rovers) 1950/1, 1951/2, 1952/3, 1953/4, 1954/5, 1955/6, 1958/9.
Gregg, H. (25) (Doncaster Rovers) 1953/4, 1956/7, 1957/8, (Manchester United) 1958/9, 1959/60, 1960/1, 1961/2, 1963/4.

Hamilton, B. (50) (Linfield) 1968/9, 1970/1, 1971/2 (Ipswich Town) 1972/3, 1973/4, 1974/5, 1975/6 (Everton) 1976/7, 1977/8 (Millwall) 1978/9 (Swindon Town).
Hamilton, W. (41) (QPR) 1977/8, 1979/80 (Burnley) 1980/1, 1981/2, 1982/3, 1983/4, 1984/5 (Oxford United) 1985/6.
Harkin, T. (5) (Southport) 1967/8, 1968/9 (Shrewsbury Town) 1969/70, 1970/1.
Harvey, M. (34) (Sunderland) 1960/1, 1961/2, 1962/3, 1963/4, 1964/5, 1965/6, 1966/7, 1967/8, 1968/9, 1969/70, 1970/1.
Hatton, S. (2) (Linfield) 1962/3.
Healy, F. (4) (Coleraine) 1981/2 (Glentoran) 1982/3.
Hegan, D. (7) (West Bromwich Albion) 1969/70, 1971/2 (Wolverhampton Wanderers) 1972/3.
Hill, C.F. (2) (Sheffield U), 1989/90.
Hill, J. (7) (Norwich City) 1958/9, 1959/60, 1960/1, (Everton) 1961/2, 1963/4.
Hinton, E. (7) (Fulham) 1946/7, 1947/8 (Millwall) 1950/1.
Hughes, P. (3) (Bury) 1986/7.
Hughes, W. (1) (Bolton Wanderers) 1950/1.
Humphries, W. (14) (Ards) 1961/2 (Coventry City) 1962/3, 1963/4, 1964/5 (Swansea Town).
Hunter, A. (53) (Blackburn Rovers) 1969/70, 1970/1, 1971/2 (Ipswich Town) 1972/3, 1973/4, 1974/5, 1975/6, 1976/7, 1977/8, 1978/9, 1979/80.

Irvine, R. (8) (Linfield) 1961/2, 1962/3 (Stoke City) 1964/5.
Irvine, W. (23) (Burnley) 1962/3, 1964/5, 1965/6, 1966/7, 1967/8, 1968/9 (Preston North End) (Brighton & Hove Albion) 1971/2.

Jackson, T. (35) (Everton) 1968/9, 1969/70, 1970/1 (Nottingham Forest) 1971/2, 1972/3, 1973/4, 1974/5 (Manchester United) 1975/6, 1976/7.
Jamison, A. (1) (Glentoran) 1975/6.
Jennings, P. (119) (Watford) 1963/4, 1964/5 (Tottenham Hotspur), 1965/6, 1966/7, 1967/8, 1968/9, 1969/70, 1970/1, 1971/2, 1972/3, 1973/4, 1974/5, 1975/6, 1976/7 (Arsenal) 1977/8, 1978/9, 1979/80, 1980/1, 1981/2, 1982/3, 1983/4, 1984/5, (Tottenham Hotspur) 1985/6.
Johnston, W. (1) (Glentoran) 1961/2, (Oldham Athletic) 1965/6.
Jones, J. (3) (Glenavon) 1955/6, 1956/7.

Keane, T. (1) (Swansea Town) 1948/9.
Kee, P.V. (1) (Oxford U), 1989/90.
Keith, R. (23) (Newcastle United) 1957/8, 1958/9, 1959/60, 1960/1, 1961/2.
Kelly, H. (4) (Fulham) 1949/50 (Southampton) 1950/1.
Kelly, P. (1) (Barnsley) 1949/50.

Lawther, I. (4) (Sunderland) 1959/60, 1960/1, 1961/2 (Blackburn Rovers).
Lockhart, N. (8) (Linfield) 1946/7, 1949/50 (Coventry City) 1950/1, 1951/2, 1953/4 (Aston Villa) 1954/5, 1955/6.
Lutton, B. (6) (Wolverhampton Wanderers) 1969/70, 1972/3 (West Ham United) 1973/4.

Magill, E. (26) (Arsenal) 1961/2, 1962/3, 1963/4, 1964/5, 1965/6 (Brighton & Hove Albion).
Martin, C. (6) (Glentoran) 1946/7, 1947/8 (Leeds United) 1948/9 (Aston Villa) 1949/50.
McAdams, W.(15) (Manchester City) 1953/4, 1954/5, 1956/7, 1957/8, 1960/1 (Bolton Wanderers), 1961/2 (Leeds United).
McAlinden, J. (2)(Portsmouth) 1946/7, 1948/9 (Southend United).
McCabe, J. (6) (Leeds United) 1948/9, 1949/50, 1950/1, 1952/3, 1953/4.
McCavana, T. (3) (Coleraine) 1954/5,1955/6.
McCleary, J.W. (1) (Cliftonville) 1954/5.
McClelland, J. (6) (Arsenal) 1960/1, 1965/6 (Fulham).
McClelland, J. (53) (Mansfield Town) 1979/80, 1980/1, 1981/2 (Rangers) 1982/3, 1983/4, 1984/5 (Watford) 1985/6, 1986/7, 1987/8, 1988/9 (Leeds U) 1989/90
McCourt, F. (6) (Manchester City) 1951/2, 1952/3.
McCoy, R. (1) (Coleraine) 1986/7.
McCreery, D. (67) (Manchester United) 1975/6, 1976/7, 1977/8, 1978/9, 1979/80 (QPR) 1980/1 (Tulsa Roughnecks) 1981/2, 1982/3 (Newcastle United), 1983/4, 1984/5, 1985/6, 1986/7, 1987/8, 1988/9 (Hearts) 1989/90.
McCrory, S. (1) (Southend United) 1957/8.
McCullough, W. (10) (Arsenal) 1960/1, 1962/3, 1963/4, 1964/5, 1966/7, (Millwall).
McCurdy, C. (1) (Linfield) 1979/80.
McDonald, A. (25) (QPR) 1985/6, 1986/7, 1987/8, 1988/9.
McElhinney, G. (6) (Bolton Wanderers) 1983/4, 1984/5.
McFaul, I. (6) (Linfield) 1966/7, 1969/70 (Newcastle United) 1970/1, 1971/2, 1972/3, 1973/4.
McGarry, J.K. (3) (Cliftonville) 1950/1.
McGaughey, M. (1) (Linfield) 1984/5.
McGrath, R. (21) (Tottenham Hotspur) 1973/4, 1974/5, 1975/6 (Manchester United) 1976/7, 1977/8, 1978/9.
McIlroy, J. (55) (Burnley) 1951/2, 1952/3, 1953/4, 1954/5, 1955/6, 1956/7, 1957/8, 1958/9, 1959/60, 1960/1, 1961/2, 1962/3, 1965/6 (Stoke City).
McIlroy, S.B. (88) (Manchester United) 1971/2, 1973/4, 1974/5, 1975/6, 1976/7, 1977/8, 1978/9, 1979/80, 1980/1, 1981/2, (Stoke City) 1982/3, 1983/4, 1984/5, (Manchester City) 1985/6, 1986/7.
McKeag, W. (2) (Glentoran) 1967/8.

McKenna, J. (7) (Huddersfield Town) 1949/50, 1950/1, 1951/2.
McKenzie, R. (1) (Airdrieonians) 1966/7.
McKinney, W. (1) (Falkirk) 1965/6.
McKnight, A. (10) (Celtic) 1987/8, (West Ham United) 1988/9.
McLaughlin, J. (12) (Shrewsbury Town) 1961/2, 1962/3 (Swansea City), 1963/4, 1964/5, 1965/6.
McMichael, A. (39) (Newcastle United) 1949/50, 1950/1, 1951/2, 1952/3, 1953/4, 1954/5, 1955/6, 1956/7, 1957/8, 1958/9, 1959/60.
McMillan, S. (2) (Manchester United) 1962/3.
McMordie, E. (21) (Middlesbrough) 1968/9, 1969/70, 1970/1, 1971/2, 1972/3.
McMorran, E. (15) (Belfast Celtic) 1946/7 (Barnsley) 1950/1, 1951/2, 1952/3, (Doncaster Rovers) 1953/4, 1955/6, 1956/7.
McNally, B.A. (5) (Shrewsbury Town) 1985/6, 1986/7, 1987/8.
McParland, P. (34) (Aston Villa) 1953/4, 1954/5, 1955/6, 1956/7, 1957/8, 1958/9, 1959/60, 1960/1, 1961/2 (Wolverhampton Wanderers).
Montgomery, F.) (Coleraine) 1954/5.
Moore, C. (1) (Glentoran) 1948/9.
Moreland, V. (6) (Derby County) 1978/9, 1979/80.
Morgan, S. (18) (Port Vale) 1971/2, 1972/3, 1973/4 (Aston Villa), 1974/5, 1975/6 (Brighton & Hove Albion) (Sparta Rotterdam) 1978/9.
Morrow, S. J. (1) (Arsenal) 1989/90
Mullan, G. (4) (Glentoran) 1982/3.

Napier, R. (1) (Bolton Wanderers) 1965/6.
Neill, T. (59) (Arsenal) 1960/1, 1961/2, 1962/3, 1963/4, 1964/5, 1965/6, 1966/7, 1967/8, 1968/9, 1969/70 (Hull City) 1970/1, 1971/2, 1972/3.
Nelson, S. (51) (Arsenal) 1969/70, 1970/1, 1971/2, 1972/3, 1973/4, 1974/5, 1975/6, 1976/7, 1977/8, 1978/9, 1979/80, 1980/1, 1981/2 (Brighton).
Nicholl, C. (51) (Aston Villa) 1974/5, 1975/6, 1976/7 (Southampton) 1977/8, 1978/9, 1979/80, 1980/1, 1981/2, 1982/3 (Grimsby T.) 1983/4.
Nicholl, J.M. (73) (Manchester United) 1975/6, 1976/7, 1977/8, 1978/9, 1979/80, 1980/1, 1981/2 (Toronto Blizzard) 1982/3 (Sunderland) (Toronto Blizzard) (Rangers) 1983/4 (Toronto Blizzard) 1984/5 (West Bromwich Albion), 1985/6.
Nicholson, J. (41) (Manchester United) 1960/1, 1961/2, 1962/3, 1964/5, (Huddersfield Town) 1965/6, 1966/7, 1967/8, 1968/9, 1969/70, 1970/1, 1971/2.

O'Doherty, A. (2) (Coleraine) 1969/70.
O'Driscoll, J. (3) (Swansea City) 1948/9.
O'Kane, L. (20) (Nottingham Forest) 1969/70, 1970/1, 1971/2, 1972/3, 1973/4, 1974/5.
O'Neill, C. (2) (Motherwell) 1988/89, 1989/90.
O'Neill, J. (1) (Sunderland) 1961/2.
O'Neill, J. (39) (Leicester City) 1979/80, 1980/1, 1981/2, 1982/3, 1983/4, 1984/5, 1985/6.
O'Neill, H.M. (64) (Distillery) 1971/2 (Nottingham Forest) 1972/3, 1973/4, 1974/5, 1975/6, 1976/7, 1977/8, 1978/9 1979/80, 1980/1 (Norwich City) 1981/2 (Manchester City) (Norwich City) 1982/3 (Notts County) 1983/4, 1984/5.
O'Neill, M.A. (12) (Newcastle United) 1987/8, 1988/9 (Dundee) 1989/90.

Parke, J. (13) (Linfield) 1963/4 (Hibernian), 1964/5 (Sunderland) 1965/6, 1966/7, 1967/8.
Peacock, R. (31) (Glasgow Celtic) 1951/2, 1952/3, 1953/4, 1954/5, 1955/6, 1956/7, 1957/8, 1958/9, 1959/60, 1960/1 (Coleraine) 1961/2.
Penney, S. (17) (Brighton & Hove Albion) 1984/5, 1985/6, 1986/7, 1987/8, 1988/9.
Platt, J.A. (23) (Middlesbrough) 1975/6, 1977/8, 1979/80, 1980/1, 1981/2, 1982/3 (Ballymena United) 1983/4 (Coleraine) 1985/6.

Quinn, J.M. (27) (Blackburn Rovers 1984/5, 1985/6, 1986/7, 1987/8 (Leicester) 1988/9 (Bradford City) 1989/90 (West Ham United)

Rafferty, P. (1) (Linfield) 1979/80.
Ramsey, P. (14) (Leicester City) 1983/4, 1984/5, 1985/6, 1986/7, 1987/8, 1988/9.
Rice, P. (49) (Arsenal) 1968/9, 1969/70, 1970/1, 1971/2, 1972/3, 1973/4, 1974/5, 1975/6, 1976/7, 1977/8, 1978/9, 1979/80.
Rogan, A. (12) (Celtic) 1987/8, 1988/9, 1989/90.
Ross, E. (1) (Newcastle United) 1968/9.
Russell, A. (1) (Linfield) 1946/7.
Ryan, R. (1) (West Bromwich Albion) 1949/50.

Sanchez, L.P. (3) (Wimbledon) 1986/7, 1988/9.
Scott, J. (2) (Grimsby Town) 1957/8.
Scott, P. (10) (Everton) 1974/5, 1975/6 (York City) 1977/8 (Aldershot) 1978/9.
Sharkey, P. (1) (Ipswich Town) 1975/6.
Shields, J. (1) (Southampton) 1956/7.
Simpson, W. (12) (Glascow Rangers) 1950/1, 1953/4, 1954/5, 1956/7, 1957/8, 1958/9.
Sloan, D. (2) (Oxford) 1968/9, 1970/1.
Sloan, T. (3) (Manchester United) 1978/9.
Sloan, W. (1) (Arsenal) 1946/7.
Smyth, S. (9) (Wolverhampton Wanderers) 1947/8, 1948/9, 1949/50 (Stoke City) 1951/2.
Smyth, W. (4) (Distillery) 1948/9, 1953/4.
Spence, D. (29) (Bury) 1974/5, 1975/6 (Blackpool) 1976/7, 1978/9, 1979/80, (Southend United) 1980/1, 1981/2.
Stevenson, A. (3) (Everton) 1946/7, 1947/8.
Stewart, A. (7) (Glentoran) 1966/7, 1967/8 (Derby) 1968/9.
Stewart, D. (1) (Hull City) 1977/8.
Stewart, I. (31) (QPR) 1981/2, 1982/3, 1983/4, 1984/5 (Newcastle United) 1985/6, 1986/7.
Stewart, T. (1) (Linfield) 1960/1.

Taggart, G.P. (2) (Barnsley) 1989/90.
Todd, S. (11) (Burnley) 1965/6, 1966/7, 1967/8, 1968/9, 1969/70 (Sheffield Wednesday) 1970/1.
Trainor, D. (1) (Crusaders) 1966/7
Tulley, C. (10) (Glasgow Celtic) 1948/9, 1949/50, 1951/2, 1952/3, 1953/4, 1955/6, 1958/9.

Uprichard, N. (18) (Swindon Town) 1951/2, 1952/3 (Portsmouth) 1954/5, 1955/6, 1957/8, 1958/9.

Vernon, J. (17) (Belfast Celtic) 1946/7 (West Bromwich Albion) 1947/8, 1948/9, 1949/50, 1950/1, 1951/2.

Walker, J. (1) (Doncaster R) 1954/5.
Walsh, D. (9) (West Bromwich Albion) 1946/7, 1947/8, 1948/9, 1949/50.
Walsh, W. (5) (Manchester City) 1947/8, 1948/9.
Watson, P. (1) (Distillers) 1970/1.
Welsh, S. (4) (Carlisle United) 1965/6, 1966/7.
Whiteside, N. (38) (Manchester United) 1981/2, 1982/3, 1983/4, 1984/5, 1985/6, 1986/7, 1987/8 (Everton) 1989/90.
Wilson, D.J. (18) (Brighton & Hove Albion) 1986/7 (Luton) 1987/8, 1988/9, 1989/90.
Wilson, K.J. (16) (Ipswich Town) 1986/7 (Chelsea) 1987/8, 1988/9, 1989/90.
Wilson, S. (12) (Glenavon) 1961/2, 1963/4 (Falkirk) 1964/5 (Dundee) 1965/6, 1966/7, 1967/8.
Worthington, N. (28) (Sheffield Wednesday) 1983/4, 1984/5, 1985/6, 1986/7, 1987/8, 1988/9, 1989/90.
Wright, T.J. (4) (Newcastle) 1988/9, 1989/90.

SCOTLAND

Aird, J. (4) (Burnley) 1953/4.
Aitken, G.G. (8) (East Fife) 1948/9, 1949/50, 1952/3 (Sunderland) 1953/4.
Aitken, R. (56) (Celtic) 1979/80, 1982/3, 1983/4, 1984/5, 1985/6, 1986/7, 1987/8, (Newcastle) 1989/90.
Albiston, A. (14) (Manchester United) 1981/2, 1983/4, 1984/5, 1985/6.
Allan, T. (2) (Dundee) 1973/4.
Anderson, J. (1) (Leicester City) 1953/4.
Archibald, S. (27) (Aberdeen) 1979/80 (Tottenham Hotspur) 1980/1, 1981/2, 1982/3, 1983/4, 1984/5 (Barcelona) 1985/6.
Auld, B. (3) (Celtic) 1958/9, 1959/60.

Baird, H. (1) (Airdrieonians) 1955/6.
Baird, S. (7) (Rangers) 1956/7, 1957/8.
Bannon, E. (11) (Dundee United) 1979/80, 1982/3, 1983/4, 1985/6.
Bauld, W. (3) (Heart of Midlothian) 1949/50.
Baxter, J. (34) (Rangers) 1960/1, 1961/2, 1962/3, 1963/4, 1964/5 (Sunderland) 1965/6, 1966/7, 1967/8.
Bell, W. (2) (Leeds United) 1965/6.
Bett, J. (25) (Rangers) 1981/2, 1982/3 (Lokeren) 1983/4, 1984/5 (Aberdeen) 1985/6, 1986/7, 1987/8, 1988/9, 1989/90.
Black, E. (2) (Metz) 1987/8.
Black, I. (1) (Southampton) 1947/8.
Blacklaw, A. (3) (Burnley) 1962/3, 1965/6.
Blackley, J. (7) (Hibernian) 1973/4, 1975/6, 1976/7.
Blair, J. (1) (Blackpool) 1946/7.
Blyth, J. (2) (Coventry City) 1977/8.
Bone, J. (2) (Norwich City) 1971/2, 1972/3.
Brand, R. (8) (Rangers) 1960/1, 1961/2.
Brazil, A. (13) (Ipswich Town) 1979/80, 1981/2, 1982/3 (Tottenham Hotspur).
Bremner, D. (1) (Hibernian) 1975/6.
Bremner, W. (54) (Leeds United) 1964/5, 1965/6, 1966/7, 1967/8, 1968/9, 1969/70, 1970/1, 1971/2, 1972/3, 1973/4, 1974/5, 1975/6.
Brennan, F. (7) (Newcastle United) 1946/7, 1952/3, 1963/4.
Brogan, J. (4) (Celtic) 1970/1.
Brown, A. (14) (East Fife) 1949/50 (Blackpool) 1951/2, 1952/3, 1953/4.
Brown, H. (3) (Partick Thistle) 1946/7.
Brown, J. (1) (Sheffield United) 1974/5.
Brown, R. (3) (Rangers) 1946/7, 1948/9, 1951/2.
Brown, W. (28) (Dundee) 1957/8, 1958/9, 1959/60 (Tottenham Hotspur) 1961/2, 1962/3, 1963/4, 1964/5, 1965/6.
Brownlie, J. (7) (Hibernian) 1970/1, 1971/2, 1972/3, 1975/6.
Buchan, M. (34) (Aberdeen) 1971/2 (Manchester United), 1972/3, 1973/4, 1974/5, 1975/6, 1976/7, 1977/8, 1978/9.
Buckley, P. (3) (Aberdeen) 1953/4, 1954/5.
Burley, G. (11) (Ipswich Town) 1978/9, 1979/80, 1981/2.
Burns, F. (1) (Manchester United) 1969/70.
Burns, K. (20) (Birmingham City) 1973/4, 1974/5, 1976/7 (Nottingham Forest) 1977/8, 1978/9, 1979/80, 1980/1.
Burns, T. (8) (Celtic) 1980/1, 1981/2, 1982/3, 1987/8.

Caldow, E. (40) (Rangers) 1956/7, 1957/8, 1958/9, 1959/60, 1960/1, 1961/2, 1962/3.
Callaghan, W. (2) (Dunfermline) 1969/70.
Campbell, R. (5) (Falkirk) 1946/7 (Chelsea) 1949/50.
Campbell, W. (5) (Morton) 1946/7, 1947/8.
Carr, W. (6) (Coventry City) 1969/70, 1970/1, 1971/2, 1972/3.
Chalmers, S. (5) (Celtic) 1964/5, 1965/6, 1966/7.
Clark, J. (4) (Celtic) 1965/6, 1966/7.
Clark, R. (17) (Aberdeen) 1967/8, 1969/70, 1970/1, 1971/2, 1972/3.

Clarke, S. (5) (Chelsea) 1987/8.
Collins, J. (4) (Hibernian) 1987/8, 1989/90.
Collins, R. (31) (Celtic) 1950/1, 1954/5, 1955/6, 1956/7, 1957/8, 1958/9, (Everton) 1964/5 (Leeds United).
Colquhoun, E. (9) (Sheffield United) 1971/2, 1972/3.
Colquhoun, J. (1) (Hearts) 1987/8.
Combe, R. (3) (Hibernian) 1947/8.
Conn, A. (1) (Heart of Midlothian) 1955/6.
Conn, A. (2) (Tottenham Hotspur) 1974/5.
Connachan, E. (2) (Dunfermline Athletic) 1961/2.
Connelly, G. (2) (Celtic) 1973/4.
Connolly, J. (1) (Everton) 1972/3.
Connor, R. (3) (Dundee) 1985/6 (Aberdeen) 1987/8, 1988/9.
Cooke, C. (16) (Dundee) 1965/6 (Chelsea) 1967/8, 1968/9, 1969/70, 1970/1, 1974/5.
Cooper, D. (22) (Rangers) 1979/80, 1983/4. 1984/5, 1985/6, 1986/7 (Motherwell) 1989/90.
Cormack, P. (9) (Hibernian) 1965/6, 1969/70 (Nottingham Forest) 1970/1, 1971/2.
Cowan, J. (25) (Morton) 1947/8, 1948/9, 1949/50, 1950/1, 1951/2 (Motherwell).
Cowie, D. (20) (Dundee) 1952/3, 1953/4, 1954/5, 1955/6, 1956/7, 1957/8.
Cox, C. (1) (Hearts) 1947/8.
Cox, S. (25) (Rangers) 1947/8, 1948/9, 1949/50, 1950/1, 1951/2, 1952/3, 1953/4.
Craig, J. (1) (Celtic) 1976/7.
Craig, J.P. (1) (Celtic) 1967/8.
Craig, T. (1) (Newcastle United) 1975/6.
Crerand, P. (16) (Celtic) 1960/1, 1961/2, 1962/3 (Manchester United) 1963/4, 1964/5, 1965/6.
Cropley, A. (2) (Hibernian) 1971/2.
Cruickshank, J. (6) (Heart of Midlothian) 1963/4, 1969/70, 1970/1, 1975/6.
Cullen, M. (1) (Luton Town) 1955/6.
Cumming, J. (9) (Heart of Midlothian) 1954/5, 1959/60.
Cunningham, W. (8) (Preston North End) 1953/4, 1954/5.
Curran, H. (5) (Wolverhampton Wanderers) 1969/70, 1970/1.

Dalglish, K. (102) (Celtic) 1971/2, 1972/3, 1973/4, 1974/5, 1975/6, 1976/7, (Liverpool) 1977/8, 1978/9, 1979/80, 1980/1, 1981/2, 1982/3, 1983/4, 1984/5, 1985/6, 1986/7.
Davidson, J. (8) (Partick Thistle) 1953/4, 1954/5.
Dawson, A. (5) (Rangers) 1979/80, 1982/3.
Deans, D. (2) (Celtic) 1974/5.
Delaney, J. (4) (Manchester United) 1946/7, 1947/8.
Dick, J. (1) (West Ham United) 1958/9.
Dickson, W. (5) (Kilmarnock) 1969/70, 1970/1.
Docherty, T. (25) (Preston North End) 1951/2, 1952/3, 1953/4, 1954/5, 1956/7, 1957/8, 1958/9 (Arsenal).
Dodds, D. (2) (Dundee United) 1983/4.
Donachie, W. (35) (Manchester City) 1971/2, 1972/3, 1973/4, 1975/6, 1976/7, 1977/8, 1978/9.
Dougall, C. (1) (Birmingham City) 1946/7.
Dougan, R. (1) (Heart of Midlothian) 1949/50.
Doyle, J. (1) (Ayr United) 1975/6.
Duncan, A. (6) (Hibernian) 1974/5, 1975/6.
Duncan, D. (3) (East Fife) 1947/8.
Duncanson, J. (1) (Rangers) 1946/7.
Durie, G.S. (7) (Chelsea) 1987/8, 1988/9, 1989/90.
Durrant, I. (5) (Rangers) 1987/8, 1988/9.

Evans, A. (4) (Aston Villa) 1981/2.
Evans, R. (48) (Celtic) 1948/9, 1949/50, 1950/1, 1951/2, 1952/3, 1953/4, 1954/5, 1955/6, 1956/7, 1957/8, 1958/9, 1959/60 (Chelsea).

Ewing, T. (2) (Partick Thistle) 1957/8.

Farm, G. (10) (Blackpool) 1952/3, 1953/4, 1958/9.
Ferguson, D. (2) (Rangers) 1987/8.
Ferguson, I. (3) (Rangers) 1988/9.
Ferguson, R. (7) (Kilmarnock) 1965/6, 1966/7.
Fernie, W. (12) (Celtic) 1953/4, 1954/5, 1956/7, 1957/8.
Flavell, R. (2) (Airdrieonians) 1946/7.
Fleck, R. (3) (Norwich) 1989/90.
Fleming, C. (1) (East Fife) 1953/4.
Forbes, A. (14) (Sheffield United) 1946/7, 1947/8 (Arsenal) 1949/50, 1950/1, 1951/52.
Ford, D. (3) (Heart of Midlothian) 1973/4.
Forrest, J. (1) (Motherwell) 1957/8.
Forrest, J. (5) (Rangers) 1965/6 (Aberdeen) 1970/1.
Forsyth, A. (10) (Partick Thistle) 1971/2, 1972/3 (Manchester United) 1974/5, 1975/6.
Forsyth, C. (4) (Kilmarnock) 1963/4, 1964/5.
Forsyth, T. (22) (Motherwell) 1970/1 (Rangers) 1973/4, 1975/6, 1976/7, 1977/8.
Fraser, D. (2) (West Bromwich Albion) 1967/8, 1968/9.
Fraser, W. (2) (Sunderland) 1954/5.

Gabriel, J. (2) (Everton) 1960/1, 1961/2.
Gallacher, K.W. (4) (Dundee United) 1987/8, 1988/9.
Gardiner, W. (1) (Motherwell) 1957/8.
Gemmell, T. (2) (St Mirren) 1954/5.
Gemmell, T. (18) (Celtic) 1965/6, 1966/7, 1967/8, 1968/9, 1969/70, 1970/1.
Gemmill, A. (43) (Derby County) 1970/1, 1971/2, 1975/6, 1976/7, 1977/8 (Nottingham Forest) 1978/9 (Birmingham City) 1979/80, 1980/1.
Gibson, D. (7) (Leicester City) 1962/3, 1963/4, 1964/5.
Gillespie, G.T. (12) (Liverpool) 1987/8, 1988/9, 1989/90.
Gilzean, A. (22) (Dundee) 1963/4, 1964/5 (Tottenham Hotspur) 1965/6, 1967/8, 1968/9, 1969/70, 1970/1.
Glavin, R. (1) (Celtic) 1976/7.
Glen, A. (2) (Aberdeen) 1955/6.
Goram, A.L. (9) (Oldham Athletic) 1985/6, 1986/7, (Hibernian) 1988/9, 1989/90.
Gough, C.R. (50) (Dundee United) 1982/3, 1983/4, 1984/5, 1985/6, 1986/7 Tottenham Hotspur) 1987/8 (Rangers) 1988/9, 1989/90.
Govan, J. (6) (Hibernian) 1947/8, 1948/9.
Graham, A. (10) (Leeds United) 1977/8, 1978/9. 1979/80. 1980/1.
Graham, G. (13) (Arsenal) 1971/2, 1972/3 (Manchester United).
Grant, J. (2) (Hibernian) 1958/9.
Grant, P. (2) (Celtic) 1988/9.
Gray, A. (20) (Aston Villa) 1975/6, 1976/7, 1978/9 (Wolverhampton Wanderers) 1979/80, 1980/1, 1981/2, 1982/3, 1984/5 (Everton).
Gray, E. (12) (Leeds United) 1968/9, 1969/70, 1970/1, 1971/2, 1975/6, 1976/7.
Gray, F. (32) (Leeds United) 1975/6, 1978/9, 1979/80 (Nottingham Forest) 1980/1, (Leeds United) 1981/2, 1982/3.
Green, A. (6) (Blackpool) 1970/1 (Newcastle United) 1971/2.
Greig, J. (44) (Rangers) 1963/4, 1964/5, 1965/6, 1966/7, 1967/8, 1968/9, 1969/70, 1970/1, 1975/6.
Gunn, B. (1) (Norwich C) 1989/90.

Haddock, H. (6) (Clyde) 1954/5, 1957/8.
Haffey, F. (2) (Celtic) 1959/60, 1960/1.
Hamilton, A. (24) (Dundee) 1961/2, 1962/3, 1963/4, 1964/5, 1965/6.
Hamilton, G. (5) (Aberdeen) 1946/7, 1950/1, 1953/4.
Hamilton, W. (1) (Hibernian) 1964/5.
Hansen, A. (26) (Liverpool) 1978/9, 1979/80, 1980/1, 1981/2, 1982/3, 1984/5, 1985/6, 1986/7.
Hansen, J. (2) (Partick Thistle) 1971/2.

Harper, J. (4) (Aberdeen) 1972/3, 1975/6, 1978/9.
Hartford, A. (50) (West Bromwich Albion) 1971/2, 1975/6 (Manchester City) 1976/7, 1977/8, 1978/9, 1979/80 (Everton) 1980/1, 1981/2 (Manchester City).
Harvey, D. (16) (Leeds United) 1972/3, 1973/4, 1974/5, 1975/6, 1976/7.
Haughney, M. (1) (Celtic) 1953/4.
Hay, D. (27) (Celtic) 1969/70, 1970/1, 1971/2, 1972/3, 1973/4.
Hegarty, P. (8) (Dundee United) 1978/9, 1979/80, 1982/3.
Henderson, J. (7) (Portsmouth) 1952/3, 1953/4, 1955/6, 1958/9 (Arsenal).
Henderson, W. (29) (Rangers) 1962/3, 1963/4, 1964/5, 1965/6, 1966/7, 1967/8, 1968/9, 1969/70.
Herd, D. (5) (Arsenal) 1958/9, 1960/1, 1970/1.
Herd, G. (5) (Clyde) 1957/8, 1959/60, 1960/1.
Herriot, J. (8) (Birmingham City) 1968/9, 1969/70.
Hewie, J. (19) (Charlton Athletic) 1955/6, 1956/7, 1957/8, 1958/9, 1959/60.
Holt, D. (5) (Heart of Midlothian) 1962/3, 1963/4.
Holton, J. (15) (Manchester United) 1972/3, 1973/4, 1974/5.
Hope, R. (2) (West Bromwich Albion) 1967/8, 1968/9.
Houliston, W. (3) (Queen of the South) 1948/9.
Houston, S. (1) (Manchester United) 1975/6.
Howie, H. (1) (Hibernian) 1948/9.
Hughes, J. (8) (Celtic) 1964/5, 1965/6, 1967/8, 1968/9, 1969/70.
Hughes, W. (1) (Sunderland) 1974/5.
Humphries, W. (1) (Motherwell) 1951/2.
Hunter, A. (4) (Kilmarnock) 1971/2, 1972/3 (Celtic) 1973/4.
Hunter, W. (3) (Motherwell) 1959/60, 1960/1.
Husband, J. (1) (Partick Thistle) 1946/7.
Hutchison, T. (17) (Coventry City) 1973/4, 1974/5, 1975/6.

Imlach, S. (4) (Nottingham Forest) 1957/8.

Jackson, C. (8) (Rangers) 1974/5, 1975/6.
Jardine, A. (38) (Rangers) 1970/1, 1971/2, 1972/3, 1973/4, 1974/5, 1976/7, 1977/8, 1978/9, 1979/80.
Jarvie, A. (3) (Airdrieonians) 1970/1.
Johnston, M. (36) (Watford) 1983/4, 1984/5 (Celtic) 1985/6, 1986/7, (Nantes) 1987/8, 1988/9 (Rangers) 1989/90.
Johnston, W. (22) (Rangers) 1965/6, 1967/8, 1968/9, 1969/70, 1970/1 (West Bromwich Albion) 1976/7, 1977/8.
Johnstone, D. (14) (Rangers) 1972/3, 1974/5, 1975/6, 1977/8, 1979/80.
Johnstone, J. (23) (Celtic) 1964/5, 1965/6, 1966/7, 1967/8, 1968/9, 1969/70, 1970/1, 1971/2, 1973/4, 1974/5.
Johnstone, L. (2) (Clyde) 1947/8.
Johnstone, R. (17) (Hibernian) 1950/1, 1951/2, 1952/3, 1953/4, 1954/5 (Manchester City) 1955/6.
Jordan, J. (52) (Leeds United) 1972/3, 1973/4, 1974/5, 1975/6, 1976/7, 1977/8, (Manchester United) 1978/9, 1979/80, 1980/1, 1981/2 (AC Milan).

Kelly, H. (1) (Blackpool) 1951/2
Kelly, J. (2) (Barnsley) 1948/9.
Kennedy, J. (6) (Celtic) 1963/4, 1964/5.
Kennedy, S. (8) (Aberdeen) 1977/8, 1978/9, 1981/2.
Kennedy, S. (5) (Rangers) 1974/5.
Kerr, A. (2) (Partick Thistle) 1954/5.

Law, D. (55) (Huddersfield Town) 1958/9, 1959/60 (Manchester City) 1960/1, 1961/2 (Torino) 1962/3 (Manchester United) 1963/4, 1964/5, 1965/6, 1966/7, 1967/8, 1968/9, 1971/2, 1973/4 (Manchester City).
Lawrence, T. (3) (Liverpool) 1962/3, 1968/9.
Leggat, G. (18) (Aberdeen) 1955/6, 1956/7, 1957/8, 1958/9 (Fulham) 1959/60.

Leighton, J. (58) (Aberdeen) 1982/3, 1983/4, 1984/5, 1985/6, 1986/7, 1987/8, (Manchester United), 1988/9, 1989/90.
Lennox, R. (10) (Celtic) 1966/7, 1967/8, 1968/9.
Leslie, L. (5) (Airdrieonians) 1960/1.
Levein, C. (6) (Hearts) 1989/90.
Liddell, W. (28) (Liverpool) 1946/7, 1947/8, 1949/50, 1950/1, 1951/2, 1952/3, 1953/4, 1954/5, 1955/6.
Linwood, A. (1) (Clyde) 1949/50.
Little, A. (1) (Rangers) 1952/3.
Logie, J. (1) (Arsenal) 1952/3.
Long, H. (1) (Clyde) 1946/7.
Lorimer, P. (21) (Leeds United) 1969/70, 1970/1, 1971/2, 1972/3, 1973/4, 1974/5, 1975/6.

Macari, L. (24) (Celtic) 1971/2, 1972/3 (Manchester United) 1974/5, 1976/7, 1977/8, 1978/9.
Macaulay, A. (7) (Brentford) 1946/7 (Arsenal) 1947/8.
Macdougall, E. (7) (Norwich City) 1974/5, 1975/6.
Mackay, D. (22) (Heart of Midlothian) 1956/7, 1957/8, 1958/9 (Tottenham Hotspur) 1959/60, 1960/1, 1962/3, 1963/4, 1965/6.
Mackay, G. (4) (Heart of Midlothian) 1987/8.
Malpas, M. (37) (Dundee United) 1983/4, 1984/5, 1985/6, 1986/7, 1987/8, 1988/9, 1989/90.
Martin, F. (6) (Aberdeen) 1953/4, 1954/5.
Martin, N. (3) (Hibernian) 1964/5, 1965/6 (Sunderland).
Martis, J. (1) (Motherwell) 1960/1.
Mason, J. (7) (Third Lanark) 1948/9, 1949/50, 1950/1.
Masson, D. (17) (QPR) 1975/6, 1976/7, 1977/8 (Derby County) 1978/9.
Mathers, D. (1) (Partick Thistle) 1953/4.
McAllister, G. (3) (Leicester C) 1989/90.
McAvennie, F. (5) (West Ham United) 1985/6 (Celtic) 1987/8.
McBride, J. (2) (Celtic) 1966/7.
McCall, S.M. (8) (Everton) 1989/90.
McCalliog, J. (5) (Sheffield Wednesday) 1966/7, 1967/8, 1968/9, 1970/1 (Wolverhampton Wanderers).
McCann, R. (5) (Motherwell) 1958/9, 1959/60, 1960/1.
McClair, B.(14) (Celtic) 1986/7 (Manchester United) 1987/8, 1988/9, 1989/90.
McCloy, P. (4) (Rangers) 1972/3.
McCoist, A. (26) (Rangers) 1985/6, 1986/7, 1987/88, 1988/89, 1989/90.
McColl, I. (14) (Rangers) 1949/50, 1950/1, 1956/7, 1957/8.
McCreadie, E. (23) (Chelsea) 1964/5, 1965/6, 1966/7, 1967/8, 1968/9.
MacDonald, A. (1) (Rangers) 1975/6.
MacDonald, J. (2) (Sunderland) 1955/6.
McFarlane, W. (1) (Heart of Midlothian) 1946/7.
McGarr, E. (2) (Aberdeen) 1969/70.
McGarvey, F. (7) (Liverpool) 1978/79 (Celtic) 1983/4.
McGhee, M. (4) (Aberdeen) 1982/3, 1983/4.
McGrain, D. (62) (Celtic) 1972/3, 1973/4, 1974/5, 1975/6, 1976/7, 1977/8, 1979/80, 1980/1, 1981/2.
McGrory, J. (3) (Kilmarnock) 1964/5, 1965/6.
McInally, A. (8) (Aston Villa) 1988/9 (Bayern Munich) 1989/90.
McInally, J. (3) (Dundee United) 1986/7, 1987/8.
McKay, D. (14) (Celtic) 1958/9, 1959/60, 1960/1, 1961/2.
McKean, R. (1) (Rangers) 1975/6.
McKenzie, J. (9) (Partick Thistle) 1953/4, 1954/5, 1955/6.
McKimmie, S. (6) (Aberdeen) 1988/9, 1989/90.
McKinnon, R. (28) (Rangers) 1965/6, 1966/7, 1967/8, 1968/9, 1969/70, 1970/1.
McLaren, A. (4) (Preston North End) 1946/7, 1947/8.
McLean, G. (1) (Dundee) 1967/8.
McLean, T. (6) (Kilmarnock) 1968/9, 1969/70, 1970/1.

McLeish, A. (72) (Aberdeen) 1979/80, 1980/1, 1981/2, 1982/3, 1983/4, 1984/5, 1985/6, 1986/7, 1987/8, 1988/9, 1989/90.
McLeod, J. (4) (Hibernian) 1960/1.
MacLeod, M. (17) (Celtic) 1984/5, 1986/7 (Borussia Dortmund) 1987/8, 1988/9, 1989/90.
McLintock, F. (9) (Leicester City) 1962/3, 1964/5 (Arsenal) 1966/7, 1969/70, 1970/1.
McMillan, I. (6) (Airdrieonians) 1951/2, 1954/5, 1955/6 (Rangers) 1960/1.
McNaught, W. (5) (Raith Rovers) 1950/1, 1951/2, 1954/5.
McNeill, W. (29) (Celtic) 1960/1, 1961/2, 1962/3, 1963/4, 1964/5, 1965/6, 1966/7, 1967/8, 1968/9, 1969/70, 1971/2.
McPhail, J. (5) (Celtic) 1949/50, 1950/1, 1953/4
McPherson, D. (7) (Hearts) 1988/9, 1989/90.
McQueen, G. (30) (Leeds United) 1973/4, 1974/5, 1975/6, 1976/7, 1977/8, (Manchester United) 1978/9, 1979/80, 1980/1.
McStay, P. (48) (Celtic) 1983/4, 1984/5, 1985/6, 1986/7, 1987/8, 1988/9, 1989/90.
Millar, J. (2) (Rangers) 1962/3.
Miller, W. (6) (Celtic) 1946/7, 1947/8.
Miller, W. (65) (Aberdeen) 1974/5, 1977/8, 1979/8, 1979/80, 1980/1, 1981/2, 1982/3, 1983/4, 1984/5, 1985/6, 1986/7, 1987/8, 1988/9, 1989/90.
Mitchell, R. (2) (Newcastle United) 1950/1.
Mochan, N. (3) (Celtic) 1953/4.
Moir, W. (1) (Bolton Wanderers) 1949/50.
Moncur, R. (16) (Newcastle United) 1967/8, 1969/70, 1970/1, 1971/2.
Morgan, W. (21) (Burnley) 1967/8 (Manchester United) 1971/2, 1972/3, 1973/4.
Morris, H. (1) (East Fife) 1949/50.
Mudie, J. (17) (Blackpool) 1956/7, 1957/8.
Mulhall, G. (3) (Aberdeen) 1959/60, 1962/3 (Sunderland) 1963/4.
Munro, F. (9) (Wolverhampton Wanderers) 1970/1, 1974/5.
Munro, I. (7) (St Mirren) 1978/9, 1979/80.
Murdoch, R. (12) (Celtic) 1965/6, 1966/7, 1967/8, 1968/9, 1969/70.
Murray, J. (5) (Heart of Midlothian) 1957/8.
Murray, S. (1) (Aberdeen) 1971/2.

Narey, D. (35) (Dundee United) 1976/7, 1978/9, 1979/80, 1980/1, 1981/2, 1982/3, 1985/6, 1986/7, 1988/9.
Nevin, P.K.F. (8) (Chelsea) 1985/6, 1986/7, 1987/8, (Everton) 1988/9.
Nicholas, C. (20) (Celtic) 1982/3 (Arsenal) 1983/4, 1984/5, 1985/6, 1986/7, (Aberdeen) 1988/9.
Nicol, S. (23) (Liverpool) 1984/5, 1985/6, 1987/8, 1988/9, 1989/90.

O'Hare, J. (13) (Derby County) 1969/70, 1970/1, 1971/2.
Ormond, W. (6) (Hibernian) 1953/4, 1958/9.
Orr, T. (2) (Morton) 1951/2.

Parker, A. (15) (Falkirk) 1954/5, 1955/6, 1956/7, 1957/8.
Parlane, D. (12) (Rangers) 1972/3, 1974/5, 1975/6, 1976/7.
Paton, A. (2) (Motherwell) 1951/2.
Pearson, T. (2) (Newcastle United) 1946/7.
Penman, A. (1) (Dundee) 1965/6.
Pettigrew, W. (5) (Motherwell) 1975/6, 1976/7.
Plenderleith, J. (1) (Manchester City) 1960/1.
Provan, D. (5) (Rangers) 1963/4, 1965/6.
Provan, D. (10) (Celtic) 1979/80, 1980/1, 1981/2.

Quinn, P. (4) (Motherwell) 1960/1, 1961/2.

Redpath, W. (9) (Motherwell) 1948/9, 1950/1, 1951/2.
Reilly, L. (38) (Hibernian) 1948/9, 1949/50, 1950/1, 1951/2, 1952/3, 1953/4, 1954/5, 1955/6, 1956/7.
Ring, T. (12) (Clydebank) 1952/3, 1954/5, 1956/7, 1957/8.

Rioch, B. (24) (Derby County) 1974/5, 1975/6, 1976/7 (Everton) 1977/8 (Derby County) 1978/9.
Robb, D. (5) (Aberdeen) 1970/1.
Robertson, A. (5) (Clyde) 1954/5, 1957/8.
Robertson, H. (1) (Dundee) 1961/2.
Robertson, J. (1) (Tottenham Hotspur) 1964/5.
Robertson, J. (28) (Nottingham Forest) 1977/8, 1978/9, 1979/80, 1980/1, 1981/2, 1982/3 (Derby County) 1983/4.
Robinson, B. (4) (Dundee) 1973/4, 1974/5.
Rough, A. (53) (Partick Thistle) 1975/6, 1976/7, 1977/8, 1978/9, 1979/80, 1980/1, 1981/2 (Hibernian) 1985/6.
Rougvie, D. (1) (Aberdeen) 1983/4.
Rutherford, E. (1) (Rangers) 1947/8.

St John, I. (21) (Motherwell) 1958/9, 1959/60, 1960/1, 1961/2 (Liverpool) 1962/3, 1963/4, 1964/5.
Schaedler, E. (1) (Hibernian) 1973/4.
Scott, A. (16) (Rangers) 1956/7, 1957/8, 1958/9, 1961/2 (Everton) 1963/4, 1964/5, 1965/6.
Scott, J. (1) (Hibernian) 1965/6.
Scott, J. (2) (Dundee) 1970/1.
Scoular, J. (9) (Portsmouth) 1950/1, 1951/2, 1952/3.
Sharp, G.M. (12) (Everton) 1984/5, 1985/6, 1986/7, 1987/8.
Shaw, D. (8) (Hibernian) 1946/7, 1947/8, 1948/9.
Shaw, J. (4) (Rangers) 1946/7, 1947/8.
Shearer, R. (4) (Rangers) 1960/1.
Simpson, N. (4) (Aberdeen) 1982/3, 1983/4, 1986/7, 1987/8.
Simpson, R. (5) (Celtic) 1966/7, 1967/8, 1968/9.
Sinclair, J. (1) (Leicester City) 1965/6.
Smith, D. (2) (Aberdeen) 1965/6, 1967/8 (Rangers).
Smith, E. (2) (Celtic) 1958/9.
Smith, G. (18) (Hibernian) 1946/7, 1947/8, 1951/2, 1954/5, 1955/6, 1956/7.
Smith, H.G. (1) (Heart of Midlothian) 1987/8.
Smith, J. (4) (Aberdeen) 1967/8, 1973/4 (Newcastle United).
Souness, G. (54) (Middlesbrough) 1974/5 (Liverpool) 1977/8, 1978/9, 1979/80, 1980/1, 1981/2, 1982/3, 1983/4 (Sampdoria) 1984/5, 1985/6.
Speedie, D.R. (10) (Chelsea) 1984/5, 1985/6, (Coventry City) 1988/9.
Stanton, P. (16) (Hibernian) 1965/6, 1968/9, 1969/70, 1970/1, 1971/2, 1972/3, 1973/4.
Steel, W. (30) (Morton) 1946/7, 1947/8 (Derby County) 1948/9, 1949/50, (Dundee) 1950/1, 1951/2, 1952/3.
Stein, C. (21) (Rangers) 1968/9, 1969/70, 1970/1, 1971/2 (Coventry City).
Stephen, J. (2) (Bradford City) 1946/7, 1947/8.
Stewart, D. (1) (Leeds United) 1977/8.
Stewart, J. (2) (Kilmarnock) 1976/7 (Middlesbrough) 1978/9.
Stewart, R. (10) (West Ham United) 1980/1, 1981/2, 1983/4, 1986/7.
Strachan, G. (43) (Aberdeen) 1979/80, 1980/1, 1981/2, 1982/3, 1983/4 (Manchester United) 1984/5, 1985/6, 1986/7, 1987/88, 1988/89 (Leeds U) 1989/90.
Sturrock, P. (20) (Dundee United) 1980/1, 1981/2, 1982/3, 1983/4, 1984/5, 1985/6, 1986/7.

Telfer, W. (1) (St Mirren) 1953/4.
Thomson, W. (7) (St Mirren) 1979/80, 1980/1, 1981/2, 1982/3, 1983/4.
Thornton, W. (7) (Rangers) 1946/7, 1947/8, 1948/9, 1951/2.
Toner, W. (2) (Kilmarnock) 1958/9.
Turnbull, E. (8) (Hibernian) 1957/8, 1950/1, 1957/8.

Ure, I. (11) (Dundee) 1961/2, 1962/3 (Arsenal) 1963/4, 1967/8.

Waddell, W. (17) (Rangers) 1946/7, 1948/9, 1949/50, 1950/1, 1951/2, 1953/4, 1954/5.

Walker, A. (1) (Celtic) 1987/8.
Wallace, I.A. (3) (Coventry City) 1977/8, 1978/9.
Wallace, W.S.B. (7) (Heart of Midlothian) 1964/5, 1965/6, 1966/7 (Celtic) 1967/8, 1968/9.
Wardhaugh, J. (2) (Heart of Midlothian) 1954/5, 1956/7.
Wark, J. (29) (Ipswich Town) 1978/9, 1979/80, 1980/1, 1981/2, 1982/3, 1983/4 (Liverpool) 1984/5.
Watson, J. (2) (Motherwell) 1947/8 (Huddersfield Town) 1953/4.
Watson, R. (1) (Motherwell) 1970/1.
Weir, A. (6) (Motherwell) 1958/9, 1959/60.
Weir, P. (6) (St Mirren) 1979/80, 1982/3 (Aberdeen) 1983/4.
White, J. (22) (Falkirk) 1958/9, 1959/60 (Tottenham Hotspur) 1960/1, 1961/2, 1962/3, 1963/4.
Whyte, D. (3) (Celtic) 1987/8, 1988/9.
Wilson, A. (1) (Portsmouth) 1953/4.
Wilson, D. (22) (Rangers) 1960/1, 1961/2, 1962/3, 1963/4, 1964/5.
Wilson, I.A. (5) (Leicester City) 1986/7 (Everton) 1987/8.
Wilson, P. (1) (Celtic) 1974/5.
Wilson, R. (2) (Arsenal) 1971/2.
Wood, G. (4) (Everton) 1978/9, 1981/2 (Arsenal).
Woodburn, W. (24) (Rangers) 1946/7, 1947/8, 1948/9, 1949/50, 1950/1, 1951/2.
Wright, T. (3) (Sunderland) 1952/3.

Yeats, R. (2) (Liverpool) 1964/5, 1965/6.
Yorston, H. (1) (Aberdeen) 1954/5.
Young, A. (9) (Heart of Midlothian) 1959/60, 1960/1 (Everton) 1965/6.
Young, G. (53) (Rangers) 1946/7, 1947/8, 1948/9, 1949/50, 1950/1, 1951/2, 1952/3, 1953/4, 1954/5, 1955/6, 1956/7.
Younger, T. (24) (Hibernian) 1954/5, 1955/6, 1956/7 (Liverpool) 1957/8.

WALES

Aizlewood, M. (17) (Charlton Athletic) 1985/6, 1986/7 (Leeds United) 1987/8, 1988/9 (Bradford C) 1989/90.
Allchurch, I. (68) (Swansea City) 1950/1, 1951/2, 1952/3, 1953/4, 1954/5, 1955/6, 1956/7, 1957/8, 1958/9 (Newcastle United) 1959/60, 1960/1, 1961/2, 1962/3 (Cardiff City) 1963/4, 1964/5 1965/6 (Swansea City).
Allchurch, L. (11) (Swansea City) 1954/5, 1955/6, 1957/8, 1958/9 1961/2, (Sheffield United) 1963/4.
Allen, B. (2) (Coventry City) 1950/1.
Allen, M. (9) (Watford) 1985/6, (Norwich City) 1988/9 (Millwall) 1989/90.

Baker, C. (7) (Cardiff City) 1957/8, 1959/60, 1960/1, 1961/2.
Baker, W. (1) (Cardiff City) 1947/8.
Barnes, W. (22) (Arsenal) 1947/8, 1948/9, 1949/50, 1950/1, 1951/2, 1953/4, 1954/5.
Berry, G. (5) (Wolverhampton Wanderers) 1978/9, 1979/80, 1982/3,(Stoke City).
Blackmore, C.G. (25) (Manchester United) 1984/5, 1985/6, 1986/7, 1987/8, 1988/9, 1989/90.
Bowen, D. (19) (Arsenal) 1954/5, 1956/7, 1957/8, 1958/9.
Bowen, M.R. (11) (Tottenham Hotspur) 1985/6 (Norwich City) 1987/8, 1988/9, 1989/90.
Bodin, P.J. (1) (Swindon T) 1989/90.
Boyle, T. (2) (Crystal Palace) 1980/1.
Burgess, R. (32) (Tottenham Hotspur) 1946/7, 1947/8, 1948/9, 1949/50, 1950/1, 1951/2, 1952/3, 1953/4.
Burton, O. (9) (Norwich City) 1962/3 (Newcastle United) 1963/4, 1968/9, 1971/2.

Cartwright, L. (7) (Coventry City) 1973/4, 1975/6, 1976/7 (Wrexham) 1977/8, 1978/9.
Charles, J. (38) (Leeds United) 1949/50, 1950/1, 1952/3, 1953/4, 1954/5, 1955/6, 1956/7 (Juventus Turin) 1957/8, 1959/60, 1961/2, 1962/3 (Leeds United) (Cardiff City) 1963/4, 1964/5.
Charles, J.M. (19) (Swansea City) 1980/1, 1981/2, 1982/3, 1983/4 (QPR), (Oxford United) 1984/5, 1985/6, 1986/7.
Charles, M. (31) (Swansea City) 1954/5, 1955/6, 1956/7, 1957/8, 1958/9 (Arsenal) 1960/1, 1961/2 (Cardiff City) 1962/3.
Clarke, R. (22) (Manchester City) 1948/9, 1949/50, 1950/1, 1951/2 1952/3, 1953/4, 1954/5, 1955/6.
Crowe, V. (16) (Aston Villa) 1958/9, 1959/60, 1960/1, 1961/2, 1962/3.
Curtis, A. (35) (Swansea City) 1975/6, 1976/7, 1977/8, 1978/9, 1979/80, 1981/2, 1982/3, 1983/4 (Southampton) 1984/5, 1985/6, 1986/7 (Cardiff City).

Daniel, R. (21) (Arsenal) 1950/1, 1951/2, 1952/3, 1953/4 (Sunderland) 1954/5, 1956/7.
Davies, A. (11) (Manchester United) 1982/3, 1983/4, 1984/5, (Newcastle United) 1985/6 (Swansea City) 1987/8, 1988/9 (Bradford C) 1989/90.
Davies, D. (52) (Everton) 1974/5, 1975/6, 1976/7, 1977/8, (Wrexham) 1978/9, 1979/80, 1980/1 (Swansea City) 1981/2, 1982/3.
Davies, G. (18) (Fulham) 1979/80, 1981/2, 1982/3, 1983/4, 1984/5 (Chelsea), (Manchester City) 1985/6.
Davies, R. Wyn (34) (Bolton Wanderers) 1963/4, 1964/5, 1965/6, 1966/7 (Newcastle United) 1967/8, 1968/9, 1969/70, 1970/1, 1971/2 (Manchester City), (Blackpool) 1972/3 (Manchester United) 1973/4.
Davies, Reg (6) (Newcastle United) 1952/3, 1953/4, 1957/8.
Davies, Ron (29) (Norwich City) 1963/4, 1964/5, 1965/6, 1966/7, (Southampton) 1967/8, 1968/9, 1969/70, 1970/1, 1971/2, 1973/4 (Portsmouth).
Davis, C. (1) (Charlton Athletic) 1971/2.
Davis, G. (4) (Wrexham) 1977/8.
Deacy, N. (11) (PSV Eindhoven) 1976/7, 1977/8 (Beringen) 1978/9.
Derrett, S. (4) (Cardiff City) 1968/9, 1969/70, 1970/1.
Dibble, A. (3) (Luton Town) 1985/6, (Manchester City) 1988/9.
Durban, A. (27) (Derby County) 1965/6, 1966/7, 1967/8, 1968/9, 1969/70, 1970/1, 1971/2.
Dwyer, P. (10) (Cardiff City) 1977/8, 1978/9, 1979/80.

Edwards, I. (4) (Chester) 1977/8, 1978/9, 1979/80.
Edwards, G. (12) (Birmingham City) 1946/7, 1947/8 (Cardiff City) 1948/9, 1949/50.
Edwards, T. (2) (Charlton Athletic) 1956/7.
Emanuel, J. (2) (Bristol City) 1972/3.
England, M. (44) (Blackburn Rovers) 1961/2, 1962/3, 1963/4, 1964/5, 1965/6, 1966/7 (Tottenham Hotspur) 1967/8, 1968/9, 1969/70, 1970/1, 1971/2, 1972/3, 1973/4, 1974/5.
Evans, B. (7) (Swansea City) 1971/2, 1972/3 (Hereford United) 1973/4.
Evans, I. (13) (Crystal Palace) 1975/6, 1976/7, 1977/8.
Evans, R. (1) (Swansea City) 1963/4.

Felgate D. (1) (Lincoln City) 1983/4.
Flynn, B. (66) (Burnley) 1974/5, 1975/6, 1976/7, 1977/8 (Leeds United) 1978/9, 1979/80, 1980/1, 1981/2, 1982/3 (Burnley) 1983/4.
Ford, T. (38) (Swansea City) 1946/7 (Aston Villa) 1947/8, 1948/9, 1949/50, 1950/1 (Sunderland) 1951/2, 1952/3 (Cardiff City) 1953/4, 1954/5, 1955/6, 1956/7.
Foulkes, W. (11) (Newcastle United) 1951/2, 1952/3, 1953/4.

Giles, D. (12) (Swansea City) 1979/80, 1980/1, 1981/2 (Crystal Palace) 1982/3.

Godfrey, B. (3) (Preston North End) 1963/4, 1964/5.
Green, C. (15) (Birmingham City) 1964/5, 1965/6, 1966/7, 1967/8, 1968/9.
Griffiths, A. (17) (Wrexham) 1970/1, 1974/5, 1975/6, 1976/7.
Griffiths, H. (1) (Swansea City) 1952/3.
Griffiths, M. (11) (Leicester City) 1946/7, 1948/9, 1949/50, 1950/1, 1953/4.

Hall, G.D. (7) (Chelsea) 1987/8, 1988/9.
Harrington, A. (11) (Cardiff City) 1955/6, 1956/7, 1957/8, 1960/1, 1961/2.
Harris, C. (24) (Leeds United) 1975/6, 1977/8, 1978/9, 1979/80, 1980/1, 1981/2.
Harris, W. (6) (Middlesbrough) 1953/4, 1956/7, 1957/8.
Hennessey, T. (39) (Birmingham City) 1961/2, 1962/3, 1963/4, 1964/5, 1965/6, (Nottingham Forest) 1966/7, 1967/8, 1968/9, 1969/70 (Derby County) 1971/2, 1972/3.
Hewitt, R. (5) (Cardiff City) 1957/8.
Hill, M. (2) (Ipswich Town) 1971/2.
Hockey, T. (9) (Sheffield United) 1971/2, 1972/3 (Norwich City) 1973/4, (Aston Villa).
Hodges, G. (13) (Wimbledon) 1983/4, 1986/7 (Newcastle United) 1987/8, (Watford) 1989/90.
Holden, A. (1) (Chester City) 1983/4.
Hole, B. (30) (Cardiff City) 1962/3, 1963/4, 1964/5, 1965/6, 1966/7, (Blackburn Rovers) 1967/8, 1968/9 (Aston Villa) 1969/70 (Swansea City) 1970/71.
Hollins, D. (11) (Newcastle United) 1961/2, 1962/3, 1963/4, 1964/5, 1965/6.
Hopkins, J. (16) (Fulham) 1982/3, 1983/4, 1984/5 (Crystal P) 1989/90.
Hopkins, M. (34) (Tottenham Hotspur) 1955/6, 1956/7, 1957/8, 1958/9, 1959/60, 1960/1, 1961/2, 1962/3.
Horne, B. (14) (Portsmouth) 1987/8, (Southampton) 1988/9, 1989/90.
Howells, R. (2) (Cardiff City) 1953/4.
Hughes, I. (4) (Luton Town) 1950/1.
Hughes, L.M. (28) (Manchester United) 1983/4, 1984/5, 1985/6, 1986/7 (Barcelona) 1987/8, 1988/9 (Manchester United) 1989/90.
Hughes, W. (3) (Birmingham City) 1946/7.
Hughes, W.A. (5) (Blackburn Rovers) 1948/9.
Humphreys, J. (1) (Everton) 1946/7.

Jackett, K. (31) (Watford) 1982/3, 1983/4, 1984/5, 1985/6, 1986/7, 1987/8.
James, G. (9) (Blackpool) 1965/6, 1966/7, 1967/8, 1970/1.
James, L. (54) (Burnley) 1971/2, 1972/3, 1973/4, 1974/5, 1975/6 (Derby County) 1976/7, 1977/8 (QPR) (Burnley) 1978/9, 1979/80 (Swansea City) 1980/1, 1981/2 (Sunderland) 1982/3.
James, R.M. (47) (Swansea City) 1978/9, 1979/80, 1981/2, 1982/3 (Stoke City) 1983/4, 1984/5 (QPR) 1985/6, 1986/7 (Leicester City) 1987/8 (Swansea City).
Jarvis, A. (3) (Hull City) 1966/7.
Johnson, M. (1) (Swansea City) 1963/4.
Jones, A. (6) (Port Vale) 1986/7, 1987/8 (Charlton Athletic) 1989/90.
Jones, Barrie. (15) (Swansea City) 1962/3, 1963/4, 1964/5 (Plymouth Argyle) 1968/9 (Cardiff City).
Jones, Bryn. (4) (Arsenal) 1946/7, 1947/8, 1948/9.
Jones, C. (59) (Swansea City) 1953/4, 1955/6, 1956/7, 1957/8 (Tottenham Hotspur) 1958/9, 1959/60, 1960/1, 1961/2, 1962/3, 1963/4, 1964/5, 1966/7, 1967/8, 1968/9 (Fulham) 1969/70.
Jones, D. (8) (Norwich City) 1975/6, 1977/8, 1979/80.
Jones, E. (4) (Swansea City) 1947/8 (Tottenham Hotspur) 1948/9.
Jones, J. (72) (Liverpool) 1975/6, 1976/7, 1977/8 (Wrexham) 1978/9, 1979/80, 1980/1, 1981/2, 1982/3 (Chelsea) 1983/4, 1984/5 (Huddersfield Town) 1985/6.
Jones, K. (1) (Aston Villa) 1949/50.
Jones, T.G. (13) (Everton) 1946/7, 1947/8, 1948/9, 1949/50.
Jones, W. (1) (Bristol Rovers) 1970/1.

Kelsey, J. (41) (Arsenal) 1953/4, 1954/5, 1955/6, 1956/7, 1957/8, 1958/9, 1959/60, 1960/1, 1961/2.
King, J. (1) (Swansea City) 1954/5.
Kinsey, N. (7) (Norwich City) 1950/1, 1951/2, 1953/4 (Birmingham City) 1955/6.
Knill, A.R. (1) (Swansea City) 1988/9.
Krzywicki, R. (8) (West Bromwich Albion) 1969/70 (Huddersfield Town) 1970/1, 1971/2.

Lambert, R. (5) (Liverpool) 1946/7, 1947/8, 1948/9.
Law, B.J. (1) (QPR), 1989/90.
Lea, C. (2) (Ipswich Town) 1964/5.
Leek, K. (13) (Leicester City) 1960/1, 1961/2 (Newcastle United) (Birmingham City) 1962/3, 1964/5.
Lever, A. (1) (Leicester City) 1952/3.
Lewis, D. (1) (Swansea City) 1982/3.
Lloyd, B. (3) (Wrexham) 1975/6.
Lovell, S. (6) (Crystal Palace) 1981/2 (Millwall) 1984/5, 1985/6.
Lowndes, S. (10) (Newport County) 1982/3 (Millwall) 1984/5, 1985/6, 1986/7, (Barnsley) 1987/8.
Lowrie, G. (4) (Coventry City) 1947/8, 1948/9 (Newcastle United).
Lucas, M. (4) (Leyton Orient) 1961/2, 1962/3.
Lucas, W. (7) (Swansea City) 1948/9, 1949/50, 1950/1.

Maguire, G.T. (5) (Portsmouth) 1989/90.
Mahoney, J. (51) (Stoke City) 1967/8, 1968/9, 1970/1, 1972/3, 1973/4, 1974/5, 1975/6, 1976/7 (Middlesbrough) 1977/8, 1978/9 (Swansea City) 1979/80, 1981/2, 1982/3.
Marustik, C. (6) (Swansea City) 1981/2, 1982/3.
Medwin, T. (30) (Swansea City) 1952/3, 1956/7 (Tottenham Hotspur) 1957/8, 1958/9, 1959/60, 1960/1, 1962/3.
Melville, A.K. (4) (Swansea C), 1989/90.
Mielczarek, R. (1) (Rotherham United) 1970/1.
Millington, A. (21) (West Bromwich Albion) 1962/3, 1964/5 (Crystal Palace) 1965/6 (Peterborough United) 1966/7, 1967/8, 1968/9, 1969/70 (Swansea City) 1970/1, 1971/2.
Moore, G. (21) (Cardiff City) 1959/60, 1960/1, 1961/2 (Chelsea) 1962/3, (Manchester United) 1963/4 (Northampton Town) 1965/6, 1968/9 (Charlton Athletic) 1969/70, 1970/1.
Morris, W. (5) (Burnley) 1946/7, 1948/9, 1951/2.

Nardiello, D. (2) (Coventry City) 1977/8.
Nicholas, P. (65) (Crystal Palace) 1978/9, 1979/80, 1980/1 (Arsenal) 1981/2, 1982/3, 1983/4 (Crystal Palace) 1984/5 (Luton Town) 1985/6, 1986/7, 1987/8 (Aberdeen), (Chelsea) 1988/9, 1989/90.
Niedzwiecki, E.A. (2) (Chelsea) 1984/5, 1987/8.
Norman, A.J. (5) (Hull City) 1985/6, 1987/8.
Nurse, M. (12) (Swansea City) 1959/60, 1960/1, 1962/3 (Middlesbrough) 1963/4.

O'Sullivan, P. (3) (Brighton & Hove Albion) 1972/3, 1975/6, 1978/9.

Page, M. (28) (Birmingham City) 1970/1, 1971/2, 1972/3, 1973/4, 1974/5, 1975/6, 1976/7, 1977/8, 1978/9.
Palmer, D. (3) (Swansea City) 1956/7, 1957/8.
Parry, J. (1) (Swansea City) 1950/1.
Pascoe, C. (7) (Swansea City) 1983/4, (Sunderland) 1988/9, 1989/90.
Paul, R. (33) (Swansea City) 1948/9, 1949/50 (Manchester City) 1950/1, 1951/2, 1952/3, 1953/4, 1954/5, 1955/6.
Phillips, D. (27) (Plymouth Argyle) 1983/4 (Manchester City) 1984/5, 1985/6, 1986/7 (Coventry City) 1987/8, 1988/9, 1989/90.
Phillips, J. (4) (Chelsea) 1972/3, 1973/4, 1974/5, 1977/8.

Phillips, L. (58) (Cardiff City) 1970/1, 1971/2, 1972/3, 1973/4, 1974/5, (Aston Villa) 1975/6, 1976/7, 1977/8, 1978/9 (Swansea City) 1979/80, 1980/1, 1981/2 (Charlton Athletic).
Pontin, K. (2) (Cardiff City) 1979/80.
Powell, A. (8) (Leeds United) 1946/7, 1947/8, 1948/9 (Everton) 1949/50, 1950/1 (Birmingham City).
Powell, D. (11) (Wrexham) 1967/8, 1968/9 (Sheffield United) 1969/70, 1970/1.
Powell, I. (8) (QPR) 1946/7, 1947/8, 1948/9 (Aston Villa) 1949/50, 1950/1.
Price, P. (25) (Luton Town) 1979/80, 1980/1, 1981/2 (Tottenham Hotspur) 1982/3, 1983/4.
Pring, K. (3) (Rotherham United) 1965/6, 1966/7.
Pritchard, H.K. (1) (Bristol City) 1984/5.

Rankmore, F. (1) (Peterborough United) 1965/6.
Ratcliffe, K. (48) (Everton) 1980/1, 1981/2, 1982/3, 1983/4, 1984/5, 1985/6, 1986/7, 1987/8, 1988/9, 1989/90.
Reece, G. (29) (Sheffield United) 1965/6, 1966/7, 1969/70, 1970/1, 1971/2, (Cardiff City) 1972/3, 1973/4, 1974/5.
Reed, W. (2) (Ipswich Town) 1954/5.
Rees, A. (1) (Birmingham City) 1983/4.
Rees, R. (39) (Coventry City) 1964/5, 1965/6, 1966/7, 1967/8 (West Bromwich Albion) 1968/9 (Nottingham Forest) 1969/70, 1970/1, 1971/2.
Rees, W. (4) (Cardiff City) 1948/9 (Tottenham Hotspur) 1949/50.
Richards, S. (1) (Cardiff City) 1946/7.
Roberts, D. (17) (Oxford United) 1972/3, 1973/4, 1974/5 (Hull City) 1975/6, 1976/7, 1977/8.
Roberts, J.G. (22) (Arsenal) 1970/1, 1971/2, 1972/3,(Birmingham City) 1973/4, 1974/5, 1975/6.
Roberts, I. W. (1) (Watford) 1989/90.
Roberts, J.H. (1) (Bolton Wanderers) 1948/9.
Roberts, P. (4) (Portsmouth) 1973/4, 1974/5.
Rodrigues, P. (40) (Cardiff City) 1964/5, 1965/6 (Leicester City) 1966/7, 1967/8, 1968/9, 1969/70 (Sheffield Wednesday) 1970/1, 1971/2, 1972/3, 1973/4.
Rouse, V. (1) (Crystal Palace) 1958/9.
Rowley, T. (1) (Tranmere Rovers) 1958/9.
Rush, I. (44) (Liverpool) 1979/80, 1980/1, 1981/2, 1982/3, 1983/4, 1984/5, 1985/6, 1986/7 (Juventus) 1987/8, (Liverpool) 1988/9 1989/90.

Saunders, D. (19) (Brighton & Hove Albion) 1985/6, 1986/7 (Oxford United) 1987/8, (Derby County) 1988/9, 1989/90.
Sayer, P. (7) (Cardiff City) 1976/7, 1977/8.
Scrine, F. (2) (Swansea City) 1949/50.
Sear, C. (1) (Manchester City) 1962/3.
Sherwood, A. (41) (Cardiff City) 1946/7, 1947/8, 1948/9, 1949/50, 1950/1, 1951/2, 1952/3, 1953/4, 1954/5, 1955/6, 1956/7 (Newport County).
Shortt, W. (12) (Plymouth Argyle) 1946/7, 1949/50, 1951/2, 1952/3.
Showers, D. (2) (Cardiff City) 1974/5.
Sidlow, C. (7) (Liverpool) 1946/7, 1947/8, 1948/9, 1949/50.
Slatter, N. (22) (Bristol Rovers) 1982/3, 1983/4, 1984/5 (Oxford United) 1985/6, 1986/7, 1987/8, 1988/9.
Smallman, D. (7) (Wrexham) 1973/4 (Everton) 1974/5, 1975/6.
Southall, N. (44) (Everton) 1981/2, 1982/3, 1983/4, 1984/5, 1985/6, 1986/7, 1987/8, 1988/9, 1989/90.
Speed, G.A. (1) (Leeds U), 1989/90.
Sprake, G. (37) (Leeds United) 1963/4, 1964/5, 1965/6, 1966/7, 1967/8, 1968/9, 1969/70, 1970/1, 1971/2, 1972/3, 1973/4 (Birmingham City) 1974/5.
Stansfield, F. (1) (Cardiff City) 1948/9.
Stevenson, B. (15) (Leeds United) 1977/8, 1978/9, 1979/80, 1981/2 (Birmingham City).

Stevenson, N. (4) (Swansea City) 1981/2, 1982/3.
Stitfall, R. (2) (Cardiff City) 1952/3, 1956/7.
Sullivan, D. (17) (Cardiff City) 1952/3, 1953/4, 1954/5, 1956/7, 1957/8, 1958/9, 1959/60.

Tapscott, D. (14) (Arsenal) 1953/4, 1954/5, 1955/6, 1956/7, 1958/9 (Cardiff City).
Thomas, D. (2) (Swansea City) 1956/7, 1957/8.
Thomas, M. (51) (Wrexham) 1976/7, 1977/8, 1978/9 (Manchester United) 1979/80, 1980/1, 1981/2 (Everton) (Brighton) 1982/3 (Stoke City) 1983/4, (Chelsea) 1984/5, 1985/6 (West Bromwich Albion).
Thomas, M.R. (1) (Newcastle United) 1986/7.
Thomas, R. (50) (Swindon Town) 1966/7, 1967/8, 1968/9, 1969/70, 1970/1, 1971/2, 1972/3, 1973/4 (Derby County) 1974/5, 1975/6, 1976/7, 1977/8 (Cardiff City).
Thomas, S. (4) (Fulham) 1947/8, 1948/9.
Toshack, J. (40) (Cardiff City) 1968/9, 1969/70 (Liverpool) 1970/1, 1971/2, 1972/3, 1974/5, 1975/6, 1976/7, 1977/8 (Swansea City) 1978/9, 1979/80.

Van den Hauwe, P.W.R. (13) (Everton) 1984/5, 1985/6, 1986/7, 1987/8, 1988/9.
Vaughan, N. (10) (Newport County) 1982/3, 1983/4 (Cardiff City) 1984/5.
Vearncombe, G. (2) (Cardiff City) 1957/8, 1960/1.
Vernon, R. (32) (Blackburn Rovers) 1956/7, 1957/8, 1958/9, 1959/60 (Everton) 1960/1, 1961/2, 1962/3, 1963/4, 1964/5 (Stoke City) 1965/6, 1966/7, 1967/8.
Villars, A. (3) (Cardiff City) 1973/4.

Walley, T. (1) (Watford) 1970/1.
Walsh, I. (18) (Crystal Palace) 1979/80, 1980/1, 1981/2 (Swansea City).
Ward, D. (2) (Bristol Rovers) 1958/9, 1961/2 (Cardiff City).
Webster, C. (4) (Manchester United) 1956/7, 1957/8.
Williams, D.G. (11) 1987/8 (Derby County) 1988/9, 1989/90.
Williams, D.M. (5) (Norwich City) 1985/6, 1986/7.
Williams, G. (1) (Cardiff City) 1950/1.
Williams, G.E. (26) (West Bromwich Albion) 1959/60, 1960/1, 1962/3, 1963/4, 1964/5, 1965/6, 1966/7, 1967/8, 1968/9.
Williams, G.G. (5) (Swansea City) 1960/1, 1961/2.
Williams, H. (4) (Newport County) 1948/9 (Leeds United) 1949/50, 1950/1.
Williams, Herbert (3) (Swansea City) 1964/5, 1970/1.
Williams, S. (43) (West Bromwich Albion) 1953/4, 1954/5, 1955/6, 1957/8, 1958/9, 1959/60, 1960/1, 1961/2, 1962/3 (Southampton) 1963/4, 1964/5, 1965/6.
Witcomb, D. (3) (West Bromwich Albion) 1946/7 (Sheffield Wednesday).
Woosnam, P. (17) (Leyton Orient) 1958/9 (West Ham United) 1959/60, 1960/1, 1961/2, 1962/3 (Aston Villa).

Yorath, T. (59) (Leeds United) 1969/70, 1970/1, 1971/2, 1972/3, 1973/4, 1974/5, 1975/6 (Coventry City) 1976/7, 1977/8, 1978/9 (Tottenham Hotspur) 1979/80, 1980/1.
Young, E. (1) (Wimbledon) 1989/90.

EIRE

Aherne, T. (16) (Belfast Celtic) 1945/6 (Luton Town) 1949/50, 1950/1, 1951/2, 1952/3, 1953/4.
Aldridge, J.W. (35) (Oxford United) 1985/6, 1986/7 (Liverpool) 1987/8, 1988/9 Real Sociedad 1989/90.
Ambrose, P. (5) (Shamrock Rovers) 1954/5, 1963/4.
Anderson, J. (16) (Preston North End) 1979/80, 1981/2 (Newcastle United) 1983/4, 1985/6, 1986/7, 1987/8, 1988/9.

Bailham, E. (1) (Shamrock Rovers) 1963/4.
Barber, E. (2) (Shelbourne) 1965/6 (Birmingham City) 1965/6.
Beglin, J. (15) (Liverpool) 1983/4, 1984/5, 1985/6, 1986/7.
Bonner, P. (43) (Celtic) 1980/1, 1981/2, 1983/4, 1984/5, 1985/6, 1986/7, 1987/8, 1988/9, 1989/90.
Braddish, S. (1) (Dundalk) 1977/8.
Brady, T.R. (6) (QPR) 1963/4.
Brady, W. L. (72) (Arsenal) 1974/5, 1975/6, 1976/7, 197/8, 1978/9, 1979/80, (Juventus) 1980/1, 1981/2 (Sampdoria) 1982/3, 1983/4 (Internazionale) 1984/5, 1985/6 (Ascoli) 1986/7 (West Ham United) 1987/8, 1988/9, 1989/90.
Breen, T. (3) (Shamrock Rovers) 1946/7.
Brennan, F. (1) (Drumcondra) 1964/5.
Brennan, S.A. (19) (Manchester United) 1964/5, 1965/6, 1966/7, 1968/9, 1969/70 (Waterford) 1970/1.
Browne, W. (3) (Bohemians) 1963/4.
Buckley, L. (2) (Shamrock Rovers) 1983/4 (Waregem) 1984/5.
Burke, F. (1) (Cork Athletic) 1951/2.
Byrne, A.B. (14) (Southampton) 1969/70, 1970/1, 1972/3, 1973/4.
Byrne, J. (19) (QPR) 1984/5, 1986/7, 1987/8 (Le Havre) 1989/90.
Byrne, P. (9) (Shamrock Rovers) 1983/4, 1984/5, 1985/6.

Campbell, A. (3) (Santander) 1984/5.
Campbell, N. (11) (St Patrick's Athletic) 1970/1 (Fortuna Cologne) 1971/2, 1972/3, 1974/5, 1975/6.
Cantwell, N. (36) (West Ham United) 1953/4, 1955/6, 1956/7, 1957/8, 1958/9, 1959/60, 1960/1 (Manchester Untied) 1960/1, 1961/2, 1962/3, 1963/4, 1964/5, 1965/6, 1966/7.
Carey, J.J. (21) (Manchester United) 1945/6, 1946/7, 1947/8, 1948/9, 1949/50, 1950/1, 1952/3.
Carolan, J. (2) (Manchester United) 1959/60.
Carroll, B. (2) (Shelbourne) 1948/9, 1949/50.
Carroll, T.R. (17) (Ipswich Town) 1967/8, 1968/9, 1969/70, 1970/1 (Birmingham City) 1971/2, 1972/3.
Cascarino, A.G. (26) (Gillingham) 1985/6 (Millwall) 1987/8, 1988/9, 1989/90 Aston Villa.
Chandler, J. (2) (Leeds United) 1979/80.
Clarke, J. (1) (Drogheda United) 1977/8.
Clarke, K. (2) (Drumcondra) 1947/8.
Clarke, M. (1) (Shamrock Rovers) 1949/50.
Clinton, T.J. (3) (Everton) 1950/1, 1953/4.
Coad, P. (11) (Shamrock Rovers) 1946/7, 1947/8, 1948/9, 1950/1, 1951/2.
Coffey, T. (1) (Drumcondra) 1949/50.
Colfer, M.D. (2) (Shelbourne) 1949/50, 1950/1.
Conmy, O.M. (5) (Peterborough United) 1964/5, 1966/7, 1967/8, 1969/70.
Conroy, G.A. (27) (Stoke City) 1969/70, 1970/1, 1972/3, 1973/4, 1974/5, 1975/6, 1976/7.
Conway, J.P. (20) (Fulham) 1966/7, 1967/8, 1968/9, 1969/70, 1970/1, 1973/4, 1974/5, 1975/6 (Manchester City) 1976/7.
Corr, P.J. (4) (Everton) 1948/9.
Courtney, E. (1) (Cork United) 1945/6.
Cummins, G.P. (19) (Luton Town) 1953/4, 1954/5, 1955/6, 1957/8, 1958/9, 1959/60, 1960/1.
Cuneen, T. (1) (Limerick) 1950/1.
Curtis, D.P. (17) (Shelbourne) 1956/7 (Bristol City) 1956/7, 1957/8, (Ipswich Town) 1958/9, 1959/60, 1960/1, 1961/2, 1962/3 (Exeter City) 1963/4.
Cusack, S. (1) (Limerick) 1952/3.

Daly, G.A. (47) (Manchester United) 1972/3, 1973/4, 1974/5, 1976/7 (Derby County) 1977/8, 1978/9, 1979/80 (Coventry City) 1980/1, 1981/2, 1982/3, 1983/4 (Birmingham City) 1984/5, 1985/6 (Shrewsbury Town) 1986/7.
Daly, M. (2) (Wolverhampton Wanderers) 1977/8.

Daly. P. (1) (Shamrock Rovers) 1949/50.
De Mange, K.J.P.P. (2) (Liverpool) 1986/7, (Hull City) 1988/9.
Deacy, E. (4) (Aston Villa) 1981/2.
Dempsey, J.T. (19) (Fulham) 1966/7, 1967/8, 1968/9 (Chelsea) 1968/9, 1969/70, 1970/1, 1971/2.
Dennehy, J. (11) (Cork Hibernian) 1971/2 (Nottingham Forest) 1972/3, 1973/4, 1974/5 (Walsall) 1975/6, 1976/7.
Desmond, P. (4) (Middlesbrough) 1949/50.
Devine, J. (12) (Arsenal) 1979/80, 1980/1, 1981/2, 1982/3 (Norwich City) 1983/4, 1984/5.
Donovan, D.C. (5) (Everton) 1954/5, 1956/7.
Donovan, T. (1) (Aston Villa) 1979/80.
Doyle, C. (1) (Shelbourne) 1958/9.
Duffy, B. (1) (Shamrock Rovers) 1949/50.
Dunne, A.P. (33) (Manchester United) 1961/2, 1962/3, 1963/4, 1964/5, 1965/6, 1966/7, 1968/9, 1969/70, 1970/1 (Bolton Wanderers) 1973/4, 1974/5, 1975/6.
Dunne, J.C. (1) (Fulham) 1970/1.
Dunne, P.A.J. (5) (Manchester United) 1964/5, 1965/6, 1966/7.
Dunne, S. (15) (Luton Town) 1952/3, 1953/4, 1955/6, 1956/7, 1957/8, 1958/9, 1959/60.
Dunne, T. (3) (St Patrick's Athletic) 1955/6, 1956/7.
Dunning, P. (2) (Shelbourne) 1970/1.
Dunphy, E.M. (23) (York City) 1965/6 (Millwall) 1965/6, 1966/7, 1967/8, 1968/9, 1969/70, 1970/1.
Dwyer, N.M. (14) (West Ham United) 1959/60 (Swansea Town) 1960/1, 1961/2, 1963/4, 1964/5.

Eccles, P. (1) (Shamrock Rovers) 1985/6.
Eglington, T.J. (24) (Shamrock Rovers) 1945/6 (Everton) 1946/7, 1947/8, 1948/9, 1950/1, 1951/2, 1952/3, 1953/4, 1954/5, 1955/6.

Fagan, E. (1) (Shamrock Rovers) 1972/3.
Fagan, F. (8) (Manchester City) 1954/5, 1959/60 (Derby County) 1959/60, 1960/1.
Fairclough, M. (2) (Dundalk) 1981/2.
Fallon, S. (8) (Celtic) 1950/1, 1951/2, 1952/3, 1954/5.
Farrell, P.D. (28) (Shamrock Rovers) 1945/6 (Everton) 1946/7, 1947/8, 1948/9, 1949/50, 1950/1, 1951/2, 1952/3, 1953/4, 1954/5, 1955/6, 1956/7.
Finucane, A. (11) (Limerick) 1966/7, 1968/9, 1969/70, 1970/1, 1971/2.
Fitzgerald, F.J. (2) (Waterford) 1954/5, 1955/6.
Fitzgerald, P.J. (5) (Leeds United) 1960/1, 1961/2.
Fitzpatrick, K. (1) (Limerick) 1969/70.
Fitzsimons, A.G. (26) (Middlesbrough) 1949/50, 1951/2, 1952/3, 1953/4, 1954/5, 1955/6, 1956/7, 1957/8, 1958/9 (Lincoln City) 1958/9.
Fogarty, A. (11) (Sunderland) 1959/60, 1960/1, 1961/2, 1962/3, 1963/4, (Hartlepool United) 1963/4.
Foley, T.C. (9) (Northampton Town) 1963/4, 1964/5, 1965/6, 1966/7.
Fullam, J. (11) (Preston North End) 1960/1 (Shamrock Rovers) 1963/4, 1965/6, 1967/8, 1968/9, 1969/70.

Gallagher, C. (2) (Celtic) 1966/7.
Gallagher, M. (1) (Hibernian) 1953/4.
Galvin, A. (29) (Tottenham Hotspur) 1982/3, 1983/4, 1984/5, 1985/6, 1986/7 (Sheffield Wednesday) 1987/8, 1988/9, 1989/90.
Gannon, E. (14) (Notts County) 1948/9 (Sheffield Wednesday) 1948/9, 1949/50, 1950/1, 1951/2, 1953/4, 1954/5 (Shelbourne) 1954/5.
Gannon, M. (1) (Shelbourne) 1971/2.
Gavin, J.T. (7) (Norwich City) 1949/50, 1952/3, 1953/4 (Tottenham Hotspur) 1954/5 (Norwich City) 1956/7.
Gibbons, A. (4) (St Patrick's Athletic) 1951/2, 1953/4, 1955/6.

Gilbert, R. (1) (Shamrock Rovers) 1965/6.
Giles, C. (1) (Doncaster Rovers) 1950/1.
Giles, M.J. (60) (Manchester United) 1959/60, 1960/1, 1961/2, 1962/3 (Leeds United) 1963/4, 1964/5, 1965/6, 1966/7, 1968/9, 1969/70, 1970/1, 1972/3, 1973/4, 1974/5 (West Bromwich Albion) 1975/6, 1976/7 (Shamrock Rovers) 1977/8, 1978/9.
Givens, D.J. (56) (Manchester United) 1968/9, 1969/70 (Luton Town) 1969/70, 1970/1, 1971/2 (QPR) 1972/3, 1973/4, 1974/5, 1975/6, 1976/7, 1977/8 (Birmingham City) 1978/9, 1979/80, 1980/1 (Neuchatel Xamax) 1981/2.
Glynn, D. (2) (Drumcondra) 1951/2, 1954/5.
Godwin, T.F. (13) (Shamrock Rovers) 1948/9, 1949/50 (Leicester City) 1949/50, 1950/1 (Bournemouth) 1955/6, 1956/7, 1957/8.
Gorman, W.C. (2) (Brentford) 1946/7.
Grealish, A. (44) (Orient) 1975/6, 1978/9 (Luton Town) 1979/80, 1980/1, (Brighton & Hove Albion) 1981/2, 1982/3, 1983/4 (West Bromwich Albion) 1984/5, 1985/6.
Gregg, E. (9) (Bohemians) 1977/8, 1978/9, 1979/80.
Grimes, A.A. (17) (Manchester United) 1977/8, 1979/80, 1980/1, 1981/2, 1982/3 (Coventry City) 1983/4 (Luton Town) 1987/8.

Hale, A. (13) (Aston Villa) 1961/2 (Doncaster Rovers) 1962/3, 1963/4, (Waterford) 1966/7, 1967/8, 1968/9, 1969/70, 1970/1, 1971/2.
Hamilton, T. (2) (Shamrock Rovers) 1958/9.
Hand, E.K. (20) (Portsmouth) 1968/9, 1969/70, 1970/1, 1972/3, 1973/4, 1974/5, 1975/6.
Hartnett, J.B. (2) (Middlesbrough) 1948/9, 1953/4.
Haverty, J. (32) (Arsenal) 1955/6, 1956/7, 1957/8, 1958/9, 1959/60, 1960/1, (Blackburn Rovers) 1961/2 (Millwall) 1962/3, 1963/4 (Celtic) 1964/5 (Bristol Rovers) 1964/5 (Shelbourne) 1965/6, 1966/7.
Hayes, A.W.P. (1) (Southampton) 1978/9.
Hayes, W.E. (2) (Huddersfield Town) 1946/7.
Hayes, W.J. (1) (Limerick) 1948/9.
Healey, R. (2) (Cardiff City) 1976/7, 1979/80.
Heighway, S.D. (34) (Liverpool) 1970/1, 1972/3, 1974/5, 1975/6, 1976/7, 1977/8, 1978/9, 1979/80, 1980/1 (Minnesota Kicks) 1981/2.
Henderson, B. (2) (Drumcondra) 1947/8.
Hennessy, J. (5) (Shelbourne) 1955/6, 1965/6 (St Patrick's Athletic) 1968/9.
Herrick, J. (3) (Cork Hibernians) 1971/2 (Shamrock Rovers) 1972/3.
Higgins, J. (1) (Birmingham City) 1950/1.
Holmes, J. (30) (Coventry City) 1970/1, 1972/3, 1973/4, 1974/5, 1975/6, 1976/7 (Tottenham Hotspur) 1977/8, 1978/9, 1980/1 (Vancouver Whitecaps) 1980/1.
Houghton, R.J. (34) (Oxford United) 1985/6. 1986/7, 1987/8 (Liverpool) 1987/8, 1988/9, 1989/90.
Howlett, G. (1) (Brighton & Hove Albion) 1983/4.
Hughton, C. (50) (Tottenham Hotspur) 1979/80, 1980/1, 1981/2. 1982/3, 1983/4, 1984/5, 1985/6, 1986/7, 1987/8, 1988/9, 1989/90.
Hurley, C.J. (40) (Millwall) 1956/7, 1957/8 (Sunderland) 1958/9, 1959/60, 1960/1, 1961/2, 1962/3, 1963/4, 1964/5, 1965/6, 1966/7, 1967/8 (Bolton Wanderers) 1968/9.

Keane, T.R. (4) (Swansea Town) 1948/9.
Kearin, M. (1) (Shamrock Rovers) 1971/2.
Kearns, F.T. (1) (West Ham United) 1953/4.
Kearns, M. (18) (Oxford United) 1969/70 (Walsall) 1973/4, 1975/6, 1976/7, 1977/8, 1978/9 (Wolverhampton Wanderers) 1979/80.
Kelly, D.T. (6) (Walsall) 1987/8 (West Ham) 1988/9 (Leicester C) 1989/90.
Kelly, J.A. (47) (Drumcondra) 1956/7 (Preston North End) 1961/2, 1962/3, 1963/4, 1964/5, 1965/6, 1966/7, 1967/8, 1969/70, 1970/1, 1971/2, 1972/3.
Kelly, J.P.V. (5) (Wolverhampton Wanderers) 1960/1, 1961/2.
Kelly, M.J. (3) (Portsmouth) 1987/8, 1988/9.

Kelly, N. (1) (Nottingham Forest) 1953/4.
Kennedy, M.F. (2) (Portsmouth) 1985/6.
Keogh, J. (1) (Shamrock Rovers) 1965/6.
Keogh, S. (1) (Shamrock Rovers) 1958/9.
Kiernan, F.W. (5) (Shamrock Rovers) 1950/1 (Southampton) 1951/2.
Kinnear, J.P. (26) (Tottenham Hotspur) 1966/7, 1967/8, 1968/9, 1969/70, 1970/1, 1971/2, 1972/3, 1973/4, 1974/5 (Brighton & Hove Albion) 1975/6.

Langan, D. (25) (Derby County) 1977/8, 1979/80 (Birmingham City) 1980/1, 1981/2 (Oxford United) 1984/5, 1985/6, 1986/7, 1987/8.
Lawler, J.F. (8) (Fulham) 1952/3, 1953/4, 1954/5, 1955/6.
Lawlor, J.C. (3) (Drumcondra) 1948/9 (Doncaster Rovers) 1950/1.
Lawlor, M. (5) (Shamrock Rovers) 1970/1, 1972/3.
Lawrenson, M. (38) (Preston North End) 1976/7 (Brighton & Hove Albion) 1977/8, 1978/9, 1979/80, 1980/1 (Liverpool) 1981/2, 1982/3, 1983/4, 1984/5, 1985/6, 1986/7, 1987/8.
Leech, M. (8) (Shamrock Rovers) 1968/9, 1971/2, 1972/3.
Lowry, D. (1) (St Patrick's Athletic) 1961/2.

McAlinden, J. (2) (Portsmouth) 1945/6.
McCann, J. (1) (Shamrock Rovers) 1956/7.
McCarthy, M. (47) (Manchester City) 1983/4, 1984/5, 1985/6, 1986/7 (Celtic) 1987/8, 1988/9 (Lyon) 1989/90.
McConville, T. (6) (Dundalk) 1971/2 (Waterford) 1972/3.
McDonagh, J. (24) (Everton) 1980/1 (Bolton Wanderers) 1981/2, 1982/3, (Notts County) 1983/4, 1984/5, 1985/6.
McDonagh, Joe (3) (Shamrock Rovers) 1983/4, 1984/5.
McEvoy, M.A. (17) (Blackburn Rovers) 1960/1, 1962/3, 1963/4, 1964/5, 1965/6, 1966/7.
McGee, P. (15) (QPR) 1977/8, 1978/9, 1979/80 (Preston North End) 1980/1.
McGowan, D. (3) (West Ham United) 1948/9.
McGowan, J. (1) (Cork United) 1946/7.
McGrath, M. (22) (Blackburn Rovers) 1957/8, 1958/9, 1959/60, 1960/1, 1961/2, 1962/3, 1963/4, 1964/5, 1965/6 (Bradford Park Avenue) 1965/6, 1966/7.
McGrath, P. (41) (Manchester United) 1984/5, 1985/6, 1986/7, 1987/8, 1988/9 (Aston Villa) 1989/90.
Macken, A. (1) (Derby County) 1976/7.
Mackey, G. (3) (Shamrock Rovers) 1956/7.
McLoughlin, A.F. (3) (Swindon T) 1989/90.
McMillan, W. (2) (Belfast Celtic) 1945/6.
McNally, J.B. (3) (Luton Town) 1958/9, 1960/1, 1962/3.
Malone, G. (1) (Shelbourne) 1948/9.
Mancini, T.J. (5) (QPR) 1973/4 (Arsenal) 1974/5.
Martin, C.J. (30) (Glentoran) 1945/6, 1946/7 (Leeds United) 1946/7, 1947/8, (Aston Villa) 1948/9, 1949/50, 1950/1, 1951/2, 1953/4, 1954/5, 1955/6.
Martin, M.P. (51) (Bohemians) 1971/2, 1972/3 (Manchester United) 1972/3, 1973/4, 1974/5 (West Bromwich Albion) 1975/6, 1976/7 (Newcastle United) 1978/9, 1979/80, 1980/1, 1981/2, 1982/3.
Meagan, M.K. (17) (Everton) 1960/1, 1961/2, 1962/3, 1963/4 (Huddersfield Town) 1964/5, 1965/6, 1966/7, 1967/8 (Drogheda) 1969/70.
Mooney, J. (2) (Shamrock Rovers) 1964/5.
Moran, K. (54) (Manchester United) 1979/80, 1980/1, 1981/2, 1982/3, 1983/4, 1984/5, 1985/6, 1986/7, 1987/8 (Sporting Gijon) 1988/9 (Blackburn Rovers) 1989/90.
Moroney, T. (12) (West Ham United) 1947/8, 1948/9, 1949/50, 1950/1, 1951/2, 1953/4.
Morris, C.B. (26) (Celtic) 1987/8, 1988/9, 1989/90.
Moulson, G.B. (3) (Lincoln City) 1947/8, 1948/9.
Mucklan, C. (1) (Drogheda) 1977/8.
Mulligan, P.M. (50) (Shamrock Rovers) 1968/9, 1969/70 (Chelsea) 1969/70, 1970/1, 1971/2 (Crystal Palace) 1972/3, 1973/4, 1974/5 (West Bromwich Albion) 1975/6, 1976/7, 1977/8, 1978/9 (Shamrock Rovers) 1979/80.

Munroe, L. (1) (Shamrock Rovers) 1953/4.
Murphy, A. (1) (Clyde) 1955/6.
Murphy, B. (1) (Bohemians) 1985/6.
Murphy, J. (3) (Crystal Palace) 1979/80.
Murray, T. (1) (Dundalk) 1949/50.

Newman, W. (1) (Shelbourne) 1968/9.
Nolan, R. (10) (Shamrock Rovers) 1956/7, 1957/8, 1959/60, 1961/2, 1962/3.

O'Brien, F. (4) (Philadelphia Fury) 1979/80
O'Brien, L. (8) (Shamrock Rovers) 1985/6 (Manchester United) 1986/7, 1987/8, (Newcastle United) 1988/9.
O'Brien, R. (4) (Notts County) 1975/6, 1976/7.
O'Byrne, L.B. (1) (Shamrock Rovers) 1948/9.
O'Callaghan, B.R. (6) (Stoke City) 1978/9, 1979/80, 1980/1, 1981/2.
O'Callaghan, K. (20) (Ipswich Town) 1980/1, 1981/2, 1982/3, 1983/4, 1984/5, (Portsmouth) 1985/6, 1986/7.
O'Connell, A. (2) (Dundalk) 1966/7 (Bohemians) 1970/1.
O'Connor, T. (4) (Shamrock Rovers) 1949/50.
O'Connor, T. (7) (Fulham) 1967/8 (Dundalk) 1971/2 (Bohemians) 1972/3.
O'Driscoll, J.F. (3) (Swansea Town) 1948/9.
O'Driscoll, S. (3) (Fulham) 1981/2.
O'Farrell, F. (9) (West Ham United) 1951/2, 1952/3, 1953/4, 1954/5, 1955/6, (Preston North End) 1957/8, 1958/9.
O'Flanagan, K.P. (3) (Arsenal) 1946/7.
O'Flanagan, M. (1) (Bohemians) 1946/7.
O'Hanlon, K.G. (1) (Rotherham United) 1987/8.
O'Keefe, E. (5) (Everton) 1980/1 (Port Vale) 1983/4.
O'Leary, D. (51) (Arsenal) 1976/7, 1977/8, 1978/9, 1979/80, 1980/1, 1981/2, 1982/3, 1983/4, 1984/5, 1985/6, 1988/9, 1989/90.
O'Leary, P. (7) (Shamrock Rovers) 1979/80, 1980/1.
O'Neill, F.S. (20) (Shamrock Rovers) 1961/2, 1964/5, 1965/6, 1966/7, 1968/9, 1971/2.
O'Neill, J. (17) (Everton) 1951/2, 1952/3, 1953/4, 1954/5, 1955/6, 1956/7, 1957/8, 1958/9.
O'Neill, J. (1) (Preston North End) 1960/1.
O'Regan, K. (4) (Brighton & Hove Albion) 1983/4, 1984/5.
O'Reilly, J. (2) (Cork United) 1945/6.

Peyton, G. (28) (Fulham) 1976/7, 1977/8, 1978/9, 1979/80, 1980/1, 1981/2, 1984/5, 1985/6 (Bournemouth) 1987/8, 1988/9, 1989/90.
Peyton, N. (6) (Shamrock Rovers) 1956/7 (Leeds United) 1959/60, 1960/1, 1962/3.

Quinn, N.J. (18) (Arsenal) 1985/6, 1986/7, 1987/8, 1988/9 (Manchester C) 1989/90.

Richardson, D.J. (3) (Shamrock Rovers) 1971/2 (Gillingham) 1972/3, 1979/80.
Ringstead, A. (20) (Sheffield United) 1950/1, 1951/2, 1952/3, 1953/4, 1954/5, 1955/6, 1956/7, 1957/8, 1958/9.
Robinson, M. (23) (Brighton & Hove Albion) 1980/1, 1981/2, 1982/3, (Liverpool) 1983/4, 1984/5 (QPR) 1985/6.
Roche, P.J. (8) (Shelbourne) 1971/2 (Manchester United) 1974/5, 1975/6.
Rogers, E. (19) (Blackburn Rovers) 1967/8, 1968/9, 1969/70, 1970/1, (Charlton Athletic) 1971/2, 1972/3.
Ryan, G. (16) (Derby County) 1977/8 (Brighton & Hove Albion) 1978/9, 1979/80, 1980/1, 1981/2, 1983/4, 1984/5.
Ryan R.A. (16) (West Bromwich Albion) 1949/50, 1950/1, 1951/2, 1952/3, 1953/4, 1954/5 (Derby County) 1955/6.

Saward, P. (18) (Millwall) 1953/4 (Aston Villa) 1956/7, 1957/8, 1958/9, 1959/60, 1960/1 (Huddersfield Town) 1960/1, 1961/2, 1962/3.

Scannell, T. (1) (Southend United) 1953/4.
Scully, P.J. (1) (Arsenal) 1988/9.
Sheedy, K. (32) (Everton) 1983/4, 1984/5, 1985/6, 1986/7, 1987/8, 1988/9, 1989/90.
Sheridan, J.J. (9) (Leeds United) 1987/8, 1988/9 (Sheffield Wed) 1989/90.
Slaven, B. (4) (Middlesbrough) 1989/90.
Sloan, J.W. (2) (Arsenal) 1945/6.
Smyth, M. (1) (Shamrock Rovers) 1968/9.
Stapleton, F. (70) (Arsenal) 1976/7, 1977/8, 1978/9, 1979/80, 1980/1 (Manchester United) 1981/2, 1982/3, 1983/4, 1984/5, 1985/6, 1986/7 (Ajax) 1987/8 (Derby County) 1987/8 (LeHavre) 1988/9 (Blackburn Rovers) 1989/90.
Staunton, S. (18) Liverpool) 1988/9, 1989/90.
Stevenson, A.E. (6) (Everton) 1946/7, 1947/8, 1948/9.
Strahan, F. (5) (Shelbourne) 1963/4, 1964/5, 1965/6.
Swan, M.M.G. (1) (Drumcondra) 1959/60.
Synott, N. (3) (Shamrock Rovers) 1977/8, 1978/9.

Thomas, P. (2) (Waterford) 1973/4.
Townsend, A.D. (17) (Norwich City) 1988/9, 1989/90.
Traynor, T.J. (8) (Southampton) 1953/4, 1961/2, 1962/3, 1963/4.
Treacy, R.C.P. (43) (West Bromwich Albion) 1965/6, 1966/7, 1967/8 (Charlton Athletic) 1967/8, 1968/9, 1969/70, 1970/1 (Swindon Town) 1971/2, 1972/3, 1973/4 (Preston North End) 1973/4, 1974/5, 1975/6 (West Bromwich Albion) 1976/7, 1977/8 (Shamrock Rovers) 1979/80.
Tuohy, L. (8) (Shamrock Rovers) 1955/6, 1958/9 (Newcastle United) 1961/2, 1962/3 (Shamrock Rovers) 1963/4, 1964/5.
Turner, A. (2) (Celtic) 1962/3, 1963/4.

Vernon, J. (2) (Belfast Celtic) 1945/6.

Waddock, G. (20) (QPR) 1979/80, 1980/1, 1981/2, 1982/3, 1983/4, 1984/5, 1985/6 (Millwall) 1989/90.
Walsh, D.J. (20) (West Bromwich Albion) 1945/6, 1946/7, 1947/8, 1948/9, 1949/50, 1950/1 (Aston Villa) 1951/2, 1952/3, 1953/4.
Walsh, J. (1) (Limerick) 1981/2.
Walsh, M. (22) (Blackpool) 1975/6, 1976/7 (Everton) 1978/9 (QPR) 1978/9 (Porto) 1980/1, 1981/2, 1982/3, 1983/4, 1984/5.
Walsh, M. (5) (Everton) 1981/2, 1982/3 (Norwich City) 1982/3.
Walsh, W. (9) (Manchester City) 1946/7, 1947/8, 1948/9, 1949/50.
Waters, J. (2) (Grimsby Town) 1976/7, 1979/80.
Whelan, R. (2) (St Patrick's Athletic) 1963/4.
Whelan, R. (39) (Liverpool) 1980/1, 1981/2, 1982/3, 1983/4, 1984/5, 1985/6, 1986/7, 1987/8, 1988/9, 1989/90.
Whelan, W. (4) (Manchester United) 1955/6, 1956/7.
Whittaker, R. (1) (Chelsea) 1958/9.

BRITISH ISLES INTERNATIONAL GOALSCORERS SINCE 1946

ENGLAND

A'Court, A 1
Adams, T.A 4
Allen, R 2
Anderson, V 2
Astall, G 1
Atyeo, P.J.W 5

Baily, E.F 5
Baker, J.H 3
Ball, A.J 8
Barnes, J. 10
Barnes, P.S 4
Beardsley, P.A 7
Beattie, T.K 1
Bell, C 9
Bentley, R.T.F 9
Blissett, L 3
Bowles, S 1
Bradford, G.R.W 1
Bradley, W 2
Bridges, B.J 1
Broadbent, P.F 2
Broadis, I.A 8
Brooking, T.D 5
Brooks, J 2
Bull, S. G. 4
Butcher, T 3
Byrne, J.J 8

Carter, H.S 7
(inc. 2 scored pre-war)
Chamberlain, M 1
Channon, M.R 21
Charlton, J 6
Charlton, R 49
Chivers, M 13
Clarke, A.J 10
Connelly, J.M 7
Coppell, S.J 7
Cowans, G 2
Crawford, R 1
Currie, A.W 3

Dixon, K.M 4
Douglas, B 11

Eastham, G 2
Edwards, D 5
Elliot, W.H 3

Finney, T 30
Flowers, R 10
Francis, G.C.J 3
Francis, T 12
Froggatt, J 2
Froggatt, R 2

Gascoigne, P. J. 2
Goddard, P 1
Grainger, C 3
Greaves, J 44

Haines, J.T.W 2
Hancocks, J 2
Hassall, H.W 4
Hateley, M 9
Haynes, J.N 18
Hitchens, G.A 5
Hoddle, G 8
Hughes, E.W 1
Hunt, R 18
Hunter, N 2
Hurst, G.C 24

Johnson, D.E 6

Kay, A.H 1
Keegan, J.K 21
Kennedy, R 3
Kevan, D.T 8
Kidd, B 1

Langton, R 1
Latchford, R.D 5
Lawler, C 1
Lawler, T 22
(inc. 6 scored pre-war)
Lee, F 10
Lee, J 1
Lee, S 2
Lineker, G 35
Lofthouse, N 30

Mabbutt, G 1
McDermott, T 3
Macdonald, M 6
Mannion, W.J 11
Mariner, P 13
Marsh, R.W 1

Matthews, S 11
(inc. 8 scored pre-war)
Medley, L.D 1
Melia, J 1
Milburn, J.E.T 10
Moore, R.F......................2
Morris, J 3
Mortensen, S.H 23
Mullen, J 6
Mullery, A.P 1

Neal, P.G 5
Nicholls, J........................1
Nicholson, W.E 1

O'Grady, M 3
Own goals......................15

Paine, T.L 7
Parry, R.A........................1
Peacock, A 3
Pearce, S. 1
Pearson, J.S 5
Pearson, S.C 5
Perry, W 2
Peters, M.......................20
Pickering, F 5
Platt, D............................3
Pointer, R........................2

Ramsey, A.E 3
Revie, D.G.......................4
Robson, B 26
Robson, R 4
Rowley, J.F 6
Royle, J 2

Sansom, K 1
Sewell, J..........................3
Shackleton, L.F 1
Smith, R.........................13
Steven, T.M.....................3
Stiles, N.P 13
Summerbee, M.G 1

Tambling, R.V 1
Taylor, P.J.......................2
Taylor, T........................16
Thompson, P.B 1
Tueart, D 2

Viollet, D.S 1

Waddle, C.R....................6
Wallace, D.L 1
Walsh, P..........................1
Watson, D.V....................4
Webb, N 3
Weller, K 1
Wignall, F.......................2
Wilkins, R.G...................3
Wilshaw, D.J 10
Withe, P..........................1
Woodcock, T 16
Worthington, F.S 2
Wright, M. 1
Wright, W.A 3

SCOTLAND

Aitken, R 1
Archibald, S....................4

Baird, S...........................2
Bannon, E 1
Bauld, W.........................2
Baxter, J.C 3
Bett, J..............................1
Bone, J 1
Brand, R 8
Brazil, A 1
Bremner, W.J 3
Brown, A.D.....................6
Buckley, P 1
Burns, K 1

Caldow, E 4
Campbell, R 1
Chalmers, S 3
Collins, J 1
Collins, R.V...................10
Combe, J.R 1
Conn, A 1
Cooper, D 6
Craig, J 1
Curran, H.P 1

Dalglish, K 30
Davidson, J.A 1
Docherty, T.H..................1
Dodds, D 1
Duncan, D.M...................1
Durie, G.S.......................1

Fernie, W 1
Flavell, R 2
Fleming, C.......................2

Gemmell, T. *(St Mirren)* ...1
Gemmell, T. *(Celtic)*.........1
Gemmill, A......................8
Gibson, D.W 3
Gilzean, A.J 10
Gough, C.R 5
Graham, A 2
Graham, G 3

Gray, A 7
Gray, E.......................... 3
Gray, F.......................... 1
Greig, J.......................... 3

Hamilton, G 4
Harper, J.M..................... 2
Hartford, R.A................... 4
Henderson, J.G 1
Henderson, W 5
Herd, D.G........................ 4
Hewie, J.D 2
Holton, J.A 2
Houliston, W 2
Howie, H 1
Hughes, J........................ 1
Hunter, W 1
Hutchison, T 1

Jackson, C 1
Jardine, A 1
Johnston, L.H 1
Johnston, M. 14
Johnstone, D.................... 2
Johnstone, J.................... 4
Johnstone, R.................... 9
Jordan, J 11

Law, D 30
Leggat, G........................ 8
Lennox, R 3
Liddell, W 6
Linwood, A.B 1
Lorimer, P....................... 4

Macari, L 5
MacDougall, E.J............... 3
MacKay, D.C................... 4
Mackay, G....................... 1
MacKenzie, J.A................ 1
MacLeod, M 1
McAvennie, F 1
McCall, S. M.................... 1
McCalliog, J.................... 1
McCoist, A...................... 6
McGhee, M 2
McInally, A 3
McKimmie, S.I 1
McKinnon, R 1
McLaren, A 4
McLean, T....................... 1
McLintock, F 1
McMillan, I.L................... 2
McNeill, W 3
McPhail, J 3
McQueen, G..................... 5
McStay, P........................ 6
Mason, J 4
Masson, D.S 5

Miller, W.......................... 1
Mitchell, R.C 1
Morgan, W 1
Morris, H 3
Mudie, J.K 9
Mulhall, G........................ 1
Murdoch, R 5
Murray, J 1

Narey, D 1
Nicholas, C...................... 5

O'Hare, J 5
Ormond, W.E 1
Orr, T.............................. 1
Own goals........................ 7

Parlane, D 1
Pettigrew, W 2
Provan, D......................... 1

Quinn, J........................... 7
Quinn, P. 1

Reilly, L..........................22
Ring, T 2
Rioch, B.D 6
Robertson, A 2
Robertson, J 8

St John, I 9
Scott, A.S......................... 5
Sharp, G 1
Smith, G 4
Souness, G.J 3
Steel, W 12
Stein, C...........................10
Stewart, R 1
Strachan, G....................... 4
Sturrock, P 3

Thornton, W 1

Waddell, W....................... 6
Wallace, I.A 1
Wark, J 7
Weir, A............................ 1
White, J.A........................ 3
Wilson, D 9

Young, A 5

WALES

Allchurch, I.J 23
Allen, M 3

Barnes, W 1

Bowen, D.L 1
Bowen, M. 1
Boyle, T 1
Burgess, W.A.R 1

Charles, J 1
Charles, M....................... 6
Charles, W.J 15
Clarke, R.J 5
Curtis, A 6

Davies, G 2
Davies, R.T 8
Davies, R.W 7
Deacy, N 4
Durban, A 2
Dwyer, P 2

Edwards, G...................... 2
Edwards, R.I 5
England, H.M 3
Evans, I 1

Flynn, B 6
Ford, T 23
Foulkes, W.I 1

Giles, D 2
Godfrey, B.C 2
Griffiths, A.T.................. 6
Griffiths, M.W 2

Harris, C.S 1
Hewitt, R 1
Hockey, T 1
Hodges, G 2
Horne, B 2
Hughes, M....................... 7

James, L.........................10
James, R 7
Jones, A.......................... 1
Jones, B.S 2
Jones, Cliff 15
Jones, D.E....................... 1
Jones, J.P 1

Kryzwicki, R.L 1

Leek, K........................... 5
Lovell, S.......................... 1
Lowrie, G........................ 2

Mahoney, J.F 1
Medwin, T.C................... 6
Moore, G 1

Nicholas, P 2

O'Sullivan, P.A 1
Own goals........................ 5

Palmer, D........................ 1
Paul, R 1
Phillips, D 1
Powell, A 1
Powell, D 1
Price, P 1

Reece, G.I 2
Rees, R.R 3
Roberts, P.S 1
Rush, I...........................16

Saunders, D 7
Slatter, N......................... 2
Smallman, D.P 1

Tapscott, D.R 4
Thomas, M 4
Toshack, J.B 13

Vernon, T.R 8

Walsh, I 7
Williams, G.E 2
Woosnam, A.P 4

Yorath, T.C 2

NORTHERN IRELAND

Anderson, T 3
Armstrong, G.................12

Barr, H.H........................ 1
Best, G 9
Bingham, W.L................10
Blanchflower, D 2
Blanchflower, J................ 1
Brennan, R.A 1
Brotherston, N 3

Campbell, W.G 1
Casey, T.......................... 2
Caskey, W 1
Cassidy, T........................ 1
Clarke, C.J 6
Clements, D..................... 2
Cocharne, T 1
Crossan, E....................... 1
Crossan, J.A 10
Cush, W.W...................... 5

D'Arcy, S.D 1

Doherty, L........................ 1
Doherty, P.D 3
(inc. 1 scored pre-war)
Dougan, A.D 8

Elder, A.R 1

Ferguson, W 1
Ferris, R.O 1
Finney, T......................... 2

Hamilton, B...................... 4
Hamilton, W 5
Harkin, J.T........................ 2
Harvey, M 3
Hughes, L.M...................... 1
Humphries, W.................... 1
Hunter, A.......................... 1

Irvine, W.J 8

Johnston, W.C 1
Jones, J 1

Lockhart, N 3

McAdams, W.J.................. 7
McClelland, J 1
McCrory, S........................ 1
McCurdy, C....................... 1
McDonald, A 1
McGarry, J.K..................... 1
McGrath, R.C 4
McIlroy, J.........................10
McIlroy, S.B 5
McLaughlin, J.C 6
McMordie, A.S 3
McMorran, E.J.................. 4
McParland, P.J 10
Moreland, V 1
Morgan, S.......................... 3

Neill, W.J.T...................... 2
Nelson, S.......................... 1
Nicholl, C.J....................... 3
Nicholl, J.M...................... 2
Nicholson, J.J................... 6

O'Kane, W.J...................... 1
O'Neill, J........................... 1
O'Neill, M......................... 1
O'Neill, M.H 8
Own goals......................... 4

Peacock, R 2
Penney, S 2

Quinn, J.M 6

Simpson, W.J 5
Smyth, S........................... 5
Spence, D.W..................... 3
Stewart, I 2

Tully, C.P.......................... 3

Walker, J........................... 1
Walsh, D.J......................... 5
Welsh, E 1
Whiteside, N 9
Wilson, D 1
Wilson, K.J........................ 2
Wilson, S.J 7

EIRE

Aldridge, J......................... 3
Ambrose, P........................ 1
Anderson, J 1

Bermingham, P................. 1
Bradshaw, P...................... 4
Brady, L............................ 9
Brown, D 1
Byrne, J. (Bray) 1
Byrne, J. (QPR) 2

Cantwell, J.......................14
Carey, J 3
Carroll, T 1
Cascarino, A 5
Coad, P............................. 3
Conroy, T.......................... 2
Conway, J......................... 3
Cummings, G 5
Curtis, D 8

Daly, G............................13
Davis, T 4
Dempsey, J....................... 1
Dennehy, M...................... 2
Donnelly, J 3
Donnelly, T 1
Duffy, B............................ 1
Duggan, H......................... 1
Dunne, J 12
Dunne, L........................... 1

Eglinton, T 2
Ellis, P............................. 1

Fagan, F........................... 5
Fallon, S........................... 2
Fallon W 2
Farrell, P........................... 3
Fitzgerald, P 2
Fitzgerald, J 1

Fitzsimons, A 7
Flood, J.J 4
Fogarty, A........................ 3
Fullam, J 1
Fullam, R 1

Galvin, A 1
Gavin, J 2
Geoghegan, M................ 2
Giles, J 5
Givens, D........................19
Glynn, D.......................... 1
Grealish, T 8
Grimes, A.A.................. 1

Hale, A............................ 2
Hand, E........................... 2
Haverty, J........................ 3
Holmes, J 1
Horlacher, A.................... 2
Houghton, R.................... 3
Hughton, C...................... 1
Hurley, C 2

Jordan, D 1

Kelly, D 4
Kelly, J 2

Lacey, W......................... 1
Lawrenson, M 5
Leech, M........................22

McCann, J 1
McCarthy, M 1
McEvoy, A...................... 6
McGee, P 4
McGrath, P...................... 4
Madden, O 1
Mancini, T....................... 1
Martin, C 6
Martin, M........................ 4
Mooney, J 1

Moore, P 7
Moran, K 6
Moroney, T...................... 1
Mulligan, P 1

O'Callaghan, K............... 1
O'Connor, T 2
O'Farrell, F..................... 2
O'Flanagan, K................. 3
O'Keefe, E 1
O'Neill, F 1
O'Reilly, J 2
O'Reilly, J 1
Own goals....................... 5

Quinn, N......................... 3

Ringstead, A................... 7
Robinson, M 4
Rogers, E 5
Ryan, G 1
Ryan, R 3

Sheedy, K........................ 6
Sheridan, J...................... 1
Slaven, B......................... 1
Sloan, W 1
Squires, J........................ 1
Stapleton, F 20
Staunton, S 1
Strahan, F........................ 1
Sullivan, J....................... 1

Townsend, A.D 1
Treacy, R 5
Tuohy, L......................... 4

Waddock, G 3
Walsh, D......................... 5
Walsh, M......................... 3
Waters, J 1
White, J.J 2
Whelan, R 3

8th UEFA UNDER-16 CHAMPIONSHIP 1990

Group 1: Iceland 0, Sweden 2; Sweden 5, Iceland 3. Sweden qualified.
Group 2: Finland 1, Denmark 3; Denmark 1, Finland 1. Denmark qualified.
Group 3: Wales 2, Northern Ireland 3; Northern Ireland 1, Wales 1. Northern Ireland qualified.
Group 4: Luxembourg 1, West Germany 5; West Germany 3, Luxembourg 0. West Germany qualified.
Group 5: Liechtenstein 0, Spain 3; Spain 7, Liechtenstein 0. Spain qualified.
Group 6: Czechoslovakia 9, Malta 0; Malta 0, Czechoslovakia 5. Czechoslovakia qualified.
Group 7: Turkey 0, Austria 1; Austria 1, Turkey 2. Turkey qualified.
Group 8: Cyprus 2, Greece 1; Greece 1, Cyprus 2. Cyprus qualified.
Group 9: Poland 1, Holland 2; Holland 0, Poland 4; Italy 1, Poland 1; Holland 1, Italy 0; Poland 1, Italy 0; Italy 6, Holland 1. Poland qualified.
Group 10: Bulgaria 0, Hungary 3; Hungary 3, Bulgaria 0. Hungary qualified.
Group 11: France 2, Switzerland 0; Switzerland 1, France 0. France qualified.
Group 12: San Marino 0, Portugal 3; Portugal 4, San Marino 0. Portugal qualified.
Group 13: Norway 1, Rumania 1; Norway 2, Scotland 0; Rumania 3, Norway 1; Rumania 2, Scotland 2; Scotland 2, Norway 0; Scotland 1, Rumania 0. Scotland qualified.
Group 14: Belgium 2, Eire 1; Eire 0, Belgium 0. Belgium qualified.
Group 15: Yugoslavia 2, USSR 0; USSR 1, Yugoslavia 0. Yugoslavia qualified.

FINAL TOURNAMENT IN EAST GERMANY

GROUP A

Denmark (2) 3, Turkey (0) 0 — Leinefeld, 17 May 1990
Northern Ireland (0) 1, Portugal (1) 2 — Arnstadt, 17 May 1990
Northern Ireland (0) 0, Denmark (4) 6 — Eisenach, 19 May 1990
Portugal (2) 2, Turkey (0) 2 — Sondersha, 19 May 1990
Northern Ireland (1) 2, Turkey (0) 0 — Weimar, 21 May 1990
Portugal (2) 3, Denmark (0) 1 — Muhlhause, 21 May 1990

	P	W	D	L	F	A	Pts
Portugal	3	2	1	0	7	4	5
Denmark	3	2	0	1	10	3	4
Northern Ireland	3	1	0	2	3	8	2
Turkey	3	0	1	2	2	7	1

GROUP B

Poland (2) 3, Cyprus (0) 0 — Kolleda, 17 May 1990
Sweden (1) 2, Hungary (1) 2 — Tambach, 17 May 1990
Cyprus (1) 2, Hungary (0) 0 — Erfurt, 19 May 1990
Poland (1) 1, Sweden (0) 1 — Nordhause, 19 May 1990
Cyprus (0) 0, Sweden (0) 3 — Heiligens, 21 May 1990

	P	W	D	L	F	A	Pts
Poland	3	2	1	0	6	1	5
Sweden	3	1	2	0	6	3	4
Cyprus	3	1	0	2	2	6	2
Hungary	3	0	1	2	2	6	1

GROUP C

Czechoslovakia (0) 0, West Germany (0) 0 — Ruhla, 17 May 1990
France (0) 1, Scotland (0) 1 — Bad Lange, 17 May 1990
Czechoslovakia (1) 2, France (0) 0 — Apolda, 19 May 1990
West Germany (1) 5, Scotland (0) 1 — Sommerda, 19 May 1990
Czechoslovakia (2) 3, Scotland (0) 0 — Ilmenau, 21 May 1990
West Germany (0) 1, France (1) 1 — Sondersha, 21 May 1990

	P	W	D	L	F	A	Pts
Czechoslovakia	3	2	1	0	5	0	5
West Germany	3	1	2	0	6	2	4
France	3	0	2	1	2	4	2
Scotland	3	0	1	2	2	9	1

GROUP D

Belgium (0) 0, Yugoslavia (0) 2 — Gera, 17 May 1990
Spain (2) 3, East Germany (0) 1 — Elsterber, 17 May 1990
East Germany (0) 0, Yugoslavia (0) 1 — Weida, 19 May 1990
Spain (0) 1, Belgium (0) 0 — Lobenstei, 19 May 1990
East Germany (1) 1, Belgium (1) 1 — Rudolstad, 21 May 1990
Spain (0) 0, Yugoslavia (1) 1 — Zeulenrod, 21 May 1990

	P	W	D	L	F	A	Pts
Yugoslavia	3	3	0	0	4	0	6
Spain	3	2	0	1	4	2	4
East Germany	3	0	1	2	2	5	1
Belgium	3	0	1	2	1	4	1

Semi-finals

Poland (1) 1, Yugoslavia (2) 4 — Sommerda, 24 May 1990
Portugal (0) 0, Czechoslovakia (0) 0 — Nordhause, 24 May 1990
Czechoslovakia won on penalty-kicks aet

Third-place match

Portugal (1) 2, Poland (1) 3 — Erfurt, 27 May 1990

Final

Czechoslovakia (0) 3, Yugoslavia (1) 2 *(aet)* — Erfurt, 27 May 1990

7th UEFA UNDER-18 CHAMPIONSHIP 1988-90

Group 1 *(Poland, Scotland, Sweden, West Germany)*

Scotland (0) 0, Sweden (0) 0 — Ayr, 21 September 1988
Scotland (0) 1, Poland (2) 2 — Hampden Park, 23 November 1988
West Germany (0) 0, Poland (0) 0 — Heilbronn, 19 April 1989
West Germany (1) 1, Scotland (0) 0 — Frankfurt, 3 May 1989
Sweden (1) 4, West Germany (0) 0 — Lomma, 24 May 1989
Sweden (2) 4, Poland (0) 0 — Ljungby, 7 June 1989
Poland (0) 2, Scotland (0) 1 — Debica, 30 August 1989
Sweden (0) 4, Scotland (0) 0 — Vaesteraa, 20 September 1989
Poland (1) 1, West Germany (0) 0 — Jaworzno, 27 September 1989
Poland (1) 2, Sweden (0) 2 — Debica, 17 October 1989
Scotland (1) 1, West Germany (1) 2 — Motherwell, 18 October 1989
West Germany (1) 2, Sweden (0) 1 — Kassel, 1 November 1989

Group 2 *(Cyprus, Holland, Norway, USSR)*

Norway (1) 2, Holland (0) 2 — Stavanger, 12 October 1988
Cyprus (0) 0, Norway (0) 0 — Paralimni, 1 November 1988
Holland (2) 2, Cyprus (0) 1 — Roosendaal, 12 April 1989
USSR (0) 2, Cyprus (0) 0 — Kishinev, 23 April 1989
Norway (0) 1, Cyprus (0) 0 — Oslo, 21 May 1989
Norway (0) 0, USSR (0) 1 — Fredrikst, 14 June 1989
USSR (1) 3, Norway (0) 0 — Kishinev, 6 September 1989
Holland (1) 1, Norway (3) 5 — Oss, 4 October 1989
Holland (0) 0, USSR (0) 3 — Almelo, 25 October 1989
Cyprus (1) 1, USSR (2) 2 — Larnaca, 19 November 1989
USSR (1) 2, Holland (0) 1 — Baku, 29 November 1989
Cyprus (0) 0, Holland (0) 0 — Aradippou, 6 December 1989

Group 3 *(Czechoslovakia, England, France, Greece)*

England (1) 5, Greece (0) 0 — Birkenhead, 20 October 1988
England (0) 1, France (1) 1 — Bradford, 15 November 1988
Greece (1) 2, France (3) 3 — Indrama, 14 December 1988
Greece (0) 0, England (2) 3 — Xanthi, 8 March 1989
Czechoslovakia (0) 0, Greece (0) 0 — Trebechovicen, 12 April 1989
Czechoslovakia (0) 1, England (0) 0 — Piovazska B, 26 April 1989
France (1) 1, Czechoslovakia (0) 0 — Orleans, 10 May 1989
France (0) 0, England (0) 0 — Martigues, 11 October 1989
Greece (1) 1, Czechoslovakia (2) 3 — Aigio, 11 October 1989
Czechoslovakia (0) 0, France (0) 0 — Senec, 28 October 1989
England (0) 1, Czechoslovakia (0) 0 — Portsmouth, 14 November 1989
France (1) 1, Greece (0) 2 — Gueugnon, 29 November 1989

Group 4 *(Albania, Italy, Portugal, Switzerland)*

Albania (0) 4, Switzerland (0) 0 — Shkodra, 12 October 1988
Portugal (2) 2, Albania (0) 1 — Lisbon, 15 March 1989
Albania (0) 1, Italy (2) 2 — Elbasan, 12 April 1989
Switzerland (0) 0, Portugal (3) 3 — Chatel-St. Denis, 19 April 1989
Albania (0) 0, Portugal (1) 2 — Tirana, 23 April 1989
Switzerland (0) 0, Italy (1) 2 — Moutier, 24 May 1989
Italy (0) 1, Albania (0) 0 — Bisceglie, 11 October 1989
Portugal (2) 2, Switzerland (0) 0 — Lisbon, 11 October 1989
Italy (0) 0, Portugal (0) 2 — Manziana, 1 November 1989
Switzerland (1) 1, Albania (0) 0 — Muri/AG, 7 November 1989
Italy (1) 5, Switzerland (0) 0 — Cremona, 22 November 1989
Portugal (0) 0, Italy (0) 0 — Lisbon, 6 December 1989

Group 5 *(Belgium, Wales, East Germany, Yugoslavia)*

East Germany (0) 0, Yugoslavia (1) 1 — Soemmerda, 12 October 1988
Belgium (1) 1, East Germany (1) 1 — Seraing, 2 November 1988
Yugoslavia (2) 4, Wales (1) 1 — Bijeljina, 9 November 1988
Wales (0) 2, Belgium (0) 0 — Newtown, 30 November 1988
Belgium (2) 2, Yugoslavia (0) 1 — Roeselare, 29 March 1989
Wales (0) 0, East Germany (0) 0 — Aberystwyth, 12 April 1989
East Germany (0) 0, Belgium (1) 2 — Hettstedt, 3 May 1989
Yugoslavia (1) 1, East Germany (0) 2 — Zavidovic, 20 September 1989
Yugoslavia (0) 1, Belgium (0) 0 — Bosanksi, 4 October 1989
Belgium (1) 5, Wales (1) 1 — Charleroi, 17 October 1989
East Germany (0) 1, Wales (1) 1 — Neustreli, 19 October 1989
Wales (1) 2, Yugoslavia (0) 0 — Newtown, 8 November 1989

Group 6 *(Bulgaria, Eire, Malta, Iceland (withdrew))*

Malta (1) 1, Bulgaria (1) 2 — Ta'qali, 12 April 1989
Eire (1) 2, Malta (0) 0 — Dublin, 27 May 1989
Bulgaria (1) 1, Malta (0) 0 — Pazardjik, 4 October 1989
Eire (1) 3, Iceland (0) 0 — Dublin, 12 October 1989
Eire (1) 3, Bulgaria (0) 0 — Dublin, 31 October 1989
Malta (0) 0, Eire (1) 3 — Corradino, 14 November 1989
Bulgaria (0) 1, Eire (0) 0 — Blagoevgr, 28 November 1989

Group 7 *(Austria, Denmark, Rumania, Spain)*

Spain (1) 4, Denmark (0) 2 — Las Palmas, 16 November 1988
Austria (0) 1, Spain (0) 2 — Lanzendorf, 19 April 1989
Austria (1) 1, Rumania (0) 1 — Kirchschl, 10 May 1989
Denmark (1) 2, Spain (0) 0 — Ronne, 31 May 1989
Rumania (0) 1, Spain (1) 3 — Ploiesti, 14 June 1989
Denmark (2) 2, Rumania (0) 2 — Roskilde, 5 September 1989

Denmark (3) 4, Austria (1) 1 — Nykobing, 20 September 1989
Spain (0) 0, Rumania (0) 0 — Talavera 4 October 1989
Austria (0) 0, Denmark (0) 0 — Ried im I 18 October 1989
Rumania (0) 0, Austria (0) 0 — Sibiu, 1 November 1989
Rumania (1) 3, Denmark (1) 1 — Ploiesti, 14 November 1989
Spain (3) 3, Austria (1) 1 — Badajoz, 22 November 1989

Group 8 *(Finland, Hungary, Luxembourg, Turkey)*
Finland (0) 0, Hungary (0) 1 — Toijala, 21 September 1988
Luxembourg (0) 0, Finland (3) 5 — Esch sur Alzette, 26 October 1988
Turkey (2) 3, Luxembourg (0) 1 — Izmir, 29 March 1989
Hungary (2) 6, Luxembourg (0) 0 — Budapest, 3 May 1989
Hungary (1) 3, Finland (0) 0 — Budapest, 10 May 1989
Finland (1) 2, Turkey (1) 2 — Uusikaarl, 7 June 1989
Turkey (1) 1, Finland (0) 0 — Kocaeli, 3 September 1989
Finland (3) 5, Luxembourg (0) 1 — Raisio, 4 October 1989
Hungary (1) 2, Turkey (0) 2 — Miske, 7 October 1989
Luxembourg (0) 0, Hungary (0) 2 — Esch, 18 October 1989
Turkey (0) 0, Hungary (0) 0 — Istanbul, 5 November 1989
Luxembourg (1) 1, Turkey (3) 4 — Lux.-Bonn, 29 November 1989

(*Final tournament in Hungary July 1990*)

7th UEFA UNDER-21 TOURNAMENT 1988–90

Group 1 *(Bulgaria, Denmark, Greece, Rumania)*
Greece (1) 2, Denmark (1) 2 — Viareggio, 18 October 1988
Bulgaria (1) 2, Rumania (1) 1 — Sofia, 18 October 1988
Denmark (0) 1, Bulgaria (0) 3 — Slagelse, 1 November 1988
Rumania (1) 2, Greece (0) 0 — 1 November, 1988
Bulgaria (2) 6, Denmark (0) 0 — 25 April 1989
Greece (0) 1, Rumania (0) 0 — 25 April 1989
Denmark (0) 3, Greece (0) 0 — 16 May 1989
Rumania (2) 2, Bulgaria (1) 1 — 16 May 1989
Denmark (0) 1, Rumania (0) 2 — Holbaek, 10 October 1989
Bulgaria (2) 2, Greece (0) 0 — Tolbukhin, 10 October 1989
Greece (0) 0, Bulgaria (0) 2 — Athens, 14 November 1989
Rumania (0) 1, Denmark (0) 2 — Bucuresti, 14 November 1989

Group 2 *(Albania, England, Poland, Sweden)*
England (1) 1, Sweden (0) 1 — Coventry, 18 October 1988
Poland (0) 0, Albania (0) 0 — Opole, 18 October 1988
Albania (0) 0, Sweden (1) 2 — Berat, 4 November 1988
Albania (1) 1, England (0) 2 — 7 March 1989
England (1) 2, Albania (0) 0 — 25 April 1989
Sweden (1) 4, Poland (0) 0 — 6 May 1989
England (2) 2, Poland (0) 1 — 2 June 1989
Sweden (1) 1, England (0) 0 — Uppsala, 5 September 1989
Sweden (1) 1, Albania (0) 0 — Eskilstun, 7 October 1989
Poland (0) 1, England (2) 3 — Jastrzebi, 10 October 1989
Poland (1) 1, Sweden (0) 1 — Opole, 24 October 1989
Albania (0) 0, Poland (1) 1 — Vlora, 14 November 1989

Group 3 *(Austria, East Germany, Turkey, USSR)*

USSR (1) 2, Austria (2) 2	Kiev, 18 October 1988
Austria (2) 3, Turkey (0) 0	St Polten, 1 November 1988
Turkey (2) 3, East Germany (2) 2	Istanbul, 29 November 1988
East Germany (0) 0, Turkey (0) 0	11 April 1989
USSR (0) 1, East Germany (0) 0	25 April 1989
Turkey (0) 0, USSR (2) 3	9 May 1989
East Germany (0) 2, Austria (0) 0	16 May 1989
Austria (0) 0, USSR (0) 2	Amstetten, 5 September 1989
East Germany (1) 3, USSR (1) 2	Grimma, 7 October 1989
Turkey (0) 1, Austria (1) 1	Istanbul, 24 October 1989
Austria (0) 0, East Germany (0) 1	Stockerau, 14 November 1989
USSR (2) 2, Turkey (0) 0	Sevastopo, 14 November 1989

Group 4 *(Finland, Holland, Iceland, West Germany)*

Finland (0) 0, West Germany (2) 3	Kouvola, 30 August 1988
Iceland (0) 1, Holland (1) 1	Reykjavik, 13 September 1988
Finland (0) 2, Iceland (1) 1	Oulu, 28 September 1988
West Germany (0) 2, Holland (0) 0	Augsburg, 18 October 1988
Holland (0) 0, West Germany (1) 1	25 April 1989
Finland (1) 1, Holland (1) 1	30 May 1989
Iceland (0) 1, West Germany (0) 1	30 May 1989
Iceland (1) 4, Finland (0) 0	Akurlyri, 5 September 1989
West Germany (2) 2, Finland (0) 0	Arnsberg, 3 October 1989
Holland (0) 2, Iceland (1) 3	Schiedam, 10 October 1989
West Germany (0 1, Iceland (1) 1	Saarbruck, 25 October 1989
Holland (1) 2, Finland (1) 1	Heerenvee, 14 November 1989

Group 5 *(France, Norway, Scotland, Yugoslavia)*

Norway (0) 1, Scotland (1) 1	Drammen, 13 September 1988
France (1) 2, Norway (0) 0	Tours, 27 September 1988
Scotland (0) 0, Yugoslavia (0) 2	Edinburgh, 18 October 1988
Yugoslavia (1) 2, France (1) 2	Titov Vrbas, 18 November 1988
Scotland (1) 2, France (0) 3	Dundee, 7 March 1989
France (0) 0, Yugoslavia (0) 1	Le Havre, 28 April 1989
Norway (0) 0, Yugoslavia (0) 1	13 June 1989
Norway (1) 1, France (1) 1	Raufoss, 5 September 1989
Yugoslavia (2) 4, Scotland (0) 1	Slavonski, 5 September 1989
France (1) 3, Scotland (0) 1	Rennes, 10 October 1989
Yugoslavia (0) 0, Norway (0) 1	Zenica, 10 October 1989
Scotland (1) 2, Norway (0) 0	Perth, 14 November 1989

Group 6 *(Cyprus, Hungary, Spain)*

Cyprus (0) 0, Hungary (0) 0	Larnaca, 11 December 1988
Cyprus (0) 0, Spain (0) 1	22 March 1989
Hungary (1) 1, Cyprus (0) 0	?2 April 1989
Spain (0) 1, Cyprus (0) 0	31 May 1989
Hungary (1) 1, Spain (0) 0	Szekesfeh, 10 October 1989
Spain (1) 1, Hungary (0) 0	Benidorm, 14 November 1989

Group 7 *(Belgium, Czechoslovakia, Luxembourg, Portugal)*

Czechoslovakia (0) 0, Belgium (2) 3	Nitra, 15 November 1988
Portugal (0) 1, Belgium (1) 1	14 February 1989
Czechoslovakia (2) 4, Luxembourg (0) 0	5 April 1989
Portugal (0) 1, Luxembourg (0) 0	25 April 1989
Belgium (1) 1, Czechoslovakia (0) 1	29 April 1989
Luxembourg (0) 0, Belgium (0) 0	26 May 1989
Belgium (0) 1, Portugal (0) 1	Beveren, 5 September 1989
Czechoslovakia (0) 1, Portugal (0) 0	Chrudim, 5 October 1989

Luxembourg (0) 0, Portugal (1) 3	Ettelbruc, 9 October 1989
Belgium (1) 1, Luxembourg (0) 0	Liege, 24 October 1989
Portugal (0) 0, Czechoslovakia (2) 3	Lisbon, 14 November 1989
Luxembourg (0) 1, Czechoslovakia (0) 1	Lux.-Verl, 29 November 1989
Group 8 *(Italy, San Marino, Switzerland)*	
Switzerland (0) 0, Italy (0) 0	26 April 1989
San Marino (0) 0, Switzerland (2) 5	6 June 1989
San Marino (0) 0, Italy (0) 2	San Marin, 4 October 1989
Italy (0) 1, Switzerland (0) 0	Padova, 25 October 1989
Switzerland (2) 3, San Marino (0) 0	Lugano, 14 November 1989
Italy (1) 2, San Marino (0) 0	Ravenna, 29 November 1989
Quarter-finals	
Italy (1) 3, Spain (0) 1	Ancona, 21 February 1990
Czechoslovakia (0) 1, Sweden (0) 2	Praha, 14 March 1990
USSR (0) 1, West Germany (1) 1	Simferopo, 14 March 1990
Yugoslavia (1) 2, Bulgaria (0) 0	Zagreb, 14 March 1990
Bulgaria (0) 0, Yugoslavia (1) 1	Sofia, 28 March 1990
West Germany (1) 1, USSR (1) 2	Augsburg, 28 March 1990
Sweden (1) 4, Czechoslovakia (0) 0	Vaxjo, 28 March 1990
Spain (0) 1, Italy (0) 0	Logrono, 29 March 1990
Semi-finals	
Yugoslavia (0) 0, Italy (0) 0	Zagreb, 11 April 1990
Sweden (0) 1, USSR (0) 1	Vaxjo, 25 April 1990
Italy (1) 2, Yugoslavia (1) 2	Parma, 9 May 1990
USSR (1) 2, Sweden (0) 0	Simferopo, 9 May 1990

Final to be arranged

LIST OF REFEREES FOR SEASON 1990–91 FOOTBALL LEAGUE

ALCOCK, P. E. (S. Merstham, Surrey)
ALLISON, D. B. (Lancaster)
APLIN, G. (Kendal)
ASHBY, G. R. (Worcester)
ASHWORTH, J. (Luffenham, Leics.)
AXCELL, D. J. (Southend)
BAILEY, M. C. (Impington, Cambridge)
BARRATT, K. P. (Coventry)
BELL, S. D. (Huddersfield)
BENNETT, A. (Sheffield)
BIGGER, R. L. (Croydon)
BODENHAM, M. J. (Looe, Cornwall)
BORRETT, I. J. (Harleston, Norfolk)
BRANDWOOD, M. J. (Lichfield, Staffs.)
BREEN, K. J. (Liverpool)
BUKSH, A. N. (London)
BURGE, W. K. (Tonypandy)
BURNS, W. C. (Scarborough)
CALLOW, V. G. (Solihull)
CARTER, J. M. (Christchurch)
COOPER, K. (Pontypridd)
COOPER, K. A. (Swindon)
COURTNEY, G. (Spennymoor)
CRUIKSHANKS, I. G. (Hartlepool)
DANSON, P. S. (Leicester)
DAWSON, A. (Jarrow)
DEAKIN, J. C. (Llantwit Major, S. Glam.)
DILKES, L. R. (Mossley, Lancs)
DON, P. (Hanworth Park, Middlesex)
DURKIN, P. A. (Portland, Dorset)
ELLERAY, D. R. (Harrow)
FITZHARRIS, T. (Bolton)
FLOOD, W. A. (Stockport)
FOAKES, P. L. (Clacton-on-Sea)
FRAMPTON, D. G. (Poole, Dorset)
GALLAGHER, D. J. (Banbury, Oxon)
GIFFORD, R. B. (Llanbradach, Mid. Glam.)
GROVES, R. G. (Weston-Super-Mare)
GUNN, A. (South Chailey, Sussex)
HACKETT, K. S. (Sheffield)
HAMER, R. L. (Bristol)
HARRISON, P. W. (Oldham, Lancs.)
HART, R. A. (Darlington)
HEMLEY, I. S. (Ampthill, Beds.)
HENDRICK, I. A. (Preston)
HILL, B. (Kettering)
HOLBROOK, T. J. (Walsall)
HUTCHINSON, D. (Marcham, Oxford)
JAMES, M. L. (Horsham)
JONES, P. (Loughborough)
KEY, J. M. (Sheffield)
KING, H. W. (Merthyr Tydfil)
KIRKBY, J. A. (Sheffield)
LEWIS, R. S. (Gt. Bookham, Surrey)
LLOYD, J. W. (Wrexham)
LODGE S. J. (Barnsley)
LUNT, T. (Ashton-in-Makerfield, Lancs)
LUPTON, K. A. (Stockton-on-Tees)
MARTIN, J. E. (Nr. Alton, Hants.)
MIDGLEY, N. (Bolton)
MILFORD, R. G. (Bristol)
MORTON, K. (Bury St. Edmunds)
MOULES, J. A. (Erith, Kent)
NIXON, R. F. (West Kirkby, Wirral)
PARKER, E. J. (Preston)
PAWLEY, R. K. (Cambridge)
PECK, M. G. (Kendal)
PHILLIPS, D. T. (Barnsley)
PIERCE, M. E. (Portsmouth)
POOLEY, G. R. (Bishop's Stortford)
REDFERN, K. A. (Whitley Bay)
REED, M. D. (Birmingham)
RUSHTON, J. (Stoke-on-Trent)
SEVILLE, A. (Birmingham)
SHAPTER, L. C. (Torquay)
SHEPHERD, R. (Leeds)
SIMMONS, A. F. (Cheadle Hulme, Cheshire)
SIMPSON, T. (Sowerby Bridge, W. Yorks.)
SINGH, G. (Wolverhampton)
SMITH, A. W. (Rubery, Birmingham)
STEVENS, B. T. (Stonehouse. Glos.)
TAYLOR, P. (Waltham Cross, Herts)
TRUSSELL, C. C. (Liverpool)
TYLDESLEY, P. A. (Stockport)
VANES, P. W. (Warley, West Midlands)
WARD, A. W. (London)
WATSON, J. L. (Whitley Bay)
WEST, T. E. (Hull)
WILKES, C. R. (Gloucester)
WILLARD, G. S. (Worthing, W. Sussex)
WILKIE, A. B. (Chester-le-Street)
WISEMAN, R. M. (Borehamwood, Herts.)
WORRALL, J. B. (Warrington)
WRIGHT, P. L. (Northwich)

GM VAUXHALL CONFERENCE

	Altrincham	Barnet	Barrow	Boston U	Cheltenham T	Chorley	Darlington	Enfield	Farnborough T	Fisher Ath	Kettering T	Kidderminster H	Macclesfield T	Merthyr Tydfil	Northwich Vic	Runcorn	Stafford R	Sutton U	Telford U	Welling U	Wycombe W	Yeovil Town
Altrincham	—	2-1	1-1	0-0	5-0	1-0	0-1	3-0	2-3	1-1	1-1	0-1	0-1	4-1	0-2	1-2	3-1	0-0	0-1	4-0	1-2	2-1
Barnet	1-0	—	1-0	1-2	4-0	5-0	0-2	2-0	4-1	4-1	4-1	2-1	0-0	4-0	1-0	2-2	1-1	4-1	2-1	1-1	2-0	1-0
Barrow	1-1	1-1	—	2-1	2-1	3-1	1-1	2-2	3-1	1-1	1-0	2-1	1-1	1-5	1-0	2-2	2-1	1-0	3-0	1-1	0-3	2-1
Boston U	2-3	1-2	2-1	—	2-1	0-1	1-3	1-0	2-2	2-0	1-2	2-3	3-0	2-2	1-3	3-2	3-0	3-1	2-2	2-1	2-0	0-1
Cheltenham T	0-0	2-0	1-0	0-0	—	2-0	0-1	3-1	4-0	0-0	1-1	2-1	2-1	0-2	2-3	2-2	1-3	2-0	1-2	3-2	1-1	2-1
Chorley	2-1	1-4	0-1	0-0	0-2	—	0-3	2-2	1-0	2-0	2-2	1-0	0-0	1-0	1-2	0-2	1-1	3-2	1-2	4-0	1-0	3-2
Darlington	2-0	1-2	0-0	6-1	5-1	3-0	—	2-1	1-1	5-0	2-1	3-0	1-1	0-0	4-0	1-1	2-1	2-0	1-1	1-0	0-1	1-0
Enfield	2-1	1-3	3-0	0-1	4-2	2-0	0-3	—	0-0	1-2	0-3	2-1	1-1	2-0	2-0	3-2	4-1	2-3	1-2	2-3	3-5	1-1
Farnborough T	0-0	0-1	3-0	1-0	4-0	1-3	1-0	2-3	—	1-1	1-1	0-1	1-2	0-1	0-1	6-3	3-3	1-3	2-1	3-1	1-1	2-4
Fisher Ath	3-0	1-2	4-0	1-0	2-5	2-0	0-2	3-2	4-2	—	3-1	1-1	1-3	1-2	1-0	0-1	0-2	1-2	1-3	1-3	3-1	1-2
Kettering T	3-0	3-2	2-0	5-0	1-0	2-1	1-3	3-2	1-1	3-0	—	0-2	0-0	2-0	3-1	1-1	0-0	2-0	1-1	0-1	1-0	1-0
Kidderminster H	1-2	0-1	2-2	1-3	1-2	3-1	3-2	2-0	3-1	1-1	2-3	—	2-2	1-2	4-0	0-0	3-0	2-2	2-4	1-1	0-2	3-2
Macclesfield T	1-0	0-1	2-1	0-0	3-0	0-0	0-0	4-0	0-0	0-1	3-1	1-2	—	3-2	3-1	4-0	2-2	1-1	3-0	3-2	1-0	1-2
Merthyr Tydfil	0-0	2-1	3-3	1-0	1-1	1-0	1-1	5-1	1-1	1-4	3-2	3-1	2-3	—	1-1	3-2	4-3	2-3	0-0	4-0	1-1	2-2
Northwich Vic	2-3	0-2	1-0	1-0	0-0	0-1	1-0	1-0	0-2	2-1	2-2	1-2	2-0	3-1	—	1-1	4-3	2-3	0-2	2-3	3-0	1-4
Runcorn	0-0	2-2	4-3	3-1	2-4	3-2	2-1	9-0	3-2	4-0	3-1	2-1	2-0	1-0	2-1	—	3-0	1-0	3-0	0-1	2-0	1-1
Stafford R	3-1	1-1	1-1	0-0	0-1	1-0	0-4	1-0	3-2	1-3	1-1	0-1	4-2	1-1	1-0	1-1	—	3-1	2-0	0-2	1-0	0-1
Sutton U	2-1	1-3	3-3	2-0	0-2	3-0	2-1	2-0	2-3	2-1	2-1	1-2	2-1	1-1	2-1	3-0	1-0	—	6-1	1-0	1-2	3-1
Telford U	1-3	1-3	3-0	4-2	0-0	0-4	0-1	1-1	4-2	3-1	1-3	1-1	1-0	1-1	2-1	2-1	0-2	1-1	—	0-0	4-1	1-1
Welling U	1-1	3-1	0-0	6-0	1-1	3-1	0-1	3-0	4-3	2-0	3-0	4-1	0-1	0-3	2-0	1-1	1-0	1-0	1-1	—	0-0	0-1
Wycombe W.	1-1	1-0	4-0	1-0	0-4	4-0	0-1	1-0	1-0	6-1	2-2	3-3	1-1	1-2	3-3	5-0	2-1	3-2	1-1	1-0	—	1-2
Yeovil Town	0-0	3-2	2-2	2-1	1-1	2-1	0-2	3-1	0-0	2-2	0-2	3-1	0-0	4-0	1-2	1-1	0-0	3-1	1-0	0-4	4-2	—

RESULTS 1989–90

Final Table for Season 1989–90

		Home			*Goals*		*Away*			*Goals*		
	P	*W*	*D*	*L*	*F*	*A*	*W*	*D*	*L*	*F*	*A*	*Pts*
Darlington	42	13	6	2	43	12	13	3	5	33	13	87
Barnet	42	15	4	2	46	14	11	3	7	35	27	85
Runcorn	42	16	3	2	52	20	3	10	8	27	42	70
Macclesfield Town	42	11	6	4	35	16	6	9	6	21	25	66
Kettering Town	42	13	5	3	35	15	5	7	9	31	38	66
Welling United	42	11	6	4	36	16	7	4	10	26	34	65
Yeovil Town	42	9	8	4	32	25	8	4	9	30	29	63
Sutton United	42	14	2	5	42	24	5	4	12	26	40	63
Merthyr Tydfil	42	9	9	3	41	30	7	5	9	26	33	62
Wycombe W	42	11	6	4	42	24	6	4	11	22	32	61
Cheltenham Town	42	9	6	6	30	22	7	5	9	28	38	59
Telford United	42	8	7	6	31	29	7	6	8	25	34	58
Kidderminster H	42	7	6	8	37	33	8	3	10	27	34	54
Barrow	42	11	8	2	33	25	1	8	12	18	42	52
Northwich Victoria	42	9	3	9	29	30	6	2	13	22	37	50
Altrincham	42	8	5	8	31	20	4	8	9	18	28	49
Stafford Rangers	42	9	6	6	25	23	3	6	12	25	39	48
Boston United	42	10	3	8	36	30	3	5	13	12	37	47
Fisher Athletic	42	9	1	11	34	34	4	6	11	21	44	46
Chorley	42	9	5	7	26	26	4	1	16	16	41	45
Farnborough Town	42	7	5	9	33	30	3	7	11	27	43	42
Enfield	42	9	3	9	36	34	1	3	17	16	55	36

Leading Goalscorers

Conf.			*FA*	*BL*	*FT*
28	Robbie Cooke (Kettering Town)	+	—	—	—
25	Efan Ekoku (Sutton United)	+	—	—	—
23	Simon Read (Farnborough Town)	+	2	1	—
21	Ian Thompson (Merthyr Tydfil)	+	3	—	—
19	John Borthwick (Darlington)	+	2	1	—
	Mark Carter (Runcorn)	+	—	1	2
18	Mick Doherty (Runcorn)	+	1	—	—
17	Gary Bull (Barnet)	+	5	3	—
	Andrew Clarke (Barnet)	+	2	—	—
	Paul Furlong (Enfield)	+	—	1	1
	Paul Gorman (Fisher Athletic)	+	—	—	—
	Terry Robbins (Welling United)	+	2	2	1
	Dave Webley (Merthyr Tydfil)	+	2	—	—
16	Steve Burr (Macclesfield Town)	+	3	—	2
	Kim Casey (Kidderminster Harriers)	+	—	6	3
15	Paul McKinnon (Sutton United)	+	1	3	—
	Mark West (Wycombe Wanderers)	+	1	2	1
14	Martin Hanchard (Northwich Victoria)	+	2	—	—
	Mark Whitehouse (Kidderminster Harriers)	+	2	2	3
12	David Cork (Darlington)	+	1	1	3
	Colin Cowperthwaite (Barrow)	+	2	1	—
	Ken McKenna (Telford United)	+	—	—	2
	Mickey Spencer (Yeovil Town)	+	1	3	1

HFS LOANS LEAGUE (PREMIER

(formerly Northern Premier League)

	Bangor C	Bishop Auckland	Buxton	Caernarfon T	Colne Dynamoes	Fleetwood T	Frickley Ath	Gainsborough Tr	Gateshead	Goole T	Horwich	Hyde U	Marine	Matlock T	Morecambe	Mossley	Rhyl	Shepshed Ch	S Liverpool	Southport	Stalybridge	Witton Alb
Bangor C	—	5-0	1-1	3-0	0-1	0-0	2-2	1-1	2-1	1-4	1-2	2-1	3-0	0-0	1-1	1-0	4-3	2-1	2-1	2-2	3-1	2-0
Bishop A	6-2	—	4-1	3-1	0-2	2-1	3-0	1-2	2-2	1-2	5-0	3-3	1-2	2-2	1-0	1-2	1-2	5-2	1-5	1-1	2-0	1-2
Buxton	2-2	3-0	—	1-1	0-0	1-3	1-0	2-1	0-4	1-0	2-0	1-2	1-4	1-0	4-0	0-3	3-0	1-1	3-3	0-1	2-1	2-2
Caernarfon T	1-2	0-2	3-1	—	1-2	0-4	1-3	1-2	1-1	0-0	1-0	1-1	0-2	0-0	3-0	3-3	3-1	3-0	2-3	0-1	0-1	1-1
Colne Dyn	2-1	2-2	2-0	1-0	—	2-2	2-1	1-2	2-1	2-1	4-2	1-3	3-1	1-0	3-1	3-2	2-1	2-1	6-1	1-0	1-0	3-2
Fleetwood T	2-0	0-2	0-3	4-3	1-1	—	1-3	4-1	0-2	2-1	2-2	3-2	0-0	3-3	1-2	2-1	4-2	1-0	6-0	1-1	1-0	1-6
Frickley Ath	1-1	2-1	4-3	0-2	1-3	0-1	—	3-1	0-1	2-4	2-0	1-1	1-1	2-1	1-0	1-3	3-1	2-0	2-2	1-2	1-0	2-1
Gainsboro	4-2	1-0	3-0	4-1	0-1	0-0	0-1	—	1-0	1-0	1-1	3-1	1-0	1-3	1-1	2-0	1-2	0-1	5-1	1-0	3-3	1-2
Gateshead	2-1	1-0	3-1	2-1	3-2	1-3	1-0	2-1	—	2-2	3-2	2-1	0-1	1-1	5-1	4-2	1-1	3-1	0-2	3-3	2-1	0-1
Goole T	0-2	1-3	1-3	1-2	1-5	2-4	0-2	2-1	1-0	—	1-1	1-2	1-3	3-0	0-5	7-2	1-2	1-3	2-1	0-1	0-2	0-2
Horwich	2-2	1-2	1-1	5-1	1-3	3-2	2-2	1-1	4-1	1-0	—	0-2	1-3	2-0	1-0	2-3	1-1	1-2	2-2	5-4	1-1	1-0
Hyde U	1-0	1-2	1-0	3-0	2-2	3-1	2-1	2-1	4-0	6-0	2-3	—	1-1	0-2	0-2	0-1	3-1	4-2	4-3	0-1	2-1	2-0
Marine	3-3	0-0	3-1	3-2	1-0	1-1	2-0	2-1	2-3	0-3	1-1	1-0	—	1-1	2-0	1-1	3-1	1-1	2-2	1-3	1-1	0-2
Matlock T	3-0	3-1	1-0	3-0	0-2	2-0	0-2	0-1	1-1	0-0	3-3	2-0	2-1	—	2-0	2-1	1-0	5-1	1-2	1-2	2-0	5-0
Morecambe	2-1	2-2	4-0	4-4	1-3	2-2	1-0	2-1	1-3	2-1	1-2	0-0	1-1	2-0	—	0-2	3-1	1-2	2-0	3-2	2-1	3-2
Mossley	1-1	1-3	1-3	2-4	1-3	1-1	1-1	0-3	2-2	1-1	1-2	1-3	1-3	0-3	2-0	—	2-2	1-1	3-3	3-1	0-1	2-1
Rhyl	0-1	0-0	1-3	1-2	0-2	1-0	1-1	1-1	1-2	0-2	1-2	2-0	2-3	1-1	4-1	3-1	—	0-4	1-5	1-1	0-0	0-1
Shepshed Ch	1-3	0-1	1-3	4-2	0-2	2-1	0-2	2-1	1-5	3-1	0-2	0-2	2-2	0-1	2-2	1-2	3-0	—	1-2	0-0	2-2	1-2
S Liverpool	2-1	3-1	2-3	4-2	1-2	1-3	5-3	3-2	1-3	3-2	1-1	0-1	2-0	1-1	4-1	2-0	2-1	4-2	—	1-1	0-1	1-1
Southport	1-1	2-1	1-0	4-0	0-0	0-0	2-0	2-0	2-2	1-3	2-1	0-0	1-0	1-1	0-1	2-4	1-0	2-0	1-3	—	2-0	0-0
Stalybridge	0-0	1-3	4-1	2-3	2-3	4-5	2-0	2-0	2-2	2-0	0-1	0-3	2-0	1-2	1-1	1-0	0-0	2-3	1-3	1-0	—	1-0
Witton Alb	0-0	1-0	3-0	2-0	0-1	3-0	3-0	1-1	0-1	0-1	2-0	2-2	2-0	2-0	2-0	2-1	2-0	3-1	0-2	5-0	4-0	—

DIVISION) RESULTS 1989–90

Final table for season 1989–90

		Home			*Goals*		*Away*			*Goals*		
	P	*W*	*D*	*L*	*F*	*A*	*W*	*D*	*L*	*F*	*A*	*Pts*
Colne Dynamoes	42	17	2	2	46	24	15	4	2	40	16	102
Gateshead	42	13	4	4	41	28	9	6	6	37	30	76
Witton Albion	42	14	3	4	39	10	8	4	9	28	29	73
Hyde United	42	13	2	6	43	24	8	6	7	30	26	71
South Liverpool	42	11	4	6	43	32	9	5	7	46	47	69
Matlock Town	42	13	3	5	39	17	5	9	7	22	25	66
Southport	42	10	7	4	27	17	7	7	7	27	31	65
Fleetwood Town	42	10	5	6	39	35	7	7	7	34	31	63
Marine	42	8	9	4	31	27	8	5	8	28	28	62
Bangor City	42	11	7	3	38	22	4	8	9	26	36	60
Bishop Auckland	42	9	4	9	46	34	8	4	9	26	30	59
Gainsborough T	42	11	4	6	34	20	5	4	12	25	35	56
Frickley Ath	42	10	4	7	32	29	6	4	11	24	32	56
Horwich*3	42	8	7	6	38	33	7	6	8	28	36	55
Morecambe	42	11	5	5	39	30	4	4	13	19	40	54
Buxton	42	9	6	6	31	28	6	2	13	28	44	53
Stalybridge Celtic	42	8	4	9	31	30	4	5	12	17	31	45
Mossley	42	3	8	10	27	42	8	2	11	34	40	43
Goole Town	42	5	1	15	26	46	7	4	10	28	31	41
Shepshed C	42	5	4	12	26	38	6	3	12	29	44	40
Caernarfon Town	42	5	6	10	25	30	5	2	14	31	56	38
Rhyl*1	42	4	6	11	21	33	3	4	14	22	44	30

* – pts deducted for breaches of rule

Goals scored – 1391 in 462 matches (average 3.010)

Leading scorers *(HFS Loans League and HFS cups only)*

26 Keith McNall (Gateshead)
25 Andy Green (South Liverpool)
24 Rod McDonald (Colne Dynamoes, inc 13 with South Liverpool)
22 Dave Lancaster (Colne Dynamoes)
21 Jim McCluskie (Hyde United, inc 11 with Mossley)
20 Steven Holden (Southport, inc 8 with Morecambe)
Graham Hoyland (Matlock Town)
19 John Coleman (Witton Albion)
Joe Olabode (Gateshead)
18 Tony Livens (Bangor City)
17 Ian Howat (Caernarfon Town)
Mark Edwards (Witton Albion)
16 Trenton Wiggan (Gainsborough Trinity)
Phil Clarkson (Fleetwood Town)

BEAZER HOMES SOUTHERN LEAGUE

	Alvechurch	Ashford Town	Atherstone United	Bath City	Bromsgrove	Burton Albion	Cambridge City	Chelmsford City	Corby Town	Crawley Town	Dartford	Dorchester Town	Dover Athletic	Gloucester City	Gosport Borough	Gravesend & Northfleet	Moor Green	VS Rugby	Waterlooville	Wealdstone	Weymouth	Worcester City
Alvechurch	—	1-2	2-3	0-5	4-2	3-3	1-2	4-2	2-2	1-1	0-4	2-0	1-6	2-2	0-1	1-2	1-2	3-5	0-0	0-2	2-3	2-0
Ashford T	1-2	—	0-5	0-2	0-3	1-1	1-1	1-1	2-3	0-3	4-0	1-3	0-2	1-2	1-0	0-1	4-0	1-1	1-7	0-1	0-0	1-2
Atherstone U	1-0	3-2	—	2-2	1-0	1-0	0-0	3-1	1-0	2-2	1-4	0-1	0-2	2-1	2-1	2-0	3-1	0-2	0-1	2-0	1-0	4-1
Bath City	2-0	4-0	1-0	—	3-1	2-0	3-1	5-1	3-1	1-1	0-0	6-0	1-0	2-0	5-0	0-1	2-1	1-0	3-2	2-1	3-3	3-1
Bromsgrove R	2-1	2-0	3-0	0-0	—	0-2	1-3	3-1	2-0	1-1	2-3	3-3	0-2	0-2	5-0	1-0	0-0	2-0	2-4	1-0	1-0	1-1
Burton Alb	2-0	2-0	1-1	1-2	0-1	—	1-0	2-0	4-1	1-1	1-1	1-1	0-1	0-0	1-0	2-2	5-2	1-1	1-0	4-0	1-0	5-4
Cambridge C	2-0	2-1	0-2	2-1	2-1	0-2	—	2-3	5-0	1-1	1-2	6-0	1-2	0-2	2-3	1-1	2-2	0-1	2-4	3-1	3-0	0-1
Chelmsford C	3-0	2-0	0-2	1-2	0-1	2-3	0-3	—	0-1	1-1	2-2	0-2	1-3	3-1	2-0	2-1	1-2	0-0	2-2	1-3	2-1	1-3
Corby T	3-1	5-0	1-3	1-2	0-1	1-0	1-4	1-1	—	1-2	1-2	3-3	0-2	1-4	2-0	3-1	2-1	2-3	2-2	0-0	8-0	1-3
Crawley T	0-1	0-2	3-0	0-1	4-0	0-1	1-2	0-3	4-3	—	2-1	0-1	3-1	2-3	2-1	1-1	0-1	1-3	5-0	0-0	1-1	0-6
Dartford	1-0	2-1	0-1	0-1	1-0	0-1	0-0	2-3	1-0	2-0	—	2-0	2-2	6-2	5-1	5-0	2-0	1-0	3-0	1-1	6-2	2-1
Dorchester T	3-1	1-2	2-2	0-1	1-0	3-1	1-2	4-1	2-1	0-1	0-1	—	0-1	3-2	4-1	0-2	0-1	1-1	2-1	1-1	0-1	3-0
Dover Ath	3-0	3-1	2-0	2-2	2-0	2-0	1-1	1-0	2-0	1-0	1-1	5-0	—	1-0	3-0	2-0	1-1	1-0	3-2	2-0	7-0	5-3
Gloucester C	5-2	5-2	3-1	0-0	1-1	0-0	3-2	3-1	3-2	1-1	0-4	0-0	0-1	—	9-0	3-0	2-3	2-3	0-1	2-2	1-1	3-1
Gosport B	2-1	0-1	1-1	0-0	0-3	0-4	3-5	2-0	0-1	0-2	0-1	0-2	1-2	2-3	—	0-1	0-3	0-1	0-3	1-0	0-3	0-0
Gravesend	2-1	1-1	1-1	0-2	3-3	1-0	1-1	0-0	1-0	2-5	1-0	2-1	0-0	1-1	1-0	—	1-0	0-0	0-0	2-0	1-0	2-0
Moor Green	1-3	1-0	1-1	1-2	2-0	3-1	1-2	2-3	3-1	0-0	1-4	3-0	0-1	4-1	0-3	1-0	—	1-0	2-0	2-2	0-0	3-0
VS Rugby	2-0	1-0	1-1	0-1	0-0	0-0	2-0	0-0	2-0	0-1	0-1	2-0	2-0	3-0	2-2	0-2	2-1	—	2-2	2-0	1-0	0-0
Waterlooville	3-1	0-5	3-2	1-0	0-3	0-4	2-7	1-1	1-0	2-1	1-2	1-2	1-3	2-4	1-1	4-0	1-3	0-3	—	4-1	1-4	1-1
Wealdstone	1-0	0-1	3-1	0-1	0-0	0-1	2-2	2-1	2-1	4-0	1-1	2-0	3-2	2-3	2-1	2-3	2-1	5-1	1-0	—	2-1	4-1
Weymouth	3-0	0-0	1-1	1-2	1-1	2-3	1-1	0-2	1-1	3-0	0-2	1-2	0-3	1-1	2-0	4-2	2-1	1-0	1-1	1-0	—	2-2
Worcester C	4-0	0-2	2-1	2-0	0-3	1-1	0-0	1-1	1-0	1-0	0-0	3-0	0-1	2-0	5-1	0-1	2-4	1-2	1-1	1-0	4-2	—

PREMIER DIVISION 1989–90

Final table for season 1989–90

	P	*W*	*D*	*L*	*F*	*A*	*Pts*
Dover Athletic	42	32	6	4	87	27	102
Bath City	42	30	8	4	81	28	98
Dartford	42	26	9	7	80	35	87
Burton Albion	42	20	12	10	64	40	72
VS Rugby	42	19	12	11	51	35	69
Atherstone United	42	19	10	13	60	52	67
Gravesend & Northfleet	42	18	12	12	44	50	66
Cambridge City	42	17	11	14	76	56	62
Gloucester City	42	17	11	14	80	68	62
Bromsgrove Rovers	42	17	10	15	56	48	61
Moor Green	42	18	7	17	62	59	61
Wealdstone	42	16	9	17	55	54	57
Dorchester Town	42	16	7	19	52	67	55
Worcester City	42	15	10	17	62	63	*54
Crawley Town	42	13	12	17	53	57	51
Waterlooville	42	13	10	19	63	81	49
Weymouth	42	11	13	18	50	70	46
Chelmsford City	42	11	10	21	52	72	43
Ashford Town	42	10	7	25	43	75	37
Corby Town	42	10	6	26	57	77	36
Alvechurch	42	7	5	30	46	95	26
Gosport Borough	42	6	5	31	28	93	23

* Denotes one point deducted

Westgate Insurance Cup

Final: Dartford 0, VS Rugby 2; VS Rugby 0, Dartford 1
(VS Rugby won 2-1 on aggregate)

LEADING GOALSCORERS

P. Randall (Bath City) 40
K. Wilkin (Cambridge City) 29
P. Moody(Waterlooville) 28
D. Hedley (Moor Green) 26
L. Lee (Dover Athletic) 25

Advance Sports Manager of the Season
Chris Kinnear (Dover Athletic)

BEAZER HOMES SOUTHERN LEAGUE

	Banbury	Barry T	Bedworth	Bilston T	Bridgnorth	Dudley T	Grantham	Halesowen	Hednesford	King's Lynn	Leicester	Nuneaton	Warwick	Redditch	Rushden	Sandwell Borough	Spalding	Stourbridge	Stroud	Sutton Coldfield	Tamworth	Willenhall
Banbury U	—	0-1	1-3	1-0	4-2	2-1	3-2	1-2	0-0	2-3	2-0	1-7	0-2	2-2	1-3	1-1	1-1	3-2	2-2	1-2	2-3	1-0
Barry T	3-0	—	1-0	0-1	2-0	1-3	4-1	1-0	3-0	1-0	2-0	3-1	1-0	0-0	1-3	1-0	2-3	2-2	2-2	4-0	2-1	1-2
Bedworth U	1-0	3-0	—	0-0	2-1	0-2	1-2	2-4	2-0	0-1	1-2	1-3	1-0	2-1	2-3	3-2	2-1	1-3	1-1	0-2	1-1	1-1
Bilston Tn	1-1	2-2	1-1	—	1-2	1-0	2-0	0-4	2-1	2-0	2-3	0-1	1-3	1-1	1-2	2-1	2-2	1-3	0-1	2-2	1-2	1-0
Bridgnorth T	6-0	1-1	0-1	1-1	—	1-0	0-3	1-1	6-1	5-2	1-3	0-4	1-4	2-1	3-2	1-0	0-2	3-5	3-1	2-2	2-2	2-2
Dudley T	3-0	0-0	0-1	0-0	0-2	—	4-2	3-1	2-1	2-2	4-1	1-0	2-0	0-0	1-2	1-2	2-1	1-2	2-1	3-2	1-4	3-0
Grantham T	1-1	0-3	1-1	0-1	1-1	2-2	—	0-0	2-0	1-0	0-3	1-1	3-1	0-0	0-0	4-2	1-0	1-3	2-1	0-1	3-1	4-1
Halesowen T	7-2	3-3	2-1	0-2	1-1	6-4	3-2	—	1-1	5-1	3-1	2-0	3-0	1-2	1-0	4-2	3-1	0-0	3-0	3-2	5-1	2-0
Hednesford T	1-0	3-1	1-1	1-1	2-2	4-0	1-2	1-1	—	1-4	4-0	0-1	1-1	1-1	0-1	1-2	3-1	1-1	2-3	1-1	0-3	1-1
King's Lynn	1-0	3-2	5-2	1-0	0-2	1-2	4-0	0-0	1-0	—	0-2	0-4	0-1	1-0	0-2	4-0	1-2	3-0	1-0	1-1	1-0	4-1
Leicester U	3-1	2-3	2-2	1-2	1-3	3-2	4-2	1-3	2-2	2-1	—	1-2	3-1	1-2	0-2	1-1	1-2	1-2	1-3	1-1	2-4	2-1
Nuneaton B	3-0	2-1	2-1	1-1	1-1	2-4	2-0	1-0	1-0	3-0	0-1	—	1-0	3-2	1-0	2-0	3-2	0-5	1-0	3-1	7-0	1-0
RC Warwick	3-2	0-0	0-1	0-1	1-2	1-0	2-1	3-4	0-0	2-0	1-0	2-2	—	0-3	1-2	3-1	1-1	3-3	1-3	1-1	1-2	1-1
Redditch U	1-1	0-3	1-0	7-1	7-1	0-0	1-1	1-2	1-2	3-0	2-1	1-2	0-0	—	0-1	1-1	4-0	0-1	0-3	2-4	0-5	2-1
Rushden T	2-1	3-0	4-0	2-0	1-1	4-0	2-1	2-1	2-0	5-2	3-0	1-2	2-0	5-0	—	4-2	2-1	2-1	3-2	1-3	0-1	2-0
Sandwell B	1-2	0-2	0-2	0-0	3-1	0-2	1-1	1-2	3-1	2-2	1-2	2-1	1-2	2-1	1-1	—	1-3	0-3	2-2	1-1	0-2	0-1
Spalding U	2-1	1-2	3-0	1-0	2-2	5-1	1-0	2-3	1-2	2-1	1-2	2-1	4-1	1-2	1-0	0-0	—	4-2	3-2	1-1	2-3	2-1
Stourbridge	1-0	1-0	2-2	0-0	1-1	1-4	0-2	0-1	2-3	4-1	3-1	1-1	0-0	4-1	0-0	2-2	1-1	—	0-1	3-1	0-3	5-3
Stroud	1-1	4-0	2-1	1-1	1-0	1-1	1-5	1-2	0-0	1-1	1-3	2-2	6-0	1-1	1-2	3-2	4-1	3-1	—	2-1	3-3	1-0
Sutton C'field	0-2	4-0	0-3	2-1	2-1	2-3	2-1	0-5	1-2	2-1	3-3	4-1	2-1	4-1	2-1	3-0	0-1	2-0	0-4	—	2-0	4-3
Tamworth	2-0	2-5	1-0	2-1	1-1	2-2	1-0	2-3	2-3	3-1	1-2	1-3	1-1	2-2	3-3	2-1	1-3	2-1	3-1	3-2	—	1-0
Willenhall T	1-0	0-1	1-0	1-0	1-0	1-1	1-2	0-3	0-1	0-2	0-1	2-2	3-0	1-0	1-0	2-2	1-3	0-2	2-2	0-0	0-3	—

MIDLAND DIVISION 1989–90

Final table for season 1989–90

	P	*W*	*D*	*L*	*F*	*A*	*Pts*
Halesowen Town	42	28	8	6	100	49	92
Rushden Town	42	28	5	9	82	39	89
Nuneaton Borough	42	26	7	9	81	47	85
Tamworth	42	22	8	12	82	70	74
Barry Town	42	21	8	13	67	53	71
Spalding United	42	20	7	15	73	63	67
Sutton Coldfield Town	42	18	10	14	72	69	64
Stourbridge	42	17	12	13	73	61	63
Dudley Town	42	18	9	15	69	64	63
Stroud	42	16	13	13	75	62	61
Leicester United	42	17	5	20	66	77	56
Bridgnorth Town	42	13	14	15	68	73	53
King's Lynn	42	16	5	21	57	69	53
Grantham Town	42	14	10	18	57	63	52
Bedworth United	42	14	9	19	50	60	51
Hednesford Town	42	11	14	17	50	62	47
Bilston Town	42	11	14	17	40	54	47
Redditch United	42	11	13	18	57	64	46
Racing Club Warwick	42	11	11	20	45	66	44
Willenhall Town	42	9	9	24	37	66	36
Banbury United	42	9	9	24	46	83	*34
Sandwell Borough	42	6	12	24	46	79	30

* Denotes two points deducted

LEADING GOALSCORERS

P. Joinson (Halesowen Town) 41
M. Twigger (Nuneaton) 28
F. Belfon (RushdenTown) 25
S. Doughty (Stroud) 24
P. Evans (Barry Town) 22
J. Muir (Dudley Town) 22

Advance Sports Manager of the Season
John Morris (Halesowen Town)

BEAZER HOMES SOUTHERN LEAGUE

	Andover	Baldock Town	Bashley	Buckingham T	Burnham	Bury Town	Canterbury City	Corinthian	Dunstable	Erith & Belvedere	Fareham Town	Folkestone	Hastings Town	Hounslow	Hythe Town	Margate	Poole Town	Salisbury	Sheppey United	Trowbridge Town	Witney Town	Yate Town
Andover	—	0-0	0-3	2-2	0-3	1-1	2-2	1-1	0-1	2-2	2-1	3-2	3-2	4-3	1-3	1-1	0-3	0-2	4-0	1-3	3-2	3-1
Baldock T	2-1	—	0-1	0-7	1-0	2-2	2-0	5-1	2-2	2-1	1-1	3-0	0-0	1-0	2-3	5-0	1-1	1-2	0-2	2-0	0-2	1-0
Bashley	2-0	2-1	—	1-1	2-3	0-0	1-0	0-3	0-1	3-0	1-1	5-0	2-2	3-0	6-2	0-0	1-2	2-1	4-1	4-1	2-0	1-0
Buckingham	3-2	1-1	3-2	—	0-5	3-1	2-1	2-1	0-1	0-1	1-0	0-2	2-1	2-0	0-0	3-1	2-0	1-1	1-0	2-2	4-1	0-0
Burnham	1-2	1-2	4-0	0-0	—	1-4	3-1	3-1	0-3	0-1	0-2	1-2	2-2	3-1	0-0	0-0	1-1	0-0	0-1	2-3	2-1	2-0
Bury T	0-0	1-0	1-2	3-0	5-1	—	0-0	2-2	0-1	2-0	0-3	3-4	2-1	5-2	3-1	3-1	4-1	1-1	2-1	1-2	3-2	1-0
Canterbury C	1-2	2-2	1-2	1-0	1-1	1-3	—	2-2	0-1	1-1	0-0	2-1	1-1	3-0	0-2	0-1	1-2	0-1	1-0	2-1	1-1	1-2
Corinthian	1-3	2-4	1-4	0-0	1-7	1-4	1-2	—	3-3	0-1	1-1	1-2	0-2	0-2	2-2	2-1	0-2	2-0	1-3	2-3	2-0	1-0
Dunstable	0-0	1-0	2-3	1-0	1-1	2-1	2-1	1-1	—	3-0	3-1	2-2	0-2	3-0	2-0	0-0	0-0	1-2	1-0	3-0	1-2	0-0
Erith	2-1	1-3	0-4	0-0	0-2	1-1	0-2	0-0	0-2	—	1-0	0-1	1-2	0-1	1-1	2-2	3-0	0-4	1-1	2-3	3-4	1-1
Fareham T	0-0	2-3	3-0	2-1	1-1	1-1	0-2	2-0	2-1	1-0	—	1-1	1-2	2-1	1-1	2-1	0-3	1-6	1-1	2-4	0-2	2-0
Folkestone	1-0	3-2	3-1	1-2	1-5	2-4	1-2	1-1	0-1	2-1	0-1	—	1-2	1-2	0-3	1-1	1-5	3-0	3-3	2-2	2-1	1-3
Hastings T	2-1	3-2	2-2	0-1	0-3	5-0	1-0	3-1	2-2	1-1	1-0	2-0	—	2-1	0-1	1-3	2-2	0-2	2-1	2-0	1-0	1-2
Hounslow	2-0	1-6	0-3	0-3	0-2	1-2	0-2	2-1	0-1	3-1	2-3	1-1	0-2	—	0-2	1-1	0-0	0-4	2-1	0-3	1-0	0-3
Hythe T	0-1	0-0	1-1	1-2	4-3	4-3	4-1	2-1	0-2	4-0	1-1	3-1	0-1	1-1	—	1-1	1-1	5-1	4-1	3-1	2-0	1-0
Margate	3-0	1-1	2-1	0-1	1-1	0-0	1-1	2-0	1-2	1-2	0-0	0-1	3-1	1-0	0-1	—	1-2	1-2	5-0	2-1	0-1	0-0
Poole T	5-0	0-2	2-0	4-2	5-4	2-1	2-5	5-1	2-1	4-1	2-0	4-0	1-1	3-1	0-1	0-2	—	2-2	3-2	1-2	2-0	3-2
Salisbury	3-0	2-2	0-1	1-3	1-5	1-1	2-1	2-0	1-1	0-1	1-1	3-4	2-0	0-1	2-0	1-2	2-0	—	2-0	3-0	3-0	2-1
Sheppey U	0-4	0-3	2-3	1-3	0-1	0-2	0-2	0-1	0-0	0-0	1-2	3-2	1-3	1-2	1-0	0-0	0-2	2-4	—	4-2	0-0	0-1
Trowbridge T	1-1	1-0	1-2	2-1	0-3	5-1	0-2	5-1	2-0	4-0	0-0	2-2	4-0	2-2	1-1	3-2	1-4	1-1	3-0	—	0-0	3-0
Witney T	1-2	2-0	0-2	2-3	0-0	1-1	0-2	3-1	2-2	2-1	2-1	1-2	2-1	4-0	2-1	1-0	3-1	2-0	4-0	1-2	—	0-1
Yate T	2-1	0-2	0-1	1-3	1-0	3-1	2-1	4-0	2-2	3-0	2-3	1-1	1-3	3-0	1-2	0-1	6-1	1-2	2-1	0-3	1-0	—

SOUTHERN DIVISION 1989–90

Final table for season 1989–90

	P	*W*	*D*	*L*	*F*	*A*	*Pts*
Bashley	42	25	7	10	80	47	82
Poole Town	42	23	8	11	85	60	77
Buckingham Town	42	22	10	10	67	46	76
Dunstable	42	20	14	8	56	38	74
Salisbury	42	21	9	12	72	50	72
Hythe Town	42	20	12	10	69	48	72
Trowbridge Town	42	20	9	13	79	64	69
Hastings Town	42	20	9	13	64	54	69
Bury Town	42	18	12	12	76	62	66
Baldock Town	42	18	11	13	69	52	65
Burnham	42	17	11	14	77	52	62
Fareham Town	42	14	14	14	49	53	56
Yate Town	42	16	6	20	53	52	54
Witney Town	42	16	6	20	54	56	54
Canterbury City	42	14	10	18	52	52	52
Margate	42	12	15	15	46	45	51
Folkestone	42	14	9	19	61	83	51
Andover	42	13	11	18	54	70	50
Hounslow	42	11	5	26	39	82	38
Erith & Belvedere	42	8	11	23	34	73	35
Corinthian	42	6	10	26	44	93	28
Sheppey United	42	6	7	29	35	83	25

LEADING GOALSCORERS

J. Lovell (Bashley) 41
J. Meacham (Trowbridge) 25
G. Manson (Poole Town) 24
I. Chalk (Salisbury) 23

Advance Sports Manager of the Season
Trevor Parker (Bashley)

VAUXHALL FOOTBALL LEAGUE

	Aylesbury Utd	Barking	Basingstoke	Bishops Stortford	Bognor Regis	Bromley	Carshalton Ath	Dagenham	Dulwich Hamlet	Grays Ath	Harrow Bor	Hayes	Hendon	Kingstonian	Leyton-Wingate	Marlow	Redbridge F	St Albans C	Slough T	Staines	Windsor & Eton	Wokingham T
Aylesbury	—	3-0	1-0	2-1	5-0	1-2	4-1	4-0	3-1	0-0	3-0	4-0	4-0	1-1	1-2	1-1	3-1	0-1	3-1	3-0	3-1	1-3
Barking	0-0	—	1-1	1-2	2-2	1-0	2-1	0-4	0-3	1-2	1-1	2-1	0-0	1-1	0-3	4-1	1-3	2-0	1-1	3-3	1-1	2-3
Basingstoke Town	0-0	2-1	—	0-0	2-1	2-0	2-0	3-1	7-0	1-1	1-0	3-1	3-2	1-2	1-1	3-0	4-0	3-1	1-3	3-1	0-0	1-2
Bishops Stortford	0-3	0-4	1-0	—	0-1	2-0	3-1	1-0	1-2	0-2	1-1	3-5	5-0	0-1	2-1	2-1	3-4	3-2	0-1	1-0	0-2	1-2
Bognor Regis T	0-2	3-2	1-1	2-3	—	2-2	2-0	1-1	2-1	0-0	0-0	1-1	0-3	0-0	0-1	0-2	1-6	3-1	1-3	1-3	0-4	0-2
Bromley	0-4	0-2	0-1	2-2	0-0	—	1-0	2-5	2-0	0-1	1-1	2-0	1-4	1-1	0-2	1-1	1-1	1-1	0-1	3-0	1-1	1-5
Carshalton Ath	1-0	4-2	2-2	1-2	3-1	1-0	—	2-0	0-1	1-2	3-3	3-0	3-1	2-0	2-0	0-1	5-1	1-2	4-4	3-1	1-1	0-2
Dagenham	1-0	1-1	3-2	1-0	0-1	1-0	0-2	—	1-1	0-0	3-0	2-1	1-1	2-0	1-0	6-1	2-2	1-3	0-3	1-1	0-0	2-2
Dulwich Hamlet	0-2	2-1	0-1	0-3	1-1	0-0	0-1	0-0	—	2-2	0-2	0-4	3-6	0-4	1-3	0-1	0-3	2-1	2-3	1-3	0-0	0-2
Grays Ath	2-1	2-1	2-3	1-1	2-0	3-0	0-1	0-0	2-1	—	4-0	2-1	3-0	3-1	1-0	2-0	1-1	0-1	1-1	4-3	3-0	0-2
Harrow Bor	1-5	3-1	3-1	2-3	1-0	2-1	0-1	1-2	4-1	4-2	—	2-0	0-2	1-3	0-2	1-1	0-0	3-2	1-5	3-2	1-3	1-4
Hayes	1-1	6-1	1-0	0-0	2-0	4-1	0-1	0-0	2-1	2-2	1-1	—	3-1	0-1	1-3	4-1	0-2	2-0	1-1	0-1	3-1	2-3
Hendon	1-1	1-0	2-1	0-1	0-1	0-2	3-1	2-1	1-0	3-0	0-1	0-2	—	3-0	0-1	0-0	2-2	1-0	1-1	1-4	2-2	0-0
Kingstonian	1-1	3-2	5-0	6-0	3-3	4-2	3-2	4-3	1-0	4-2	2-1	1-0	3-0	—	2-3	4-2	3-1	4-2	1-2	3-0	2-0	4-2
Leyton-Wingate	1-3	2-1	4-1	0-3	1-1	3-1	1-0	0-1	1-0	1-1	1-0	2-2	2-3	1-0	—	0-0	2-1	0-1	1-2	2-4	1-3	2-1
Marlow	0-3	4-1	3-1	1-3	2-0	0-0	3-0	0-0	2-1	0-1	3-1	2-2	1-2	1-1	0-1	—	0-2	1-1	0-0	1-3	1-0	0-0
Redbridge F.	1-2	3-1	4-0	3-1	0-2	0-1	3-1	1-1	2-1	2-1	3-1	1-2	1-1	1-2	0-1	2-1	—	1-1	2-0	1-1	1-1	1-1
St Albans C	0-1	3-1	1-1	2-1	0-0	2-0	1-2	0-1	1-1	1-2	2-1	3-0	2-1	0-0	2-0	1-1	1-0	—	0-3	0-2	2-4	1-2
Slough T	1-2	4-2	2-1	1-1	0-0	1-0	3-2	0-1	2-0	2-0	4-0	1-0	3-1	2-1	3-2	3-0	5-0	3-3	—	1-0	1-1	2-0
Staines	0-3	4-1	0-2	0-2	1-2	2-0	2-3	0-2	1-0	0-0	3-1	2-2	0-2	0-4	1-0	1-0	0-1	1-1	0-4	—	0-1	0-1
Windsor & Eton	2-1	1-1	0-2	0-2	2-1	4-0	0-0	1-2	1-2	0-0	1-1	0-1	3-0	1-1	0-0	0-2	4-1	1-0	0-1	0-3	—	3-0
Wokingham T	1-1	2-1	2-1	1-0	2-0	1-0	0-1	0-0	1-1	2-0	1-1	1-1	1-1	2-0	1-0	1-0	1-0	2-0	1-1	2-0	3-1	—

PREMIER DIVISION RESULTS 1989–90

Final table for season 1989–90

		Home			*Away*						
	P	*W*	*D*	*L*	*W*	*D*	*L*	*F*	*A*	*GD*	*Pts*
Slough	42	15	4	2	12	7	2	85	38	47	92
Wokingham	42	13	7	1	13	4	4	67	34	33	89
Aylesbury Utd	42	14	3	4	11	6	4	86	30	56	84
Kingstonian	42	17	2	2	7	7	7	87	51	36	81
Grays Ath	42	13	4	4	6	9	6	59	44	15	70
Dagenham	42	9	8	4	8	7	6	54	43	11	66
Leyton-Wingate	42	9	4	8	11	2	8	54	48	6	66
Basingstoke	42	13	5	3	5	4	12	65	55	10	63
Bishops Stortford	42	9	1	11	10	5	6	60	59	1	63
Carshalton*	42	11	4	6	8	1	12	63	59	4	59
Redbridge F	42	9	6	6	7	5	9	65	62	3	59
Hendon	42	8	6	7	7	4	10	54	63	–9	55
Windsor & Eton	42	7	6	8	6	9	6	51	47	4	54
Hayes	42	9	6	6	5	5	11	61	59	2	53
St. Albans	42	8	5	8	5	5	11	49	59	–10	49
Staines	42	6	3	12	8	3	10	53	69	–16	48
Marlow	42	7	7	7	4	6	11	42	59	–17	46
Harrow Borough	42	9	2	10	2	8	11	51	79	–28	43
Bognor Regis	42	4	7	10	5	7	9	37	67	–30	41
Barking	42	5	9	7	2	2	17	53	86	–33	32
Bromley	42	4	8	9	3	3	15	32	69	–37	32
Dulwich Hamlet	42	2	5	14	4	3	14	32	80	–48	26

*Carshalton –3 points by order of the League

Leading goalscorers

		Lge	*AC*	*CC*
20	John Neal (B Stortford)	18	1	1
	Includes 9, 1, 1 for Barking)			
19	Devon Gayle (B Stortford)	15	4	0
18	Cliff Hercules (Aylesbury Utd)	17	1	0
	Dave Pearce (Wokingham T)	15	3	0
	Neal Stanley (Slough T)	16	1	1
17	Conrad Kane (Carshalton Ath)	16	1	0
	Francis Vines (Kingstonian)	17	0	0
	Leroy Whale (Basingstoke T)	16	1	0
16	Uche Egbe (Hendon)	15	1	0
	Paul Clarkson (Basingstoke T)	16	0	0
	Scott Young (B Stortford)	13	2	0
	Jim Bolton (Carshalton Ath)	16	0	0
	Neil Fraser (Hayes)	15	1	0
	Robin Lewis (Kingstonian)	16	0	0
	Tommy Langley (Slough T)	15	1	0

VAUXHALL FOOTBALL LEAGUE

	Boreham Wood	Chalfont St Peter	Chesham Utd	Croydon	Dorking	Hampton	Harlow Town	Hitchin	Kingsbury	Leatherhead	Lewes	Metropolitan Police	Purfleet	Southwick	Tooting & Mitcham	Uxbridge	Walton & Hersham	Wembley	Whyteleafe	Wivenhoe Town	Woking	Worthing
Boreham Wood	—	2-1	2-0	2-1	0-2	1-1	1-3	0-1	3-2	3-0	1-5	1-1	1-1	0-0	0-0	1-0	3-1	3-2	2-2	1-1	0-4	2-1
Chalfont St Peter	1-0	—	0-0	1-1	0-2	3-1	4-1	0-5	3-1	2-2	2-1	1-0	3-0	0-0	1-0	2-2	0-2	0-4	1-2	2-1	1-1	0-2
Chesham Utd	2-2	2-1	—	1-1	0-1	0-1	1-0	1-1	2-2	1-0	4-1	2-1	2-0	2-0	0-0	1-5	0-1	1-0	0-1	0-1	2-4	2-1
Croydon	0-0	2-1	2-0	—	0-1	1-1	0-1	1-1	3-0	3-3	0-3	1-1	3-1	0-0	1-0	1-2	1-1	0-2	0-0	0-1	0-2	0-0
Dorking	2-0	2-3	2-1	2-0	—	3-0	1-1	0-0	2-1	1-1	2-2	0-1	5-1	0-0	3-0	2-1	1-1	1-2	3-2	1-2	0-0	1-1
Hampton	0-1	2-0	1-2	1-0	1-0	—	0-2	0-1	1-0	0-0	0-1	1-2	1-1	1-2	4-2	1-1	0-0	0-1	2-2	0-3	0-1	0-1
Harlow Town	1-1	1-2	5-1	0-0	0-0	1-1	—	0-1	4-0	0-2	3-1	2-2	0-1	0-3	0-1	3-1	3-2	3-2	2-2	1-2	2-2	4-1
Hitchin Town	2-2	2-0	1-0	2-1	3-1	2-1	1-1	—	1-1	2-0	1-0	2-0	0-1	0-0	3-0	3-0	1-0	2-1	0-1	1-3	1-3	2-1
Kingsbury	0-1	0-0	0-0	4-1	1-4	4-1	0-3	1-1	—	2-0	0-1	2-2	1-0	2-3	0-1	2-2	0-3	2-2	3-1	0-1	1-3	2-1
Leatherhead	2-3	1-0	0-1	0-1	0-2	0-0	1-2	0-3	2-0	—	1-1	1-0	2-1	1-4	2-3	0-2	1-1	1-2	1-2	0-1	0-2	1-3
Lewes	2-1	0-1	0-1	1-3	2-2	0-0	0-2	1-2	3-3	0-0	—	0-1	2-2	0-0	3-1	3-1	2-4	3-1	4-1	0-0	0-3	0-1
Metropolitan Police	3-1	1-1	1-5	2-1	2-1	0-1	0-1	1-1	1-0	1-1	3-0	—	1-0	0-4	1-2	4-2	0-4	2-0	0-0	1-3	3-3	2-1
Purfleet	1-2	2-2	0-0	3-0	0-4	1-0	2-3	1-1	0-5	2-0	1-3	1-2	—	2-3	0-0	0-1	1-2	2-1	0-1	1-2	0-1	0-0
Southwick	1-0	0-2	1-1	3-1	2-0	3-1	0-0	0-0	6-0	3-0	1-0	2-0	2-1	—	1-0	0-0	3-2	1-0	4-0	1-1	1-1	1-1
Tooting & Mitcham	0-1	0-0	2-0	0-0	2-1	0-0	0-1	0-4	1-1	0-0	3-1	1-1	4-0	5-1	—	0-3	2-1	2-1	0-0	2-1	2-2	2-1
Uxbridge	2-2	0-0	1-2	1-2	0-3	0-0	2-2	0-2	1-0	3-0	0-3	2-0	3-1	0-4	0-0	—	0-1	2-6	0-1	0-3	2-3	1-1
Walton & Hersham	1-4	1-1	0-0	1-5	2-1	0-0	1-0	2-1	1-0	4-2	0-0	2-1	3-0	1-2	4-0	2-1	—	4-1	1-1	1-3	1-1	3-0
Wembley	1-2	1-1	1-1	1-1	1-3	3-1	0-0	0-0	1-2	3-1	0-1	0-1	3-0	2-3	2-2	2-1	1-0	—	0-0	1-5	0-3	1-2
Whyteleafe	3-2	2-3	2-2	1-1	1-1	0-1	5-2	1-1	3-0	2-3	2-2	1-3	1-2	1-1	1-0	0-2	0-3	1-1	—	0-4	0-0	1-2
Wivenhoe Town	3-2	3-1	3-1	3-2	1-1	2-1	0-0	1-0	3-0	4-0	2-1	2-2	2-0	1-1	0-1	5-2	4-1	4-1	4-1	—	1-2	3-1
Woking	1-2	4-1	1-0	5-0	3-0	2-0	4-0	3-0	3-0	6-0	6-0	1-0	4-0	1-0	2-0	6-1	3-1	2-1	0-1	1-2	—	2-1
Worthing	2-2	3-2	0-2	2-2	0-2	2-0	2-0	0-2	3-0	1-2	3-2	2-4	2-0	0-1	3-1	1-2	0-2	2-2	2-1	1-3	2-1	—

DIVISION ONE RESULTS 1989–90

Final table for season 1989–90

		Home			*Away*						
	P	*W*	*D*	*L*	*W*	*D*	*L*	*F*	*A*	*GD*	*Pts*
Wivenhoe Town	42	15	4	2	16	3	2	94	36	58	100
Woking	42	18	0	3	12	8	1	102	29	73	98
Southwick	42	13	7	1	10	8	3	68	30	38	84
Hitchin Town	42	13	4	4	9	9	3	60	30	30	79
Walton & Hersh	42	11	6	4	9	4	8	68	50	18	70
Dorking	42	9	8	4	10	4	7	66	41	25	69
Boreham Wood	42	9	7	5	8	6	7	60	59	1	64
Harlow Town	42	7	7	7	9	6	6	60	53	7	61
Met Police	42	9	5	7	7	6	8	54	59	–5	59
Chesham Utd	42	9	5	7	6	7	8	46	49	–3	57
Chalfont St. Peter	42	9	6	6	5	7	9	50	59	–9	55
Tooting & Mitcham	42	9	8	4	5	5	11	42	51	–9	55
Worthing	42	9	3	9	6	5	10	56	63	–7	53
Whyteleafe	42	4	8	9	7	8	6	50	65	–15	49
Lewes	42	5	7	9	7	4	10	55	65	–10	47
Wembley	42	5	7	9	6	3	12	57	68	–11	43
Croydon	42	5	9	7	4	7	10	43	57	–14	43
Uxbridge	42	4	6	11	7	4	10	52	75	–23	43
Hampton	42	5	5	11	3	8	10	28	51	–23	37
Leatherhead	42	4	3	14	3	7	11	34	77	–43	31
Purfleet	42	4	5	12	3	3	15	33	78	–45	29
Kingsbury*	42	6	6	9	2	4	15	45	78	–33	25

*Kingsbury –9 points by order of the League

Leading goalscorers

		Lge	*AC*
39	Tim Buzaglo (Woking)	33	6
26	Steve Clark (Wivenhoe T)	26	
22	Phil Coleman (Wivenhoe T)	22	
21	Terry Worsfold (Dorking) *(Includes 1 for Woking)*	21	
	Paul Mulvaney (Woking)	18	3
19	Jeff Wood (Harlow)	18	1

VAUXHALL FOOTBALL LEAGUE

	Aveley	Barton Rovers	Basildon Utd	Berkhamsted Town	Billericay Town	Clapton	Collier Row	Finchley	Hemel Hempstead	Hertford Town	Heybridge Swifts	Hornchurch	Letchworth Garden City	Rainham Town	Royston Town	Saffron Walden Town	Stevenage Borough	Tilbury	Tring Town	Vauxhall Motors	Ware	Witham Town
Aveley	—	3-0	0-1	3-1	0-0	0-0	0-0	1-1	1-1	1-1	1-0	0-0	3-0	3-1	3-0	2-2	1-1	3-2	4-1	0-0	0-0	1-0
Barton Rovers	3-1	—	0-0	1-3	0-0	1-0	1-2	1-0	1-0	1-2	0-1	3-0	3-1	3-1	2-0	0-0	0-2	1-0	2-2	1-0	2-0	1-0
Basildon Utd	1-2	0-1	—	2-3	1-0	0-0	1-1	3-3	4-0	0-1	1-1	0-0	0-0	2-2	0-1	1-1	1-1	2-1	1-0	1-1	0-2	1-1
Berkhamsted Town	2-1	2-2	0-2	—	1-4	0-2	0-1	1-1	2-2	2-2	0-3	0-3	2-0	2-1	0-2	3-0	2-2	0-1	2-0	0-3	2-2	2-2
Billericay Town	0-3	4-2	1-1	2-0	—	0-4	2-1	0-0	1-1	4-0	0-1	0-2	1-2	5-0	1-1	2-1	0-0	0-2	0-1	1-2	5-0	0-3
Clapton	1-2	0-2	0-0	1-1	2-2	—	0-2	2-1	1-1	3-2	0-2	1-2	3-1	1-2	4-1	1-1	2-0	3-0	0-1	3-0	2-0	3-0
Collier Row	0-3	1-3	0-2	1-3	2-1	0-0	—	1-1	2-1	1-1	0-1	0-0	2-0	0-3	1-4	0-3	0-0	1-3	2-1	1-1	1-0	5-1
Finchley	0-1	0-3	0-2	2-1	1-1	2-3	0-3	—	1-0	0-3	2-3	1-2	4-0	1-0	5-1	1-1	0-4	2-1	0-3	1-1	2-3	1-0
Hemel Hempstead	1-1	1-0	3-1	2-1	1-0	4-0	1-1	4-1	—	1-4	1-4	3-1	1-1	0-1	2-2	0-0	0-4	3-1	1-1	1-1	0-3	0-1
Hertford Town	1-1	1-0	0-0	6-0	4-0	4-2	0-3	1-1	3-2	—	3-1	2-0	3-1	5-1	1-2	5-2	2-3	2-2	4-1	4-3	1-0	2-0
Heybridge Swifts	1-1	2-1	1-0	0-0	5-0	0-0	0-2	5-0	4-0	0-0	—	0-1	0-0	1-0	0-1	6-0	1-0	6-1	4-1	5-1	0-2	3-1
Hornchurch	0-0	2-4	1-1	0-0	1-1	1-0	1-0	4-2	1-1	0-2	1-4	—	1-1	4-3	3-4	1-2	0-2	2-3	0-2	1-2	1-4	2-1
Letchworth Garden C	0-3	2-3	0-1	2-2	0-1	0-0	0-0	3-0	0-1	0-4	0-2	0-3	—	1-1	0-3	0-0	0-0	1-2	1-3	0-1	2-1	1-0
Rainham Town	0-0	2-1	1-2	1-1	1-2	1-1	3-0	0-2	2-4	1-1	2-2	1-0	0-2	—	0-2	2-3	1-1	0-1	2-1	0-3	1-2	1-0
Royston Town	0-1	0-4	1-1	2-0	1-3	1-2	2-1	2-3	3-3	1-2	1-2	2-2	1-3	2-2	—	1-2	0-0	0-0	2-1	2-2	2-4	2-2
Saffron Walden	1-4	2-0	2-2	2-0	2-0	2-2	0-2	1-0	2-0	3-2	2-0	3-1	3-2	2-0	1-2	—	1-2	1-2	1-3	1-1	0-5	2-1
Stevenage Town	0-3	2-0	3-3	0-0	1-0	5-0	0-1	2-0	2-1	2-1	2-2	1-0	0-0	1-1	4-0	4-1	—	1-1	1-1	3-1	4-1	0-0
Tilbury	0-2	1-2	4-1	0-1	5-2	0-0	0-0	2-1	3-3	1-3	1-1	2-0	1-0	3-1	3-0	3-3	0-1	—	3-1	0-1	5-0	1-0
Tring Town	0-4	0-1	2-3	0-0	0-1	0-0	0-0	2-3	2-2	1-2	0-1	1-1	5-0	3-0	0-5	2-1	1-3	0-2	—	1-3	1-2	1-1
Vauxhall Motors	0-2	3-1	1-2	4-1	2-0	0-0	0-1	3-1	1-2	3-3	0-1	0-2	1-1	2-1	1-2	2-1	1-3	0-1	3-0	—	0-2	0-0
Ware	1-2	1-1	1-1	0-0	0-1	0-0	1-0	1-1	2-3	1-1	0-2	1-1	3-1	1-3	0-1	2-1	0-3	1-2	0-1	0-0	—	2-2
Witham Town	0-1	1-2	1-2	1-1	1-1	2-1	1-1	0-2	3-0	0-1	0-1	4-1	0-1	2-2	1-1	4-1	1-0	2-2	2-1	1-1	1-2	—

DIVISION TWO NORTH RESULTS 1989–90

Final table for season 1989–90

		Home			*Away*						
	P	*W*	*D*	*L*	*W*	*D*	*L*	*F*	*A*	*GD*	*Pts*
Heybridge Swifts	42	12	5	4	14	4	3	79	29	50	87
Aveley	42	9	11	1	14	5	2	68	24	44	85
Hertford Town	42	14	4	3	10	7	4	92	51	41	83
Stevenage Boro	42	11	8	2	10	8	3	70	31	39	79
Barton Rovers	42	12	4	5	10	2	9	60	45	15	72
Tilbury	42	10	5	6	10	4	7	68	54	14	69
Basildon Utd	42	4	11	6	9	9	3	50	44	6	59
Collier Row	42	6	6	9	9	7	5	43	45	-2	58
Royston Town	42	3	8	10	12	3	6	63	72	–9	56
Saffron Walden	42	11	3	7	4	8	9	60	73	–13	56
Vauxhall Motors	42	7	4	10	7	9	5	55	54	1	55
Clapton*	42	9	5	7	4	11	6	50	46	4	54
Ware	42	3	9	9	11	2	8	53	59	–6	53
Hemel Hempstead	42	8	7	6	4	8	9	58	70	–12	51
Billericay	42	7	5	9	6	6	9	49	58	–9	50
Hornchurch	42	5	6	10	7	6	8	49	64	–15	48
Berkhamsted	42	5	7	9	4	9	8	44	68	–24	43
Finchley	42	7	3	11	4	7	10	50	75	–25	43
Tring Town	42	3	6	12	7	3	11	48	70	–22	39
Witham Town	42	6	7	8	2	7	12	44	56	–12	38
Rainham Town	42	5	6	10	4	5	12	48	75	–27	38
Letchworth G.C.	42	3	6	12	4	6	11	30	68	–38	33

*Clapton –1 point by order of the League

Leading goalscorers

		Lge	*AC*
30	Paddy Butcher (Royston T)	30	
	Kevin Newbury (Heybridge Swifts)	28	2
29	Micky Fredericks (Hertford T)	29	
23	Robert McComb (Stevenage Bor.) *(Includes 5 for Hertford T)*	23	
21	Robert Smith (Barton Rovers)	20	1

VAUXHALL FOOTBALL LEAGUE

	Abingdon Town	Banstead Athletic	Bracknell Town	Camberley Town	Chertsey Town	Eastbourne United	Egham Town	Epsom & Ewell	Feltham	Flackwell Heath	Harefield United	Horsham	Hungerford Town	Maidenhead United	Malden Vale	Molesey	Newbury Town	Petersfield	Ruislip Manor	Southall	Yeading
Abingdon Town	—	5-3	2-0	1-0	1-0	4-0	2-1	2-1	4-2	3-2	2-0	1-1	2-2	1-0	1-0	0-0	2-0	7-0	1-1	0-1	2-3
Banstead Athletic	0-1	—	1-1	7-1	0-2	0-0	1-0	0-1	4-1	2-2	1-0	1-0	1-0	3-0	0-1	0-2	1-3	0-1	1-2	0-0	0-1
Bracknell Town	0-3	1-1	—	2-3	0-2	1-2	0-2	0-3	3-1	7-0	1-0	1-0	0-1	2-3	3-1	0-2	0-2	1-1	0-0	0-2	2-3
Camberley Town	2-1	1-0	0-0	—	1-0	1-1	1-2	0-0	4-0	3-2	0-1	1-3	4-1	0-3	0-1	0-7	2-0	3-3	1-2	2-0	0-2
Chertsey Town	1-2	3-1	0-0	0-0	—	1-2	2-0	1-1	4-1	1-3	1-3	1-1	2-2	2-6	2-0	2-1	1-0	2-0	0-1	1-2	2-3
Eastbourne Utd	0-0	1-2	1-2	2-0	1-2	—	1-1	1-0	0-1	2-0	1-3	2-1	2-1	1-1	2-2	3-5	0-1	3-1	0-4	2-0	1-1
Egham Town	0-1	0-0	4-0	1-1	3-2	3-2	—	1-1	1-0	0-2	0-1	3-0	0-0	0-1	4-1	0-1	1-0	2-2	1-1	2-2	0-1
Epsom & Ewell	3-0	1-1	2-3	1-0	1-2	3-1	0-0	—	0-2	2-2	0-2	4-1	1-0	0-2	0-1	0-0	0-1	2-1	0-5	0-2	1-2
Feltham	1-3	2-1	1-0	2-2	1-1	2-1	1-1	0-3	—	3-4	0-1	3-1	2-0	0-1	1-0	1-4	0-3	1-3	3-2	0-1	2-1
Flackwell Heath	2-1	1-1	3-1	1-0	4-2	1-1	1-1	1-1	0-2	—	2-0	3-0	1-1	3-0	3-1	1-1	0-2	4-0	1-0	3-5	0-2
Harefield United	1-1	0-1	1-1	2-0	0-3	3-0	0-1	2-3	1-1	3-3	—	1-0	0-1	0-1	0-1	3-2	0-0	3-2	0-0	0-1	3-2
Horsham	0-2	0-1	0-0	0-2	0-1	1-4	0-1	0-3	3-0	0-0	0-4	—	2-2	1-3	2-4	1-2	0-1	1-2	2-3	0-2	0-1
Hungerford Town	1-0	3-2	0-3	3-3	3-2	1-1	0-0	3-1	2-0	3-2	0-0	2-1	—	1-3	1-1	2-1	1-1	4-0	1-1	2-1	0-1
Maidenhead United	0-0	1-2	0-0	1-0	1-1	1-0	0-0	1-0	5-2	4-3	0-0	1-1	2-0	—	2-3	1-1	0-0	5-2	0-0	1-0	2-1
Maiden Vale	0-0	0-2	2-0	1-3	1-0	0-3	1-0	0-5	2-0	1-2	1-1	0-1	1-1	0-6	—	0-2	2-0	3-0	0-2	0-1	0-5
Molesey	2-0	1-0	0-1	2-0	3-0	1-1	2-0	3-1	4-1	2-2	1-0	2-1	1-1	0-0	3-0	—	1-1	2-1	3-1	0-0	1-0
Newbury Town	1-2	1-0	1-0	1-0	3-1	5-1	1-1	3-0	3-2	1-0	1-0	0-1	2-4	2-1	1-1	2-1	—	2-0	0-2	1-1	1-2
Petersfield	1-1	1-3	2-4	2-0	2-2	2-1	0-1	3-2	2-2	3-0	3-2	2-1	0-0	0-4	2-2	0-3	1-2	—	0-2	0-2	1-3
Ruislip Manor	4-1	2-0	2-0	2-2	1-1	2-0	1-0	0-0	3-1	1-0	2-1	1-1	0-1	1-1	2-0	2-2	2-0	0-1	—	1-0	2-3
Southall	0-1	1-2	2-0	4-1	1-0	2-0	1-0	4-0	2-2	1-3	3-0	2-0	2-1	1-0	0-1	0-3	0-1	4-0	2-0	—	1-2
Yeading	3-1	3-0	1-0	2-0	2-0	3-0	4-1	1-2	0-0	1-2	3-2	1-1	2-2	5-2	4-0	1-2	2-0	7-1	1-0	1-0	—

DIVISION TWO SOUTH RESULTS 1989–90

Final table for season 1989–90

		Home			Away						
	P	*W*	*D*	*L*	*W*	*D*	*L*	*F*	*A*	*GD*	*Pts*
Yeading	40	14	3	3	15	1	4	86	37	49	91
Molesey	40	13	6	1	11	5	4	76	30	46	83
Abingdon Town	40	14	4	2	8	5	7	64	39	25	75
Ruislip Manor	40	11	6	3	9	6	5	60	32	28	72
Maidenhead Utd	40	9	9	2	11	3	6	66	39	27	72
Southall	40	12	1	7	10	4	6	56	33	23	71
Newbury	40	12	3	5	9	4	7	50	36	14	70
Flackwell Heath	40	10	6	4	6	5	9	69	65	4	59
Hungerford	40	10	7	3	4	9	7	54	51	3	58
Egham Town	40	7	7	6	5	7	8	39	38	1	50
Banstead Athletic	40	7	4	9	7	4	9	46	47	–1	50
Harefield	40	6	6	8	7	3	10	44	46	–2	48
Chertsey Town	40	7	5	8	6	4	10	53	58	–5	48
Epsom & Ewell	40	6	4	10	7	5	8	49	54	–5	48
Malden Vale	40	6	3	11	7	4	9	36	67	–31	46
Eastbourne Utd	40	7	5	8	4	5	11	47	65	–18	43
Camberley	40	8	4	8	3	5	12	44	66	–22	42
Feltham	40	8	3	9	3	4	13	47	80	–33	40
Bracknell	40	5	3	12	5	6	9	40	57	–17	39
Petersfield	40	6	5	9	4	3	13	48	93	–45	38
Horsham	40	1	3	16	3	5	12	29	70	–41	20

Leading goalscorers

		Lge	*AC*
23	Michael Rose (Moseley)	21	2
	Paul Sweales (Yeading)	23	
21	Tony Wood (Flackwell H)	21	
19	Victor Schwartz (Yeading)	18	1

Ovenden Papers Football Combination

	P	W	D	L	F	A	Pts
Arsenal	38	26	6	6	84	51	84
Tottenham Hotspur	38	25	6	7	93	47	81
Chelsea	38	22	6	10	78	47	72
Millwall	38	20	11	7	58	36	71
Norwich City	38	20	7	11	66	41	67
Wimbledon	38	18	9	11	69	46	63
West Ham Utd	38	18	7	13	83	59	61
Oxford Utd	38	16	9	13	73	58	57
Brighton & HA	38	15	6	17	52	66	51
Portsmouth	38	12	13	13	47	57	49
Swindon Town	38	15	3	20	58	68	48
Luton Town	38	13	8	17	68	70	47
Q.P.R.	38	14	5	19	65	93	47
Crystal Palace	38	11	10	17	56	50	43
Southampton	38	10	12	16	45	58	42
Ipswich Town	38	12	5	21	60	75	41
Watford	38	11	8	19	59	79	41
Reading	38	11	8	19	64	86	41
Charlton Athletic	38	11	6	21	49	70	39
Fulham	38	4	7	27	25	95	19

The Bass North West Counties League – First Division

	P	W	D	L	F	A	Pts
Warrington Town	34	22	6	6	69	31	72
Knowsley United	34	21	6	7	68	45	69
Colwyn Bay	34	16	12	6	79	50	60
Vauxhall G.M.	34	16	9	9	50	42	57
Clitheroe	34	17	6	11	48	47	57
Darwen	34	15	9	10	40	34	54
Nantwich Town	34	13	5	16	50	52	44
St. Helens Town	34	10	13	11	50	48	43
Ashton United	34	11	10	13	39	45	43
Prescot Cables	34	10	11	13	49	54	41
Bootle	34	11	8	15	44	58	41
Flixton	34	11	7	16	37	47	40
Leyland Motors	34	10	7	17	55	64	37
Atherton L.R.	34	8	13	13	43	58	37
Skelmersdale United	34	8	11	15	48	59	35
Salford	34	8	11	15	31	47	35
Burscough	34	8	12	14	38	41	*33
Chadderton	34	7	12	15	39	55	33

* Denotes points deducted for breach of rules.

Central League – First Division

	P	W	D	L	F	A	Pts
Liverpool	34	24	4	6	74	42	76
Nottingham Forest	34	19	6	9	79	48	63
Aston Villa	34	17	7	10	84	42	58
Manchester United	34	17	7	10	54	39	58
Manchester City	34	18	3	13	64	51	57
Leicester City	34	16	8	10	51	48	56
Derby County	34	16	7	11	64	47	55
Everton	34	16	5	13	58	53	53
Leeds United	34	14	8	12	62	49	50
Blackburn Rovers	34	14	8	12	69	59	50
Newcastle United	34	15	5	14	42	50	50
Sheffield United	34	14	5	15	47	46	47
Coventry City	34	12	5	17	50	64	41
Huddersfield Town	34	11	5	18	40	64	38
Notts County	34	8	9	17	44	90	33
Bradford City	34	8	6	20	41	64	30
Hull City	34	6	6	22	47	74	24
Oldham Athletic	34	6	6	22	34	74	24

Central League – Second Division

	P	W	D	L	F	A	Pts
Sunderland	34	20	8	6	68	32	68
Rotherham United	34	20	6	8	61	31	66
Sheffield Wednesday	34	19	6	9	69	36	63
Wolverhampton Wanderers	34	17	10	7	91	43	61
West Bromwich Albion	34	16	10	8	64	36	58
Stoke City	34	14	8	12	50	44	50
Middlesbrough	34	12	13	9	48	34	49
Barnsley	34	15	4	15	54	50	49
Scunthorpe United	34	14	7	13	48	47	49
Port Vale	34	13	9	12	58	63	48
York City	34	13	5	16	43	53	44
Bolton Wanderers	34	10	11	13	47	55	41
Mansfield Town	34	12	5	17	36	55	41
Wigan Athletic	34	11	7	16	41	49	40
Blackpool	34	10	9	15	40	60	39
Preston North End	34	10	5	19	30	71	35
Grimsby Town	34	6	8	20	35	65	26
Burnley	34	7	3	24	30	69	24

Skol Northern League – First Division

	P	*W*	*D*	*L*	*F*	*A*	*Pts*
Billingham Synthonia	38	29	4	5	87	35	91
Gretna	38	23	6	9	79	44	75
Tow Law Town	38	22	7	9	78	57	73
Newcastle Blue Star	38	19	10	9	77	48	67
Stockton	38	18	8	12	73	64	62
Consett	38	16	9	13	57	61	57
Guisborough Town	38	16	8	14	59	46	56
Alnwick Town	38	16	6	16	59	54	54
Blyth Spartans	38	15	8	15	58	58	53
Seaham Red Star	38	15	7	16	62	66	52
Spennymoor United	38	14	8	16	58	53	50
Whitby Town*	38	15	8	15	74	73	50
Ferryhill Athletic	38	14	4	20	63	79	46
Shildon	38	12	10	16	58	75	46
Whickham	38	11	7	20	48	69	40
South Bank	38	10	10	18	40	65	40
Durham City	38	9	12	17	64	77	39
Brandon United	38	9	12	17	46	60	39
Billingham Town	38	10	9	19	52	67	39
Easington Colliery	38	6	9	23	29	70	27

Division Two

	P	*W*	*D*	*L*	*F*	*A*	*Pts*
Murton	38	27	8	3	86	33	89
Northallerton Town	38	26	9	3	82	32	87
Peterlee Newtown	38	24	10	4	71	24	82
Langley Park Welfare	38	24	8	6	67	35	80
Chester-le-Street Town	38	23	8	7	62	34	77
Crook Town	38	20	7	11	70	45	67
Evenwood Town	38	19	8	11	77	52	65
Prudhoe East End	38	17	10	11	63	49	61
Bedlington Terriers	38	17	5	16	67	72	56
Washington	38	16	4	18	50	58	52
Ryhope Community	38	14	6	18	68	67	48
Darling Cleveland Bridge*	38	13	7	18	45	72	43
Ashington	38	10	6	22	62	85	36
Willington	38	10	5	23	51	86	35
Hebburn	38	8	8	22	56	76	32
Horden Colliery Welfare	38	8	8	22	34	66	32
Shotton Comrades*	38	8	10	20	51	69	31
Norton & Stockton Ancients*	38	7	9	22	43	71	30
West Auckland Town	38	5	13	20	43	72	28
Esh Winning*	38	7	5	26	41	91	23

Nene Group United Counties League – Premier Division

	P	*W*	*D*	*L*	*F*	*A*	*Pts*
Holbeach	42	29	5	8	94	46	92
Rothwell	42	27	8	7	72	38	89
Raunds	42	20	10	12	67	42	70
Bourne	42	19	13	10	71	47	70
Cogenhoe	42	20	10	12	57	46	70
Stotfold	42	19	9	14	66	52	66
N'ton Spencer	42	19	9	14	63	51	66
M. Blackstone	42	18	12	12	73	63	66
Arlesey	42	17	10	15	55	60	61
Long Buckby	42	16	9	17	58	61	57
Hamlet S & L	42	12	17	13	46	42	53
Irthlingborough	42	14	10	18	64	66	52
Baker Perkins	42	14	9	19	50	63	51
Potton	42	12	14	16	54	48	50
Stamford	42	13	11	18	55	63	50
Desborough	42	13	11	18	65	77	50
Burton PW	42	12	12	18	48	67	48
M Wootton	42	12	11	19	52	71	47
Wellingborough	42	13	7	22	59	70	46
Brackley	42	12	10	20	46	67	46
Eynesbury	42	8	14	20	30	68	38
Kempston	42	8	9	25	41	78	33

Banks's Brewery League – Premier Division

	P	*W*	*D*	*L*	*F*	*A*	*Pts*
Hinckley Town	40	24	10	6	87	30	82
Rocester	40	25	7	8	85	44	82
Gresley Rovers	40	24	8	8	89	42	80
Blakenall	40	24	5	11	78	52	77
Lye Town	40	22	10	8	68	35	76
Hinckley Athletic	40	18	10	12	58	47	64
Wednesfield	40	16	14	10	60	44	62
Oldbury United	40	18	8	14	62	60	62
Halesowen Harriers	40	17	10	13	79	55	61
Chasetown	40	16	12	12	57	36	60
Paget Rangers	40	18	6	16	74	63	60
Harrisons STS	40	15	11	14	55	54	56
Malvern Town	40	15	10	15	62	62	55
Rushall Olympic	40	15	5	20	65	56	50
Stourport Swifts	40	12	10	18	40	59	46
Wolverhampton Casuals	40	10	9	21	41	80	39
Westfields	40	10	7	23	44	84	37
Oldswinford	40	10	5	25	39	82	35
Tividale	40	8	8	24	42	80	32
Millfields	40	6	9	25	39	90	27
Tipton Town	40	4	12	24	30	99	24

Great Mills League – Premier Division

	P	*W*	*D*	*L*	*F*	*A*	*Pts*
Taunton Town	40	28	8	4	80	41	92
Liskeard Athletic	40	28	7	5	91	30	91
Mangotsfield United	40	27	7	6	96	42	88
Tiverton Town	40	26	6	8	92	51	84
Exmouth Town	40	24	5	11	74	37	77
Weston Super Mare	40	20	8	12	86	56	68
Plymouth Argyle	40	19	10	11	75	47	67
Saltash United	40	19	9	12	62	41	66
Swanage & Herston	40	18	7	15	77	67	61
Clevedon Town	40	16	8	16	58	60	56
Paulton Rovers	40	16	7	17	51	52	55
Bristol Manor Farm	40	13	12	15	49	59	51
Chippenham Town	40	14	7	19	36	46	49
Dawlish Town	40	12	7	21	55	78	43
Chard Town	40	8	14	18	50	74	38
Bideford	40	8	14	18	37	76	38
Torrington	40	8	11	21	48	74	35
Barnstaple Town	40	8	10	22	38	75	34
Radstock Town	40	7	12	21	43	82	33
Frome Town	40	4	14	22	43	77	26
Welton Rovers	40	3	5	32	30	106	14

Highland League

	P	*W*	*D*	*L*	*F*	*A*	*Pts*
Elgin City	34	26	3	5	103	33	81
Caledonian	34	23	7	4	103	35	76
Peterhead	34	23	4	7	77	35	73
Inverness Thistle	34	23	4	7	69	31	73
Forres Mechanics	34	20	5	9	79	53	65
Cove Rangers	34	17	8	9	72	59	59
Fraserburgh	34	17	6	11	58	51	57
Huntly	34	17	5	12	72	46	56
Lossiemouth	34	15	5	14	77	67	50
Buckie Thistle	34	14	7	13	63	53	49
Ross County	34	13	5	16	54	54	44
Keith	34	11	8	15	49	45	41
Fort William	34	12	4	18	59	73	40
Brora Rangers	34	9	6	19	52	80	33
Nairn County	34	9	6	19	51	90	33
Deveronvale	34	6	2	26	42	102	20
Rothes	34	4	6	24	36	84	18
Clachnacuddin	34	0	3	31	26	151	3

FA CHALLENGE VASE 1989–90

Third Round

Droylsden	3	Rossendale United	3

(tie awarded to Rossendale United as Droylsden played a suspended player)

Harrogate Town	3	Chester-le-Street Town	0
Warrington Town	3	Netherfield	1
Guiseley	4	Northallerton Town	2
Emley	3	Denaby United	1
Curzon Ashton	1	Bridlington Town	2
Darwen	1	St Helens Town	2
Peterlee Newtown	0	Farsley Celtic	1
Spalding United	1	Lye Town	0
Heanor Town	3	Paget Rangers	2
Hucknall Town	2	Boldmere St Michaels	1
Bourne Town	1	Eastwood Hanley	0
Raunds Town	1	Hinckley Athletic	0
Rushden Town	3	Wisbech Town	0
Yeading	1	East Thurrock United	0
Billericay Town	3	Aveley	1
Stotfold	0	Great Yarmouth Town	2
Walthamstow Pennant	1	Collier Row	2
Potton United	2	Stevenage Borough	0
Sudbury Town	4	Haverhill Rovers	1
Whitstable Town	1	Greenwich Borough	2
Bracknell Town	0	Harefield United	2
Eastleigh	1	Thatcham Town	2
Deal Town	0	Hythe Town	1
Hailsham Town	1 2	Hastings Town	1 5
Vale Recreation	0	Merstham	1
Chertsey Town	0	Molesey	2
Chard Town	2	Dawlish Town	1
Exmouth Town	0	Bashley	4
Abingdon Town	3	Brislington	2
Paulton Rovers	2	Yate Town	1
Falmouth Town	2	Newbury Town	1

Fourth Round

Guiseley	3	Rossendale United	1
Harrogate Town	1	Bridlington Town	3
Emley	2 3	Warrington Town	2 0
Farsley Celtic	1 0 1	St Helens Town	1 0 0
Bourne Town	1 1	Spalding United	1 3
Heanor Town	1	Rushden Town	2
Raunds Town	1	Hucknall Town	4
Sudbury Town	3	Great Yarmouth Town	4
Potton United	2 3	Hastings Town	2 1
Harefield United	1 5	Greenwich Borough	1 4
Yeading	1	Molesey	0
Merstham	2	Billericay Town	3
Hythe Town	1 3	Collier Row	1 1

Falmouth Town	0	Paulton Rovers	2
Bashley	1	Chard Town	0
Thatcham Town	0	Abingdon Town	1

Fifth Round

Farsley Celtic	1	Guiseley	3
Rushden Town	2	Emley	0
Great Yarmouth Town	0	Spalding United	2
Bridlington Town	5	Hucknall Town	2
Billericay Town	2	Potton United	1
Paulton Rovers	1 1	Yeading	1 2
Abingdon Town	1 1	Hythe Town	1 3
Harefield United	2	Bashley	1

Sixth Round

Rushden Town	0	Hythe Town	1
Yeading	2	Harefield United	0
Spalding United	1	Guiseley	3
Billericay Town	0	Bridlington Town	1

Semi-Finals *(2 legs)*

Hythe Town	3 0	Yeading	2 2
Guiseley	0 0	Bridlington Town	3 1

FINAL at Wembley, 5 May, att. 7932

Bridlington Town	(0) 0	Yeading	(0) 0

Replay at Leeds, 14 May, att. 5000

Yeading	(1) 1 *(Sweales)*	*Bridlington Town*	*(0) 0*

FA CHALLENGE TROPHY 1989–90

First Round Proper

Colne Dynamoes	5	Altrincham	0
Spennymoor United	1	Leek Town	2
Shepshed Charterhouse	1 0	Nuneaton Borough	1 1
Billingham Synthonia	2 1	Darlington	2 3
Stafford Rangers	2	Guisborough Town	1
Telford United	2	Burton Albion	1
Gretna	2 1 1	Hyde United	2 1 2
Northwich Victoria	1 3	Bishop Auckland	1 2
Sutton Coldfield Town	2 1	Tow Law Town	2 3
Barrow	1	Bangor City	0
Witton Albion	2	Blyth Spartans	0

(at Northwich Victoria FC)

Seaham Red Star	2	Marine	0
Newcastle Blue Star	0 1	Runcorn	0 4
Boston United	0 0	Macclesfield Town	0 3
Welling United	2	Fisher Athletic	0
Wivenhoe Town	2	Hendon	1
Kettering Town	0	Wokingham Town	2
Slough Town	1 0	Redbridge Forest	1 3

Wycombe Wanderers	1	Metropolitan Police	3
Leyton-Wingate	0	Kidderminster Harriers	3
Weston-Super-Mare	2	Windsor & Eton	3
Enfield	3	Merthyr Tydfil	2
Sutton United	0	Dover Athletic	1
Dartford	1	Yeovil Town	2
Farnborough Town	1	Staines Town	0
Ashford Town	0	Bath City	4
Weymouth	2	Barnet	0
Aylesbury United	2 1	Worcester City	2 0
Cheltenham Town	5	Gravesend & Northfleet	1
Wealdstone	1 0	Harrow Borough	1 1
Dagenham	2	Kingstonian	5
Woking	3	Bromsgrove Rovers	0

Second Round

Woking	3	Seaham Red Star	1
Leek Town	1 1	Nuneaton Borough	1 0
Kingstonian	2	Hyde United	1
Wokingham Town	0 1	Stafford Rangers	0 3
Darlington	1	Macclesfield Town	0
Barrow	1	Metropolitan Police	0
Harrow Borough	0 0	Redbridge Forest	0 2
Witton Albion	0 1	Kidderminster Harriers	0 2
Bath City	2	Tow Law Town	0
Cheltenham Town	3	Enfield	1
Farnborough Town	2	Windsor & Eton	1
Dover Athletic	2	Weymouth	1
Wivenhoe Town	1 2	Runcorn	1 3
Telford United	0 2	Welling United	0 0
Colne Dynamoes	1	Northwich Victoria	0
Yeovil Town	2	Aylesbury United	0

Third Round

Colne Dynamoes	2	Farnborough Town	1
Kingstonian	3 3	Cheltenham Town	3 0
Yeovil Town	1 1	Barrow	1 2
Stafford Rangers	1 2	Redbridge Forest	1 1
Telford United	0 0	Leek Town	0 3
Kidderminster Harriers	3	Dover Athletic	0
Darlington	1	Runcorn	0
Woking	1 1	Bath City	1 2

Fourth Round

Kingstonian	2 0	Barrow	2 1
Leek Town	1	Darlington	0
Kidderminster Harriers	0 1	Colne Dynamoes	0 2
Bath City	0	Stafford Rangers	2

Semi-Finals *(2 legs)*

Stafford Rangers	0 0	Leek Town	0 1
Colne Dynamoes	0 1	Barrow	1 2

FINAL at Wembley, 19 May, att. 19,011

Barrow	(1) 3	Leek Town	(0) 0

(Gordon 2, Cowperthwaite)

FA YOUTH CUP 1989-90

Second Round

Everton	0	Doncaster Rovers	2
Port Vale	4	Blackburn Rovers	0
Newcastle United	1 2	Tranmere Rovers	1 0
Oldham Athletic	0	Liverpool	1
Leeds United	4	Carlisle United	1
Sheffield Wednesday	5	Sheffield United	1
Wigan Athletic	4	Darlington	0
Scunthorpe United	1 0	Middlesbrough	1 2
Burnley	0	Manchester United	2
Wrexham	1	Manchester City	6
Coventry City	2	Birmingham City	0
Watford	2	Aston Villa	1
Cambridge United	1	Wolverhampton Wanderers	2
Kingsbury Town	1 0	Leicester City	1 8
Ipswich Town	11	Rothwell Town	1
Derby County	1	West Bromwich Albion	2
Grimsby Town	1	Colchester United	2
Stoke City	1	Southend United	2
Notts County	3	Nottingham Forest	0
Arsenal	2 4	Luton Town	2 2
Bristol City	0	Plymouth Argyle	4
Whyteleafe	2	Wokingham Town	3
Chelsea	5	Maidenhead United	1
Portsmouth	3	Millwall	1
Southampton	0	Crystal Palace	2
Swansea City	6	Carshalton Athletic	1
Queen's Park Rangers	3	Reading	1
Exeter City	1	Gillingham	2
Leyton Orient	2 2	Brighton & Hove Albion	2 1
Tottenham Hotspur		AFC Bournemouth	

(tie awarded to Tottenham Hotspur FC as AFC Bournemouth failed to fulfil fixture)

Oxford United	4	Charlton Athletic	0
Brentford	1	Wimbledon	0

Third Round

Liverpool	5	Newcastle United	0
Wolverhampton Wanderers	3	Leeds United	2
Doncaster Rovers	2	West Bromwich Albion	4
Notts County	0	Middlesbrough	2
Sheffield Wednesday	2	Wigan Athletic	0
Port Vale	0	Manchester United	3
Manchester City	0 6	Coventry City	0 1
Colchester United	0	Tottenham Hotspur	3
Oxford United	1	Arsenal	5
Ipswich Town	1	Chelsea	0
Wokingham Town	2 1	Swansea City	2 3
Crystal Palace	1	Brentford	1 0
Watford	3	Southend United	0

Portsmouth	1 3	Queen's Park Rangers	1 2
Leyton Orient	1 1	Gillingham	1 2
Leicester City	5	Plymouth Argyle	0

Fourth Round

Tottenham Hotspur	4	Wolverhampton Wanderers	1
Watford	1	Leicester City	5
Manchester City	3	Crystal Palace	0
Manchester United	3	Sheffield Wednesday	1
Arsenal	0	Portsmouth	1
West Bromwich Albion	3	Gillingham	0
Middlesbrough	2	Ipswich Town	0
Swansea City	0	Liverpool	1

Fifth Round

Middlesbrough	2	West Bromwich Albion	0
Manchester City	1	Tottenham Hotspur	2
Manchester United	2	Leicester City	0
Liverpool	2 1	Portsmouth	2 2

Semi-finals *(2 legs)*

Portsmouth	0 1	Middlesbrough	1 3
Tottenham Hotspur	2 1	Manchester United	0 1

Final *(2 legs)*

Middlesbrough (0) 1 *(Tucker)* — Tottenham H (1) 2 *(Houghton, Potts)*
att. 8000

Tottenham H (1) 1 *(Morah)* — Middlesbrough ...... (0) 1 *(Fletcher)*
att. 5579

FA SUNDAY CUP 1989–90

Second Round

Annfield Plain Morrison S	3	Framwellgate Moor	1
Humbledon Plains Farm	2	Queens Arms	0
Sir Robert Peel	0	Gibraltar	3
Blyth Waterloo SC	2	Nicosia	3
Northwood	4	Almithak	1
Royal Oak	4	Overpool United	1
Clubmoor Nalgo	2	East Levenshulme	5
Lobster	1	Baildon Athletic	0
East Bowling Unity	3 1	Blue Union	3 3
Iron Bridge	1	East & West Toxteth	2
Broadoak Hotel	1	Avenue Victoria Lodge	4
Sandwell	1	Railway Hotel	0
Woodpecker	2	Oakenshaw	1
Marston Sports	4	Inter Volante	2
Brereton Town	1	Cork & Bottle	0
Hallen Sunday	1	FC Coachman	4
Brookdale Athletic	1	Goodwin Lock	0
Shouldham Sunday	1	Grosvenor Park	3

Lodge Cottrell	3	Welwyn Youth	1
Kettering Odyssey	2	Newey Goodman	1
Olympic Star	4	Chequers	2
Hazel Tennants	3	Poringland Wanderers	5
Girton Eagles	0	Ford Basildon	2
Slade Celtic	4	Norbridge	1
Oak Hill United	1	Ranelagh Sports	0
Concord Rangers	0	Lee Chapel North	1
Santogee 66	2	Whittingham	1
St Josephs (Sth Oxley)	1	Leyton Argyle	3
Merton Admiral	5	Broad Plain House	0
Lebeq Tavern Easton	3	ABP	1
AFC Bishopstoke	0	Artois United	2
Bedfont	4	Inter Royalle	1

Third Round

Royal Oak	1	Lobster	2
East Levenshulme	0	Humbledon Plains Farm	1
Blue Union	0	Nicosia	3
Northwood	2	Annfield Plain Morrison Sports	3
East & West Toxteth	3	Gibraltar	0
Lebeq Tavern	2	Olympic Star	3
Slade Celtic	0	Brookvale Athletic	1
Sandwell	2	Woodpecker	1
Avenue Victoria Lodge	3	FC Coachman	1
Kettering Odyssey	1	Marston Sports	3
Grosvenor Park	1	Brereton Town	5
Leyton Argyle	5	Artois United	0
Merton Admiral	2	Ford Basildon	3
Bedfont	0	Lee Chapel North	1
Santogee 66	1	Poringland Wanderers	3
Lodge Cottrell	4	Oak Hill United	2

Fourth Round

Sandwell	2	Annfield Plain Morrison Sports	0
Nicosia	2	Lobster	0
East & West Toxteth	3	Brereton Town	1
Avenue Victoria Lodge	2 0	Humbledon Plains Farm	2 3
Lee Chapel North	2 3	Leyton Argyle	2 1
Marston Sports	3	Olympic Star	1
Ford Basildon	2 1 0	Lodge Cottrell	2 1 2
Poringland Wanderers	3	Brookvale Athletic	1

Fifth Round

Sandwell	2	East & West Toxteth	3
Nicosia	0	Humbledon Plains Farm	1
Lee Chapel North	2	Lodge Cottrell	0
Marston Sports	3	Poringland Wanderers	2

Semi-Finals

East & West Toxteth	0	Humbledon Plains Farm	2
Marston Sports	1	Lee Chapel North	0

Final

Marston Sports	1	Humbledon Plains Farm	2

(at West Bromwich Albion FC, 6 May)

FOOTBALL AWARDS 1989–90

Footballer of the Year

The Football Writers' Association this year voted the Liverpool and English player John Barnes Footballer of the Year.

Past winners: 1947–8 Stanley Matthews (Blackpool), 1948–9 Johnnie Carey (Manchester U), 1949–50 Joe Mercer (Arsenal), 1950–1 Harry Johnston (Blackpool), 1951–2 Billy Wright (Wolverhampton W), 1952–3 Nat Lofthouse (Bolton W), 1953–4 Tom Finney (Preston NE), 1954–5 Don Revie (Manchester C), 1955–6 Bert Trautmann (Manchester C), 1956–7 Tom Finney (Preston NE), 1957–8 Danny Blanchflower (Tottenham H), 1958–9 Sid Owen (Luton T), 1959–60 Bill Slater (Wolverhampton W), 1960–1 Danny Blanchflower (Tottenham H), 1961–2 Jimmy Adamson (Burnley), 1962–3 Stanley Matthews (Stoke C), 1963–4 Bobby Moore (West Ham U), 1964–5 Bobby Collins (Leeds U), 1965–6 Bobby Charlton (Manchester U), 1966–7 Jackie Charlton (Leeds U), 1967–8 George Best (Manchester U), 1968–9 Dave MacKay (Derby Co), Tony Book (Manchester C), 1969–70 Billy Bremner (Leeds U), 1970–1 Frank McLintock (Arsenal), 1971–2 Gordon Banks (Stoke C), 1972–3 Pat Jennings (Tottenham H), 1973–4 Ian Callaghan (Liverpool), 1974–5 Alan Mullery (Fulham), 1975–6 Kevin Keegan (Liverpool), 1976–7 Emlyn Hughes (Liverpool), 1977–8 Kenny Burns (Nottingham F), 1978–9 Kenny Dalglish (Liverpool), 1979–80 Terry McDermott (Liverpool), 1980–1 Frans Thijssen (Ipswich T), 1981–2 Steve Perryman (Tottenham H), 1982–3 Kenny Dalglish (Liverpool), 1983–4 Ian Rush (Liverpool), 1984–5 Neville Southall (Everton), 1985–6 Gary Lineker (Everton), 1986–7 Clive Allen (Tottenham H), 1987–8 John Barnes (Liverpool), 1988–89 Steve Nicol (Liverpool).

PFA Player of the Year

The Professional Footballers' Association chose David Platt (Aston Villa) as their Player of the Year.

Past winners: 1974 Norman Hunter (Leeds U), 1975 Colin Todd (Derby Co), 1976 Pat Jennings (Tottenham H), 1977 Andy Gray (Aston Villa), 1978 Peter Shilton (Nottingham F), 1979 Liam Brady (Arsenal), 1980 Terry McDermott (Liverpool), 1981 John Wark (Ipswich T), 1982 Kevin Keegan OBE (Southampton), 1983 Kenny Dalglish (Liverpool), 1984 Ian Rush (Liverpool), 1985 Peter Reid (Everton), 1986 Gary Lineker (Everton), 1987 Clive Allen (Tottenham H), 1988 John Barnes (Liverpool), 1989 Mark Hughes (Manchester U).

PFA Young Player of the Year 1989–90: Matthew Le Tissier (Southampton).

Barclays Manager of the Year 1989–90: Kenny Dalglish (Liverpool).

Scottish Football Writers' Association Player of the Year 1990: Alex McLeish (Aberdeen).

Past winners: 1965 Billy McNeill (Celtic), 1966 John Greig (Rangers), 1967 Ronnie Simpson (Celtic), 1968 Gordon Wallace (Raith R), 1969 Bobby Murdoch (Celtic) 1970 Pat Stanton (Hibernian), 1971 Martin Buchan (Aberdeen), 1972 Dave Smith (Rangers), 1973 George Connelly (Celtic), 1974 Scotland's World Cup Squad, 1975 Sandy Jardine (Rangers), 1976 John Greig (Rangers), 1977 Danny McGrain (Celtic), 1978 Derek Johnstone (Rangers), 1979 Andy Ritchie (Morton), 1980 Gordon Strachan (Aberdeen), 1981 Alan Rough (Partick Th), 1982 Paul Sturrock (Dundee U), 1983 Charlie Nicholas (Celtic), 1984 Willie Miller (Aberdeen), 1985 Hamish McAlpine (Dundee U), 1986 Sandy Jardine (Hearts), 1987 Brian McClair (Celtic), 1985 Paul McStay (Celtic), 1989 Richard Gough (rangers).

Scottish PFA Player of the Year 1989–90: Jim Bett (Aberdeen).

Past winners: 1978 Derek Johnstone (Rangers), 1979 Paul Hegarty (Dundee U), 1980 Davie Provan (Celtic), 1981 Sandy Clark (Airdrieonians), 1982 Mark McGhee (Aberdeen), 1983 Charlie Nicholas (Celtic), 1984 Willie Miller (Aberdeen), 1985 Jim Duffy (Morton), 1986 Richard Gough (Dundee U), 1987 Brian McClair (Celtic), 1988 Paul McStay (Celtic), Theo Snelders (Aberdeen).

Scottish PFA Young Player of the Year 1989–90: Scott Crabbe (Aberdeen).

European Footballer of the Year 1989: Marco van Basten (AC Milan).

Previous winners
1956 Stanley Matthews (Blackpool), 1957 Alfredo Di Stefano (Real Madrid), 1958 Raymond Kopa (Real Madrid), 1959 Alfredo Di Stefano (Real Madrid), 1960 Luis Suarez (Barcelona), 1961 Omar Sivori (Juventus), 1962 Josef Masopust (Dukla Prague), 1963 Lev Yashin (Moscow Dynamo), 1964 Denis Law (Manchester United), 1965 Eusebio (Benfica), 1966 Bobby Charlton (Manchester United), 1967 Florian Albert (Ferencvaros), 1968 George Best (Manchester United), 1969 Gianni Rivera (AC Milan), 1970 Gerd Muller (Bayern Munich), 1971 Johan Cruyff (Ajax), 1972 Franz Beckenbauer (Bayern Munich), 1973 Johan Cruyff (Barcelona), 1974 Johan Cruyff (Barcelona), 1975 Oleg Blokhin (Dynamo Kiev), 1976 Franz Beckenbauer (Bayern Munich), 1977 Allan Simonsen (Moenchengladbach), 1978 Kevin Keegan (SV Hamburg), 1979 Kevin Keegan (SV Hamburg), 1980 Karl-Heinz Rummenigge (Bayern Munich), 1981 Karl-Heinz Rummenigge (Bayern Munich), 1982 Paolo Rossi (Juventus), 1983 Michel Platini (Juventus), 1984 Michel Platini (Juventus), 1985 Michel Platini (Juventus), 1986 Igor Belanov (Dynamo Kiev), 1987 Ruud Gullit (AC Milan), 1988 Marco van Basten (AC Milan).

BRITISH FOOTBALL RECORDS

HIGHEST SCORES
First class match
Arbroath 36 Bon Accord 0 *Scottish Cup 1st Rd, 12.9.1885.*
International match
England 13 Ireland 0 *Belfast, 18.2.1882*
Football League Tranmere R 13, Oldham Ath 4, *Division 3 (N) 26.12.1935*
FA Cup
Preston NE 26 Hyde U 0 *1st Rd, 15.10.1887*
League Cup
West Ham U 10 Bury 0 *2nd Rd, 2nd leg, 25.10.1983*
Liverpool 10 Fulham 0 *2nd Rd, 1st leg, 23.9.1986*
Scottish League
East Fife 13 Edinburg C 2 *Division 2, 11.12.1937*

MOST GOALS IN A SEASON
Football League
128 in 42 games, Aston Villa *Division 1, 1930–31*
128 in 42 games, Bradford C *Division 3 (N), 1928–29*
134 in 46 games, Peterborough U *Division 4, 1960–61*
Scottish League
142 in 34 games, Raith R *Division 2, 1937–38*

FEWEST GOALS IN A SEASON
Football League *(minimum 42 games)*
24 in 42 games, Stoke C *Division 1, 1984–85*
24 in 42 games, Watford *Division 2, 1971–72*
27 in 46 games, Stockport Co *Division 3, 1969–70*
Scottish League *(minimum 30 games)*
18 in 39 games, Stirling A *Division 1, 1980–81*

MOST GOALS AGAINST IN A SEASON
Football League
141 in 34 games, Darwen *Division 2, 1898–99*
Scottish League
146 in 38 games, Edinburgh C *Division 2, 1931–32*

FEWEST GOALS AGAINST IN A SEASON
Football League *(minimum 42 games)*
16 in 42 games, Liverpool *Division 1, 1978–79*
21 in 46 games, Port Vale *Division 3 (N), 1953–54*
Scottish League *(minimum 30 games)*
14 in 38 games, Celtic *Division 1, 1913–14*

MOST POINTS IN A SEASON
Football League *(2 points for a win)*
72 in 42 games, Doncaster R *Division 3 (N), 1946–47*
74 in 46 games, Lincoln C *Division 4, 1975–76*
Football League *(3 points for a win)*
76 in 38 games, Arsenal *Division 1, 1988–89*
76 in 38 games, Liverpool *Division 1, 1988–89*
90 in 40 games, Liverpool *Division 1, 1987–88*
90 in 42 games, Everton *Division 1, 1984–85*
102 in 46 games, Swindon T *Division 4, 1985–86*
Scottish League
72 in 44 games, Celtic *Premier Division, 1987–88*
69 in 38 games, Morton *Division 2, 1966–67*
76 in 42 games, Rangers *Division 1, 1920–21*

FEWEST POINTS IN A SEASON

Football League *(minimum 34 games)*
8 in 34 games, Doncaster R *Division 2, 1904–05*
8 in 34 games, Loughborough T *Division 2, 1899–1900*
11 in 40 games, Rochdale *Division 3 (N), 1931–32*
17 in 42 games, Stoke C *Division 1, 1984–85*
19 in 46 games, Workington *Division 4, 1976–77*
Scottish League *(minimum 30 games)*
6 in 30 games, Stirling A *Division 1, 1954–55*
7 in 34 games, Edinburgh C *Division 2, 1936–37*
11 in 36 games, St Johnstone *Premier Division, 1975–76*

MOST WINS IN A SEASON

Football League
33 in 42 games, Doncaster R *Division 3 (N), 1946–47*
Scottish League
27 in 36 games, Aberdeen *Premier Division, 1984–85*
33 in 38 games, Morton *Division 2, 1966–67*
35 in 42 games, Rangers *Division 1, 1920–21*
Home
Brentford won all 21 games in Division 3(S) in 1929–30
Away
Doncaster R won 18 out of 21 games in Division 3(N) in 1946–47

FEWEST WINS IN A SEASON

Football League *(minimum 34 games)*
1 in 34 games, Loughborough T *Division 2, 1899–1900*
2 in 46 games, Rochdale *Division 3, 1973–74*
Scottish League *(minimum 22 games)*
0 in 22 games, Vale of Leven *Division 1, 1891–92*
1 in 38 games, Forfar Ath *Division 2, 1974–75*

MOST DEFEATS IN A SEASON

Football League
33 in 40 games, Rochdale *Division 3(N), 1931–32*
Scottish League
30 in 36 games, Brechin C *Division 2, 1962–63*
31 in 42 games, St Mirren *Division 1, 1920–21*

FEWEST DEFEATS IN A SEASON

Football League *(minimum 20 games)*
0 in 22 games, Preston NE *Division 1, 1888–89*
0 in 28 games, Liverpool *Division 2, 1893–94*
2 in 40 games, Liverpool *Division 1, 1987–88*
2 in 42 games, Leeds U *Division 1, 1968–69*
3 in 46 games, Port Vale *Division 3(N), 1953–54*
Scottish League *(minimum 20 games)*
1 in 42 games, Rangers *Division 1, 1920–21*

MOST DRAWS IN A SEASON

Football League
23 in 42 games, Norwich C *Division 1, 1978–79*
23 in 46 games, Exeter C, *Division 4, 1986–87*
Scottish League
19 in 44 games, Hibernian *Premier Division, 1987–88*
21 in 44 games, East Fife *Division 1, 1986–87*

MOST GOALS IN A GAME
Football League
10, Joe Payne, for Luton T v Bristol R *Division 3(S), 13.4.1936*
Scottish League
8, Jimmy McGrory, for Celtic v Dunfermline Ath *Division 1, 14.9.1928*
8, Owen McNally, for Arthurlie v Armadale *Division 2, 1.10.1927*
8, Jim Dyet, for King's Park v Forfar Ath *Division 2, 2.1.1930*
8, John Calder, for Morton v Raith R *Division 2, 18.4.1936*
FA Cup
9, Ted MacDougall, for Bournemouth v Margate *1st Rd, 20.11.1971*
Scottish Cup
13, John Petrie, for Arbroath v Bon Accord *1st Rd, 12.9.1885*

MOST LEAGUE GOALS IN A SEASON
Football League
60 in 39 games, W.R. "Dixie" Dean (Everton) *Division 1, 1927–28*
59 in 37 games, George Camsell (Middlesbrough) *Division 2, 1926–27*
Scottish League
66 in 38 games, Jim Smith (Ayr U) *Division 2, 1927–28*
52 in 34 games, William McFadyen (Motherwell) *Division 1, 1931–32*

MOST LEAGUE GOALS IN A CAREER
Football League
434 in 619 games, Arthur Rowley *(WBA, Fulham, Leicester C, Shrewsbury T, 1946–65)*
Scottish League
410 in 408 games, Jimmy McGrory *(Celtic, Clydebank, Celtic, 1922–38)*

MOST CUP WINNERS' MEDALS
FA Cup
5, James Forrest (Blackburn R) *1884, 1885, 1886, 1890, 1891*
5, Hon. A.F. Kinnaird (Wanderers) *1873, 1877, 1878,* (Old Etonians) *1879, 1882*
5, C.H.R. Wollaston (Wanderers) *1872, 1873, 1876, 1877, 1878*
Scottish Cup
7, Jimmy McMenemy (Celtic) *1904, 1907, 1908, 1911, 1912, 1914,* (Partick Th) *1921*
7, Bob McPhail (Airdrieonians) *1924,* (Rangers) *1928, 1930, 1932, 1934, 1935, 1936*
7, Billy McNeill (Celtic) *1965, 1967, 1969, 1971, 1972, 1974, 1975*

RECORD ATTENDANCES
Football League
83,260, Manchester U v Arsenal, Maine Road, 17.1.1948
Scottish League
118,567, Rangers v Celtic, Ibrox Stadium, 2.1.1939
FA Cup-tie (other than the final)
84,569, Manchester C v Stoke C, 6th Rd at Maine Road, 3.3.1934 *(a British record for any game outside London or Glasgow)*
FA Cup final
126,047*, Bolton W v West Ham U, Wembley, 28.4.1923 **The figure stated is the official one. Perhaps as many as 70,000 more got in without paying.*
European Cup
135,826, Celtic v Leeds U, semi-final at Hampden Park, 15.4.1970

TRANSFER MILESTONES
First four-figure transaction
Alf Common: Sunderland to Middlesbrough £1,000, February 1905.
First five-figure transaction
David Jack: Bolton W to Arsenal £10,340, October 1928.
First six-figure transaction:
Alan Ball: Blackpool to Everton £112,000, August 1966.
First £200,000 transaction
Martin Peters: West Ham U to Tottenham H £200,000, March 1970.

First seven-figure transaction
Trevor Francis: Birmingham C to Nottingham F £1,000,000, February 1979.
First £2,000,000 transaction
Paul Gascoigne: Newcastle U to Tottenham H £2,000,000, July 1988.
Highest British transaction
Chris Waddle: Tottenham H to Marseille £4.5 million July 1989.

MOST GOALS IN AN INTERNATIONAL MATCH

England
5, Malcolm Macdonald (Newcastle U) v Cyprus, Wembley, 16.4.1975
5, Willie Hall (Tottenham H) v Ireland, Old Trafford, 16.11.1938
5, G.O. Smith (Corinthians) v Ireland, Sunderland, 18.2.1899
5*, Steve Bloomer (Derby Co) v Wales, Cardiff, 16.3.1896 *(*one of which was credited to him in only some sources)*
5, Oliver Vaughton (Aston Villa) v Ireland, Belfast 18.2.1882
Scotland
5, Charles Heggie (Rangers) v Ireland, Belfast, 20.3.1886
Ireland
6, Joe Bambrick (Linfield) v Wales, Belfast, 1.2.1930
Wales
4, James Price (Wrexham) v Ireland, Wrexham, 25.2.1882
4, Mel Charles (Cardiff C) v N. Ireland, Cardiff, 11.4.1962
4, Ian Edwards (Chester) v Malta, Wrexham, 25.10.1978

MOST GOALS IN AN INTERNATIONAL CAREER

England
49 in 106 games, Bobby Charlton *(Manchester U)*
Scotland
30 in 55 games, Denis Law *(Huddersfield T, Manchester C, Torino, Manchester U)*
30 in 102 games, Kenny Dalglish *(Celtic, Liverpool)*
Ireland
12 in 25 games, Billy Gillespie *(Sheffield U)*
12 in 63 games, Gerry Armstrong *(Tottenham H, Watford, Real Mallorca, WBA, Chesterfield)*
12 in 11 games, Joe Bambrick *(Linfield, Chelsea)*
Wales
23 in 38 games, Trevor Ford *(Swansea T, Aston Villa, Sunderland, Cardiff C)*
23 in 68 games, Ivor Allchurch *(Swansea T, Newcastle U, Cardiff C)*
Republic of Ireland
20 in 70 games, Frank Stapleton *(Arsenal, Manchester U, Ajax, Derby Co, Le Havre, Blackburn R)*

HIGHEST INTERNATIONAL SCORES

World Cup Match: New Zealand 13, Fiji 0, 1981
Olympic Games: Denmark 17, France 1, 1908; Germany 16, USSR 0, 1912
Friendlies: Germany 13, Finland 0, 1940; Spain 13, Bulgaria 0, 1933
European Cup: Feyenoord 12, Reykjavik 2, 1969
Cup Winners' Cup: Sporting Lisbon 16, Apoel Nicosia 1, 1963
Fairs/UEFA Cup: IFC Cologne 13, Union Luxembourg 0, 1965

GM VAUXHALL CONFERENCE FIXTURES 1990–91

	Altrincham	Barnet	Barrow	Bath C	Boston U	Cheltenham T	Colchester U	Fisher Ath	Gateshead	Kettering T	Kidderminster H	Macclesfield T	Merthyr Tydfil	Northwich Vic	Runcorn	Slough T	Stafford R	Sutton U	Telford U	Welling U	Wycombe W	Yeovil T
Altrincham		30-3	10-11	25-8	4-5	1-12	19-1	9-2	13-10	8-12	2-10	1-1	16-2	6-4	21-8	8-9	29-12	16-3	16-4	22-9	2-3	6-10
Barnet	27-8		1-9	26-1	11-9	15-12	1-1	13-10	3-11	4-9	13-4	9-2	16-3	19-1	2-3	21-8	6-10	8-12	1-4	27-4	18-9	23-2
Barrow	5-1	16-2		29-9	19-1	25-8	8-9	3-11	1-1	13-10	18-8	18-9	13-4	15-12	8-12	2-3	11-9	27-4	2-2	4-5	23-3	24-11
Bath City	23-3	22-9	1-4		13-4	23-2	20-10	20-11	27-4	18-8	29-12	4-5	11-9	2-2	3-11	19-2	9-3	5-1	27-8	16-10	8-12	26-12
Boston U	27-2	20-2	6-4	8-9		9-2	19-9	22-8	10-10	1-1	30-3	5-1	8-12	3-11	27-3	27-4	24-11	9-3	16-3	25-8	20-4	26-1
Cheltenham T	27-10	2-10	16-3	6-4	17-11		22-12	5-3	18-8	16-2	11-9	20-10	27-4	27-8	26-1	8-12	20-4	29-12	24-11	19-1	1-1	23-3
Colchester U	20-4	26-12	27-10	2-3	29-12	22-9		23-3	8-12	2-2	4-5	9-3	25-8	1-9	16-2	5-1	3-11	13-10	15-9	9-2	24-11	30-3
Fisher Ath	18-8	4-5	20-4	6-10	15-12	10-11	27-8		19-1	29-12	16-2	8-12	25-3	9-3	6-4	2-2	2-3	29-10	1-9	1-1	17-11	20-10
Gateshead	12-9	9-3	26-12	17-11	10-11	5-1	1-4	13-4		22-12	2-2	23-3	4-5	1-12	19-9	1-9	15-12	22-9	9-2	6-10	20-10	8-9
Kettering T	1-4	23-3	23-2	20-4	26-12	21-8	10-11	22-9	25-8		5-1	1-9	6-10	24-11	8-9	2-10	20-10	9-2	6-4	15-12	5-3	4-5
Kidderminster H	15-12	8-9	9-2	20-8	22-9	6-10	6-4	25-8	23-2	27-4		3-9	1-1	20-10	10-11	23-3	29-9	20-4	8-12	1-4	19-1	2-3
Macclesfield T	26-12	18-8	26-3	9-4	23-2	2-3	6-10	1-4	27-8	16-3	16-10		8-9	20-4	15-12	22-9	22-1	2-2	29-12	24-11	25-8	3-11
Merthyr Tydfil	3-11	20-10	15-9	9-2	23-3	30-3	15-12	24-11	6-4	9-3	26-12	10-11		18-8	5-1	27-8	23-2	29-9	20-4	26-1	22-12	4-9
Northwich Vic	9-10	25-8	21-8	15-9	2-3	4-5	23-2	5-1	29-12	13-4	26-1	2-10	1-4		26-12	9-2	8-12	10-11	13-10	16-3	27-4	22-9
Runcorn	2-2	24-11	29-12	16-3	6-10	9-3	29-9	27-4	26-2	19-1	15-9	13-4	1-12	1-1		30-3	27-8	1-9	11-9	20-10	18-8	9-2
Slough T	13-4	20-4	20-10	1-12	18-8	1-4	16-3	22-12	16-2	11-9	24-11	26-1	29-12	6-10	25-8		19-1	1-1	3-11	23-2	16-10	15-12
Stafford R	27-4	5-1	2-10	1-9	5-3	18-9	1-12	8-9	26-1	30-3	16-3	13-10	22-9	9-4	1-4	10-11		25-8	26-12	16-2	9-2	13-4
Sutton U	24-11	15-1	6-10	16-2	20-10	8-9	26-1	23-2	27-10	27-8	3-11	15-9	2-3	23-3	4-5	26-12	6-4		18-8	13-4	30-3	25-9
Telford U	20-10	10-11	22-9	15-12	16-2	13-4	27-4	26-1	9-4	1-12	9-3	29-9	21-8	30-3	23-2	4-5	1-1	19-1		8-9	6-10	25-8
Welling U	9-3	29-12	1-12	10-11	2-2	3-11	22-8	26-12	30-3	15-9	1-9	6-4	13-10	29-9	20-4	19-9	18-8	20-2	2-3		27-3	5-1
Wycombe Wanderers	1-9	6-4	26-1	26-2	2-10	26-12	13-4	9-10	16-3	3-11	1-12	16-2	2-2	8-9	22-9	9-3	4-5	15-12	5-1	27-8		10-11
Yeovil Town	22-12	1-12	9-3	1-1	1-9	2-2	18-8	16-3	20-4	29-9	27-8	27-4	19-1	16-2	13-10	6-4	15-9	1-4	17-11	8-12	29-12	

BARCLAYS LEAGUE DIVISION ONE

	Arsenal	Aston Villa	Chelsea	Coventry C	Crystal Palace	Derby C	Everton	Leeds U	Liverpool
Arsenal..........	—	2.4	15.9	11.5	23.2	26.12	19.1	16.3	1.12
Aston Villa.....	22.12	—	11.5	8.9	1.1	2.2	30.3	27.10	12.1
Chelsea..........	2.2	3.11	—	22.12	8.12	25.8	1.1	20.3	4.5
Coventry C.....	3.11	19.1	1.4	—	2.3	13.4	29.8	24.11	17.11
Crystal Palace .	10.11	13.4	28.8	1.12	—	16.3	20.4	6.10	29.12
Derby Co	30.3	15.9	15.12	1.1	29.9	—	6.4	16.2	23.3
Everton	8.9	26.12	13.4	8.12	20.10	29.12	—	25.8	22.9
Leeds U.........	29.9	4.5	26.12	9.3	23.3	17.11	15.12	—	13.4
Liverpool	2.3	1.9	27.10	16.2	6.4	6.10	9.2	1.1	—
Luton T	8.12	24.11	29.12	22.9	25.8	11.5	27.10	8.9	23.2
Manchester C..	1.1	5.9	9.2	6.10	22.12	20.4	1.9	10.11	9.3
Manchester U .	20.10	29.12	24.11	25.8	3.11	23.2	2.3	8.12	2.2
Norwich C......	23.3	17.11	23.2	6.4	8.9	22.9	22.12	12.1	20.10
Nottingham F..	22.9	23.2	20.4	12.1	2.2	9.3	7.10	11.5	8.12
QPR	24.11	9.2	1.9	16.3	17.11	1.4	11.5	17.4	26.12
Sheffield U	6.4	2.3	16.3	27.10	12.1	8.12	10.11	23.9	25.8
Southampton ..	16.2	15.12	6.10	20.4	24.11	27.10	16.3	2.3	1.4
Sunderland	4.5	23.3	19.1	10.11	30.3	1.12	15.9	23.12	29.9
Tottenham H ..	12.1	29.9	2.3	30.3	22.9	8.9	16.2	2.2	3.11
Wimbledon.....	25.8	20.10	17.11	2.2	4.5	12.1	24.11	6.4	8.9

FIXTURES 1989–90

and have been reproduced with their permission under Licence.

Luton T	Manchester C	Manchester U	Norwich C	Nottingham F	QPR	Sheffield U	Southampton	Sunderland	Tottenham H	Wimbledon
29.8	13.4	20.4	6.10	9.2	9.3	29.12	17.11	27.10	1.9	15.12
9.3	8.12	6.4	16.2	10.11	22.9	1.12	25.8	6.10	16.3	20.4
6.4	22.9	9.3	10.11	20.10	12.1	29.9	23.3	8.9	1.12	16.2
9.2	23.3	15.12	29.12	1.9	29.9	4.5	20.10	23.2	26.12	15.9
16.12	1.4	11.5	19.1	15.9	16.2	1.9	9.3	26.12	9.2	27.10
3.11	20.10	10.11	9.2	24.11	23.12	29.8	4.5	2.3	19.1	1.9
4.5	12.1	1.12	1.4	23.3	31.1	23.2	29.9	2.2	17.11	9.3
19.1	23.2	28.8	1.9	3.11	20.10	9.2	1.12	2.4	15.9	29.12
10.11	24.11	15.9	20.4	28.8	30.3	15.12	22.12	16.3	11.5	19.1
—	17.11	4.9	16.3	2.3	2.2	26.12	12.1	20.4	1.4	13.4
16.2	—	27.10	15.9	6.4	1.12	19.1	30.3	11.5	15.12	16.3
23.2	4.5	—	26.12	29.9	8.9	17.11	22.9	12.11	13.4	2.4
29.9	2.2	30.3	—	2.1	4.5	3.11	8.12	25.8	9.3	1.12
1.12	29.12	16.3	13.4	—	25.8	1.4	8.9	17.11	27.10	26.12
15.9	2.3	19.1	27.10	15.12	—	13.4	23.2	29.12	6.10	29.8
30.3	8.9	16.2	11.5	22.12	1.1	—	2.2	24.11	20.4	6.10
1.9	26.12	9.2	28.8	19.1	10.11	15.9	—	13.4	29.12	11.5
20.10	3.11	1.9	15.12	16.2	6.4	9.3	1.1	—	28.8	9.2
22.12	25.8	1.1	24.11	4.5	23.3	20.10	6.4	8.12	—	10.11
1.1	29.9	22.12	2.3	30.3	8.12	23.3	3.11	22.9	23.2	—

BARCLAYS LEAGUE DIVISION TWO

	Barnsley	Blackburn R	Brighton & HA	Bristol C	Bristol R	Charlton Ath	Hull C	Ipswich T	Leicester C	Middlesbrough
Barnsley	—	2.2	25.8	1.1	8.12	16.3	6.4	2.10	10.11	11.5
Blackburn R	15.9	—	29.9	15.12	12.3	13.4	28.8	19.1	18.9	1.4
Brighton & HA	15.12	16.3	—	9.2	26.12	15.9	24.10	11.5	29.12	27.10
Bristol C	13.4	25.8	22.9	—	12.2	1.12	17.11	9.3	12.3	29.12
Bristol R	7.11	3.10	30.3	19.9	—	1.9	15.9	9.2	15.12	20.4
Charlton Ath	29.9	1-1	2.2	2.3	12.1	—	22.12	6.4	13.10	23.2
Hull C	29.12	8.12	27.4	16.2	2.2	1.4	—	10.11	23.11	2.3
Ipswich T	12.3	8.9	3.11	24.11	22.9	29.12	23.2	—	4.5	26.12
Leicester C	23.2	13.2	6.4	3.10	25.8	20.3	9.3	27.10	—	16.3
Middlesbrough	3.11	22.12	4.5	6.4	20.10	10.11	1.12	30.3	29.9	—
Millwall	1.9	11.5	9.3	24.10	1.12	9.2	19.9	15.9	26.12	20.3
Newcastle U	17.11	12.1	8.12	16.3	1.4	24.10	11.5	20.4	2.3	3.10
Notts Co	18.9	30.3	1.1	22.12	29.9	11.9	15.12	16.2	23.3	19.1
Oldham Ath	19.1	6.10	1.12	20.4	9.3	18.9	19.3	23.10	28.8	9.2
Oxford U	23.3	6.4	20.10	10.11	27.4	16.2	30.3	1.1	3.11	24.11
Plymouth Arg	26.12	20.4	23.2	19.1	29.12	11.5	27.10	6.10	15.9	1.9
Portsmouth	13.10	22.9	12.2	30.3	4.5	9.3	1.1	21.12	20.10	17.11
Port Vale	9.2	9.3	22.12	27.10	23.2	6.10	16.3	18.3	1.9	17.9
Sheffield W	27.4	23.2	13.2	7.11	23.3	19.1	1.9	15.12	9.2	13.4
Swindon T	4.5	1.12	2.3	2.9	13.10	15.12	19.1	28.8	27.4	15.9
Watford	1.12	19.3	8.9	11.5	17.11	20.3	2.10	16.3	1.4	6.10
WBA	20.10	17.11	13.10	15.9	3.11	26.12	9.2	1.9	13.4	7.11
West Ham U	1.4	24.10	17.11	20.3	13.4	27.10	6.10	19.9	19.1	15.12
Wolverhampton W	9.3	27.10	12.1	6.10	8.9	2.10	20.4	1.12	16.2	23.10

FIXTURES 1989–90

and have been reproduced with their permission under Licence.

Millwall	Newcastle U	Notts Co	Oldham Ath	Oxford U	Plymouth Arg	Portsmouth	Port Vale	Sheffield W	Swindon T	Watford	WBA	West Ham U	Wolverhampton W
12.1	16.2	12.2	8.9	6.10	30.3	19.3	22.9	23.10	27.10	2.3	20.4	22.12	24.11
3.11	1.9	26.12	23.3	29.12	20.10	9.2	23.11	10.11	2.3	13.10	16.2	27.4	4.5
24.0	7.11	13.4	2.3	20.4	10.11	19.9	3.4	3.10	6.10	19.1	20.3	16.2	1.9
27.4	29.9	1.4	20.10	23.2	8.9	26.12	4.5	8.12	12.1	3.11	2.2	13.10	23.3
2.3	22.12	16.3	24.11	24.10	6.4	27.10	10.11	6.10	20.3	16.2	11.5	1.1	19.1
22.9	27.4	8.12	12.2	17.11	3.11	24.11	23.3	8.9	25.8	20.10	30.3	4.5	12.3
12.2	3.11	25.8	13.10	26.12	4.5	13.4	29.9	12.1	8.9	12.3	22.9	23.3	20.10
2.2	20.10	17.11	27.4	13.4	22.3	2.4	13.10	25.8	8.12	29.9	12.1	12.2	2.3
30.3	1.12	6.10	8.12	11.5	2.2	20.4	12.1	22.9	24.10	23.12	1.1	8.9	17.11
13.10	12.3	8.9	22.9	9.3	12.1	16.2	12.2	1.1	2.2	23.3	8.12	25.8	27.4
—	19.1	20.4	29.12	7.11	16.2	3.10	13.4	27.10	16.3	15.10	6.10	10.11	3.4
8.9	—	29.12	13.4	20.3	25.8	6.10	2.2	13.2	26.12	24.10	27.10	22.9	23.2
20.10	6.4	—	4.5	1.9	27.4	15.9	12.3	2.3	24.11	9.2	10.11	3.11	13.10
6.4	1.1	27.0	—	15.9	21.12	1.9	16.2	11.5	2.10	10.11	16.3	29.3	15.12
8.12	13.10	12.1	2.2	—	13.2	2.3	25.8	22.12	22.9	4.5	8.9	13.3	29.9
17.11	16.12	23.10	1.4	18.9	—	16.3	2.3	19.3	13.4	28.8	2.10	24.11	9.2
12.1	23.3	2.2	12.1	1.12	29.9	—	8.9	6.4	23.2	27.4	25.8	8.12	3.11
1.1	15.9	1.10	17.11	15.12	1.12	19.1	—	20.4	11.5	30.5	22.10	6.4	28.8
4.5	19.9	1.12	3.11	1.4	13.10	29.12	20.10	—	17.11	15.9	9.3	29.9	26.12
30.9	30.3	9.3	12.3	9.2	1.1	10.11	3.11	16.2	—	6.4	22.12	20.10	18.9
25.8	9.3	22.9	23.2	27.10	8.12	23.10	26.12	2.2	29.12	—	12.2	12.1	13.3
23.3	4.5	23.2	29.9	19.1	13.3	15.12	27.4	24.11	1.4	5.12	—	2.3	29.12
23.2	9.2	11.5	26.12	3.10	9.3	29.8	29.12	16.3	20.4	1.9	1.12	—	15.9
22.12	10.11	19.3	25.8	16.3	22.9	11.5	8.12	30.3	12.2	1.1	6.4	2.2	—

BARCLAYS LEAGUE DIVISION

	Birmingham C	Bolton W	Bournemouth	Bradford C	Brentford	Bury	Cambridge	Chester C	Crewe Alex	Exeter C
Birmingham C	—	29.12	24.11	5.1	26.12	15.9	19.1	23.2	27.4	18.9
Bolton W..............	6.4	—	1.1	1.9	5.2	19.3	22.12	11.5	15.9	5.1
Bournemouth	16.2	13.4	—	18.9	19.1	1.9	5.1	2.3	20.10	5.2
Bradford C............	13.2	12.1	2.2	—	6.10	1.1	15.12	3.10	16.2	20.3
Brentford.............	29.3	22.9	25.8	23.3	—	10.11	14.10	8.9	6.4	16.2
Bury	26.1	13.10	12.1	13.4	23.2	—	23.3	25.8	29.9	15.12
Cambridge	25.8	1.4	12.2	8.3	19.3	6.10	—	21.9	30.11	16.3
Chester C	10.11	3.11	1.12	12.3	9.2	19.1	5.2	—	4.5	1.9
Crewe Alex...........	23.10	25.1	20.4	24.11	29.12	16.3	1.3	27.10	—	13.4
Exeter..................	2.2	13.2	22.9	13.10	24.11	9.3	29.9	12.1	1.1	—
Fulham.................	2.10	15.12	16.3	26.12	5.1	23.10	1.9	29.12	19.1	27.10
Grimsby T	20.4	24.11	22.12	15.9	16.3	5.1	6.4	19.3	9.2	11.5
Huddersfield T.......	11.5	8.9	23.10	1.12	20.4	22.12	10.11	16.3	9.3	2.10
Leyton O..............	12.1	20.10	6.4	29.9	3.3	30.3	12.3	26.1	22.12	10.11
Mansfield T...........	1.1	12.3	30.3	20.10	1.9	5.2	18.9	15.12	3.11	15.9
Preston NE	16.3	2.2	27.10	23.2	2.10	6.4	1.1	23.10	30.3	6.10
Reading................	6.10	23.2	2.10	9.2	23.10	20.4	15.9	13.4	18.9	19.1
Rotherham U	9.3	27.4	23.2	3.11	18.9	9.2	4.5	26.12	5.1	1.4
Shrewsbury T	27.10	25.8	11.5	2.4	13.4	2.10	16.2	20.4	9.11	29.12
Southend U..........	19.3	26.12	5.10	28.12	11.5	27.10	8.2	2.4	1.9	23.10
Stoke C................	8.9	23.3	26.1	27.4	16.12	16.2	20.10	2.2	13.3	2.3
Swansea C	1.12	4.5	9.3	5.2	15.9	18.9	3.11	24.11	13.10	8.2
Tranmere R	21.12	1.3	18.3	18.1	26.10	11.5	29.3	6.10	4.2	20.4
Wigan Ath	22.9	28.9	8.9	4.5	1.4	1.12	27.4	12.2	23.3	26.12

THREE FIXTURES 1989–90

and have been reproduced with their permission under Licence.

Fulham	Grimsby	Huddersfield T	Leyton O	Mansfield T	Preston NE	Reading	Rotherham U	Shrewsbury T	Southend u	Stoke C	Swansea C	Tranmere R	Wigan Ath
12.3	20.10	3.11	1.9	13.4	29.9	23.3	15.12	4.5	13.10	9.2	2.3	1.4	5.2
9.3	16.2	9.2	20.4	2.10	18.9	10.11	23.10	19.1	30.3	6.10	27.10	1.12	16.3
29.9	2.4	27.4	29.12	26.12	30.4	12.3	10.11	3.11	23.3	15.9	14.12	16.10	8.2
30.3	26.1	2.3	16.3	20.4	10.11	8.9	11.5	22.12	6.4	24.10	22.9	25.8	27.10
12.2	29.9	20.10	2.12	12.1	12.3	27.4	2.2	1.1	4.1	9.3	26.1	4.5	23.12
27.4	12.2	1.4	26.12	22.9	29.12	20.10	8.9	12.3	4.5	24.11	2.2	3.11	2.3
12.1	29.12	23.2	2.10	1.2	3.4	26.1	27.10	24.11	9.9	20.4	11.5	26.12	23.10
6.4	13.10	29.9	15.9	9.3	27.4	1.1	30.3	20.10	22.12	18.9	16.2	23.3	5.1
25.8	8.9	15.12	1.4	11.5	26.12	1.2	12.2	22.2	12.1	2.10	19.3	21.9	6.
4.5	3.11	13.3	23.2	26.1	23.3	25.8	22.12	6.4	27.4	1.12	8.9	20.10	30.3
—	13:4	15.9	11.5	1.4	5.2	2.3	6.10	9.2	23.2	19.3	20.4	24.11	18.9
1.1	—	18.9	23.10	1.12	19.1	30.3	2.10	5.2	9.3	27.10	6.10	23.2	1.9
26.1	2.2	—	6.10	27.10	16.2	22.9	19.3	30.3	25.8	6.4	12.1	12.2	1.1
4.11	27.4	23.3	—	8.9	15.12	4.5	22.9	13.10	12.2	1.1	25.8	2.2	16.2
22.12	2.3	4.5	9.2	—	13.10	6.4	16.2	23.3	29.9	5.1	10.11	27.4	19.1
22.9	25.8	24.11	9.3	19.3	—	12.1	20.4	1.12	26.1	22.12	12.2	8.9	11.5
1.12	26.12	5.2	27.10	29.12	1.9	—	16.3	5.1	24.11	11.5	1.4	9.3	19.3
23.3	12.3	13.10	5.2	24.11	20.10	29.9	—	1.9	1.12	19.1	13.4	29.12	15.9
8.9	22.9	26.12	19.3	6.10	2.3	12.2	12.1	—	2.2	16.3	23.10	25.1	15.12
10.11	15.12	19.1	4.1	15.3	15.9	15.2	1.3	18.9	—	5.2	2.10	12.4	19.4
13.10	4.5	29.12	13.4	13.2	1.4	3.11	25.8	29.9	22.9	—	26.12	12.1	10.11
20.10	23.3	1.9	19.1	23.2	5.1	22.12	1.1	27.4	12.3	30.3	—	28.9	6.4
16.2	10.11	5.1	17.9	22.10	8.2	14.12	5.4	14.9	1.1	31.8	15.3	—	1.10
2.2	12.1	13.4	24.11	25.8	3.11	13.10	26.1	9.3	20.10	23.2	29.12	12.3	—

BARCLAYS LEAGUE DIVISION

	Aldershot	Blackpool	Burnley	Cardiff C	Carlisle U	Chesterfield C	Darlington	Doncaster R	Gillingham	Halifax
Aldershot	—	23.2	5.2	18.9	13.4	5.1	26.12	2.3	27.4	2.11
Blackpool	10.11	—	18.9	5.1	2.4	5.2	13.10	16.2	20.10	30.4
Burnley	22.9	2.2	—	1.12	16.3	30.3	12.1	12.2	9.3	24.11
Cardiff C	1.2	12.2	1.3	—	26.12	10.11	13.4	23.10	15.2	29.12
Carlisle U	1.1	23.12	28.9	30.3	—	20.10	12.2	25.8	12.3	13.10
Chesterfield	12.2	22.9	26.12	23.2	20.4	—	1.4	27.10	1.12	9.3
Darlington	30.3	19.3	1.9	1.1	5.1	22.12	—	16.3	19.1	15.9
Doncaster R	1.12	24.11	5.1	27.4	19.1	4.5	29.9	—	3.11	9.2
Gillingham	23.10	20.4	15.12	24.11	2.10	2.3	25.8	11.5	—	22.2
Halifax T	11.5	27.10	16.2	6.4	19.3	15.12	26.1	8.9	9.11	—
Hartlepool U	2.10	16.3	1.4	1.9	5.2	19.1	23.2	19.3	9.2	13.4
Hereford U	9.3	1.12	13.10	20.10	15.9	9.2	23.3	6.4	19.9	27.4
Lincoln C	6.10	6.4	19.1	15.9	11.5	19.9	24.11	20.4	22.12	1.9
Maidstone	16.2	9.3	27.4	3.11	9.,2	1.1	20.10	30.3	6.2	5.1
Northampton T	26.1	8.9	12.3	21.12	9.3	23.3	27.4	1.1	6.4	29.9
Peterborough U	6.4	30.3	20.10	4.5	1.9	3.11	12.3	10.11	5.1	18.9
Rochdale	25.8	12.1	4.5	12.3	24.11	13.10	3.11	15.9	23.3	1.4
Scarborough	16.3	3.10	9.2	19.1	24.10	1.9	29.12	7.10	15.9	26.12
Scunthorpe U	12.1	25.8	13.4	29.9	29.12	27.4	4.5	15.12	13.10	23.3
Stockport Co	19.4	22.10	14.9	4.2	17.9	6.4	1.12	21.12	1.1	18.1
Torquay U	19.3	6.10	29.12	8.2	27.10	15.9	9.3	2.10	31.8	5.2
Walsall	27.10	11.5	10.11	9.3	6.10	16.2	8.9	2.2	30.3	1.12
Wrexham	8.9	26.1	3.11	22.3	1.12	29.9	22.9	12.1	4.5	12.3
York C	21.12	1.1	23.3	13.10	23.2	12.3	2.2	22.9	29.9	20.10

FOUR FIXTURES 1989–90

and have been reproduced with their permission under Licence.

Hartlepool U	Hereford U	Lincoln C	Maidstone U	Northampton T	Peterborough U	Rochdale	Scaborough	Scunthorpe U	Stockport Co	Torquay U	Walsall	Wrexham	York C
12.3	15.12	23.3	24.11	14.9	29.12	19.1	29.9	1.9	19.10	12.10	4.5	9.2	1.4
29.9	2.3	29.12	15.12	9.2	26.12	1.9	12.3	19.1	27.4	23.3	3.11	15.9	13.4
22.12	19.3	25.8	23.10	2.10	20.4	27.0	8.9	1.1	26.1	6.4	23.2	11.5	6.10
12.1	20.4	26.1	11.5	1.4	27.10	2.10	25.8	16.3	22.9	8.9	15.12	5.10	19.3
22.9	16.1	3.11	8.9	15.12	12.1	16.2	27.4	6.4	2.2	4.5	23.3	2.3	10.11
25.8	8.9	2.2	13.4	6.10	11.5	19.3	12.1	23.10	29.12	26.1	24.11	16.3	2.10
10.11	6.10	16.2	20.4	23.10	2.10	11.5	6.4	27.10	2.3	15.12	9.2	5.2	18.9
13.10	29.12	20.10	26.12	13.4	22.2	26.1	24.3	8.3	1.4	12.3	18.9	1.9	5.2
8.9	2.2	1.4	22.9	29.12	12.2	6.10	25.1	19.3	13.4	11.1	26.12	27.10	16.3
1.1	23.10	12.1	12.2	15.3	1.2	21.12	30.3	6.10	25.8	21.9	2.3	2.10	19.4
—	27.10	15.12	6.10	11.5	23.10	18.9	24.11	5.1	26.12	2.3	29.12	20.4	14.9
4.5	—	13.3	23.2	25.8	24.11	5.1	3.11	22.12	29.9	1.1	6.2	30.3	1.9
9.3	3.10	—	16.3	27.10	20.3	24.10	1.12	6.2	23.2	30.3	5.1	1.1	9.2
23.3	10.11	29.9	—	1.9	1.12	6.4	4.5	15.9	13.3	22.12	13.10	19.9	19.1
3.11	19.1	30.4	12.1	—	22.9	1.12	1.2	30.3	13.10	12.2	19.10	9.11	15.2
27.4	16.2	13.10	2.3	5.2	—	1.1	22.12	9.2	23.3	29.9	15.9	19.1	15.12
2.2	12.2	27.4	29.12	2.3	13.4	—	22.9	23.2	8.9	20.10	29.9	15.12	26.12
16.2	11.5	2.3	27.10	19.9	3.4	6.2	—	20.4	15.12	9.11	13.4	20.3	5.1
12.2	1.4	22.9	26.1	26.12	8.9	10.11	20.10	—	3.11	2.2	12.3	16.2	2.3
29.3	16.3	10.11	1.10	18.3	6.10	9.2	8.3	11.5	—	15.2	1.9	4.1	26.10
1.12	13.4	26.12	2.4	4.1	15.3	20.4	22.2	18.9	23.11	—	19.1	23.10	11.5
6.4	22.9	12.2	19.3	20.4	26.1	16.3	1.1	2.10	12.1	25.8	—	21.12	23.10
20.10	26.12	13.4	2.2	23.2	25.8	9.3	13.10	24.11	12.2	27.4	1.4	—	29.12
26.1	12.1	8.9	25.8	24.11	9.3	30.3	12.2	1.12	3.5	3.11	27.4	6.4	—

INTERNATIONAL AND CUP FIXTURES 1990–91

August
11 Sat Official Opening of Season
18 Sat Tennent's FA Charity Shield
25 Sat Football League Season starts
29 Wed Littlewoods Cup 1st Round (1st Leg)

September
1 Sat FA Cup Preliminary Round
5 Wed Littlewoods Cup 1st Round (2nd Leg)
8 Sat FA Vase Extra Preliminary Round
FA Youth Cup Preliminary Round*
11 Tue Hungary v England (U21)
12 Wed Hungary v England (F)
Scotland v Romania (EC)
N.Ireland v Yugoslavia (EC)
Iceland v England (U17)
15 Sat FA Cup 1st Round Qualifying
19 Wed European Cups 1st Round (1st Leg)
22 Sat FA Trophy 1st Round Qualifying
26 Wed Littlewoods Cup 2nd Round (1st Leg)
29 Sat FA Cup 2nd Round Qualifying
FA Youth Cup 1st Round Qualifying*

October
3 Wed European Cups 1st Round (2nd Leg)
6 Sat FA Vase Preliminary Round
10 Wed Littlewoods Cup 2nd Round (2nd Leg)
13 Sat FA Cup 3rd Round Qualifying
FA Youth Cup 2nd Round Qualifying*
14 Sun FA Sunday Cup 1st Round
16 Tue England v Poland (U21)
England v Belgium (U17)
17 Wed England v Poland (EC)
Scotland v Switzerland (EC)
N. Ireland v Denmark (EC)
Wales v Belgium (EC)
20 Sat FA Trophy 2nd Round Qualifying
FA County Youth Cup 1st Round*
24 Wed European Cups 2nd Round (1st Leg)
27 Sat FA Cup 4th Round Qualifying
31 Wed Littlewoods Cup 3rd Round

November
3 Sat FA Vase 1st Round
7 Wed European Cups 2nd Round (2nd Leg)
10 Sat FA Youth Cup 1st Round Proper*
11 Sun FA Sunday Cup 2nd Round
13 Tue Rep of Ireland v England (U21)
14 Wed Rep of Ireland v England (EC)
Bulgaria v Scotland (EC)
Austria v N. Ireland (EC)
Luxembourg v Wales (EC)
17 Sat FA Cup 1st Round Proper
24 Sat FA Vase 2nd Round
28 Wed UEFA Cup 3rd Round (1st Leg)
Littlewoods Cup 4th Round

December
1 Sat FA Trophy 3rd Round Qualifying
FA County Youth Cup 2nd Round*
8 Sat FA Cup 2nd Round Proper
FA Youth Cup 2nd Round Proper*
9 Sun FA Sunday Cup 3rd Round
12 Wed UEFA Cup 3rd Round (2nd Leg)
15 Sat FA Vase 3rd Round
22 Sat
29 Sat

January
5 Sat FA Cup 3rd Round Proper
12 Sat FA Trophy 1st Round Proper
FA Youth Cup 3rd Round Proper*
16 Wed Littlewoods Cup 5th Round
19 Sat FA Vase 4th Round
FA County Youth Cup 3rd Round*
20 Sun FA Sunday Cup 4th Round
26 Sat FA Cup 4th Round Proper

February
2 Sat FA Trophy 2nd Round Proper
6 International Date
9 Sat FA Vase 5th Round
FA Youth Cup 4th Round Proper*
13 Wed Littlewoods Cup Semi-Finals (1st Leg)
16 Sat FA Cup 5th Round Proper
17 Sun FA Sunday Cup 5th Round
23 Sat FA Trophy 3rd Round Proper
FA County Youth Cup 4th Round*
27 Wed Littlewoods Cup Semi-Finals (2nd Leg)

March
2 Sat FA Vase 6th Round
FA Youth Cup 5th Round Proper*
6 Wed European Cups Quarter Finals (1st Leg)
9 Sat FA Cup 6th Round Proper
England v Scotland (Schoolboys)
16 Sat FA Trophy 4th Round Proper
20 Wed European Cups Quarter Finals (2nd Leg)
23 Sat FA Vase Semi-Finals (1st Leg)
FA County Youth Cup Semi-Final*
24 Sun FA Sunday Cup Semi-Finals
26 Tue England v Rep of Ireland (U21)
27 Wed England v Rep of Ireland (EC)
Scotland v Bulgaria (EC)
Yugloslavia v N. Ireland (EC)
Belgium v Wales (EC)
30 Sat FA Vase Semi-Finals (2nd Leg)
FA Youth Cup Semi-Final*

April
6 Sat FA Trophy Semi-Finals (1st Leg)
10 Wed European Cups Semi-Finals (1st Leg)
13 Sat FA Trophy Semi-Finals (2nd Leg)
14 Sun FA Cup Semi-Finals
20 Sat
21 Sun Littlewoods Cup Final

24 Wed European Cups Semi-Finals (2nd Leg)
27 Sat FA County Youth Cup Final
Rugby League Final
30 Tue Turkey v England (U21)
Wales v England (U17)

May
1 Wed Turkey v England (EC)
San Marino v Scotland (EC)
East Germany v Wales (EC)
4 Sat FA Vase Final
FA Youth Cup Final*
5 Sun FA Sunday Cup Final
8 Wed UEFA Cup Final (1st Leg)
11 Sat FA Trophy Final
15 Wed European Cup Winners' Cup Final
18 Sat FA Cup Final
22 Wed UEFA Cup Final (2nd Leg)
England v Wales (U17)
29 Wed European Champion Clubs' Cup Final

June
5 Wed Wales v West Germany (EC)
8 Sat England v West Germany (Schoolboys)

* Closing date for Rounds

USEFUL ADDRESSES

Football Association: R.H.G. Kelly, FCIS, 16 Lancaster Gate, London W2 3LW.
Scottish FA: J. Farry, 6 Park Gardens, Glasgow G3 7YF.
Irish FA: D. Bowen, 20 Windsor Avenue, Belfast BT9 6EG.
Welsh FA: A.E. Evans B.Sc., 3 Westgate Street, Cardiff CF1 1JF.
FA of Ireland (Eire): 80 Merrion Square South, Dublin 2.
League of Ireland: E. Morris, 80 Merrion Square, Dublin 2.
Fedération Internationale de Football Association (FIFA): J. Blatter, FIFA House, 11 Hitzigweg, CH-8032 Zurich, Switzerland.
Union des Associations Européenes de Football (UEFA): G. Aigner, Jupiterstrasse 33 PO Box 16, CH-3000 Berne 15, Switzerland.
Football League: J.D. Dent, Lytham St Annes, Lancashire FY8 1JG.
Scottish League: 188 West Regent Street, Glasgow G2 4RY.
Irish League: M. Brown, 87 University Street, Belfast BT7 1HP.
Welsh League: K.J. Tucker, 16 The Parade, Merthyr Tydfil, Mid-Glamorgan CF47 0ET.
GM Vauxhall Conference: P.D. Hunter, 24 Barnehurst Road, Bexley Heath, Kent DA7 6EZ.
Beazer Homes League: D.J. Strudwick, 11 Welland Close, Durrington, Worthing, W. Sussex BN13 3NR.
Northern Premier League: R.D. Bayley, 22 Woburn Drive, Hale, Altrincham, Cheshire WA15 8LZ.
Vauxhall League: N. Robinson, 226 Rye Lane, Peckham, London SE15 4NL.
The Association of Football League Referees and Linesmen: J.B. Goggins, 1 Tewkesbury Drive, Lytham St Annes, Lancs FY8 4LN.
The Football League Executive Staffs Association: P.O. Box 52, Leamingston Spa, Warwickshire.
Women's Football Association: Miss L. Whitehead, 448/450, Hanging Ditch, The Corn Exchange, Manchester M4 3ES.
English Schools FA: C.S. Allatt, 4a Eastgate Street, Stafford ST16 2NN.
Professional Footballers' Association: G. Taylor, 2 Oxford Court, Bishopsgate, off Lower Mosley Street, Manchester, M2 3W2.
The Association of Football Statisticians: R.J. Spiller, 22 Bretons, Basildon, Essex.
England Supporters' Association: David Stacey, 66 Southend Road, Wickford, Essex SS11 8EN.
The Football Programme Directory: Editor, David Stacey, 66 Southend Road, Wickford, Essex SS11 8EN.
National Federation of Football Supporters' Clubs General Secretary: 69 Fourth Avenue, Chelmsford, Essex.
Football Trust Second Floor, Walkden House, 10 Melton Street, London NW1 2EJ.